THE UNKNOWN BLACK BOOK

THE UNKNOWN BLACK BOOK

THE HOLOCAUST IN THE GERMAN-OCCUPIED SOVIET TERRITORIES

EDITED BY
JOSHUA RUBENSTEIN
AND ILYA ALTMAN

Introductions by
Yitzhak Arad, Ilya Altman,
and Joshua Rubenstein

Translated by Christopher Morris
and Joshua Rubenstein

*Published in association with the
United States Holocaust Memorial Museum*

INDIANA UNIVERSITY PRESS
BLOOMINGTON AND INDIANAPOLIS

This book is a publication of

Indiana University Press
601 North Morton Street
Bloomington, Indiana 47404-3797 USA

www.iupress.indiana.edu

Telephone orders	800-842-6796
Fax orders	812-855-7931
Orders by e-mail	iuporder@indiana.edu

First published in Russian as *Neizvestnaia chernaia kniga: Svidetel'stva ochevidtsev o katastrofe sovetskikh evreev (1941–1944)*, compiled and edited by Y. Arad, T. Pavlov, and I. Altman (Jerusalem and Moscow: Yad Vashem and State Archive of the Russian Federation, 1993).

First paperback edition published 2010
© 2008 by Indiana University Press
Published in association with the United States Holocaust Memorial Museum

The assertions, arguments, and conclusions contained herein are those of the author or other contributors. They do not necessarily reflect the opinions of the United States Holocaust Memorial Museum.

All rights reserved

No part of this book may be reproduced or utilized in any form or by any means, electronic or mechanical, including photocopying and recording, or by any information storage and retrieval system, without permission in writing from the publisher. The Association of American University Presses' Resolution on Permissions constitutes the only exception to this prohibition.

∞ The paper used in this publication meets the minimum requirements of the American National Standard for Information Sciences—Permanence of Paper for Printed Library Materials, ANSI Z39.48-1992.

Manufactured in the United States of America

The Library of Congress catalogued the hard copy edition as follows:

The unknown black book : the Holocaust in the German-occupied Soviet territories / edited by Joshua Rubenstein and Ilya Altman ; introductions by Yitzhak Arad, Ilya Altman, and Joshua Rubenstein ; translated by Christopher Morris and Joshua Rubenstein.
   p. cm.
"Published in association with the United States Holocaust Memorial Museum."
Includes bibliographical references and index.
  ISBN-13: 978-0-253-34961-3 (cloth : alk. paper) 1. Jews—Persecutions—Soviet Union. 2. Holocaust, Jewish (1939–1945)—Soviet Union. 3. Soviet Union—History—German occupation, 1941–1944. 4. Jews—Soviet Union—History. 5. Soviet Union—Ethnic relations. I. Rubenstein, Joshua. II. Al'tman, I.
  DS135.R92U55 2007
  940.53'180947—dc22

2007023537

ISBN 978-0-253-22267-1 (pbk.)

  6 7 8 9   15 14 13 12 11 10

Book design: David Alcorn, Alcorn Publication Design

Contents

Preface	vii
Acknowledgments	ix
The Destruction of the Jews in German-Occupied Territories of the Soviet Union Yitzhak Arad	xiii
The History and Fate of *The Black Book* and *The Unknown Black Book* Ilya Altman	xix
Note on Translation	xl
The War and the Final Solution on the Russian Front Joshua Rubenstein	3
I • Ukraine	51
II • Belorussia	233
III • Lithuania	277
IV • Latvia	316
V • Estonia	331
VI • The Crimea	337
VII • Russia	383
VIII • Prisoners of War	406
Detailed Table of Contents	421
Index	427

Preface

The Unknown Black Book provides a compelling set of testimonies from Jews who survived open-air massacres and other atrocities carried out by the Germans and their allies in the occupied territories of the Soviet Union during World War II. The testimonies in this volume are raw, first-hand accounts from survivors of work camps and ghettos, forced marches, beatings, starvation, and disease. They are stories from Jews who lived in pits, in walled-off corners of apartments, in attics, in basement dugouts, unable to walk outside. They are the stories of people too afraid to talk to fellow human beings, fearful of the Germans, of neighbors, "afraid of the slightest sound, of footsteps on the street,"[1] not so much camouflaged as concealed, even buried—until they went mad, were betrayed, or miraculously survived until liberation.

In his thoughtful study of Holocaust testimonies, Lawrence Langer observed that "from the point of view of the witness, the urge to tell meets resistance from the certainty that one's audience will not understand."[2] But unlike so many memoirs and collections of oral testimony compiled in recent years in North America, Europe, Israel, and elsewhere, the stories in *The Unknown Black Book* were recorded almost immediately after liberation, near the very place where these Jews endured their suffering. Under the direction of two renowned Soviet-Jewish journalists—Ilya Ehrenburg and Vasily Grossman—the interviews were conducted by soldiers or journalists who were often Jews themselves and spoke the language of the survivors: Russian, Yiddish, or Ukrainian. They too were survivors, had fought the Germans and lost loved ones of their own. They were determined to collect these testimonies so that the crimes of the Germans and the suffering of the Jews would not be ignored, forgotten, or denied. The close identification between the survivor and the interviewer helps to give these accounts an immediacy that present-day oral testimonies—taken in well-equipped video studios or comfortable living rooms, in an acquired language, decades after liberation, and inevitably informed by broad intervening knowledge of the Holocaust—do not convey. Ultimately, though, these are not stories about human resilience or the overcoming of adversity. They are about the victims who did not survive, who are the shadows on the page.

JOSHUA RUBENSTEIN

---

1. See "The story of Anna Morgulis from Odessa," p. 118.
2. Lawrence Langer, *Holocaust Testimonies: The Ruins of Memory* (New Haven, 1991), p. xiii.

Acknowledgments

Numerous people helped me to complete this book, and I would like to acknowledge their assistance and encouragement.

My friend and co-editor Dr. Ilya Altman, who founded and remains the Co-Chairman of the Russian Research and Educational Holocaust Center in Moscow, deserves substantial recognition for discovering the long-lost material that led to the publication of *The Unknown Black Book* in Moscow in 1993. Ilya worked with the State Archive of the Russian Federation (GARF) and with Yad Vashem in Jerusalem (The Holocaust Martyrs' and Heroes' Remembrance Authority, which is the official Israeli national institution for commemoration of the Holocaust) to produce the original volume. Their cooperation has been indispensable to the publication of this English-language edition. Following the reforms of Mikhail Gorbachev and the broadened access to archives that had formerly been out of reach, Ilya and his colleagues continue to carry out research and bring to our attention the full scale and horror of the Holocaust on German-occupied Soviet territories during World War II. Ilya was especially helpful to me during my visit to Russia in 2002 and during his visit to the United States in 2004, when we were able to spend time together going over these documents. Dr. Yitzhak Arad, the long-time director of Yad Vashem, who is now retired, also contributed to this volume and to our understanding of the magnitude of the catastrophe in a substantial way. Even with all that scholars and survivors have related, there is still much to be learned about a major dimension of the Holocaust that Western audiences are only beginning to fathom.

I want to especially express my gratitude to Benton Arnovitz, Director of Academic Publications at the Center for Advanced Holocaust Studies of the United States Holocaust Memorial Museum in Washington, D.C., and to Janet Rabinowitch, Director of Indiana University Press, for asking me to take on this project. I hope the book lives up to their confidence and expectations. I also wish to acknowledge the contribution of Christopher Morris, who produced the initial translation of *The Unknown Black Book* and also translated the introductions by Ilya Altman and Yitzhak Arad.

A number of people lent me their energy and expertise in order to deepen my understanding of how leaders of the Einsatzgruppen were brought to justice in Nuremberg. It was a privilege for me to interview Benjamin Ferencz at his home in New Rochelle, New York; Mr. Ferencz was the chief prosecutor at their trial in 1947 and even decades later retains a vivid memory of what took place and an equally vivid anger over their crimes. Hannah Wartenberg saw me on several occasions in New York, where she generously allowed me to examine the papers of her late husband, Rolf Wartenberg, who interrogated leaders of the Einsatzgruppen.

I would also like to acknowledge the support of several Western scholars, most notably Hilary Earl of Nipissing University in Ontario, Canada, who was especially generous with her time and attention; her study of the Einsatzgruppen trial proved to be especially helpful to me. John Barrett of St. John's University School of Law helped orient me when I first began to look into the Nuremberg trials. And Francine Hirsch of the University of Wisconsin provided needed information and feedback about the Soviet role at Nuremberg. My friend Michael Berenbaum read portions of the manuscript and was always willing to lend me his energy and thoughtful suggestions. Ilya Bourtman, a student at Johns Hopkins University, shared his work on the trials of German war criminals and Soviet collaborators in the former Soviet Union. Michael Gelb, an editor at the United States Holocaust Memorial Museum, helped to sharpen the translation, answered questions about history, and provided invaluable assistance as I neared completion of the manuscript. Pavel Ilyin, of the United States Holocaust Memorial Museum, also proved to be extremely helpful in making the translation more accurate, particularly with regard to questions of geography and unusual Russian-language terms; he and his colleague Liliya Meyerovich prepared the map for this volume. Zvi Gitelman read some of the material, and I am grateful for his helpful suggestions. And Boris and Natalya Katz were tireless in their willingness to help me produce as accurate and readable a translation as possible. I could not have imagined back in the spring of 1978, when we first met in Moscow and they were soon permitted to emigrate, how much I would come to rely on their friendship and good judgment.

Mark Kuchment, once again, assisted me with his knowledge of Soviet history. Aleisa Fishman of the United States Holocaust Memorial Museum provided invaluable technical assistance.

Among Russian colleagues, my friend Boris Frezinsky was always prepared to answer questions about Ilya Ehrenburg, the war, and the Final Solution. Lev Lazarev, the editor of *Voprosy literatury* (Problems of Literature), discussed the career of Vasily Grossman with me.

The preparation and publication of this volume was made possible by a grant from the Memorial Foundation for Jewish Culture. This support helped me to pursue research in various libraries, among them the New York Public Library; the library of Hebrew College in Newton, Massachusetts; Harvard University's Widener Library; and the library of the YIVO Institute in New York; as well as in the archives of the United States Holocaust Memorial Museum. Staff members of each of these institutions were consistently attentive. I am also grateful for the encouragement and support of my colleagues at Amnesty International USA and the Davis Center for Russian and Eurasian Studies at Harvard University, where I enjoy the privileges of an Associate. I would like to thank my agent, Robin Straus, as well, for her longstanding friendship and support.

Thankfully, I have been blessed with a patient and understanding family who permit me to invest so much energy into scholarly marathons when, at least some of the time, my wife, Jill, and our son, Benjamin, would prefer I open my study and come out to play.

Finally, I would like to acknowledge the special contribution of Irina Ilinichna Ehrenburg. She died in May 1997, several years before I started work on this volume. Studying these documents, I was constantly aware of her selfless efforts to honor the work of her father by undertaking an accurate and comprehensive edition of *The Black Book* in Russian, which she was able to see published in 1993, following the collapse of the Soviet Union. This was a suitable tribute to her father's determination, under the most terrible conditions, that the murder of two and a half million Jews by the Germans during their occupation of Soviet territories not be overlooked or forgotten.

JOSHUA RUBENSTEIN

The Destruction of the Jews in German-Occupied Territories of the Soviet Union

YITZHAK ARAD

World War II marked one of the most tragic periods in the history of the Jewish people. One third of all the Jews who were alive on the eve of the conflict—approximately six million men, women, and children—were savagely murdered by Nazi Germany, its allies, and their local collaborators. The entire populations of the countries occupied by Germany suffered terribly, but the fate of the Jews, including those living in the occupied territories of the former Soviet Union, was unique; the Jewish people alone were condemned by Hitler to total extermination.

The "Final Solution of the Jewish Question," alongside expansion to the East (*Drang nach Osten,* as the Germans called it) and the enslavement of the Slavic peoples, lay at the foundation of Nazi ideology. According to these notions the Germans, as members of a superior race, had the right to rule over other nations. The Jews, whom Hitler defined not only as the lowest of all peoples but also the most dangerous obstacle to achieving German rule over Europe, were to be annihilated entirely.

The Final Solution was implemented by Nazi Germany in several stages: forced emigration of the Jews from the Third Reich in the years 1933–1939; ghettoization of the Jews after the occupation of Poland in the years 1939–1941; total extermination of the Jews beginning in June 1941 after the German invasion of the Soviet Union. Soviet Jews were the first to be targeted for systematic mass murder. This policy was then applied to the Jews in the other countries occupied by Germany and in countries allied to Germany.

That the decision totally to exterminate the Jews was made simultaneously with the attack on the Soviet Union, code-named Operation Barbarossa, or within a few months after the attack, was not a mere coincidence. Having declared himself an enemy of communism, Hitler maintained that the Soviet state and its communist ideology were the instruments with which the Jews (the rulers of the USSR, according to Hitler) were using to establish their dominance over the world. Consequently, the physical destruction of the Soviet Jews, as a part of the Final Solution of the Jewish Question, became a means of simultaneously annihilating communism and the Soviet state, and of preparing its East European lands for German colonization.

Before Operation Barbarossa around 4,000,000 Jews, among them as many as 250,000 refugees from German-occupied Poland, lived in territories of the Soviet Union, including those areas annexed in the years 1939–1940, that would soon be overrun by the German army. (Another million lived in areas that the Germans failed to reach.) Part of the Jewish population managed to escape or was evacuated in time, particularly from eventually occupied areas farther to the east, but as many as 2,610,000 to 2,745,000 Jews remained under Hitler's power. They became immediate targets for total extermination.

A directive of March 13, 1941, associated with Operation Barbarossa and issued by the supreme command of the German armed forces, stated: "In the sphere of military operations, the Reichsführer SS [Himmler] receives from the Führer special assignments for the preparation of political operations arising from the total struggle of two opposing political systems." These "special assignments" included the mass extermination of the Soviet Jews. Hitler had determined that the war against the USSR was to be total and unrestrained. Even international agreements on the treatment of POWs—agreements that had not been signed by the Soviet Union, for that matter—or of the civilian populations would have no significance. Supplementing these directives, Wehrmacht commanders issued three orders in May and June 1941 creating a "legal" basis for the Nazi terror on the occupied territory of the Soviet Union: the first, dated May 13, is concerned with military jurisdiction in the zone of the implementation of the Barbarossa plan; the second, dated May 19, refers to the adoption on the territory of the Soviet Union of severe and decisive measures against "Bolshevik agitators," partisans, saboteurs, and Jews; the third, dated June 6, is known as the "commissar decree." These documents emphasize that combatants and civilians alike suspected of hostile activities—which automatically included communists, commissars, and Jews—would be subject to execution without trial or investigation. The inclusion of Jews in the category of "enemies" alongside partisans and saboteurs signaled a death sentence for all of Soviet Jewry.

These directives gave the SS terror organs complete freedom of action on the territory under the control of the Wehrmacht. The German armed forces became an accomplice and bore full responsibility for the crimes committed in regions that it controlled. Orders given after the attack on the Soviet Union drew the military even further into the commission of war crimes and crimes against humanity.

To carry out the "special assignments" given to Himmler, four operational groups, known as the Einsatzgruppen, were created. The four Einsatzgruppen numbered three thousand people altogether. Their duty was the extermination of Jews, commissars, and all other "enemies" of the Third Reich. In the interests of complete secrecy, these groups received oral orders for the annihilation of the Jews. Einsatzgruppe A operated in the Baltic states in the direction of Leningrad (now Saint Petersburg); Einsatzgruppe B operated in Belorussia in the direction of Moscow; Einsatzgruppe C operated in Ukraine in the direction of Kiev and Kharkov; and Einsatzgruppe D operated in Bessarabia and southern Ukraine, in the direction of the Crimea and the North Caucasus.

In addition to the Einsatzgruppen, some brigades of Waffen SS, subordinated directly to Himmler, and some dozens of battalions of the German Order Police under the command of the Higher SS and Police Leaders, took part in the regime of terror and the murder of the Jews in the occupied territories of the Soviet Union.

All these German forces were reinforced by auxiliary police units recruited from local inhabitants who volunteered to serve the Germans. Depending on where and how they were recruited and deployed, units were comprised of Lithuanians, Latvians, Estonians, Ukrainians, Russians, Belorussians, Crimean Tatars, and members of other nationalities.

As a rule, the Jews in the occupied territories of the Soviet Union were shot and buried close to the localities where they had been living. The most well-known of these killing sites, at which tens of thousands of Jews perished, included the Ninth Fort in Kaunas; Ponary near Vilnius; the Rumbula Forest near Riga; Maly Trostyanets near Minsk; Babi Yar in Kiev; Drobitsky Yar near Kharkov; and Bogdanovka in Transnistria.

The occupied territories of the Soviet Union were divided into two main administrative areas. One of them, close to the frontline and taking into account the need for military operations from Leningrad in the north to the Caucasus mountains in the south, was under military administration. The second area, farther toward the rear, was handed over to a German civilian administration headed by Alfred Rosenberg as Minister for the Occupied Eastern Territories. This civilian administrative area was divided into two Reichskommissariats: Reichskommissariat Ostland, which included Estonia, Latvia, Lithuania, and parts of Western Belorussia (including the city of Minsk); and Reichskommissariat Ukraine, which included southwest Belorussia (Polesye) and parts of Ukraine up to the Dniepr River. Bessarabia and Northern Bukovina, annexed by the Soviet Union in 1940, were returned to Romania. Parts of Moldavia and southern Ukraine between the rivers Dniestr and Southern Bug, including the city of Odessa, were handed over to Romanian administration. Romania called this latter area Transnistria. Southwest Ukraine (East Galicia), including the city of Lvov (Lviv), was attached to the General Government, the name given to German-occupied territories in central Poland.

The Wehrmacht gave a free hand to the SS Einsatzgruppen in areas under military administration, and almost all of the Jews in them were exterminated by the end of 1941. At the outset of the occupation, the Germans created ghettos in some cities and regions under military control. The Jewish prisoners in these ghettos were killed in the spring and summer of 1942. Thus the German military administration and its army units were criminally complicit with the organs of the SS in the annihilation of the Jews on occupied Soviet territory.

In sectors under German civilian administration, more than 80 percent of the Jews of Lithuania, Latvia, and Estonia were wiped out by the end of 1941, while the majority of the Jews in Western Belorussia and Western Ukraine were killed in the spring and summer of 1942.

The majority of the Jews in Bessarabia and Northern Bukovina were exterminated by German and Romanian forces in the first months of the occupation (between June and September 1941); at least another 125,000 were exiled to Transnistria. Most of the

Jews who had been living in Transnistria, including those of Odessa, perished in the final months of 1941 and in early 1942. The rest, along with the Jews expelled from Moldavia and Bukovina, were imprisoned in ghettos and labor camps. Most of the Jews living in the regions of Western Ukraine annexed to the General Government were killed in the Belzec death camp between the spring and autumn of 1942. Those remaining were imprisoned in ghettos and camps.

Owing to a shortage of labor, and of specialists in particular, the German civilian administration gave orders for the partial temporary preservation of ghettos and labor camps in Vilnius, Kaunas, Riga, Minsk, Lvov, and several other locations. Life in the ghetto meant hunger, disease, forced labor, and unbearable living conditions. The Germans regularly carried out so-called *Aktionen* during which anyone unable to work—children, old people, and the sick—were sent to the camps to be killed. The prisoners in the ghettos were forbidden any form of social activity, as well as the observance of religious rites or the bearing of children.

The Jews in such ghettos courageously resisted the barbarous actions of the Nazis. Ignoring the orders of the Germans, they organized medical services and schools, tried to maintain religious traditions, provided public assistance, and obtained foodstuffs by illegal means. Hidden radios brought news of the war. Behind the barbed wire, ghetto residents distributed forbidden printed matter. In some ghettos, residents maintained underground archives in order to preserve written testimonies and other evidence of this dreadful time. All of this was done at great risk, and thousands of Jews paid with their lives in the struggle to preserve their human dignity under intolerable circumstances.

After the spring of 1943, when the German army was beginning to retreat under pressure from Soviet forces, the Germans liquidated the ghettos and labor camps that still existed in the Red Army's path. Some inhabitants of the ghettos perished where they were living, some were deported to concentration camps in Germany, and some were taken to the gas chambers at Sobibor and Treblinka. Any remaining labor camps were eradicated before the final German retreat in 1944.

The small number of Jews who managed to escape from the ghettos and the camps sought refuge, but generally could not find support among the local populations. A substantial number of people, particularly in the Baltic countries and in Ukraine, collaborated with Hitler's troops, and many participated in the murder of the Jews. Without the active support of the local inhabitants, tens of thousands of whom served in police units, the Germans would not have been able to identify and exterminate as many Jews in the occupied territories of the Soviet Union. Large segments of the local population were indifferent to the fate of their former neighbors who were condemned to death. The reasons for such attitudes varied: for some sheer antisemitism sufficed, while for others a desire to claim the apartments and household goods left behind by Jews was reason enough. Yet almost everywhere in the occupied territories, in Lithuania and in Ukraine, in Latvia and in Belorussia, there were a few individuals—the Righteous among the Nations as designated by Yad Vashem—who, at the risk of their own lives, helped Jews and tried to rescue them.

Many Jews who remained in the occupied territories offered resistance to Hitler's forces and fought back. Jewish underground groups existed in many ghettos and camps and included members of youth organizations of diverse political movements. Jews from Vilnius, Kaunas, Minsk, and other ghettos entered bravely into an unequal struggle with the Germans.

Members of these underground groups carried out acts of subversion in the German rear area. Many Jews, both alone and in groups, managed to break out of the camps and ghettos to join the partisans. In the forests of Belorussia, in northern Ukraine, and in eastern Lithuania, tens of thousands of Jews fought in Jewish and multi-ethnic partisan detachments. They attacked German and local police posts, prepared ambushes on the roads, laid mines, and derailed trains. Approximately half a million Soviet Jews served in the ranks of the Red Army and partisan units during World War II. Many Soviet Jews distinguished themselves, and more than 150 received the country's highest honor—the Order of Hero of the Soviet Union.

When Soviet forces liberated the occupied territories, they found very few surviving Jews. For the overwhelming majority, liberation came too late. Of the approximately 2,610,000 to 2,745,000 who had been trapped in the German-occupied territories, somewhere between 2,460,000 and 2,600,000 were murdered; probably only 100,000 to 120,000 Jews survived. Over half of the survivors were in Transnistria, which had been under Romanian administration. The second-largest group of survivors were Jewish partisans and Jews in the family camps in the forests. Several thousand Soviet Jews survived using Aryan documents to hide their Jewish identity, or survived with the help of local people—the Righteous among the Nations.

In addition to the number of victims mentioned above, between 75,000 to 80,000 Jewish prisoners of war were murdered in POW camps. Many Soviet POWs perished from hunger and diseases in these camps. But the Jewish POWs, alongside the political commissars, were shot according to German orders, not because they were POWs or commissars, but because they were Jews.

To the total number of Soviet Jews murdered directly by Nazi Germany and its collaborators, we could add close to 120,000 Jewish soldiers who fell in battle and tens of thousands of Jews who succumbed, during the siege of Leningrad and in the Soviet rear areas, to German bombs and artillery shells or to hunger and disease brought on by wartime conditions.

All told, of the five million Jews who lived in the Soviet Union on the eve of the German attack on June 22, 1941, about half lost their lives as a result.

The History and Fate of *The Black Book* and *The Unknown Black Book*

ILYA ALTMAN[1]

The history of *The Black Book* and the material constituting *The Unknown Black Book* form part of the tragic legacy of the Jewish Anti-Fascist Committee (JAC). Established in February 1942—less than a year after the German invasion of the Soviet Union, at a time when the Wehrmacht was still advancing into Soviet territory—the JAC was one of five anti-fascist committees whose principal purpose was to appeal to various constituencies in the West—and for the Slavic committee, to appeal to Bulgaria and parts of what was soon to become Yugoslavia—to support the war-time alliance of the Western democracies with the regime of Joseph Stalin. All five committees—for women, young people, scientists, Slavs, and Jews—were expected to publish articles, make radio broadcasts, arrange for visits by Soviet representatives, and host foreign dignitaries in Moscow, all with the overriding purpose of highlighting German atrocities and the valor of Soviet forces who were battling the Wehrmacht on the Eastern Front.

The chairman of the JAC was the famous actor and director of Moscow's State Jewish Theater, Solomon Mikhoels. A number of distinguished Yiddish writers and poets joined Mikhoels on the committee, among them David Bergelson, Peretz Markish, Leyb (Lev) Kvitko, Itsik Fefer, and David Hofshteyn. Other Jewish cultural figures, such as the writers Ilya Ehrenburg and Vasily Grossman, wrote in Russian, but they still played prominent roles in the JAC's work and deliberations, particularly when it came to the question of how the JAC should respond to the systematic mass murder of Soviet Jews by the occupying Germans.

---

1. From the time work on *The Black Book* began over sixty years ago, several versions of how the book was to be published have appeared in Russia and abroad. This account will rely primarily on the stenographic records of the meeting of the Literary Commission of the Jewish Anti-Fascist Committee (JAC) on October 13, 1944, and the meeting of the JAC Presidium on April 25, 1946. Other documents and the extensive correspondence of members of the Literary Commission and of the JAC itself, which can be found in the JAC archive housed in the State Archive of the Russian Federation (GARF), and in Ilya Ehrenburg's papers in the archives of Yad Vashem in Jerusalem, are also of substantial interest. In addition, the testimony of the defendants in the JAC trial of 1952 and documents from the Central Committee of the Communist Party, which are currently held in the Russian State Archive of Social and Political History (RGASPI), help elucidate this history. For a collection of documents in English on the history of the Jewish Anti-Fascist Committee, see Shimon Redlich, ed., *War, Holocaust and Stalinism: A Documented History of the Jewish Anti-Fascist Committee in the USSR* (Luxembourg, 1995). For an abridged, English language version of the transcript of the secret 1952 trial of the JAC, see Joshua Rubenstein and Vladimir Naumov, eds., *Stalin's Secret Pogrom: The Postwar Inquisition of the Jewish Anti-Fascist Committee* (New Haven, 2001, in association with the United States Holocaust Memorial Museum).

For a time, the JAC carried out its activities within the framework established by the regime. Under the close supervision of the Central Committee of the Communist Party, JAC members sent a continuous stream of articles to newspapers outside the country, particularly in the West and of course to the Jewish press. As expected, they emphasized Jewish suffering and often highlighted the frontline exploits of Jewish soldiers who were fighting in the ranks of the Red Army.

The high point in the history of the JAC came in the spring and summer of 1943, when two of its leading figures, Solomon Mikhoels and the poet Itsik Fefer, traveled to North America, Mexico, and England. They were in the West for almost eight months and raised millions of dollars for the Red Army. During their stay in New York, where they met Mayor Fiorello La Guardia and a host of Jewish and non-Jewish dignitaries, they were the honored guests at a mass rally at the Polo Grounds on July 8. Hosted by several leading Jewish organizations, the rally drew fifty thousand people and generated passionate support for the two emissaries who represented the largest Jewish community outside the United States, a community that was enduring terrible losses.

Mikhoels and Fefer returned to a country different from the one they had left in the spring. By the winter of 1943, the Red Army had already liberated a great deal of Soviet territory. The Germans were retreating and sustaining dramatic losses of their own. As the Red Army advanced, it found massacre sites where Soviet Jews had been systematically slaughtered. Members of the JAC could not ignore such evidence. While the committee had been established for propaganda purposes, JAC members felt tremendous pressure to respond to the Final Solution not only as Soviet patriots but as Jews. For many of them, the decision was also a personal one. Itsik Fefer lost his father, who had once been a Hebrew teacher in the Ukrainian town of Shpola. Vasily Grossman lost his mother in Berdichev. Dr. Boris Shimelyovich, who was the medical director of Moscow's Botkin Hospital, lost his brother. The actor Benjamin Zuskin, who performed alongside Mikhoels at the State Jewish Theater, lost his first wife in Lithuania. The Yiddish poet David Hofshteyn lost his mother and younger brother at Babi Yar outside Kiev. Colonel David Dragunsky, one of the most decorated Soviet Jewish war heroes, lost his parents, his brothers, two sisters, and seventy other relatives.

Faced with such a national and personal tragedy, JAC members began looking for ways to help survivors, to document their suffering, and even to appeal to Western Jewish organizations to send material aid. *The Black Book* project fit into this initiative.

This was intended to be the first joint Soviet-American documentary collection devoted to World War II. The idea evolved through several stages following the German invasion of Soviet territory on June 22, 1941. In mid-August a group of Jewish writers, actors, and literary scholars developed a plan for a shortwave radio broadcast, which aired on August 24. In the course of the broadcast, Solomon Mikhoels warned that the Nazis planned "the total annihilation of the Jewish people." Mikhoels was thus the first individual to speak publicly in the Soviet media about the mass murder of the Jews. Ilya Ehrenburg, speaking in highly personal terms, invoked the image of his mother: "I grew up in a Russian city. My mother tongue is Russian. I am a Russian writer. Like all Russians, I am now defending my homeland. But the Nazis have reminded me of something else—my mother's name was Hannah. I am a Jew. I say this proudly. Hitler hates us more than anything, and this makes us proud."[2] Nazi attacks against Jews in Germany and the rest of Europe meant that Soviet Jews came under a universal threat, a theme that was repeatedly made clear by the broadcast's participants.

Jews around the world responded to this appeal by their Soviet brethren, particularly in the United States where, in the words of the Soviet ambassador, Konstantin Umansky, "the Jewish broadcast aroused the most tremendous reaction." One hundred thousand copies of the transcript of the broadcast were published in America—fifty thousand in English and fifty thousand in Yiddish.[3] In the fall of 1941, the American Committee of Jewish Writers, Artists, and Scientists was formed as a direct result of the appeal from Moscow, with branches in many large American cities. On October 26 the American Committee organized a similar radio broadcast. In response, a group of Soviet writers and artists (including Mikhoels and Ehrenburg) sent a congratulatory telegram to the American Committee on December 8, 1941. For the Kremlin, playing the "Jewish card" proved to be such a propaganda success that, as early as 1942, the Soviet Information Bureau (Sovinformburo), under whose supervision the radio broadcast had been carried out, initiated plans to publish pamphlets about the massacres of Soviet Jews and the heroism of Jewish soldiers. The collection and editing of these documents and eyewitness statements were supposed to be carried out by the JAC, founded in February 1942 under the direction of the Sovinformburo, whose chairman, Alexander Shcherbakov, was one of the Secretaries of the Central Committee of the Communist Party.[4]

But the official who was actually in charge of the JAC's work was Shcherbakov's lieutenant, Deputy People's Commissar (or Deputy Minister) of Foreign Affairs of the USSR Solomon Lozovsky. It is worth recalling the 1942 press conference, at which Lozovsky explained the creation of the JAC. "Hitler made it his goal to destroy the Jewish people, and that is what he is doing in the occupied countries and regions—annihilating the Jewish population. It's no wonder that the Jews created the Anti-Fascist Committee to help the Soviet Union, the United States, and England put an end to Hitler's bloody insanity."[5]

---

2. Redlich, *War, Holocaust and Stalinism*, pp. 177–183, for excerpts from several speeches at the rally. The speeches were also widely quoted in the Soviet press; see *Pravda*, August 25, 1941, pp. 3–4; *Izvestia*, August 26, 1941, p. 3.
3. N. K. Petrova, *Antifashistskie komitety v SSSR* (The Anti-Fascist Committees in the USSR) (Moscow, 1999), pp. 67, 77.
4. Ibid., pp. 77–78.
5. Redlich, *War, Holocaust and Stalinism*, p. 71.

One of the leaders of the JAC, the poet Itsik Fefer, later recalled that "from the very beginning the Jewish Anti-Fascist Committee kept a running count of the victims. This then served as the basis for *The Black Book*. . . . Lozovsky told us that we should emphasize this because in America . . . people did not believe that fascist atrocities had really taken place. He said that we must definitely talk about that and that we should also talk about how the Soviet Union had saved many Jews."[6]

The idea for the publication of *The Black Book* as a collection of documents about the murder of the Jews in German-occupied Europe—and thus an indictment of fascism—originated with the American Committee of Jewish Writers, Artists, and Scientists, whose honorary chairman was Albert Einstein. This proposal emerged after the Joint Declaration by the Allied Powers Concerning Nazi Crimes against the Jews. (The declaration appeared on the front page of *Pravda* on December 18, 1942.) Fefer stated at the meeting of the JAC Presidium on April 25, 1946, that Einstein, together with the writer Sholem Asch and the journalist B. Z. Goldberg, the son-in-law of Sholem Aleichem, had approached the JAC "in late 1942" with a proposal to start collecting materials on the Germans' destruction of the Jewish population of the USSR. Fefer's claim that "the possibility of publishing a Russian-language edition of *The Black Book* was raised later by Ilya Ehrenburg" is especially pertinent.[7]

The book—or more precisely, the collection of documents, including material supplied from Moscow—was originally intended to be published only in the United States. For a few months this proposal received no answer from the Soviet side. A decisive moment came in the spring and summer of 1943 when Mikhoels and Fefer were in the United States. Lozovsky later maintained that he did not know anything about *The Black Book* before Mikhoels and Fefer left for the United States in the spring.[8] Another member of the JAC, Solomon Bregman, the Deputy People's Commissar of State Control for the RSFSR, tried to dispute the idea that the American side initiated *The Black Book* project. Both Lozovsky and Bregman claimed that it was Mikhoels and Fefer who asked the Americans in the summer of 1943 to send their proposal directly to Soviet officials. The Lozovsky-Bregman interpretation is partially confirmed by the fact that their American partners knew about the collected materials in the hands of the JAC. On the other hand Mikhoels and Fefer probably would not have acted on such a sensitive matter without the approval of the Central Committee and the Sovinformburo.

A letter dated April 23, 1943, over the signature of Mikhoels and JAC executive secretary Shakhno Epshteyn to Shcherbakov confirms that the JAC was already assembling pertinent documents. Their letter quoted the words of the American Committee: "The Soviet Union is the only country that has gathered concrete data

---

6. Rubenstein and Naumov, *Stalin's Secret Pogrom*, pp. 81, 100.
7. Ibid., 178–179.
8. Ibid., 275.

about all the pogroms of the fascists against the Jews. These documents are presently located in the archives of the Jewish Anti-Fascist Committee and other official organizations of the Soviet Union. It is essential that these facts become known to the government of the United States and the governments of all countries fighting against fascism, as well as to the Jews of the entire world. To accomplish this, it is essential that all this valuable material be collected, processed, and published in an official document under the title of *The Jewish Black Book.*"[9]

The JAC letter to Shcherbakov spoke of attracting Jewish organizations in Great Britain and Palestine to join a coordinated project. This likely had been a suggestion of the committee's American partners. Nine members of the JAC were nominated for the editorial board of the publication by the JAC Presidium: Mikhoels, Epshteyn, General Yakov Kreyser, the poets and writers Ilya Ehrenburg, David Bergelson, Itsik Fefer, Peretz Markish, and Leyb Kvitko, along with Academician Lina Shtern.[10] Five of these individuals—Bergelson, Fefer, Markish, Kvitko, and Shtern—were subsequently arrested as part of the crackdown against the JAC in the late 1940s.

But the question of the JAC's participation in the project was decided only while Mikhoels and Fefer were in the United States. The American Committee continued to insist on producing a joint work, evidently in English. Mikhoels and Fefer obtained the necessary clearance after long telephone conversations with Moscow. Lozovsky informed Shcherbakov of this proposal and received a positive reply.[11]

But the first steps to produce *The Black Book* were not easy. Soviet propaganda often obscured the annihilation of Soviet Jews by the Germans, referring to the killing of unnamed "Soviet civilians." The Communist Party leadership used a double standard with regard to the so-called "Jewish Question": inside the country it was to its advantage not to emphasize the Final Solution and the military service of Soviet Jews in order to limit how the Germans could play upon the antisemitic attitudes of the Soviet population. At the same time the need for moral and financial support by Jewish organizations abroad compelled the Kremlin to permit the collection and transmission of material about the Final Solution to the West, as well as information describing the exploits of Jews at the Front and their contribution behind the lines.[12]

It was no accident that on July 27, 1943—while Mikhoels and Fefer were still in the United States—*Eynikayt*, the newspaper of the JAC, appealed to its readers for documentary material on the German massacres of the Jews. In addition, everyone

---

9. Redlich, *War, Holocaust and Stalinism*, p. 347.
10. Ibid., p. 348.
11. Rubenstein and Naumov, *Stalin's Secret Pogrom*, p. 275. As did Bregman, Lozovsky stated that the initiative for the Soviet side to take part came not from the Americans but from Fefer and Mikhoels. Fefer denied this categorically. Ibid., p. 285.
12. For a more thorough discussion of official Kremlin attitudes toward the Final Solution, see Ilya Altman, *Zhertvy nenavisti: kholokost v SSSR, 1941–1945* (Victims of Hatred: The Holocaust in the USSR, 1941–1945) (Moscow, 2002), pp. 373–399.

who worked with the committee and correspondents traveling to regions that had been liberated from occupation also were asked to gather documents and conduct interviews with survivors.[13] To a great extent, the political state of affairs within the country and abroad determined the fate of the Soviet *Black Book*. The JAC leadership did obtain permission to collect materials and to cooperate with the American editors. But the question of an analogous edition of the book in the USSR remained unresolved for more than a year.

It was here that Ilya Ehrenburg played a decisive role. He considered it an issue of fundamental principle to publish inside the Soviet Union a book dedicated to the murder of the country's Jews. But the objectives of the American edition were much broader; material relating to the USSR was to be only one part of this book. Ehrenburg, in the meantime, began the work of preserving the memory of the victims of the Final Solution and the heroes of the resistance independently of this project. As early as 1943, Jews who had miraculously survived and had escaped across the frontlines strove to see Ehrenburg in person and to hand him their notes. In his memoir, *People, Years, Life,* Ehrenburg recalled a diary written by Sara Gleykh of Mariupol. She had made her way over hundreds of kilometers of occupied territory.[14] Another woman, Basya Pikman of Minsk, told the author of these lines how Ehrenburg wept when he met her in the JAC office in Moscow and listened to her story about escaping from the Minsk ghetto and her subsequent sojourn in occupied Smolensk. Other people remember piles of letters in Ehrenburg's apartment from Jews who wanted him to know about their experiences and their suffering.

As things turned out, Ehrenburg was not only the prime mover behind *The Black Book* in Russian and the organizer of its collective authorship; he was also its first editor. He personally wrote thirty-three articles, half of all the literary contributions that went into the final text of the book. Most of the letters, diaries, and memoirs on which future articles were based had been sent directly to Ehrenburg. He also prepared fourteen of the twenty-eight entries in the section devoted to his native Ukraine, and co-authored another one with Raisa Kovnator.

By early 1944 the editors of *Eynikayt* publicly named Ehrenburg as "one of the most active initiators of *The Black Book*."[15] At the beginning of that same year material from the future collection was published in the journal *Znamya* (Banner).[16] In the spring, Ehrenburg passionately condemned antisemitism at a JAC plenum that was held in Moscow's Hall of Columns, one of the capital's largest and most prestigious auditoriums. In the spring of 1944 a Literary Commission of the JAC was established to compile *The Black Book*. Ehrenburg sponsored the commission's creation and was its first

---

13. Rubenstein and Naumov, *Stalin's Secret Pogrom,* p. 106.
14. See Ilya Ehrenburg, *Lyudi, gody, zhizn* (People, Years, Life), vol. 2 (Moscow, 2005), p. 430.
15. *Eynikayt,* January 27, 1944, as cited in Shimon Redlich, *Propaganda and Nationalism in Wartime Russia: The Jewish Anti-Fascist Committee in the USSR, 1941–1948* (Boulder, Colo., 1982), p. 67.
16. *Znamya,* no. 1–2, 1944, pp. 185–196.

chairman. He intended the book to help counteract the effects of Nazi propaganda inside the Soviet Union.

Thus, the JAC organization and the staff and contributors of *Eynikayt* on the one hand, and the Literary Commission under the leadership of Ehrenburg on the other hand, conducted parallel work on both the American and Soviet editions. What was lacking, however, was the required degree of coordination and cooperation. Nor was there any definitive, official decision in favor of compiling a Soviet edition of the book.

On August 23, 1944, Mikhoels and Epshteyn cautiously informed Shcherbakov about the preparation of *The Black Book* in Russian under the guidance of Ehrenburg and Vasily Grossman, and "under the leadership of the JAC," and about the formation of the Literary Commission several months earlier. The formal pretext for the letter was a request for permission to underwrite the work of four technical employees for the organization of the volume. In passing, they also mentioned agreements concluded with their American partners to publish it in French, Spanish, German, and Yiddish in addition to English.[17]

No answer was forthcoming. Evidently, supplementary information had been requested orally. Ehrenburg prepared it. In order to bring the Soviet version of *The Black Book* to life, the Soviet leadership had to recognize the importance of the theme and the enormous authority of Ilya Ehrenburg. On September 6, 1944, Ehrenburg sent a memorandum entitled *The Black Book Project* through proper bureaucratic channels. He did not address this document to a specific individual or office, but meant it to be read by the Central Committee. Ehrenburg may have assumed that the fate of the project would be decided at the highest level—by Stalin himself. At the beginning of his memorandum, Ehrenburg focused on the unique and compelling material he and his colleagues were assembling: "the stories of escaped Jews, witnesses to the atrocities, German orders, diaries and statements of the butchers, notes and diaries of those in hiding. Not declarations, not transcripts, but real-life stories must show the depth of the tragedy."

Ehrenburg also anticipated the concern that the collection would focus too closely on the fate of the Jews. As he put it in his letter, "It is extremely important to show the solidarity of the Soviet population, the rescue of individual Jews by Russians, Belorussians, Ukrainians, and Poles." He also added that it was "essential to show that Jews died bravely, highlighting all the instances of active or passive resistance; the underground organizations of the ghetto; the escapes and uprisings; and the Jewish partisans, who, after escaping death, took vengeance on the murderers of their loved ones." He went on to provide the names of likely contributors, including the Jewish writers Vasily Grossman, Margarita Aliger, and Veniamin Kaverin, as well as popular non-Jewish poets and war correspondents such as

---

17. Redlich, *War, Holocaust and Stalinism*, p. 348.

Konstantin Simonov (he had written about the Final Solution, and his articles on the Majdanek death camp had been published a few weeks before Ehrenburg's letter);[18] the poet Alexander Tvardovsky; and the writers Marietta Shaginyan and Lidia Seyfullina.[19] For various reasons, with the exception of Seyfullina, these non-Jewish figures did not contribute to *The Black Book,* but another well-known Russian writer, Vsevolod Ivanov, later joined. Relying on his own astute judgment, in the memorandum Ehrenburg did not mention working with any foreign organizations.

The Central Committee did not respond directly to Ehrenburg's report. The initiators of the Soviet *Black Book* found themselves in an awkward position. In his speech at the second meeting of the *Black Book* Literary Commission on October 13, 1944, Ehrenburg referred to this confusion: "I did not know for a long time whether or not the publication of this book would be approved. Even now its final status is not clear to me. I was asked to write a report describing the purpose and contents of this book. On the basis of our first meeting, I wrote and presented a report. No direct answer followed, but I was told through the Jewish [Anti-Fascist] Committee: 'Do the book and if it's good it will be published.'"

The regime expected "good" work from the compilers, that is, a book that was needed for propaganda purposes, but with no guarantee that it would be published. This could not but dismay Ehrenburg. "Since the Germans, not we, are the authors of the book, and since the purpose of the book is clear, I don't understand the meaning of: 'if it's good.' This is not a novel whose contents are unknown," he declared at the same meeting on October 13. "It seems to me that inasmuch as we had the chance to put together a manuscript, we should fight to have it printed. The question is becoming more and more important as the German capitulation draws nearer."[20]

Without waiting for an official decision on the fate of the book, Ehrenburg agreed to the JAC's suggestion that some of the materials be published in Yiddish. They appeared in two printings at the end of 1944 and the beginning of 1945 under the title *Merder fun felker* (Murder of Peoples), a title similar to what was used for material that had earlier appeared in the Russian-language *Znamya*. Ehrenburg also used information that reached him in his articles and publications, for both the domestic and the foreign press.

Meanwhile the JAC obtained agreements from the World Jewish Congress (WJC) that each side was to organize the collection and exchange of materials that were intended for later publication in several languages. Also in 1944 an executive committee in charge of publishing *The Black Book* was formed in the United States under the chairmanship of B. Z. Goldberg and Nahum Goldman of the WJC. An international editorial board was created; it included representatives of the Jewish National

---

18. See Konstantin Simonov, "Lager Unichtozheniia" (Extermination Camp), *Krasnaya zvezda,* August 10–12, 1944.
19. For the text of Ehrenburg's memorandum, see Redlich, *War, Holocaust and Stalinism,* p. 248.
20. Ibid., p. 351.

Council of Palestine as well as the JAC (Ehrenburg was not among them) and the WJC, in addition to representatives of the American Committee of Jewish Writers, Artists, and Scientists. The JAC maintained contact with this editorial board through its Literary Commission.

On October 19, 1944, only six days after the meeting of the Literary Commission, Itsik Fefer and Shakhno Epshteyn sent to the United States 552 pages of documentary material that had been gathered in the USSR. Fefer later recounted that this urgent shipment of materials, *which had not been cleared in advance with Ehrenburg,* resulted from a demand by Andrei Gromyko, the Soviet ambassador to the United States. Fefer added that the material had been transmitted via the People's Commissariat of Foreign Affairs. He maintained that "there was a telegram from Gromyko to the effect that *The Black Book* was about to be published in the USA without any material from us." Another member of the JAC, Joseph Yuzefovich, confirmed that Solomon Lozovsky knew the material had been sent.[21]

Ehrenburg was furious. He immediately understood that by sending the material to America, the JAC was undermining its chances of appearing in the Soviet Union, which always had been his intended priority. His ensuing conflict with the JAC leadership moved Lozovsky to form a special commission headed by Solomon Bregman. Dated February 26, the commission's report described how these collections differed from one another and spoke for the first time of "two versions" of *The Black Book*. Conceding the merit of the literary essays compiled under the editorship of Ilya Ehrenburg, the members of the commission nonetheless considered that the "editor-selected path of constructing free literary revisions of documentary and factual documents diverges from the profile of *The Black Book* as a collection of documents whose significance lies in the authenticity of its contents."[22]

Ehrenburg, in fact, is the last person to whom this reproach should be directed. At the October 13, 1944 meeting of the Literary Commission Ehrenburg and Grossman discussed how to work with eyewitness accounts. Grossman called for a generalized approach and insisted that the chief objective of the book was "to speak in the name of people who are lying in the ground and cannot say anything." Ehrenburg, however, believed that the "emotional effect of a human document borders on art." As for his method of working with documents, Ehrenburg observed: "You get a story in a letter, and you retain what the author wanted to say, but you cut it down in length. This is the work that I did on the documents. . . . Your conscience and the need to be selective must tell you that when the document is interesting, keep it. If it is inherently uninteresting, put it aside, look at other documents, then bring them together, perhaps on the territorial principle."[23]

---

21. Rubenstein and Naumov, *Stalin's Secret Pogrom*, p. 90.
22. Redlich, *War, Holocaust and Stalinism*, p. 355.
23. GARF, f. 8114, op. 1, d. 967, from the meeting of the Literary Commission on October 13, 1944.

Bregman's commission saw another substantive "deficiency" in the materials compiled by Ehrenburg: In the stories that appear in the book, "too much is recounted . . . about the vile activity of traitors among the Ukrainians, Lithuanians, and others. This diminishes the force of the main accusation against the Germans, which should be the primary and decisive purpose of the book." [24]

Bregman may have been the first to advance this fundamental criticism of *The Black Book*, one that had a material influence on the selection of eyewitness accounts for the final text as well as on the fate of the project as a whole. The commission recommended, however, after revision and approval "of a single authoritative political editor," that both collections—a literary reworking of accounts and an anthology of documents—be published, at least in part. As for the materials prepared under Ehrenburg's editorial direction, however, still another potential variant was envisioned—the publication of a series of pamphlets, but not a special collection.[25]

These suggestions were conveyed to Ehrenburg on March 5, 1945, with a cover letter from Solomon Lozovsky. In support of the commission's conclusions, Lozovsky emphasized that two books would be better than one, for then "enemies" in Britain and America could not accuse the Soviet side of presenting literary revisions rather than the documents themselves. It is easy to imagine that these documents, as well as Lozovsky's proposal that they continue the work with the promise of publishing the collection "in all the languages of the world," did not persuade Ehrenburg. He demanded clarification of how materials for *The Black Book* were sent to America, insisting that they should have appeared in the USSR first. Ehrenburg's feelings could not be assuaged; he resigned from the leadership of the JAC's Literary Commission as a direct result of this dispute. Moreover, he believed that work on a parallel edition and the idea of editing a series of separate pamphlets could only mean that the work of the Literary Commission would stop altogether. That same month he sent identical letters to each of the writers he had recruited, offering them a free hand to dispose of the materials on which they had worked. Still, he concluded his letter on a hopeful note: "I am deeply convinced that the work that you have accomplished will not be lost to history." [26]

That spring, Ehrenburg came under intense pressure from another source. Georgy Alexandrov, no doubt inspired by Stalin himself, published in *Pravda* a prominent article in which he accused Ehrenburg of "simplifying" the political situation and argued, in response to Ehrenburg's famously harsh rhetorical attacks on Germany and his call for justice, that the Red Army "never intended and would never have as its goal the extermination of the German people." [27] Suddenly, Ehrenburg became the target of attacks from people who would never have dared to criticize him before.

---

24. Redlich, *War, Holocaust and Stalinism*, pp. 355–356.
25. Ibid., p. 357.
26. Ibid., pp. 358–359.
27. *Pravda*, April 14, 1945, p. 2. For a full discussion of the controversy surrounding this article, see Rubenstein, *Tangled Loyalties*, pp. 222–226.

As can be seen from the transcript of the meeting in Lozovsky's office on May 22, 1945, the question of the JAC's relationship with Ehrenburg was a central focus. Ehrenburg's stature seemed to have diminished, at least in the eyes of some of the participants. The head of one department at the Sovinformburo, A. A. Severin, charged Ehrenburg with bringing "forces to life that revealed a centrifugal tendency," while the leaders of the JAC "did not appear able to govern the forces that they had put in motion."[28]

Solomon Bregman directly accused Ilya Ehrenburg of "holding up the materials," and he went on to state the following about Ehrenburg and the Literary Commission that he had headed: "There were a lot of tempests in a teapot in this commission; they quarreled, they swore at each other, and no one knew anything about it. . . . If this had been known, steps could have been taken in time. In my opinion, you lost your nerve. How could that be? Ehrenburg, this great man, is quarreling with us, so we have to give in. We all respect Comrade Ehrenburg, but even he should have been called to order." At the same time Bregman admitted that the material handed over by "Ehrenburg's group" was completely satisfactory and certainly deserved to be sent to the United States. The JAC's conflict with Ehrenburg had reached a fever pitch; joint work was out of the question.[29]

Later that spring, a new *Black Book* editorial board was formed, consisting of JAC members Mikhail Borodin (chairman), A. A. Severin, Solomon Bregman, Vasily Grossman, Shakhno Epshteyn, Joseph Yuzefovich, and Alexander Troyanovsky.[30] Ehrenburg was left off this editorial board. Only Grossman had earlier connections with the preparation of *The Black Book*. He was directly responsible for continuing all the organizational work, collecting further material, and preparing the manuscript for publication. Bregman later emphasized that JAC documents directly "stated that individual Ukrainians and Belorussians participated with the Germans in annihilating the Jews, whereas Grossman's material emphasized the opposite, that no small number of incidents were cited of Ukrainian and Belorussian citizens saving and hiding Jews."[31]

---

28. See transcript of May 22, 1945 meeting. GARF, f. 8581, op. 1, d. 1161, ll. 2–3.
29. See Bregman's letter of May 13, 1945. Ibid., l. 8.
30. Mikhail Borodin (Grunzenberg) (1884–1951) was a Soviet diplomat, secret agent, and editor. He had been a member of the Bund before joining the Bolsheviks in 1903. He lived in the United States from 1907 to 1918. After the Revolution, he became an important figure in the People's Commissariat of Foreign Affairs, later serving as ambassador to Mexico and then, from 1923 to 1927, as Soviet adviser to the Guomindang in China. He was chief editor at the Sovinformburo from 1941 to 1949. Arrested in 1949, he died in prison in 1951. A. A. Severin headed a department at the Sovinformburo. Joseph Yuzefovich (Shpinak) (1890–1952) was born in Warsaw and was a member of the Bund from 1905 to 1917. After the Revolution, he worked closely with Solomon Lozovsky in the official trade union movement. Yuzefovich was a member of the JAC and was among the defendants at the trial in 1952. Alexander Troyanovsky (1882–1955) was a veteran Soviet diplomat; he served in Japan and worked at the Soviet embassy in Washington, D.C., in the 1930s.
31. Rubenstein and Naumov, *Stalin's Secret Pogrom*, p. 319.

This served as the basis for a thorough editing of parts of the text that were already prepared, and the selection of new materials for the book. The decision was made to supplement the volume with documents from the Extraordinary State Commission, a process that prolonged preparation of the manuscript.[32] It was also proposed to print two supplementary articles: an introductory political article (Solomon Lozovsky was asked to write it, but in the end Vasily Grossman wrote the introduction) and a "final juridical" article projected as a kind of closing statement based on the materials in *The Black Book*. (At the request of the editorial board, this article was written by Academician Ilya Trainin, a member of the JAC.)

It was in the summer of 1945 that the idea of preparing two versions of *The Black Book* was abandoned. The participants decided to add short clarifications concerning the origin of the materials and their authenticity. Early in 1946 the manuscript, supplemented and edited in conformity with necessary corrections, was reprinted and circulated to Australia, Great Britain, Bulgaria, Hungary, Italy, Mexico, France, Poland, Romania, the United States, and Czechoslovakia, as well as to Palestine. Another set of the documents also went to Soviet prosecutors at Nuremberg.

At the end of 1945 and early in 1946 the Literary Commission (now under the leadership of Vasily Grossman) stepped up its work, sending to several dozen correspondents a letter that asked them to submit documents touching on the Final Solution. As Grossman explained, materials soon began to arrive, including "over 200 eyewitness testimonies by people of different occupations and in various age brackets."[33]

Meanwhile, the problems surrounding the publication of the American version of *The Black Book* found resolution in Moscow over the winter of 1945–1946. After several months of waiting—B. Z. Goldberg sent numerous telegrams to Moscow insisting on knowing if the JAC had any problems with the manuscript—the Americans learned of the JAC's objections on January 23, 1946; these focused on the proposed

---

32. On November 2, 1942, the Kremlin created the Extraordinary State Commission for the Investigation of Atrocities Committed on Soviet Territory by the German Fascists and Their Accomplices. Known by its Russian initials, ChGK, the commission collected a massive amount of information based on interviews with survivors, eyewitnesses, and even perpetrators. Some of this evidence was used during the thousands of trials that were held by Soviet officials; some evidence was also submitted at Nuremberg. See a recent study of the ChGK in Marina Sorokina, "People and Procedures: Toward a History of the Investigation of Nazi Crimes in the USSR," *Kritika* (new series) 6, no. 4 (fall 2005), pp. 797–831. One particular criticism of its reports substantiates the ambivalent attitude of the regime toward the Final Solution: the initial interviews and documents from the field explicitly mentioned Jewish victims, but as the reports were edited and moved up the bureaucratic chain, the terminology was changed to "Soviet civilians," in effect camouflaging the fundamental nature of the Final Solution.

33. See transcript of the meeting of the JAC Presidium of April 25, 1946. GARF, f. 8114, op. 1, d. 967, l. 13. See Ilya Altman, "Toward the History of *The Black Book*," in *Yad Vashem Studies* 21 (Jerusalem, 1999), pp. 240–249.

foreword by Albert Einstein. As Lozovsky explained during the trial of fifteen JAC members in court in 1952, "The book contained a foreword by Einstein in which our commission discovered Zionistic tendencies and a number of issues about the history of the Jewish people, starting from the destruction of Jerusalem. This material had nothing to do with combating fascism."[34] Einstein agreed to withdraw his piece; the American *Black Book* could now proceed, and it appeared in English in 1946 (*The Black Book: The Nazi Crime Against the Jewish People,* New York, 1946. The volume includes 59 sections based on Soviet sources). Only a handful of JAC documents appeared in it. By 1952, however, the very participation of the JAC in the preparation of this joint edition was an important part of the indictment against Lozovsky, Fefer, and the others. As the court would conclude:

> A glaring example of the collusion in terms of nationalist activity between the JAC leaders and the Jewish nationalists of the United States is the publication in 1946 of the so-called *Black Book,* which was accomplished by the JAC with Lozovsky's concurrence in league with Jewish nationalists in the United States and Palestine. In this book the Jews set themselves apart in a separate category, in opposition to other peoples. The contribution of Jews to world civilization is exaggerated, and attention is focused exclusively on the sacrifices borne by the Jews in World War II; the thought is dragged in that fascism presented a threat to the Jews alone and not to all peoples and to world civilization.[35]

Even in 1946, the JAC's participation had an ambivalent quality. The committee received ten copies of the book from the United States for distribution to members of the editorial board. But Boris Shimelyovich asserted in court in 1952 that he not only had not received his copy, he had "learned only a few days ago" that the book in fact had been produced. Leyb Kvitko rebuked Fefer directly for not informing the members of the presidium that the JAC supported the idea of the publication and that the book had been published in the United States. Fefer, however, observed that "this question had been discussed in the presidium. The publication of the [American] *Black Book* was not a secret; ten thousand readers of *Eynikayt* knew about it." He reminded Kvitko that he had been collecting materials in the Crimea for the project. Kvitko answered that he had collected them for the Soviet edition, failing to foresee that the material would be sent to America.[36]

The complicated process of obtaining bureaucratic clearances to contribute to the American version of *The Black Book* did not put the JAC leadership on its guard. It appeared to them that the committee's manuscript was also close to publication, an impression shared by all participants in the discussion of *The Black Book* at the JAC

---

34. Rubenstein and Naumov, *Stalin's Secret Pogrom*, p. 276.
35. Ibid., p. 487.
36. Ibid., pp. 102, 105, 178.

meeting on April 25, 1946. Already there were galley proofs prepared for most of the book. The creative and financial work on the book was detailed. Even the continued collection of information for future volumes was recommended. Solomon Mikhoels, the chairman of the JAC, called *The Black Book* a memorial to the dead and to all Jews who had miraculously survived, along with their rescuers. Indeed, he brought up the question of publishing it in Yiddish.[37]

However, these hopes were not destined to bear fruit. In the summer and fall of 1946 work on publication of *The Black Book* in Moscow came to a virtual halt. Nevertheless, in reply to Kvitko's question at a meeting of the JAC on November 16, 1946, Mikhoels optimistically answered: "*The Black Book* will come off the presses soon."[38] It seemed that there were no problems (at least not technical ones). But only twelve days later, the initiators of the edition appealed to the country's chief ideologue, member of the Politburo and Secretary of the Central Committee of the Communist Party Andrei Zhdanov, "with a fervent plea to help speed up publication of *The Black Book*."[39] Ehrenburg was one of the signatories of this letter on behalf of the JAC Presidium, together with Mikhoels, Fefer, and Grossman. Ehrenburg and Grossman signed as editors of *The Black Book*; even after leaving the Literary Commission, Ehrenburg remained committed to the fate of his offspring.

With their letter, they were hoping to learn the status of *The Black Book*. The Department of Agitation and Propaganda, though, to which the letter was forwarded, insisted on seeing the full text of the manuscript. Comments by the head of the department, Georgy Alexandrov, delivered to Zhdanov on February 3, 1947, categorically affirmed that it would be "inexpedient" to publish *The Black Book*. Alexandrov's arguments were curious. First, he blamed the JAC for circulating the text of the manuscript to various countries around the world without the knowledge of the department. He particularly emphasized that the manuscript had been "sent" to the United States and "published" there, which was a gross misrepresentation, since only a fragment of the manuscript had appeared. But at the start of the Cold War, any connection with America already looked criminal. These arguments were to be lodged against the JAC leadership during the interrogations leading to the JAC trial in 1952, where *The Black Book* occupied a significant place.

Alexandrov, moreover, claimed that *The Black Book* provided "a false picture of the true nature of fascism" because it created the impression that "the Germans fought against the USSR for the sole purpose of destroying the Jews." Referring to cases in the book in which Jews escaped death by pretending to be Russians, Alexandrov came to the paradoxical conclusion that *The Black Book* falsified history: the misdeeds of

---

37. Redlich, *War, Holocaust and Stalinism*, p. 363.
38. Cited in Vadim Dubson, "Rukopisi ne goriat" (Manuscripts do not burn), V*estnik evreiskoi sovetskoi kultury* (Bulletin of Jewish Soviet Culture) 11 (September 13, 1989), p. 4.
39. Redlich, *War, Holocaust and Stalinism*, p. 365.

the Nazis against the people of other nationalities were not shown. "Hitler's ruthless slaughters were carried out equally against Russians, Jews, Belorussians, Ukrainians, Latvians, Lithuanians, and other peoples of the Soviet Union," he concluded. His commentary ended with the statement, "the Propaganda Department considers the publication of *The Black Book* to be inexpedient."[40]

Nevertheless the JAC leadership kept on searching for ways to print the manuscript, determined to overcome bureaucratic and ideological hurdles. They placed an order for publication with the press of the Higher Party School of the Central Committee in July 1947, for a total printing of thirty thousand copies. Evidently no official prohibition against publishing the book had come from Zhdanov, and the galley proofs (later kept in the personal archives of Ehrenburg's daughter Irina) were stamped "To the Printer" with the date of July 14, 1947. But a comparison of the galleys with the manuscript as prepared in 1946 reflects new editorial changes in the spirit of Alexandrov's instructions.

We know about the subsequent fate of the book from Mikhoels's second letter to Zhdanov on September 18, 1947. Mikhoels reported that "having obtained the appropriate instruction of the Propaganda Department and the approval of Glavlit," the JAC began to print *The Black Book*. On August 20, 1947, however, after thirty-three sheets of print had been produced, "an order came down from Glavlit" to stop work.[41] (It is unclear why Glavlit and the Propaganda Department seem to have approved publication and then quickly reversed their decision.)

In his letter Mikhoels argued that the book had not lost its urgency and warned of the rebirth of fascism. However, the fate of the book was already determined. A new group of Party bureaucrats had "worked it over"—among them Mikhail Suslov,[42] Alexandrov's replacement, to whom Zhdanov had forwarded Mikhoels's letter, and Dmitri Shepilov,[43] who on Suslov's instructions was to examine the petition of the JAC leaders.

An "expert" evaluation of the manuscript was quickly prepared by M. Morozov, the chief of the publications branch of the Department of Agitation and Propaganda. Dated October 7, 1947, it read: "*The Black Book* has been meticulously examined in the Propaganda Department. The book contains serious political errors. Publication

---

40. Ibid., pp. 365–366.
41. Ibid., p. 367. Glavlit is the Russian acronym for Glavnoe upravlenie po delam literatury i izdatelstv (Main Administration for Literary and Publishing Affairs); this was, in effect, the offices of the Soviet censorship. Official censorship itself was long denied.
42. Mikhail Suslov (1902–1980) was a veteran Party official who was famous for his strict approach to ideological questions. He became head of the Foreign Relations Department of the Central Committee in 1946 and then was appointed to lead the Department of Agitation and Propaganda the following year. He later became a member of the Politburo.
43. Dmitri Shepilov (1905–1995) was a veteran Party official. He was an editor at *Pravda* in 1946–1947, and became editor-in-chief in 1952. Between 1947 and 1952, he was a leading figure in the Department of Agitation and Propaganda.

of the book in 1947 is not approved by the Propaganda Department. Accordingly, *The Black Book* cannot be published."[44]

On November 15, 1947, the press suggested that the JAC take back the galley proofs.[45] Less than two months later, Solomon Mikhoels was killed in Minsk on Stalin's personal orders; his death was blamed on a traffic accident. Mikhoels had become too visible and outspoken a supporter of an independent Jewish state in Palestine. The murder was a precursor to the crackdown on the JAC and Yiddish culture that would accelerate in the fall of 1948. With Mikhoels gone, Itsik Fefer undertook a final, highly peculiar attempt to obtain permission to publish *The Black Book*. On February 13, 1948, he sent a letter marked "secret" to the Propaganda Department of the Central Committee with the following proposals: permit the printer to finish printing the final portions of the manuscript and then distribute 150–200 copies of *The Black Book* to an officially approved list of libraries and anti-fascist committees, and to the Extraordinary State Commission to be kept in their "special collections."[46] Fefer's letter exemplifies the dramatic fate not merely of *The Black Book* but of the JAC in its entirety: from the original idea of publishing the book in several languages to a timid request for a tiny printing for "special collections" that would be closed to the public.

The JAC archives do not contain a response to this letter. The end of the JAC itself was fast approaching. On November 20, 1948, the committee was officially closed. By the end of the year, the secret police began to arrest its leaders and staff members, including many who had been involved with *The Black Book*. The JAC case lasted from 1948 to 1952 and culminated in the execution of thirteen defendants in the case, including former deputy foreign minister Solomon Lozovsky and five Yiddish writers and poets: David Bergelson, Itsik Fefer, David Hofshteyn, Leyb Kvitko, and Peretz Markish. (These may have been the last executions of political prisoners during the Stalin years.) The court highlighted involvement in the *Black Book* project as material evidence of "bourgeois nationalism" on the part of the defendants, "a vivid example of how the leaders of the Jewish Anti-Fascist Committee joined ranks with Jewish nationalists in the United States in their nationalistic activity."[47]

Although connected with *The Black Book,* neither Grossman nor Ehrenburg was arrested. Ehrenburg may have been saved because he had openly protested against sending the manuscript to the United States and then resigned from the committee. But at the peak of the investigation Ehrenburg was included (together with Vasily Grossman and other well-known writers and public figures) in an extensive list of people against whom material for a public campaign of defamation was being gath-

---

44. Redlich, *War, Holocaust and Stalinism,* p. 368.
45. Ibid., p. 369.
46. Ibid., p. 370.
47. Rubenstein and Naumov, *Stalin's Secret Pogrom,* p. 487.

ered. Luckily, Stalin was not ready at that moment to destroy the entire flower of the assimilated Soviet Jewish intelligentsia.

At the close of the JAC trial, the presiding judge used the word "nationalism" to signify speaking in the name of a particular people and emphasizing its exclusive nature. During the proceedings, many defendants exposed the absurdity of accusing Jews of "bourgeois nationalism" because they had emphasized the mass murder of the Jews by the Germans. Lozovsky said,

> Let us say that this is nationalism, then I ask the court to take the following circumstances into account: Did the Nuremberg trials take place under my supervision? No, there were six prosecutors who spoke at the Nuremberg trials, and the main one was Rudenko. . . . After Rudenko and four other prosecutors had spoken, prosecutor Sheynin spoke, and he talked about the Hitlerites' atrocities against the Jews. What, was this a nationalistic speech? The writer Sutzkever was flown over there. He, too, spoke about atrocities committed against the Jews. Why did the Soviet government arrange such speeches? Was this really nationalism?

Lozovsky later told the judges that he considered the American edition of *The Black Book* especially important for the prosecution at the Nuremberg trial, where it "really did play a big role" and, "from that standpoint, *The Black Book* was useful for the Soviet Union." At the same time Lozovsky agreed with the banning of the book in the USSR "because Soviet people did not need such a book. In our country all peoples endured suffering from the Hitlerites' invasion."[48]

Fefer as well, in spite of the fact that he turned state's witness at the outset of the trial as part of the court's effort to intimidate the other defendants, still spoke up about Jewish suffering, as this dramatic exchange revealed:

> **Presiding Officer:** You still keep on spreading the exceptionally nationalistic idea that the Jews suffered more than anyone, don't you?
> **Fefer:** Yes, I feel that the suffering of the Jewish people has been exceptionally great.
> **Presiding Officer:** Were the Jews really the only ones to suffer during the Great Patriotic War?
> **Fefer:** Yes, you will not find another people that has suffered as much as the Jewish people. Six million Jews were destroyed out of a total of eighteen million—one-third. This was a great sacrifice. We had a right to our tears, and we fought against fascism.
> **Presiding Officer:** But you did not simply weep over this. You used it as anti-Soviet activity. The committee became a center for nationalistic struggle.[49]

---

48. Ibid., pp. 248–249, 276–277.
49. Ibid., pp. 93–94.

The Russian manuscript of *The Black Book* survived in a form somewhat different from that in which it was distributed in eleven countries around the world. All the materials on which it was based (twenty-seven volumes comprising 6,211 pages) were carefully stored at the Ministry of State Security and were later transferred to a closed government archive. The archived documents contain typewritten pages of the text of *The Black Book* prepared in the summer of 1945. All the places that gave rise to objections in the proofreading of the book before its text was printed early in 1946 were crossed out with a red or blue pencil. These usually were references to the assistance provided by the local population to the Germans and to other manifestations of antisemitism. The editing of the manuscript went through a second stage in late 1946 and early 1947. It is curious that wherever the term "*zhid*" (or kike) appeared—a word that came naturally to the lips of an antisemite—it was replaced by "Jew."

The Soviet *Black Book* did not appear during the lifetimes of its editors or principal authors—Ilya Ehrenburg and Vasily Grossman. Ehrenburg kept the original letters addressed to him in two special albums. He donated them to the State Jewish Museum of Lithuania in Vilnius on the condition that they would be returned to him should the museum be closed. Ehrenburg's request proved to be prescient: soon after the closing of the JAC, the museum was also shut down, and it required substantial effort on Ehrenburg's part to get his documents back. They are now kept in the archives of Yad Vashem because his daughter, Irina Ehrenburg, in accordance with her father's wishes, arranged for them to be discreetly sent there in 1985, "at a time when to do such a thing was still relatively dangerous."[50]

In the mid-1960s Ehrenburg himself made several attempts to publish the book by approaching the Novosti Press Agency, but still there was no hope for publication in the USSR. In 1980, Yad Vashem finally published the Russian text of *The Black Book* that had arrived in Palestine as early as 1946, but without the section on Lithuania. The edition mentioned that it had been "compiled under the editorial direction of Vasily Grossman and Ilya Ehrenburg." A more complete variant of the book appeared in Yiddish in Jerusalem in 1981. Also, 1981 saw publication of *The Black Book* in English in the United States as part of the Holocaust Library series.

---

50. *Sovietskie yevrei pishut Ilye Ehrenburgu 1943–1966* (Soviet Jews Write to Ilya Ehrenburg) (Jerusalem, 1993), p. 107, from the contribution by Shmuel Krakowski of Yad Vashem. Irina Ehrenburg (1911–1997), the only child of Ilya Ehrenburg, was born in Nice; her mother was a Russian émigré named Yekaterina Shmidt, who later took her to Moscow. Irina Ilinichna received her secondary and college-level education in France after her father formally adopted her and brought her to Paris in 1924. After returning to live in Moscow in 1933, she worked as a translator and journalist. During World War II, she was assigned to a frontline army newspaper, which was eventually closed because it had too many Jewish staff members. Her husband, Boris Lapin, was a talented writer and journalist assigned to *Krasnaya zvezda* (Red Star); he disappeared at the Front near Kiev in the opening months of the war. Irina Ehrenburg helped to publish many of her father's works before and during the Gorbachev era, and was particularly devoted to *The Black Book* and her father's efforts to document the Final Solution on German-occupied Soviet territory.

The existence of *The Black Book* became more generally known in the Soviet Union in the 1960s with the publication of Ehrenburg's controversial memoir, *People, Years, Life*.[51] Until then, only a narrow circle of people knew about the idea of publishing during the war a book of documentary articles by leading writers of the country, exposing the tragedy of Soviet Jews. Ehrenburg stated mournfully in his memoir that *The Black Book*, though completely ready for publication, had been banned in the late 1940s and its type broken up.

In the late 1980s, during the period of reform (or perestroika) directed by Mikhail Gorbachev, I was working at the Central State Archive of the October Revolution of the USSR (now the State Archive of the Russian Federation, known as GARF). Archivists and scholars were just beginning to explore collections located in secret or semi-secret storage. My eyes chanced to fall on an inventory of material connected to the Jewish Anti-Fascist Committee. A section bearing the title *The Black Book* immediately caught my attention. This collection had come to the archive from the Soviet KGB after the rehabilitation of the condemned defendants in the JAC case in 1955. The authors and editors had used only a portion of the collection's eyewitness accounts, letters, and diaries in the preparation of *The Black Book*.

This very collection allowed us to make selections and carry through preparations for the first complete Russian-language edition of *The Black Book*, which was published in Lithuania in 1993 with inserted material printed in a special script to show where Soviet censors had earlier made deletions. Translations of this edition were republished in Germany (1995), Italy (1999), and the United States (2002). It includes almost sixty printed pages that were deleted from the text of the manuscript of *The Black Book* in 1945–1947 by various editors and censors.[52]

In Moscow in 1993, Tekst Publishers issued a collection named *The Unknown Black Book*, prepared by GARF and Yad Vashem.[53] It contained documentary materials that the editors of *The Black Book* had rejected for censorship reasons when they were selecting testimonies for the volume. They are being published in English for the first time in this volume. The present book contains ninety-three documents,

---

51. Ehrenburg's chapter about *The Black Book* was excluded from the original publication of the memoir in *Novy mir*; it only appeared in censored form when his *Collected Works* were published in nine volumes in 1966–1967; see *Sobranie sochinenii*, vol. 9 (Moscow, 1967), pp. 411–418. The full text was published in the first posthumous edition of the memoirs in 1990; see *Lyudi, gody, zhizn* (People, Years, Life), vol. 3 (Moscow, 1990), pp. 351–359.
52. *Chornaya kniga* (The Black Book) (Vilnius, 1993). This edition was initiated by Irina Ehrenburg. She produced it on the basis of a 1947 galley-proof kept in a personal archive. It was in this form that *The Black Book* was published in Paris in French in 1996, and it included a foreword I had written to the 1993 Russian-language edition and the text of Irina Ehrenburg's introduction. Unfortunately, the forewords to the American edition contain several factual inaccuracies, and the history of the preparation of the complete edition of the text is also incorrectly set forth.
53. *Neizvestnaya chornaya kniga* (The Unknown Black Book), compiled by Ilya Altman and Shmuel Krakowski and edited by Yitzhak Arad and Tatyana Pavlova (Moscow and Jerusalem, 1993).

including forty records of eyewitness accounts written by twenty-seven authors. Among them are Soviet officers such as Major Z. Ostrovsky, whose materials came to the JAC from Ukraine and Lithuania; teachers (Kruglyak in Ukraine and A. Yerusalimsky, a former secretary of a Judenrat in Shaulyay, Lithuania); correspondents of *Eynikayt* such as Miriam Zheleznova; and the writer Dmitry Stonov, who was attached to the Sovinformburo. An especially large number of items were produced by the poet Matvey Grubian and the frontline correspondent Savva Golovanivsky, who were both Jewish. The American foreign correspondent R. A. Davis also contributed. The materials prepared by the writers Vladimir Lidin and Leyb Kvitko are of special interest. Lazar Lagin, who had written a popular book for Soviet youngsters, *Starik Khottabych* (Old Man Khottabych), also wrote one of the contributions, based on his experiences as a war correspondent in the Crimea.

Twenty-one of the documents consist of accounts by survivors. Lev Rozhetsky contributed poems. A few people sent their reports to Ehrenburg in somewhat fictional style, affirming both the authenticity of their work and uncertainty about their own literary abilities. One of the apparent motives for sending these materials to the JAC or to the editors of *The Black Book* was the hope that they would be published.

Sixteen letters are included in the book (for the most part addressed to Ehrenburg). Four of these were written by witnesses to events that engulfed their relatives. There are also four diaries from people who were living in Ukraine, Latvia, and Lithuania, along with notes jotted down before the writer's death at the hands of the Germans. Five documents were selected from materials compiled by the Extraordinary State Commission, including statements by German soldiers and officers. The report by the Kantarovich sisters about the Odessa underground, along with a letter addressed to Solomon Mikhoels, are especially compelling.

In the sixteen years following my initial publications about *The Black Book*, I had the opportunity to meet with a number of the heroes of this edition and with their relatives, and to discover additional documents about what had befallen them. The following are some of my most vivid encounters.

In her memoirs, Ida Belozovskaya of Kiev (her husband and his parents were awarded the title Righteous among the Nations by Yad Vashem) speaks about the children of her sisters, whom none of her husband's friends had agreed to hide and who were killed. In a Moscow Jewish school run by ORT,[54] I was able to find a photograph of these two boys. I also came to know the father of Stepan Shenfeld, a former inmate of the Yanovsky camp in Lvov. In his account, he does not mention that he and his father went into hiding with fake documents, first in Zaporozhe and then in Warsaw. Soviet troops liberated them in Kharkov. Military counterintelligence units

---

54. Founded in Russia in 1880, ORT is an abbreviation of three Russian words meaning "Society for Rehabilitation and Training." It is an international organization promoting skilled trades and agricultural development work among Jews.

planned on smuggling them back into Warsaw before it was liberated. But Stepan left for the Front and was killed. His father later emigrated to Canada and died in Toronto at the age of 101 after writing his memoirs.

The report of the Kantarovich sisters in the Odessa underground refers to a counterfeit Romanian seal (for "authenticating" documents) that Lyusya Kalika devised and then concealed in the basement of their apartment building. She was eighteen years old at the time, and she stayed in hiding for 820 days. After the war she wrote a memoir in the form of a diary. She worked as a doctor in Odessa for many years, and she now lives in Israel. Another account concerns the partisan Raisa Dudnik, concluding with her trying to locate her little sister, Khaya; that was in 1944. Khaya (Valentina) Dudnik currently lives in Novosibirsk Oblast. We became personally acquainted after she wrote to the Holocaust Center in Moscow proposing the establishment of a Memorial Day for Victims of the Holocaust in Russia on January 27, the day that Red Army troops liberated Auschwitz in 1945.

After a lecture I gave in Saint Paul, Minnesota, I met the brother of David Rozenfeld, whose fate is described in this book. Nadezhda Tereshchenko hid David after he had been released by the Germans, who did not realize he was a Jew. This was near Kirovograd in Ukraine. After the Red Army liberated their town, David went to the Front and was soon killed. Nadezhda, who was his common-law wife, later moved to the village where he had fallen. She never married again, and tended his grave for the rest of her life.

In 1994 I met Sara Gleykh when she was a featured speaker at one of the first Holocaust memorial meetings in Russia. Sara is referred to as a college student in the text of *The Black Book* and in Ehrenburg's memoirs. In reality, Sara never went on to higher education; she worked as a draftsman. It was a privilege to speak with her.

These were all unexpected encounters. None of the heroes in *The Black Book* whom I have mentioned here had heard of it or had known about the publication of *The Unknown Black Book* before I was able to inform them.

Note on Translation

The Unknown Black Book was first published jointly by Yad Vashem in Jerusalem and the State Archive of the Russian Federation (GARF) in 1993. Its editorial board included Ilya Altman (compiler), Yitzhak Arad (editor-in-chief), Tatyana Pavlova (editor-in-chief), Aron Vays, the late Boris Kaptelov, Shmuel Krakowski (compiler), and Shmuel Spector.

For the present volume, Christopher Morris and Joshua Rubenstein translated the Russian documents into English.

In the footnotes accompanying the documents, the reader will also come across references to *The Complete Black Book of Russian Jewry* by Ilya Ehrenburg and Vasily Grossman. This is the most recent English-language edition of *The Black Book;* it was translated and edited by David Patterson and published by Transaction Publishers in 2002. There are also references to Ilya Ehrenburg's archive consisting of two volumes of material which are currently held at Yad Vashem in Jerusalem.

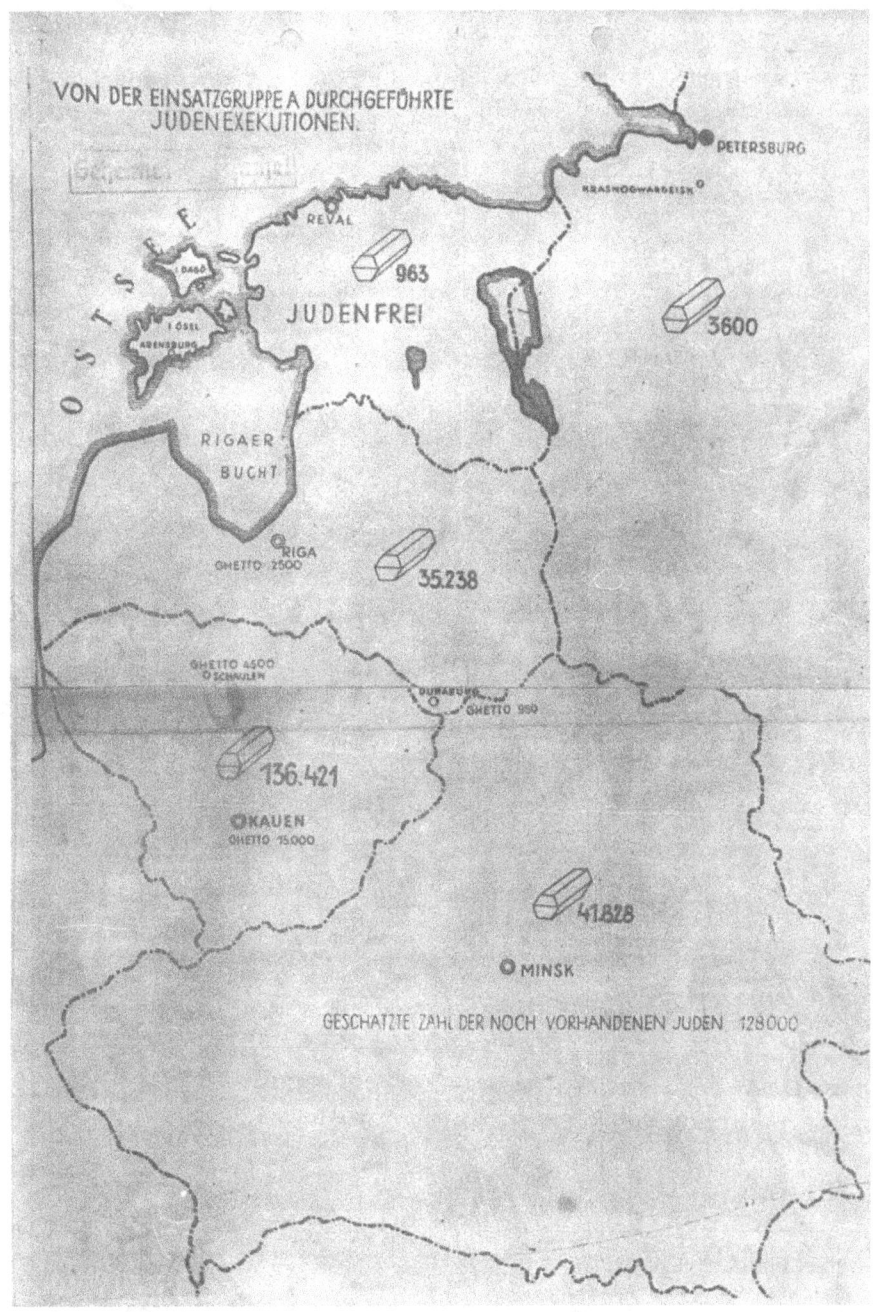

Entitled "Jewish Executions Carried Out by Einsatzgruppe A" and stamped "Secret Reich Matter," this map accompanied a secret, undated report on the mass murder of Jews submitted by Franz Stahlecker, the commander of Einsatzgruppe A. Symbolizing the victims by coffins, the map shows the number of Jews executed in the Baltic states, Russia, and Belorussia by late 1941. The legend near the bottom indicates that "the estimated number of Jews still on hand [was] 128,000." The document was used as evidence by both the American and British prosecution teams during the International Military Tribunal war crimes trial at Nuremberg. USHMM, courtesy of National Archives and Records Administration, College Park.

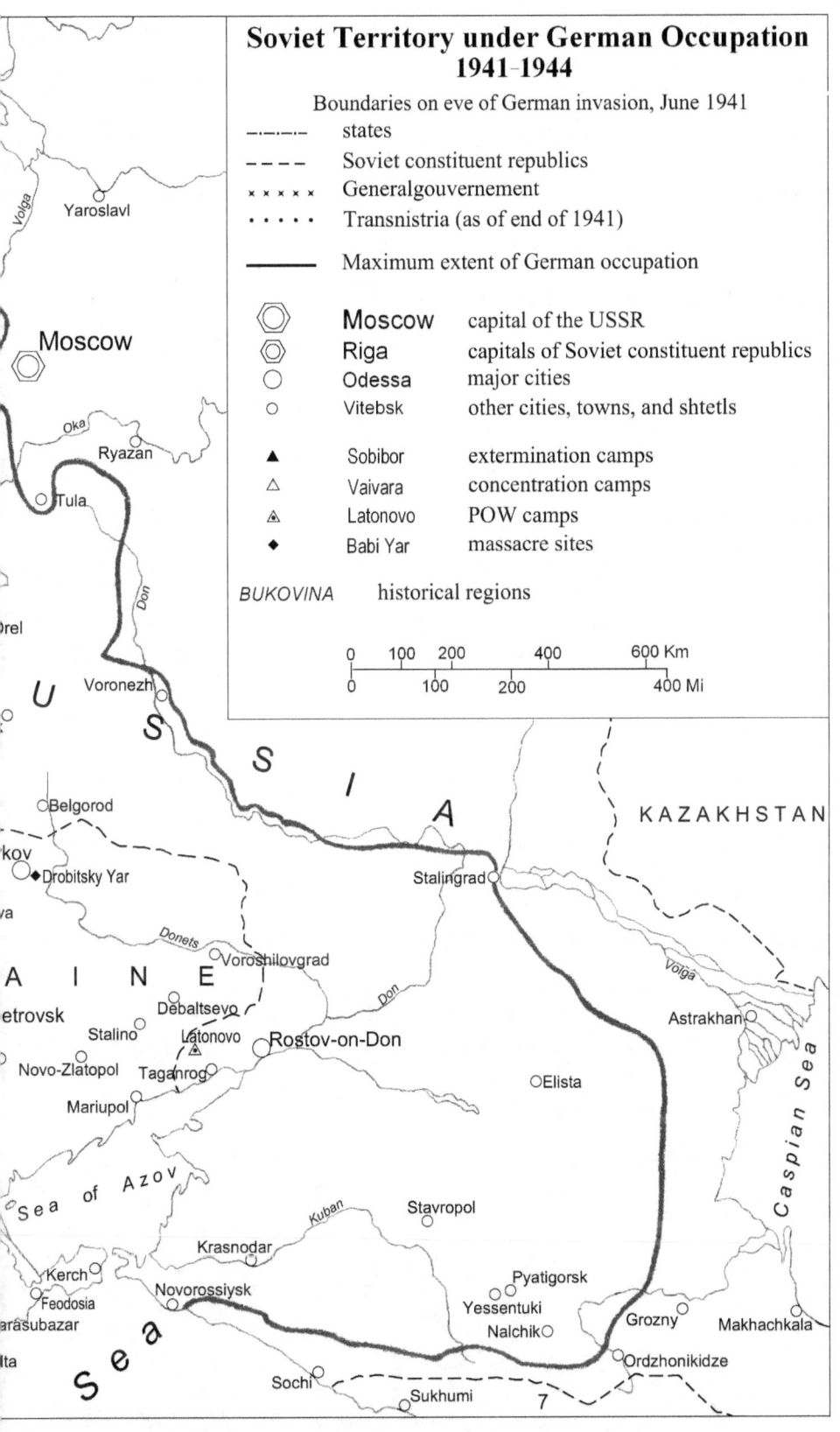

THE UNKNOWN BLACK BOOK

The War and the Final Solution on the Russian Front

Joshua Rubenstein

The terrible images associated with Adolf Hitler and the Nazis are engraved in our collective memory. Once that regime came to power in Germany, each of its crimes created the momentum for a more destructive act of cruelty. From the burning of books in 1933 to the Nuremberg laws of 1935, from Kristallnacht in 1938 to the creation of the Warsaw ghetto in 1940, the murder of as many as six million Jews appears to have been an inevitable consequence of Nazi racial hatred. In the initial months of the German occupation of Soviet territory—between June and December of 1941—the Germans murdered nearly a million Jews.[1] It was here, before a single Jew was killed in the gas chambers of Treblinka, that the Nazis first manifested the breadth of their murderous intentions.

Adolf Hitler, Heinrich Himmler, and Reinhard Heydrich—the principal architects of the Final Solution—may not have grasped the full logic of their hatred until military victories gave them opportunities to realize their vision of a Europe rid of Jews. Between 1939 and 1941—when the Wehrmacht invaded Poland, and then targeted Western Europe and the Balkans—the Nazi dictator was still planning to "cleanse" Europe by expelling the Jews to Madagascar or some other far-off location. After the invasion of Poland, there were plans to create a kind of reservation for the Jews in the Lublin region of southeastern Poland. But this idea was soon put aside. More ominously, the Germans began to single out Jews for humiliating persecution,

---

1. Jurgen Matthäus estimates that between 500,000 and 800,000 were murdered by the end of 1941— "on average 2,700 to 4,200 per day." See Christopher R. Browning, with contributions by Jürgen Matthäus, *The Origins of the Final Solution: The Evolution of Nazi Jewish Policy, September 1939–March 1942* (Lincoln, Neb., and Jerusalem, 2004), p. 244.

expulsion from their homes, and random murder. Still, the Germans began to push Jews over the demarcation line into Eastern Poland, which was occupied by Soviet troops, or to compel them to live in sealed-off urban districts—ghettos—where their labor could be exploited while their numbers were severely reduced through starvation and disease.

One of the first ghettos was established in the spring of 1940 in Lodz, the second largest city in Poland, and over the four years of its existence came to house more than 200,000 Jews; there was not even a sewer system to connect it to the outside world. Hermetically closed off, the Jews were forced to work, subjected to random shooting, starvation, and disease. In Warsaw, too, after several months of construction, a ghetto was officially established in fall 1940, enclosed behind high walls. At one point, the population of the ghetto reached 400,000. As in Lodz, thousands of Jews succumbed to starvation and disease. But as awful as life was in the ghettos of Eastern Europe, the Nazis had yet to embark on their plan of systematic mass murder.

By spring 1940, the Germans found themselves in control of 4,000,000 Jews, far more than the mere 550,000 who had been living in Germany on the eve of Hitler's coming to power. At this point the Nazi leadership was apparently still considering shipping them to the island of Madagascar, a French colony off the eastern coast of Africa, a kind of "territorial Final Solution."[2] With the defeat of France in June 1940, the Germans assumed they would gain control of its colonial empire. And with the (presumably) impending defeat of Great Britain, Hitler expected to have its merchant marine at his disposal, which would make it possible to transport so many people to such a remote location.

Hitler confided his plan to Mussolini in June 1940, and a month later the Germans even halted work on the Warsaw ghetto because, in the words of one German official, "according to the plan of the Führer, the Jews of Europe were to be sent to Madagascar at the end of the war and thus ghetto building was for all practical purposes illusory."[3] Britain's unexpected and effective resistance, however, rendered shipping Jews to the Indian Ocean impractical.[4]

It was not until Hitler initiated the planning of Operation Barbarossa, the invasion of the Soviet Union, that the Nazis finally abandoned the idea of making Europe *judenfrei* (free of Jews) through expulsion. On the eve of invading the Soviet Union, where Bolshevik ideology and a Jewish population numbering over five million people (after Germany and the Soviet Union's division of Europe into "spheres of

---

2. Ibid., p. 83, where Browning cites a phrase attributed to Reinhard Heydrich.
3. Christopher R. Browning, "The Madagascar Plan," *The Holocaust Encyclopedia* (New Haven, 2001), pp. 408–409.
4. See Philip Friedman, "The Lublin Reservation and the Madagascar Plan: Two Aspects of Nazi Jewish Policy During the Second World War," *Roads to Extinction: Essays on the Holocaust* (New York, 1980), pp. 34–58.

influence") awaited them, Hitler made clear to the military leadership that this conflict would be "very different from the war in the West."[5] Writing in *Mein Kampf* in 1924, Hitler had declared that "we must regard Russian Bolshevism as Jewry's attempt to achieve world rule in the twentieth century."[6] For the Nazis, "Eastern Jewry was the reservoir of Bolshevism."[7] These Jews "endangered the security of the German Reich," according to SS General Otto Ohlendorf, who at his postwar trial in Nuremberg admitted to supervising the murder of ninety thousand of them. "The carriers of this blood became especially suitable representatives of this Bolshevism. That is not on account of their faith, or their religion, but because of their human makeup and character."[8]

Wehrmacht commanders soon understood that Jews would be systematically killed. The Germans deployed four paramilitary agencies to carry out the slaughter: a private army under Heinrich Himmler's personal command known as the Kommandostab Reichsführer-SS brigades; the Order Police; any number of army units; and most important, special mobile killing units—the Einsatzgruppen.[9]

Many of the commanding officers in the Einsatzgruppen were highly educated, including lawyers and other intellectuals. Otto Ohlendorf, the leader of Einsatzgruppe D, had studied at three universities—he never finished his doctoral degree in law—and for a time in the 1930s held a responsible position in the Institute for World Economy and Maritime Transport in Kiel.[10] Ernst Biberstein, one of the commanders of Einsatzgruppe C, was a World War I veteran and Protestant minister; he was a theologian by training and worked as a church official under the Nazis. Paul Blobel, also of Einsatzgruppe C, had been trained as an architect. Other officers included the doctor Erwin Weinmann and the opera singer Waldemar Klingelhofer. Their orders were chilling in their simplicity: to follow the Wehrmacht into Soviet territory, occupy towns and cities along the way, separate out Jews, Gypsies, communist officials, and anyone else regarded as an enemy of the Germans, and then to murder them.

What took place in the initial months after June 22, 1941, staggers the imagination. Soviet defenses collapsed, allowing the Wehrmacht to advance 350 miles in the

---

5. Speech by Hitler on March 30, 1941, as cited by Browning, *The Origins of the Final Solution*, p. 218.
6. Cited in Andreas Hillgruber, "War in the East and the Extermination of the Jews," *Yad Vashem Studies* 18 (1987), p. 106.
7. *Trials of War Criminals Before the Nuernberg Military Tribunals Under Control Council Law No. 10*, IV (October 1946–April 1949), U.S. Government Printing Office, Washington, D.C., p. 244, from the affidavit by Dr. Walter Blume, one of the Einsatzgruppen leaders; hereafter *Einsatzgruppen Trial Account*.
8. Ibid., pp. 274–275.
9. See Yehoshua Büchler, "Kommandostab Reichsführer-SS: Himmler's Personal Murder Brigades in 1941," *Holocaust and Genocide Studies* 1, no. 1 (1986), pp. 11–25.
10. Hilary Camille Earl, *Accidental Justice: The Trial of Otto Ohlendorf and the Einsatzgruppen Leaders in Nuremberg Germany, 1945–1958*, unpublished Ph.D. dissertation, University of Toronto, 2002, pp. 101–108, for a comprehensive study of Ohlendorf's education and career before the war.

first ten days. Vilnius (Vilna) was taken on June 24; Minsk on June 28; Riga on July 1; Kiev on September 19. The 900-day siege of Leningrad began on September 8. By December German troops had reached the suburbs of Moscow. Soviet losses were enormous. Around Kiev alone, five Soviet armies were destroyed, leading to the capture of more than half a million troops.

The vast majority of Soviet Jews were living in the westernmost regions of the country, and most of them were quickly trapped. They had no idea of what awaited them. Between August 1939 and June 1941, while Germany and the Soviet Union were in effect allies, the Soviet press had remained silent about Nazi attacks on Jews in Poland.[11] German officers were amused at how uninformed some Jews appeared to be. An intelligence official reported from Belorussia on July 12, 1941, that

> the Jews are remarkably ill-informed about our attitude toward them. They do not know how Jews are treated in Germany, or for that matter in Warsaw, which after all is not so far away. Otherwise, their questions as to whether we in Germany make any distinctions between Jews and other citizens would be superfluous. Even if they do not think that under German administration they will have equal rights with the Russians, they believe, nevertheless, that we shall leave them in peace if they mind their own business and work diligently.[12]

And yet in spite of this one officer's observation, it is difficult to believe that many Jews would have harbored even cautious hope in regard to the Germans' intentions. Although they could not have imagined the full horror of the Final Solution—including the murderous hatred of their non-Jewish neighbors—most of them certainly knew enough about Nazi antisemitism to be apprehensive in the extreme.

Indeed, the violence of war was immediately overtaken by the carnage of mass murder. By July 11, 1941, Einsatzgruppe A could report that "up to now a total of 7,800 Jews have been liquidated, partly through pogroms and partly through shooting by [non-German] Lithuanian Kommandos." Einsatzgruppe B reported on July 13 that in Minsk "1,050 Jews were . . . liquidated," while in Vilnius "about 500 Jews, saboteurs among them, are liquidated daily." The author of the same report complained that "only 96 Jews were executed in Grodno and Lida during the first days. I gave orders to intensify these activities," he assured his superiors in Berlin. From Latvia Einsatzgruppe A reported on July 16 that it "[had] shot 1,150 Jews in Daugavpils," while "outside Riga . . . an additional 1,600 Jews were liquidated." By August 20, Einsatzgruppe B proudly claimed to have liquidated 16,964 people. The murders only escalated. On September 11, Einsatzgruppe C reported that in the town of Kamenets-Podolsky, "23,600 Jews were shot in three days by a

---

11. Ben-Cion Pinchuk, "Soviet Media on the Fate of Jews in Nazi-Occupied Territory (1939–1941)," *Yad Vashem Studies* 11 (1974), pp. 221–233.
12. Cited in Raul Hilberg, *The Destruction of the European Jews* (Chicago, 1967), p. 207.

Kommando of the Higher SS and Police Leaders." And at Babi Yar outside of Kiev, in two days of continuous shooting on September 29 and 30, the Germans and their accomplices killed 33,771 Jews.[13] According to the testimony of Lieutenant Erwin Bingel, Himmler once ordered the slaughter of 10,000 Jews for each of six German officers who had been killed and mutilated by partisans outside of Vinnitsa. "Even the child in the cradle must be trampled down like a poisonous toad," Himmler made clear. "We are living in an epoch of iron during which it is also necessary to sweep with iron-made brooms."[14]

Five years after the initial assault, when German leaders were in the dock at the International Military Tribunal, the actions of the Einsatzgruppen were described in a graphic and realistic manner. Telford Taylor recalled in *The Anatomy of the Nuremberg Trials* an affidavit about a massacre "as horrifying as any in the annals of Nazism." It came from Hermann Friedrich Graebe, a German construction boss in occupied Ukraine and the only German civilian who volunteered to testify in Nuremberg against the Nazis. Graebe had observed several massacres organized by the SS with assistance by Ukrainian militiamen. This episode was the murder of all of Dubno's Jews on October 5, 1942. That morning near his building site 5,000 people were being shot and buried in large pits. Graebe's affidavit continued:

> I drove to the site . . . and saw near it great mounds of earth, about 30 meters long and 2 meters high. Several trucks stood in front of the mounds. Armed Ukrainian militia drove the people off the trucks under the supervision of an SS man. The militiamen acted as guards on the trucks and drove them to and from the pit. All these people had the regulation yellow patches on the front and back of their clothes, and thus could be recognized as Jews.
>
> . . . Now I heard rifle shots in quick succession, from behind the earth mounds. The people who had got off the trucks—men, women, and children of all ages—had to undress upon the order of an SS man, who carried a riding or dog whip. They had to put down their clothes in fixed places, sorted into piles of shoes, outerwear, and undergarments. I saw a heap of shoes of about 800 to 1,000 pairs, great piles of underwear and clothing. Without screaming or weeping these people undressed, stood around in family groups, kissed each other, said farewells and waited for a sign from another SS man, who stood near the pit, also with a whip in his hand. During the fifteen minutes that I stood near the pit I heard no complaint or plea for mercy. I watched a family of about eight persons, a man and a woman, both about 50 with their children of about 1, 8 and 10, and two grown-up daughters of about 20 to 24. An old woman with snow-white hair was

---

13. Yitzhak Arad, Shmuel Krakowski, Shmuel Spector, eds., *The Einsatzgruppen Reports: Selections from the Dispatches of the Nazi Death Squads' Campaign Against the Jews in Occupied Territories of the Soviet Union July 1941–January 1943* (New York, 1989), pp. 17, 22, 23, 28, 29, 124, 129, 168.
14. "The Extermination of Two Ukrainian Jewish Communities, Testimony of a Germany army officer Oberleutnant Erwin Bingel," *Yad Vashem Studies* 3 (1959), pp. 308–309.

holding the one-year-old child in her arms and singing to it, and tickling it. The child was cooing with delight. The couple were looking on with tears in their eyes. The father was holding the hand of a boy about 10 years old and speaking to him softly; the boy was fighting his tears. The father pointed to the sky, stroked his head, and seemed to explain something to him. At that moment the SS man at the pit shouted something to his comrade. The latter counted off about twenty persons and instructed them to go behind the earth mound. Among them was the family, which I have mentioned. I well remember a girl, slim and with black hair, who, as she passed close to me, pointed to herself and said, "twenty-three." I walked around the mound, and found myself confronted by a tremendous grave. People were closely wedged together and lying on top of each other so that only their heads were visible. Nearly all had blood running over their shoulders from their heads. Some of the people shot were still moving. Some were lifting their arms and turning their heads to show that they were still alive. The pit was already two-thirds full. I estimated that it already contained about a thousand people. I looked for the man who did the shooting. He was an SS man, who sat at the edge of the narrow end of the pit, his feet dangling into the pit. He had a tommy gun on his knees and was smoking a cigarette. The people, completely naked, went down some steps which were cut in the clay wall of the pit and clambered over the heads of the people lying there, to the place to which the SS man directed them. They lay down in front of the dead or injured people; some caressed those who were still alive and spoke to them in a low voice. Then I heard a series of shots. I looked into the pit and saw that the bodies were twitching or the heads lying already motionless on top of the bodies that lay before them. Blood was running from their necks.[15]

Coming from a German civilian, Graebe's testimony was particularly significant. It described organized, cold-blooded mass murder at close range that could have been possible only with the full support of the Wehrmacht.

This kind of slaughter was psychologically troublesome for many soldiers and officers, and German commanders grew concerned over its effect on their men. Himmler decided to watch a massacre in order to understand its full impact. On a visit to Minsk in September 1941 he asked Artur Nebe, leader of Einsatzgruppe B, to arrange an execution of a hundred people so he could observe it for himself. Except for two women, they were all men. As one German officer, Erich von dem Bach-Zelewski, later recounted,

---

15. Telford Taylor, *The Anatomy of the Nuremberg Trials, A Personal Memoir* (New York, 1992), pp. 244–245. Graebe's affidavit was read into the record on January 3, 1946. Graebe did more than testify at Nuremberg. During his years in Ukraine, he helped to save several hundred Jews by arranging for them to work on various building sites. After the war, he and his family faced ostracism, even death threats in Germany, compelling them to find refuge in America. In 1965, Yad Vashem recognized Graebe with the title Righteous among the Nations. See Douglas K. Huneke, *The Moses of Rovno* (New York, 1985) for details about Graebe's life and wartime activities.

Himmler spotted in the group a youth of about twenty who had blue eyes and blond hair. Just before the firing was to begin, Himmler walked up to the doomed man and put a few questions to him. "Are you a Jew?" "Yes." "Are both of your parents Jews?" "Yes." "Do you have any ancestors who were not Jews?" "No." "Then I can't help you!" As the firing started, Himmler was even more nervous. During every volley he looked to the ground. When the two women could not die, Himmler yelled to the police sergeant not to torture them.

When the shooting was over, Himmler and a fellow spectator engaged in conversation. The other witness was Obergruppenführer von dem Bach-Zelewski. Von dem Bach addressed Himmler: "Reichsführer, those were only a hundred." "What do you mean by that?" "Look at the eyes of the men in the *Kommando*, how deeply shaken they are! These men are finished . . . for the rest of their lives. What kind of followers are we training here? Either neurotics or savages!"

Himmler acknowledged that "he hated this bloody business and that he had been aroused to the depth of his soul." It was "a repulsive duty" and "he would not like it if Germans did such a thing gladly."[16]

But he was still proud of accepting this "necessary" and "historic" burden. In his notorious speech to veteran SS officers at Posen (Poznan) in 1943, Himmler acknowledged how difficult it must be to commit mass murder and remain a normal human being. "Most of you will know what it means when 100 corpses are lying side by side, when 500 are lying there or when 1,000 are lying there. To have stuck this out and at the same time—apart from exceptions due to human weaknesses—to have remained decent, that is what has made us hard."[17]

Not all soldiers or officers overcame their human feelings. Von dem Bach-Zelewski could barely tolerate supervising such carnage. He broke down in early 1942 and had to be hospitalized with serious stomach and intestinal distress. When he failed to recover, Himmler ordered Ernst Grawitz, the chief physician of the SS, to evaluate him. The latter reported that "von dem Bach was suffering from hallucinations in which he relived his experiences in the East, particularly the shooting of Jews."[18] The unrelenting job of killing unarmed and innocent men, women, and children at close range exacted a psychological toll on many of the killers. Lieutenant Bingel told his captors that in September 1941, he "was compelled to send twenty percent of [his] men on leave of absence, since, as a result of their recent experiences, they were quite incapable of performing any duty."[19] Such a statistic may well have been typical for many units.

---

16. Cited in Hilberg, *The Destruction of the European Jews*, p. 218. The story was originally told by von dem Bach-Zelewski and appeared in *Aufbau* (New York), August 23, 1946, pp. 1–2.
17. Cited in Gerhard Schoenberner, *The Yellow Star* (New York, 1973), p. 121.
18. Ibid., p. 216.
19. "The Extermination of Two Ukrainian Jewish Communities," p. 309.

Faced with the trauma of their own men, German commanders decided to find a way of murdering women and children that spared the soldiers emotional suffering. One alternative was the use of mobile gas vans—trucks whose tailpipe vented through the floor into the rear cabin. Depending on the size of the van, the Nazis could asphyxiate up to sixty people at one time by this means. After picking up the victims at a collection point, the van would arrive fifteen minutes later at a pit, its passengers conveniently dead. It is now believed that three trucks were used in the murder of 97,000 Jews in Ukraine between December 1941 and June 1942. By the close of 1944, the Germans employed fifteen gas vans in the occupied Soviet territories, killing 350,000 people by means of this device.[20] The presence of the vans in many areas became so noticeable and their purpose so well-known "that not only the authorities but the civilian population referred to them as 'Death Vans,'" according to SS Untersturmführer August Becker, who helped to design the mobile gas vans and supervised their use. In response to this problem, Becker ordered the vans "disguised as housetrailers by having a single window shutter fixed to each side of the small vans, and on the large ones, two shutters, such as one often sees on farm houses in the country."

There were still emotional complications for the killers. When soldiers opened the trucks, they were confronted by corpses covered in vomit and excrement, making the task of unloading the victims too unpleasant for the killers' sensitive natures. Becker ordered German soldiers not to unload the vans because such work was having an "enormous psychological and physical harm" on them.[21] Other military officers had different objections. At least one Einsatzgruppe leader, Karl Rudolf Werner Braune, rejected the use of gas vans as a matter of principle. As he told his judges at Nuremberg, "In my opinion, an execution by shooting is more honorable for both parties than killing by means of a gas truck."[22]

Such declarations were consistent with the peculiar moral boundaries Nazis set for themselves. Wilhelm Kube, the Gauleiter of Belorussia, opposed the murder of German Jews who were being "re-settled" to the region he commanded. "People who come from our cultural sphere just are not the same as the brutish hordes in this place," he told one colleague.[23] But such qualms did not stop Kube from killing them. And he continued to oversee the mass murder of Soviet Jews. The Einsatzgruppe

---

20. "Gas Chambers," *The Holocaust Encyclopedia* (New Haven, 2001), pp. 230–231.
21. Yitzhak Arad, Yisrael Gutman, and Abraham Margaliot, eds., *Documents on the Holocaust: Selected Sources on the Destruction of the Jews of Germany and Austria, Poland, and the Soviet Union* (Jerusalem, 1981), pp. 419–420; this is from a report from Kiev by Becker to officials in Berlin dated May 16, 1942.
22. *Einsatzgruppen Trial Account*, p. 214.
23. Arad, Gutman, and Margaliot, eds., *Documents on the Holocaust*, p. 409; Kube sent the letter from Minsk on December 16, 1941. For more on this subject, see Shalom Cholovsky, "The German Jews in the Minsk Ghetto," *Yad Vashem Studies* 17 (1986), p. 242.

officer Eduard Strauch offended the sensibilities of his superiors by ordering the removal of gold from the teeth of his victims "before they were executed, not afterward." Strauch justified his practice by claiming it had been carried out by "expert physicians."[24]

Even while the Einsatzgruppen and other killing units were under instructions to kill all Jews, certain categories of skilled workers were identified as useful to German industry; these were kept in ghettos or in a number of slave-labor camps until they were of no more use. The ghettos in the Soviet Union were different from those in Poland in one essential respect. In Poland ghettoization preceded the mass murders. In occupied Soviet territories, the murders came first; survivors of the first round of killing were the ones herded into ghettos. The largest, in Minsk, held at its peak as many as one hundred thousand Jews and functioned for over two years. Other sizable ghettos were located in Vilnius, Kaunas (Kovno), and Pinsk. There were hundreds of smaller ones. The dependence on Jewish labor created a degree of tension between elements in the army primarily concerned with economic needs and the forces of outright extermination, who grew impatient with anything less than immediate killing. A sensible solution was quickly found. The Nazis understood that there were enough Jewish workers and artisans on hand to make it possible to work them to death and still sustain productivity.

In spite of their military victories, the Germans understood the need to keep their crimes secret. Soldiers were forbidden to take photographs of the massacres (although some did) and there were orders to carry out the shootings as far away as practical from population centers.[25] Nonetheless, Western governments and the Kremlin were beginning to understand the scale of the atrocities. On January 6, 1942, Soviet Foreign Minister Vyacheslav Molotov issued an official diplomatic note citing specific massacres of Jews on Soviet territory.[26]

Many of the mass graves had been covered with only a thin layer of earth. After the winter, "running water from melting snow" uncovered some. Such gruesome evidence was becoming too easy to locate, while in some places the "local population and

---

24. Earl, *Accidental Justice*, p. 269. Strauch was an efficient killer. In a report dated July 31, 1942, Wilhelm Kube discussed the struggle against Jewish partisans and went on to praise Strauch as an "exceedingly capable leader" because he had led the way in killing "about 55,000 Jews . . . in the past ten weeks"; see Arad, Gutman, and Margaliot, eds., *Documents on the Holocaust*, p. 411.
25. During the trial of the German High Command at Nuremberg, the prosecutors entered a handwritten letter dated July 22, 1941 (a month after the German invasion of Soviet territory) in which soldiers were forbidden to take photographs of "abominable excesses." Photographs like these could undermine their "decency and discipline." As the letter concluded, "It is beneath the dignity of a German soldier to watch such incidents out of curiosity." *Trials of War Criminals Before the Nuernberg Military Tribunals Under Control Council Law No. 10*, X (October 1946–April 1949), U.S. Government Printing Office, Washington, D.C., p. 1209.
26. *Pravda*, January 7, 1942, pp. 1–2.

German army units ... complained about the stench." [27] Something had to be done. In spring 1942, Himmler decided to order the corpses of the murdered Jews incinerated, intending to erase the most conclusive evidence of Nazi crimes. The project was called Aktion 1005. Paul Blobel, who had overseen the massacre at Babi Yar, was ordered to supervise the process. At concentration camps throughout Poland and in still-occupied Soviet territory, teams of Nazis forced their prisoners to erect enormous open-air furnaces and started experimenting on the best way to stack corpses to burn them in the most efficient manner. They even employed special machines to grind human bones. They obliterated many mass graves and put enormous efforts into hiding their crimes, as if hoping to avoid the judgment of history or an investigation by a resurgent enemy.

Local Collaborators and Romanian Allies

The Germans could not have achieved all this killing on their own. Local collaborators, at times with the instigation and encouragement of the occupiers, carried out pogroms throughout Belorussia, Western Ukraine, and the Baltic region. After Einsatzgruppe A moved into Kaunas on June 28, it reported to Berlin that "during the last 3 days Lithuanian partisan groups have already killed several thousand Jews." [28] Lithuanians, in fact, carried out nearly five hundred separate pogroms before the Germans began their own, more systematic roundups.

The violence in Ukraine was equally grotesque. On July 6 Einsatzgruppe A reported to Berlin, this time from Tarnopol, that the day before "about 70 Jews were assembled by the Ukrainians and finished off with concentrated fire [machine gunned]." Ten days later, on July 16, Einsatzgruppe A had further encouraging news. "In the first hours after the Bolshevik withdrawal, the Ukrainian population displayed commendable activity against the Jews. For example, the Dobromil synagogue was set on fire and 50 Jews were killed by the enraged crowd at Sambor. Maltreating them, the Lvov inhabitants rounded up about 1,000 Jews and took them to the GPU prison, which has been occupied by the Wehrmacht." And from Kremenets, not to be outdone, "Ukrainians killed 130 Jews with clubs" in retaliation, it was claimed, for the murder of Ukrainians by retreating Soviet forces. By August 3 Einsatzgruppe A could report with satisfaction that "in the self-cleansing actions in Lithuania, Latvia, and Estonia over 20,000 communists and Jews were liquidated by the self-defense [sic] organizations." [29]

The outright killing by auxiliary military and police units was made worse by the hatred, sadism, and greed of ordinary neighbors. Reading the accounts preserved

---

27. Shmuel Spector, "Aktion-1005: Effacing the Murder of Millions," *Holocaust and Genocide Studies*, 5, no. 2 (1990), pp. 157–158.
28. Arad, et al, *The Einsatzgruppen Reports*, p. 1.
29. Ibid., pp. 12, 31, 39, 62.

in *The Unknown Black Book,* again and again one comes across stories of neighbors waiting to take over an apartment, of people arguing among themselves over who was entitled to Jewish property, about people taunting the Jews, and about people betraying Jews to the Germans. As the survivor Sara Gleykh observed in her diary, "The neighbors waited like vultures for us to leave the apartment."[30] What must have been most terrifying to the Jews was the realization that their neighbors wanted not just their clothing, furniture, and apartments; they wanted the Jews dead. The fact that Lithuanian and Ukrainian militias in particular helped to guard ghettos, camps, and prisons, to forcibly herd Jews and others to execution sites, to carry out massacres, and even to loot the corpses, has long been known. It is the frequency of spontaneous civilian collaboration that stands out so conspicuously in this collection.

Throughout the Baltic region and Western Ukraine in particular, it was as if the population understood, without much prodding by the Germans, that there were no limits on what they could do to their Jewish neighbors. In Lithuania, Latvia, and Estonia, the population had lived for barely a year under direct Soviet control, and there were feelings of resentment against the Jews because many of them had welcomed Soviet power as a counterweight to the Germans.

During World War II the Germans also received substantial assistance from their Romanian allies. On the eve of the war, Romania had the third-largest Jewish population in Europe, over 750,000, exceeded only by the Jewish communities of the Soviet Union and Poland. By the late 1930s antisemitic political parties had gained significant influence inside the country, leading to severe restrictions on Jews similar to those imposed by Germany's Nuremberg Laws. Tens of thousands of Jews who had become Romanian citizens after World War I were now deprived of their citizenship.

But the situation turned murderous in summer 1940. In July, nearly a year after the Hitler-Stalin Pact, the Soviet Union forced Romania to cede the provinces of Bessarabia and Northern Bukovina, while northern Transylvania was transferred to Hungary (at the insistence of Germany). Although Hitler and Stalin compelled these transfers, many if not most Romanians held the Jews responsible, leading to the massacre of hundreds of Jews in Moldavia by retreating Romanian soldiers. On September 6 General Ion Antonescu came to power in alliance with the fascist and deeply antisemitic Iron Guard. When this coalition collapsed in January 1941, however, the Iron Guard, which had been suppressed by General Antonescu, turned on the Jews of Bucharest. What followed was one of the most horrifying episodes of the war. The American journalist Robert St. John was in the city where friends reported the gruesome details to him: About 150 Jewish men and women were taken "to the abattoir on the edge of the city. There they were stripped naked, forced to get down on all fours, and were driven up the ramp of the slaughterhouse. Then they were put

---

30. See "The destruction of the Jews of Mariupol—The diary of the student Sara Gleykh," p. 216 in this volume.

through all the stages of animals at slaughter until finally the beheaded bodies, spurting blood, were hung on iron hooks along the wall. As a last sadistic touch the legionnaires took rubber stamps and branded the carcasses with the Romanian equivalent FIT FOR HUMAN CONSUMPTION."[31]

Six months later, Romania joined Germany in the invasion of the Soviet Union. Within a few days, Romanian army units, police, and civilians, joined by German soldiers, killed as many as 13,000 Jews in Yassy (Iasi), a city in northeastern Romania.[32] The Romanians were only getting started. Under instruction from officials in Bucharest, army units once again in control of Bessarabia and Bukovina killed 30,000 Jews. In August Romania joined her German allies in occupying parts of Ukraine, a sizable area between the Dniestr and Southern Bug rivers—called Transnistria during the war—in which the Romanians carried out further massacres of their own, and forced tens of thousands of Jews from Moldavia and Northern Bukovina into Transnistria, where they would then face gradual extermination.

As testimonies included in *The Unknown Black Book* make clear, it was the Romanians who rounded up and killed 25,000 Jews in Odessa after the Romanian army headquarters was blown up in October 1941, killing fifty officers. General Ion Antonescu personally ordered these killings as an act of reprisal. It was the Romanians, joined by Ukrainian militiamen between the end of December 1941 and February 1942, who killed 70,000 Jews in the ghettos of Bogdanovka, Domanyovka, and Akmechetka within the confines of Transnistria,[33] which "served Romania as a giant killing field for Jews." Recent scholarship now concludes "that between 280,000 and 380,000 Romanian and Ukrainian Jews were murdered or died during the Holocaust in Romania and the territories it controlled." After Germany, no other country was more involved in the wholesale slaughter of Jews.[34]

Still, the Germans had reasons of their own to be dissatisfied with the Romanian approach to solving the "Jewish problem." As the historian Jean Ancel has shown,

---

31. Robert St. John, *Foreign Correspondent* (New York, 1957), pp. 216–217.
32. There is a curious incident in literary history connected to the Yassy pogrom. The Italian writer Curzio Malaparte was in a nearby city at the time. In an initial dispatch for *Corriere della Sera* in Milan, he echoed the Romanians' contrived claim that they had attacked the Jewish quarter in response to rifle shots, as if the Jews were a "Soviet fifth column." But in 1944, in his famous novel *Kaputt*, Malaparte wrote a compelling description of the pogrom and its terrifying violence, an account that is sympathetic to the Jews; this was among the first literary treatments of the Holocaust. The original Italian text of his dispatch, which first appeared in *Corriere della Sera* on July 5, 1941, along with a French translation, can be found in Pierre Pachet, *Conversations à Jassy* (Paris, 1997), pp. 94–95 and pp. 193–196. See also Curzio Malaparte, *Kaputt* (New York, 2005).
33. See Dora Litani, "The Destruction of the Jews of Odessa in the Light of Rumanian Documents," *Yad Vashem Studies* 6 (1967), p. 140.
34. See the *Executive Summary of the Final Report of the International Commission on the Holocaust in Romania*, presented to Romanian President Ion Iliescu in Bucharest, Romania on November 22, 2004, p. 2.

"each time the Romanians proceeded without any plan, without erasing traces of the mass murder, killing, robbing, raping, and shooting on the streets, . . . or allowed themselves to be bribed by Jews, they aroused the anger of their Nazi comrades."[35] Even the Nazis could be appalled by the grotesque brutality of their Romanian allies. Later on, however, the Nazis became disappointed when Antonescu grew overly mindful of Romania's interests. Beginning in 1942 and even more following the German defeat at Stalingrad, his government distanced itself from German policies, refusing to deport Romanian Jews to Auschwitz and curtailing the widespread murder of Jews in Transnistria. This reversal in official policy helped 290,000 Romanian Jews primarily from Bucharest and the central provinces of the country (known as "Old Romania") to survive the war. As accounts in *The Unknown Black Book* make clear, corrupt Romanian officials in Odessa readily accepted bribes, permitting Jews to save themselves, to survive incarceration in prisons, even to organize clandestine networks of resistance.

Nonetheless, Antonescu and other Romanian leaders were too steeped in blood to be forgiven. The new government formed after the Soviets occupied Romania conducted trials in Bucharest after the war that condemned Antonescu and three of his closest colleagues to death. The courts sentenced hundreds of other officials to long prison terms. Later on, both the communist regime and the more democratic leadership that came to power in 1989 were reluctant to acknowledge the extent of Romania's involvement in the Holocaust. The communist dictator Nicolae Ceaușescu tried to "to cleanse the war-time record of Romania" and "gradually rehabilitate Marshal Ion Antonescu," in the words of the historian Randolph Braham. This meant minimizing the numbers of Jews killed in Romanian-led pogroms and virtually denying Romanian complicity as a military ally to Germany and as an enthusiastic accomplice to mass murder in Ukraine. The post-communist government tolerated efforts to rehabilitate Antonescu, including the erection of statues in his honor in at least two cities. In reaction, U.S. officials reminded President Ion Iliescu in 1995 that "no other European nation has erected statues of a war criminal since the end of World War II."[36] The statues are now gone. Still, in 2003, there was a disheartening incident of Holocaust denial by Romania's Minister of Information Vasile Dancu, who declared that "within the borders of Romania between 1940 and 1945 there was no Holocaust."[37]

The response to such a provocation was immediate and effective. The government quickly agreed to appoint an independent commission, which included the writer and Nobel Peace Prize laureate Elie Wiesel as chairman, himself from the Romanian town

---

35. Jean Ancel, "The Solution of the 'Jewish Problem' in Bessarabia," *Yad Vashem Studies* 19 (1988), p. 229.
36. Randolph L. Braham, "Romanian Nationalists and the Holocaust: A Case Study in History Cleansing," *Holocaust and Genocide Studies* 10, no. 3 (1996), pp. 211, 236.
37. "Double Dividend," *Jerusalem Report,* January 10, 2005, p. 30.

of Sighet. After two years of work, and building on the contributions of scholars such as Jean Ancel, Randolph Braham, and Radu Ioanid (who served as vice-chairman), the commission issued the nearly 500-page report in which it confirmed the full scale of official and popular complicity. The government of Ion Iliescu accepted the findings at an official ceremony in Bucharest in November 2004.

The Challenge of Resistance

Reading *The Unknown Black Book* provokes a question that has often troubled observers of the Holocaust. How could hundreds, thousands, even tens of thousands of people "resign" themselves to their fate—to stand at the edge of pits, to undress and walk into gas chambers? Nazis and their sympathizers sometimes portrayed their Jewish victims in this light. But the similar fate of millions of Soviet POWs who also perished and appear to have been equally compliant compels us to look at this question in a different way.

In the decades after the war, there was much discussion over the supposed behavior of the Jews, particularly the lack of organized, armed resistance. Such assumptions ignore the victims' grim reality. In his novel, *In the Days of Simon Stern*, Arthur A. Cohen admonished readers that "the pride of the living may not be salvaged from the conduct of the dead."[38] The victims did not suffer from moral paralysis, but from overwhelming terror and intimidation. As one account after another confirms, the Nazis had a genius for demonstrating that being shot and made to fall into a ditch was not the worst thing that could happen. "Resistance was often an act of desperation," in the words of the scholar Michael Berenbaum, "a decision about how to die, not how to live."[39] A witness at Eichmann's trial, Dr. Leon Wells, described the fate of one mother who spat in the face of an SS man. "They took her child away from her and smashed its head against a tree, then hung her by her feet as the other prisoners looked on."[40] Such cruelty overwhelmed the prisoners and instilled a kind of incapacitating terror that surpassed any ordinary category of intimidation.

For the Nazis, there was a definite purpose to fully gratifying their sadism. During one roundup in the Kaunas ghetto, as recounted in *The Unknown Black Book*, an officer named Wilhelm Goecke ordered the Jews to relinquish all children, announcing that severe punishment awaited those who evaded the order. A couple named Zeller was publicly executed for failing to hand over their child to the butchers. The unfortunate parents were beaten, forced to sit on a red hot stove, and had needles shoved under their fingernails. When they lost consciousness, they were carried to the gallows. Holding their victims in the nooses in a way that was calculated not to kill them, the Germans took them down and put off completing the execution until the

---

38. Arthur A. Cohen, *In the Days of Simon Stern* (New York, 1973), p. 197.
39. From a review of Gideon Greif, *We Wept Without Tears: Testimonies of the Jewish Sonderkommando from Auschwitz* in *Yad Vashem Studies* 29 (2001), p. 442.
40. Haim Gouri, *Facing the Glass Booth: The Jerusalem Trial of Adolf Eichmann* (Detroit, 2004), p. 40.

next day. Then they lashed the father to a stake and lit a fire beneath his feet. They stripped the mother naked and continued to torture her. "That's how it will go with anyone who puts up resistance to us," Goecke announced through a megaphone.[41]

Unarmed, responsible for children and the elderly or sick, isolated from their neighbors, cut off from either partisans or a sympathetic army, the Jews were helpless and on their own. Nonetheless, to hold a child's hand, to embrace a parent, to console a friend, to tickle an infant, as accounts in *The Unknown Black Book* frequently report—all in the face of imminent, violent death—was to remain human even if one could not remain alive. These were genuine acts of courage.

Moreover, the historical record contains numerous examples of desperate resistance, of young men and women attacking soldiers and policemen with their bare hands, trying to throttle them, to tear out their eyes, to grab a gun. Herman Graebe witnessed how the Jews of Rovno refused to go quietly when they were ordered out of their homes.

> On the evening of [July 13, 1942] I drove to Rovno.—Shortly after 22.00 hours the ghetto was encircled by a large S.S. detachment and about three times as many members of the Ukrainian militia. Then the electric arclights that had been erected in and around the ghetto were switched on. S.S. and militia squads of 4–6 men entered or at least tried to enter the houses. Where the doors and windows were closed and the inhabitants did not open to their knocking, the S.S. men and militia broke the windows, forced the doors with beams and crowbars, and entered the houses. The people living there were driven on to the street just as they were dressed, even from their beds. Since the Jews in most cases refused to leave their houses and resisted, the S.S. and militia applied force. They finally succeeded, with strokes of the whip, kicks, and blows with rifle butts in clearing the houses. . . .
>
> Since several families or groups had barricaded themselves in especially strong buildings, and the doors could not be forced with crowbars and beams, these houses were now blown open with hand grenades. The ghetto was near the railroad tracks and the younger people tried to escape across the tracks and over a small river to get away from the ghetto area. . . .
>
> All through the night these beaten, hounded, and wounded people moved along the lighted streets. Women carried their dead children in their arms down the road toward the train. Again and again the cries "Open the door! Open the door! Echoed through the ghetto."[42]

In the town of Tulchin as well, in the fall of 1942 ghetto residents prepared ahead of time for the final assault. They managed to buy a handful of weapons, including rifles,

---

41. See "Extermination of the Jewish children in Kaunas, Account of Maria Ilinichna Yarmovskaya," p. 295 in this volume.
42. Cited in Nathan Eck, "Historical Research or Slander," *Yad Vashem Studies* 6 (1967), pp. 409–410.

pistols, and hand grenades, then set fire to the ghetto before attacking the Nazis and Ukrainian policemen. As many as 2,000 of the ghetto's 3,000 residents reached a nearby forest, but most of them were hunted down and killed.[43]

It should be emphasized that evasion of the perpetrators was the most effective way to avoid murder. While 4,000,000 Jews resided in the Soviet territories that would be overrun by the Germans, an estimated 1,500,000 were able to get away. As the Germans moved further eastward, they found proportionally fewer Jews.

And the record of armed resistance includes the exploits of the Bielski brothers, who led a large group of mostly Jewish partisans in the forests of Belorussia, and of Hirsh Smolar, who was among the leaders of a partisan organization that saved 10,000 Jews from the Minsk ghetto. Somewhere between 20,000 and 30,000 Jews participated in the Soviet partisan movement. The Generalkommissar for White Ruthenia (Belorussia), Wilhelm Kube, was killed in Minsk on September 22, 1943, by a member of a partisan unit under a Jew named David Keimach. But the Soviets did little, if anything, to make this history known and, at times, refused to acknowledge that it ever really happened. There was the famous incident involving Masha Bruskina, a seventeen-year-old Jewish partisan who was captured and publicly hanged with two of her comrades in Minsk on October 26, 1941. These were the first public executions of Soviet partisans. Photographs taken by a Lithuanian policeman were widely circulated after the war. But while the identities of her two comrades, both men and both Slavs, were quickly established, the woman was not identified. In 1968 journalists in Moscow conducted an investigation, locating classmates, neighbors, and relatives, including people who had witnessed the executions; their statements established the identity of the young woman being executed as Masha Bruskina. But her Jewish background apparently made it too difficult for Soviet officials to acknowledge her courage or her sacrifice.[44]

Jews in fact earned the most disproportionate number of military awards of any Soviet nationality during the war, distinguishing themselves in every branch of the armed forces. Between 450,000 and 470,000 served and about 40 percent were killed, either at the Front or in German captivity.[45] About 150 Jews received the title of Hero of the Soviet Union, while another 160,722 were decorated, the fourth largest number, just after Russians, Ukrainians, and Belorussians.[46]

---

43. Shmuel Spector, "The Jews of Volhynia and their Reaction to Extermination," *Yad Vashem Studies* 15 (1983), pp. 169–170.
44. See Nehama Tec and Daniel Weiss, "A Historical Injustice: The Case of Masha Bruskina," *Holocaust and Genocide Studies* 11, no. 2, Fall 1997, pp. 366–377. See also *New York Times*, September 15, 1987, p. 1, for a front-page story on this controversy; and *Forward*, November 15, 1996, p. 1, about a recent controversy in Belarus and reprisals against journalists who publicly identified her.
45. See Yitzhak Arad, "Soviet Jews in the War," *Yad Vashem Studies* 23 (1993), p. 125. Arad believes this is proportionately "the highest percentage of the fallen among all national groups in the Soviet army."
46. Ibid., p. 84.

The Kremlin and the Final Solution

The Soviet regime responded to the slaughter of its Jewish citizens and the heroic loyalty of its Jewish soldiers in an inconsistent and inadequate manner. Lapses into silence and deliberate distortions of what actually occurred figure in the historical record. But as Zvi Gitelman has observed, "If there was a policy of repressing the Holocaust, it was applied unevenly at best."[47] After Hitler gained power in Germany in 1933, the Soviet press made frequent references to antisemitic developments in Germany. In a speech on November 25, 1936, to mark the new Soviet constitution, Vyacheslav Molotov condemned the Nuremberg laws and fascism in general for its support of antisemitism. Indeed, five years earlier Stalin himself had declared that "antisemitism, like any form of racial chauvinism, is the most dangerous vestige of cannibalism."[48] But Stalin had made his remark in a written response to a question from the Jewish Telegraphic Agency in New York, and it was only when Molotov cited it in his speech in 1936 that it appeared in the Soviet Union. Molotov went so far as to express sympathy for the people who had given birth to Karl Marx and many of the "greatest figures in science, engineering, and art." Speaking of "brotherly feelings for the Jewish people," Molotov emphasized that these "will define our attitudes toward antisemites and antisemitic atrocities wherever they occur."[49]

Soviet propaganda and popular culture reflected this attitude and occasionally focused on the plight of Jews in Germany. In 1938 two Jewish filmmakers, Adolf Minkin and Herbert Rappaport, produced the movie *Professor Mamlock*, which was based on the 1933 play by the German-Jewish writer Friedrich Wolf and is regarded as the first Soviet film to depict Nazi antisemitism. *Professor Mamlock* appeared widely in the Soviet Union and in the West, including the United States, where critics hailed it as "engrossing" and "sincere."[50] The Soviet press also provided extensive coverage of Kristallnacht, when the Nazis carried out systematic attacks on Jews and Jewish properties during the night of November 9–10, 1938. *Pravda* carried prominent articles for more than a week, often on the front page, with vivid descriptions of synagogues being burned, stories of Jews forced half-naked from their homes, and information on thousands of arrests and scores of outright murders and suicides. As *Pravda* lamented, this was "a massacre of a defenseless Jewish population," creating "an incredible fear" among Jews throughout Germany.[51]

---

47. Zvi Gitelman, "The Soviet Union," in David S. Wyman, ed., *The World Reacts to the Holocaust* (Baltimore, 1996), p. 307.
48. Cited in the introduction by Vasily Grossman to Ilya Ehrenburg and Vasily Grossman, eds., *The Black Book* (New York, 1981), p. xxx.
49. *Pravda*, November 30, 1936, pp. 1–3.
50. *New York Times*, November 8, 1938, p. 26. A few days later, there were front-page headlines about the pogroms of Kristallnacht.
51. *Pravda*, November 13, 1938, p. 5, November 18, 1938, p. 5.

With the signing of the Soviet-German Non-Aggression Pact in August 1939, however, Soviet propaganda did an about-face. The Soviet media remained silent about antisemitic attacks by the Nazis in Poland. At the same time, with the annexation of Western Ukraine and Western Belorussia (Eastern Poland), the Baltic states, and Bessarabia and Northern Bukovina, the Jewish population under Soviet control grew by 2,000,000, to 5,000,000 people. They would all be in jeopardy after the German invasion on June 22, 1941.

After the invasion, Stalin and the supreme leadership were quickly informed about atrocities against the Jews. Pantaleymon Ponomarenko, First Secretary of the Central Committee of the Belorussian Communist Party and soon to be official head of the partisan movement, wrote to Stalin on June 25 that "an animal fear has taken hold of [the Jews]; in place of fighting, they are running away." He then went on to report that "all of the Nazis' propaganda, oral and written, is carried out under the banner of a struggle with the Yids and communists, which are used as if they were synonyms." Two months later, Ponomarkenko provided Stalin with graphic details of massacres in the cities and towns of Belorussia, concluding that "the Jewish population is undergoing ruthless destruction."[52]

By August, Stalin was ready to enlist Jewish voices and use Jewish suffering in an appeal to Jews in Britain and the United States. On August 16, several leading Jewish cultural figures approached the Kremlin with a proposal to stage a rally "with the participation of Jewish academicians, writers, artists, and Red Army soldiers."[53] The regime accepted the idea and arranged for an international radio broadcast and a mass rally in Moscow's Park of Culture on August 24. All the speakers, in carefully screened remarks later published in leading newspapers, emphasized Jewish unity and the terror of Nazi persecution.

This meeting was the first step in the creation of the Jewish Anti-Fascist Committee (JAC), one of five such committees set up to engage in propaganda directed toward the West to generate support for the wartime alliance with the Soviet Union.[54] Until the end of the war, the JAC would collect information about atrocities and distribute news articles and essays, primarily in the West, about Jewish suffering. All the speakers at the 1941 event, most notably Mikhoels, several Yiddish-language writers, and figures such as Ehrenburg, became leading voices within the JAC.[55]

---

52. Cited in Ilya Altman, *Zhertvy nenavisti: Kholokost v SSSR* (Victims of Hate: The Holocaust in the USSR) (Moscow, 2002), pp. 385–386.
53. Russian State Archive of Social and Political History (hereafter RGASPI), f. 17, op. 125, d. 35, ll. 62–65. The letter is dated August 16, 1941. A full translation can be found in Shimon Redlich, *War, Holocaust and Stalinism: A Documented History of the Jewish Anti-Fascist Committee in the USSR* (Luxembourg, 1995), pp. 173–174.
54. The other anti-fascist committees were directed toward scientists, young people, women, and Slavs who were living in the West, primarily in Canada and the United States.
55. See Joshua Rubenstein and Vladimir Naumov, eds., *Stalin's Secret Pogrom: The Postwar Inquisition of*

On occasion, Soviet officials also made references for domestic audiences to the massacre of the Jews. On November 6, 1941, Stalin gave a defiant speech in Moscow commemorating the twenty-fourth anniversary of the Bolshevik Revolution, at a time when the Wehrmacht was threatening the capital. Among German atrocities, Stalin explicitly accused them of "happily organizing medieval pogroms against the Jews, just as the tsarist regime had done before." [56] Twelve days later, *Izvestia* cited a New York news source that claimed that 52,000 Jewish men, women, and children had been killed in Kiev. [57] Then Molotov, in an official diplomatic statement a year later, to protest German atrocities, included an explicit reference to the massacre in Kiev; the text of his message began on the front page of *Pravda*. [58] The Soviet press carried two front-page denunciations of the massacres of Jews. On December 18, 1942, *Pravda* provided the full text of a joint declaration by eleven nations and the French National Committee condemning the persecution and murder of Jews in every territory occupied by the Germans, and declared that "such events can only reinforce the determination of freedom-loving peoples to overthrow Hitler's barbaric tyranny." And the next day *Izvestia* carried a prominent article under the grim headline: "On the Fulfillment of the Hitlerite Plan to Exterminate the Jewish Population of Europe." In three long columns, it described the deportation and massacre of Jews throughout Europe East and West, including Scandinavia and the occupied Soviet territories. It left no doubt that the plan was to rid Europe of all its Jews. [59]

But these public references to Jewish suffering came almost entirely in the first years of the war, when Stalin was anxious to curry favor with the West. By 1944 and 1945, when Soviet troops were already liberating the concentration camps, news articles hardly mentioned Jewish victims. In reports about massacres and concentration camps the word "Jew" was replaced by vague references to "peaceful civilians."

This kind of deceit—especially the denial of Jewish resistance, both officially and among the population—disturbed Ilya Ehrenburg and Vasily Grossman. The writer Mikhail Sholokhov told Ehrenburg in Kuybyshev in November 1941 that "You are fighting, but Abram is doing business in Tashkent." Ehrenburg was furious and shouted that he could not "sit at the same table with a pogrom-monger." [60] Later that month, Grossman sent Ehrenburg a detailed letter about antisemitism, about

---

the Jewish Anti-Fascist Committee (Yale University Press, New Haven, 2001, in association with the United States Holocaust Memorial Museum) for a history of the JAC and an abridged transcript of the secret trial of fifteen of its members in 1952.

56. Iosif Stalin, *O velikoy otechestvennoy voyne Sovetskogo Soyuza* (On the Great Patriotic War of the Soviet Union) (Moscow, 1950), pp. 50–51.
57. *Izvestia*, November 19, 1941, p. 4
58. *Pravda*, January 7, 1942, pp. 1–2.
59. *Pravda*, December 18, 1942, p. 1, and *Izvestia*, December 19, 1942, p. 1.
60. Commentary by Boris Frezinsky in Ilya Ehrenburg, *Lyudi, gody, zhizn* (People, Years, Life) (Moscow, 2005), vol. 3, p. 495–496. The canard usually ran: "Ivan is at the Front, while Abram is in Tashkent."

the many Jews he encountered at the Front, and about Sholokhov's disreputable behavior:

> I think about Sholokhov's antisemitic slander with pain and contempt. Here on the Southwestern Front, there are thousands, tens of thousands of Jews. They are walking with machine-guns into snowstorms, breaking into towns held by the Germans, falling in battle. I saw all of this. I saw the illustrious commander of the First Guards Division Kogan, tank officers, and intelligence men. If Sholokhov is in Kuybyshev, be sure to let him know that comrades at the Front know what he is saying. Let him be ashamed.[61]

Ehrenburg anguished over such slanders and did what he could to counteract them. In one article entitled "Jews," he described the heroic exploits of three fallen Jewish officers and their attacks on German positions. "Hitler wanted to turn the Jews into a target," he wrote in *Krasnaya zvezda* (Red Star) in November 1942. "The Jews of Russia showed him that a target shoots. . . . Once upon a time, the Jews dreamed of a promised land. Now a Jew has a promised land: the main line of defense. There he can take revenge against the Germans for wives, for the elderly, for the children.[62]

In April 1944 it was Ehrenburg who placed an unprecedented article in *Pravda* itself about the Yiddish-language poet and resistance fighter from Vilnius Abram Sutzkever. They had met that spring when both spoke before three thousand people at a rally organized by the Jewish Anti-Fascist Committee. Ehrenburg immediately befriended him. "He became closer to me than all my acquaintances, Jewish and non-Jewish writers and artists in Moscow," Sutzkever recalled years later.[63] Ehrenburg's article "The Triumph of a Man" described Sutzkever's leadership in the Vilna ghetto, his saving of precious manuscripts from a Jewish museum, and his partisan activity after he escaped the ghetto into the forests. Ehrenburg concluded the piece with a summary of Sutzkever's famous poem, "Kol Nidre," about an elderly Jew who kills his son to save him from torture at the hands of the Nazis.[64]

Such articles exemplify the role that Grossman and Ehrenburg assumed during the war—to give a face to Jewish suffering and Jewish resistance and to assure that the Jews would not be portrayed solely as victims. Their unique prestige, earned through their reporting on the war, made it possible to broaden the limits of what could be conveyed in the Soviet press. It was altogether natural, if not inevitable, that Ehrenburg and Grossman were the preeminent voices opposing the standard Soviet depiction of the Final Solution. No other figures during the war or in the

---

61. Letter of Vasily Grossman to Ilya Ehrenburg near the end of November 1941. From the archive of the late Irina Ehrenburg.
62. *Krasnaya zvezda,* November 1, 1942, p. 3.
63. Abraham Sutzkever, *Moznayim* (Balance), May–June, 1985, p. 53.
64. *Pravda,* April 29, 1944, p. 4.

immediate postwar period enjoyed the combined courage and stature to initiate such a challenge to the Kremlin's official, limited version of German atrocities.

Vasily Grossman was the most important correspondent on the German-Soviet Front. He witnessed the full fury of the fighting and the destruction. As his biographers John and Carol Garrard observed, Grossman

> spent over 1,000 days with the Red Army at the Front during their struggle against the Wehrmacht from 1941 to 1945. Arguably, Grossman thus witnessed more action than any other correspondent in any theater of World War II. He was present at the decisive battles on the Eastern Front: the sudden Soviet counterattack before Moscow in the winter of 1941; Stalingrad, the most savage hand-to-hand battle in human memory, in the fall and winter of 1942; Kursk, the greatest clash of armor in the history of warfare, in the summer of 1943; and many other battles of the Red Army's blood-soaked advance to Berlin."[65]

His reports from Stalingrad were a vivid source of information for the Soviet public until his editor, David Ortenberg, abruptly withdrew Grossman from Stalingrad and assigned the reliable Russian journalist Konstantin Simonov to report the victory on the Volga. Ortenberg was a Jew himself; he used the pen name Vadimov at *Krasnaya zvezda*. It is hard to know whether Ortenberg was following the order of Stalin, who may not have wanted Grossman to cover the victory, or whether Ortenberg was acting on what he thought might be Stalin's wishes. For Ehrenburg, Grossman's transfer out of Stalingrad was a gross injustice. Soviet troops at Stalingrad "did not look on Grossman as a journalist, but saw him as one of their fighting comrades, [who] could convey all of the tragedy" of the battle.[66]

Later that year, as Grossman followed the Red Army chasing the Wehrmacht out of Soviet territory, he came to understand the full magnitude of the massacres. His piece "Ukraine Without Jews," which he hoped to publish in *Krasnaya zvezda*, was rejected and only appeared that November in Yiddish translation in *Eynikayt* (Unity), the newspaper of the Jewish Anti-Fascist Committee. By then Grossman had witnessed the liberation of many Ukrainian towns and villages. He was stunned by the absence of Jewish survivors. "There are no Jews in Ukraine," Grossman wrote. "Nowhere—Poltava, Kharkov, Kremenchug, Borispol, Yagotin—in none of the cities, hundreds of towns, or thousands of villages will you see the black, tear-filled eyes of little girls; you will not hear the sad voice of an old woman; you will not see the dark face of a hungry baby. All is silence. Everything is still. A whole people have been brutally murdered."[67]

His own mother was among the fallen. Trapped by the Germans in the summer of 1941, she was among the twelve thousand Jews killed outside Berdichev on

---

65. John and Carol Garrard, *The Bones of Berdichev* (New York, 1996), p. xvii.
66. Ehrenburg, *Lyudi, gody, zhizn*, vol. 2, p. 424.
67. Garrard, *The Bones of Berdichev*, p. 170.

September 15, 1941. Throughout the war, his mother's fate weighed heavily on Grossman, but it was only in January 1944 that he was able to reach Berdichev and to retrace his mother's forced march from the ghetto to an airstrip outside of town where two large mounds covered thousands of Jews who had been shot and buried.[68] Determined to clarify the details of what had taken place, Grossman interviewed survivors and witnesses. This material formed the basis for his essay "The Murder of the Jews of Berdichev," which became part of *The Black Book*.[69]

Grossman did not spare himself. In the summer of 1944 he was reporting from Poland. When he reached Lublin, he observed that when the Germans wanted to annihilate the general population, they always "began with the Jews." And in Lublin, "with [its] sizable Jewish population, I did not meet a single Jew."[70] In the fall of 1944 he followed Soviet troops to the site of the now-destroyed extermination camp at Treblinka, sixty kilometers east of Warsaw. He was among the first to write about the systematic mass murder of Jews in Poland. His piece "The Hell of Treblinka" originally appeared in *Znamya* (Banner) and later was to assume a central place in *The Black Book*.[71] There was nothing veiled in Grossman's language. Treblinka was "a slaughterhouse for Jews" where "the animals" forced the camp's regulations "upon the humans." It was a heartless enterprise "operated as if they were raising cabbage or potatoes."[72] Grossman continued to visit killing sites in order to insure the vividness and reliability of his reporting. Soon after his return to Moscow in summer 1944, Ehrenburg invited him to meet with several people, including Western journalists, to press on them the gravity of what was being discovered in the camps. But Grossman was suffering from uncontrollable nausea and was forced to stay in bed.[73]

During Grossman's final years he was in conflict with the regime, which had confiscated the manuscript of *Life and Fate*, his great novel about the war. Upon Grossman's death in 1964, Ehrenburg was among the principal speakers at the funeral. "One need

---

68. See Antony Beevor and Luba Vinogradova, *A Writer at War: Vasily Grossman with the Red Army, 1941–1945* (New York, 2006), p. 113, for a diary entry in spring 1942 expressing his despair over his mother's likely fate.
69. The essay can be found in Ilya Ehrenburg and Vasily Grossman, eds., *The Complete Black Book of Russian Jewry* (New Brunswick, N.J., 2002), translated and edited by David Patterson, pp. 12–20.
70. Vasily Grossman, "V gorodakh i selakh Polshi" (In the cities and towns of Poland), *Literaturnaya gazeta*, August 6, 1944, p. 3. Lublin, which had a pre-war Jewish population of 40,000, and the nearby extermination camp of Majdanek, were liberated by the Red Army on July 24. In the article Grossman went on to describe how the gas chambers worked in Majdanek. See as well Beevor and Vinogradova, *A Writer at War*, pp. 280–306 for a full chapter about Grossman's visit to Lublin, Majdanek, and Treblinka.
71. *Znamya*, no. 11 (November 1944), pp. 121–124.
72. Ehrenburg and Grossman, *The Complete Black Book of Russian Jewry*, "Treblinka," pp. 465, 463, 470.
73. See Jean Cathala, *Sans fleur ni fusil* (Paris, 1981), p. 371.

not learn from Grossman how to write," Ehrenburg declared. "But one needs to learn from him what to write."[74]

It would be difficult to overstate the contribution to the Soviet war effort of Ilya Ehrenburg, the initiator and principal editor of *The Black Book*. Ehrenburg's prestige during the war was astonishing and unexpected. He had lived virtually his entire adult life in Western Europe. After imprisonment in a tsarist jail as a Bolshevik organizer, Ehrenburg fled into political exile in 1908, quit the Bolshevik movement, then returned to Russia in 1917, only to leave again in 1921. For the next two decades, although he held a Soviet passport, Ehrenburg forged a career as a writer and journalist living in France, publishing widely, and traveling throughout Europe. But he relinquished his independence in 1932 when he became *Izvestia*'s correspondent in Paris. After covering the Spanish Civil War and witnessing the German occupation of Paris, he returned to Moscow in summer 1940. In the eyes of many people he fell into suspicious categories: he was an intellectual, an ex-Bolshevik, a Jew, and someone who had lived in the West. Ehrenburg did not know it at the time, but in 1938 and 1939, when he was still in Spain and France covering the rise of fascism, the Soviet regime was forcing arrested friends such as the writer Isaac Babel to provide testimony that Ehrenburg was a "Trotskyite spy" involved in a plot to overthrow the regime. But no charges were ever brought against him.[75]

Within days of the German invasion in June 1941, Ehrenburg was invited to write a column in *Krasnaya zvezda,* the paper of the Red Army. Ultimately he would contribute more than two thousand articles to the Soviet press and for Western newspapers during four years of war. Ehrenburg believed that the Soviet people had not been readied for this conflict, many of them expecting to face civilized Germans as in World War I. Ehrenburg knew better; he knew they were facing Nazified Germans and would have to learn to hate them in order to overcome the invasion. Soviet troops were especially drawn to his writing; officers were known to read Ehrenburg's columns to the troops before battles. There was even a decree that his columns had to be cut out before the newspapers could be used to roll cigarettes.

Ehrenburg also consistently devoted time and attention to the plight of the Jews. He wrote about atrocities, about Jewish military heroes. Reading his pieces, Jewish soldiers and families across the country saw him as an "address" to whom to send countless letters, pouring out their hearts. Ehrenburg tried to share this material as well. One project, *100 Letters,* was to contain correspondence from soldiers at the Front and to appear in French and Russian in 1943. But after Soviet victories,

---

74. Commentary by Boris Frezinsky to Ehrenburg, *Lyudi, gody, zhizn,* vol. 2, p. 562. Ehrenburg also wrote a famous tribute to Grossman in *Literaturnaya gazeta* on February 23, 1946, p. 3, entitled "Glazami Vasiliia Grossmana" (Through the Eyes of Vasily Grossman).
75. For a discussion of this incident and other issues relating to Ehrenburg's complicated and sometimes contradictory career, see Joshua Rubenstein, *Tangled Loyalties: The Life and Times of Ilya Ehrenburg* (Tuscaloosa, Ala., 1999).

bureaucrats and editors began to censor his work more frequently, often targeting his references to Jews and Jewish suffering. *100 Letters* did appear in French translation, but the Russian volume was never published.[76]

There were times when Ehrenburg's articles were so outspoken and so explicit about Jewish suffering—and so out of step with Soviet propaganda—that the censors would not permit them to appear in the central press, though they did allow some to appear in Yiddish translation in an obscure newspaper like *Birobidzhaner shtern* (Birobidzhan Star) or in *Eynikayt*. In the article "Our Place," for example, Ehrenburg expressed his full identification with the Jewish people. "Yes," he wrote, "there are fewer Jews than there once were, but every Jew is greater than he was before. . . . We will die, but we will destroy the hated butchers."[77] And in another article in the same newspaper entitled "Why do the fascists so hate the Jews?" Ehrenburg condemned the Nazis and indirectly rebuked the Kremlin as well. "In order to justify the annihilation of the Jews," Ehrenburg wrote, "the fascists scream that the Jews have always been hostile to the national culture of the people among whom they are living. This is a lie. Who besides Heine expressed the German spirit during the romantic age? Who besides Disraeli, with such wisdom and knowledge, defended the interests of Victorian England?"[78]

Within a year of the Soviet victory at Stalingrad, Party bureaucrats began a quiet purge of Jews from the country's leading cultural institutions, such as the Bolshoi Opera. And in 1949, during the infamous anti-cosmopolitan campaign, Jews were targeted again, this time publicly and in the harshest and crudest of terms, for their indifference to Russian culture. Ehrenburg was beginning to understand how the murderous antisemitism of the Germans could infect Soviet culture as well.[79]

---

76. Ehrenburg was able to publish without such restrictions for foreign audiences. On August 2, 1943, the Soviet embassy in Washington, D.C., distributed his article "The Murder of the Jewish People" in a special supplement to its *Information Bulletin*.
77. "Nashe mesto" first appeared in *Birobidzhaner shtern* on August 11, 1943. It is reprinted in the collection *Voina 1941–1945* (War 1941–1945) (Moscow, 2004), pp. 457–459; the collection is edited and introduced by the Saint Petersburg scholar Boris Frezinsky.
78. "Pochemu fashisty tak nenavidyat evreev?" *Birobidzhaner shtern*, July 17, 1942. I am grateful to Boris Frezinsky for sharing the text of this article with me.
79. Ehrenburg was always sensitive to the suspicion that Jews could not identify with the plight of their fellow Jews anywhere and still remain loyal to the country in which they are living. In April 1917, in an article entitled "French Jews and the War," he described seeing Jews from many different countries at the Front, and he went on to refer to the satisfaction of French Jewish soldiers who welcomed the decision of the newly installed Provisional Government in Russia to abolish the Pale of Settlement, where the tsar's Jews had been forced to live. As he wrote at the outset of this article, "the Greco-Roman world indicted the Jews, claiming that in a cosmopolitan society they remained nationalists, while the modern world indicts them by claiming that among nationalists, [the Jews] are cosmopolitans"; see *Birzhevie vedomosti* (The Stock Exchange Gazette), April 15, 1917 (April 28), morning ed., p. 5.

Ehrenburg persisted. Shortly after the German occupation of Hungary in March 1944, Ehrenburg understood that hundreds of thousands of Jews who had survived under a Hungarian fascist regime were now in grave danger. Writing in the mass circulation journal *Voina i rabochii klass* (War and the Working Class), Ehrenburg appealed on behalf of Hungarian Jewry.[80] Later that year, two articles in *Pravda* further exemplified his unique stature. By August 1944, Soviet troops were approaching the German border. Thousands were taken to Majdanek and Treblinka as part of their preparation for the final assault on the Germans. In "On the Eve," an article for the August 7 issue of *Pravda*, Ehrenburg described how trains carried Jews from France, the Netherlands, and Belgium to extermination centers in German-occupied Poland. "We are not only on the German border," he wrote, "we are on the threshold of a trial. . . . It is not revenge that is driving us, but a longing for justice."[81]

Five months later, with Soviet armies poised to invade East Prussia, Ehrenburg focused again in *Pravda* on the Nazis' greatest crime. "Ask a captured German why his countrymen destroyed six million innocent people and he will answer: 'They are Jews. They are black or red-haired. They have different blood'. . . . All this began with stupid jokes, with the shouts of street kids, with signposts, and it led to Majdanek, Babi Yar, Treblinka, to ditches filled with children's corpses."[82] This may have been the first reference in print to the number six million. It is not clear how Ehrenburg reached this figure, but there is little doubt that he was the first journalist to grasp the full magnitude of the Final Solution.

Nor could the Nazis fail to take note of Ehrenburg's voice. In March 1943, the leading Nazi newspaper, the *Volkischer Beobachter* (People's Observer), lashed out at him on its front page, claiming that his articles were "an appealing mixture, lumping sentimental caricatures of soft-hearted and magnanimous Soviet soldiers with genuine slander about the behavior of German troops on the Eastern Front. It is all a lie from beginning to end."[83] Hitler himself signed an order complaining on January 1, 1945, that "Stalin's court lackey, Ilya Ehrenburg, declares that the German people must be exterminated."[84]

The Black Book project exemplified Ehrenburg's commitment to documenting the Final Solution on German-occupied Soviet territory. Through the Jewish Anti-Fascist Committee, he assembled a group of two dozen Jewish and non-Jewish writers and journalists to follow the Red Army as it pushed the Germans out of the country and beyond. They found massacre sites, desperate notes and letters in former ghettos, as well as diaries on the corpses of German soldiers. Ehrenburg himself

---

80. See Ilya Ehrenburg, "Spravedlivost" (Justice), *Voina i rabochii klass* (War and the Working Class), 12 (June 15, 1944), p. 8.
81. *Pravda*, August 7, 1944, p. 3.
82. *Pravda*, December 17, 1944, p. 3.
83. *Volkischer Beobachter*, March 25, 1943, p. 1.
84. As cited by Ilya Ehrenburg in his memoirs; see *Lyudi, gody, zhizn*, vol. 2, p. 304.

carried out many interviews and edited a large proportion of the material they gathered. He hoped to see a volume published in the Soviet Union, not only as a means to commemorate the dead but to counteract the antisemitism he saw flourishing during the second half of the war.

The Black Book fell victim to the Kremlin's growing indifference to Jewish suffering and to its own promotion of antisemitism. In late 1944 an official review of the manuscript concluded, "Too much is recounted in the sketches about the vile activity of the traitors among the Ukrainians, Lithuanians, et al. This diminishes the force of the main accusation against the Germans, which should be the primary and decisive purpose of the book." [85] So reports of collaboration were removed, much to Ehrenburg's chagrin. It was only decades later that Ilya Altman found these testimonies in a Moscow archive, and collected them in *The Unknown Black Book*.

Ehrenburg quit the project in anger, handing it over to Vasily Grossman. But the regime did not relent. In 1947 the Central Committee issued a definitive judgment, confirming *The Black Book*'s "grave political errors" and making it impossible to publish. [86] In January 1948, Stalin ordered the killing of the famous theater director Solomon Mikhoels (his murder was camouflaged as a traffic accident). The following November saw the official closing of the Jewish Anti-Fascist Committee and the arrests of many of its leading members. The typeset of *The Black Book* was broken up. *The Black Book* never appeared in the Soviet Union. But it was published by Yad Vashem in Jerusalem three decades later.

The mass killings throughout Ukraine, Belorussia, Bessarabia and Bukovina, and the Baltic region still haunt these lands. Although Stalin permitted memorial services in the main Moscow synagogue in 1945 and 1946, subsequent appeals to hold memorial assemblies were ignored or suppressed by local officials. [87] The famous Soviet Jewish general David Dragunsky, who had lost scores of relatives to the Nazis, asked the Jewish Anti-Fascist Committee in 1946 to set up "memorial stones for the executed children, old people, and women. . . . We must erect fences, monuments, and plaques everywhere and show dates." [88] But his plea led nowhere. Even when families took it on themselves to place modest memorials at massacre sites, the regime would dismantle them or erase any direct reference to the fact that the victims were Jews. On the twentieth anniversary of the slaughter at Babi Yar, Yevgeny Yevtushenko's famous poem, decrying the lack of a proper memorial at the ravine outside Kiev, provoked a severe backlash by the Kremlin. In the 1980s there were reports of mass graves being looted for jewelry and other valuables. [89] Now, after the

---

85. Redlich, *War, Holocaust and Stalinism*, p. 355.
86. Ibid., p. 368.
87. See Mordechai Altshuler, "Jewish Holocaust Commemoration Activity in the USSR Under Stalin," *Yad Vashem Studies* 30 (January 2002), pp. 271–295.
88. Redlich, *War, Holocaust and Stalinism*, p. 231.
89. The poet Andrei Voznesensky came across a group of people in Simferopol who were digging up a

liberalization and then the collapse of the Soviet Union, Jews have been free to discover this history, to examine material in formerly closed archives, and to remember their dead in public.

There has even been a heroic, ongoing project led by the French Catholic priest Father Patrick Desbois to locate "all sites where Jews murdered by the Nazis were buried in Ukraine." By his own estimate, Father Desbois is looking for 1,200 mass graves. Appealing to local priests, he has been able to gain concrete information from elderly people who witnessed their Jewish neighbors being taken away. Father Desbois and his colleagues make narrow openings at sites to verify they are actually mass graves, estimate the number of bodies based on the size and depth of the pit, and find forensic and ballistics evidence to prove the grave dates from the war. At that point, they arrange for a proper memorial stone to mark the site.[90]

The Soviet Trials Begin

Judicial proceedings against Nazi perpetrators and their collaborators did not begin at Nuremberg. Already in the summer of 1943, following the victories at Stalingrad and Kursk, the Soviet regime held the first trial of collaborators, in Krasnodar, in the southeastern part of European Russia east of the Black and Azov Seas, an area that had been occupied between August 1942 and February 1943.[91] In the surrounding region, the Germans had killed over twenty thousand Jews.[92] This was the first trial in which the mass murders of the Einsatzgruppen and the use of gas vans were made known to the broader world. Hoping to deter further collaboration, prosecutors indicted eleven Soviet civilians for working with the Germans; eight were publicly executed immediately after the trial in front of a crowd of thousands. Five months later another significant trial was held in Kharkov, where the Germans had murdered twenty thousand Jews. In spite of their vivid recounting of atrocities, such trials did not always identify the Jews as the Germans' principal victims. In Krasnodar and Kharkov, for example, the fate of the Jews was not mentioned explicitly at all. But this did not deter Ehrenburg. Covering the Kharkov trial for *Krasnaya zvezda*, he wrote explicitly about the Jewish victims and described with contempt how German officers spoke without emotion about

---

mass grave on the outskirts of town. He wrote several poems about the incident, which appeared in the journal *Yunost* (Youth). But the accompanying article could only refer to "civilians" and deliberately avoided saying that the victims were Jews. According to *Yunost*, the authorities dispatched an official commission, convicted the criminals, and arranged to place a memorial at the site. See *Yunost*, July 1986, pp. 6–15.

90. See Roey Cohen, "Saint Patrick," *Haaretz*, May 1, 2006. *Haaretz* is a daily newspaper published in Tel Aviv.
91. I would like to acknowledge the assistance of Ilya Bourtman and his paper "Blood for Blood, Death for Death! History, Mechanism and Portrayal of Soviet Investigations and Military Tribunals (1943–1946)," Johns Hopkins University history thesis, May 2005.
92. Altman, *Zhertvy nenavisti*, p. 286.

killing helpless women and children, as if hoping they could "emerge dry from the water."[93]

Subsequent trials in the Soviet Union reflected a similar ambivalence over how to acknowledge the Jewish victims. In Smolensk, Minsk, Riga, and Kiev in the immediate post-war period large-scale trials were held, with scores of defendants, including high-ranking Nazi officers and their civilian collaborators. Charged with committing atrocities, many were in fact asked specifically about "the murder of Soviet citizens of Jewish nationality."

In Riga, on February 3, 1946, SS general and police leader Friedrich Jeckeln was one of the defendants. Units under his command had killed hundreds of thousands of Jews in Ukraine, Belorussia, and the Baltic region. (Himmler held Jeckeln in great esteem and made a point of assigning him to liquidate large Jewish populations in Latvia.) Convicted by a people's court, Jeckeln was hanged on the afternoon of the day he was tried.

The Kremlin deliberately mounted a number of trials just when the International Military Tribunal against leading Nazis was getting underway in Nuremberg in the fall of 1945. According to Alexander Prusin, who has studied these Soviet trials, "the Soviet press and the prosecution in the courtrooms repeatedly stressed that the trials in the Soviet Union were part and parcel 'of the unified international campaign to punish war criminals. The reports from the trials were published alongside the headlines from Nuremberg."[94] Publicity for the Soviet trials played a major role in revealing "to the Soviet public the scope of the Jews' tragedy," even when press reports referred to all victims with the more neutral and deliberately misleading phrase "Soviet citizens."[95]

Nuremberg

It was at Nuremberg that the Allies settled their accounts.

The trials at Nuremberg, for all their success and the rich and enduring inspiration they continue to provide, still leave a legacy of uneven justice. The first trial—the International Military Tribunal, or IMT—remains the most familiar in our collective memory. Its twenty-two defendants included several of the most infamous political and military leaders of Nazi Germany: Hermann Goering, Rudolf Hess, Albert Speer, Joachim von Ribbentrop, Alfred Rosenberg, Ernst Kaltenbrunner, Wilhelm Keitel, and others.

This was the most elaborate of the thirteen trials that took place at Nuremberg, and the only one to involve judges and prosecutors of all four major Allied powers—

---

93. See *Krasnaya zvezda,* December 17, p. 3; December 18, p. 3; and December 19, 1943, p. 3 for a series of three articles by Ehrenburg about the Kharkov trial.
94. Alexander Prusin, "'Fascist Criminals to the Gallows!': The Holocaust and Soviet War Crimes Trials, December 1945–February 1946," *Holocaust and Genocide Studies* 17, no. 1 (2003), p. 7.
95. Ibid., p. 9.

the United States, the Soviet Union, Great Britain, and France. But contrary to what most people assume about justice at Nuremberg, the mass murder of the Jews was not the driving force behind the prosecution, although this was the first time that the crime of genocide was included in a criminal indictment. The principal charges involved initiating a war of aggression, war crimes (against soldiers and civilians), and crimes against humanity. The IMT, after all, opened on November 20, 1945, just six months after the end of the war in Europe, when the Allies were still absorbing the scale of the Nazis' crimes. Telford Taylor, who served as assistant to Justice Robert Jackson during the IMT and then as Chief Prosecutor for all twelve subsequent trials, acknowledged in his memoirs that in 1945 he "remained ignorant of the mass extermination camps in Poland and [that] the full scope of the Holocaust did not dawn on me until several months later." [96]

The IMT, nonetheless, succeeded in presenting "the first comprehensive definition and documentation to a non-Jewish audience of the persecution and massacre of European Jewry," as Michael Marrus has noted. [97] In his famous opening statement, Justice Jackson devoted an entire section to crimes against the Jews, "the most savage and numerous crimes planned and committed by the Nazis." [98] Over the year that followed, more than eight hundred documents and thirty witnesses substantiated the charges regarding the fate of the Jews.

About six weeks into the trial the Americans summoned SS general Otto Ohlendorf to testify. Ohlendorf had commanded Einsatzgruppe D, which had operated in southern Ukraine and the Crimea. His testimony was "a real blockbuster," as Taylor recalled in his memoirs. "Ohlendorf was small of stature, young-looking, and rather comely. He spoke quietly, with great precision, dispassion, and apparent intelligence," even as he admitted that under his command the five hundred men of Einsatzgruppe D had killed ninety thousand people between June 1941 and June 1942, including men, women, and children. [99] Similar testimony that linked the army to the atrocities of the Einsatzgruppen was heard from General Erich von dem Bach-Zelewski. Their statements stunned the courtroom, provoking even Hermann Goering, who always tried hard to preserve his equanimity. Following Ohlendorf's testimony, Goering was heard to denounce him as a "swine" who was "selling his soul to the enemy." And when Bach-Zelewski left the witness stand, Goering "glared at him and snarled, 'swine and traitor.'" [100]

---

96. Taylor, *The Anatomy of the Nuremberg Trials*, p. xi.
97. Michael R. Marrus, "The Holocaust at Nuremberg," paper prepared for a conference, "Political Justice in Europe in the Aftermath of World War Two," Institut für die Wissenschaften vom Menschen, Vienna, November 1995, revised in February 1996, p. 1.
98. *Trial of the Major War Criminals Before the International Military Tribunal, Nuremberg, 14 November 1945–1 October 1946* (Nuremberg, Germany, 1947), vol. 2, p. 18.
99. Taylor, *The Anatomy of the Nuremberg Trials*, pp. 246, 248.
100. Ibid., pp. 248, 260. Ohlendorf testified on January 3, 1946; his testimony can be found in *IMT*, vol. 4,

The Soviet prosecutors also decided to focus on the persecution of the Jews. They called three witnesses on February 27, 1946: the poet Abram Sutzkever; Severine Shmaglevskaya, a Polish woman who described the murder of Jewish women and children at Auschwitz; and Samuel Rajzman, one of the few Jews who had miraculously survived for nearly a year in Treblinka. Sutzkever had been among the partisans in the Vilna ghetto; he provided vivid testimony about the fate of Lithuanian Jewry and the extermination of nearly eighty thousand Jews in Vilna alone. [101]

The Soviet press responded favorably to their testimonies. Writing in *Pravda* a week later, the well-known journalist Boris Polevoy identified Sutzkever as a "Yiddish poet" with a European reputation, who had survived "the Jewish ghetto" in Vilna. Polevoy was most impressed by Sutzkever's description of his family's destruction at the hands of the Germans. [102]

Following the IMT, Telford Taylor and his colleagues planned to hold as many as eighteen subsequent proceedings, focusing on the leaders of important sectors of German society—bankers, industrialists, doctors—who had been directly complicit in the crimes of the Nazis. The trial of the Einsatzgruppen leaders was not originally among them. But then in 1946 an American officer working under the supervision of a young war-crimes investigator named Benjamin Ferencz came across a large trove of documents in the basement of the German Foreign Ministry. Looking them over, he immediately understood their disturbing value. He hurried to share them with Ferencz. [103] Recruited by Telford Taylor, Benjamin Ferencz was serving as chief of the Berlin branch of the Office of Chief of Counsel for War Crimes. It was his responsibility to help prosecutors gather material evidence from captured Nazi documents as they proceeded with cases against a wide variety of government, military, and industrial leaders. [104]

---

pp. 311–354. Bach-Zalewski testified on January 7, 1946; his testimony can be found in *IMT*, vol. 4, pp. 475–496.

101. *IMT*, vol. 8, pp. 301–321. These three witnesses all appeared on February 27, 1946. Sutzkever is referred to in the trial transcript with the spelling Suzkever. Ilya Ehrenburg, with the help of Solomon Mikhoels, arranged for Sutzkever to testify at Nuremberg. Sutzkever confided to Ehrenburg that he intended to smuggle a gun into the Palace of Justice to shoot Goering, but Ehrenburg dissuaded Sutzkever from carrying out such a desperate act. See Joseph Leftwich, *Abraham Sutzkever: Partisan Poet* (New York, 1971), pp. 10 and 51.

102. Boris Polevoy, "Ot imeni chelovechestva" (In the Name of Humanity), *Pravda*, March 4, 1946, p. 4. Polevoy repeated these observations in his book on the trial *V kontse kontsov* (In the End) (Moscow, 1969), pp. 167–68; there is also a drawing of Sutzkever from Nuremberg in the book. When Sutzkever returned to Moscow, he visited Ehrenburg. In his memoirs, Ehrenburg made a point of recalling Polevoy's coverage of Sutzkever's testimony in *Pravda* and how the judges were shaken by his story; see *Lyudi, gody, zhizn*, vol. 3, p. 37.

103. Earl, *Accidental Justice*, pp. 122–123.

104. Ibid., p. 122. See also the oral history interview with Benjamin B. Ferencz conducted by the United States Holocaust Memorial Museum, on August 26, 1994, and October 21, 1994 (RG-50.030*269).

Ferencz was brought twelve loose-leaf notebooks containing "top secret daily reports from the Eastern Front itemizing the carnage of the mobile security and killing units."[105] Gestapo Chief Heinrich Müller had ordered the heads of all four Einsatzgruppen to send Hitler reports about their work "in the East."[106] What Ferencz examined was a set of duplicates—the only set ever found—one of approximately one hundred that had been broadly distributed within the German government and military bureaucracy. As *New Yorker* writer Andy Logan observed, such precise reports reflected "the weakness of the members of the erstwhile super-race for keeping *Protokolle*, or records, elaborately indexed, of everything they did, thought, or hoped for."[107]

Ferencz read them carefully, using an adding machine to tally up the murders. He stopped when he reached one million. When he showed them to Taylor, the general was horrified, but felt perplexed over what to do: they were planning to hold more trials, but there were neither personnel nor a budget for yet another. Ferencz persisted, insisting that the murder of over one million Jews could not be ignored and that the documents provided such compelling and dramatic evidence that a way had to be found to hold the perpetrators accountable. Taylor reconsidered. He was already planning on bringing Ohlendorf to justice, and intended to try other members of the SS. If Ferencz believed he had the time, Taylor would permit him to organize a trial specifically for leaders of the Einsatzgruppen.[108]

The Einsatzgruppen Trial opened on September 29, 1947 (six years to the day after the massacre at Babi Yar), and lasted for eight months. There were twenty-three defendants, including six SS generals. (One additional defendant committed suicide before the start of the trial.) From all the perpetrators in custody, Ferencz deliberately chose to prosecute only those of genuinely high rank and education; there were to be no enlisted men in the dock. At trial, they were all charged with "the murder of more than one million persons, tortures, and atrocities, and other inhumane acts."[109] The indictment went on to list nearly one hundred separate incidents or patterns of incidents associated with each Einsatzgruppe, what the prosecution called "a systematic program of genocide," only the second time the term was used as part of an actual indictment.[110]

Ferencz presented the prosecution's case in two days, relying on the Einsatzgruppen reports as his principal evidence. His only witness was the chief interrogator, Rolf

---

105. Earl, *Accidental Justice*, pp. 124–125.
106. Cited in Saul Friedländer, "From Anti-Semitism to Extermination: A Historiographical Study of Nazi Policies toward the Jews and an Essay in Interpretation," *Yad Vashem Studies* 16 (1984), p. 31.
107. Andy Logan, "Letter from Nuremberg," *The New Yorker*, December 27, 1947, p. 45. Logan spent two years in Nuremberg with her husband, Charles Lyons, who was serving as an American prosecutor.
108. Author interview with Benjamin Ferencz, New Rochelle, N.Y., June 4, 2005.
109. *Einsatzgruppen Trial Account*, p. 13.
110. Ibid., p. 15.

Wartenberg, who assured the court that the defendants had been questioned properly, without the use of any "third degree" tactics. [111]

Faced with overwhelming evidence of their guilt, several defendants tried to mitigate their culpability by assuring the court that they did all they could to avoid gratuitous violence. Heinz Schubert (a direct descendant of the composer Franz Schubert) sought to establish his humanitarian credentials by explaining that he "took care that the condemned persons were not beaten while the loading [into gas vans] was going on." [112] And Ernst Biberstein, who also oversaw the use of gas vans, assured the judges that he himself "saw the unloading of the dead bodies, [that] their faces were in no way distorted, [and that] death came to these people without any outward signs of spasms." [113] Or as Otto Ohlendorf claimed, "it was my wish that these executions be carried out in a manner and fashion which was military and suitably humane under the circumstances." [114]

These Nazi officers, in fact, had been more concerned over the psychological impact of such killing on their own men than by any scruples about the murders. Ohlendorf, for example, "never permitted shooting by individuals in Group D, but ordered that several of the men should shoot at the same time in order to avoid direct personal responsibility." [115] Blobel too adjusted his practice by arranging for his men to shoot for only one hour at a time before being replaced.

Otto Ohlendorf was the central figure in the case. His readiness to testify—he had already appeared at the IMT in January 1946 and would later testify at the trial of the German High Command in August 1948 as a witness for the defense—and to confess to his actions (but not his guilt) made him stand out from virtually all the other defendants at Nuremberg. [116] Ohlendorf's testimony reflected how an intelligent, well-educated German could participate in mass murder out of sheer ideological conviction.

During the final years of the war Ohlendorf had been "instrumental in shaping and refining Nazi intelligence-gathering practices," Hilary Earl has noted. "He saw this work as important and was so arrogant and deluded that he actually believed that the Allies would utilize his expertise when they realized his intellectual strengths as an opinion researcher." [117]

Ohlendorf gave himself up to British forces on May 24, 1945, more than two full weeks after the unconditional German surrender. Over the next two years, he was

---

111. Author interview with Hannah Wartenberg, New York, N.Y., May 6, 2005.
112. *Einsatzgruppen Trial Account*, p. 208.
113. Ibid., p. 210
114. Ibid., p. 134.
115. Ibid., p. 206.
116. Ohlendorf's testimony at the trial of the German High Command on August 6, 1948, can be found in *Trials of War Criminals Before the Nuernberg Military Tribunals*, pp. 1277–1280.
117. Earl, *Accidental Justice*, p. 96.

interrogated on thirty-six different occasions by the Americans, who had obtained his extradition from the British Zone; they were hoping to use him as a witness against other Nazi leaders.[118] Ohlendorf did not disappoint them and identified hundreds of other war criminals who otherwise would have been difficult if not impossible to track. Ohlendorf's attitude baffled his interrogators. "His moral compass was so skewed that he genuinely believed that what he had done, supervise the murder of 90,000 innocent civilians, was not wrong," as Hilary Earl pointed out in *Accidental Justice*, her study of the trial.[119] One prison psychologist had to conclude that Ohlendorf must have been "a sadist, a pervert or a lunatic" to have participated so intimately in genocide and then talked in such a matter-of-fact way about his crimes without the slightest hint of remorse.[120] For Ohlendorf, though, obedience to Hitler and Himmler was the highest ideal. Even when the prosecutor and Judge Michael Musmanno, determined to grasp the full measure of Ohlendorf's ideological commitment, challenged him to answer if he would kill his own sister if ordered to by a superior, Ohlendorf felt compelled to say "yes."[121]

Not all the defendants were as articulate or as ideologically committed as Ohlendorf. Several claimed they experienced inner conflicts but still had to obey orders. One defendant, Gustav Nosske, in the face of overwhelming corroborating evidence, stubbornly maintained his innocence until, pressed by Judge Musmanno, he admitted that his unit "might be" responsible for killing 244 people.[122] Another defendant, Walter Haensch, who was a lawyer by training, denied doing anything illegal or immoral; he claimed that he learned about the murder of the Jews only when he reached Nuremberg in July 1947. And when prosecutors showed reports confirming his unit's massacres, Haensch had the audacity to declare under oath that he had been "in Berlin, attending a birthday party, having his photograph taken, and visiting his dentist."[123]

Paul Blobel offered a different kind of defense. He had supervised the killings at Babi Yar, earning a reputation among the Nazis as one of their most efficient killers. One witness claimed that Blobel "lost patience with the pace of the operation and frequently yelled at his men to speed it up."[124] Judge Musmanno later recalled that

---

118. Ibid., p. 81.
119. Ibid., p. 99.
120. Ibid., p. 100. This same psychologist, Dr. Leon Goldensohn, described Ohlendorf as looking "like a burned-out ghoul, and his conscience, if it can be called such, is clean as a whistle and as empty. There is a dearth of affect, but nothing clinically remarkable. His attitude is 'Why blame me? I didn't do anything wrong.'" See Robert Gellately, ed., *The Nuremberg Interviews*, conducted by Leon Goldensohn (New York, 2004), p. 390.
121. See Michael A. Musmanno, *The Eichmann Kommandos* (Philadelphia, 1961), pp. 117–121, for a compelling account of how the court pressured Ohlendorf to respond on whether or not he would execute his sister.
122. Cited in Earl, *Accidental Justice*, p. 253; Nosske gave this testimony on December 9, 1947.
123. Ibid., p. 256.
124. Ibid., pp. 258–259.

Blobel "sat in the front row in the defendant's dock with his square red beard jut[ting] out ahead like the prow of a piratical ship commanded by himself. His blood-shot eyes glared with the penetrating intensity of a wild animal at bay."[125] During the pre-trial investigation, Blobel initially denied killing anyone. But Rolf Wartenberg persisted. "I questioned him about his sleep," Wartenberg once recalled. "I wanted to know if his conscience permitted him to sleep or if the memory of the Jews he had killed had disturbed his sleep. Now, he confessed, I was correct, he was directly involved in the execution of 10–15,000 Jews."[126] But Blobel insisted that he had not killed as many as his own reports had claimed, as if this alleged discrepancy could amount to mitigating evidence.

With the trial over, Judge Musmanno grappled with how to punish the defendants. He was a devout Catholic and the idea of imposing the death penalty "filled [him] with a sense of disquietude and sadness."[127] But he also understood the full scale and horror of the massacres. More important, as Andy Logan observed in December 1947 (while the trial was still underway), "with each succeeding war-crimes case in Germany, the sentences become less formidable (prisoners who would have been hanged a while back now get off with ten years)."[128] Judge Musmanno decided to ignore this trend toward increasing leniency. Of the twenty-three defendants in the Einsatzgruppen case, fourteen were sentenced to death, more even than were executed after the International Military Tribunal in 1946.

Andy Logan witnessed the reading of the sentences.

> The guard unit in the Nuremberg courthouse changed recently when Company C of the 370th Infantry Battalion took over the job. As the Einsatz Kommandos—most of them rather small, thin-nosed, pale-eyed men . . .—stood up to hear their sentences, they were flanked on one side by Staff Sergeant J. L. Henderson, of Houston, Texas, and on the other by Pfc. Joe Dodds, of Baton Rouge, Louisiana. Sergeant Henderson and Private Dodds are both nearly six and a half feet tall, proud, alert, and colored. They did not by the barest smile offend the terrible dignity of the occasion, but one could not escape the impression that they were enjoying their work.[129]

Justice, it seemed, was sure to be carried out.

But as trials continued to unfold in various parts of Europe, led by American, British, and Soviet prosecutors, a dispiriting pattern began to emerge: there was

---

125. Musmanno, *The Eichmann Kommandos*, p. 145.
126. Author interview with Hannah Wartenberg, New York, N.Y., May 6, 2005; the quotation is from the personal papers of Rolf Wartenberg, which have been deposited with the United States Holocaust Memorial Museum.
127. Musmanno, *The Eichmann Kommandos*, p. 259.
128. Andy Logan, "Letter from Nuremberg," *The New Yorker*, December 27, 1947, p. 44.
129. Andy Logan, "Letter from Germany," *The New Yorker*, May 8, 1948, p. 82.

less and less determination to hold Nazis accountable for their crimes. In the spring of 1948—just three years after the end of the war—Andy Logan wrote that "on the barbed-wire fence surrounding the crematorium and the mass grave at Dachau, there is a sign that reads, 'This Really Happened.' It appears to be in some danger of being replaced by one that reads, 'So What?'"[130] In the Soviet Union, as Alexander Prusin has shown, during the period 1945–1952 fewer than five hundred Axis personnel received death sentences. The Kremlin actually abolished the death penalty in May 1947, but the military tribunals still applied it on occasion, though after its abolition defendants in war crimes cases received lengthy sentences of up to twenty-five years. Nonetheless, by the mid-1950s, "those who had survived Soviet prisons and camps were repatriated or extradited to the German Democratic Republic, where some found employment with the state police and other government institutions."[131]

The British as well grew faint-hearted when faced with the challenge of what to do with several high-ranking German officers remaining in their custody, including field marshals Albert Kesselring and Erich von Manstein, and Colonel-General Nikolaus von Falkenhorst. Already in 1945, the same Winston Churchill who had once countenanced the idea of summarily shooting thousands of German leaders now stated, at least in regard to senior military figures, that he did not "like to see the German admirals and generals, with whom [the British] had made arrangements, being made to stand with their hands above their heads."[132]

For the British, there was a thoroughly unsubstantiated belief that the Wehrmacht, led by a professional officer corps, had fought honorably, while it was the SS who had carried out atrocities against civilians. This flew directly in the face of a mountain of evidence. The Wehrmacht, after all, was fully complicit in the crimes of the Einsatzgruppen and was charged with coordinating the work of the shooting units. It helped to set up ghettos, issued yellow badges, and commanded forced labor brigades, especially after December 1941, when the failure to capture Moscow made it necessary to exploit Jewish labor for what the army knew would turn into a much longer and more uncertain campaign. At Babi Yar, it was the army that helped to place explosives along the face of the ravine in order to cover up the mass grave. In the Crimea, it was the army that called upon Einsatzgruppe D to kill the Jews of Sebastopol before Christmas 1942. According to the Sonderkommando commander Werner Braune, "The army, at the time, was afraid that hundreds of thousands of people might starve to death." Based on such motives, some Wehrmacht leaders may have believed it would be more "humane" to murder them outright.[133]

---

130. Ibid., p. 81.
131. Prusin, "'Fascist Criminals to the Gallows!'" p. 30, n. 104.
132. Cited in Donald Bloxham, *Genocide on Trial: War Crimes Trials and the Formation of Holocaust History and Memory* (Oxford, 2001), p. 166.
133. *Einsatzgruppen Trial Account*, p. 546.

Field Marshal von Manstein, who led forces in the Crimea and Ukraine in 1941, had expressed his own belief in the necessity of annihilating the Jews.

> Since [the invasion of the USSR] the German people has been involved in a life-and-death struggle against the Bolshevik system. . . . This struggle is not being conducted . . . solely according to the European rules of war. . . . Jewry forms the middleman between the enemy in the rear and the part of the Red Army still fighting and the Red leadership. More strongly than in Europe [Jewry] holds all the key points of political leadership and administration, occupies commerce and trade, and further it forms the cell for all unrest and potential uprisings. The Jewish-Bolshevik system must be annihilated once and for all. . . . The soldier must comprehend the necessity for harsh atonement by Jewry, the spiritual bearer of the Bolshevik terror.[134]

But the British seemed indifferent to this stunning complicity. General von Falkenhorst, who had led German forces in Norway, was convicted of war crimes in August 1946—he had ordered the killing of British POWs—and sentenced to death by firing squad. But within months the sentence was reduced to twenty years, and he was released altogether in 1953. A similar process saved Field Marshal Kesselring. A British court convicted him of war crimes in May 1947 and condemned him to death. But the sentence was quickly commuted to life in prison and he was sent home in 1952.

As for von Manstein, whom many regarded as the Wehrmacht's most brilliant field commander, leading military figures worked hard to avoid bringing him to trial. A defense fund was established on von Manstein's behalf in England to which even Winston Churchill contributed twenty-five pounds. For Churchill, it now seemed foolish "to make a feature of such squalid long-drawn vengeance when the mind and soul of Germany may once again be hanging in the balance."[135] (This was in October 1948, just three years after the fall of Berlin and the liberation of the concentration camps.) But once the British turned down a request from the Kremlin to extradite von Manstein (his crimes had been committed against Soviet citizens on Soviet territory), the British decided to proceed with a trial.

It opened in Hamburg in August 1949. Von Manstein was acquitted of several of the most serious charges, but still was sentenced to eighteen years. By this time, Cold War realities and pressure from the government of the new German Federal Republic had grown stronger. There was the perceived need to appeal to West German public opinion in order to facilitate the country's integration into NATO.

---

134. Cited in Donald Bloxham, "Punishing German Soldiers during the Cold War: The Case of Erich von Manstein," *Patterns of Prejudice* 33, no. 4, 1999, p. 30, from von Manstein to Armeeoberkommando 11, November 20, 1941, reproduced in Leon Poliakov and Josef Wulf (eds.), *Das Dritte Reich und seine Diene: Dokumente* (Berlin: Volk und Welt, 1995), pp. 459–461.
135. Cited in Bloxham, "Punishing German Soldiers during the Cold War," p. 36.

Chancellor Konrad Adenauer explicitly linked these questions to "cessation of the defamation of the German soldier and a satisfactory settlement of sentences for war crimes."[136] Adenauer wanted leniency and was not afraid to link rearmament to clemency for condemned Nazis. By August 1952, von Manstein was released to a hospital for treatment of cataracts. Using his medical condition as a pretext, and taking into account reductions in his sentence already in effect, the British government effectively released him in the spring of 1953. By 1958, British jails had been cleared of all German war criminals.

The record of the United States grew equally uneven and troubling. Following the Einsatzgruppen trial, where fourteen defendants had been sentenced to death, the Americans were in no hurry to carry out the executions. As months went by, the mood in Germany began to harden, and pressure to commute the death sentences grew stronger. It became fashionable to quote Abraham Lincoln to the Americans, as if Lincoln's magnanimous attitude toward the defeated South could be applied to German war criminals.[137]

There were still more questionable tactics and claims. Ohlendorf's defense attorney filed a request for a pardon. One of his principal arguments was that the "Einsatzgruppen had not killed one million people as the indictment charged, but only 450,000. This . . . was a distortion of history and given [that] one of the stated purposes of the trial was to create an historical record" his client should be released altogether.[138] German Catholic and Protestant clergy often led efforts for commutation and were not above advancing unfounded claims. Bishop Hans Meiser, a leader of the Evangelical Church of Bavaria, accused Benjamin Ferencz of "threatening potential defense witnesses with the promise of extradition to the Soviet Zone if they testified in behalf of a defendant." He also claimed that Rolf Wartenberg had abused the defendants and altered their affidavits in order to confirm confessions of guilt. But Meiser failed to cite any corroborating evidence for his denunciation, while the defendants themselves never charged the prosecution with any mistreatment.[139]

General Lucius Clay headed the American Military Government in Germany until 1949, when the country was officially divided and West Germany regained a measure of sovereignty. He and his staff conducted a thorough review of the capital cases and confirmed the death sentences in spite of growing pressures within the country. But they were not carried out before Clay returned to America; the final decision was left to his successor, the Wall Street lawyer and former War Department

---

136. Ibid., p. 36, as cited from Konrad Adenauer, *Memoirs, 1945–1953* (London, 1966), p. 300.
137. Bruce M. Stave and Michele Palmer, with Leslie Frank, *Witnesses to Nuremberg: An Oral History of American Participants at the War Crimes Trials* (New York, 1998), interview with Andy Logan, p. 204.
138. Cited in Earl, *Accidental Justice*, pp. 454–455.
139. Ibid., p. 463.

official John J. McCloy, who came to Europe to serve as high commissioner in the new Federal Republic of Germany.

McCloy assumed his position at a time when the Cold War was growing more acute. Benjamin Ferencz, the only Nuremberg prosecutor who remained in Germany, recalled that "at the time there was a sense of panic about the Russians, a feeling that there was an urgent need for an understanding with the Germans. McCloy couldn't detach himself from that atmosphere."[140] West Germany needed to be "a bulwark against the communist East."[141]

Gradually, the Americans began looking for ways to avoid executions and to review the cases of scores of convicted Nazis. There were ninety cases of imprisoned Nazis to deal with, including that of the industrial magnate Alfried Krupp, who had employed slave labor in factories at Auschwitz; Oswald Pohl, the leader of the entire SS concentration camp system, who had been condemned to death; a group of doctors who had carried out experiments on concentration camp inmates; and fourteen Einsatzgruppen leaders who had supervised the slaughter of a million or more Jews on occupied Soviet territory and now awaited execution in Landsberg prison.

Soon after becoming high commissioner, McCloy appointed a clemency panel to review the sentences. It was led by David W. Peck, Presiding Judge of the New York Supreme Court's Appellate Division. Its work could not be insulated from Cold War pressures. Appointed in the spring of 1950, it deliberated for six weeks during the initial period of the Korean conflict, which had broken out that June. The Peck Commission read the final judgments but failed to read the trial transcripts or even consult with the prosecutors; when Benjamin Ferencz offered to meet with them, they turned him down.

From the outset, Telford Taylor had warned McCloy of the controversy he would face if he granted clemency to these men. Referring to Oswald Pohl and the Einsatzgruppen commanders, Taylor reminded McCloy that "they are, without any question, among the most deliberate and shameless murderers of the entire Nuremberg list, and any idea of further clemency in their case seems to be out of the question."[142]

But the Peck Commission's report and McCloy's ultimate decision confirmed Taylor's worst fears. The commission recommended to McCloy in August "the reduction of sentence or immediate clemency in seventy-seven of the ninety cases, including commutation of seven of the fifteen death sentences."[143] For example, the Commission urged that Alfried Krupp's sentence be reduced from twelve years to seven and that he be allowed to regain control of his property and businesses,

---

140. Cited in Kai Bird, *The Chairman: John J. McCloy, The Making of the American Establishment* (New York, 1992), p. 368.
141. Ibid., p. 330.
142. Ibid., p. 331.
143. Ibid., p. 361.

contrary to the judgment at Nuremberg. But McCloy was more concerned over the proposed clemency for men who had directly participated in atrocities. As McCloy's biographer, Kai Bird, made clear, "Inevitably, word leaked that the high commissioner was weighing the merits of a general or partial clemency."[144] The rumors galvanized supporters of the defendants. Adenauer appealed against the death sentences and asked for a broad clemency. A group called the Christian Aid Committee organized a campaign of letters and cables on behalf of all the prisoners. Others appealed solely against the death sentences, pointing out that capital punishment had been outlawed under the new West German constitution. At the end of January 1951, after much soul-searching and deliberation, including support from President Harry Truman, McCloy announced that only five of the pending fifteen executions would be carried out, while the sentences of sixty-four of the other seventy-four Nazi war criminals would be reduced. Alfried Krupp, among others, would be released immediately. "No other decision McCloy made in his years in Germany aroused greater furor than this mass clemency," McCloy's biographer observed.[145]

Most Germans welcomed the commutations and continued to reject the impending execution of five participants in mass murder. Outside of Germany, McCloy faced withering criticism. Eleanor Roosevelt wrote to ask him, "Why are we freeing so many Nazis?"[146] Telford Taylor publicly castigated McCloy. For Taylor, the clemency decision was an act of "political expediency."[147] Looking back, it seems unavoidable to conclude that the Americans and the British chose, in the words of one historian, to "pander to demands of nationalist and militaristic elements in the Federal Republic of Germany."[148]

But Otto Ohlendorf, Paul Blobel, Werner Braune, and Erich Naumann seemed to McCloy to be "beyond the pale." For them, at least, the clemency process offered no reprieve. Joined by Oswald Pohl, they were hanged on June 7, 1951. The other ten condemned prisoners from the Einsatzgruppen trial had their sentences commuted; in place of the death penalty, they received new sentences ranging from life in prison to twenty years in prison.

Even so, the political will of the Americans continued to dissipate. By 1958, the remaining Einsatzgruppen commanders still in jail were granted parole. The attitude of Robert Karicher, the director of Landsberg prison in Bavaria, reflected the prevalent mood. Characterizing Ernst Biberstein, a former Protestant minister and the commander of Einsatzkommando 6 of Einsatzgruppe C, whose men had killed tens of thousands of Jews in Ukraine, Karicher wrote in August 1957 as if Biberstein were a petty criminal who had reformed his ways and deserved to return to society. "The inmate is

---

144. Ibid., p. 362.
145. Ibid., p. 364.
146. Ibid., p. 365.
147. *Nation*, February 24, 1951, p. 171.
148. Bloxham, "Punishing German Soldiers during the Cold War," p. 42.

somewhat reserved," Karicher wrote. "He is at no time a troublemaker and endeavors to make the best of things. He seems devoted to his faith and his family; he is anxious to get released, reestablish his home, and pursue his profession. He is a model inmate and possesses the qualifications to make a good adjustment in a free society."[149]

In May 1958, after U.S. officials released the last four Nazi war criminals in their custody, including Martin Sandberger and Adolf Ott—*who had been sentenced to death at the Einsatzgruppen trial for the murder of one million Jews*—the New York Times claimed, in a shocking understatement, that they had been "judged responsible for the death of hundreds of Nazi persecuted victims."[150] The brief article also failed to mention that their victims were primarily Jews. Seven years earlier, when McCloy announced his clemency decision, the *Times* had responded critically, uncomfortable with this "compromise between justice and expediency."[151] By 1958, the "paper of record" too seemed to be afflicted with moral amnesia.

Many years later McCloy expressed some regret to Ferencz, writing to him in a personal letter, "If I had all the facts I now have, I might have reached a more just result. It was an ordeal," he explained to Ferencz, "that I would not care to repeat."[152] But the facts had all been confirmed by the Nuremberg trials and by the mountains of material evidence amassed by the prosecutors, the same evidence that the Peck Commission had neglected to consult. Just a few years after the Holocaust, the international community, including the governments of the United States, Great Britain, and the Soviet Union, were morally exhausted.

Fate of the Defendants in the Einsatzgruppen Trial[1]				
Defendant	Original Sentence	Advisory Board	McCloy	Ultimate Fate
Paul Blobel	Death	Death	Death	Hanged, June 8, 1951
Ernst Biberstein	Death	15 years	Life	Released, May 6, 1958
Walter Blume	Death	20 years	25 years	Released, March 15, 1955
Werner Braune	Death	Death	Death	Hanged, June 8, 1951
Lothar Fendler	10 years	Time Served	8 years	Released, March 1951
Matthias Graf	Sentenced to time served. The court determined that he was neither a commander nor an officer in a killing unit; he was released at the close of the trial.			
Walter Haensch	Death	15 years	15 years	Released, August 26, 1955

---

149. Cited in Earl, *Accidental Justice*, p. 449.
150. *New York Times*, May 10, 1958, p. 3. See also Laurel Leff, *Buried by The Times: The Holocaust and America's Most Important Newspaper* (New York, 2005) for a critique of how poorly the *Times* covered the Holocaust during the war itself.
151. *New York Times*, February 2, 1951, p. 22.
152. From the archive of Benjamin Ferencz. The letter was dated April 10, 1980. In December 1944, McCloy, still undersecretary of war, reportedly wondered aloud to one Jewish journalist, "Do you

Emil Hausmann	Committed suicide on July 31, 1947, two months before the trial opened.			
Heinz Jost	Life	10 years	10 years	Released, December 1951
Waldemar Klinglhofer	Death	Death	Life	Released, December 21, 1956
Erich Naumann	Death	Death	Death	Hanged, June 8, 1951
Gustav Nosske	Life	10 years	10 years	Released, December 1951
Otto Ohlendorf	Death	Death	Death	Hanged, June 8, 1951
Adolf Ott	Death	Death	Life	Released, May 6, 1958
Waldemar von Radetzky	20 years	Time Served	Time Served	Released, February 1951
Otto Rasch	Died in custody on November 1, 1948			
Felix Rühl	10 years	Time Served	Time Served	Released, February 1951
Martin Sandberger	Death	Death	Life	Released, August 6, 1958
Heinz Schubert	Death	Time Served	10 years	Released, December 1951
Erwin Schulz	20 years	10 years	15 years	Released, July 12, 1952
Willy Seibert	Death	Time Served	15 years	Released, May 12, 1954
Franz Six	20 years	Time Served	10 years	Released, October 2, 1952
Eugen Steimle	Death	15 years	20 years	Released, June 28, 1954
Eduard Strauch	Death	Transferred to Belgian authorities for further trial, where he was again sentenced to death. He died there on September 15, 1955.		

1. This information is drawn from Earl, *Accidental Justice*, and the papers of Rolf Wartenberg.

Nonetheless, the trials, the executions, the premature release of so many Nazi war criminals did not bring an end to the search for accountability. Of all the post-war cases after Nuremberg, the Jerusalem trial of Adolf Eichmann in 1961 was the most famous. The Soviet Union, West Germany, and on occasion the United States, France, and Israel, held trials of increasingly older and feebler defendants accused of wartime atrocities. In West Germany, in spite of several well-publicized and significant trials, the prosecution of perpetrators has been inconsistent. In April 1958, ten former perpetrators were brought to trial in Ulm for the killing of more than five thousand Jews in Klaipedia, a port city in Lithuania and the site of one of the first mass shootings. At the time this was the largest trial in post-war Germany, and it helped to galvanize officials to create a central office "to expedite the discovery and prosecution of Nazi criminals."[153] Up until 1992, just over 6,400 Nazis were legally

---

really believe that those terrible things happened?" See "Criminal State vs. Moral Society," by Aryeh Leon Kubovy, *Yad Vashem Bulletin* 13 (October, 1963), p. 7.

153. *New York Times*, April 29, 1958, p. 59, for news about the Ulm trial; *New York Times*, October 7, 1958, p. 10, on the creation of a central office to prosecute Nazi criminals in Germany.

tried and convicted for murder in German courts, while at the same time untold thousands of others were able to live out their lives in peace.[154]

Innumerable historical studies and memoirs by survivors continue to shed light on a crime so enormous that sometimes it seems the facts alone do more to confound than to clarify our understanding. As the historian Isaac Deutscher wrote in the 1960s, "I doubt that in a thousand years people will better understand Hitler, Auschwitz, Majdanek and Treblinka than we do today."[155]

Reading *The Unknown Black Book* can only bring a meager degree of consolation. Lawrence Langer once cautioned us not to transform "personal stories of unredeemable atrocity back into triumphant accounts of survival."[156] Every Jew who survived marked a moment of failure on the part of the Nazis; every murder was a representative event. *The Unknown Black Book* contains the testimonies of individuals of remarkable resilience who could not have imagined before the catastrophe how they would choose to behave. Then afterward, overcome with the "contaminated joy of liberation,"[157] they could not fathom how what they had endured could really have happened, or if it was in fact that person, themselves, who had survived a sojourn in the valley of death. Watching their loved ones be killed all around them, "Every human being was broken, shattered, and envious of the dead," one survivor recalled.[158] We should celebrate each life that was spared but not allow ourselves the comfort of being distracted from the harsh reality the Nazis fashioned: they murdered six million Jews and would have been happy to kill more. On the eve of his death, Hitler boasted that he regarded the killing of the Jews as the greatest service rendered by National Socialism to humanity.[159] And Adolf Eichmann remarked that he "would leap laughing into the grave because the feeling that he had five million people on his conscience would be for him a source of extraordinary satisfaction."[160] The only banal quality to their bloodthirsty satisfaction was that it was so widely and enthusiastically shared.

---

154. See Katharina von Kellenbach, "Vanishing Acts: Perpetrators in Postwar Germany," *Holocaust and Genocide Studies* 17, no. 2 (Fall 2003), p. 305, for a personal account by a German woman whose uncle had supervised the massacre of thousands of Jews on occupied Soviet territory.
155. Isaac Deutscher, *The Non-Jewish Jew* (New York, 1982), p. 16.
156. Langer, *Holocaust Testimonies*, p. 109.
157. Ibid., p. 85.
158. See "In Uman. The recollections of Manya Feingold," p. 192 in this volume.
159. Cited in Friedländer, "From Anti-Semitism to Extermination," p. 32.
160. Cited in Taylor, *Anatomy of the Nuremberg Trials*, p. 248.

Portrait of Yevgenia Golovataya Peretiatko, a Jewish sniper in the Red Army, Rostov, ca. 1943. USHMM, courtesy of YIVO Institute for Jewish Research.

Group portrait of Jewish partisan leaders from the Minsk ghetto soon after the liberation in 1944. Pictured seated from right to left are: Hirsh Smolar, commissar of the 'Sergei Lazo' Battalion; Sh. Zorin, commander of Family Camp 106; and B. Khaymovich, commissar of Battalion 1 of the 208th Brigade. Standing from right to left are: Naum Feldman, commissar of the '25 Years of Belorussia' Battalion; Y. Krachinsky, leader of a demolition unit of the 'Marshal Budyonny' Battalion; and K. Feygelman, commissar of Family Camp 106. USHMM, courtesy of Beit Lohamei Haghettaot.

During a war crimes trial in Kiev, Dina Pronicheva, a Jewish survivor of the Babi Yar massacre, testifies about her experiences, January 24, 1946. USHMM, courtesy of Babi Yar Society.

Ilya Ehrenburg (at left with pipe) and Vasily Grossman (right) visit the Front near Kiev to collect evidence of German war crimes, 1944. USHMM, courtesy of Irina Ehrenburg.

SS General Friedrich Jeckeln stands in the dock during his trial for atrocities committed in the Baltic states, Riga, probably February 3, 1946. USHMM, courtesy of the Russian State Documentary Film and Photo Archive.

Thousands of spectators pack a square in Kiev during the execution of twelve Germans convicted of perpetrating war crimes against the Soviet people, January 29, 1946. USHMM, courtesy of the Russian State Documentary Film and Photo Archive.

I
UKRAINE

On the eve of the German invasion of Soviet territory in June 1941, Ukraine was home to 2.4 million Jews, one of the highest concentrations in Europe. After Russia, Ukraine was the second most populous of the constituent republics of the former Soviet Union, with sizable cities and vast areas of land under cultivation. Within its pre-1939 borders, or Eastern Ukraine, the Jews constituted a significant minority in major cities such as Kiev, Kharkov, Zhitomir, Berdichev, Dnepropetrovsk, and Odessa, and in much smaller cities and towns such as Shpola, Uman, Khmelnik, and Sumy. Following the Hitler-Stalin Pact of August 1939, parts of Eastern Poland, including much of Galicia and Volhynia, were absorbed by the USSR as Western Ukraine. This western portion was very different from its eastern counterpart. The West included a population that was more supportive of Ukrainian nationalism and generally more antisemitic in its outlook. Galicia was a territory that long had been disputed between Poland and Ukraine. It, too, contained a high concentration of Jews in places such as Lvov, Tarnopol, and Rovno. Their pre-war population was swelled by tens of thousands of Jews who had fled the German occupation of western Poland in September 1939, preferring to live under Soviet rule. Finally, in June 1940, the Soviet Union also took control of Bukovina and Bessarabia from Romania—areas with significant Jewish communities—and attached them to Ukraine.

The Germans had captured all of Ukraine by the end of 1941, and though the Red Army began to liberate parts of its territory just over a year later, it did not expel the Germans altogether until the summer of 1944. A significant number of Jews succeeded in escaping. As many as 800,000 Jews in Eastern Ukraine were evacuated or escaped on their own. Another 50,000 managed to get away from the newly absorbed western territories.

Hundreds of places throughout Ukraine soon became the sites of large, open-air massacres in which thousands and sometimes tens of thousands of Jews were killed by Einsatzgruppen C and D. At the end of August 1941, the Germans killed 23,000 Jews in Kamenets-Podolsky; of those killed, somewhere between 14,000 and 18,000 had been expelled from Hungary to occupied Ukraine because they were considered "alien" Jews (many were actually of Polish background), while the remainder were Ukrainian Jews. This was the first German massacre of more than 10,000 people at one time. It paved the way for many others that soon followed. In 1942, the Germans began to set up ghettos and labor camps as well, intending to exploit Jewish labor. During the occupation, Ukraine also had as many as 442 ghettos and 81 separate labor camps. All of these were liquidated on Himmler's orders in 1943, their inmates systematically murdered.

The massacre at Babi Yar, outside of Kiev, has long been recognized as an emblematic atrocity. Ilya Ehrenburg wrote about it in his postwar novel *The Storm*, which was awarded the Stalin Prize in 1948. In 1961, on the twentieth anniversary of the massacre, the poet Yevgeny Yevtushenko published his "Babi Yar" in *Literaturnaya gazeta*, the weekly newspaper of the Soviet Writers' Union.[1] The poem not only commemorated the killings but also rebuked the Kremlin for its failure to acknowledge Jewish suffering; as Yevtushenko noted in the first line, "No monument stands over Babi Yar." Yevtushenko was officially criticized for his poem. Soon after, the composer Dmitri Shostakovich set Yevtushenko's verses to music in his *Thirteenth Symphony*. The premiere took place in Moscow on December 18, 1962, and though the audience responded with a passionate ovation, the regime responded differently. By February, when the piece was played once again in Moscow, Yevtushenko had made changes in the verses, adding lines to confirm that non-Jewish civilians had also been killed at Babi Yar and specifically honoring the heroism of the Russian people in defeating fascism.

The massacre at Babi Yar remained the focus of conflicting passions. In 1966, during an unofficial ceremony to commemorate the killings, the Ukrainian activist Ivan Dzyuba called for Ukrainian-Jewish reconciliation and decried the fact that "silence [can become] a partner to falsehood and enslavement." For him, "Babi Yar is a tragedy of all mankind, but [one that] happened on Ukrainian soil. And, therefore, a Ukrainian has no more right to forget it than a Jew has."[2]

Three years later, in July 1969, the Soviet writer Anatoly Kuznetsov defected during a visit to England. He had survived the German occupation of Kiev as a teenager. In 1966, his novel *Babi Yar*, which drew on his war-time experiences, appeared

---

1. "Babi Yar" appeared in the issue of September 19, 1961.
2. "Babyi [sic] Yar Address by I. Dzyuba," in Abraham Brumberg, ed., *In Quest of Justice: Protest and Dissent in the Soviet Union Today* (New York, 1970), pp. 200–204; Dzyuba spoke on September 29, 1966, the 25th anniversary of the massacre.

in the Soviet press, but in a highly censored and expurgated form. Following his defection, he was able to publish the complete text in the West. Once again, Soviet officials could not bring themselves to permit an honest account of the massacre to appear. One of the first gestures of post-Soviet Ukraine was to acknowledge the truth about Babi Yar and its Jewish victims, and to allow proper commemorations to take place.

In southwestern Ukraine the Romanians worked closely with the Germans in an area they called Transnistria. Its largest city, Odessa, had a pre-war population of 180,000 Jews, making it a major center of Jewish life. The Romanians carried out massacres on their own, for example at Domanyovka, Bogdanovka, and Akmechetka, where they murdered about 70,000 Jews in December 1941 and January and February 1942.

Transnistria also contained the largest concentration of Volksdeutsche, or ethnic Germans, in Ukraine, with more than thirty German villages having populations exceeding one thousand.[3] These Germans also organized killing units of their own, called the Selbstschutz, which were organized by the SS. The Romanians coordinated attacks on the Jews with these ethnic German units, which helped them to carry out large-scale massacres.

The Jewish population of Ukraine in 1939 was about 1.5 million, a figure that rose to 2.4 million after the absorption of territories from Poland and Romania following the Hitler-Stalin Pact. Possibly 850,000, almost all in the pre-1939 part of Ukraine, were evacuated before the occupation. Of those who remained, virtually all perished during the Holocaust.

Kiev
1. Life in occupied Kiev
THE RECOLLECTIONS OF IDA S. BELOZOVSKAYA

It would be difficult to talk about why I stayed in occupied Kiev, and perhaps it would serve no purpose. Earlier, before the occupation, it was for a commonly held reason, but now it seems unimportant and insignificant. Nobody believed that this nightmare would really descend on us. Like drowning people, we were clutching at straws, eagerly listening to the radio: "Kiev will never be surrendered," and we believed and hoped. On September 17, 1941, when our armies all began retreating, the roar of pursuing German shells and the fire and smoke from burning buildings still did not entirely convince me that the catastrophe had come, that life would soon be over. At that moment, the word "life" had its own meaning. The result was that its meaning faded. Too often, or even constantly, it meant being close to death, and because of that, it lost its usual colors.

---

3. See the *Final Report of the International Commission on the Holocaust in Romania* (Presented to Romanian President Ion Iliescu, November 11, 2004), p. 28.

On September 19, when the Germans began entering the city, people stood along both sides of the street (Krasnoarmeyskaya Street, beside the Vladimir market) with servile, eager-to-please expressions that pretended to be joyful. They greeted their "liberators," the Germans, who were bringing a "great life." But I already felt that life was slipping away from us and that suffering was coming. We were all caught in a mousetrap. Where could we go? All the roads were closed.

I went to Podol, to my five-year-old son, who was with my husband's family. My relatives included two younger sisters with three children (one had two sons—ages five and a half and three and a half, while the other had one boy three and a half years old). My mother and father were moving from one apartment to another—now they were at my sister's place on Gershun Street, now at mine at 13 Tverskaya Street. They stayed near my husband, thinking that he would save them from the inevitable (he was a Russian).

A few days later, my father went out onto the street for some reason and did not come back; they had already begun snatching male Jews on the street, as though they were sending them to work. The next day, after the order for the collection of all Jews at a specific place for transport somewhere had been published, my husband's sisters came and dragged him to their place by force—they feared for his life. Perhaps you can imagine the scene when my sisters, three small boys, my mother (my father was no longer with us) were begging and wailing for my husband to rescue them. They were clutching at the last shred of hope, but he could do nothing to help them. He left for Podol. When he arrived, it seemed to me too that they had lost their last chance to be saved.

A nightmarish, uncertain death arrived. I was not alive during the Middle Ages, and in our century had not seen what people did when they experienced inescapable despair. But I was pulled down to earth and made to sit on a low stool. I felt a strong desire to sprinkle my head, my whole self, with ashes, to hear nothing, to be changed into dust. But no, I was alive. I was still in a condition to hear and to notice that people were living around me, that they had the *right to live*. Why should some individuals who had the bad fortune to be a different people have to die a violent death—children, the innocent, small ones, not knowing why, not understanding what life and death are? Why should my child, who has a Russian father, have people defending his life?

On September 28, my husband and his sister, a Russian, came to accompany my unfortunate ones on their long journey. It seemed to them, and we all wanted to believe, that the German barbarians would send them away, and for four or five days people moved in whole columns to "safety." The Germans could not take them all and ordered them to come back the next day (they did not overburden themselves with work). So people came for several days; the Germans did not manage to send them all off to the next world, but eventually their turn came. Not far from their common destination—historic Babi Yar—my husband left my relatives and went off to see for himself how the Germans were receiving people. And he saw: behind a high fence (there was a hole in it to look through), they were sorting them: men to one side, women and children separately.

Naked (their things had been taken away to a separate place), they were killed on the spot by submachine guns and machine guns, while shouts and cries of horror were drowned out.

My husband came back to my sisters and mother, and said: "Get away from here, wherever you can." What happened over there I do not know, but he went back to his people in Podol where I was with our son, and he brought three doomed little boys with him. He thought that he would save them. His mother told him that we had all gone, since there was no way of saving everyone anymore, and that the only thing that was going to happen was that everyone would be shot. I had no right to accuse them. After all, my husband's father, mother, and sisters had the right to live, and they wanted to live.

The children came and stayed with me for another six days—they extended their lives six more days. For those six days, they did not leave my side, holding onto my skirt from both sides. They did not play, nothing interested them. They had big, innocent eyes that did not understand what life and death were. They asked: "Auntie Ida, tell us, Mama's going to come, isn't she? Tell us! When's she coming?" Silently, their eyes filled with tears and they cried with stifled sobs. They could not cry loudly because people might have heard them and that would have been the end for everyone. I did not cry. I just moved around automatically as if I were made of wood. I comforted them, trying to convince them that it would all be over soon and that their mama would come.

I had nightmarish thoughts. Why does my child have the right to only half a life? I can live for the time being because they want to save the mother of my son, Igor, their grandson, and anyway, it is easier to hide me, a grownup. These children who do not understand anything, what are they guilty of? Why should their lives be taken away? My husband approached all our Russian friends, whomever it was possible to talk to, pleading with them to save at least one child, but the Germans were searching thoroughly and everyone feared for their lives.

One of my old co-workers from the laboratory, a woman who prepared specimens, came to see me at my invitation. She was a simple woman, but with a big heart. In answer to my request to take at least one of the children temporarily (it seemed to us that all of this was temporary, that light and life would soon return), she told me about what happened in her apartment building when the Germans arrived. One of the neighbors had come back from captivity, a Jew swollen from hunger, in a dreadful state. He asked the other residents to let him back into his old apartment (his family was no longer there). He wanted to hang himself with everyone watching. He did not want to go into hiding and save his own life. The tenants would not let him, though. He left, and had not reached the end of the block before he was handed over to the Germans.

"As you can see," said my co-worker, "they'll hand me and my children over along with your child." That was the end of that hope. On the eve of the sixth day, my husband was at our place on Tverskaya and found my mother there. She, along with my sisters, had escaped from near Babi Yar, then headed in the direction of Stalinka.[4] But mother had a heart condition, coronary sclerosis, and she had not been able to keep up with her young daughters. She had stayed sitting on a little square in Stalinka, and some "good people" had picked her up there and taken her to a German command post, but the Germans, taking her age into account, had let her go home. So she went home, climbed in through a window and sat there, not quite alive and not quite dead. A neighbor brought her something to eat, quietly, through the window. When no one was watching, she reached her with a ladle. Mother did not turn on the light, but her unlawful existence in the building was discovered, and they began debating whether or not she should live.

On the sixth day, we decided to take the children to their grandmother's on Tverskaya Street. We were afraid to keep them in Podol. I knew that if they appeared on Tverskaya Street, it would hasten the end of Mama and the children. I paced up and down the room the entire night. I kept asking myself the same questions: "What should I do? Why should I live? Have I got the right to live while those around me, who mean the most to me, have to die such a horrible, violent death?" I could not be of any help to them except by my own death, out of solidarity. But what about Igor, who had the right to live? Should I deliberately deprive him of his mother? He is only five, after all! So I stayed alive.

For three days and nights I paced up and down the small room and counted the hours. At what time would their death come? I did not notice being hungry or tired. I tried to burn into my memory what the weather was like on the other side of the drawn curtains, along with everything about how they led them out to death.

I pleaded with my husband's relatives to go and see, so that I could know: were they still in agony or had the end come on Tverskaya Street? They were afraid to go, but on the third day they finally went and had a look. The evening before, the landlords (it was a private building) had invited the Germans into our apartment, and they led Mama and the children out to the end of their lives. When she left the place, Mama locked the door and gave the key to the landlady. She knew that my husband was still alive, and that maybe I was, too, and so, what was in the apartment might be of use to us. The landlady gave the key back, but there was nothing left in the apartment anyway.

I was not able to see mother's face when she went to her death, but I felt as though I were there and will never forget her expression. It was windy that day, snowflakes were clinging to her eyes. She was holding a child in each hand and walking deliberately, without crying or indignation, into the world of non-existence. I was the only one of our family who survived. How many times for more

---

4. Stalinka was a nickname for the Stalin District in Kiev.

than two years of hopeless captivity did I curse the circumstances that I should live until a violent death came? How many times did I feel sorry that I had not taken Igor there where my mother had gone, to the place where there is no human suffering? I stayed alive to fight for this strange life.

I was buried, I no longer existed, I had disappeared from among the living. I stayed off the street for two years, not seeing the sun or breathing fresh air. The curtains were drawn in the windows of the apartment. When a stranger appeared in the courtyard, I had to hide in a place where I would not be discovered during a search. At every hour, death waited outside the door, death for everyone, for the whole family that was hiding me.

I cannot complain about the way my husband behaved toward me during the first year. The death of my relatives had an effect on him, too. He tried to obtain another passport for me so that we could live anywhere at least semi-legally, but these attempts came to nothing. When the question of whether or not I should leave was coming to a head because everyone was threatened with execution, he would tell my relatives that he would leave with me, that there was only one way out. It would have been enough for me to open the door and step out onto the landing for death to rush to meet us. All the neighbors were curious to discover my whereabouts. They knew that I was somewhere since they had seen me on the day the Germans arrived, but they no longer knew where I was. They only guessed and constantly kept an eye out.

After some time had passed, when there was no longer any hope for a life within the law, and no hope that the Red Army would soon come to liberate us, it came down to the three of us—myself, my son, Igor, and my husband—committing suicide by hanging ourselves. The question was how to manage it technically, whether or not to hang the child first, and then which of us would go last. My husband said this quite seriously and thoughtfully. He felt responsible that we had not been evacuated, so he was sacrificing his own life.

But I had greater strength of will than my husband and insisted that if it was a matter of Igor's life, then we still had to fight, so we remained alive and continued to struggle. The building superintendent raised the question of Igor's life—his mother was a Jew, after all (I did not exist)—saying he needed to be handed over to the Germans. The men in our family somehow came up with proof, genuine or otherwise, that Igor had been baptized, and so saved him. They coached the child at home to say that he had no mother, that she had left. Everyone in the building tried to catch him off guard, suddenly asking: "Where's your mama?" Outside the apartment, he was forbidden to say the word "mama," and at home, only quietly, so that no one would hear.

He would ask me, "Mama, tell me, what's a Jew? A kike? And how come the Germans killed Borya and Marik (my sister's children)?" But he sensed without any special explanations what it was all about. In the courtyard, the superintendent's children would call him a kike and he would go out into the street only with grown-ups. He was always waiting for the Red Army who would bring freedom and then he would be able to say "mama" in a loud voice and walk alongside her.

I was alive, but it was a bitter, hopeless life. Loneliness was destroying me, even though my husband was there. I had to realize that every living creature had a right to exist, but I, obviously, was doing poorly at recognizing it. As far as life was concerned I was buried and yet remained alive. It so happened that my husband was alive, he had the right to live, and, like every living creature, should enjoy life. I was in no condition to raise myself above commonplace things and not react to my surroundings. So I reacted painfully and life became hell. I began to burden myself with all kinds of housework, something that I had never done before, but I was still left with a great deal of free time. I slept badly and very little. I was afraid to fall asleep. The death of those dear to me and those around me, particularly the children, constantly haunted me. I felt indirectly responsible for their deaths. If I had not been in the city, they would never have stayed in Kiev.

I used to read a lot, but now there was nowhere to get books and I suffered terribly from that. In my free time, when I had absolutely nothing to do and nothing to read, I could not find a place to hide from myself. (Often there was no one at home; everyone would leave, then lock the door.) I would climb the tile stove in the small room and bang my head against it in order to deaden the pain inside me. I could not scream, after all! It seemed that things were easier when the pain was physical. How many times would I go to that same stove, where the rope ladder was hanging, the ladder that I would use to scramble to the very top in case of a raid. There was still a hollowed-out space under the ceiling. I would curl up in a ball and pull the ladder up behind me. I would want to end this senseless life. But there was Igor. I forced myself to summon hope and go on living.

The thought that Igor would grow up and look at peoples' lives, as so many did during the Occupation, compelled me to live. I want to bring him up so that he will treat all people equally without any prejudice.

The only person from the outside world who came to visit me during the time of my involuntary captivity was the husband of one of my girlfriends (she herself came rarely). He provided me with books. When he came by, I well understood the feeling prisoners have when a ray of sunshine peeps into the cell. I would breathe the air which he brought from the other side of the world. We would discuss the successes of the Red Army as reflected in the German press. I did not lose hope that Soviet power would survive, that the Red Army would come, but I had no hope that I would live to see it. It was too difficult.

But I did live to see that day. A month and a half before the arrival of the Red Army, the Germans chased everyone out of their houses. Podol was declared a forbidden zone and my husband's relatives had to leave it. We were the last family to leave the building. When I emerged onto the street, I thought the air would knock me down, it was moving so strongly. We lived on the outskirts of the city for a month and a half, hidden in a pit. (I will send the next part of the story by mail).[5]

Belozovskaya, I. S.
Kiev, 13/7 Tverskaya Street

GARF, f. 8114 (Jewish Anti-Fascist Committee or JAC), op. 1, d. 965, ll. 68–75. A typewritten manuscript.

2. A list of members of the Jewish intelligentsia, with their families, who perished at Babi Yar

Compiled by A. Kagan
January 15, 1945

No.	Last Name and First Name	Specialty
	Doctors	
1)	Zalivansky	Urologist
2)	Gimelfarb, Isaak	Gynecologist
3)	Radbil	Venereologist
4)	Markovich	Gynecologist
5)	Saltanov	Neuropathologist
6)	Reicher	Venereologist
7)	Rabinovich, Semyon	Surgeon
8)	Rotenberg (prof.)	Laryngologist
9)	Ioselevich, David	Epidemiologist
10)	Frenkel (prof.)	Laryngologist
11)	Zvonitsky	Therapist
12)	Ayzin, Sigizmund	"
13)	Boyarsky, Semyon	Physiotherapist
14)	Taberovsky	Therapist
15)	Boskis (Medical doctor)	Stomatologist
16)	Shapiro, Nikolai (prof.)	"
17)	Mogilyansky	"
18)	Berenshteyn	"
19)	Kodinsky	"
20)	Shmorginsky	"
21)	Maydan	"
22)	Pliner	"
23)	Tovbin	Surgeon
24)	Dukelsky, Vladimir	Pediatrician
25)	Vaysbreyt, Arkady	Therapist
26)	Rybakov, Semyon	T.B. Specialist
27)	Sheynis-Rybakova, Sofia	Stomatologist
28)	Benyash, Moisey (prof.)	Bacteriologist
29)	Vaysblat, Aron	Stomatologist
30)	Sklovsky, Grigory	Pediatrician
31)	Mitinsky, David (docent)	Neuropathologist
32)	Turok	Therapist

---

5. The second part of I. S. Belozovskaya's memoir has not been found in the archives of the Jewish Anti-Fascist Committee or in the papers of Ilya Ehrenburg at Yad Vashem.

33)	Kaplinskaya, Yekaterina	"
34)	Podgaets, Sara	Neuropathologist
35)	Dolberg	Therapist
36)	Kanevsky, Lev	Therapist
37)	Deych, Yakov	"
38)	Rabinovich	Immunologist
39)	Burshteyn, Lidia	Stomatologist
40)	Cherkassky	Therapist
41)	Reyderman, Isaak	Pediatrician
42)	Shampaner (woman)	Therapist
43)	Ikhelzon	"
44)	Gimelfarb (Director, Kiev City Health Dept.)	"

Jurists

1)	Babat	"
2)	Leytman	"
3)	Kogan, Ya.	"
4)	Kogan, Ye.	"
5)	Shakh	"
6)	Tsiperovich	"
7)	Gorenshteyn	"
8)	Tseytlin	"

Engineers

1)	Gorenshteyn	"
2)	Levin	"
3)	Polonsky (prof. at Industrial Inst.)	"

Various

1)	Levit	Composer
2)	Berenshteyn, Sofia	Librarian
3)	Volman, Rakhil	Teacher
4)	Satanovsky	Pianist (with a family of 14)

They all perished with their families.

A. KAGAN, KIEV, JANUARY 15, 1945

GARF, f. 8114, op. 1, d. 965, l. 134–134ob. A typewritten manuscript with a postscript and the signature of the author.

3. Nineteen months in a coffin

THE STORY OF THE MIDWIFE SOFIA BORISOVNA AYZENSHTEYN-DOLGUSHEVA[6]

Sofia Borisovna is small, active, and too lively for her age. It is hard to believe that Sofia Borisovna is fifty-five. But it is even harder to believe that this energetic, animated old lady lived for nineteen months in a coffin, buried alive. And yet, that is just what happened. It was only in this way that her husband Grigory Dolgushev was able to save her life.

Sofia Borisovna Ayzenshteyn, a Jew by nationality and a midwife by profession, was married to Grigory Dolgushev. It was her second marriage. By her first

---

6. The author's name is not indicated in the document.

husband, a Jew, she had three children: two sons and a daughter. She had no children with Dolgushev, but Sofia Borisovna's children by her first husband became his children.

They did not live badly at all. Sofia Petrovna was widely known as a good midwife. She did not have so much as a minute to spare; they were tearing her to bits, as it were—they said that she had "golden hands." Her husband had worked for many years in a sausage shop and then for the Southwestern Railroad Line. They raised their children, who became engineers and brought all their pay home. So the Dolgushev-Ayzenshteyn family made their way in the world, enjoying a full and happy life. But then the war with Hitler broke out and the whole life of this family, as it did for thousands and thousands of others, suddenly collapsed. The children were evacuated deep into the interior of the country, while Sofia Borisovna remained in Kiev. Where was an old woman like her supposed to go? Isn't it all the same, where I die? she reasoned. Here almost the whole city knows her and her husband. Who will touch her? Why would anyone want to bother her?

But it happened that she had visitors in the first days following the entry of the Germans into Kiev. The door was locked. The Germans tore out the lock, took everything that caught their eye, and left. The Dolgushevs realized that things were turning out badly and began to think of various ways in which they might save the life of Sofia Borisovna.

When announcements were posted in the city that all Jews should go to Lukyanovka, Sofia Borisovna decided to go there. "Whatever happens to all the Jews will happen to me, too," she thought. But her husband was categorically against it. "As long as I live, you will, too," he declared to his wife. He looked for an attic for his wife and made a show of beginning to prepare her for the trip to Lukyanovka. She got dressed, took food and clothing for five days in keeping with the order, said goodbye to the neighbors, and left the apartment in which she had lived for decades. Her husband went with her to Lvovskaya Street, and then, with a glance over his shoulder, took her up to the attic at No. 2. She could not stay there long, though. She soon had to move to a second apartment, then to a third. Once she had to live sewn into a mattress, but the mattress-grave proved unreliable. They were starting to shoot people for hiding Jews so the residents told her to go. Then the husband took his wife to "his own place" which he had been preparing for her for several weeks in the depths of a rear courtyard on Bulvarno-Kudryavskaya Street, not far from their home, so that he could visit her more often. He settled on a concealed corner and rigged up something like a dugout. He brought in clothes, a little bench, provisions. He dressed his wife as a beggar and she attended her own burial in a grave. Her husband walked ahead of her, while she followed some distance behind. He went along the back streets so as not to run into anyone he knew. It was already dark by the time they reached the appointed place. They looked around. Not a living soul in sight. The husband said a hasty goodbye to his wife, let her down into the dugout and walled her in. He left only a narrow chink which was heavily overlaid with bricks to pass food through.

Her husband would go there walking the dog. Chepa lives with the Dolgushevs even now. He would go there accompanied by Chepa. Chepa was the only friend with whom he could share his thoughts about the terrible secret. Chepa was the only witness to his terrible anxiety when the time would come to go to his wife; the dog was also his assistant in the risky undertaking. Dolgushev would talk to Chepa, knowing that his wife was listening. Sharing his thoughts with Chepa in some code language, he passed on his thoughts and hopes to his wife, and in this way gave her encouragement and bravery, which were vital to her to survive the ordeal, that of being buried alive. Dolgusheva begged her husband many times to give her poison. Her husband, of course, did not want to hear anything about it. He consoled and encouraged her with the thought that the time of liberation was coming and in this way he kept her alive with a ray of hope without which existence in such conditions would have been impossible.

But now the long-awaited moment came: the Red Army entered Kiev on November 6. Dolgushev went to see his wife, and, in the code language to which they were accustomed, shouted to her: "Sonya, our sun has risen! Kiev is free!" But Sonya did not believe it. How many times had her husband reassured her, only to have it turn out that there was still no freedom. But now her husband was beginning to break apart the dugout. Dolgusheva was all but blinded by the bright light. She could not see a thing and she did not want to move from where she was; fear continued to shackle her. Perhaps joy hampered her thinking? More likely she had lost the use of her legs (as later proved to be the case). She felt it, but she did not yet know it. When after a great deal of convincing she arose from her place, it turned out that she could no longer stand on her legs. They carried her back to the apartment and she walked on crutches for a long time before she recovered.

Fear pursued her for a long time. She felt calm again only after they moved to a new apartment. Then her husband collected the children and brought them to Kiev and the Dolgushev-Ayzenshteyn family began to live happily again. But when Sofia Borisovna remembers her entombed life, her eyes involuntarily fill with tears and her hands tremble, as on her first day of freedom.

GARF, f. 8114, op. 1, d. 965, ll. 36–38. A typewritten manuscript with corrections.

4. A stranger from the other world
THE STORY OF THE ARTIST FELIX ZINOVEVICH GITERMAN[7]

Comrade Felix (Yefim) Zinovevich Giterman was born in 1906. He was an artist and set designer by trade. By the way, he worked on the design of the buildings on Kreshchatik and Sverdlov Streets, among others.

---

7. The name of the author of this story is not indicated in the document.

From the beginning of the war with the Germans, comrade Giterman took part in the defense work of the Leninsky District Executive Committee. His wife was a Ukrainian woman named Lyudmila Filippovna Gusak (b. 1906), and they had two children, a daughter, Larisa, born in 1932, and a son, Oleg, born in 1940. At the start of the war, the boy fell ill, which prevented the family from being evacuated. Comrade Felix Giterman himself left Kiev on September 16, 1941, along with a group of functionaries of the district executive committee. The Germans were already quite nearby and all the roads out of Kiev were under constant aerial attack by the enemy. It was only possible to get out of the city by night, and then with great difficulty.

It was not until September 19 that the car arrived in Borispol under heavy bombardment. One bomb had scored a direct hit on the car. Comrade Giterman was about ten meters from the car at the time—someone's hat ended up in his hands, along with a severed head. Many of the functionaries who were leaving with him perished. Those who were still alive managed to find another car and tried to get out of Borispol, but it was already too late. The Germans surrounded them and locked them up in a concentration camp. Some of them began destroying their papers on the sly. Comrade Giterman decided to keep his with him.

The first question that the Germans asked the prisoners was: "*Jude?*" Investigator Lorman, along with a Jewish prosecutor who was among the captives, were shot on the spot. A third functionary, a Jew named Zilbershteyn, answered the question in the negative. Comrade Giterman, then, immediately replied "Yes, a Jew." They led him off to one side.

Soon a large group of prisoners had formed. They were all driven to Brovary. In a few days' time, there were more than thirty thousand assembled there—among them were two thousand Jews, who were separated from the rest. They were fenced in with a dense barbed wire entanglement; machine guns were placed around them. They were given nothing to eat (the Ukrainians got only raw potatoes). All were gripped by fear and did not even think about food. Their horror increased with nightfall. The Germans amused themselves by building fires right in front of the concentration camp, then burning portraits of Soviet leaders. This spectacle made a terrible impression on the prisoners. All were overcome by a feeling of terror and by a realization of their own helplessness. No one had any hope of rescue.

They brought a new group of prisoners on the second day. Again, they separated the Jews. Some of the Ukrainian captives began taking the Jews' boots, watches, jackets, and so on. The half-naked Jewish prisoners were driven into a separate camp.

In the evening, the Germans selected thirty men for a work detail and they returned in the morning. Then, a correspondent and a photographer turned up in the camp and they took pictures chiefly of half-naked and starving prisoners, with the aim of using the pictures to illustrate how the Soviet army looked. After the photographer left, another large group of prisoners was taken away. It turned out that they were digging broad ditches near the camp. The job took three days. On the fourth day, they lined up all the Jews on the edge of a forest near the ditches. Corpses could already be seen at the bottom. Then they began to machine gun the prisoners. Those still standing were struck with gun butts and flung into the pit. Comrade Giterman also fell into the pit, half dead. All day he lay unconscious. It was already dark when he came to. The pits were still uncovered. Cries, moans, and the wheezing that comes before death could be heard. Blood was oozing from comrade Giterman's legs. He bound his wound with a rag from his shirt as best he could and began to clamber carefully across the bodies of the dead and half-dead. Suddenly, though, he stumbled: it seemed to him that someone in the heap was pulling him by the leg.

He awoke at dawn. He put on a sweater that he had hidden beneath his trousers and set off down the road. He went by the forest in the opposite direction from the camp. From a distance, Giterman noticed some peasants digging potatoes. He went up to one of them, a woman, and began to ask for the way to Kiev. The woman, looking around in fright, silently struck him on the hand and pointed at the potatoes: dig with me, she was saying, and keep quiet. Giterman obeyed her. After a little while, she filled a good-sized sack with potatoes, and, tying it up, loaded it onto his back. Then, cautiously looking around, she pointed out the direction to him. He trudged off, and soon caught up with others who were fleeing the camp; they were Ukrainians. They recoiled from him in fear. Giterman had to leave them. But not letting them out of his sight and keeping a certain distance he followed them. Soon he noticed that the Gestapo was checking papers. He hid in the forest and waited. Somehow or other he finally made his way to Trukhanov Island. Avoiding the German guards by the headquarters, which was surrounded by machine guns, he ran into a fisherman, who took him to the city in exchange for the sack of potatoes.

In this way, Giterman again found himself in his hometown, which he had abandoned ten days earlier. But, sad to say, Giterman felt as though he were in a completely alien city. On Kirov Street, he saw a group of Jews being taken somewhere by the Gestapo, all the while beating their heads with rubber truncheons. There were almost no passers-by in sight. Here and there he came upon old men and women apprehensively crossing the street with hurried steps. Comrade Giterman somehow made his way to Kreshchatik. Looking around, he spotted a Jewish woman with a child some distance off. He approached her and started a conversation. She told him that they were frequently killing Jews who had done nothing at all and that it was not a good idea for Jews, particularly men, to be walking on the street since at best they would be taken off to do hard, dirty labor. Giterman kept going. He came to the place where until recently had stood the building in which he lived (13/25 Sverdlov Street)—only smoky, naked walls remained. What to do? Where to seek a hiding place? Suddenly he saw an old acquaintance, Mikhaylenko, who told him that his

(Giterman's) wife was living in Solomenka at her father's place. The house in which Mikhaylenko lived had also burned down, and so Mikhaylenko led Giterman to a courtyard where he kept his things. Mikhaylenko supplied him with some provisions and gave him a cup of tea. After several days of hunger such a treat seemed like the height of refinement to Giterman. Unbelievably tired, he lay down to sleep. In the evening, Mikhaylenko covered him with a blanket.

Around 1:00 AM, the radio came to life. All residents were ordered to leave the city. They did not forget about the Jews, against whom they were mounting a pogrom. Giterman decided to make his way to Solomenka immediately. His father-in-law, with whom his wife was now living, was a long-time railroad worker, a Party member. His son was at the Front, the rest of the family had been evacuated; he himself had been digging trenches and did not manage to get away. And here was Giterman arriving at his father-in-law's apartment. Not a living soul around. Here and there, the decaying ruins of houses. Right there, the House of Scientists had almost completely rotted away. Hardly any passers-by could be seen on the street. But now the Gestapo showed up. They had been stopping pedestrians and herding them into a large courtyard on Karavaevskaya Street, where they had begun checking papers. This went on for more than two hours. Those who had "good" Ukrainian papers in their possession—like the majority of those detained—hurried to press themselves against the gates as quickly as possible; those like Giterman who held back, stayed somewhere a bit farther away. The Germans finally got fed up with the whole business. They opened the gates wide and chased everyone out onto the street. Giterman continued on and managed to make his way to Solomenka. It was not easy for him to enter his father-in-law's house, though: the driver of the car that had taken Giterman out of Kiev had seen with his own eyes how they had led him off to be shot, and he had informed Giterman's wife of this. As a result, they greeted him like a stranger from the other world.

A day or two later, all Jews were notified in the newspapers that they had to report to Melnik Street with warm clothing and food to last five days. "That means," Giterman reasoned, "they are getting ready to ship us off." He was already deciding to appear as ordered. But his wife was categorically against it. She went off to Lukyanovka herself and toward evening burst into the house in hysterics. It turned out that they were taking people to be slaughtered there. The next day, she went to town again in order to learn more about the fate of the Jews rounded up on Melnik Street. Giterman, who was left alone, decided to shave for want of anything else to do. Sitting facing the mirror, he saw a German come through the unhinged door. He froze. The German glanced around the room. In reply to his question *"Jude?"* Giterman barely managed to shake his head. The German went away. In this way, Giterman skirted death for the third time when it seemed unavoidable.

As for staying any longer in his father-in-law's house, it was out of the question. Giterman's wife dug a deep hole near the Baykovo cemetery, lined it with sheepskin and stored dry biscuits there, and buried her husband, leaving a hole to pass food through.

Living in this hole for a month and a half, Giterman swelled up all over. To stay there any longer would have meant certain death. Lyudmila Filippovna decided to find some kind of apartment. At the time, there were many empty, luxuriously furnished apartments in the city. But that wasn't what Giterman needed. He settled on a basement apartment on Krasnoarmeyskaya Street with a back entrance, so that in the event of any danger he could slip out into the depths of the courtyard.

He came back to life here. By day, everyone would leave, locking the apartment from the outside, as if to say "no one at home here." Giterman stayed inside. In the evening, everyone would come together and share news. Giterman would entertain the children. The word "papa" was banned so that a child would not unintentionally betray his father during a possible search. Everyone in the house called Giterman "grandma." Mother and daughter would gather the necessary food from among their friends. Mother took care of the washing and somehow obtained bread and potatoes. The cold was incredible because the windows were not entirely closed in order to open them more easily in case of an emergency. Still, suffering from hunger and cold, they somehow lived. However, the season of frequent searches and dragnets was coming. What to do now? Through friends of hers, Lyudmila Filippovna managed to get the chief physician of the Kirillovskaya Hospital to admit her husband as a lunatic. But the plan did not come off: the Germans came to the hospital and shot all the patients. Giterman was forced to stay at home for the time being. Then one day, the Germans unexpectedly arrived with the local police. The daughter managed to get her father out the back entrance into the yard in time. "Any men here?" a policeman asked. "No," Larochka replied, "father was killed at the Front." The Germans and the police left. Giterman came back to the apartment and noticed to his horror that he had left his papers on a pillow.

Meanwhile, the dragnets were becoming more and more frequent. They were taking the remaining Jews through the streets to be shot; along with them they were shooting Ukrainians who had hidden Jews in their homes. One day, as she was doing the washing, Giterman's wife heard a knock at the door. The raid did not turn up anything this time either. Giterman had had the presence of mind to take all the underwear to the attic; otherwise, the sight of a man's underwear would have betrayed his presence in the house. Even so, the danger increased, the raids became more frequent. Then the father-in-law was called in, so they made a barricaded corner in the attic, so artfully camouflaged that it would have been impossible to find it. Giterman came down only rarely, preferring to remain in his hideaway.

Twenty months passed in this way. And then the Germans declared Krasnoarmeyskaya Street a "forbidden zone." The inhabitants were given forty-eight hours to move beyond the boundaries of the zone.

They had to move to Solomenka, back to the father-in-law's house, although things were going badly there, too. Someone had denounced the old railroad man as a Party member and he had been shot alongside eight other Ukrainians. Giterman's wife walled her husband up in the cellar, where, truth be told, there were mice and rats, but where there was also enough air to breathe. Here it was comparatively safe. But the Germans soon gave the order to clear out Solomenka. Where could they go now?

Lyudmila Filippovna had a friend—the wife of Colonel Pichugin, who was active in the partisan movement. She hid partisans in the ruins of houses on Kreshchatik Street. In one of those houses she kept reserves of potatoes and water. She proposed to the Giterman family that they go there. It was not so easy to walk there from Solomenka. They dressed Giterman as an old woman again. With little Oleg in his arms, he set off on this risky journey along with his wife and daughter. Along the way, at the sight of the first German, he dropped the child. They picked up the little one and put him back in the trembling arms of the "old woman." In this way, they finally reached their "new apartment."

At 1:00 AM on the night of November 6, 1943, our tanks appeared on Kreshchatik Street. At 11:00 AM, Comrade Giterman came out onto the street, where he met comrade Mazur, an NKVD agent. On November 7, he met comrade Bazhan.[8] The latter kissed him on both cheeks and introduced him to Nikita Sergeyevich Khrushchev. Comrade Giterman could barely stand and was unable to get a word out. Nikita Sergeyevich held him up and consoled him: "That's all right, friend, you'll be able to design another Kreshchatik soon."[9]

They soon provided Giterman with work and he received Order No.1 for an apartment (6 Lvovskaya Street, no. 51). It had a lovely view of the Dniepr, something which particularly attracted comrade Giterman, the artist-designer.

GARF, f. 8114, op. 1, d. 965, ll. 39–45. A typewritten manuscript with corrections.

5. How I was saved from Hitler
THE RECOLLECTIONS OF THE TEACHER EMILIA BORISOVNA KOTLOVA

From letters to Ilya Ehrenburg
1945
Kiev, January 13, 1945
Our own dear Ilya Ehrenburg!

I received your letter on January 12, for which I am very grateful. I waited a whole year for it. Yesterday was the second happiest day of my life, when I read the letter

---

8. Mykola Bazhan was a prominent Ukrainian writer; after the war, he represented the Ukrainian Soviet Socialist Republic at the United Nations.
9. Khrushchev always recalled his arrival in Kiev with great emotion. Others who were with him that day in early November 1943 remember Khrushchev "repeatedly wiping tears from his eyes with his handkerchief" as people came and embraced him; see William Taubman, *Khrushchev: The Man and His Era* (New York, 2003), pp. 177 and 695.

from you. The happiest day of my life was December 25, 1943, when I saw our glorious Red Army on the streets of our village. The third happiest day of my life would come when I could speak with you personally.

I could give you some very valuable material for *The Black Book,* and you would not manage to write it all down. Although I do not have a gift for words, I hope that you will understand me. I am already old—forty-three. My children are still small. My older daughter, Mary, is ten, and Svetlana, the younger one, is eight. My husband has been in the Red Army since June 23, 1941. We have no news of him.

First I will write down my own experiences and then those of other people. I started to write a book about Hitlerism, but I stopped.

The book is divided into three parts: 1. My autobiography. 2. How I was saved from Hitler. 3. I am alive again.

In three years of wandering around with two children (one was six years old and the other four), I saw and lived through such sorrow that it seems to me that no human being could either tell it or write it down. No mind can grasp what happened at Babi Yar. When I remember the past, I get scared. I feel dreadful and cold. It is as though I am all alone in the woods at night. Just seeing how those innocent Jews went to the place set out for their execution (consciously). Then, how they led the Jews out of Kharkov in formation, the ones who had managed to get away from Babi Yar (how they beat them!). Bloody, exhausted, starving, undressed, all skin and bones, barefoot, tortured, they moved along in columns: youngsters, old women, men of thirty-five or thirty-six in the prime of life, children of different ages, even infants. (I am crying bitterly as I write to you.) There were posters on every pole saying that Hitler had killed sixty-two thousand Jews at the request of various other nationalities,[10] but that was a lie. It was all his own initiative. I was among the Germans in Kiev for a month, then I was handed over by neighbors who had lived in the same house with me for many years. We were the best of friends the day before Hitler came, then ten days later they turned me in and brought the Gestapo to the house. These are the sorts of roots that Hitler has put down. These roots will stay for years to come. Then I left with the children for Zhitomir. I was arrested there and taken to the Gestapo. I will describe my interrogation briefly. On the way to Gestapo headquarters, a Ukrainian policeman gave Svetlana a kick in the back (she was four and getting over the measles). She was walking slowly, crying in pain. "Go! Get a move on, you dirty kike. It's execution time for you." I answered: "We don't know which of you is going to be executed, you or her." They brought us in and locked us in a dark storeroom with a cement floor. A fine, cold autumn rain was coming down. As Pushkin wrote: "A rather gloomy time would now betide/ 'Twas November in the yard outside." That is how it was for us. I had left Kiev in just my summer coat and shoes. I had not had time to take anything with me, since the Gestapo came for me with the directions given

---

10. According to German statistics, 33,771 Jews were killed at Babi Yar in two days of continuous executions. No other source, besides this testimony of Emilia Kotlova, mentions these announcements.

them by the neighbors. (Someone got something out of it.) The children and I were worn out by the journey, and then in Zhitomir I found out that my sister and her family had been buried alive.[11] I fell to the floor from all that I had been through and slept with the children on the bare, cold cement. Suddenly I heard the door to the room open; someone was calling me and the children out for interrogation. A Gestapo agent was sitting there with an interpreter beside him (I quote):

"You are accused of being a Jew."

My reply: "Who is accusing me?"

The interpreter: "The German government."

My question: "And not of anything more? Not of stealing?" "No." "Of murder?" "No." "Then I'm not a Jew. Have you got any evidence? Show it."

They left me for a while. The interpreter turned to Mary (my older girl): "Tell me, little girl, does your mama like the Germans?"

Mary's answer: "My mama hates the fascists, but she's afraid to say that to you."

They ask my younger girl: "Jew?" "Oh, I'm not hungry." (She thought that it was something to eat).

Then they turned back to Mary: "Are you a Jew?" "No." "A Russian?" "No." "A Pole?" "No." "A German?" "No." "A Czech?" "No." "A Ukrainian?" "No."

Then he shouted: "Who are you then?" "I'm Mary," came the little girl's answer. My interrogation was painful, long, and exhausting. Without finding out who I was, the Gestapo questioned us (they took several pictures of me). In those very days, when I was with the Gestapo, I found out where the partisans were, and in what forest (from people arriving). I'm going to draw a terrible picture of my time with the Gestapo. Jews were executed by firing squads right before my eyes. The door opens and in tumbles a band of men and one girl of about seventeen or eighteen. I looked at them and realized right away that they were Jews.

I asked the girl: "Where did they bring you from?" She answers: "From Korostishev, thirty-five kilometers from Zhitomir. They found the men in the forest and they grabbed me today." Again I ask: "What for?"

The girl's answer was quiet, disjointed. She had been staying with an old peasant woman in the village. A Ukrainian policeman made passes at her and wanted to sleep with her, but she refused. "Better that they kill me, but I won't give in to him."

The crowd of Jews asked those already under arrest in Yiddish: "*Sukht, khaverim, vus ken zein mit uns?*" [Tell us, comrades, what will happen to us?]

When suddenly, out of nowhere, the executioner burst in; I already knew him well because he kept looking in my direction, wondering how many bullets it would take for me. "Eh, dirty kikes, and everything in kike language, too." He began beating these Jews with the butt of his gun, wherever the blows fell: in the mouth, the face, the stomach,

---

11. The Germans carried out their first actions in Zhitomir in July and August 1941, when approximately 5,000 Jews were killed; on September 19 another 5,000 were killed.

the nose, and even the legs. I fainted on the spot and the children were shrieking and crying out something awful. What a shame I am not an artist or I would draw their faces. The interrogation was a short one. The executioner didn't think for long. I saw him take a rifle, bullets, and a black shawl. He took the clothes from the dead back to the Gestapo in this shawl. And he drove the crowd of Jews along, like a flock of submissive sheep, through the long Gestapo courtyard.

I heard shots and in twenty-five minutes he came back happy and contented that there were lots more bloody Jewish rags in his black shawl. A modest young woman told me goodbye, saying: "Be alive with your children. I want so much to live. I'm only eighteen." Now she's no more. I did not even ask what her name was. The next day, they brought in a woman who was a Jewish communist. She slept next to me and gave the children bread. In the night I asked her why they had picked her up and where. She had been working somewhere in Zhitomir and some scoundrel had wanted her only coat. (It was a man's.) The girl had refused because it was the middle of a cold autumn and she couldn't have gotten along without her overcoat. He turned her in for this. They sang to her when they led her off to interrogation: "Ah, you've been caught, little bird. You'll not get out of the net. We'll never part with you in this world." I never saw her again. What happened to her, I don't know, but I can guess. Of all those arrested, I met only one of them later, a girl named Charna, in Zhitomir in the summer of 1942. (She survived by some accident.) She recognized me and I recognized her. She did not admit to me that she was a Jew, and I did not admit it to her, either. She was afraid of me and I was afraid of her. And how many other scenes I saw there, I could not tell or describe. Not only was I arrested that one time, I was also arrested twice without the children. The third time, a Gestapo car came for me in the village of Pokostivka, in the Zhitomir District and Region in August 1943. (The Gestapo took my picture.) I have still not written anything about my life and my sufferings. Those are even more terrible. It is already two in the morning. I am writing by the light of an oil lamp; I will write about myself later. If it were warm and if I had a winter coat, then I would go to Moscow. My brother lives there on 3/5 Friedrich Engels Street, apartment 4; his name is A. B. Kotlov.

The other day, the daughter of my old nursemaid from Fastov (a peasant) arrived. She told us this story. In 1941, when the Germans killed all the Jews in Fastov, they left the children. There were about eight hundred of them. They gave the order that every villager had to take one child each and feed it and bring it up well. And if so much as one child were to die, then the whole family would answer for it. They fed these children for three months. When that period of time was up, when the children were in better health, the Germans gave the following order: "All the children of Jews are to be returned to a designated place. Refusal will mean death." The children were brought, then taken to a hospital. There they were tied down to beds and their blood sucked out for wounded Germans. And the fate of the children was sealed.[12]

---

12. This story has not been corroborated by other sources.

My personal request to you: I have been living in Kiev since April 28, 1944. All told, I have lived in Kiev for a quarter of a century and worked in the schools for twenty-four years. At the moment, I am working as a kindergarten teacher because of the apartment. I am spending the night on two cots in the kindergarten because I am writing. I have yet to receive my own apartment. Seven people wallow in a wet cellar which belongs to someone else and we sleep on the bare floor. I stopped writing for these reasons: I had no place to call my own, no table to write on, no chair to sit on.

My case, number 8985, is under review by comrade Lozin, the city prosecutor. It is already winter and my apartment is occupied by other people even though according to the law of August 5, 1941, I should receive my own living space as a member of the family of active duty military personnel. The lady who turned me over to the Gestapo has settled in my apartment and taken all my property. She is enjoying the luxury of the belongings that I earned through honest labor and I am lying about with no bed. We have been in the courts since May 1944. The case has already gone into the criminal courts, as a case of theft of another's property. Everyone is promising that there will be a trial soon. My case file has been in the Leninsky District prosecutor's office with comrade Samsonova for a long time, but it has yet to move. I myself am defenseless and would like your help in this matter. It seems to me that after so many torments I ought to have a corner of my own in my old age, and the children of a Red Army officer deserve it as well. And my neighbor, an enemy of the people, just as satisfied as she can be, lives and deals in kerosene at the outdoor market. If there is the slightest chance, help me.

Now I want to ask you, dear Ilya Ehrenburg, about the book that I have thought of. Your instructions and direction. I am writing for the first time in my life. I loved to write about nature when I was young. I have a strong desire to write that sort of book, but I am in a bad frame of mind and over the last few days I have begun to feel that my left hand is becoming paralyzed from the damp. Under Hitler, I did not see bread for two years and my room was unheated in the coldest part of winter. My children still have frostbitten hands and feet.

Be well!
Emilia Borisovna

Why do I have to suffer even now?

My nephew, Abrasha Kostovetsky, will send his verses about the Jewish people for *The Black Book*. The boy is still young, only twenty-three. He reads a lot and loves to write.

All the best,
Kotlova

My neighbor, the enemy of the people who took everything from me, is now writing fairy tales about me and gratuitously pouring all kinds of dirt on my head. I have walked the path that I have as an honest worker. She says to me that Soviet power will shoot me like a dog if she wants it to. Please answer me.

Dear writer Ilya Ehrenburg!
I am sending material for *The Black Book*.
Some facts I will not write. If possible, I will tell them to you in person.

How did I come to stay in Kiev, and why? There was a time when there was no chance to get out of Kiev, and by the time the possibility came, my younger daughter had fallen ill and there was no way to move a sick child. No sooner had she gotten free of one sickness then they both came down with the measles on the very day of that cannibal Hitler's arrival. There is no need to write about Hitler's arrival in the city, everyone knows about it. A black cloud hung over the city. There were posters and orders for death (or "death penalties") posted at every intersection and in every shop window. The people said: "If it's death for everything, then what was life given for?" Three days later Kiev was on fire. It felt like Judgment Day. In that terrible time, when houses were collapsing, burning beams were flying through the air, chunks of stone and macadam were raining down on living people, glass was showering down from windows like a fine rain. People were rushing around like singed rats in a cage while absolutely everywhere you heard people crying and screaming. At that very time, in the smoke, Hitler's people were looting apartments and hauling off phonographs, typewriters, and clothes, and did not even think about saving people. In those days, Hitler showed his true face. (How rotten he was, how insolent. He had not yet shown, however, what a beast he was—that was still under wraps.) He killed many young Jews, accusing them of arson. Exactly ten days later, on Yom Kippur—Judgment Day according to Jewish tradition—on September 29, 1941, one of Hitler's infamous atrocities was committed.[13] He offered a sacrifice to his ideal of "fascism." He swallowed up 62,000 Jews—innocent inhabitants. He gorged himself on Jewish blood until his veins were bursting. This memorable day will go down in the history of humanity. At the break of day, the "Nazi order," not signed by anyone, on the unprecedented destruction of Jews (I am writing this down word for word) appeared in all its splendor. The order was printed in two languages: in German and in Ukrainian. "All Jews of the city of Kiev and its environs must present themselves on Monday, September 29, 1941 at 8:00 AM on the corner of Melnik [Melnikov] and Dokterivsky [Degtyarovskaya] Streets (near the cemetery). Documents, money, and valuables, as well as warm clothing, underwear, and so on are to be brought."[14]

---

13. The author is mistaken here; Yom Kippur fell on October 1, 1941.
14. The full text of the order read: "All Jews in the city of Kiev and its surroundings will present themselves on Monday, September 29, 1941, at 8:00 AM at the corner of Melnik and Dokterivskaya Streets (besides the cemetery). Documents, money, and valuables, as well as warm clothing, underwear, and so on are to be brought. Any Jew not carrying out this order and found elsewhere will be shot. Any citizen entering premises vacated by Jews and appropriating property for themselves will be shot."

Already on the day before Yom Kippur, on September 28, 1941, Hitler assembled all the Jewish men in Kiev and took them out to Babi Yar to dig ditches, then shot them all toward evening. All the Jews were sure that Hitler was taking them to a ghetto, but none of them could imagine that it would be the end for them there. How difficult it was to look at those unhappy, defenseless Jews and at their procession to the place appointed for their execution! Fear and horror! They went along like a wave: young people, old people, women, men, and children of all ages, and each of them hurried to get the most comfortable place in the wagon. They took their household belongings (clothing, pots and pans, samovars, and food) on carts and little wagons. The procession began at eight in the morning on September 29, 1941, and for three straight days, the Jews went off, on foot and in transport. But to where? They did not know themselves. Babi Yar lies near the Jewish cemetery; one of its walls is practically built in Babi Yar. The ditches had been prepared ahead of time. They stopped around the edges of the ditches. They shot them with machine guns and they fell into the ditches. They took the children aside and killed them separately, bayoneted them, tore newborns in half. There weren't enough ditches, so they blew up the earth with landmines to make new ones, at the same time burying Jews alive. The ground shook from the movement of people in one ditch, while a crack appeared in another one, Jewish blood oozing from it. The area was surrounded by the Gestapo. All identity papers, clothing, valuables, and food were taken away at the entrance; farther along in Babi Yar they sorted them and tossed them into heaps. Howls, cries, wails, prayers and the piercing shrieks of children did not touch the animal souls of the loathsome fascist executioners. Everything was being done "on the orders" of Hitler. Old Jews were praying to God and crying out: "*Shma Yisroel adenoi ekhod*" [Words from the Hebrew prayer: "Hear, O Israel, the Lord our God, the Lord is one."]

Young people fought with the executioners, shouting, "The people will avenge us." Before killing them, they still had time to rape the women. Standing at a distance, it was possible to die from fright, but a man is stronger than iron and does not die before his time; he lives and withstands everything. (I am abbreviating here.) Some Jews did not go to Babi Yar; they committed suicide. Doctors poisoned themselves and their children with morphine; there were cases of people pouring kerosene over themselves and their children, and not handing themselves over to the butchers. This was how one of our pupils, Riva Khazan, in the fifth grade at School No. 47, living at 43 Korolenko, apartment 13, went to her death. Mother and daughter poured kerosene over themselves and set themselves on fire, and everything went up with them. In our building, at 12 Lenin Street, they killed the old man Stolyarov, and when the residents threw him out into the courtyard, they, Hitler's men, trampled on the face of the murdered Jew with their dirty, hobnailed boots, gloating and yelling: "*Kaput Jude!*" The face of the dead man became covered with small holes. They shot him twice more in the mouth and eyes, then went away. Seeing that, what sort of revenge could I take? None, sad to say! How I cursed that moment, that I had lived to see it.

Five days after Babi Yar, another order was issued: all Jewish apartments were to be sealed off and all Jewish belongings handed over by the building superintendents at the place indicated. What was the point? To drive the Jews out once and for all and be done with them. Hitler fulfilled his goal. The Jews were chased out, their property seized. Hitler still had Jews in captivity. Eight hundred thousand prisoners had been taken near Kiev.[15] They were still [in camps] for the time being (Borispol, Nezhin, Pereyaslav). Among them were four thousand Jews (including my husband). For nearly two weeks, they herded prisoners toward Kiev. It was autumn and the evenings were already quite cold. A column of Jews marched in the front: unclothed and barefoot, exhausted, emaciated, bound, and bloody. When they fell out along the road, Hitler's people beat them badly. The prison camp was on Kerosinnaya Street. There were pits in the courtyard and in these pits were captive Jews. They would not give them food for three days at a time. They were dying of hunger. Once they pointed out a Jew, saying that he was a commissar. They pulled him out of the pit in just his underpants, put him in the middle of the yard and began to torture him. Four of Hitler's people surrounded him with daggers. "Are you a commissar?" Then a knife in the back. Another: "Are you a *Jude*?" A knife in the stomach. A third: "Are you a communist?" A knife in the right side. A fourth: "Are you NKVD?" A knife in the left side. The execution was carried out in the presence of others. The Jew managed to yell twice: "Butchers! They'll avenge me and all of us!" The remaining Jews were also shot at Babi Yar. In the summer of 1942, I saw many western Jewish men from the ages of fourteen to sixty working on grave-digging duty outside Zhitomir. They worked the entire summer and toward winter they were shot, while many others died of hunger. And that was the fate of all the Jews.

I will describe my life under Hitler briefly. After this order, our neighbors would no longer let me into my apartment; these were people with whom I had lived in the same apartment for eight years in great friendship. Kristina Stepanovna Artemenko, the wife of a Party member, was always profiting actively from my "death." She turned me in and set herself up in my room. She took all my belongings, which she is using to this day. She is living in the calmest way that you can imagine in the capital city of Kiev, at 10 Lenin Street, apartment 3. It seems she works somewhere and is now an honest Soviet citizen. She knew that I was still alive and would get in her way; it is obvious that she thought so. She built her well-being upon my unhappiness. She is openly involved in stealing and looting, and feels on top of the world (no children, a former kulak). But I lie on a bare, cold floor with two children, in a cellar where water streams down from the walls, just as Hitler spilled Jewish blood (without a bed, without a table, without a chair), because I do not have the means to acquire new belongings, and this good-for-nothing of an enemy of the people lives in luxury with

---

15. According to German sources, approximately 650,000 Soviet prisoners of war were captured near Kiev.

my things that I earned through years of honest, hard work. Where is human justice, then? Perhaps my mind has not got to that point yet? History says nothing about it. (I am writing about the past.)

Because I had these sorts of neighbors, I had to move with my sick children to another house on Lenin Street, number 29, since no one there knew that I was a Jew. Then I would go to the outdoor market every day to get something for the sick children (one was six, the other four). One day at the Jewish market,[16] a vendor whom I knew came up and said out loud to me: "How is it she's not afraid to be gallivanting around the market? She ought to be sitting at home, not showing her face." It was hard trying to buy food since the Germans were taking everything from the villagers without paying them, and the villagers had stopped bringing provisions to the city. There were days when my sick children were almost dying of hunger and no one wanted to help (not with so much as a crust of bread), and everything was left in the apartment. And so I lived for a month in the Kiev of the Germans in hunger and fear. The neighbors were looking for me, they did not know where I was. One fine morning, one of our neighbors caught up with me, none other than Baran, the stoker at our school. He followed me and found out where I was staying, then he told Artemenko about it. That hooligan Artemenko, she turned up at our place, and at the front door of the building harangued the neighbors: why were they hiding me at such a dangerous time? I was a Jew, after all. One neighbor was the wife of a professor and her grandson had been my student. She replied: "Emilia Borisovna isn't a Jew, that's not so." Another neighbor answered: *"Khiba vona zhidivka? Vona ludina, yak třeba."* [How can she be a Jew? She's a person just like you.] (It turns out that Jews are not human.) But my neighbors were not satisfied with this. Baran met me again in the morning, he was going on his merry way to work for Hitler, and I was coming from the market. This time he could not stand it any longer. He found out what apartment I had entered, and thirty minutes later he brought the Gestapo to my building. He told them that I was a Jew—a *Jude*—and that I was hiding here. He was shouting at me, stamping his feet and swearing away: "Kike, show your passport!" I showed him a document that I will say more about later. Of course, I denied everything that Baran said. They went away saying that they would be back, since both children were in bed sick. They must have been thinking "Where would she go with them?" A little while later I heard them in the corridor asking where the Jew lived. The neighbors were horrified that a Jew—a *Jude*—was in their building. A cry went through the whole place, and when it reached me, I grabbed my two sick children and darted out the back entrance onto Shevchenko Boulevard, then down to Turgenev Street to the place of a teacher whom I had known for only ten days. That was Saturday and on Sunday I left Kiev.

---

16. In cities or towns with sizable Jewish populations, an outdoor market could have been known as the place where Jewish produce sellers had stalls and where other Jews liked to shop.

Baran and Artemenko led the police to me, but I saved myself by fleeing. There were still a few medical professors left in Kiev. Rabinovich was a surgeon, a professor of childhood diseases. Dukelsky was a Jew. They were killed a year later, in 1942. The wife of old Dukelsky (he was seventy-two) told me a great deal—his wife was Russian—about how she tried to save him, but it did not help.

How did I leave Kiev and set off for Zhitomir? New ordeals befell me on the road to Zhitomir. Why had I chosen Zhitomir? I will tell you why. During the first month of the German occupation of Kiev, I was witness to many terrible and painful scenes of the suffering of Jews who were being marched back into Kiev under guard. They had run off toward Kharkov or closer to the Front in order to get to our people. Often they failed. There was a "death office" at the Jewish cemetery. When I asked our building superintendent, still the "Soviet" Polonsky, to come with me into our apartment to pick up the evidence of my graduation from the Institute, he told me that I should bring a certificate from this "death office" confirming that I was a person harmless to the Germans, but when I offered my husband's coat, he left without this certificate.

Once when I was walking along Korolenko Street near the Bogdan Khmelnitsky monument, I saw Germans leading a column of Jews somewhere. They were blacker than black. Imagine the state I was in when I spotted a teacher I knew. I must have been dreadful to look at. I broke into a cold sweat from fear. I walked along behind them, staying off to one side. The teacher was still wearing the dark blue autumn coat that I knew, her kerchief had slipped from her head, and in her hands she was holding a small dictionary, as usual (she probably slept with it). She noticed me. I shall never forget how she asked me to spare her life, thinking that I was Russian. The difference between us was that I was still free, while they were leading her to the "death office." Then I thought to myself: "My dear friend! Tomorrow I'll meet you in the same place because there is no way for me to avoid this path." Every so often the guards would hit old women with the butts of their rifles because they were walking too slowly to the place of death. One woman was moaning loudly and crying: "*Oi vey iz mir, vus hob ich zich derlebt.*" [Oh, how terrible. Why have I lived to reach this?] Her son-in-law picked her up but he could only carry her a short way since he was already exhausted. They were taken to the police precinct at 15 Korolenko Street. The officer in charge came out. The guards reported: "What do we do with the Jews?" The commander answered (he wasn't a German): "Take them to the 'death office' for shooting!" So I followed them to Lukyanovka.

How I counted the hours of life. Every knock at the door meant they were coming for me. I felt sorry only for my two little ones. After all, they had not known life yet, had only just gotten over being sick. I pictured the death of my children before my eyes. The bandits liked to kill children in the presence of their mothers. Oh, how hard the suffering of a mother is when she sees her children killed. (I'm crying bitterly.)

I often changed markets so that people would not recognize me. I went to the Bessarabka market. An old Jewish woman sat behind the counter at the newspaper kiosk; she could not get up anymore. The passers-by were giving her things: money, bread, or fatback. She would not take food and shouted: "*Yiden, bnei rakhmunes, ratevet mich fun dem toit.*" [Jews, merciful people. Save me from death!] They drove her out of her apartment, took everything from her; she was in nothing but rags. It was the depths of a cold autumn. Slush, a cold rain, and she was trembling from the cold. She was telling everyone that her daughters and grandchildren had already left for the ghetto, and that they had left her, a single old woman, all alone, and that she was very angry with them. The next day I went to see what had become of the old woman, but she was already dead. She had frozen to death. An old lady hid in an attic for an entire month, having stocked up on sugar and water. When they found her and took her off to the "death office," she told everyone that she had lived an extra month. Autumn. Cold. I saw a woman of thirty-eight or so sitting in the Zolotovorotsky Gardens. She had been thrown out of her home. I kept an eye on her for two days and then that was the end of her. I hope you never live to see a time like the one that I had to see and live through.

My departure from Kiev. After the order, all the teachers were afraid of me like they were of fire. They were scared to cross the street with me, they even asked me not to meet with them. How hard that was and how insulting that people who were my friends the day before, whom I had worked with for ten years in the same school, where we had worked miracles together, today did not want to see me and help me in a difficult moment. Only one Russian teacher, Vera Petrovna Sukhozanet—she is now working in Kiev as a teacher and has been my friend for many years—saved my life. She gave me papers marked with another nationality, Russian, written on them, but with everything else as before. (I still have all the documents from that time.) She also advised me to leave Kiev right away because she was afraid for her life. With a pain in my heart, I left Kiev, the school that I loved and the house that I was born in. With two little ones, I set off in awful weather without a crust of bread or any belongings. I was wearing a summer coat and dress shoes because I had not managed to take anything with me. (The neighbors had seen to that.) After all, I had studied and worked in Kiev for many years, and brought up children, both other people's and my own. I had lived in Kiev for a quarter of a century, had worked in the schools for twenty-four years. I gave the children my youth and my soul. I had always worked two shifts, only night forced me to part with the school. In the summer I worked in children's camps. I always liked the ringing voice of a child. I never got tired or felt fatigue. I could always be found among children. Children are my whole life. By the time I was eighteen, I was already in charge of a large class of them. Then suddenly I had to leave everything and find refuge for myself. But where? I didn't know myself. My children remained unsteady on their feet from illness and the red spots were still on their faces. Early one Sunday morning, we took to the road on foot. Svetochka picked up her favorite doll since it was too hard for her to say goodbye to it, and when her hands turned numb with the cold, she gave it to me and said: "Mama, take it and don't lose it!" I thought then: "All of this is the work of that enemy of mankind, the cannibal Hitler." (How painful it is to remember the ugly past.)

What happened to me along the way? A little bag with bits of bread, my new identity papers, and two small children. We saw a cart on the road, and hitched a ride to the Mylo farm twenty-five kilometers from Kiev. There was slush in the yards and a fine rain was coming down. Along the way we had gone stiff with cold and were very hungry. There were a few scattered huts on the farm. We went into the first one. We warmed up, and they offered us baked potatoes. The first question was, "Who are you? And where are you headed?" The answer: "I lost everything in a fire so I'm headed for my family's place." And where this family was, I did not know myself.

It was impossible to stay the night because it was already crowded for the farmer and his own family, never mind us. So the children and I trudged along in the dreadful weather to the village of Spitki, but there was not a single hut that would take us in for the night. In the huts there was an order not to take in strangers because they could be partisans. I was standing, numb with cold, in the middle of a field with the children. Where could we go to sleep? A dark, cold night was closing in. That moment was worse than death. Finally, I went to see a hunchbacked woman who was the former head of the collective farm. I asked her to sell us some milk for the children. She promised it for later, but for the time being there was the chance to get warm. The children fell asleep sitting up, from fatigue, cold, and hunger. In the evening, the woman told me to clear out of her hut. No matter how I pleaded with her to let us stay the night, she would not agree to it. I shook the children, but they did not wake up; they were in a deep sleep. An old man, the woman's father, who was sleeping by the stove, heard my weeping and pleading. I had not even noticed him at first. He yelled at his daughter in Ukrainian: "Let her and her children spend the night. Nothing will happen because of Hitler." A young woman then brought some straw into the kitchen and we stayed the night.

In the morning, there was rain, and impassable mud in the village, yet there I was in my dress shoes. They showed us out and we went on our way. We walked through almost the entire village. No one wanted to take in a stranger, especially one with children. Everyone looked at me with distrust. One village woman said to me in Ukrainian: "You're a Jew, I guess? From Kiev, since you're wearing a long coat, and the kids have caps on, even if you talk like our women." (That was her conclusion.) Finally, one family let us in, but I had to show my passport to the village elder and my passport had stayed behind for Hitler to remember me by. I could tell that the mayor could not read, so instead of my passport I showed him a membership booklet with my photo. He scrawled out a permit saying that these people were honest and could stay in the village. I took this document to the lady of one house and we stayed for a couple of days until the weather got better. That evening, my daughter came down with angina. We were lying on the bare floor and then they gave us some straw. The woman did not want to keep me with a sick child and sent us packing into the street. We moved on from that village. We passed through Soviet fields that stretched as far as the eye could see, through forests, meadows, and hundreds of villages occupied by the fascists.

How much grief and suffering I went through on the way with the children, I couldn't describe or tell. We made it to Zhitomir in a few days. On the way, we met a man from Kiev who had been living in Glubochitsa Street. He was on his way to Zhitomir to ransom his two sons from captivity. He told me about how enthusiastically he had taken part in the killing of Jews at Babi Yar. He went to Babi Yar every day to help the Germans and for that the Germans gave him junk belonging to the Jews and food that Jews had left behind in heaps. He had even collected 43,000 rubles in Soviet money, and now wanted to buy back his sons. I asked him: "Are you happy that they killed so many Jews?" He smiled pleasantly and quickly answered: "I'm very glad about it!" I had already figured out whom I was walking alongside. We traveled for a few kilometers in a car, and by the time we got to my sister's place (at 11 Malovilskaya Street), it was dark. We spent the night in my sister's apartment, and there the neighbors told us that she had been buried alive along with her family for showing resistance. Our "good" traveling companion spent the night with us. In the morning, I went to a neighbor in the opposite house, the Polish woman in number 12, to cook potatoes for the children. It turned out that the son of this Polish lady was working for the Germans; he arrested us and took us to the Gestapo.

I already wrote about my first arrest. At the Gestapo post, I had learned from others under arrest that there were partisans in the Pokostovsky forest, near the Korosten station. When I came out of the Gestapo post onto the street, my eyes went dark from the sunlight, which I wasn't used to. I stood there and thought: "Where do I go?" I decided to go to the Narobraz [the regional office for education] to learn about any nearby orphanages. I had decided to leave my children in a home, then join the partisans in the Pokostovsky forest. That is what I did. At the Narobraz, I learned there was an orphanage on Kurbatovka Street. When I went into the reception office, an old, sooty icon and a famous portrait of the cannibal Hitler caught my eye. My heart even skipped a beat at the sight of a worker with his little fascist flags. Here, I thought, one has to keep up with the fashion. The rank-and-file workers were Ukrainians. The boss was a German. They would not take my children and answered: "If you're the mother, then be one, and feed your kids." It was there that I found out the address of another orphanage. I took my hungry children and we trudged off to the other side of town. I brought them into the orphanage. I asked the director for a place to stay for the night and said that I would bring a request form for their admission in the morning. The home made a depressing impression on me. They were beating up the children. They were real riffraff. From the ages of four to eighteen. Before my eyes, they locked a village child in the cellar for having stolen money from a teacher. He spent the night locked up and was very frightened. When they let him out in the morning, he looked out of his mind from fear. The children told me that not long before, the Germans had taken all the Jewish children, led them away and killed them, and that four Jewish boys, ages ten and eleven, had been hanged in the garden of the orphanage two days earlier. They had been handed over by the doctor who worked in the home. I got to know her. She was a real hooligan, all right. She told me that there were a lot of Jews and that you could not kill them all. The next day, I asked the director to take the children, or at least to let me leave them there for a couple of days while I got set up; in the meantime, I took off for the Pokostovsky forest and the partisans.

The forest was fifty-nine kilometers from Zhitomir. In nothing but my summer coat and dress shoes, in a biting cold, I went. I left my dear children to sure death, but there was no other way out for me. How sorry I was that I had not died at Babi Yar.

I did not know the road. I kept getting lost. Finally, I came to the village of Pokostivka, and beyond the village, another four kilometers farther along, the forest started. I went into the woods and did not see any partisans. I wandered around in the forest for a long time and only when I was on my way out did I see two men sitting under a tall tree. One was quite young, the other was older. I was afraid of them. My left leg was really hurting me because I had given it a chill sitting on the cement floor in the Gestapo post. One asked me: "Hey, lady, you limping?" I plucked up my courage and approached him since in his voice I heard the voice of our people. When they asked me: "Got any kids?" I burst into tears, and they understood right away who I was. They told me that they were getting ready to head for the Korostensky forest since the partisans were there, but that I would not get far with a bad leg. So they advised me to return to my children.

I headed back to Zhitomir. I came across a school in Pokostivka. The villagers told me that the school was not running because there was no teacher. I talked to the school principal. He told me that they needed a first grade teacher and what the conditions would be. I found out everything and in seven days went back to my children. The children had come down with scabies by then; their bodies were covered with boils from dirt and hunger. They were not accepting my children in the orphanage. I was afraid to go to the school, the principal was the son of a priest, and besides, I would stand out before everyone. So what should I do now? Winter was closing in and I had no roof over my head. No one was letting me into their hut. I wanted to join the collective farm and work there, but they were not taking any workers. So I decided to go in the completely opposite direction, to Berdichev, where the Reya Collective Farm was located.

I set off. I traveled on foot for a long time. I passed through hundreds of villages (wherever I spent the day, I did not stay the night), but I could not find a place to settle down. Winter was getting closer and they were cutting back on the workforce. Finally, I made it to the Reya Collective Farm, which was ten kilometers from

Berdichev. They wanted to put me to work in the office and sent me to see the head agronomist. (I learned he was a German.) I did not say a word, but instead headed back to Zhitomir because I was afraid to have him see me. I lost another week going back. The director of the orphanage was very unhappy that I was leaving the children each time. My meeting with the children cannot be described. The way they pleaded with me and cried for me to take them out of the orphanage. "Mummy, you're not going away without us, are you?" And they followed me round the whole day. I decided that if we were going to die, then it was going to be all together. I gathered up the children and took to the road. I got an appointment at the school in Zhitomir. Even though I had the position, I did not want to go to the school—I was afraid. I thought that wherever there was the possibility of staying, I would stay there with the children. But no village wanted to take us in, as if we were carrying some disease.

Going from village to village with the little ones without a crust of bread, I cried so much that if you collected all my tears, you could give a man a bath in them. So we came to the village of Pokostivka; I knew it well. For the sake of saving my children, I went to work in the village school as a first grade teacher. They gave me a room with no stove and a broken window. There was a narrow iron bed. I got some straw. After a month they gave me a small stove, I promised to pay for it myself. There was school firewood, made ready by our government for the 1941–1942 school year, but the principal had taken it for himself and did not want to share it; I did not dare argue with him. In 1941, there was a terrible cold, but the room was not heated since there was no fuel. The children now had frozen hands and feet, too. We did not see bread for more than two years.

Hitler had taken away all the bread and the villagers themselves went hungry. We lived for a whole winter on unsalted potatoes. There was no pot for boiling the potatoes. The water froze in the well. We had nothing to cover ourselves with. We slept in our overcoats for six months, not undressing, because none of our things were left. I was covered with boils; having nothing was eating away at us. My life was just one long nightmare. No human tongue could tell about all that came crashing down on all the Jews and on me in particular. It was something unheard of in human history, the tortures and sufferings inflicted by Hitler on me and on all the Jewish people. The school was shut down. There were no pupils, books, or fuel, and I was blissfully happy because of that. Hitler would answer the villagers that he did not need educated people, he needed slaves, beasts of burden and manpower. He always wrote that Europe would triumph.

After the New Year of 1942, religious education became mandatory in the schools. How was I supposed to know anything about religious education? Had I ever studied it? And the priest's son (the principal) knew straight away that I was not Russian (in their way of thinking, Orthodox). They gave out a form with several questions to answer. The main thing was that nationality appeared there and this was important to Hitler. At the village council, they asked me about my religious faith. I nearly answered Jewish instead of Orthodox. Even though it was so revolting to me that it made me cry, I had to keep silent. The priest's son, a first-class hooligan, began interrogating me. Who was I? Why didn't I recognize any holidays or even know their names? Why didn't I go to church and teach the children to pray? The whole village already knew that I wasn't Orthodox. On the last Sunday in May 1942, the principal of the school, the son of a priest (lame in one leg) learned from the village council that there was a new decree from Hitler: anyone turning in a Jew, a communist, a partisan, or a deputy to the Supreme Soviet would receive a reward of one thousand rubles and ration cards for food at a low price. On that day the principal came to see me with the absolute certainty that I was a Jew and that he would get a thousand rubles for my head. He started to tell me that he loved the Jews so much that he had almost married a Jewish schoolteacher once. Right after that he proposed that I give him a thousand rubles to conceal my Jewish identity. I was sick at heart, but I did not let it show. I answered: "Let someone who fits into this category be worried." I only said that if I went to where I came from, I would bring some of my things. I saw so much disgusting behavior on his part toward me, but I had to keep quiet about all of it. Our lives were hanging by a thread, after all, and I still had not lost hope that I would see my loved ones again and survive Hitler besides (and so it happened).

His wife would always tell me that her husband, that is, the principal, had never been a Soviet teacher, and that he had worked in a school in the Soviet Union for more than twenty years in disguise. But when Hitler came to power, he showed his real face. How painful it was to see how happily people lived and live. (I am not writing much about the village.) The days of Hitler dragged by, long, dull, and gloomy. The principal grew impatient that I did not go to my hometown. He went to Zhitomir and announced that there was a kike woman living in his village. The village elder had promised to give me official proof that I was living in the village. And without a stamp, the document was not valid, and the mayor did not have the stamp yet. Finally, the happy moment came, and the mayor gave me the necessary paper with a seal. It was June 1942. The school director went to Zhitomir and brought a memo from the education department saying that they were summoning me there. He gave it to me conditionally.

I set off for Zhitomir in answer to the summons. I walked for fifty-five kilometers, but it turned out that it was not the education department but the Gestapo who wanted to see me. It was no longer possible to get away. My interrogation was long, painful, and dreadful. Hitler kept on accusing me of having been born a Jew. But living for forty years as a Jew had been a lot easier than two and a half years as a Russian. I denied everything, of course, just as I had done the first time. They took my picture again and printed it in the papers and searched me. (I got to keep my photo identification.) They asked me when my birthday was and when my name day was. I answered that I was Mary Magdalene and not Mary the Egyptian. And still other stupid questions. This time, I was particularly calm and composed, like never before. They released me conditionally, with personal responsibility to show them my passport.

Barefoot, without a crust of bread, I set out for Kiev to ask Vera Petrovna Sukhozanet for advice. My heart felt like it was being squeezed tightly within me from pain, anger, and agitation, like a lemon peel on a hot roadway. I went along on foot slowly and tediously. I could not even see light in front of me. It was very hot at that time of year. I wanted to lie down and not get up any more. I was terribly anxious about the children. Before I left, while I was still in Zhitomir, I wrote out a note with the address of my brother, who lives in Moscow, and sewed it into the lining of my older girl's coat. I asked her: "Daughter of mine, when our people come, the Red Army, then ask to send this bit of paper to Moscow so that my brother will come for you, if you're still alive. It could be that I won't come back to you anymore. You'll be living without a mama and a papa." I stood there for a long time looking at them and weeping. My older girl was saying to me: "Mama, you'll come back and you'll live with us." The younger one kept clinging to me and would not let me go.

I tore myself away from them and moved off. In Pokostivka, there were friends as well. In the Mushinsky family there was a doctor, an old lady; they had taken her son off to Germany (he was deaf, but they took him anyway). This old lady came to see me every day with her grandson, a six-month-old child, to find out when Hitler would meet his end. I entrusted my children to them. I arrived in Kiev in the morning and found Vera Petrovna at home. She was living on Reiterskaya Street, number 25 in apartment 3. She did not believe that I was still alive. I stayed the night. That evening I told her my whole story and asked her for advice: what to do and where to go? After our discussions it seemed to me that she had changed and it was as if she was afraid of me. We did not come to any result. This time, Vera Petrovna could not help me at all. I woke up early, took a few things and went back to the village.

The city of Kiev under Hitler. Dirty, cheerless, emptied of people. Instead of magnificent flowers on the streets, potatoes were growing everywhere. Green overcoats wandered the streets with tall cockades. Gloomy, dull, hungry people roamed along the Svyatoshinsky highway with sacks and wheelbarrows in the direction of the villages to make trades. The city was weeping. Although I was dressed like a village woman and it was difficult to recognize me, the mother of one of my pupils recognized me just the same and stopped (they were Germans named Tsoll; her daughter had studied with me for three years). Truth be told, I was afraid of her. I trembled on the street. It seemed to me that I was being followed. Everyone seemed like an enemy to me. How I wanted to see my home! I did not go; I was afraid. In the rest home in Svyatoshin, where we had once lived, Germans and their families were living there now. Each one had a detached house or a dacha. I looked at them with so much burning hatred. Their voices were repulsive to me. They were building their happiness on our bones. They were drinking their fill of our blood. The whole world was weeping and they, the butchers, were gloating. (I thought that it would soon be the end of them.)

I looked for a long time at the rest home where I had stayed long before. In 1940, I had been rewarded for good work, but now I was poor, without rights, defenseless.

I was a living corpse. Walking along, I would ask myself: "And when are our people going to come?" It was as though someone in my soul was answering: "Soon, soon." I went faster. Seven days later I returned to the village.

While I was away, they had decided in the village that I really was a Jew and that they had hanged me in Zhitomir for carrying out a deception. Now they were getting ready to send my children to the city. The children were sobbing and refusing to go. They were saying to everyone: "Our mama will come back soon. She's just got to come to us." (A child's heart does not deceive children.) Out of nowhere, I showed up in the village. Everyone ran out to see the "hanged woman," and it was only then that they became convinced that I really was a Russian. It would be hard to describe our meeting. We were crying from joy at being together again. Although I was very tired, I did not sleep the whole night. I only wondered why that Hitler was wasting his culture, his intellect, and his time, and for what? Searching for one defenseless Jewish woman. The village calmed down. I went to work in the fields. I left the school. I did not want to work anymore. I was in a dreadful mood. I suffered from fears of what was to come. A heavy stone was lying on my heart. After work, the children and I would gather wheat. I would grind the grains and make watery dumplings for the children instead of bread and potatoes; there was no money to buy a pood of potatoes.[17] (They were 150–200 rubles a pood.) One Tuesday morning, after bringing in the harvest at the end of August, the director came to me and proposed that I go to some district to get some quicklime to whitewash the school. I refused since I would not be working there. Lately he had been ingratiating himself with me in order to get my husband's leather coat, which he had borrowed from me on permanent loan.

I used to walk through the village looking for scraps to boil something for the children. It was already eleven in the morning and the children had not had breakfast yet. I saw a big, magnificent German car pull up to the village council building. I realized it was coming for me. Three Gestapo agents and one interpreter. The interpreter was from Czechoslovakia. The mayor was in Zhitomir at that moment and there was only one clerk in the building. The Gestapo men demanded to see me and the school principal. The clerk pointed at me, as if to say "Here she comes." I heard them calling me: "Kotlova! Kotlova!" (I threw down the scraps and hurried over to them.) The first thing that caught my eye were the medals on their chests—the skull and crossbones. I had been arrested twice and had sat there for days and I had never noticed these pins.

One of the agents took out my photo identification and showed it to the others, saying: "Yes, this is her; she's *kaput* here and now." He tried his rifle to see if it was firing properly. The whole scene was happening on the street outside the council office. The entire village came running to see them execute me. I stood there firmly, but the villagers told me later that I was as pale as death. One Gestapo agent said to me:

---

17. One pood is equal to just over thirty-six pounds.

"Get in the car." They wanted to take me to a field and kill me there. I got ready to get in. But another one says: "*Kaput!*" (in other words, why take the trouble). In my heart, I was thinking: "No, you bastards! Butchers, monsters, you won't kill me! I'll go on living for a long time yet!" The translator insisted that I be interrogated in the principal's presence. The first one kept on yelling: "*Kaput!*" He ordered me to take a few steps, and then he fired twice. It was so close that I went deaf. "You're going to tell the truth. Otherwise, we'll kill you right now." I answered calmly: "I've been telling you the truth all along." To myself, I thought: "And are you living by the truth?" It was all a lie, one lie after another. Blood for blood. Death for death. I remembered the wise words of our great Stalin. I was just glad that the children would not see the death of their mother.

They talked together for a long time, then decided to finish the interrogation at the village council in the presence of the principal and the villagers. They all went in and I did, too. They were sitting, I was standing. "Show us your papers!" I showed them. "Show the proof that you graduated from the Pedagogical Institute in 1930." It showed where I was born and who I was. The interpreter looked at my photo identification, which was part of the evidence, then he showed it to the Gestapo agents, saying: "See how you used to look, and now you're an old woman." I thought to myself: "You're the ones who made me this way, you scum!" "How old am I?" "Thirty-nine." Then a third man, still young, who had been silent the entire time, now said: "My mother's fifty-two, but she isn't as old as you are." (That is, me.) I said nothing. Then I showed them my new papers in place of my passport. It said that the certificate had been issued in 1938 and gave my nationality as Russian. Then they stopped and put their heads together for a long time. The Soviets had been in power in 1938, after all, so why would I have changed my nationality? Back then, all the Jews had been living very well, and, as they saw things, Soviet power was kike power.

They asked the principal if he knew for a fact that I was a Jew. He answered: "Maybe some other nationality, but she's not Orthodox." How could he be so sure? The principal replied: "She doesn't know the Scriptures, the names of the holidays, she doesn't go to church, and she doesn't teach her children the prayers." The interpreter answered: "It doesn't make any difference if she doesn't know or doesn't want to!" Then they started to ask the people of the town what sort of woman I was. The head of the first kolkhoz, Mr. Shevchenko, answered that I was not a Jew. "She's one of our folk, you know, Orthodox." One old woman gave this definition: "Are Jews really people? One like that, how can she be a Jew? That one there is one of our women." In a word, my life was hanging in the balance. I thought: "What scale of justice are they using?" Then they asked me a question in a reproachful tone: Why didn't I have a passport for two years? I answered by saying that everyone in the village was living without a passport. And to myself I thought: "I don't want to show it to your faces, you bandits. Your passport is disgusting to me, just like you Germans. I'm waiting every day for our husbands and brothers." They told me that I would have to go to

Zhitomir, to the office of the district bürgermeister [the head of the district administration] for a new passport. If I fell into their hands without a passport again, they would kill me. I said: "Why kill me? I'm always in your hands, after all, and I'm not going anywhere." (Where would you hide from the butchers?) I asked them to give me a certificate that I had been arrested three times, but a Gestapo agent answered that it was enough that they had given me back my papers and my life. And the interpreter added; "Especially your life."

They went away in the evening. I was not myself anymore when I left them. I came home. The children were already asleep on the famous bed. At first I nodded off from exhaustion and alarm, and then I thought: How can I get out of this village? And what measures do I take?

I went to see the Mushinskys to ask where to find sugar processing plants. I found out. Two days later, under the pretext of having to go to Zhitomir for a passport, I left for Andrushovka (in the Andrushovka District of the Zhitomir Region). I got there, but the factories were not running. They sent me even farther, to Chervonoe (and all that time I had to walk, without a crust of bread). After a week of walking, I was blacker than black. I felt that I had no more strength to fight, that I had no way out. The first month of autumn. Warm. They were hiring at the sugar works in Chervonoe, but they were not offering housing. There were no apartments and out of fear they were not taking in strangers. Plus, you needed a passport to work in a factory and I did not have one. Another tough situation. Regardless of where you put a sick person, things are still bad for him. No, I could not make up my mind. Better to find a collective farm among the villagers. I was already used to them and they were better as bosses.

The collective of the sugar beet factory was in the village of Yaropovichi, in the Andrushovsky District of the Zhitomir Region. I went there. There was lots of work and they needed bodies. They were hiring, but there was no housing at all. I worked there for two days. The conditions were awful. There was nothing to eat and no place to live. I spent the night in a shed. We worked in the fields from morning until it was past dusk, stacking up beets. The work was too much for me because I had no more strength and could barely drag my legs along. We were paid twenty kilos of grain in the winter for a workday.[18] The villagers had their farms and their huts but could barely exist, so what about me? Neither house nor home. How could I get by with children? It was typical Hitler pay for human labor. Hitler issued a proclamation at the beginning of the war: "You, villagers, serve the Soviet state for a kilo of chaff." It was of no use to him, Hitler, to see how villages prospered under Soviet power and so he took everything out of the villages in advance. The population of the villages that had any sense struggled against Hitler, like we did.

I was terribly worried about the children. I thought the Gestapo would come to the village and take the children away instead of me. So I decided to send the children to

---

18. More than likely, this is a mistake in the text. They could have received two kilograms.

the Kiev orphanage, where my former children's home director had worked. When I was at school, we had worked together. (Her name was Alexandra Gnatieva Yershova.) We were good friends at that time. I thought that she would help me out at this difficult hour, that she was truly a Soviet person, but things turned out differently.

When I came to Kiev solely to see her at the orphanage (at 3 Belitskaya Street)—now it is a special home for the children of frontline soldiers—she was not there, of course. I went to her room, and I saw an icon—the Mother of God—hanging over her bed. There were icons on the wall in the dining room and the children were on their knees praying to God. She was in front of them, praying as well. At that moment I became terribly afraid seeing her in that position. The thought went through my head that perhaps she had been in disguise for twenty-three years. I was not mistaken. When I asked her: "Alexandra Gnatieva, I don't recognize you!" (Not long ago, she had been preparing to join the Party.) She replied with a smirk: "Emilia Borisovna! You've got to trim your sails to the wind." I regretted seeking her help in Kiev. I was even afraid to stay overnight with her.

I went to see Vera Petrovna. This time I walked the streets with more confidence. I walked along Lenin Street and even stopped by the Academy of Sciences and looked at the building where I had lived for so many years. I thought to myself that I would live in Kiev again. I was on Kirov Street across from the First of May Park, where my sister once lived. She had been evacuated in 1941 with the children's home. (Lucky her.) I went to Podol and there I saw the apartment of my other sister, who had also been evacuated with her institution. (Lucky her as well.) I came back to life for a moment at the sight of my beloved city. It would be evening soon, and it would be forbidden to walk about (movement on the streets was allowed only until nine in the evening). I hurried to Vera Petrovna's to find a place to stay for the night. She let me in and locked the door behind me, since our former English teacher lived there and her husband worked for the city council, and Vera Petrovna did not want them to know that I was spending the night. We talked all night about what I should do about the passport, but nothing came of it. At dawn, I set off again for the village. Four days later I was with my children. I had quite a few adventures along the way. What I saw, what I heard, what I went through, I will not describe. (I am not capable of putting it down on paper. If I had been born talented or some kind of genius, then that would be different.)

Arriving at the village, I hurried to leave with my children because it was not possible to stay in the village any longer. It was my luck that some profiteers were coming from Zhitomir in a car. I pleaded with them and they took us to Zhitomir. I left the children at the orphanage again since the director was already an acquaintance of mine. I myself went to the village of Yaropovichi to rent a hut for the children and settle in for the winter. It was after great effort that I rented a place from an old woman. I went back to Zhitomir for the children. From Zhitomir to Yaropovichi, it was fifty kilometers. I went from Zhitomir on foot, and on the way I met a car and caught a ride the rest of the way to the village. For the first few days I went into the fields to dig potatoes for the villagers. After two weeks, we were tossed out onto the street. The reason was that my older daughter came down with the mumps and the old lady demanded fifty rubles from me for firewood and I did not have it.

I started making the rounds of the huts. There were days when no one wanted to so much as let us into a shed. Our situation was dreadful. Winter was closing in. Finally, we moved in with a young woman named Anna Perepecheva who had a second hut from the Church. We promised her the moon. This Anna was just like Vera Chibiryak[19] in person. I had already sensed everything then and there. It wasn't the end of my suffering. Both girls fell ill from cold, hunger, and deprivation, and they were marked for death. How many nights did I stay up weeping, sitting beside them.

Soon the mayor and the commandant of the village were summoning me to the council building. The mayor was trying the whole time to find out where my husband worked. In a slaughterhouse, I said. He said that all Jews were working in a slaughterhouse. And the commandant said: "That explains everything then." That meant that we were Jews. (My husband had been a military man almost his whole life.) In a little while, the children got better. I let everyone know that I was a good seamstress. All the villagers were afraid that I would steal the rags that they gave me to sew since I was in real need. I sewed by hand, all of it rough material, on cotton wadding. I sewed slowly, patiently. After a short time they were convinced that I was a genuinely honest worker, that I even returned the rough peasant threads that were left on the ball after sewing. I took every bit of work that was offered me just to feed my hungry children. And so I spent the whole winter of 1943 with this Anna. I was swollen from hunger. The children wasted away to the point where they had no faces. They were as translucent as wax candles.

The spring came and I went out to the fields again to work for the villagers planting potatoes. Then the mayor made me plant potatoes under the plough. I did not work much in the collective's fields since the labor was not paid. When I worked for the peasants, they at least gave me something to eat and some bread for the children. Unfortunately for me, visitors from Kiev came to stay with Anna so I had to leave the hut. Again they made me abandon the corner that I had. Again things were bad. There was no roof over our head, but at least it was getting to be spring. The children and I slept on the ground for a long time, anywhere we could. One fine day, another village woman, Maria Mashtaler, took me in.

There, my cup of sorrows ran over. I sent my eight-year-old Mary to work in a pigsty. She looked after five pigs and a dozen piglets. She would leave at five in the morning and return at nine at night. The villagers fed her. My younger girl envied the older, but no one in the village wanted to hire six-year-old Svetlana. Svetlana

---

19. Vera Chibiryak testified against Mendel Beilis in the infamous "blood libel" trial that took place in Kiev in 1913; he was acquitted.

cried bitterly because Mary was eating while she went hungry. It was comforting to see that Mary shared the last of what she had. Whatever the lady of the house gave her she would hide and bring home to Sveta. She would frequently offer some to me: "Take this, Mama!" I felt as though some sort of protection was growing up around me. It wasn't for nothing that I had given myself so much trouble to save their lives for the time being. So we worked throughout the summer (the children and I were in the fields from dawn to dusk). I never saw anything of the world at all. The mayor and the commandant were keeping a close eye on us.

More to follow. I am writing late at night by the light of an oil lamp.[20]

GARF, f. 8114, op. 1, d. 960, ll. 138–175ob., 191–198ob. The original manuscript.

Lvov

6. A forced labor camp
THE RECOLLECTIONS OF STEPAN YAKIMOVICH SHENFELD
[1943][21]

It was the autumn of 1942. Rain clouds hung over the city of Lvov. The beginning of November brought frost as well.

Early in the morning of Saturday, November 14, I got up as always from my folding cot (because of the close quarters we used fold-up beds), washed up, and began to put on my ragged overalls. All my roommates got up as well. (Two families were living in the small room.) My poor mother gave me breakfast, then I left the house for work. It was still dark out. The smelly, dirty puddles on the streets of the Jewish quarter were frozen, but the air was relatively clean; the smell that was always hanging in the air was hardly noticeable. In the darkness, one could see the silhouettes of people on their way to work. Everyone was hurrying. Someone was finishing his skimpy breakfast while walking. On their right arm, each of them wore a white armband with a blue six-pointed star, the distinguishing mark of the Jews.

I was walking quickly. I went through a door in the fence that ringed the Jewish quarter and was immediately surrounded by people offering bread, blini, and dumplings at unbelievably high prices. Since the residents of the Jewish quarter were given only one hundred grams of bread per day, the population was starving. They lived only on what they could buy from non-Jewish profiteers with connections to the villages for the clothing or other valuables which they had to sell at outrageously low prices. One of those coming out of the quarter, the so-called ghetto, was buying something

---

20. The archives of Ilya Ehrenburg contain additional materials for *The Black Book* sent by E. B. Kotlova on September 29, 1945. They contain lists of people who rescued Jews in the Kiev and Zhitomir Regions and the names of those who were saved.
21. Stepan Yakimovich Shenfeld was taken to a labor camp at the age of sixteen. His brother Zigmunt and their mother perished. Stepan escaped in 1943, then joined the Red Army. He wrote his reminiscences in the autumn of 1943. He also appended the letter from his father, which appears at the end of his story.

and hurrying on his way. I blended in with the crowd of workers from other parts of town. Almost all of them had the same expressions of exhaustion from eleven- or twelve-hour workdays. Now there were already a few white armbands in sight.

I quickly walked up the steep rise of Yanovskaya Street, turned onto Peratskaya Street and found myself at the entrance to the establishment where I worked. The early morning light revealed a green uniform, a steel helmet, and under it the fat, animal face of the sentry. In fright, I raised my hand to my cap and pulled it from my head. I remember that morning well [. . .].[22] Not suspecting anything, I go up to the guard, but he grabs me by the shoulder, throws my cap into the dirty street and with his hands and feet begins to teach me about the rules of behaving "with respect" toward German soldiers. Mechanically, I take my photo identification for my place of work out of my pocket. The soldier looks at me, at the photograph, and finally waves his hand. The gesture means that I have permission to enter. I am on the grounds of so-called GAP 547 (an automobile repair pool). I go to the department for repairing cars, metals, and the like. The workday begins at six. The workers are bustling around on the lot, occupied with the business of separating and moving rusty metal car parts from place to place without rhyme or reason, "so that the German doesn't notice that you're taking a break." One by one the hours tick by. The only thing you'd think about was making it to the break. It was already seven, eight, nine, closer and closer, already ten, eleven, twelve, only a half hour to go.

The bell rang at a quarter to twelve. Surprised, we dropped our work. How was this possible? They made us a present of fifteen minutes? We looked around and saw something unusual: all the entrances and exits were closed, and the soldiers, our bosses, had submachine guns in their hands. A few minutes later, they formed us up into three ranks and ordered us out onto the lot where some workers were already standing—Jews from other departments. The officers in charge of the motor vehicle pool soon arrived, led by a major. Everyone recognized him right away by his height and by his face, which looked like the mug of a racist, English bulldog. "As of today, you will no longer return to the ghetto after work. My soldiers will take you to an SS forced labor camp," he said, and walked away, with the officers behind him.

Marching in ranks of five, we were led along Yanovskaya Street in the direction of the concentration camp. Soon we saw a brick barrier on our right, with people wearing black uniforms with gray collars and cuffs, and armed with rifles, walking back and forth along it. These were "Cossacks,"[23] the camp guards. At the end of the barrier towered a big, broad entrance, topped by a sign with many little electric bulbs; it read "SS Forced Labor Camp." They led us into the camp. The "Cossacks" standing guard at the entrance greeted us with vulgar jokes. We were standing in a broad square covered with snow. The area was lined on two sides with buildings, and next

---

22. A few words in the text are not decipherable.
23. Non-German guards were called "Cossacks" by the prisoners.

to them were working dirty people in rags with yellow stripes on their backs and chests. On the third side one could see buildings containing the camp offices. And on the fourth side stood a double row of barbed wire fences with guard towers manned by "Cossacks" with machine guns. A gate and a booth were in one corner of the yard. The clock over the booth read 1:00 PM.

They ordered us to stand. We stood in the snow and looked around, expecting something to happen. At three o'clock we saw a horse ridden by SS Untersturmführer Gustav Wilhaus, the bloodthirsty camp commandant who was well known to everyone. He drew up near to us and halted his horse. He counted us. Some five hundred or more. The officer was not happy; he had expected eight hundred. Almost three hundred had managed to escape along the way. After counting us, he turned and made a speech in German: "From this moment on, you are residents of an SS forced labor camp. You will leave the camp for work only under guard. You are bound by the most iron discipline. Death on the scaffold or by shooting awaits you for the smallest infraction. You will be divided up into brigades. The foreman will answer for your conduct. Is that clear to everyone?" We answered, "Understood." Wilhaus left.

Two SS troops with submachine guns came up to us. In addition to their weapons, each one had a leather whip with a piece of lead at the end. They took us into the buildings with the offices. Each man entering the office was met by SS trooper Bitner: "If you have any money, hand it over!" He looked in pockets and bags, patted down our clothing. If anyone had so much as a kopeck hidden, he whipped him until blood flowed, then stomped on him with his feet. He took away all identity papers, watches, rings, and so on. He threw all the papers in a sack. (We later found out that they were burned.) He also collected all the white armbands. Clerks took down last names, first names, and other information. After that they sewed on yellow stripes with numbers. At that moment I felt that I had stopped being myself and had become simply a member of concentration camp No. 14.

Then they led groups of fifty men at a time into a hall where prisoners were working as barbers. Everyone had their head shaved. Even though the haircut was being done for the sake of hygiene, I am quite sure that the barbers left each "customer" with no small quantity of insects, since the hall was full of hair clippings, and who knew how long they had been lying there? Moreover, the barbers themselves were not exactly clean. In the same hall, they painted a red stripe on the back of the "candidates'" clothing. This entire ceremony was carried out in the presence of SS men who beat their victims, laughed, and taunted them every way they could.

They led us into the barracks. The barracks were a long, low building containing two halls with a corridor between them. These halls resembled peculiar storerooms with six rows of shelves stacked five high.

We were surprised to learn that these shelves were the bunks on which we were supposed to sleep. We took our places. The space was very tight and our bones ached from contact with the hard boards. It was impossible to sit straight up because the space between the berths above and below was too small. Every time the comrade above me moved, some dust from his bunk sprinkled into my eyes. Even though it was freezing outside, it was unbearably hot inside from the breath of hundreds of chests. They turned out the lights at ten in the evening. Everyone was lying in their bunks.

The so-called *Ordnere,* meaning those who oversaw the barracks, stood beside the doors. Their commander was a camp guard who had been promoted from among the prisoners; he was armed with a rubber truncheon. At the time, there were about five thousand men in the camp, including some fifteen hundred Poles and Ukrainians; the rest were Jews. There were ten policemen, whose power extended only to Jews. Some of them felt right at home in their jobs—they beat, robbed, and jeered. But some of them helped the prisoners as best they could. All of them, good and malicious alike, knew the same fate awaited them that awaited all Jews under fascist rule. And, in fact, the commanders of the police force were frequently replaced, one after another. That was what happened to Sheffler, whom the Germans used when they buried their victims in sand dunes near Lvov, the place of execution for all the people who were a bother to them and guilty of nothing at all. After one round of executions, where the victims were women and children and which Sheffler attended, the SS, afraid of having a living witness to their crime, shot him as well.

On the second day of my imprisonment, at half past three in the morning, the booming voice of camp guard Ormlyand woke up everyone in the barracks: "Get up, get up!" The lights came on. Movement began in the bunks. The prisoners crawled down the ladders. Naturally, because of the close quarters, they stepped on the heads of those standing in the narrow passages between the rows of bunks. Quarrels broke out, and curses. I climbed down carefully from the fourth tier, where I had spent the night. After making a fortunate landing and not hitting anyone, I made my way toward the exit, helping myself along with my voice and my elbows. I crossed the corridor where a policeman was entertaining someone with a taste of a club. I went outside. It was still the middle of the night. A warm wind was blowing, and the square in the midst of the barracks was covered with deep, repulsive muck. Hopping along the less swampy places, I went up to the door of a small building. A vivid stench penetrated everything. In front of the door of this place—as you all probably guessed, this was the latrine—crowded ragged, skinny, stooped, wind-chilled creatures that had once been human beings.

After waiting in line, I went into the stinking hall. And here, just as outside, people were crowding and shoving each other. As a result, it often happened that prisoners who were barely able to stand slipped and fell into the muck. Almost all the others had hearts that were so turned to stone that the majority relieved themselves, ignoring those who had fallen down. It was in this unbelievably disgusting atmosphere, in the middle of stinking filth, in view of dirty bodies performing their functions, that most meetings between friends took place, along with the business dealings of the camp. Here they sold bread, kasha, fruits, sugar in cubes, and pills.

Sometimes you could even find small and dirty meat pies, compressed by soiled hands. I got out of there as soon as I could and went back to the barracks. Fortunately, before getting there, I spotted danger: my comrades were all running out. The already familiar form of a lead-tipped leather whip was rising and falling over their heads with blinding speed, while a German voice rang out: "Faster, faster. What, you're still here? Still not out? Go wash yourselves!" We headed for the long building where there were taps with a trickle of water. Inside, a crowd of human shadows. Wash yourselves—easy to say, only hard to do. A raw wind blew through the barracks. People were packed in so tightly that not only was it impossible to take off your jacket, but you could not even raise a hand to the tap or rinse the sleep out of your eyes. Finally, with the help of my elbow, I "washed." I feel it is necessary to explain the meaning of this word, namely, that "wash" meant to rinse your hands and with damp fingers touch your eyelids and a part of your face. Naturally, no one even dreamed about soap. So, already "cleaned up," I went out into the yard and, feeling the cold of the morning on my face, dried myself with a handkerchief in the absence of a towel. With absolute confidence, I can say that whole swarms of insects of all imaginable kinds were hopping and crawling back and forth on everyone who had visited one of the two "hygienic" institutions that I mentioned above; they were looking for new, food-rich territory.

Coming out of the washroom, I was in the small square. I saw the kitchen building on the left, with its small windows, where they were serving a thin, black liquid, so-called "coffee," to long lines of prisoners. A gallows stood on the other side of the square, probably to improve the appetite of those being fed.

Not having a cup, I headed for the barracks, which stood a bit farther along. The paltry light of the gloomy autumn morning showed two rows of identical yellow barracks standing at right angles to each other, about ten to twelve meters long and wide. Every two barracks were connected by a passage, thereby forming one low building about twenty-five meters long and ten or twelve meters wide. The kitchen, washroom, and the oldest and ugliest barracks, along with the barracks I have just described, formed a horseshoe surrounded on three sides by a large, filthy square where little streams of muck flowed through its ridges and bumps. A thick barbed wire fence some three meters or so high wrapped around all the buildings and squares. There was another identical fence one and a half meters beyond it.

A "Cossack," the traitor, patrolled between the fences, in the same uniform as the ones I had seen coming into the camp the day before. Guard towers rose in the fields and on the hills beyond the fences surrounding the camp.

"Cossacks" were in the towers armed with machine guns. Powerful searchlights were mounted on every tower and rocked in the wind. Lamps shone on the fences as well. Snug, attractive little dachas built not long before the war stood on the left outside the camp. The SS commanding the camp lived there. They were probably sleeping peacefully in warm beds. Tall mounds with withered grass stood behind me.

To the right and opposite, a railway line, and farther along in a thicket of rails, the Central and Kleparovo stations.

Steam engines crawled along the rails, pulling behind them rows of loaded cars, breathing in a whistle and letting clouds of steam out of their stacks.

One of them was moving quickly to the right, but was hidden for a minute or two in the gully beside the camp. The cars disappeared one after the other. Only clouds of black smoke rose from the invisible locomotive. And there it was, its black, gleaming body showing up farther along to the right, and again a file of red cars, big and small, were moving through the snow. The train turned to the right and was finally hidden behind the hills. Again, car after car sank down as if they were going underground. Another ten cars, five, two, one, and then they all disappeared.

Where was this long row of cars heading? Somewhere to the east, to the east where the brave fighters of the country of freedom, the country of flowering life, the country of happiness and joy, were fighting for our Motherland, for our wise, dear father, leader and friend, for Stalin.

And suddenly my chest rose in a melancholy sigh. I felt sad that I was a poor prisoner in a severe-regime concentration camp[24] with the whips of SS troopers whistling over it, and where machine guns thundered, and that I could not go along that road to the east! To the east, to the fighters for socialism, in order to join the ranks for the common cause. But I knew that my dream would come true in the near future.

I headed for "my" barracks. I arrived there just at the moment when the foreman was dividing up the bread. Each prisoner got one piece. A piece was supposed to weigh 175 grams according to the norm. But in most cases it weighed no more than 120 grams. The bread was black, full of bran, and very difficult to swallow. I took my bread and climbed to my place on the fourth tier of bunks because it was unbearably cramped down below and people were pushing one another. I was still eating my piece of bread when down below I heard the voice of a camp guard: "Come and run to formation. In ten minutes this barracks had better be empty." I slipped the uneaten bit of bread into my pocket and began to wait for the moment when it would be possible to let myself down without hurting anyone. Having waited my turn, I thrust myself out in one push, still afraid that someone would block my way. By the time I was standing on the floor, I heard the loud voice of the guard: "Come to attention! Hats off!" In the door appeared the green uniform and mug of a professional bandit. A submachine gun rested on his shoulder, while a whip was in his raised hand. It was Scharführer Epler. All voices grew silent. The only sound that could be heard was the stamping of hundreds of feet on the floor on their way out of the barracks, and the whistling of the whip hitting the shoulders and heads of those leaving.

---

24. He is using Soviet terminology when he refers to this German labor camp as a "severe-regime" camp.

After a minute I reached the door, too. The whip whistled again and I felt a sharp, burning pain on my shaved skull. I leapt out into the yard, put my hand to my head and felt a broad welt beneath my fingers. Upon contact with the cold air it became very painful for me, and I quickly covered my head. I made for the main compound of the camp, where the brigades were already forming up in five ranks. The shouts of men looking for their units could be heard. I found my group and got into line. We stood for a long time in the muck. I finished my piece of bread. With nothing better to do, I began to look at my surroundings. I noticed with surprise that the whole huge compound lying between the horseshoe of buildings and the fence of the camp was filled with a crowd of ragged, sickly creatures. It was almost impossible to understand where all these people disappeared to at night. But all you had to do was remember those rows of five-tiered bunks in the barracks and the unbearably close quarters in the berths to understand this surprising and improbable, yet quite true fact.

Suddenly the familiar sound of a whip on human backs reached my ears. From behind the ranks of prisoners with their backs turned to the barracks and their faces to the fence, Scharführer Schenback appeared unnoticed and began to give a taste of the whip to everyone who was near him, with the aim of instilling discipline and order into the ranks of those who had been weakened by the long wait. The group that I was standing in was a long way from where Schenback was "working" and managed to bring order to its ranks by itself, so we took a relatively small number of blows.

Soon after, the so-called morning Appel began under the command of Scharführer Kolanko with the help of Schenback. "Hats off!" rang out the command. We took off our hats. "Hats on!" the German shouted. We put them back on. "Hats off!" came the order. "Hats on!" was repeated. These exercises were repeated several dozen times in the course of a morning Appel, regardless of the weather, summer or winter, in the rain, snow, heat, and frost, until the director of this "show" himself grew tired of it. Meanwhile, the SS walked up and down the rows teaching the inmates the rules of the exercise. Instructions were given mainly with the aid of whips and rods, and the role of the tongue was included only in curses and all sorts of screaming in German, which was understandable to a greater or lesser degree. Then would come some sort of speech about what was not allowed and what was categorically and strictly forbidden, but never about what was permitted. Standing in a more distant section of the compound, we only understood one thing: "most strictly forbidden," said in a voice hoarse from shouting. Later on, only the voice could be heard, but it was impossible to make out the words, except for the last one: "Understood?" and then the whole crowd loudly answered: "Understood!" Then, those who were standing closer and could hear better, relayed in a whisper what the Germans had said to those who had not been able to hear. Then they read out a few names—the names of those who were to be punished or transferred from one brigade to another. In most cases, the man called could not hear his name. The Germans called him again or ordered the clerks of the camp office to do it until the prisoner heard it. They punished him on the spot with the whip for not having come running at the first summons and would not allow him to explain himself.

Quite often, death sentences were carried out immediately during the Appel as an example to all the other prisoners of the fate that awaited them for the slightest disobedience. Regardless of the sort of "crime," the guilty man was either executed immediately or given twenty-five lashes across his bare buttocks before death. The bodies of those shot were taken away on ordinary, small stretchers to the sand or the stones, so that the legs and the upper part of the body of the dead man dangled beside the legs carrying the stretcher. Sometimes the condemned were led between the fences by the exit out of the camp. Everybody knew that anyone who went to that place, that is, "between the barbs," as they called it, would only come out dead. It was not unusual for the Germans to kill prisoners standing in the rows for no reason at all, or to injure them with a whip. The exercise was over.

Finally, a voice of command rang out: "Even step, forward, march!" The columns moved out of the camp. Several brigades had already gone out before our turn arrived. We could hear music ahead of us, some march being played. The camp bosses had formed a brass ensemble of musically talented inmates, including well-known musicians. The foreman called out the command: "Brigade, forward, march! Hats off!" We took several steps. We were at the gates of the camp. A yellow booth on the left with several SS carrying whips stood nearby. To the right were two barbed wire fences. Between them were several men. Some of them were lying in the dirt, others were sitting or standing. Looking at one lying down, I could tell that he was dead. Later on I was told that the Germans had tossed him there the night before because he was ill and that he had died during the night. The dead eyes were looking off somewhere into endless space with a glassy stare, looking calmly and, you might even say, joyfully. The deceased had probably been happy just before death because for the first time in several months he could stop being afraid of the whip, that nobody would be jeering at him, that his body would feel no pain, exhaustion, cold, or hunger, and that for the first time he would get a rest—an eternal, well-earned rest. Another body lay there not quite alive and not quite dead, resting against the dead man. His chest was breathing with loud groaning sounds. His face was thin, with a growth of fine gray stubble. It seemed that the poor sick man was already dying, only his eyes denied it, nervously casting their glance from one object to another and burning with some strong, strange gleam. His eyes drew so much attention to himself that they seemed to the observer to take up half his face. Two prisoners were standing, leaning against the fence, and looking sadly at the formations marching out of the camp. They knew that they would cross that threshold only once, when, several hours later, they would be loaded onto a truck and taken to the opposite end of town, to the sand dunes, where the course of their lives would come to an end. The faces of the others were not visible.

Pale and trembling, the foreman stood at attention before Scharführer Kolanko: "Scrap brigade, fifty-three men." In a hoarse voice, the German gave the command:

"Even step, forward, march!" We moved off. The SS troopers counted us. Up front, beside the building with the office, the brass ensemble was standing, and, blowing with all their might, they played the very same march. We turned to the right. The foreman, a few paces in front, shouted an order: "Hats on!" Since our camp did not work on Sundays, we stayed in the open space beside the camp. The remaining brigades came through the gates. Some proceeded straight ahead, making for the work areas. Because it was Sunday, some of them turned to the right and took their places next to us. We could see through the fences how the crowd in the compound in the camp was growing smaller and smaller. Brigade after brigade filed past the SS men at the gates. Several times they removed someone from his column. The Germans beat him from all sides with their whips and pushed him "between the barbs." The group between the fences was growing. Finally, the last brigade came out. The ensemble set off and, still playing the same march, returned to the camp area.

A policeman came up to us and announced that we would be working on clearing the space that we were standing on, and also on sorting out the boards, beams, and other materials that were scattered around the area.

The "work" began. Foremen attached to that location directed us. We ended up working here only on that day, that is, Sunday. Our job consisted of taking piles of things from one place to another since there was no other work, and a prisoner, after all, had no right to time off. A friend of mine and I picked out a light but long board, lifted it onto our shoulders, and carried it at a slow pace around the whole area. Then my friend yelled at the top of his lungs: "One, two, heave!" We threw the board. We picked up another one and returned with it, and again: "One, two, heave!"

We repeated this game until we were tired of it. Then we hid behind one of the piles. After waiting for a bit, we came out and continued "working." All of the others used this method as well. The foremen were shouting loudly and going from place to place, as if showing us where to throw things, where to take things from, and how to stack them. To someone watching, the whole crowd seemed to be busy and thinking only about how to work better. All of this continued until some German arrived on horseback. The SS men beat everyone within reach of their whips. They beat one worker for having lifted too little, for working too slowly. Even though everyone tried not to give any grounds for punishment, they beat men for no other reason than to satisfy their sadistic desires. Since the clearing was located outside the camp area, it was guarded by "Cossacks." Counting on the fact that winter was closing in, these fine young men walked among the workers and got themselves ready for the frost by stealing gloves. In a few minutes, everyone knew about it. We hid gloves in our pockets, but even that did not help. The "Cossacks," when they did not find them on our hands, were not ashamed to go into our pockets, leaving only those gloves that were in tatters. After this kind of workday, you could not find anyone with a pair of good, or even not so ragged, gloves.

There was a break at 11:30. We stopped working, formed up in groups, and proceeded to the kitchen. They counted us beside the booth at the gates to the camp.

There were long lines at the little windows of the kitchen. Our brigade waited in line for soup. I borrowed a mess tin from someone I knew who had already eaten. At the bottom of the tin was a spoonful of sand. I went to wash the container. As I was coming back, I saw something that I had missed noticing before. The body of a man was hanging on the gallows beside the kitchen, but it was hanging by his legs. His face was red and swollen. His hands, also puffy, were hanging downward, twisting in the wind. His cap was lying in the dirt beneath his body. I felt a shudder. But hunger was nagging at me too much, and, after finding my spot, I took my place in line. Finally, my turn came. I went up to the little window and put my tin on the metal plate over the large pot from which dense steam was rising. The cook took out the serving spoon and poured soup into my tin. He poured the soup with a sweep of his arm, so that some splashed out and back into the pot, spattering my hand. Looking into the tin, I saw a grey liquid, with a few potatoes boiled with their skins still on.

Leaving the kitchen, I took another look at the gallows. SS trooper Rozenov was standing beside it; he had appeared unnoticed. The beast picked up the dead man's hat from the dirt, and, laughing, placed it on the foot of the corpse. Then he began beating the dead body with his whip, laughing insanely the whole time. I did not see anymore because I rushed back to the barracks. I downed the soup, even though it was giving off a stench of rotting potatoes; I found nothing else in it. I had such a fierce hunger that I gobbled down even the potato peelings. At the bottom of the tin there was a spoonful of sand.

I was already thinking about leaving the barracks when I spotted two men coming from the kitchen with their soup. Their faces were covered with blood, and they looked as if they had been cut with a knife. In answer to my question, one of them told me that Rozenov, after playing with the body, had started to beat the living. Most of those waiting for the soup had caught it.

The break ended at 12:30. We returned to work. In the evening after work, we went back to the barracks. No matter how we had shirked and avoided doing real work, we were exhausted all the same. We received the same amount of bread as in the morning. We lay down in the bunks. At ten o'clock, the lights went out. My second night in the camp began.

The morning of the next day was generally similar to the one before. The only difference was that the horrors of the camp regime did not make such a vivid impression on me. Just as on the first day, there were calisthenics, and we removed our hats at the gates trembling in the same way. We stood there waiting for a group of "Cossacks," and then a little longer for a "special detachment" of Jews, whose members worked as guards. Two men broke off from this second group and walked alongside us. This was our escort. We proceeded with the very same ensemble playing the very same march and came out onto Yanovskaya Street. It was our first time out of the camp! Solitary people were moving along the sidewalks. How we envied their relative freedom. After all, they had only just gotten up from their beds, washed, dressed, and, after saying goodbye to their families, left their homes. They hoped to return to those homes, where their families would be waiting for them with love. True, they did not know what might happen to them in the next ten minutes, since the black clouds of Hitler's power, of Hitler's new order in Europe, were hanging over them, as well. They, too, could be arrested, deported to Germany or to a concentration camp. They could be shot, as well. But we felt that our situation was worse than anyone else's.

When we had reached a bit farther away from the fences of the camp and its attendant workshops, we noticed a few people with white armbands among the passers-by. These were relatives of the prisoners; they had come here in order to at least glimpse us passing along the street, to bring us money or packages of food. I began to look around, searching their eyes. I actually saw my father. He saw me, too.

I will not go into a description of our meeting. I will say only that I received a package of bread and butter and a little money. Just when I had managed to collect all of this and had started to tell my father about what had happened to me in the last two days, a "Cossack" guarding one of the brigades behind us ran up from somewhere.

The bandit grabbed my father, dragged him off to one side, threw him to the ground and began going through his pockets. He took the money that he found (not much, fortunately), then went after his gloves. Taking the gloves from my father's hands, he noticed a watch on his arm, and that object also fell victim to the thief. He was beating my father the whole time, leaving him with several head wounds. From that day on, my father, who did not stop meeting me every day, was careful to avoid the "Cossacks."

My dear, beloved son!

I do not know if you are alive or dead. If you are not among the living, I can only be consoled by the fact that you did not die a slave, that you fell like a hero for the freedom and the independence of our Motherland.

If you are alive, receive my greetings as your father. Remember your dear mother, your brother, Zigmunt, who both perished at the hands of the fascists, and bring revenge and death to the Germans.

Your father.

GARF, f. 8114, op. 1, d. 960, ll. 16–30. Typewritten with corrections.

Kharkov
7. The story of one individual who was saved from the Kharkov ghetto
THE RECOLLECTIONS OF THE ENGINEER S. S. KRIVORUCHKO

I, a resident of Kharkov, by nationality a Jew, by training an engineer, could not be evacuated from the city in October 1943, due to illness. From the very first hours after the Germans captured the city, the Jews could sense that the Germans were paying particular attention to them. It began with individual murders, expulsion from apartments, and frequent visits by Germans to private Jewish dwellings, during which they confiscated whatever caught their eye. In addition to unorganized thievery, they also carried out pillaging, so to say, according to a plan. For this purpose a so-called Jewish elder was designated by them, the old Dr. Gurevich, whose job it was to collect the taxes imposed upon the Jewish population. One exaction followed another, in ever-increasing amounts.

On the morning of December 14, a decree was posted throughout the city from the German commandant of Kharkov ordering all Jews to move to barracks on the grounds of the tractor factory within two days; persons found in the city after December 16 would be shot on the spot.

Starting on the morning of December 15, whole columns of Jews headed out of the city. Many were on foot with bundles in their arms, others were dragging small wagons and handcarts with the negligible household belongings that they had managed to take with them. Some were also riding on privately owned carts. In the rush to relocate, almost all belongings were left behind.

For many of the elderly and the handicapped, the journey from the city to the barracks of the tractor factory was the last of their lives. The corpses of no fewer than thirty old people lay on the road. The pogrom began at about twelve o'clock, along with the robbing of the Jews who were on the move. As a result, many Jews arrived at the barracks without anything to their name and, more importantly, with barely any food, which began to make itself felt on the second day.

The barracks in which they proposed that we should settle were one-story, ramshackle structures, with smashed windows, torn away floors, and holes in the rooftops. The floor areas were about eight to ten times smaller than would have been required for a minimum standard of sanitation. In the room in which I found myself, more than seventy people had arrived by evening, whereas no more than six to eight people would have been able to live in it under normal circumstances. People stood compressed against each other. On the second day, with some difficulty, we found pieces of ten iron beds in a dump. Three or four people slept on each bed. In spite of the cold weather and the smashed windows, it was warm in the room from all our breath. On the third day, the barracks were surrounded by German sentries, who allowed no contact between us and the outside world.

There was no provision for meals. People ate whatever food that they had managed to bring. Starvation set in. Some twenty to thirty people a day were dying from hunger. We were also suffering from lack of water. Between noon and one o'clock each day, a limited number of women were allowed to go under guard to a nearby well and to draw water, or rather not water, but a dirty, murky liquid. Men were not allowed to go for water. Water was soon in very short supply, and was selling for 100 rubles per bottle. Fortunately for us, there was a snowfall, and we used the snow instead of water.

From the dreadful overcrowding, hunger, and lack of water, an epidemic of gastro-intestinal diseases broke out, which led to an even greater sanitation problem. We were permitted to go out of the barracks between 8:00 AM and 4:00 PM. Anyone who went out at any other time was shot on the spot. By morning, the corridors of the barracks were befouled to an unimaginable degree. Then there began a cleanup by hand, since there were no shovels or brooms, and the Germans threatened us with the firing squad if it wasn't all picked up within an hour. The morning was also the time for removing the bodies of those who had died the night before. The bodies were stacked in nearby anti-tank ditches. In a week, these ditches were already full.

Robbery and murder were daily occurrences. Usually, the Germans would burst into the room on the pretext of searching for weapons and would steal anything that came to mind. In the event of any resistance, they dragged people out into the yard and shot them. The day before Christmas and New Year's, they demanded that we gather supplies to organize parties for the people who were guarding us and money to buy vodka. Ragged, half-starved people tore the last lumps of sugar or fat out of their children's hands and gave them to the bandits to arrange parties. That was still not enough. The Nazi scoundrels demanded that we give them watches and valuables. These demands were met, backed up as they were by the threat of shooting.

There were many cases of killings, for example, for moving from one barracks to another, for the discharge of a bodily function against a wall instead of in the latrine, and for picking up a woodchip lying outside the zone of the camp. We witnessed fifteen to twenty murders of innocent people each day.

I lived under these conditions of hunger, cold, filth, overcrowding, absolute lawlessness, and savage murder until January 2, 1942. Some five days before that, the Germans posted flyers announcing a voluntary evacuation to Poltava. Until then, people were so naïve that they still believed the Germans. About five hundred signed up; they were loaded into trucks and driven off in an unknown direction. During the boarding, belongings were loaded onto another vehicle. When there were not enough passengers for the last truck, the Germans began grabbing people from those who had come to see off those moving. They forcibly put them in the truck and drove off. The fate of those who were "evacuated" was clear—they were exterminated.

On January 2, 1942, at 7:00 AM, in the corridor of the barracks where I was staying, a German sentry shouted out an order for everyone to gather their things and be outside in ten minutes. Collecting my things in a bag and stuffing a few pieces of bread into my pocket, I went outside, where one hundred to two hundred people from several barracks had gathered. Next we were ordered to leave all bags and belongings on the ground. Then German sentries and policemen formed a tight ring around us and announced that we were being evacuated to Poltava. We marched out onto the Chuguyev-Kharkov highway but then were directed away from the city, although the road to Poltava ran through town. It was obvious that they were not taking us to Poltava, but where exactly we *were* going, nobody knew. Along the way, we met many Germans who had run out of their homes to see us on our way with laughs and malicious smiles. Two kilometers past the last houses of the tractor factory workers' quarters, they turned us in the direction of a ravine. The whole ravine was strewn with bits of rags and the remains of torn clothing. It became clear why they had brought us here. The ravine was sealed off by a double row of sentries. On the edge of the ravine stood a truck with machine guns. Terrible scenes erupted when people understood that they had been brought here to be slaughtered. Dreadful cries filled the air. Some mothers smothered their children rather than hand them over to the executioners. Some went out of their minds. There were cases of people poisoning themselves. Many said goodbye to each other, embracing, kissing, exchanging the last supplies they had. Others took valuables from their pockets and broke them, trampled them into the snow, tore up money, slashed their outer clothing, anything so long as their things did not fall into the hands of the killers.

From the standing column, the Germans began using clubs to drive groups of fifty to seventy people one hundred paces or so forward, then forcing them to strip down to their underwear. It was -20° or -25° C. Those undressed were driven down to the bottom of the ravine, from which were heard occasional shots and the chattering of machine guns.

I was in a daze and did not notice the screaming behind me. The Germans began driving forward the group that I was part of. I moved off, ready to die within a few minutes. But just then, something happened: the Germans brought up the aged and handicapped to be executed. The belongings of those who had been killed had been loaded onto these trucks and brought back to the city. I moved along behind one of these vehicles. Two young Jews were in the truck; the Germans had assigned them to do the loading. In a flash, I jumped into the truck and asked the youngsters to cover me. Then they hid themselves as well. When the truck was full, the German drivers took off with it and in this way took me and the two boys away from the awful ravine. After an hour, they brought us to the Gestapo post, where, in unloading the truck, they discovered us.

In the compound, the belongings were piled up beneath a newly constructed awning. It was later that I learned that everything was being sorted for shipment to Germany.

After the unloading, they locked us in the truck again and took us back to the ravine. On the way there, we managed to remove the window frame without making any noise. I was the first to jump from the vehicle. The fall turned out to be a lucky one. I received some serious bruises, but my bones remained intact. I was knocked out by the fall, but someone must have pulled me off the road and revived me. I went to find my wife (she is not a Jew and had stayed behind in the city with our adopted daughter) who hid me with a girlfriend of hers. I stayed with her for six and a half months. For four months after that I wandered from village to village with a false passport and, in this way, held on until February 16, 1943, when Kharkov was liberated for the first time from the German occupiers.

GARF, f. 8114, op. 1, d. 958, ll. 241-246. Typewritten document with author's corrections.

8. Pages from Dante
FROM THE DIARY OF KHARKOV RESIDENT N. F. BELONOZHKO [25]
PREPARED BY VLADIMIR LIDIN [26]
[1941–1942]

On December 15, 1941, more than ten thousand Jews were herded onto the grounds of the Kharkov tractor factory; in January, all of them were shot near Rogan. The only ones who managed to survive were those who had escaped or had gone into hiding under false names. One woman residing in Kharkov, N. F. Belonozhko, kept brief notes. We are preserving them all in their tragic, documentary character. "I carry them to outcast villagers, I carry them where groaning is eternal, I carry them to perished generations." These words from Dante's *Inferno* could serve as the epigraph to the notes of sorrow presented here.

A harsh wind blows along the streets of the city. It sways the corpses of the hanged, tears away the scraps of the menacing orders posted on the houses. "For the giving of aid to the partisans—death; for hiding Red Army soldiers—death." Death, death. Everywhere, death.

In these terrible days, we move from a destroyed house to a new apartment on Sumskaya Street. Lots of people live in it, but I don't know that yet. Frightened, they all sit in separate rooms. The Germans wander through the rooms and take the ones that catch their eyes. People have gathered in our room, lots of them, and they are all women. Over there sits Riva, a lovely girl with big, dark eyes, beautiful skin, her hair elegantly arranged on her head, her voice pleasant, throaty. Beside her, a small, chubby little boy of about two and a half named Shurik. She also has two sisters—Sofa, a little girl, and Margarita, older, about twelve, with a stern face and the same large eyes as her sister. Their mother has died. They say that their brother is in the Red Army. He graduated from the Academy in Moscow. Where is he now? Terrified, they listen for every knock at the door. The Germans have already taken the best of what they have, so what is next?

The Gershelman family also lives in the apartment. A mother and two daughters. The mother is a superb pianist; she used to work at the conservatory. In the evenings,

---

25. N. F. Belonozhko graduated from an institute before the war and was the wife of a soldier. There is no further information about her fate in the archives of the Jewish Anti-Fascist Committee.
26. Vladimir Lidin (1894–1979) was a well-known Soviet writer and a correspondent for *Izvestia* at the outset of the war. Lidin and Ilya Ehrenburg were close friends. In his memoirs, Ehrenburg mentions how Lidin was demoted from *Izvestia* to a frontline army newspaper because one of his articles "angered Stalin"; see *Lyudi, gody, zhizn* (People, Years, Life) (Moscow, 2005), pp. 315, 390.

by the light of an oil lamp, she reads and the girls sew. The daughters, Shura and Sonya, have been to the university. Sonya came from Lvov, where she was the director of a library.

I live with my mother. My husband is in Saratov, in military training. I did not manage to get away. Everyone was expecting him to come for me. Winter began fiercely this year. No one had a stove. There was no firewood either. I am already working in a cafeteria. Today it's borscht from frozen beets without bread, then came *kozein,* a glue-like, repulsive, white substance [made from bones]; it tasted like rubber. I do not know to this day what it was for. They say that it was used in building airplanes. I spend the whole day in the kitchen freezing. There is shouting: there isn't enough kozein. People are dropping in the doorways. I am still alive. I can eat a few helpings of kozein and still bring a bit home, but at home things grow worse every day. The stove in the kitchen is still smoldering; they are chopping up the furniture for fuel. The stove is surrounded by people.

Lyuba and Vera make matchboxes. One hundred boxes for a glass of bran. The oil lamp is still smoldering. The Mordukhaev girls sit on the floor by the stove. They don't say anything. There's no end to the evening. The other day, a worker named Nadya, after gathering her things, went to the flea market. She came back five days later all beaten up. The Germans had taken everything, leaving only a sackful of peas. Nadya went on and on with her story of how she had eaten bread with borscht in the village. And so all the youngsters decide to go with her. It's freezing outside, there's nothing to wear. Riva wears sandals and old galoshes. They've left. It's quiet. I've got the best place, right by the stove.

New orders were posted in the streets: all Jews had twenty-four hours to leave the city. Terrible processions formed. I come running home at four o'clock. There is panic and weeping in the apartment. The building superintendent says that the Mordukhaevs have to clean the apartment right away since they're Jews. The girls have only just got back from the village. They've brought nothing, everything was taken away from them, while Shurik wants a cookie. What to do? I dash with Margarita to 100 Sumsky, to the commandant's offices, and say that I've known the Mordukhaevs for many years, and that they're Armenians (I know a little German, since it was not long ago that I graduated from the institute). It worked. They let them stay until they can get a guarantee. They stay, but they've no more strength. No one wants to take them on, since they're Jews, and everyone shouts *Jude* after them. They have nothing to live on. In their large room with the windows facing north, it is colder than it is outside.

The first to get sick in our room is Shura and Sonya's mother. Sonya would go to a village to the south to get her milk. Her mother dies slowly. And now in our apartment is the first coffin, made from a chest of drawers.

In the kitchen in the evenings, everyone looks nervously at their legs, squeezing them. Are they swollen? Sonya's and Nyura's are very swollen, and the Mordukhaev girls are just wasting away. They look like they are made of wax. They don't comb their hair, they don't wash, they make something out of potato peelings and snow and eat it on the spot, raw. People live by selling things, but they've got nothing left to sell. Lice are crawling around the apartment, they're everywhere. Sofa and Nyura have gotten sick. Shurik as well. He doesn't cry anymore and doesn't even want the soup that I bring from the cafeteria. There's a second body in the apartment; Nyura has died and then a week later Riva is gone, too. Margarita goes begging, she's staggering from weakness. Her eyes are wild. I can't think about those eyes without being horrified. She falls, gets up, and falls again. She needs to give Shurik and Sofa something to eat. She is older, she's twelve. Sofa and Shurik are crying from the next room, demanding something to eat from her. The room stinks and is dirty, it's dreadful to enter. I'm still working at the cafeteria. It's cold as the devil, the soup freezes in the plates. I hold on. One has to live.

Another one of us has died. Sonya died in the hospital. Her feet became infected and she died of blood poisoning. They buried her in a common grave. There's no one left to recall the past, our life before the Germans. There's no one to dream about. Margarita has gotten sick, too.

Yesterday, Shurik asked for a cookie. "Mama gave me one," he said, then smiled, and, toward evening, died. Margarita got up and with great difficulty said that Shurik should be taken to his relatives to be buried. She moves along, ragged, in a terrible state. The cold keeps on getting more bitter. Shura's not here, she's gone to Lyubotin. Nadya went off to the village as well and hasn't come back. It's obvious that she's died. Sofa and Margarita are getting sick. I brought them soup, but they do not want to eat. They ask for tea. It is terrible to look at them. Kozha is all bones and huge, dark eyes. In the morning, I poked my head into their room. They're dead. Both are dead. Sofa on the bed, Margarita on the floor. How to bury them? I went to the bürgermeister repeatedly. He says: "We don't bury Jews." They've been lying there for ten days now. It's a good thing that it's cold, but the bodies smell all the same. They lie there for another twelve days. Finally, they come to pick them up. They need to tidy up the room. The Petrovna woman comes. She wants to lift up the feather bed. I hear an awful, heartrending cry. Shurik lies under the bed where Margarita slept. Had he died then, or did she deliberately put him there in order to bring an end to his sufferings? Who can say? He lay there for a month and a half. When will this end? When?

The notes end here.

GARF, f. 8114, op. 1, d. 953, ll. 38–42. A typewritten manuscript.

9. The destruction of the Jews of Kharkov
THE RECOLLECTIONS OF NINA MOGILEVSKAYA, WIFE OF A WELDER
RECORDED BY S. GOLOVANIVSKY

It is difficult, painful to remember Kharkov. December 14, 1941.

My husband Yalovsky, a welder, and I were going to the market; we needed to trade some of our belongings for food.

There was a crowd on the street. In an oppressive silence, people were reading flyers in which the Germans announced that "All Jews, regardless of sex, age, confession, or state of health are required to resettle in the Losevo District behind the Kharkov Tractor Factory by December 16. All those discovered outside of that area will be shot on the spot."

The next day I, along with my husband, went to the Tractor Factory. A huge crowd of sixteen thousand Jews was winding its way through the streets. The young, the old, teenagers, small children were all walking. The healthy were carrying the sick.

An older woman was walking alongside us carrying her palsied, aged mother. In front of us was a family—a husband and wife and two small children. The man had one leg in a cast and was walking on crutches. It was slippery, he fell several times. They shot him at the Electro-Chemical Plant.

It was very cold. Those who were freezing lagged behind, and if they caught the eye of the Germans they were killed.

The robberies began in the city center. They robbed people at every bridge and at every spot where the column slowed its pace. Hardly anyone reached the tractor factory with what they had been permitted—were forced—to bring with them.

The barracks were waiting for us beyond the tractor factory. The windows were knocked out, the stoves smashed. In a room of about twenty or twenty-five square meters, some fifty or sixty people piled in. They locked the barracks. The doors opened when the Germans, on the pretext of searching for weapons, came to steal. They took everything: valuables, clothes, food.

People were dying from hunger and the cold. The first to go were the elderly and the children. But all this is known from other witnesses. I will tell about myself and my sorrow.

On December 25, 1941, when it was already obvious that nothing but death awaited us, I said to my husband (he is a Russian) that he should not die because of me, that he should go home. My husband refused, so I promised him that I would escape.

There was a girl named Marusya in my barracks. Her husband, also a Russian, was at the Front. I convinced her to escape as well.

There was no water in the barracks. The Germans needed water, too. They sent the women for water to a pump located some three kilometers away from the barracks.

On December 27, going out for water, we didn't return to the barracks. Convinced that they wouldn't come after us, we made for the village of Kaplunovka, where the parents of my new friend's husband lived. A hundred ten kilometers in the cold and drizzle, poorly dressed (the Germans had taken away all our warm clothing) we walked, not stopping anywhere.

They offered us help in the villages, but we were afraid to stay the night. So we went on, day and night, we walked and walked.

The parents of Marusya's husband, the Serdyukovs, welcomed us and gave us food. Serdyukov told us that if we had money, he could buy documents for us from the commandant's office and in that case we could live without fear.

But we did not have any money. The next day, when we came to Kaplunovka, I remembered that my husband's uncle lived seven kilometers from that village. I decided to ask him for help and I invited Marusya to come with me. But she was worn out by our wanderings and decided to go stay with her in-laws.

I went away. I did not get any money and on the same day went back to Kaplunovka. Approaching the village, I saw a crowd. I took a few more steps and saw Marusya, hanging from a crossbar. There was a sign hanging on her that said "This kike woman is a Bolshevik."

It later turned out that she had been betrayed by her father-in-law, Serdyukov. I went back to my husband's relatives. He was summoned to the commandant's office where they beat him and demanded that he tell them where I had gone, but he kept silent. I had to stay for days on end in the cellar, coming to the hut only at night.

I was pregnant. The time was coming for me to give birth. To have the child here was unthinkable. The cry of a child could be heard by any neighbor who happened to come by. I did not want to be the undoing of people who were protecting me so bravely. One night, I left for Kharkov.

The road to Kharkov was hard, but in Kharkov itself life was even more difficult. A policeman was standing on almost every street corner, checking papers. I would hide in the entranceways of buildings and in three days made my way through the city to Mt. Kholodnaya, where my husband's parents lived.

They told me that my husband had gone off to join a partisan unit. These old people, knowing that it might cost them their lives, nevertheless took me in. A few hours later, I gave birth to a boy.

The neighbors agreed that I should come back and though there were no scoundrels among them who would turn in my child and me it was still too dangerous to stay. Two weeks later, with my child and a birth certificate in the name of Valentin Yalovsky on which I dribbled a few drops of ink in the necessary places, I left Kharkov to look for work and a roof over my head.

I had a child with me: everywhere, people let me stay the night. Sometimes they let me bathe the child, but in the morning, I had to go, and there was no end in sight to my wanderings.

I was already close to despair when they told me about a sugar beet farm called Ekonomia in Parkhomovka that was taking on workers. But I had to get in touch with the "boss," and the "boss" came by the motor pool every day. I waited for the "boss" for a whole day, but he never turned up. And the next day, all confused, I went down to the railroad tracks to throw myself and my child under the engine. Suddenly, someone jerked me by the shoulder: "Stop, where do you think you're going?" he asked me. (He was dressed in city clothes.) "I'm hungry. My child is dying. I can't find any work." The questions followed: where was I from, where was my husband, and so on. I was quite used to all this and I answered as usual.

"You're a city girl and we do hard work here."

"I can handle any sort of work."

The "boss" put me in a cart and we went off. The "boss lady" met us.

"Look at this Katerina with a knapsack on her shoulders and a kid in her arms that I've brought back," he said to her.

The "boss lady" muttered, "You've always got some wild idea in your head."

The "boss" looked at me and said in an embarrassed voice, "Seems she wanted to throw herself under some vehicle. When she was suffering, her face was beautiful."

Thanks to his fantasy, I got a roof over my head, even though my papers were not entirely in order. The work was very hard, and for me, a city girl, even harder. My child was always with me. He lay on some rags not far from me, but I could not tear myself away from my work long enough to feed him.

My son died by my side. I kept on working, stupidly, like a machine, which filled the people around me with hostility and irritation against me.

My husband arrived toward the end of the summer. He asked for work and they took him on. A few days later, someone dug up a few potatoes from the garden of one of the Germans. Someone said that I had done it for my husband. We were called in to see the commandant. They beat me unconscious. The scars remain on my body to this day. Then they took us out to be shot.

Don't be surprised: they killed the old and the young for a spool of thread or a cigarette stolen from the Germans.

We were walking and I thought to myself: it is obviously my fate to die at the hands of a German executioner. And why had I been fighting so hard for my life? It was good that my son had died; he was better off.

Suddenly we saw that a woman had come up to the commandant. She was young and beautiful and had been living with him for several days. She was saying something to him and we managed to hear: "Well, of course, that's not them. I know them very well. These are very honest people."

I don't remember what happened after that. All I know is that they let us go. I went down on my knees before this woman and she stroked my hair and whispered: "Don't worry, I'm one of you." I think she was a partisan. How my husband and I would like to see our rescuer, whose name we don't even know!

My husband soon went back to his unit, while I stayed in Ekonomia until the arrival of our troops. I am twenty-two now, but I've seen so much sadness in my life that it would be enough for several human lives.

Mind you, I'm not the only one!

GARF, f. 8114, op. 1, d. 961, ll. 24–29. A typewritten manuscript.

Odessa and Transnistria
10. Why did it happen to us?
The recollections of Dr. Lidia Maximovna Slipchenko (Kozman)[27]
[1944]

Deeply respected Comrade,

I am sending you an article written by my cousin, Lidia Maximovna Kozman, Slipchenko by marriage.

L. M. is a young woman of thirty, a Jew, who was on the threshold of death when she was with the Germans, but who was saved and is now living with her family in Novosibirsk. She sent me her article with the request that I look it over. In forwarding the article to you, I am guided by the following considerations: the dramatic odyssey of my cousin and the literary capabilities that one could employ to create a document bearing witness against the Germans.

In the autumn of 1941, L. M. found herself alone in the Odessa ghetto. Having become convinced that death was inescapable, she, along with several other comrades in the ghetto, took poison, from which she did not die, but rather fell seriously ill. In the hospital to which she was sent, she managed to obtain a passport with a Russian name and to escape. Over the next two and a half years until the arrival of the Red Army, she worked in some cattle yards.

L. M. was a doctor, the mother of an eight-year-old son, and the wife of a Ukrainian. She grew up in an assimilated family, was not a Party member, and could not be suspected of any kind of chauvinism or prejudice.

Her notes and recollections, corrected and edited in a suitable manner, could be useful both within and outside our country.

I ask you to advise me of your opinion on this matter. My telephone at work is K0-21-90, ext. 42.

Luiza Petrovna Skupnik

Why did it happen to us?

Hundreds and thousands of individuals who were not guilty of any crime, including weak old people, women and children, perished with this question on their lips. All of them dreamed of posing this question out loud, of receiving an answer, so as to learn what they were guilty of, if anything, and to disprove the absurd accusations which rained down on their heads like a hail of bullets. But they received no answer, and so with that question on their lips they departed for a world in which there were neither accusers nor accused, nor nations having a right to life nor those without such a right.

A modest number managed to break out of the gruesome ring of death and to live to speak of their pain and sorrow out loud. I am such an individual, and I consider it my duty to ask, at last, in the name of those who went to their graves and who will never again have the opportunity to speak: Why did it happen to us?

---

27. A portion of these recollections appear in *The Black Book,* p. 57.

Odessa, October 1941. A frightful atmosphere of repression, killings, and torture. The corpses of the hanged could be seen in the windows of almost every store, kiosk, and shop. Bodies dangled on every corner, bearing signs that said: "This will be the punishment for anyone who dares to resist the Romanian-German command."

Frightened, pale inhabitants hid in the courtyards, fear dominating their faces. Orders said: "For every soldier killed, one hundred inhabitants will be shot. For an officer, two hundred."[28] Vigilant sentries stood at the gates, looking for spies, communists, and Jews.

October 23: The large NKVD building on Marzlievskaya Street is blown sky high. Eight Romanian generals are blown up with it. Afterward, provocateurs spread rumors throughout the city that Odessa Jews blew up the building.

A momentous decree will be published: "All individuals of Jewish ancestry—men, women and children—must present themselves for registration at the village of Dalnik." The order must be fulfilled and building superintendents and custodians actively help to do so.

Hundreds and thousands of Jews, having gathered up their most essential "things," flowed toward the registration point. This registration was finished at the brick factory opposite the artillery depot, which was burned to the ground with all the people in it. Those who managed to get away, to break out of the flames, were killed straight away by machine guns posted around the building.

For a considerable time, people avoided passing by because of the stench of decaying bodies. The "considerate" Romanian command had to order hostages, who were being held in a school on Bolgarskaya Street, to dig a ditch in order to bury the bodies of the Jews that had not been burned entirely.

But the Jews who perished at that time were much luckier than the rest of their brothers and sisters. They perished immediately, not having experienced the full horror of persecution, hounding, and humiliation, not having fallen into the cattle-like state of a pitiable, hungry animal gnawed at by parasites, without even the appearance of being human.

Others were still waiting their turn.

At the same time, the newspapers were full of articles about racial purity and the Jewish peril, and published the "inspired" speeches of the Führer, saying that in the New Europe that he would create, skeletons of Jews would be great rarities in archeological museums. "The Jewish race," they wrote in the papers, "must be wiped entirely from the face of the earth because the Jews want to rule the whole world, which is why they began the war." A great deal more nonsense was written and said about the Jews, but it was impossible to object.

Another order appeared in December stating that all individuals of Jewish ancestry would have to be interned in a ghetto, and that as a socially dangerous element, it

---

28. This order was given after the bombing of the NKVD building.

would be necessary to isolate them from the rest of the population. It was indicated in the decree that all property was to remain in the apartments of the resettled Jews and that they would be permitted to take with them only what they could carry.

Streams of naïve people flowed away, hoping that they would be given the possibility of living—even if it was in isolation and even under oppression—but the right to live would be left to them all the same.

How people clung to life, how they wanted to hope and believe in spite of what they read in the newspapers, in spite of being trampled, plundered, persecuted, and given over to be torn apart by anyone who wished to indulge in such a pleasure. They were outside the law, after all. How they hoped, nevertheless, that they would be left the last thing remaining to them—their lives.

People walked about marked like criminals with yellow six-pointed stars on their chests. Seeing such a star, anyone who wished could go up and beat such a person, spit in their face, or strip them naked. They hunted the Jews like beasts at bay. It was enough for any of them to appear on the street or at the market for some scoundrels, out of greed or hatred, to point them out to a Romanian policeman with the words: "There's a kike," and the policeman would deal with them according to whatever mood he was in. There were even some who brought the Romanians to Jewish apartments that had been inhabited before the expulsions to the ghetto, and who along with the Romanians or the Germans would plunder the property of that person, whether he was a worker or a clerk, a doctor or an artist, a thief or an honest man—just so long as he was a Jew. Even among the most advanced part of the local population, for example, an intellectual like Professor Ch., to whom the Soviet government had provided such wide-ranging possibilities for scientific work and a good life, very quickly became imbued with Hitler's national theory and his entire program. When one of his former prize students, a woman whom he knew well and whom he had treated with respect, came to him with a request for help, he found it impossible to honor her with an answer and turned away from her arrogantly, surrounded as he was by resplendent Romanian officers. She, of course, was a Jew.

The most credulous or self-deceived people obeyed the orders of the Romanians unconditionally. The Romanians originally designated Slobodka for the Jewish ghetto, and crowds of people moved slowly in that direction. There were no exceptions. Even paralytics who had not risen from their beds in years, cripples, patients suffering from severe infections, the mentally ill, and women on the point of giving birth had to show themselves in the ghetto. All, without exception, were Jews. They all went along obediently. Some walked, others led their loved ones, and still others carried them in their arms. Some had the good fortune to die in their own beds. Those who did not go were driven out by their vigilant neighbors who had betrayed them to the police.

On the first day, people realized that they had been deceived, that there would be no ghetto in Slobodka, and that they would be driven farther on. But to where?

There were not enough apartments in Slobodka. People crowded into the streets. The sick moaned and lay directly on the ground; the Romanians rode their horses right onto them. The wails of hungry, freezing children, cries of horror and pleas for mercy rang out all around. All of this was drowned out by the shouts of the Romanians: "*Jidan, dei drumu!*" [Move it, kike!]. People would clear out of the way like a frightened flock of sheep. The Odessa winter was particularly severe that year and it was almost evening on the first day when frozen corpses appeared on the streets of Slobodka. Slobodka was strewn with frozen corpses. On the first night, the desperate cries of people being expelled and driven onto another train for transport onward rang out. Some managed to remain in Slobodka longer, trying to put off their departure for as long as possible in the hope that the "gracious" government would have pity on them.

But the government was implacable. With each passing hour there were fewer and fewer Jews. They were driving columns of ragged, beaten, and starving people along the streets: they were driving them to their death.

Who are these people?

Here comes a man of short stature. His head is hunched deeply into his shoulders. He has the high and thoughtful forehead of a learned man, with sad, brown eyes. His whole expression is one of incomprehension, profound sorrow, and childlike submission to fate. He is leading a small old woman with silver hair and rosy cheeks by the hand. Who is he, who has sinned so grievously against "great Germany" and its Führer, against the creators of a new, "cultured" Europe? Who is he? A barbarian, a killer, a criminal? No, it is the renowned scientist and neuropathologist Dr. Blank, who had dedicated himself entirely to science and who had remained with his patients in a clinic until the last moment.

Here is another one: a tall, thin man with a white beard and bright, intelligent eyes. Why are women accompanying him with looks of gratitude and furtively wiping away tears? What mother does not know him? Which of them is not thankful to him for the life of a child whom he had saved? This is Dr. Petrushkin, an old pediatrician, who had not managed to get out of Odessa in time. Alongside walks another, with a Red Cross armband. This doctor is no longer young, a portly, ill man dragging his legs with difficulty. He has lagged behind, for which he is hit over his head with a stick wielded by a Romanian. Summoning up all his strength, he walks faster and catches up with the crowd of Jews in front of him, but his strength fails him again, his legs will not obey him. And again, blow after blow rains down on his head. He stumbles and falls to the ground with the full weight of his heavy body.

"Have mercy, kill me," he says in a pleading voice. And they have mercy: two bullets to the forehead and he falls, lifeless, spared from torture, mockery, and humiliation. But what is it that his lips are whispering as they go cold? Still one and the same question: "Why is it happening to us?"

Here comes a man who is not more than twenty-five, handsome and in the prime of life. He is a qualified lathe operator at the head of his profession and until recently was working at the military factory, where he had stayed because he was exempted from the draft. His work is finished, no one needs his specialty anymore. There cannot be any distinctions. He is a Jew and that says it all.

In front is a woman, still young. There does not seem to be anything that distinguishes her from those around her; her walk is obedient, her thoughts far away. She thinks that she hears music; it is as though she does not see, does not understand her surroundings. When one looks at her, it seems that she is walking while her whole being is hovering somewhere in the air. This is the only woman conductor of a symphony orchestra in the Soviet Union—at the Odessa Jewish Theater.

There are so many that you cannot count them all: young, old, clever, stupid, honest, dishonest—all sorts. Hitler has bound them all together. In accordance with his orders, everything is being done consistently, methodically, gradually. Just as a cat does not let a mouse out of its paws and amuses itself with its sufferings, so these people are caught in a giant mousetrap. There is nowhere for them to go. There is no exit. Gendarmes, collaborating Ukrainian police, building superintendents, the whole network of fascist investigators are everywhere.

And they all walk. They stumble, they fall, but they continue walking. After several days in a closed building surrounded by sentries (a former school in Slobodka), with broken windows, drafts, without water and almost without food, they are at the end of their strength. The weakest of blows is enough to make them fall and be trampled by crowds and horses, and, in the best case, be put out of their misery with a bullet.

They do not know where they are being driven. They feel death breathing upon them, but they cling to hope, to life any way that they can. Finally they have arrived. Before them is the sorting station and the freight cars. Before they board the train, a band of predators descends on them from somewhere—teenage robbers, they fling themselves on the defenseless, exhausted people—on those who have their belongings in one hand and a child or a helpless old person in the other. In a rage, they throw themselves upon these people, tearing baskets with their remaining provisions out of their hands. One hears the heartrending wails of people deprived of their last crumbs. But it is like a cry in the wilderness. No one defends the insulted and humiliated.

Before boarding, they rush to ask the engineer: "Where are they taking us?" From the reply of the sleepy engineer they learn that the previous train was abandoned several kilometers from Odessa and that the people in them froze to death in the securely sealed boxcars. Others were taken to Beryozovka and then driven until the exhausted and hungry people collapsed to the last man.

The advice "Run!" sounded out from those who did not understand that there was no escape.

They squeeze the people into the boxcars. There are so many of them that it is possible only to stand, pressed tightly against each other. The wagons are securely sealed from the outside, leaving the people in darkness. Gradually their eyes grow accustomed to the dark and they begin to make out terrified faces with eyes where pupils are wide from fear, the haggard faces of old people, of weeping women and children. But the train has moved off. The faces light up again in hope and old women exclaim: "God help us!" People begin to believe that they are really being taken someplace where they will be given the opportunity to hope for happier times—this is all that is left to them.

But gradually their faces cloud over. The train is moving slowly and, as it seems, endlessly. Where they are going is unknown. Every jolt, every halt arouses fear. What if the train derails or catches fire? Their only hope is that they will take pity on the train. On the Jews, of course, they will have no pity.

But where are they taking them? The people are growing more and more numb from the cold. They remain motionless, they suffer from thirst. Children wail, they ask for something to eat or drink, and their mothers suffer both for themselves and for them. The boxcars are not opened. Gradually, children first, then the adults, begin performing their natural bodily functions on the spot. On one side, the moans of women are heard. Little by little they turn into cries for help. A woman is in the pangs of childbirth, but who can help her? The boxcars still do not open and with each passing minute the conviction grows in these people that they never will. The train stops, nonetheless. There is a scraping of bolts and people are driven out of the boxcars. In each car there are five to ten corpses of those who perished from sickness, cold, and hunger.

But this suits the plans of the Romano-German authorities. Nothing is left to chance. The bodies, along with human waste, are tossed out of the boxcars and remain on the steppe without even being buried.

✳✳✳

Now, in this half-animal existence full of trembling expectation, a cry of alarm bursts out: the village is surrounded by Romanians, while German colonists from Kartakay have also arrived. With lightning speed, this news goes through the whole village. Ukrainian mounted police soon turn up and drive all the Jews who were living in apartments into Jewish dormitories. They still know nothing about it there; old women are cooking and going about their business. But the young are not deceiving themselves any longer. People huddle together in frightened herds, keep themselves in small groups. Mortal fear is on some faces, on others, determination. They will die proudly, not allowing the enemy to see them trembling in the face of death! But there is little time for thinking. The Germans are acting quickly and with organization. They chase the Jews out of the dormitories, up to the trenches, where they undress them beforehand, out of the goodness of their hearts handing out the clothing to the locals and even allowing them to rip things from the Jews awaiting death.

Groups of people move up to the trenches, where they are shot with machine guns and rifles.

The more thrifty Germans, in order to save on bullets, grab the small children and smash their heads against poles and trees. One dekulakized colonist from Kartakay distinguished herself in particular: as if she were drunk on cruelty, with wild cries she took hold of children and smashed a rifle butt into their heads with such force that their brains were spattered for some distance around.

In other cases, people were not shot: they simply flung them down into pits, covered them with gas, and set them on fire. Then they checked to see that there was no one left alive, loaded their things into trucks, and with cries of "Heil Hitler!" drove off to their colonies, leaving a portion of the belongings to the Romanians who had been active participants in the slaughter. The killing was a thorough extermination, and so, even if any of those who had not been finished off had managed to crawl out of the pit under the cover of darkness, it was only a temporary reprieve, because there was no possibility of escaping the iron vise of the hellish fascist machine of annihilation.

GARF f. 8114, op. 1, d. 960, ll. 38–49. A typewritten manuscript, along with the letter of L. P. Skupnik and her signature (from the archive of Ilya Ehrenburg, vol. 1, ll. 129–130).

11. The story of Anna Morgulis from Odessa [29]
Recorded by R. A. Davis
Translated by M. Bregman
[1944]

I would like to present the story of Anna Yakovlevna Morgulis of 21 Gogol Street, Odessa. I will convey it just as she herself related it to me in this martyr city on the fifth day after the Germans were driven out. There is no need to embellish her story. It speaks for itself. No, it shouts for itself and cries out for revenge.

Anna Morgulis is fifty-four years old. She looks young for her age. But her hair has turned gray quickly, her face is wrinkled, her eyes reflect the horror that she endured for the last two and a half years (less five days) in Odessa under the authority of the Germans and the Romanians. Her husband and one of her sons are in the Red Army. Her other son is in the Red Navy.

Like all Jews, she has relatives in America: Jack Meyer and Garry Bromberg, who live somewhere on Grand Street in New York, and Jack Charenin, who also lives in the same city.

Before the war, Anna Morgulis was a secretary at the Martí Shipyard.

"The Romanians entered Odessa on October 16, 1941," she begins her story, "and the following day, our sufferings began. On October 17, 1941, we saw hundreds of people on the street who had been shot or hanged. Anyone who looked like a Jew

---

29. Part of Anna Morgulis's story appears in *The Black Book*, p. 57.

or a worker was seized and executed on the spot. Then on October 23, there was an explosion in the building that had formerly been the offices of the NKVD; forty Romanian officers were killed. In response to this, a savage terror began. The Romanians posted flyers in which they announced that they would kill two hundred people for every officer killed and one hundred for every soldier. That same day there appeared an order for the general registration of the Jews.

"On October 24, 1941, Romanian gendarmes appeared under the leadership of an officer. 'Everyone out!' they shouted. 'Come out of the buildings!' They dragged us out of our apartments. In the meantime, the gendarmes shoved everything that they could lay their hands on into their pockets."

Anna Morgulis and the other Jews in her district were taken to 19 Sofyskaya Street.

"When I arrived," she goes on, "around two hundred people were already there. We were all supposed to be sent to Dalnik (a village about eighteen kilometers away) for 'registration.'"

But this time, Anna Morgulis managed to escape. After half an hour, she was freed by a Romanian commissar because she managed to prove that she had converted to Christianity thirty years earlier.

"When I returned home," she continues, "I found the front door open. I decided that they had taken everything from me, but no! They gave me the keys, so I lived for a time in my own apartment. Soon, my father came back from Dalnik. He was eighty-four and he seemed on the verge of death. The next day I set out to look for my mother. I hired a cart and drove along the road to Vygoda station, where, as I had heard, they had taken all the Jews. I did not find my mother, but I did see an enormous number of bodies of old people, of children, and of girls who had been raped.

"Afterward, I found out from a Russian woman—the wife of a Jew, who had come to look for her husband—that the Jews had been taken to the village of Bogdanovka, herded into a large barn, and burned alive. Her husband had perished there.

"I went back to Odessa. My mother had disappeared."

When I heard all this, delivered with almost stone-like calm, I felt a shiver run down my back. The facts themselves and the calm with which they were related were profoundly shocking to me.

"On October 29, 1941," Anna Morgulis goes on, "my dying father tried to light a lamp. He lit a match, but was in no condition to hold it up any higher so his blanket caught fire. I put everything out in a second. But that evening one of our neighbors, a Romanian, told the police that I had wanted to burn down the building. I was arrested the next morning, on the thirtieth, and thrown into a cold, damp jail cell in which there were thirty women, Jews and non-Jews."

"Where was this?" I asked.

"At 7 Krasny Lane."

They took her for interrogation that very night. "Naturally, I denied my guilt," she said. "They started beating me. Oh how they beat me! With clubs! With rifle butts! With a rubber hose! I passed out.

"That night, with impenetrable darkness all around us, thirty Romanian soldiers burst into our cell and, after throwing their coats to the damp floor, threw themselves on us. We were all raped, even the old women. Some of the younger girls were driven insane. We, the older women—and there were women there even older than I was—sat there and wept."

The next day, they were all taken and handed over to female guards. Still, there were daily beatings. The officers would send two gendarmes every night who would call out: "Valya, Manya, come spend the night with the officers." No one could do anything. Refusal meant instant death.

"Are there any living witnesses to this?" I asked. "Yes," she answered. "Valya Nefedova and Olga Orlova. Both of them live at 42 Khersonskaya Street."

The living want to live. And Morgulis did everything that was in her power to survive. She sent out statements, offered bribes, presented witnesses, and in the end, after two months of imprisonment, was released, on December 26, 1941.

"On January 10, 1942," she continues her story, "the Romanians issued a new order: all Jews, including those professing the Christian faith, must report to the ghetto (somewhere in Slobodka)."

But since the Romanians were systematically hanging and shooting Jews every day, the Jews understood perfectly well what this meant. According to Anna Morgulis, on the firing range by the field artillery depot—and this is confirmed by others—no fewer than fifteen thousand people were burned to death.

"Every Jew knew that to go to Slobodka meant going to their death. For this reason, many committed suicide, particularly intellectuals."

"Can you name some people?" I asked.

"Yes! The jurists Pyotr Polishchuk—he hanged himself—and Shaya Weiss, who took poison; Dr. Petrushkin; a seventy-four-year-old writer named Arnold Giselevich, who hanged himself in his room when he saw the Romanians coming for him, and many, many others."

Later on I met Arnold Giselevich's daughter, who had survived by some miracle. She was married to a Russian and did not look like a Jew herself. She told me that relatives on her mother's side, by the name of Lovitz, lived in America.

But the Golgotha of Anna Morgulis did not end there.

"I had a relative, a Polish woman, Stanislava Kraevskaya," she went on. "On January 11, she came to see me at the very moment when the police were coming through the gate. She hid me in washrooms and cellars, in attics, in her own apartment, in the apartments of Russian friends, both hers and mine, who because of this were risking their lives. One day, during a raid on the house where I was staying, I climbed into a barrel. I lived this way for an entire year, until December 1942."

After that, Anna Morgulis lived for half a year with a false passport bought for a fur coat, a blanket, and a dress in the workers' district of Moldavanka, the center of partisan activity in Odessa.

"Lots of Russians knew or suspected that I was a Jew," she said, "but no one turned me in. This was how I survived."

But thousands did not. I talked with her about the fate of other Jews. The figures are not clear to this day. But it is already known that all rabbis and even the sick, the decrepit, elderly people on the verge of death, were especially sought out and shot, while the synagogues were destroyed. The Slobodka Jews were taken out onto a frozen estuary nearby (a salt lake); the ice gave way and the unfortunate ones drowned.

When the Romanians captured Odessa, there were, by the reckoning of Anna Morgulis, 135,000 Jews in the city. Now, she supposes that only a few hundred remain. Nevertheless, the total number is unknown and the number of those who were saved is perhaps higher because some have been living on false passports. Others are in the catacombs, while still more are in surrounding villages.

It is doubtful that it will be possible to provide a complete description of everything that happened to the Jews of Odessa. Some people have simply vanished. The Giselevich girl with whom I spoke told me that her sister, Dr. Polina Arnoldovna Giselevich, had been taken away along with her three-month-old son by the gendarmes and that nothing had been heard from her since. Citizen Giselevich does not know anything about her two aunts, a grandfather, or a seventeen-year-old cousin; they have vanished.

Our conversation was coming to an end. I quickly jotted down my notes, turning my face so as not to betray my feelings as I listened to this awful human document.

"I didn't know, having lived fifty years," Anna Morgulis told me as we were saying our goodbyes, "that it would be possible to live to see the day when you would be afraid of the slightest sound, of footsteps on the street. The faintest knock at the door could make you experience mortal fear. And the most terrible thing of all is that the people whom you have known your entire life turn away from you like you're a stranger, an enemy, a pariah, like you're the lowest of the low.

"Before the war, we could not imagine that such a thing could happen. Now we know. When the Red Army arrived, when the first moment of amazement and disbelief had passed, and I saw that dear, beloved uniform, the garrison caps, the insignia, I leaped out into the street and threw my arms around the first Red Army soldier that came along. I wanted to go down on my knees before him: to kiss his feet, to cry, to shout. And the only thing that I want is to give everything that is left to me to my dear Motherland."

What can be added to that?

GARF f. 8114, op.1, d. 964, ll. 52–57. A typewritten manuscript.

12. In prison for concealing Jews
THE TESTIMONY OF NURSE ALEXANDRA YAKOVLEVNA VOLOVTSEVA
MAY 10, 1944
FROM THE FILES OF THE EXTRAORDINARY STATE COMMISSION FOR THE INVESTIGATION OF ATROCITIES COMMITTED ON SOVIET TERRITORY BY THE GERMAN-FASCIST INVADERS AND THEIR ACCOMPLICES

I, Alexandra Yakovlevna Volovtseva, a nurse in the First Hospital for Infectious Diseases, live with my mother, Maria Antonovna Sandul, at 13 Komsomol Street.

During the enemy occupation, we were arrested on August 1, 1942, for concealing the Jew Alexander Borisovich Zaksman, the former Komsomol secretary at the Odessa Streetcar Trust.

A. Zaksman was discovered in a wardrobe during a search by a police officer of the fourth district named Chervinsky, who lives at 9 Baranov Street, as he did before the enemy occupation. When I asked officer Chervinsky what he was looking for, he replied: "Partisans are concealed in your apartment, along with weapons and a radio receiver."

Instead of all of that, he found a Jew.

In spite of our pleas to spare us (we promised that Zaksman would leave our home), Chervinsky would hear none of it, assigning two policeman he had with him to guard us while he went to the station to report his discovery, and also to carry out a thorough search since he suspected an armed ambush could take place. The two men assigned to us, clearly afraid to stay in the apartment, went out to the courtyard.

I took advantage of this and hid Zaksman in the opening high in the outside wall of our apartment; this wall gave onto a dark corridor.

Three quarters of an hour later a heavy truck with a squad of policemen pulled up. They searched our apartment and the entire building. Not finding anyone or anything, they took my mother and me to the police station. They led us down into the cellar where those under arrest were kept. Two hours later they summoned us for interrogation. They threw themselves on me with their fists and crude swearing: "What did you do with the kike? We'll teach you to hide kikes. You'll be where all the kikes are." I was ready for anything, for any torture right up to the electric chair, which was so favored by the savage butchers, particularly the Jewish ones, who, having escaped reprisals by the fascists, had renounced their own people.

Failing to learn about Zaksman from us, they sent us on the third day to the military field tribunal (the court martial tribunal at 27 Kanatnaya Street). Here they spoke in slightly lower tones. After my interrogation, they asked me if I had anything to add. I answered: "I ask you to release my mother, who has not done anything, and to do with me whatever you like."

After some discussions in Romanian, the interpreter turned to Mama: "We're letting you go for now. Here's a note. Go to the address written there. They'll tell you what to do, but remember, you have to keep your mouth shut about this."

They sent me to jail under guard along with other prisoners, in spite of the fact that my guilt in concealing a Jew had not yet been established, neither by my declarations nor by those of my neighbors.

When Mama, coming out of the military field tribunal, presented herself at the address indicated, 5 Kanatny Lane, she was received by a woman calling herself Fyodorova, a lawyer for the military field tribunal. Fyodorova, in her turn, interrogated Mama, saying that Mama would have to tell the whole truth: had we hidden a Jew, and where had he gone? After taking down Mama's testimony, she said that the matter could be taken care of for two thousand marks and that she would help us.

She ordered us to bring the first thousand the next day so that supposedly she could begin working on our behalf. The second thousand Fyodorova would allow us to bring in weekly installments of five hundred marks, since Mama complained that it would be very difficult for her to hand over so much and in such a short space of time; we had no savings, we would have to sell some things. And in addition to everything, Fyodorova ordered Mama to come the next day for another interrogation. These interrogations were completely exhausting. She was afraid that if they found anyone at our place, we would be condemned.

A month later, that is, on September 1, 1942, they let me out of jail, but Fyodorova still would not leave me in peace. She ordered me, and Mama as well, to come to her office in the next day or two for interrogation. She told me: "You're not free. Your case still has to examined by the general. Everything depends on him. You could still be convicted. In that case, we'll also help you. We'll hire a Romanian lawyer." All told, this affair was still costing us another thousand marks.

Not two weeks had gone by before they arrested us again. They sent us to 13 Bebel Street, to the gendarmerie. Here they treated us like animals: they beat our legs, smashed our heads into walls, thrashed us about the head with iron rods. My aunt, Sofia Antonovna Levchenko, brought us food. But they kicked her in the stomach so hard that she lay in bed for a week or two. They released us two days later, beaten and tortured. A month later, the police came for us again, but let us go after the interrogation.

In spite of all these torments and suffering, we managed to save Zaksman and to live to see the arrival of our dear liberators and of Soviet power, so dear to our hearts.

GARF, f. 8114, op. 1, d. 940, ll. 261-263. A typewritten, notarized copy. The original text is preserved in the archive of the Extraordinary State Commission (GARF, f. 7021, op. 69, d. 342, ll. 94-95).

13. To avenge my children
A LETTER FROM TATYANA REKOCHINSKAYA TO HER BROTHER, ABRAM, ON ACTIVE DUTY IN THE ARMY
[1944]

Hello, my dear, beloved brother Abrasha!

I've waited so long for the moment when I would receive news from you that you're still alive. I came to Odessa on April 25, 1944, the very same day when the people who live in our building received your letter. Just think, today you're the only relative left to me—only you.

When the invaders occupied the city, they drove me and the two children out of our apartment and into the severe, freezing winter, then deported us to Southern Bug, 160 kilometers from Odessa. Massacres took place there, in the village of Bogdanovka. My nursing child, a girl, died along the way, while my boy, along with the other children in the convoy, was shot. But when my turn came to be executed, the shootings stopped.

They set up a death camp in which people dropped like flies from cold, hunger, and filth. We lay beside the bodies, and everything that you can imagine happening in a nightmare took place in that camp. I escaped twice. I went into the villages, doing any work for people that I could, and they fed me. But each time the gendarmes caught me, beat me, and sent me back to the camp. I suffered this way for two and a half years, but the hope that our boys would free us never left me.

Now I've come back to my hometown and to the place where I used to live, of which nothing is left except bare walls and not one of our family. Our Rosa was evacuated at the last minute along with the communists from the Cafeteria Trust. About three years ago, I got word from her that she had arrived safely at the port of Tuapse near Novorossiysk. I don't know what became of her after that. I don't know anything about our Sara. Nothing about our Polya either. My husband, Boris Stratievsky, has been at the Front for three years. I don't know whether or not he is still alive. I have not had a letter from him yet.

At the moment I am not working anywhere. Manufacturing has been destroyed, but rebuilding efforts continue.

My dear brother, write to me about yourself. Are you wounded? Where is your family?

I beg you, as a member of the family, avenge my children and avenge all the atrocities that they inflicted on us without mercy.

Write to me, dearest. Your letters will make my life easier. I kiss you affectionately.

Tanya Rekochinskaya. My address is still the same—37 Lazarev Street, no.1. Write.

GARF f. 8114, op. 1, d. 964, ll. 7–8. A typewritten manuscript.

14. My life in a fascist prison
THE RECOLLECTIONS AND VERSES OF THE SCHOOLBOY LEV ROZHETSKY [30]
APRIL 4–AUGUST 16, 1944

---

30. Part of this text appeared in *The Black Book*, pp. 59–60, 65.

Dear Comrade Ehrenburg!

I received your letter, and I am very grateful for it. I wrote a great deal while I was a prisoner of the fascists. In the spring, comrade Major Faynerman, a pilot, took my poem "In Exile" and delivered it by hand to comrade Marshak's son.[31] He wrote me several times that he had had no reply from comrade Marshak. The actress, comrade Vanshteyn, visited Odessa (her address: 12 Bolotnaya Street, no. 1a), and she also took a copy of my poem. A good deal of time has gone by, but there has been no answer.

As you requested, I have written a few sketches describing what I endured. There are probably a few mistakes in syntax and other things. Look them over. I would very much like to send you my long poem since it provides a broader perspective, but I have only one handwritten draft left. If you take an interest in my poem "In Exile," you can get it from comrade Marshak. This is, to be sure, a rough version, but it is written powerfully and clearly. I await your response.

Yours truly,
Lev Rozhetsky
August 16, 1944, Odessa

Two years we were wrapped in chains,
Two years the enemy trampled our native ground,
Two years we were despised slaves,
Well, we knew what captivity was!
In the sanguinary darkness of killing and of the baseness of evil,
Oh, no, I did not cast my weapons aside,
I encouraged the hearts of others with my verse.
I wrote justly of the suffering of peoples.
The desired hour of liberty and retribution came to pass,
The world will remember it for a thousand years to come!
And the Soviet soldiers rumbled like thunder,
And "courageous" Fritz fled without his trousers.
Our people fought, by liberty inspired,
And the warrior giant brought it to us.
Oh, how easily my reborn voice sounds:
I am a free man! I am a young citizen!
We traveled a long road of struggle and sufferings,
We must avenge our brothers and sisters!
"Beat the vile butchers!" is our united cry,

---

31. Samuil Marshak (1887–1964) was a writer especially revered for his stories for children. He was among the prominent Jewish cultural figures who participated in an international broadcast in Moscow on August 24, 1941, appealing to Jews around the world to join the struggle against Nazi Germany.

And I am ready to trade my pen for a rifle.
For a group of gray-heads and children burned,
For maids and women violated in their honor,
For the enemy—holy vengeance!
April 4, 1944

Sketches of life in a fascist prison

I have been interested in literature since childhood. I write poetry and work to improve myself. Two years before the war, when I was not yet eleven, I read my epic poem about Stalin at the all-republic Olympiad in Kiev and won a prize. The war broke out. We could not be evacuated and remained in Odessa: my mother, my seven-year-old brother, and I.

1

After the heat of battle.
The battle of the giants,
We abandoned Odessa
To the Romanian filth.
Thus the she-eagle abandons
Her young
In order later, with the mighty eagle,
To rescue the young.
(From my poem).

The Romanians marched in on October 16, and on October 22 a bloody terror began.

The day of terror
Rivers of blood
Thousands executed
This was the housewarming
For the stinking butchers.
(From the poem).

After this, bloody and dreadful events did not let up even for a moment. Soon there came the order: "All persons of Jewish origin are to report for registration in the village of Dalnik. Those who conceal themselves, as well as those who conceal them, will be turned over for execution." In a second order it was explained that the phrase "individuals of Jewish origin" also meant baptized Jews, even if the father and mother had been baptized. Tens of thousands of Soviet citizens were hounded to the "registration point" in Dalnik (several kilometers outside of Odessa). We decided not to go to Dalnik, whatever the cost. Later, we learned that all those people were taken onward to the village of Bogdanovka (180 kilometers from Odessa), and burned and shot there.

All those who did not submit to the orders of the Romanians were gathered and taken off in some unknown direction. We were among them. They herded us for a long time, until evening, in a column through the streets.

2
Prison

For a long time the Romanians drove us on,
Tortured and beat us.
Children are crying, mothers are crying:
"It would be better if they shot us."
And in the sky, the moon wept,
Looking on with pity,
Bathing passers-by
With loving radiance.
Here they crammed us in
Like herring into a barrel
Barely, barely did we find shelter
We sat in one corner.
Night fell, outlining
Golden stars,
And covered with darkness
Human suffering.
(From the poem)

Thousands of peaceful citizens, women, the elderly, and children were herded into prison. Here we saw no small number of horrors. At night there was the constant sound of shots and soul-rending, inhuman cries. They would gather people every day and take them off somewhere unknown. The Romanians taunted the women. The beasts tossed one girl into a latrine, cursing her all the while. They told the Bessarabian Jews that they were sending them home. Four thousand Bessarabians were taken out and shot.

Lice-infested, dirty, one after another, we sat in the cells. Every day they took corpses from the cells. The Romanians not only did away with us, they humiliated us in all kinds of ways. Polishchuk had been a well-known lawyer in Odessa. He had been baptized in childhood many years earlier. The Romanians dragged him into the jail. They put him in the middle of the yard. The commandant of the prison took out his revolver and growled: "So, you're a Russian?" "Yes," the lawyer replied. "Then pull your pants down!" the Romanian yelled in a rage.

The next morning, the lawyer hanged himself. That was how people lived in jail, bound hand and foot, in fear of death. Having tortured and plundered us to their hearts' content, the Romanians released us "into freedom."

3
Sortirovochnaya Station

Before long, the Romano-German butchers arranged a so-called ghetto in an isolated part of the city called Slobodka. Right away, an order was posted: "Jews are to be sent to work in the districts of Beryozovka and Ochakov."

This meant death.

On January 11, Anatoly (who was just getting over typhus), Mama, and I were forcibly taken to Slobodka. They took us and led us off at three in the morning. Temperatures were well below freezing. The snow was up to our knees. They drove us along in a crowd. Many people—the elderly and children—died right there in the streets of Peresyp (on the outskirts of the city) in a howling blizzard. The Germans were laughing and taking pictures. Those who could made it to Sortirovochnaya Station. The dam had been blown; there was a huge river along the way. Wet people were freezing. They were pulling us along in carts. At the yard there was a train. I will never forget the scene: pillows, blankets, overcoats, boots, saucepans, fur coats, and other objects were strewn the length of the platform. Freezing old men were unable to stand up and were moaning quietly and pitifully, mothers were losing children, children their mothers, there were cries, wails, and shots. A mother is wringing her hands, tearing her hair out and crying out: "Where are you, darling?" A child is running back and forth on the platform in tears: "Mama!" She is freezing and falls.

I remember the indifferent expressions of the Germans. It was if they were driving livestock into cattle cars. The whistle hooted and the train moved off.

4
Beryozovka (100 kilometers from Odessa)

The train does not stop. It keeps going, but where? We do not know. The freight car is in total darkness. Children are crying. Bodies are shuddering. You can hear the wind howling. Night. Suddenly, the train begins slowing down. A stop. What's next? Horror. Death. The doors creak. A clatter of rifle butts.

Thoughts flashed through our minds as quickly as an electrical current. We heard them throwing people out of the neighboring cars. Wails, weeping, shouts. It was dreadful, taking people against their will. What would happen? Suddenly, the doors open with a scraping sound, there is a glow from a fire, the flames of a bonfire. I see people, the elderly, women, and children, running around enveloped in flames. How the children's screams cut to the heart! I see piles of objects, bodies, frozen people. The sharp smell of gas. The immense glow of a bonfire. The faces of the killers set in stone. They were burning people here. It is easy to say "they were burning." They were burning children alive, burning people alive!

This slaughter took place at the Beryozovka train station. There seemed to be no way out! But we were fated to remain alive. Suddenly, there was a powerful jolt and the train began moving farther and farther away from the bonfire. All the living were being driven on again. Really, it was a miracle!

5
Sirotskoe (125 kilometers from Odessa)

Endless snowfalls, drifts, utility poles. People moving from village to village in long columns. The road from village to village was strewn with bodies. Bullets whistling overhead. They were killing those who lagged behind. It wasn't easy for us to walk. My brother could barely stay on his feet. Just like the rest of us.

How many times in a burst of grief
Sadness overcomes,
How many times does the unfortunate fool
Decide to perish!
But when he is in the clutches of death,
Then he realizes
That life, after all, is dearer than everything,
What can replace it!
(From the poem)

And we walked. It should be said that walking became easier: they took all the things that we had been carrying. They looted everything: the dead were seen off by Romanians and policemen. I remember many awful scenes. I'll not talk about them. I described this march clearly and vividly in my poem "In Exile."

Finally, toward evening, those of us who were still alive were herded into the village of Sirotskoe. I saw long, half-fallen down stables. Crowds of people rushed toward them—anywhere, after all, but on the street!

One unusual thing after another happened to us. Maybe it was a game of chance or maybe something else, but that's how it turned out.

We had a heavy feeling of foreboding. No, the guards had not brought us here to rest. We decided not to sleep in the stables. It was growing dark. We went off in another direction. We knocked at one hut; afraid, they would not let us in. At another one, the same thing. We wandered for a long time through the snowdrifts and then knocked at the door of the last hut. An old woman lived there, the sister of a village policeman. After taking our last blanket and two spools of thread, she let us in.

At night, drunken Romanians, policemen, and local bandits armed with shotguns, knives, and clubs burst into the stables, stabbing, killing, robbing, raping.

In the morning we decided to run away, anywhere. Death was all the same to us!

But we did not manage to take more than a few steps from the hut before we were surrounded by a crowd of hooligans. They yanked the hat from my head and dragged us toward the stables. I saw an awful sight: many nude corpses were lying around the stables. One could hear moaning. I saw a bandit remove boots from a dead old woman. I saw them take a jacket off a dying girl.

As for us, who once again remained alive, they made us form a column (it was quite small by now) and drove us farther on.

6
Domanyovka (150 kilometers from Odessa)

I want every letter of these names to be remembered with particular clarity. All these names: Sortirovochnaya, Beryozovka, Sirotskoe, Domanyovka, Bogdanovka, Gorka, Stavki—they are historic names. These were death camps. Here the fascists exterminated thousands of civilians, thousands of Soviet citizens in these places. I will describe Domanyovka in detail because it occupies a "place of honor" among all the camps.

Domanyovka is a district center, a small town. It is enclosed on two sides. Fields stretch all around. There is a beautiful little forest. Rags and scraps of clothes hang from shrubs and branches to this day. In these parts, there is a grave under every tree. Thousands of people were shot here.

Here is a large cemetery for animals. Thousands of horses, cows, and Jews are buried here. Look at this broad, deep ditch—the fascists shot four hundred Jews here. The skeletons of animals and human beings are visible. Here are the sizable ruins of the former club. There was a concentration camp there. Domanyovka is a bloody and black word. Domanyovka was a center of all kinds of killings and deaths. Thousands of groups of people were herded to their deaths from all over. The columns followed one another without letting up.

We did not get there directly, however. From Sirotskoe they marched us to Mostovoe, and from Mostovoe to Lidievka. We numbered three thousand when we left Odessa and five hundred when we arrived in Lidievka. We spent a month and five days there. People were again housed in ruined stables. I will not describe the horrors of Lidievka; I will say only that they drove just a tiny handful of people out to Domanyovka. Almost no one besides our family was left of the whole group.

7
Gorka

There were two half-fallen-down stables on the outskirts of Domanyovka. They began herding Jews into them in April 1942. They did not allow them out of the barracks, they were in filth up to their knees, people were executed on the spot. Corpses lie there as though at the morgue. Hungry children are crying, women are sobbing. The prolonged, dreadful moans of the dying.

Typhus. Dysentery. Gangrene. Death.

Black marketers took advantage of the helpless condition of these martyrs. They sold soup in mugs and collected an extraordinarily high price for a few spoonfuls of some disgusting slop. A hungry man will give everything for a few crusts of bread.

And to others, so as not to lie,
It was simply a blessing!
For a bowlful of porridge—
A new dress, a shirt.
For a piece of bread
A first-rate jacket!
(From my verses)

People were dying by the thousands, rotting alive in the barracks. The corpses were tossed into heaps. Half-mad people stripped them naked so they could exchange clothing for rusks later. And there gradually arose such mountains of bodies that it was horrible to look at them. I do not put the word—mountains—in quotation marks. I remember those bodies piled on top of one another as though they were before me now. Old people, men, women, children entirely naked and gone blue lay there in various poses. A dead mother held her dead child in an embrace. The wind ruffled the gray beards of old men.

I wonder today: How is it that I did not lose my mind? It is not by chance that they say that nothing is stronger than a man! Day and night, dogs came here from every direction. The dogs of Domanyovka got as fat as rams! Day and night these dogs gnawed at human meat and human bones! The smell in the air was unbearable.

One day, the praetor deigned to take a drive past these places and glimpsed this "magnificent" spectacle. Of course, this gentleman became nauseated. The gentleman could not stand it.

It was only after this that he gave the order to remove the bodies. The traitors Nikora and Kozakevich were the police of the Domanyovka District. One of the policemen, petting his dog, said: "What do you say, Polkan, eaten enough kikes?" That is what was happening at this famous Gorka. Even now one can see the remains of the barracks and mass graves.

8
Bogdanovka

Bogdanovka is located on the banks of the Southern Bug (twenty-five kilometers from Domanyovka). It used to be a state pig farm. Some of these famous barracks have been preserved to this day. There is a small forest or rather a park on one side. Its pathways lead to the well-known Bogdanovka pit. About one hundred thousand civilians were herded here from all over, from Bessarabia, Kishinev, Akkerman, Bukovina, from the cities and villages of Ukraine, from Odessa and Tiraspol.[32] The principal aim of the killers was to seize everything of value and then destroy the people.

Having caught the scent of booty, all sorts of dirty scoundrels came running from every direction.

The killers were under the direction of the Germans. The commander of the gendarmerie was a Romanian named Malinescu. The traitors Slivenko and Kravets were in charge of the police. Nikora and Kozakevich took part in the shootings.

There is no point in describing the horrors that took place in the barracks. Disease. Death. Many attempted to flee. Caught, they were killed on the spot.

Mass killings and shootings began on December 21. At first, they stripped the condemned naked, then led them up to the pit. They went down on their knees, facing the Bug. A cask of wine stood nearby. The killers fortified themselves with wine and, foaming at the mouth, took aim. They used only explosive bullets and took aim only at the back of the head. The corpses were thrown into the pit.[33]

---

32. According to recent scholarship, about 54,000 Jews were herded into Bogdanovka.
33. The Germans did not use exploding bullets; military weapons fired at close range would have produced a shocking visual effect.

Howls. Cries. Pleas for mercy. Curses. A woman was killed before her husband's eyes. He was supposed to throw her down. Then they killed him. The killers hauled away everything they had plundered on carts. The bodies were burned.

A few people from among the prisoners of Bogdanovka were left alive. They forced them to work and did not manage to shoot them. The bodies of the dead were transformed into an enormous heap of ashes.

A monument has been raised over the well-known Bogdanovka pit. It reads: "To the victims of fascism." Perhaps they will inscribe the words from my poem:

Whoever you are, stop,
Draw near, gentle traveler,
To this grave gloomy and cold,
Look around, in the lap of sorrow.
Embraced by anger and disquiet,
Do not let a tear cloud your eye,
Honor the incinerated ash of people
With silent worship.

9
Stavki—The Death Camp

Twelve kilometers from the village of Akmechetka, like an island in the wastes of the steppe, is the former state pig farm of Stavki—three half-fallen-down barracks. They were surrounded by deep drainage ditches. The water was far away, almost two kilometers.

On May 10, 1942, the Romanian butchers forcibly brought the Jews from the Domanyovka District here. Those left alive from Gorka—the crippled and the ill— were also brought to the death camp. A new epic of horrors began. The barracks were divided up into narrow cells where the pigs had once lived. The unhappy martyrs were not allowed to take a step out of the camp. They were condemned to death by starvation. Epidemics of lice and disease broke out. The camp was guarded by local police. Anyone who dared to cross over the ditches was shot on the spot. The camp commandant was the traitor, murderer, and sadist Pirozhenko. The following incident was generally known: As a column of Jews was being led into the camp, a young girl hid behind a bush to relieve herself. Pirozhenko saw this. He took aim and fired. The wounded girl summoned up all her strength, got to her feet and, covered in blood, cried out "Mama, they've killed me!" The butcher, not wasting any time, finished her off with a bayonet. What those monsters did not do! How they taunted us! One was allowed to relieve oneself only at specific times, and the rest of the time, even if you were about to burst, they would not let you go. Children cried, yelling at the top of their lungs, but crying wasn't permitted either, so they beat them. One elderly Jew could not stand it; he hanged himself. A lawyer named Fuks tried to hang himself and soon died. Ten people were allowed to line up for water. One day, Pirozhenko saw that "order had been violated"; instead of ten, eleven had gone. Not wasting a minute, the animal took aim and fired. Two women at the end of the line were wounded. One went off to one side, while the other, named Doba, took her kerchief from her head and started to dress her wounded leg. The sadist fired a second shot, then went up to her and finished her off with his rifle butt.

On the third day of the Jews' stay in the camp a Romanian engineer arrived and took eight hundred of them out to work. The beasts forcibly separated fathers and mothers from their children. They needed working people; as for the children, let them have a rest, they said.

Mothers hid their children under their skirts, pleaded, and wept. But what could touch the heart of a fascist? The selected ones were taken to the village of Karlovka to do convict labor. The orphans left behind perished. People were dying like flies. Typhus, dysentery, scurvy, the bullets and whips of the Romanians, and death, death, death. People were covered with boils, scabies, many had frostbitten hands and feet.

Thousands of people died from gangrene. Bits of flesh were dropping from the bodies of the unfortunates. The number of deaths continued to increase. Sometimes they gave out "rations"—half a spoonful of gruel. Only forty people survived among all the martyrs of the death camp.

10
Life in the ghetto

The fascist monsters did not always kill people right away. They took pleasure in prolonged agony and used the condemned for all kinds of convict labor. Besides that, they were thinking about the fact that their bloody work would not go unpunished. They needed to cover up the traces of their crimes, to camouflage them. An order arrived at the gendarmerie: no shootings. In fact, the damn Romanians turned out to be very clever. Why shoot the Jews when they can die on their own?

So they began putting the Jews behind barbed wire in concentration camps, to wear them out with hunger, hard labor, to keep them in filth, and naked in the freezing cold, to beat them, while shooting them on the sly. This was an exceptionally successful method. In the Odessa newspapers one could read that Jews were working in labor colonies, living in private apartments, and were even receiving two marks a day!

See, they were saying: How kind we are! All of this was cleverly arranged.

Everything that I went through seems like some sort of nightmare today.

I remember barracks, stables, shouts, moans, gunshots. Soon the Romanians allowed Jews who were able to work to be taken to collective farms. The director of the Domanyovka collective farm, Radyansk, took pity on us and took us in. It was a rare bit of luck!

We started to work on the collective farm, living in two damp, small rooms. We were dirty, lice-infested, and hungry. We lived just opposite the Gorka camp. There were fifty of us, and half died. Several times, the Romanians and the police wanted to have us shot. We suffered from typhus and dysentery, but we stayed alive. Our bodies were all covered with scabies and boils. In addition to doing all sorts of work, they forced us to bury the dead and to carry corpses.

I remember how we approached the barracks with a cart. I led the horse by the bridle, while Mama pushed the cart from behind. We took the bodies by the legs, by the arms, tossed them up onto the cart, and when we had filled it, we took our load to the pit and dumped it in.

Everyone was made to wear a six-pointed star on their caps, their chests, and their backs.

One day they beat me half to death because they found a copy of Pushkin's verse on me. They wanted to kill me, but they didn't. I describe this incident in my poem "In Exile."

Exile—here is the crown of all sorrows,
A murderous word, a dreadful poison!
We were convicts outside the law,
And human life turned into hell.
Deprived of the rights of a man, stripped of all
A man becomes a toy,
And the word "kike" sounds like "leper,"
And life is worth nothing then, a pathetic cheque.
Only in this savage hour of cruel persecution,
Did I recognize my origins.
(from my verses)

But I have said very little. It is impossible to recount everything I went through.

11
Struggle and Freedom

We were in the clutches of the fascists for two and a half years. For two and half years, in hellish conditions, we lived in fear of death. Thousands of people died an excruciating death before our eyes. But we did not want to give up. We wanted to resist with everything at hand. And I resisted. I chose as my weapon of war the only means available to me—the word. Under these circumstances, I wrote. You ask: "How? How did you manage it?" I told of this in my poem "In Exile." We were working as field laborers. This helped me. With great effort, having gotten hold of a pencil, on a small board or a piece of plywood, on a bit of brown wrapping paper or on any scrap I could find, I wrote, often after concealing myself in the grass. Most of the time I had to write, then memorize my verses. Of course, this put me under the threat of death. I wrote many pieces, sketches, poems, and songs. Two anti-fascist songs of mine, "The Sky Stretched High Above" and "Nina" (in memory of a woman who lost her mind) reached a wide audience. Once again I became convinced of the enormous role that the free, living word can play in any circumstance. I was inspired only by the word "freedom." Often, when there was a chance to do so, I would read verses to my comrades in unhappiness. How good it felt when people sang my songs and read my poems, even through groans and tears! But it all seemed very little to me. I decided to write a large-scale work which would reflect all the horrors we had seen.

I wrote the long poem "In Exile." No doubt it has many shortcomings from an artistic point of view, but every line is written in blood, every line is written with a burning anger toward the murderers.

The Red Army was coming closer and closer to us. The cowardly Romanians, hearing the muffled rumbling of guns, began to retreat. Immediately, all the Jews in the concentration camps and collective farms made their escape, in whatever direction they could. But then the Germans moved in.

We hid out for two weeks, moving from village to village. We waited. Our people arrived. Hurrah! Freedom!

Now I can freely walk the streets without any distinguishing marks. I can freely write, study, work. I would like for my poor verses to become an eternal mark upon the fascist butchers. I want to tell, I will tell everyone, the whole world, what fascism is.

LEV ROZHETSKY, PUPIL IN THE 7TH CLASS, SCHOOL NO. 47 OF THE CITY OF ODESSA.

AUGUST 16, 1944

GARF f. 8114, op. 1, d.964, ll. 21–39. A typewritten manuscript.

15. In occupied Odessa and Transnistria

THE RECOLLECTIONS OF DR. ISRAEL BOROVICH ADESMAN[34] AND THE LIST HE COMPILED OF ODESSA DOCTORS WHO PERISHED

RECORDED BY HIS WIFE, RAKHIL IOSIFOVNA GOLDENTAL

[1944]

The Romanian occupiers carried out the task that they had set for themselves in Odessa, namely the extermination of the Jewish population according to the following plan.

On October 17, 1941, the day after the Romanian army entered Odessa, the gendarmes surrounded all the houses and forced all the Jews out to be forcibly registered, demonstrating along the way in the most shameless fashion the thieving tendencies proper to all Romanians.

There were several registration points. At the one to which my wife and I were taken, it required about four hours to register some five to six hundred people. Several such groups made up a column of three or four thousand people, including old people, cripples on crutches, and women with infants in their arms, who were sent to the outskirts of the city under the escort of gendarmes. They pushed stragglers with their rifle butts and used sticks and whips to beat anyone who stepped out of formation.

---

34. Dr. Israel Borisovich Adesman was born in 1862 and worked as a doctor for fifty-six years. A portion of his reminiscences was published in *The Black Book*, pp. 55–58.

At this new gathering point our entire column was herded onto the premises of a school. It was dark. Pushing each other, driven on by impatient gendarmes, we took our places standing. We spent the entire night this way. Fatigue, stifling air, pangs of hunger and thirst, the groans and cries of children—all of this put off not only any feelings of resentment, but also any fear of what awaited us.

It was only early in the morning, when, contrary to an obviously false promise to return us to apartments in the city, they moved us in the direction of the prison, that this feeling was awakened. A Russian woman, overcome by pity, had the nerve to bring some water to a child in our group; she received a resounding slap before our eyes, a clear demonstration of the hatred that the occupiers had for us.

My wife and I did not remain in the prison for long—two or three hours. We were among a small number of people who managed to escape. As to the subsequent fate of those who remained, I received more or less precise information from doctors who were later evacuated to the ghetto. Almost all those who remained in the prison after our departure perished, some from hunger and exhaustion, others by suicide. The majority, however, paid with their lives in reprisal for the blowing up of Romanian headquarters on December 23, 1941, during a meeting of the army staff. It was decided that for each dead officer, three hundred Russians or five hundred Jews should be shot (actually, they were hanged).[35] The reprisals for this explosion went on for several days. Jews who had remained in the city after the registration also paid with their lives, including even those who were bedridden. This group included a palsied professor of mathematics named Fudim, who was hanged.

The majority of those who, in obedience to the orders that were issued three or four days after the explosion, set out for Dalnik (a small village some four or five kilometers from the city) perished as well. Many of them were shot on the spot, while others were taken to Bogdanovka, where a common grave awaited them.

After the Romanians' desire for vengeance had subsided, the life of the surviving Jews proceeded over the next two and half months without the fear of being shot. But they were subjected to robbery and extortion on the part of the Romanian civilian authorities, who blackmailed them, kindly offering their services to Jews who wanted to protect themselves against the difficult consequences that would result from anticipated decrees. Representatives of Romanian civilian authority had already managed to line their pockets with Jewish savings even days before the publication of the order on the handing over of valuables.

The decree ordering all Odessa Jews to leave the city on January 11, 1942, at 8:00 AM for the ghetto was published on January 9. The large village of Romanovka, just

---

35. The explosion took place on October 22, 1941. Sixty-six Romanian soldiers, including the commandant of the city, were killed, along with several German officers. As was noted earlier, according to a subsequent decree, two hundred people were hanged for every dead officer, and one hundred for every dead soldier.

outside of Odessa, served as the staging area for the ghetto. It was from there that those who had undergone preliminary registration, which was also the occasion for humiliations and cynical tricks, were dispatched in groups of two to three thousand in the direction of Domanyovka. The groups headed off every day or every other day, depending upon how much the rail network could handle. The route to the ghetto hardly looked promising. Many, therefore, tried to linger in Romanovka as long as possible, where, it is true, it was possible through great effort to maintain contact with friends and with the slightly more fortunate part of the population. These efforts served as a source of income for the Romanian gendarmes.

Along with petty acts of extortion, to which the Jews were subjected in the village, "Hitler's falcons" took advantage of the lawless situation. This was a group of young soldiers who by night raided Jews temporarily living in private apartments and, under the cover of the law forbidding the keeping of arms, stole anything that struck their fancy. At the same time, the criminal youth of the village also carried out raids in the company of Romanian soldiers on the same pretext.

My wife and I (both of us having experienced the scrupulous observance of the law on the keeping of weapons by both groups) succeeded, with the permission of the Romanian authorities (and this was not done free of charge), to become consultants to the ghetto hospital; we managed to prolong our stay in Romanovka until February 11, 1942, when the final column was dispatched.

The ghetto hospital, where we saw the most extreme cases of frostbite and exhaustion, was evacuated. Patients who had managed to stay alive were transferred to the water transport workers' hospital.

The assembling point for dispatch to the ghetto was the textile mill, a cold, damp structure without windows or doors, from which, after spending the night, one was sent to the village schoolhouse, which conceded nothing to the factory in its lack of sanitation.

At midday on February 11 our column moved to Sortirovochnaya, where we were transferred to the train that took us in freight cars to Beryozovka station by ten o'clock that evening.

Our subsequent journey resembled earlier marches. We trudged with packs on our backs for twenty-five kilometers into the dark, cold night, along a road covered in some places with deep snow, in some with ice. Along the way, we had to throw away many of the things that we had brought with us. The rest stops that we were allowed by our guides (in exchange for bribes, naturally) were very brief. We also came across the frozen bodies of our comrades in suffering. This, in turn, inspired the disheartening idea that such a fate awaited us as well.

After our group reached Sirotskoe on February 12, we were given the chance to rest. I do not know how many comrades we lost along the way.

Our experience in Sirotskoe, which many other Jews were forced to endure at the hands of the Romanian occupiers, was the most difficult one for me personally.

The savagery displayed toward my wife and me surpassed anything that I had seen and gone through on my way to the ghetto, sown as it was with nothing but thorns. Romanian soldiers looted us in such a merciless, cynical fashion on the night of February 13 that we arrived in Domanyovka as paupers.

We arrived in Domanyovka on February 14, 1942; this was the final destination for the majority of the last group of Jews expelled from Odessa. Small groups from this final convoy remained in the villages of Mostovoe and Lidievka, where our group spent the night of February 13 in a pigsty. Domanyovka, where my wife and I lived out our exile in a ghetto for almost two and a half years, will not occupy the foremost place in the history of the cruelties perpetrated by the Romanians against the Jews. It is true, though, that here, too, local residents witnessed the shooting of totally innocent people.

It is claimed that the total number of Jews murdered in Domanyovka reached as high as fifteen thousand. The record number, however, is cited by the inhabitants of the village of Bogdanovka, where the number of those shot or burned alive reached almost sixty thousand. The cruelty displayed in such a fashion continued until February 1942, until one or two days before our arrival, when an order was issued forbidding the physical destruction of the Jews. Such an understanding, however, in keeping with the thinking of Romanian officials, did not include such deprivations as cold and hunger, which could not fail to cause physical destruction. Incidents of shootings took place even after the publication of this order, but they were isolated, and the Romanians blamed them on German colonists.

With regard to the living conditions in which most of the ghetto exiles were placed, it would be hard to imagine any more conducive to the physical destruction of a living human being. The right to live in private apartments was enjoyed by only a few Jews in Domanyovka. The majority were offered half-ruined buildings with neither windows nor doors, barns, or cowsheds, to live in. If one adds to that overcrowding and malnutrition, then it becomes easy to understand the frightful prevalence of illness and the high death rate from infectious diseases and exhaustion.

Among the camps producing the highest numbers of physically destroyed Jews—not by means of shooting, but due to the absence of elementary conditions for existence—Akmechetka takes first place. Transfer to the Akmechetka camp was regarded as the supreme measure of punishment. In order to justify the severe measures which were designed to hasten the death of Jews who remained alive—who had already been robbed and reduced to such penury that they were no longer of any interest either to Romanian authorities or to the criminal part of the population that had attached itself to them—the occupiers resorted to the services of the Russian-language newspapers that were coming out in Transnistria, *Molva* (Common Talk) and *Pribugski krai* (The Bug Region), which, not stopping at any foul or vulgar invention, sowed hostility and hatred toward the Jews.

The majority of the inhabitants of the ghetto were easy to distinguish not only by the symbols decorating their chests and backs (whose absence would result in corporal punishment), but also by their clothes, which, thanks to the fact that they had to exchange their more or less presentable clothing and undergarments for bread and other edibles, came more and more to resemble those of prehistoric man.

The outward appearance of a ghetto Jew produced the most painful impression. This explains why, on a summer day in 1942 when the governor of Transnistria was scheduled to visit Domanyovka, all the Jews had to leave the town and stay five or six kilometers away, then return only in the evening.

All the Jews living on the territory occupied by the Romanians (Transnistria) found themselves in ghetto conditions. Contact with any Russian friends was strictly punished. Help, however, made its way illegally from there. All of it was still not enough to cover our needs. For the most part, the typical inhabitant of the ghetto remained a beggar.

In the spring of 1944, with the approach of the Front to the ghetto, there were many such people on the territory of Transnistria, and there arose, more and more clearly before us, the horrors experienced by the Jews upon the arrival of the Romanian army. Rumors of the acts of savagery committed by the Germans on their way through the Soviet Union reached us, as well.

Romanian authorities left Domanyovka on March 13, 1944. The ghetto was turned over to the Germans, from whom there seemed to be no escape. Some of us were able to hide in Domanyovka itself. The majority scattered throughout the area, moving from village to village, from farm to farm, or concealing themselves in haystacks. Fortunately, at the time when we were saving ourselves from the Germans, the Germans were not walking away from the Reds, but running. This saved us.

The official documentation of the murder of fifty-four thousand Jews in Bogdanovka was established by representatives of the Red Army, local authorities, and the population on March 27, 1944, and published in the Odessa newspaper *Chernomorskaya kommuna* (Black Sea Commune) on April 30, 1944.

Odessa doctors who perished

Professors
1) Ya. S. Rabinovich — Neuropathologist
2) M. Fayngold — Dermatologist
3) L. P. Blank — Neuropathologist
4) B. G. Rubinshteyn — Histologist

Doctors
5) E. M. Bikhman — Stomach Ailments
6) A. F. Goldenberg — Therapist
7) N. A. Goldenberg (his daughter) — Neuropathologist
8) Petrushkin — Pediatrician
9) Filler — Venereologist
10) Chatskin — Public Health Doctor
11) Brodsky — Public Health Doctor

12)	Brodskaya	Dentist
13)	Varshavskaya	Therapist
14)	Varshavskaya	Dentist
15)	Zinger	Therapist
16)	Zusman	Therapist
17)	Gurfinkel	Urologist
18)	Orlyuk	Dentist (woman-doctor)
19)	Shkolnik	Dentist (woman-doctor)
20)	Kamenetsky	Therapist
21)	Kamenetskaya	Laryngologist
22)	M. L. Chernyavker	Pediatrician
23)	E. L. Chernyavker	Gynecologist
24)	E. I. Revich	Pediatrician
25)	S. I. Revich	Pediatrician
26)	Khuvo	Therapist
27)	G. M. Rubinshteyn	Neuropathologist
28)	Svoren	Malaria Specialist
29)	Shapiro	Venerologist
30)	Chudnovsky	Gynecologist
31)	Zaynfeld	Gynecologist
32)	Guz	Lecturer-Therapist
33)	Kirbis	Neuropathologist
34)	Pasternak	Therapist
35)	Gorovitz	Surgeon-Urologist
36)	Bronfman	Therapist
37)	Goldberg	Venerologist
38)	P. M. Furman	Epidemiologist
39)	Galbershtadt	Stomach Ailments
40)	Fishberg	Therapist
41)	Frak	Pediatrician
42)	Teplitsky	Therapist
43)	Velderman	Therapist
44)	Birbraf	Venerologist
45)	Fayngersh	Therapist
46)	Levi	Dentist (woman)
47)	Levi	Dentist (man)
48)	Bronshteyn	Dentist
49)	Gaukhman	Dentist
50)	Gauzenberg	Dentist
51)	Frenkel	Doctor-Biochemist
52)	P. I. Polyakova	Doctor-Laboratory Researcher
53)	N. M. Moshkovich	Doctor-Laboratory Researcher
54)	Zhvier	Laboratory Researcher
55)	Burman	Doctor-Laboratory Researcher
56)	Mikman	Laboratory Researcher
57)	Gorn	Pharmacist
58)	Elzon	Pharmacist
59)	A. A. Zaydelbern	Public Health Doctor
60)	Kan	Tuberculosis Specialist
61)	A. M. Zamels	Venerologist

with their families, including twenty-four women doctors.

GARF f. 8114, op. 1, d. 959, ll. 1–8; GARF f. 8114, op. 1, d. 956, ll. 165–167. *A typewritten manuscript.*

16. The camp at Bogdanovka
THE TESTIMONY OF FILIPP BORISOVICH KLINOV, PAVEL IVANOVICH STONOGA,
KARP KORNEEVICH SHEREMET, AND VERA PAVLOVNA KABANETS
MAY 1–2, 1944
FROM THE ARCHIVES OF THE EXTRAORDINARY STATE COMMISSION

Klinov, Filipp Borisovich, born in 1912, native of Golovanevsk of the same District of the Odessa Region, office worker, a Jew, last place of residence in Odessa.

Testified:

On October 23, 1941, on the order of Professor Aleksianu, the governor of Transnistria, a column consisting of 25,000 Jews, including elderly people and children, was sent from Odessa to Dalnik, ostensibly for the purpose of registration.

There was no registration in Dalnik, though, and they sent us from there along the banks of the Bug river to Bogdanovka guarded by Romanian soldiers.[36] Many stragglers were shot on the way there, while the rest were robbed by those same guards. Our column, which now numbered about 10,000, down from 25,000, arrived in Bogdanovka on November 10, where we were turned over to the local gendarmerie under the command of platoon leader Melinescu and sent to the sheds of the state pig farm, Bogdanovka. We were kept under guard in the sheds and forbidden to go anywhere outside the camp area. We were given no food. From December 10 to 21, new shipments of Jews—from 900 to 5,000 people—arrived in the camp under guard, from the Odessa and the Vinnitsa regions and from Moldavia.

On December 21, 1941, 54,000 people were in the camp, according to the records of Shoykhet Kopyl, the camp overseer. Around December 13 or 14, 1941, the county prefect of the city of Golta, Lieutenant Colonel Modest Ionescu, came to Bogdanovka.[37] He ordered the inhabitants to bake bread, which was subsequently sold in the camp at the price of five gold rubles for a half kilo. He then took gold and valuables away with him. Where 200 pigs had once lived, approximately 2,000 human beings were now staying. In place of litter for the pigs there remained only the rotten straw on which people lay, while a significant number of people, including the elderly and children, were out in the yard under the open sky. Those who happened to make their way by night or even by day out of the camp area and into town for provisions were badly beaten or shot.

On December 17 or 18, 1941, the police, acting on orders, set fire to two barracks in which there were more than 2,000 people. They were all burned; only a tiny number managed to save themselves. Approximately two days before the shootings, the prisoners of the camp were forbidden to draw water for drinking from the Bug River.

---

36. The described route of the column was roundabout. Rather than directly north, the victims traveled northeast to the Bug and then northwest to Bogdanovka.
37. Golta is the name of the right bank district of the city of Pervomaysk, which is located on both sides of the Southern Bug River.

In the early morning of December 21, 1941, one of the barracks was surrounded and some fifty people were led out in pairs. They were taken to the edge of the woods on a forestry collective. There, they were stripped naked, sent to a ravine outside the collective, made to kneel in groups of ten to fifteen, and shot at a distance of approximately fifteen meters.

Those shot or often only wounded fell into the ravine. Then a work detail, formed from that same group of prisoners, piled the bodies into the form of a cross and set it on fire. So it went every day until December 24, when there was a three-day break for the Christmas holiday. The execution detachment set off for Golta. From December 28 until January 10, they carried out similar mass shootings; at the same time, the Golta prefect issued his hypocritical order to halt such mass shootings. In this way, between January 10 and 15, 1942, around 52,000 people were shot, and within two weeks after that approximately 2,000 more people died from the cold and exhaustion. In all, no fewer than 54,000 people were destroyed.

The property of those killed was divided among the police and the Romanian gendarmes, while a portion of it was transported to the prefect in Golta. I myself was taken up to the edge of the ravine for shooting thirteen times. I fell into the ravine prematurely and then walked away with the work detail in the evening. Six members of my family were shot before my eyes. I was put into a work detail of 127 men who survived. Another detail was formed from a group of 50 women. So only 177 prisoners of all those who had been in the camp remained alive.

This testimony has been correctly recorded from my words. May 1, 1944. Klinov.

Stonoga, Pavel Ivanovich. Born in 1882. Native and resident of Bogdanovka, Domanyovka District of the Odessa Region, worker in the Path of Lenin Collective Farm.

Testified:

Beginning around September 1941, the Romanians began bringing large columns of Jews under guard into the camp they had set up for the Jewish population on the Bogdanovka collective farm and housed them in the farm's pigsties. They were allowed to walk around the village for the first few days and to barter for food, but soon after they were strictly forbidden to go beyond the perimeters of the camp. Those who tried to get outside of the camp area were shot on the spot. I remember an incident when one day a Jewish woman came to my home to ask for bread. I gave her some bread, then she went into the street. A car full of Romanian soldiers came toward her; one of the soldiers jumped out and executed that citizen right there in the street with his revolver. The shooting of the prisoners began around December 21, 1941, and continued on a mass scale until December 25, after which there was a break for the Christmas holidays until December 27. The mass shootings began again on December 27 and continued until January 10, after which the shootings were halted. Shots were heard in the village for days on end; the flames of a campfire were visible day and night and the wind brought the odor of burning human flesh to the village.

The clothing and the valuables of those shot were systematically taken off to Golta in six or seven carts escorted by Romanian soldiers. Worn-out clothing was burned.

This testimony has been correctly recorded from my words. May 2, 1944. Signed, Stonoga.

Sheremet, Karp Korneevich, born in 1910. Native of Bogdanovka, Domanyovka District, Odessa Region, Ukrainian, from a peasant family. Prior to the occupation was deputy director of a state pig farm, at present director of the same farm.

Testified:

Around the end of September 1941, the first group of 640 members of the Jewish population was herded under guard onto the territory of the farm. They were housed in the barn, but before they were put there, the Romanian gendarmes took various things from them. Until December 21, groups of people numbering from 500 to 5,000 arrived daily and were put in the pigsties. Because the pigsties were overcrowded, in spite of the fact that there were more than twenty-two of them, not counting other accommodations, a significant number of the people stayed out in the open. On December 18 an automobile arrived at the camp; it carried two German officers and a third man in civilian clothes. They took pictures of the camp area, including a ravine. On December 21, 1941, an execution detachment commanded by a German named Hegel arrived from Golta. All the laborers were driven off the territory of the camp, while those with necessary skills were isolated. The execution detachment was evidently made up of German colonists since they were all in civilian clothes. There were sixty of them in all.

On December 21, the butchers set about their dirty work. They led people out of the barracks in groups of forty or fifty, stripped them, and then led them to the ravine, forced them to kneel, and shot them with rifles. A large bonfire was built at the bottom of the ravine, into which the bodies fell and were burned. The executioners even competed among themselves to see who could shoot the most people. The mass shooting went on every day from the morning of December 21 until December 24, and then from December 28 until January 10. There was a break for the Christmas holidays from December 24 to 27. During this time, a work detail, formed from among the prisoners who had been burning bodies, made an earthen dam in the ravine so that blood would not flow into the Bug River. The mass shootings were halted on January 10. By February 1, however, another 2,000 people or so died from cold and hunger. All in all, 54,000 out of 65,000 were destroyed. The rest, who had escaped from the camp, were shot in the steppe. In addition to them, 177 remained alive and attached to work details: 127 men and 50 women.

This testimony has been correctly recorded from my words.

May 1, 1944. Signature.

Kabanets, Vera Pavlovna. Born in 1921 in Bogdanovka, Domanyovka District, Odessa Region, state farm worker, Komsomol member.

Testified:

In September 1941, the Romanians began bringing group after group from the Jewish population into the camp that they had opened for them on the collective farm of Bogdanovka; they housed them in the pigsties. All the sheds were overflowing with prisoners. They gave them nothing to eat. At first they were allowed to exchange their belongings for food, but then it was forbidden, and they were strictly isolated. There were around 60,000 people in the camp. Mass shootings started on December 21, 1941, and continued for days on end. They shot them beside the ravine outside the forestry collective, then they burned them right away. There was a pause from December 24 to 26 because the execution detachment went to Golta to celebrate Christmas. During that time, some people from the camp went to the village to exchange a few things for food and to get water. Around December 27, I was drawing water from the well when a Jewish woman from the camp approached to draw water. At the same time, a cart came by in which there were three Romanians. One of them jumped down from the cart and began to draw his gun to shoot her. She did not beg him to have mercy on her, but asked him to let her go back to the camp; evidently she had children there. She was killed there and then, however, and her body lay beside the well for five days.

This testimony has been correctly recorded from my words.

May 1, 1944. Signed, Kabanets, Vera.

GARF f. 8114, op. 1, d. 940, ll. 72–77. A typewritten copy. The original can be found in the archives of the Extraordinary State Commission (GARF, f. 7021, op. 69, d. 342, ll. 70–71, 74–75).

17. Resistance

A REPORT ON THE ACTIVITIES OF AN UNDERGROUND GROUP IN ODESSA [38]

[1944]

On October 11, 1941, the following weapons were left by the head of the Armed Communications Guards Detachment to comrade F. G. Skuli: twenty rifles, three thousand rounds of ammunition, one revolver, one mine with a fuse, three thousand sheets of carbon paper, wax paper, twenty kilos of white paper, a mimeograph machine, and one typewriter.

All of this was concealed by comrade Skuli, with the assistance of the electrician Mikhail Yurkulov (17 Studencheskaya Street); the baker Nikolai Andronov (8 Stieglitz); and the toolmaker Fyodor Sidelnikov (1 Second Vodoprovodny Lane) in the boiler room of a post office (10 Sadovaya Street) for use by an underground detachment in the city.

---

38. This report was presented to the Odessa Regional Committee of the Communist Party.

On October 13, 1941, the leadership of the administrative and economic section of the communications and postal system was entrusted to comrade Skuli. With the assistance of the above-named comrades, comrade Skuli concealed motors and hoses—which had been left in the post office following the evacuation—in the same boiler room.

On October 15, at 8:00 PM, a group of sappers, headed by comrade Major Kalinin, arrived at the post office building. While we provided security under the supervision of comrade Skuli, the following buildings were blown up at midnight after evacuating all persons from the establishments ahead of time: the central post office, the central telephone exchange, and a laboratory complex at 16 Komsomolskaya Street, in accordance with the orders of the front commander comrade Lieutenant-General Vorobyov.

After the implementation of the order to blow up the above-mentioned buildings, when comrade Skuli's team returned to these targets, the demolition team of comrade Kalinin departed in an unknown direction, and comrade Skuli and his group of comrades went underground.

On October 25, 1941, comrade Skuli, in the course of his underground organizational work, came into contact with the sisters Olga and Yelena Kantarovich. By this time he had created an underground group consisting of the following comrades: Mikhail Yurkul; Alexander Kushch; Georgy Buzanov (perished at the hands of the Gestapo, having been caught in the outdoor market with Sovinformburo reports);[39] Yevgeny Stritinin; Feodosy Vladimirov; Ivan Zhuravlyov; Viktor Budnik; Ivan Dovbnya; Fyodor Sidelnikov; Georgy Pozdnev; Mikhail Nikandrov; Ivan Syrtsov; Nikolay Gaynevich; Ivan Prokopovich; Georgy Sidelnikov; and Fyodor Pogorelov.

On January 19, 1942, Skuli learned through comrades Olga and Yelena Kantarovich that there was a group of nine Jews hiding in the cellar of their apartment building. They had in their possession a Telefunken radio receiver which could receive Sovinformburo bulletins and propaganda, which, in turn, could be distributed through the Kantarovich sisters and the group of comrades under the leadership of comrade Skuli.

With the entry of the Romanians into Odessa, they assumed responsibility for repairing the city's damaged communications systems, for which purpose they needed to employ communications workers, including engineers. Comrade Skuli began to carry out appropriate work among these people, seeking to sabotage orders of the Romanian authorities for the re-establishment of communications. He relied

---

39. The Soviet Information Bureau, or Sovinformburo as it was universally called, was created in June 1941 from the Comintern, or Communist International, a few days after the German invasion of the Soviet Union. Its primary responsibilities included supplying information about the war effort to the international press and the holding of press conferences for foreign journalists. Alexander Shcherbakov served as its chairman; Solomon Lozovsky served as the deputy chairman.

on the support of comrade engineers Vladimirov, Shestopal, Vasiliev, Voznyak, and others. As a result, Skuli, Vladimirov, and Shestopal were arrested on January 30, 1942, by the 4th Police Detachment of the Romanian secret police.

In the course of his propaganda work, comrade Skuli made use of radio receivers (in the Kantarovich and Radionov apartments) to obtain materials and bulletins from the other side of the frontlines.

On January 31, 1942, the 4th Police Detachment of the Romanian secret police brought comrade Skuli to his apartment for the purpose of carrying out a search. At that moment they came upon comrades Sidelnikov, who were disassembling the typewriter.

Thanks to a bribe paid to Radionov, an inspector of the 4th District Police, Skuli and the Sidelnikovs were freed. On February 5, 1942, Skuli was arrested by gendarmes upon entering the courtyard of his building and sent to the Romanian secret police office which was located in the prefecture of police (29 Pushkinskaya Street); comrade engineers Shestopal and Vladimirov were being interrogated there.

After interrogation, Shestopal was freed, while comrades Skuli and Vladimirov were transferred to the Romanian military secret police at 12 Bebel Street, where they were charged with blowing up the post office, with ties to the partisans, and with sabotage of the communications network in their role as agents left behind by the NKVD for diversionary operations. One of the pieces of evidence presented against Skuli supposedly showed that he had evacuated his own family deep into the rear.

Following interrogations by the military secret police at 12 Bebel Street, comrades Skuli and Vladimirov were led down into the nearby basement at 13 Bebel Street. Here, Skuli was able to have contact for a certain time with the partisan leader Volodya Bodayev-Molodetsky (code-named Smolny), from whom Skuli learned of the existence of a partisan organization concealed in the catacombs in the village of Usatovo, and also with Pyotr Nikolenko, Pyotr Dobrov, and Ivan Platov.

With such a group of comrades, and by bribing the commandant, they managed to establish a connection with the outside. Newspapers reached the basement; they were read in the cells and passed from the bottom floor to the top and back. After six interrogations accompanied by beatings, Skuli, along with Vladimirov, was sent to the Central Odessa Prison for attempting to bribe Seulescu, the inspector of the Romanian secret police.

As of May 12, 1942, still in the central prison, comrade Skuli was able to contact Belmak, Mogila, and Tokarenko; after bribing the guards, Skuli was able to receive messages and sustain contact with organization members Yelena Kantarovich and Yelena Sidelnikova, who were at liberty. Through them, he received Sovinformburo bulletins and newspapers, distributing the latter in the cells (the bulletins orally). In September 1943, he, Skuli, established contact with comrade Yefim Tokarenko at a secret rendezvous—at the corner of Lekkert and Preobrazhenskaya Streets.[40]

---

40. The report does not explain how he got out of prison.

In December 1943, Skuli concealed four Red Army prisoners of war in private apartments; he had helped to arrange their escape (Lapushinskaya, Prokopovich, Kanonko, residing in Odessa, Second Vodoprovodny Lane, nos. 1a and 1b, and no. 2 Vodoprovodny Lane).[41]

In February and March of 1944, Skuli contacted a village group through Ivan Syrtsov at the bakery, and then in a meeting at a conspiratorial apartment on Lavochnaya Street—the house of the Teryaevs, Tatyana Teryaeva's apartment—where work on the distribution of flyers was being organized.

On March 28, 1944, comrade Skuli and his group (using the password "39–52") made contact with a detachment under the command of comrade Major Volgin, located in the catacombs. And on March 30, 1944, Skuli was in contact with the group of Andrei Renk of the Canal Trust in the same catacombs. During the retreat of the Romano-German occupying forces, Skuli served as assistant to the leader of the Special Tasks Group, working in the catacombs until April 10, 1944.

As of January 12, 1942, Olga and Yelena Kantarovich (14 Shmidt Avenue) concealed four Jewish families numbering nine people in the basement of their apartment. They also had a Telefunken radio receiver in the cellar. At the same time, Robert Kantarovich, having received Sovinformburo bulletins, passed them on to Olga and Yelena for distribution on the outside (after each reception of bulletins, the receiver was concealed in the basement). This radio receiver was used for two and a half years. Olga, Yelena, and Robert forged stamps, passports, and certificates for the purpose of concealing their (ethnic) Jewish origins. For a Russian seal, a Khimpromprodukt seal and a copper five-kopeck coin were used; and Lyusya Kalika devised a Romanian seal in the Kantarovich cellar (Lyusya Kalika, 10 Avchinkovsky Lane).

Robert Kantarovich, with the help of his sisters Olga and Yelena, worked in the cellar on a collection of all the newspapers that came out in Odessa during the occupation. The newspapers have been preserved.

In February 1942, Olga and Yelena Kantarovich were arrested by the gendarmerie. They were accused of being Jewish and of having been left behind by the NKVD supposedly for sabotage work in the city. A search was carried out in the apartment for the purpose of detaining Robert Kantarovich (witness Isaev, 14 Shmidt Avenue), but he was not discovered.

Olga and Yelena were subjected to beatings at the gendarmerie, but were released in exchange for a bribe. As of May 22, 1942, from the moment Olga Kantarovich was transferred from the field military tribunal to the Central Odessa Prison in connection with a new arrest and her indictment following the discovery of material evidence—a false passport and a stamp for her stay in Lvov—more communication between the prison and the outside began through Yelena Kantarovich, who, being at large, received Sovinformburo bulletins from her brother, Robert.

---

41. The report does not mention the fourth soldier.

By means of visits and parcels, which she passed along through Olga Kantarovich, she delivered the bulletins and local newspapers to the prison every day. Once the guards were bribed, the Sovinformburo bulletins were delivered in the folds of clothing, at the bottoms of baskets, and inside dumplings. Yelena Kantarovich also organized assistance to partisans, Jews, and prisoners of war who were in the prison, under the guise of food parcels. Olga Kantarovich then distributed these parcels among this category of comrades.

Through her sister Yelena, Olga Kantarovich passed a large number of messages to the outside, and these messages were delivered to their addressees.

Olga Kantarovich distributed Sovinformburo bulletins within the prison itself through comrades Skuli, Bochkovsky, Dobrov, Borovsky, and Natasha Felyuva, in cells in the first as well as in the second block of the prison. All this work continued until October 25, 1942, that is, until Olga Kantarovich was released from prison in exchange for a bribe (paid to Kormush, the secretary of the prison).

Yelena Kantarovich, being at liberty, distributed Sovinformburo bulletins in markets, in streetcars, beside the prison, and by word of mouth wherever the possibility presented itself, and assisted women in the vicinity of the prison to bribe officers and soldiers to allow visits and to pass on parcels (witnesses thereto are Klavdia Kuchuk, 45 Troitskaya, and Nina Kalashnikova, 1 Raskidaylovskaya).

From October 28, 1942, onward, immediately following the release of Olga Kantarovich from prison, already knowing the needs of the partisans, Jews, communists, and prisoners of war who were wasting away in the prison, she organized, along with her sister, Yelena, the women living in buildings near the prison to render aid to those starving and dying in the prison (one hundred grams of hominy and watery gruel per day were being given out).

Along with Sovinformburo bulletins and newspapers that were arriving in the prison for the hungry, they also brought food, passing it through comrade P. Dobrov, and continued to maintain contact with Misha Bochkovsky and Fyodor Skuli, to whom they also passed along literature. There were times on the days of their deliveries (and there were many of them) when Olga and Yelena Kantarovich, with the help of the women they had organized, in exchange for bribes to the officers and prison guards, brought food and clothing directly to the prison, both to the yard and to the vestibule. Moreover, through the same P. Dobrov, who had learned in advance from Misha Bochkovsky that they were coming, they distributed food and clothing to the starving partisans, Jews, and communists (helping Jewish children in particular) who were brought by Dobrov from their cells out into the yard and into the entry hall by bribing the Romanian police who were on duty at the time.

On December 23, 1942, and February 8, 1943, there were two transports of prisoners from the prison. Olga and Yelena Kantarovich, having learned from comrades Bochkovsky and Skuli of these transports, and having received an assignment from them, organized the delivery of food, clothing, and money for those who were being dispatched, bringing all of this to the vicinity of the prison and distributing some of it there. In the prison, the distribution was carried out through Misha Bochkovsky and P. Dobrov, while in the vicinity of the prison through the Kantaroviches and the women organized by them.

It goes without saying that all this effort to provide material aid, carried out over an extended period of time for the starving in the prison, carried out from the outside by Olga and Yelena Kantarovich with the help of other women and in the prison with the help of Bochkovsky, Skuli, and P. Dobrov, entailed considerable risk and a series of dangerous encounters. There were occasions when Misha Bochkovsky was placed in solitary confinement, when Dobrov was beaten by the gendarmes and the Romanian police (those who had not been bribed). None of this, however, stopped anyone. Comrades Skuli, Bochkovsky, and Dobrov, receiving bulletins and newspapers from Olga and Yelena Kantarovich, who were at liberty, passed all of this from cell to cell, from floor to floor, from block to block, giving support to the starving (witnesses: Shura Raykis, who works at the port; Maria Obodzinskaya, 15 Baranov Street; Yakers, 18 Karl Marx Street; P. Z. Nikolenko, 3/43 Voenny Slope).

In February 1943, materials pertaining to the anniversary of the Red Army were passed into the prison by Olga and Yelena Kantarovich, through Bochkovsky and Skuli; the materials had been received by Olga and Yelena Kantarovich in their home from comrade V. F. Mironenko (8 Uyutnaya Street), who was working in the underground organization of comrade Vasilkov. One set of these materials was taken by the Kantaroviches to Dr. Stoyanova so that the workers of the Medical Institute could read them on a "Read it and pass it on" basis (witness: Dr. Stoyanova, 49 Torgovaya Street). Olga and Yelena Kantarovich continued distributing Sovinformburo bulletins by word of mouth in the markets and in the vicinity of the prison, regardless of the fact that Misha Bochkovsky had been sent to the Vapnyarok camp, and that Fyodor Skuli had been released (witness: Novitsky, 6 Lekkert Street).

From June 1943 onward, in order to establish more effective communications with the prison, Olga and Yelena Kantarovich went to work as clerks in a grocery store that was located opposite the prison; it was owned by Jadwiga Bobrovskaya. Through long-time prisoners whom they knew from the jail—comrades Mikhail Selinov and Mikhail Gabrilian—they recommended their contact and work, which assumed even greater proportions, since Selinov and Gabrilian were permitted to go outside the prison gates and into the shop (for passing on deliveries from the street to the cells).

These conditions made it possible to continue passing Sovinformburo bulletins into the prison, along with newspapers, messages, and correspondence with the outside, and indeed on a greater scale back into the prison. (All the messages basically passed through the shop.) During the time when the prison was under quarantine and was not accepting any deliveries, women brought messages into the shop, and the Kantaroviches, already having connections with gendarmes and members of the Romanian police by means of having bribed the latter, passed on deliveries to prisoners and organized visits (since visits were forbidden), carrying on this work particularly for a group of rural partisans from the villages of Varvarovka and Alexandrovka (witnesses to this: P. Nikolenko, 3 Voenny Slope; A. Savelev and wife, 29 Petropavlovskaya Street; Ivan Katrich and Smirnov, inhabitants of the village of Varvarovka).

Comrade Yelena Zabora was also receiving food and money from the Kantaroviches in the store. She used to come to the prison and pass along to those starving in the prison what she had gotten at the store and what she had brought herself. In addition to that, M. Borovsky (Lagernaya Street, beside the prison) was receiving Sovinformburo bulletins from the Kantaroviches for distribution wherever it was possible. Borovsky also helped Olga Kantarovich rescue Tatyana Zaslavskaya, who had escaped from the prison (where she was serving a twenty-five-year sentence); they gave her new clothes in the store, then brought her to Borovsky's home (witnesses: the lawyer Brodsky, 20 Karl Marx Street, and Savelev, 29 Petropavlovskaya Street).

Along with the work that was being carried out in the prison, Yelena and Olga Kantarovich organized work among Soviet prisoners of war who were in a camp not far from the prison. It was, in fact, to a prisoner of war who came into the shop that Sovinformburo bulletins were passed on by word of mouth. They also passed along food to the prisoners of war. This led to a denunciation on the part of Dimitry Vasilievich at Volunteer Center No. 117, in which he accused the Kantaroviches of being Jews and of carrying out underground work in the shop to the detriment of the existing order. A search was then conducted of the Kantarovich apartment, but no evidence was found, and in exchange for a bribe, the Kantaroviches learned the source of the denunciation from the agent. The denunciation was burned in the presence of the agent right there in the Kantarovich apartment.

On February 5, 1944, Yelena Kantarovich was arrested as a Jew and sent to the prison, where she continued, after receiving Sovinformburo bulletins and newspapers from her sister Olga via Misha Selinov, to distribute the materials among the women of the fifth block.

Her sister, Olga Kantarovich, continued to maintain contact with comrade Skuli on the outside, receiving instructions from him.

On February 29, 1944, Yelena Kantarovich was freed from prison by a prosecutor of the field military tribunal named Colonel Saltan in exchange for a bribe (a certificate of national origin was given to her). But on February 30 [sic; the following day], 1944, the police of the first district carried out a search on the basis of an accusation against the Kantaroviches of being Jewish, but the case was again dropped in exchange for a bribe.

Upon exiting the prison, Yelena Kantarovich, along with her sister Olga, organized the escape of Mikhail Selinov, who during all this time had continued to distribute mail (bulletins, newspapers, and so on) from the store to the prison and back, right up until his escape on March 16, 1944, through Pyotr Dobrov in the first block, P. Nikolenko in the third block, and Soyfer in the second block (shot).

On the evening of March 16, 1944, Mikhail Selinov escaped with the aid of the Kantaroviches. They sent him to an apartment in the city, where he stayed until the arrival of the Red Army. On April 11, he was sent to the lines in the Red Army.

Before handing over the prison to the Germans, the Romanians freed many prisoners in exchange for bribes, in particular with the aid of the Kantaroviches; comrade Dobrovolsky, sentenced to twenty-five years for weapons possession (ransomed by his uncle, Kamenchuk, 10/35 Stanovaya Street); and Timchenko, sentenced to six years' imprisonment for flyers of Soviet content (47 Lagernaya Street). In addition to this, the Kantaroviches helped women make contact with the secretary in order, through bribes, to gain the release of their relatives (witnesses: Valentina Timchenko, 47 Lagernaya Street, and Dragomiretskaya, 13 Lagernaya Street).

In the first days of April 1944, after the departure of the German punitive detachment from the prison, the Kantaroviches left the store near the prison, having transferred the distribution of Sovinformburo bulletins to the outdoor market (by word of mouth in the course of selling pastries off a tray), and this work was carried out until April 8, 1944.

Upon the retreat of the Romano-German forces, an additional six people were found to have been hiding in the Kantarovich apartment for two and half years; these people were afraid of being caught in citywide dragnets or of being either deported to Germany or exterminated (witnesses: Anatoly Kochuk, 45 Troitskaya Street; Andrey and Mikhail Deonchenko; and Kvanin and sons, 7 Avchinikovsky Lane).

In 1942, during the time when comrades Skuli, Nikolenko, and Dobrov were being kept in the cellars of the Romanian secret police at 13 Bebel Street, a political hunger strike was conducted by Lida Mashkovskaya. She was soon freed. The same comrades organized a prison-wide, political hunger strike, which was conducted by Yevgenia Glovatskaya (she was freed by the prosecutor Colonel Saltan) and Alexandra Bantysheva (also released).

In February 1943, comrades Nikolenko and Skuli organized a protest called the "tobacco uprising" following the confiscation of tobacco and matches; everything was returned to the prisoners. In March 1943 all delivery of parcels was forbidden in connection with escapes that had taken place, whereupon, as a result of another protest, comrades Skuli and Nikolenko obtained permission for all the prisoners to buy food with the help of the guards.

After the Red Army entered Odessa, comrade Skuli turned over to the 110th Armed Communications Guards Detachment sixteen rifles, two thousand rounds of ammunition, one revolver with ammunition, one typewriter, one radio apparatus, motors, and pumps for the reestablishment of communications, all of which was concealed during the occupation and removed from the boiler room.

At the request of the regional committee, we can turn over sets of newspapers that came out in Odessa, German and Romanian seals, poems and letters written in prison and preserved to this day, and a forged passport, as part of this report.

Skuli
Kantarovich O.
Kantarovich Ye.

Dear Comrade Mikhoels:

How happy I am today to be able to write a few lines to you without fear of the Gestapo.

You will probably be surprised that I am writing to you. It is very difficult to feel humiliation, but even more so when, over the course of three years, in spite of the risks, you carried on the struggle against the Romanian occupation.

And now they are trying to push you aside. They could have given me an education, they could teach me how to behave, but they could not arrange for me to be born into a different nationality.

And now I have to be patient and see how the work and the risk are being wiped out.

You yourself will read the report, and something of this will become clear to you.

I have a great favor to ask of you, and I think that you will be able to do it. I ask you to send me a temporary pass so that I may come to see you, and then I will be able to tell you more of what I have to say.

If you cannot manage it, then do not harm your position. Thanking you in advance.[42]

GARF f. 8114, op. 1, d. 965, ll. 148–151ob. A typewritten manuscript; the letter bears her signature.

18. The escape of twenty-five Jewish girls from the Tulchin ghetto
REMINISCENCES OF THE PARTISAN FIGHTER GOLDA VASSERMAN
[1944]

In the autumn of 1942, there were more than three thousand Jewish families from Ukraine, Bukovina, and Bessarabia in the Tulchin ghetto. Each morning at first light, everyone, old and young alike—in short, anyone who could stand—was pushed out to work. Antonescu's bandits paid them nothing for this work, nor did they feed them. They had to get food for themselves, even though it was strictly forbidden for Jews to leave the ghetto. When, however, the Romanian gendarmes caught a farmer in the ghetto, they would savagely beat him, then take away his provisions. It was only on the way to and from work that the Jews managed to obtain anything from the farmers or to exchange their last article of clothing for food and smuggle it into the ghetto. Every day, new shipments of Jews would arrive in the ghetto. They were in part people who

---

42. This letter by Olga Kantarovich was attached to the copy of the report that was sent to the Jewish Anti-Fascist Committee. She sent a letter with similar content to Ilya Ehrenburg; it can be found in the Ehrenburg archive at Yad Vashem, vol. 1, p. 152.

had been hiding in the forests for a long time, had made their way to the partisans and had then fallen into the hands of the fascist cutthroats, and in part Jews from various countries in Europe that had been occupied by Hitler's forces.

Every day in the ghetto, some fifteen or twenty people would die from hunger, typhus, bleeding ulcers, and other illnesses. On top of that, Antonescu's bandits, day in, day out, would shoot on the job anyone who, as a result of total exhaustion, could barely drag themselves along. Corpses would lie there untouched, often for a whole week—there simply was not time to get around to it. As for verbal abuse and beatings, even of children, they were the normal order of things.

Fifteen kilometers or so from the ghetto, there were Italian and Hungarian reserve units. At the demand of the commanders of these units, the chief of the Romanian gendarmes in Tulchin would select healthy young girls from the ghetto and send them, according to the official version, to serve in the kitchens and bakeries of the Italian and Hungarian detachments. The girls usually returned after being raped and infected with all kinds of venereal diseases. The majority of the girls committed suicide while still at the barracks, or on their way home; some of them were shot while resisting rape or while attempting to escape.

Each time, the commander would take new girls "out to work." They were led from the ghetto to the commander of the gendarmes, and there they would be turned over to Hungarian and Italian scoundrels.

The selection took place almost every fifteen or twenty days. The things that went on in the ghetto—the desperate wailing of the girls, of their parents—beggar description. En route, the girls, risking their lives, would try to take advantage of the smallest opportunity to save themselves by escaping. The fascist scum would shoot at their backs, and those they did not hit would sooner or later fall into the hands of the butchers and be shot. Only a few here and there managed to hide out in the villages by disguising themselves as peasant girls, or be rescued by partisans after wandering for a long time in the forests.

I belong to the latter category.

I, along with twenty-five Jewish girls, was selected to be sent "out to work" in the Hungarian and Italian reserve units. We were led by two soldiers, a Hungarian and an Italian. The road led through a swamp over narrow bridges. More by glances than by words, Zhenya Fuks, Sore Vital, Klara Meydler, and I made the unanimous decision to shove these scoundrels into the swamp and to run. Unfortunately, the plan only partially succeeded. One soldier was immediately sucked under by the swamp, but the other managed to pull himself out. He grabbed hold of a rotten stump and began to fire at us as we ran. One of the girls, Blyuma Krieger, was hit by a bullet as she was crossing the bridge. She fell into the swamp and was sucked under. The soldier had fired all his bullets. When he set about reloading, we rained a hail of stones on him. He lost his balance and fell, but this time was unable to grab hold of the stump; it was too far from him, and he was sucked into the bog.

We wandered for two weeks in the woods around Tulchin, eating berries and other things that grew in the forest. After that, we found our way to some godforsaken village, but we decided not to enter it; you could hear the roar of cars and tanks. In the fields adjoining the woods, we gathered potatoes and corn on all fours while steadily going deeper and deeper into the forest. We were found, barely alive, by the scouts of a partisan detachment and saved from sure starvation. Of the wounded girls, only Berta Kimelman was still alive. Sonya Fuks and Regina Zalkind died from loss of blood.

Sima Khabad from Sikureny, Roza Grinberg from Chernovitsy, and Leah Kuperman from Kishinev all died heroically in the ranks of the partisans. All three of them were twice decorated. Regina Kotesman, Khannah Beker, Lili Shekhter, Sonya Kurtz, and Golda Vasserman also received the highest decorations and now live in different cities of the Soviet Union, where they are carrying on their studies in Soviet institutions of higher education.

GARF f. 8114, op. 1, d. 959, ll. 194–196. A typewritten manuscript. The text was originally written in Yiddish.

19. Mama, save me!
A LETTER FROM BLYUMA ISAAKOVNA BRONFIN, KHMELNIK, VINNITSA REGION, TO ILYA EHRENBURG
[1944]

Dear Comrade Ilya Ehrenburg:

I received your letter in which you ask me to write down what I experienced during the German occupation. Comrade Ehrenburg, it would be difficult for me to describe what I went through, since all the horrors that I saw with my own eyes cannot be told.

I shall begin with January 9, 1942. Early that morning, we, the Jews, were surrounded by Ukrainian police and an SS detachment. A panic began, no one could grasp what awaited us. Around eight in the morning, the local police and the Germans went on a rampage: they smashed windows, fired their guns, and finally began driving people from their homes. They formed them into groups and drove them out into the pine forest. I did not know what to do or where to go with the children. I hid my older son, Misha. My three-year-old, Isaiah, and I were beaten and driven out onto the street, where I saw an awful sight. Corpses were strewn everywhere, the snow was red with blood, the barbarians were running around and shouting like wild animals: "Beat the kikes! *Jude kaput!*" Then they fired into the crowd. They only had to see a small child before throwing themselves upon it and cutting it to pieces with daggers. The cries of the children: "Mama, I'm afraid, Mama, hide me!" ring in my ears to this day.

When they had gathered about two hundred people together, they drove us into the pine forest. The whole way they were beating and shooting anyone who even thought to step out of the crowd. A large pit had been dug in the forest, and a mound of clothing was lying to one side. One by one, people were forced to undress, then take their places on the edge of the pit, where a burst of machine gun fire awaited them. It was a dreadful scene: the wild cries of the children and the moans from the pit of those who had been shot made me think about escaping. I grabbed my terrified son by the hand and broke into a run, thinking that they would quickly kill me. But a heavy snowfall helped me. I ran, not knowing where, and felt as if my strength would leave me at any moment, and that I would fall with my child and freeze to death in an open field since there was a heavy frost. But just then, I spotted a broken-down, empty barn. I made my way up to the loft, wrapped my headscarf around my child, and sat there like that until the evening of January 11. That evening I decided to go back into town to see if my older son was still alive. With great effort, I managed to get across the stream unnoticed by the barbarians, who were standing guard by the bridge.

Late that evening, I found myself back in my apartment. The windows were smashed, as they were everywhere. The door was open and everything had been looted down to the last coin. I did not find my son. On the morning of January 12, I was spotted in the building by a woman named Kurta, who was coming by regularly to steal, and who turned me over to the local police. They led my child and me to the station. On the way there, I met a Russian woman of my acquaintance named Lunina, who was carrying a large sack full of things on her shoulders, and who asked me: "Where are they taking you, to the women's section?" Then she burst into loud laughter, at the same time winking at the policeman, Zhuk, who was escorting me. After that came two powerful blows of a gun butt to the back of my head, and blood poured from my nose and mouth. My poor little boy looked at me and asked: "Mama, are you hurt?" And he burst into tears. By the way, Lunina is in Khmelnik at this moment, working for a distribution center for privileged bureaucrats. During the German occupation, she worked for the gendarmes.

I was thrown, covered in blood, into a cell. I made the acquaintance of people who were just as unfortunate as I was. I stayed at the police station from January twelfth until the fifteenth, and what I saw there cannot be put into words. I cannot imagine anyone who could describe this persecution. They would not let us sit down. Every ten minutes the local police and the Germans would turn up and take people out to work, shouting: "Come out, you kike!" They would go into a cell, set up a phonograph, and put on a record of a popular Jewish tune, and they made people run around a table to this music where policemen were standing with rubber whips. They beat them unconscious. After that, they poured water over them and tossed them back into the cell. The cries and moans could be heard all around. Children were crying, asking for food. The Germans would come with bread and ask: "Who wants to eat?" The children, of course, would rush up to them to ask for bread, but all they got was a beating from their nightsticks. In the evening, the Germans and the local police would come, select young women, and then take them away only to throw them back in the cell after torturing and abusing them.

On January 15, I managed to escape from the police station with my child. On January 16, they shot all the suffering Jews in the station house. From January 16, 1942, until June 12, I lived on a Jewish street set aside for specialists. We lived in constant fear the entire time. On June 12, an SS detachment, along with the local police, surrounded the ghetto; on that day, they killed 320 people, for the most part the elderly, women, and children: my child and I were hidden in a secret place dug underground. After this pogrom, I spent most nights out in the fields, but when the cold weather came, I was forced to go home, that is, to the ghetto, where I stayed until March 1943. A pogrom began on March 8 and lasted a whole month. The barbarians wanted to use this pogrom to wipe out all the Jews in Khmelnik.

My child and I crossed the river by night. Soaking wet, I hid out in a haystack in a field, where I stayed without food for three days. On the fourth day, at night, I felt that my strength was leaving me. My child began to beg me: "Mama, save me, I want to eat!" I decided to walk, where, I did not know. I walked without any hope of finding shelter. At the first crossing, I was met by a man who said to me: "I understand everything. Come with me, but be quiet about it." I was terribly frightened, but there was no other way out for me, so I followed him. He brought me to a little house and knocked at the door. The door was opened by a woman who looked at me in surprise, as if to say, who are you, you poor dear? They let us into the house, gave us food, warmed us up, and allowed us to stay the night. My child and I lived at the home of this man—Ivan Alexandrovich Bartkevich—until April 20, and then I was forced to leave, since a local policeman named Alvinsky lived in the neighborhood; he was always finding fault with my hosts and keeping an eye on them.

I went to the area temporarily occupied by the Romanians, to the city of Zhmerinka. In Zhmerinka, I lived in a Jewish labor camp, working for the German firm of Walther-Schiffler. They gave us food once a day. I suffered from hunger and cold, but I lived by the hope that the time would come when we would settle accounts with the fascists, and, finally, the long-awaited day of liberation arrived. The Red Army freed us, the suffering Jews, from the yoke of fascism.

I went back to my hometown of Khmelnik. On June 25, 1944, a captain, who everyone thought had been killed long ago, came to see his father, Voyner, my neighbor. I went to see him. Standing there, I thought: "How good it is to lose, and then to find." At that point, my neighbor's daughter ran in and said: "Auntie Blyuma, go home. Your boy's arrived!" I did not know what boy she meant, but I ran home. And what did I see? There in the kitchen stood a boy, my son, Misha, whom I had lost on January 9, 1942, a ragged, barefoot shepherd. When he saw me, he only managed to say: "Mama, my happiness!" then passed out. In general, I am not able to put our meeting into words. There would hardly be enough colors in the whole world to paint a picture of it. After a few days, when he had calmed down a bit, he told me the following story.

On January 9, after he had seen them chase me and the child out onto the street, he had followed us down the street and then decided to take off, for where, he did not know. Since he was ten at the time, he made his way across the stream, where he was shot at. He fell and played dead. When the Germans had gone, he got to his feet and continued along an unknown road. On the second day, he found himself in the village of Staraya Guta. From there, he went on the following day to the village of Roshkovtsy, where he lived like a vagrant for three months until the village elder began to harass him. He had to move on. He came to the village of Dashkovtsy, where the tractor driver Kovalenko gave him a place to stay. He lived with him for a whole year. After that, he went to another farm in the same village because his host, Kovalenko, was accused of contact with the partisans, and he was afraid that it would be discovered that he was a Jew. My boy worked for someone else on the farm as a shepherd and stayed there until the arrival of the Red Army.

When the Red Army liberated Khmelnik, he was afraid to go there right away since he knew that his mama and little brother no longer existed. He had seen us led off to be shot. Even so, on June 25 he decided to try his luck and went to Khmelnik, where he found me and his little brother and letters from his papa at the Front. This is real Jewish happiness! Comrade Ilya Ehrenburg, everything that I am writing to you in this letter is a thousandth part of what I and my son went through. There is no possible way to write about everything.

Now I am working as a foreman in a clothing workshop and trying to work productively for the good of our motherland. The children are going to school. My husband, from whom I receive letters, is at the Front with the hope of coming home soon after total victory over the most evil enemy of our humanity and culture.

I am waiting for an answer from you. In my next letter,[43] I will try, dear comrade Ilya Ehrenburg, to explain the behavior and attitude of the workers toward the Jews.

Blyuma Isaakovna Bronfin

My address: Khmelnik, 74 Respublikanskaya Street

GARF f. 8114, op. 1, d. 960, ll. 79–82ob. *The letter bears the original signature.*

Cities and Shtetls of Ukraine
20. Avenge us!
FAREWELL INSCRIPTIONS ON THE WALLS OF THE SYNAGOGUE IN KOVEL, VOLYN REGION. LETTER FROM SERGEANT S. N. GRUTMAN TO ILYA EHRENBURG
DECEMBER 2, 1944

At the beginning of September of this year, I had occasion to be in Kovel while searching for my mother and mother-in-law. I already knew their fate, but I wanted to find at least something to remember them by, perhaps a photograph or something else. I arrived in Kovel at night. Soon after, when dawn broke, the ruins of the town

---

43. This additional letter has not been found in the Ehrenburg archive. There is only a brief letter from Blyuma Bronfin to a relative in Moscow which was passed along to the Jewish Anti-Fascist Committee.

began to appear in outline. My heart was oppressed by sadness and pain. I had come to Kovel in 1940 and had worked there until the beginning of the war as the headmaster of a Jewish school. What a lively, industrious city it was! And now, ruins!

I walked toward the "neighborhoods" where only laborers and craftsmen had lived, where I had lived too, where my mother had stayed, where my students had lived, but I did not find the place. The inhabitants had pulled down their own houses on the orders of the German military authorities. Not one stone was left standing on another stone. Not a trace of the houses remained; it was just like a wasteland, overrun with weeds as tall as a man. Only one large synagogue was still standing, outwardly untouched, as though it were mocking me. Without even wanting to I entered the building where people had spent their lives, cradle to grave, where people had worshipped, blessed their labors and the fruits of their labors. What did I see before my eyes? A huge, empty two-story structure that could accommodate a thousand or fifteen hundred people. The altar had been pulled down. The Torah scrolls were burned. There were no benches and the walls had been pockmarked by bursts of automatic weapons fire. Two huge lions were the only "living" witnesses to the terrible savagery perpetrated by the Nazis in what had once been God's temple.

In spite of myself, I remained standing on the very threshold, seeing the desolation, the desecration of the holy house, and was already thinking about leaving, but I wanted to have a closer look and to examine the holes in the walls: Had there been a battle here? Perhaps this had been a fortified position for the Germans? When I approached the walls, I was filled with horror. The walls began to speak.[44]

It turned out that the walls were covered with writing in pencil. There was not a single empty spot on the wall. These were the last words of the doomed, their farewell to this world. The Nazis had driven people in here, and then, after robbing them of everything down to their last stitch of clothing, had led them out naked to be shot somewhere outside of Kovel, in the city cemetery, in the swamps or forests, or maybe in Majdanek, which had a direct rail connection to Kovel. They had also killed people right here, those who were too weak, or who had cursed their murderers. My heart began pounding, and it ached. I had seen a lot of sadness, had been through the whole of the Great Patriotic War from day one, had seen the grief and suffering of evacuated [sic] people, stretching their hands out to us, pleading with us not to go, not to leave them, when we were forced to retreat. I had seen many towns and villages burned down by the Germans. I remained firm, I knew that we would be back, that we would drive out the Germans and pay them back for everything and for everyone. But now I could no longer contain myself. Perhaps my mother's last

---

44. The Jews of Kovel were destroyed on August 19, 1942. Many of them were herded into the Great Synagogue and from there were taken in groups to their deaths. It was only then that the farewell inscriptions were scrawled on the walls. They number about ninety-five. The full text of all the inscriptions can be found in the *Memorial Book for the Jews of Kovel* (Tel-Aviv, 1957), pp. 487–498.

pleas were here? I began to read the inscriptions carefully. I was hurrying because I could feel my legs giving way, while tears were choking me and getting in the way of my reading. I had been strong for three and half years of war, then I burst into tears. Somehow, the walls made me feel ashamed, as though they were saying or thinking about me: "You went away and left us. You did not take us with you. You knew that this would happen to us and you left us all alone."

The inscriptions were packed so closely together that each writer had tried to draw a line around their own so as to make their cry for help, for vengeance, stand out the more strongly. They were written in different languages: in Yiddish, Polish, and Russian. In every inscription, the words for revenge—"*Nekome!*" [Yiddish], "*Pomsti!*" [Polish (sic)] and "*Otomstite!*" [Russian] were written clearly. I did not find an inscription from my mother: either I could not find it or she had joined in these calls silently.

The names of entire families were written out, dates of executions, and words addressed at the heads of the inscriptions to various people who had managed to get away and join the partisans or the Red Army, or who had been driven by Polish reactionaries out of their own country to far-away America, Palestine, or other countries, with the slogan "Kikes to Palestine!" In every inscription were the words "Avenge us!"

Here are some of their words:

In Yiddish: "Leyb Sosna! Know that they killed all of us. Now I'm going with my wife and children out to die. Be well. Your brother Avrum. August 20."

"Dear Sister! Maybe you managed to save yourself, but if you're ever in the synagogue, read these words. I'm in the synagogue and waiting for death. Be happy, and survive this bloody war. Remember your sister. Polya Friedman."

"September 21 Bar Khana, Bar Zeidik, Avrum Segal, Petl Segal, Falik Bar—they died eight weeks ago along with their brother-in-law. David Segal."

"Ida Soyfer, Zelig Friedman, Friedman with wife and children. Tserun Leyzer with his daughters and Sroul Katz died at the hands of the German murderers. Avenge them!"

"Gitl Zafran from 6 [. . .][45] Street, Rina Zafran had her throat cut on Thursday, August 19, 1942. Take revenge!"

In Polish:

"Borya Rosenfeld and wife Lama died August 19, 1942."

"August 20, 1942, Zelik, Tama, Jela Kozen perished. Avenge us!"

"*Nevinna krev zhidovska nekhai splyne na vshistskikh nemtsov. Pomsty! Pomsty! Nekhai ikh porun zabie. Kurva ikh mat.*" [Let innocent Jewish blood pour down on all Germans. Avenge us! Avenge us! May lightning strike them. Their mothers are whores.] Srul Vaynshteyn. August 23, 1942." (I reproduce it in Polish for better effect, and also because I simply do not know some of the words.)

---

45. The name of the street is illegible.

In Russian:

"Liza Rayzen, wife of Leybish Rayzen. The dream of every mother, to see her only daughter Beba, living in Dubno, did not come true. With great pain she goes to her grave."

There were no inscriptions on the second floor, in the corridors, or on the stairs. Obviously, the condemned had not been allowed up there, so that they could not throw themselves from the windows or from the balconies.

Let our allies know that these calls are also addressed to them and to their armies and peoples, since the fathers and mothers, brothers and sisters, sons and daughters of those who died at the hands of Hitler's people are in their midst. Let the Polish reactionaries in London know that they are the accomplices of these beasts, that they supported Hitler. They let him into their country and they carried out their disgusting antisemitic policies, disarming the people against Hitler.

Let the whole world know that they are being called to vengeance, that Lady Gibb [46] is a fifth and maybe a sixth column that is preparing a new war.

I still do not know the whole story of the Kovel tragedy, but I know that it will be a tragedy for many nations and for humanity if mercy triumphs on behalf of the murderers.

Let Lady Gibb know that no diplomatic notes, no conferences, congresses, committees, societies, white, brown, or black books will save the world and humanity from a new war and from barbarism, but that it is only by fire that we must smoke out, burn out the thieves' dens, only with "Katyushas" and love for humanity.

Let Lady Gibb also know that Hitlerism is not just a weapon against the Jewish people, but against her own.

GARF f. 8114, op. 1, d. 960, ll. 6–9. A typewritten manuscript.

21. The fate of the Jews of the shtetl of Yedintsy, Khotin District, Chernovitsy Region [47]
FROM A LETTER BY RAKHIL FRADIS-MILNER TO RAKHIL KOVNATOR
SEPTEMBER 25, 1944 [48]

---

46. In the fall of 1944, just as Soviet troops were about to enter German territory, the prominent Quaker Lady Dorothy Gibb appealed to Ehrenburg to leave justice to God and stop calling for revenge against the Germans. Ehrenburg included her letter in a column in *Krasnaya zvezda* on October 15, 1944, which provoked a deluge of mail to her English village from Soviet troops who shared Ehrenburg's thirst for justice. See the pamphlet *Soviet Russia Today* (December 1944), pp. 9–10.
47. Beginning in 1941, Yedintsy was in the Moldavian SSR. Today it is in the Republic of Moldova.
48. A portion of this letter was used in *The Black Book*, pp. 70–76. Rakhil Fradis-Milner was able to move to Israel in 1960. She sent her first letter to Ilya Ehrenburg in 1944, when she provided biographical information about herself and her family; see Ehrenburg archive, vol. 1, pp. 108–117. The reworked text of this letter, entitled "Shura's Mother," along with the signature of Rakhil Milner, can be found there as a typewritten manuscript, pp. 119–122.

Dear Comrade Kovnator!

I received your letter and am hurrying to reply, with gratitude for your attentive consideration toward my family.

On July 5, 1941, the enemy occupied the shtetl of Yedintsy in Khotin County. The people were caught unawares, having neither the time nor the opportunity to get away. Until July 28, savage terror reigned in the shtetl, during which eight hundred people were shot and numerous young girls, practically children, were raped, and this is without even mentioning the cruel beatings and the plundering. On July 28, the entire Jewish population was driven out of the shtetl; the Jews of neighboring shtetls had been gathered there as well. My parents, my older brother with his wife and two young children, the mother and sister of my husband, and many other relatives and people close to me were among them. Tens of thousands of people were driven out like cattle, struck with whips and rifle butts, and very often hit by bullets. They drove them without any rest, cruelly, not giving them anything to drink or allowing them to stop to help a dying mother or child. They drove them over hundreds of kilometers from Bessarabia to Ukraine, back to Bessarabia, then back to Ukraine. The whole way was strewn with corpses. Convoy after convoy walked along and left behind dying children, the elderly, the sick, and those who had simply lost the will to live from the madness they had been through; the following convoy would find only naked corpses.

The first victim in my family was Reyza Milner, the seventy-five-year-old mother of my husband. She stayed behind, dying, sixty kilometers from home. Her daughter wanted to stay with her, but they beat her [the daughter] badly, so her neighbors made her go farther on. They laid the poor mother beneath a tree, she said goodbye to her daughter, whom she herself asked to move on, and she stayed there alone. The second victim was Manya, the daughter herself. She was left in the Kosoutsy Forest, somewhere in the Soroki area. She starved to death stoically, without complaining, not wishing to accept any help. They stopped in the forest for several days, and the butchers brought a bit of water and food in exchange for valuables. But now they moved them on farther, and again it was the same scene: screams, beatings, horror and death. My mother, Tseytel Fradis, fell; she had dislocated her knee and was seen lying frozen to death along the road. My healthy, vivacious, active mother who had dedicated her whole life to helping the sick and the indigent, who was an ideal mother, had to end her life in this way. They went on.

The children of my brother went down. His two beautiful little daughters and his wife, Pesya Bronshteyn. They told me that she asked God, when the children fell asleep, that they should no longer wake up, that she should not be the first to die and the children left alone to go through these horrors. My father's two sisters fell with their husbands. The last stops were the villages and collective farms around Bershad, in Balta County. The remains of the convoys were herded together there and housed in filthy pig and cow sheds with neither doors nor windows. Here, typhus spread from filth, cold, and hunger, and hundreds of people were dying each day without help. After a few days, the dead were lying among the living.

There was a well-known dairy farm near Obodovka where tens of thousands of people died. The last greeting that I received from that camp was the following: an acquaintance from Chernovitsy who had been taken away in November 1941 saw my father in Bondarovka. He was a ragged, decrepit old man with a long beard. He was out looking for leeches for my older brother, Yakov.[49] They were the last remaining members of the family. My brother had gone to the well for a bucket of water without permission. They had beaten him on the head for this so badly that he had suffered a brain hemorrhage. Father had been told that leeches were good for this, and he was asking people for them. When our acquaintance told him that we were alive, he could not stop asking: "And Shurik too, it's true, true?" My brother soon died, and my father after him from hunger, cold, and the loss of hope and any interest in life. My brother once had the strength of Hercules, with muscles like iron. I had left my father in 1940 as a healthy, handsome man full of energy and vitality. Shmil Fradis, who had lived such a wonderful life, respected by everyone, who would have predicted such an end for him?

My younger brother, Ksilik, was a responsible employee of the State Bank in Chernovitsy, a stalwart worker, young, capable, handsome, a musician. He was evacuated along with the State Bank, and, as far as we were told, his fate was as follows: The train was bombed. It was his task to destroy some important documents or money. He carried out the assignment and was the last to jump from the train, without any belongings, and fell into German hands. They sent him to a concentration camp, transferred him from one camp to another, and, finally, shot him in Bar, where he lies in a mass grave. I am writing about all of this, and my heart is like a stone. It seems to me that if they had sliced open my heart, blood would not have flowed. You ask what we are doing. We both work, my husband is an engineer in the state transport authority, while I am the manager of a pharmacy in a railroad hospital. At the moment, we are not having an easy time of it materially. We have been in Chernovitsy for only three months. My husband finds himself in a collective which is still organizing; its staff has not yet been confirmed, and for three months he has yet to receive a ruble in salary. I started work, but a few days later the hospital shut down for repairs, so now I am working part-time. I am sending you a photograph of my son, but I do not have one of the people who saved him. I will write to them and ask them to send you one directly, if they can manage it.

I want to describe a few more episodes and scenes for you from the German concentration camp worthy of the pen and the movie screen of, naturally, greater specialists than I.

---

49. Many people still treated illnesses by applying leeches.

Our friend, David Lerner, from Yedintsy, along with his wife, his six-year-old daughter, and some of his wife's relatives, the Axelrods, were in the village of Chukov, four kilometers from our camp. During the killing of children in September, they managed to hide the little girl in a sack. The girl was clever and quiet, and she was saved. Over the course of three weeks, the father took the little girl to work with him, and the child lived in the sack the whole time. After three weeks, that beast Genig[50] came to their place to steal some valuables. He went up to the bag and gave it a kick; the little girl shrieked and was discovered. Vicious spite took hold of the murderer. He beat the father, beat the child, and took all their belongings, leaving the whole family with almost no clothes. Still, he did not kill the little girl. She remained in the camp and spent the whole winter in mortal fear, expecting death any day. On February 5, during a second Aktion, the little girl was taken along with her grandmother. The child was seized by a mad fear. She screamed so much on the sled along the way that her little child's heart could not take it and gave out. The child was carried to the common grave already dead in the arms of her grandmother. The local police who were present during the Aktion told us this story. The mother lost her mind after finding out what happened. She was shot. The father and the rest of the family were killed shortly after.

In Nemirov, there were two old men from Chernovitsy with us, Morgenshtern and Vizel. Old, helpless, alone, they soon became infested with lice and lay by themselves in the straw. One of them was so weak that he soon died. When they came to bury them, there was an order to take them both. Poor Vizel begged, pleaded, promised to clean himself up. With a gentle smile, he was ordered to turn around; they shot him in the back of the head and both were thrown into the common grave.

The Zarudnitsy camp.[51] Jews from Pechora were taken there. It was also a death camp, but from hunger and disease. The healthier and younger ones were taken from there, while the remainder stayed in Pechora. In this way, they tore mothers away from their infant children, children away from their aging parents, wives from their husbands, and so on. These people, who had already spent a year in the camp, were in a dreadful state, without any belongings or money. On February 1, 1943, I came to the camp to visit with the sick, and this was the scene that met my eyes: people with dull faces that had lost all human expression, who were covered by rags, barefoot, with bodies tormented by scabies and with the most varied kinds of sores that medicine never meets with in normal times, who were sitting on the floor in some tatters or other, anxiously picking off lice. They were so occupied with this work that they barely paid attention to my arrival; only those who were in particular need of my help got to their feet. And suddenly, there was a rush, there were shouts, people were running, their eyes gleaming, some were crying. What was

---

50. Genig was the head of the German police unit and of the concentration camp in the region.
51. The village of Zarudnitsy, Zhitomir Region.

going on? They had brought some bread. Just picture it, they were giving a whole loaf to each person. This was something new; salvation is probably near, the unfortunates thought. It turned out that our good-hearted, efficient Germans, knowing that the Aktion would take place on February 5, and that in a few days it would be impossible to know the precise quantity of bread that was needed, and that since it would be necessary to make the calculation, had given an advance on the total amount of bread. We found this out after the tragedy.

After February 5, they took us, too, to this camp.

A severe winter dawn, it was still dark outside, when they drove us out to work with whips. The unfortunates bound sacks over the decrepit shoes on their feet with straw, so as not to lose their feet to frostbite. They put old blankets on their heads and wound them around.[52]

GARF f. 8114, op. 1, d. 960, ll. 362–364ob.

22. The boy from Berdichev
THE STORY OF KHAIM ROYTMAN[53]

They named me Misha Ostapchuk. But I am Khaim Roytman. I come from Berdichev. I am now thirteen years old. The Germans killed my father and my mother. I had a younger brother named Borya. A German killed him with a submachine gun, right before my eyes. It was awful, the earth shook!

I was standing on the edge of the pit, waiting. Any second now they are going to shoot. A German came up to me, squinting. And I point for him: "Look, a watch." There, on the ground, a bit of glass was glinting. When the German went to pick it up I took off running. He blazed away after me with his submachine gun, putting a hole in my cap. I ran, ran, and then collapsed. Then I do not remember what happened. An old man picked me up, Gerasim Prokofevich Ostapchuk. He said to me: "Now you're Misha, my son." He had seven of his own and I became his eighth.

One time, the Germans came around, drunk, and started to yell. They noticed that I was dark. They asked Gerasim Prokofevich: "Whose is he?" He said: "Mine." They swore and said that he was lying because I was quite dark. And he answered them calmly: "It's because he has the looks of my first wife. She was a gypsy."

When Berdichev was liberated, I went to the city. I found my older brother, Yasha. He had escaped as well. Yasha is big; he is sixteen, and he is fighting. When the Germans left, Yasha found the scoundrel who had killed our mother, and shot him.

Khaim Roytman

GARF 8114, op. 1, d. 962, l. 170. A typewritten manuscript.

---

52. The continuation of her letter has not been found.
53. This story is used in Vasily Grossman's essay "The Murder of the Jews of Berdichev," which can be found in *The Black Book*, pp. 12–20.

23. At the family grave
The fate of the Jews of the shtetl of Chudnov, Zhitomir Region
Recorded by P. Zozulya
February 15–16, 1944

On the territory of our beloved Old and New Chudnov and its surrounding areas, 5,500 people of the shtetl population, for the most part women, children, and the elderly, were savagely tortured and exterminated, buried in pits.

From the stories of eyewitnesses, I learned that the first victim was the town rabbi, the eighty-seven-year-old Iosif Yakovlevich Mosuk, killed on September 8, 1941, just before evening (on a Friday, it would seem). They mocked this God-fearing old man by forcing him to put on religious garb, then arranged for two old women neighbors to lead him down the street by the hand, with candles in their hands, as if they were going to the altar. To the accompaniment of the rubber whip of the German butcher Zapevaylo, the old women were forced to sing, walking through the whole shtetl until they reached the garden, where, after these so-called "ceremonial" mockeries, they were killed and buried in the same pit right there in the garden, and a cross was put over their grave. Summoning her courage, a girl (named Chirashner, they say) discreetly removed the cross; nonetheless, she immediately paid for this with her young life.

The first mass shooting committed by the German monsters took place on September 9, 1941. Some nine hundred people were summoned by the so-called "special messengers" Eli Sherman and Nuty Zilberman and herded together by the Gestapo onto the premises of the cinema as if they were being sent off to work. From there they were shipped off to the park in trucks filled to overflowing. Lazar Kharitonovich was in the first vehicle (no one knew yet what route the trucks were taking). He was waving his hat, bowing, and shouting: "I'm going to a certain death, but for an idea!" What he meant by this, of course, you cannot understand any more than you would understand a madman. The vehicle made no fewer than forty turns between the cinema and the park. People formed lines in front of ditches that had been dug ahead of time. There was a narrow board over each ditch, and moving toward this board was a long line of no fewer than five hundred petrified people who were barely able to stay on their feet. Standing alongside each other in one of those lines that day were my beloved mother, Auntie Sura, her daughter, and, pressing himself up to them, the brother of Yankel's wife with a hunk of bread in his hand since he had been preparing to go to work. By the butchers' orders, people were stepping one by one onto the board. An exploding round was immediately shot into the back of the head of each one of them. Skulls flew off along with their hair and lodged on the branches of pine trees, while brains sprayed around and bodies quickly fell into the pit. Waiting her turn, Liza Gnip (the daughter of Yankel Simkhes, the shoemaker), went into labor before she even reached the pit. With his own dirty hands, a German butcher tore the baby out of the womb of its mother along with her innards, and then took the newborn by its little leg and smashed its head against the trunk of an old pine tree—that was how he awakened its life—and then tossed the infant to its bullet-riddled mother in the common grave.

The first group was wiped out in this way, although to make the humiliation all the more painful, an entire family was not exterminated all at once. Rather, the husband or wife or a member of the family would be killed. There was no limit to the humiliations visited on those left alive for the time being. Blackened, bearded shadows emaciated by overwork and hunger were wandering around as captives of the treacherous fascists. They forced master tailors to sew, to alter, and to make things from looted goods for the needs of the butchers. The monsters gave the order that skilled workers would not be killed since they were necessary labor, and suggested to surviving widows and those who wanted to save their lives the chance to marry skilled workers. Naturally, all of this was done by force. For example, the wife of Fuka Ulman, immediately after he was killed, registered her marriage to Nusya Britan, since his wife had been killed as well, and there were other similar forced unions. Vyest Moyshe-Meyer, left alone after the murder of his family, could not stand it and lost his mind. There he was, running through Chudnov, filthy, with an overgrown beard, like an animal, emaciated, looking for something. He was not the only one to go crazy: the wife of Libov followed his example. The daughter-in-law of Aron Kilup got dressed up and went to the scaffold singing and dancing. The old man Shmil-Duvid from Guralna put on religious garb and went to the pit on his own, and there were other such cases.

The second mass shooting took place around October 15 or 16, 1941. At this time my father was killed. He had been in hiding from the rabid beasts: he stayed in water for three days, he lay in pits and graves before he was picked up half alive by the commandant's people. They made him work as a servant to the commandant for several days, and then Father was beaten to death. The shoemaker Lizogub had kept him going for some time with food. I made a special trip to see him and to thank him for helping my father before his death. At the same time, the wife of Yankel Freydl was killed along with her three innocent children. I was told that Freydl, her head wrapped in a white kerchief, carried one infant and led her five-year-old daughter by the hand, while eight-year-old Fima clutched at her skirts. The executioner pushed her in the shoulder to make her go faster, and she said: "Well, I'm going." And so she and her children walked their last journey.

On that day, Yankel Barshtman came to the park in a truck. He was holding Dimka, Sara's little boy, in his arms. His wife Sheyndl stood alongside him holding a swaddled three-week-old child—another little boy of Sara's—while Sara herself, or more accurately her skeleton, standing, or rather leaning on them, arrived in the park, and in this way they went to the slaughter. One of the butchers took the three-week-old child, tossed it up by the leg like a football, and shot it in midair. This sort of stunt and others were photographed by the German fiends. They led Khanys, a beautiful nineteen-year-old teacher, the daughter of Itsik Bludy, up to the pit. The soldiers made her strip naked and let her long hair down. They themselves just could not get enough of such beauty. They took her out of the line and told her to get dressed and walk away, leaving her alive. "*Zurück!*" [Move back!] the German beast shouted. She stubbornly refused, demanding immediate death, in order to take her place alongside her loved ones. So then an explosive bullet took away the upper part of her skull, which flew up in the air along with her long, luxuriant golden hair and landed in the branches of a pine tree. It hung there for a long time until it was carried away by a gust of wind.

The third mass killing, and the concluding one, so to speak, came in the middle of November 1941. This time, the eighty-three-year-old Dr. Libov, beloved by everyone, was killed along with his little daughter, as well as Dr. Frenkel and his family. So here is the handsome old man who had saved thousands of lives in his time. He was throwing little notes with the words "Save us, save us," but he was saved from German captivity by another one of those same explosive rounds, and the brains of this learned man, like those of the other doctors, flew in all directions into the branches of the pines and hung there to dry until dispersed by the wind. While waiting in line, Dr. Libov gave a speech in German and Russian before he reached the pit. He said: "I was a Bolshevik and I am going to my death as a Bolshevik." The first bullet toward the back of his head did not hit its target; he still managed to turn around and say: "Well, come on now, if you're going to shoot, shoot straight."

The population almost done with, the rest were picked up, even Khuma the hunchback, Yankel Elis with a baby and her crippled husband, who said: "If you kill my dear wife and child, kill me as well." And he threw himself after them into the pit, where they killed him. I counted twelve large pits in the park, but there were even more of them; now they have been smoothed over with earth and snow, and it would be impossible to tell where they were. But it was not only here that these unfortunates were buried. They are lying on the territory of the old-new shtetl and its surroundings. Seventy-eight people from New Chudnov are lying there. Not far from the center, on the rock, lies Moyshe-pampushka, who, with a cry of: "Listen to me, listen, I have ten children!" jumped from the moving truck and made for the rock, where he was killed on the run. The body of Arka Tutinyker lay on the road for a long time. He fell there in 1942, his body wasted away by privations. Buried beneath the soil of Krasnogurka is Moshko Khanys, who did not die until the autumn of 1943; he was wandering through the fields and was spotted by these savages. Goendek sits in the Gvozdyarenski Forest over an extinguished campfire, frozen and filthy like a beast. Not reaching Guralnya,[54] Aron, who made a living delivering moonshine, was killed on a small bridge in November 1943 along with his wife and son.

And Ruzya Furman, that splendid girl. Ruzya did not hand herself over to the Germans. Along with Pupa Barshtman, she hanged herself in the cellar of the

---

54. Guralnya refers to a distillery in Ukrainian.

Barshtman house and stayed there for a long time, until the residents of the house took a look in the cellar. A dead boy was also found there; it must have been Pupa Barshtman. They buried Ruzya beside the house, in the middle of the town. May she rest in peace. Uka Gilshteyn wandered the fields of the Yanushpolsky District with her wonderful child for some time, and she perished there. But Lyusya, her daughter, by some miracle survived. And so, they all perished, there are no more good Jewish cobblers and tailors [...][55] who used to take their rest on Saturdays in that very park in which they now lie.

I was at the graves of many relatives, close friends and acquaintances. On that day there was a terrible snowstorm. I pressed my ear to one of the pits, and I heard my own mother whispering: "*Kinder meine, Kinder meine.*" [My children, my children.] This whisper was echoed by the evergreen trees, bending their branches ever lower and lower. The pine trees told the story of how skulls had hung from their branches for a long time and of how brains had dried on them. Yes, do not doubt it, in this case, the pine trees speak as living witnesses. In spite of the winter season, even the Teterev did not freeze this year for some reason; currents of blood still seethe in it. They flowed in streams from the rocks of the park and will not let it freeze over. Over these two and a half years, the rocks on either side of the Teterev have vividly raised themselves up and become overgrown with moss. Darkness had already fallen when I made my way rapidly from the park to the spot where the dwellings of these dead had once been. But, sad to say, the 248 homes of those killed had been entirely taken to pieces by the Germans. Now imagine this place, all the streets merging into one; it was difficult for me to make out the location of my parents' house. There was nothing but heaps of stone and clay.

Yes. All those dear to me!

This is not a legend about King Ahasuerus and his minister, Haman.[56] I have described evil deeds and bestial actions of the Nazis in just one little town. This is how Hitler brought about his new order in Europe, that is, in our Chudnov.

P. Zozulya

GARF 8114, op. 1, d. 960, ll. 85–90. The original text of P. Zozulya.

24. Tragedy in the shtetl of Slavuta, Kamenets-Podolsky Region
THE STORIES OF DR. VOITSESHCHUK, THE CATHOLIC PRIEST MILEVSKY, THE TEACHER VYSOTSKAYA, THE WORKER FYODOROVA, AND THE METALWORKER YENIN
RECORDED BY MAJOR Z. G. OSTROVSKY
FEBRUARY 14, 1944

---

55. A few words in the original text are illegible.
56. This is a reference to the Biblical Book of Esther, which is read on the Jewish holiday of Purim. It tells the story of how the Jews of Persia were saved through the intervention of Mordechai and his niece, Esther, who is married to King Ahasuerus.

Slavuta is a small town in the Kamenets-Podolsky Region. Before the war, it was populated mostly by Jews. About a month ago, Slavuta was liberated by the Red Army from the German-fascist bandits. We looked here painstakingly for a single Jew who had survived the shootings. Within a month it was possible to establish a more or less complete picture of the savage treatment meted out by the German butchers on a defenseless Jewish population that was not guilty of anything.

Everything that we learned has been confirmed with documentation and attested to by credible inhabitants of the town of Slavuta, including the Russian doctor and long-time resident of Slavuta, Voitseshchuk; the priest Milevsky; Vysotskaya, a teacher in the Slavuta school; Fyodorova, a worker in the dairy; and Yenin, a metalworker.

Here is what we found out.

The German occupants began their bandits' work in Slavuta with the persecution and destruction of the Jews. All the Jews were made to wear special armbands. They were driven out to do the heaviest physical labor and were often shot there on the spot. Shootings were carried out both in an organized manner, by the orders of the German commandant of the town of Slavuta, and in a disorganized manner—at the whim of any soldier or officer.

In this way, by the close of September 1941, the Germans had killed around five thousand Jews in Slavuta. Among them were women, old people, and children. Those that survived—around seven thousand people—were wiped out by the Germans through mass shootings near the water tower of a military base. This water tower was a silent witness to how, for several days, the fascist butchers mocked and humiliated the Jews whom they had gathered from throughout the town and from surrounding villages and shtetls. Those who were to be shot were made to undress and to lie down alive in pits half-filled with corpses. Victims out of their minds with fear often fell into these pits as though dead. They were fired on with submachine guns. There is documentation to show that many dozens of Jews were buried alive.

The fascist officers overseeing this hellish work would say to the soldiers: "No point in wasting ammunition on them, bury them!" The metalworker Yenin, who was working in the prisoner of war camp located on the army base where the shootings were taking place, tells of seeing with his own eyes how they threw Jewish children into the pits alive and buried them.

Altogether, as many as twelve thousand Jews were exterminated in and around Slavuta. A living witness, the Polish Catholic priest Milevsky, told us:

"Before shooting the Jews, they herded them together into a separate area, fenced off with barbed wire, and then led them out in groups to be executed. Many people were driven into cellars in groups of twenty-five to fifty. Here they were starved to death. In the first days after the arrival of the Red Army, the bodies of sixteen Jews put to death by the Germans were discovered in the cellar of the house at 8 Bolnichnaya Street."

I have not added a word to what the living witnesses to these monstrous crimes, committed by the Germans in a peaceful Ukranian town against defenseless people—my people—told me. No imagination would be capable of making up the things that the Germans did and continue to do in the places that they occupied. May they be cursed forever and ever! Jews! No court, human or divine, would be capable of finding the right measure of punishment for these enemies of the human race. Let not a single Jewish soul find rest until these butchers of the Jewish people have been wiped from the face of the earth and destroyed to the last man.

Major Z. Ostrovsky. Active army, February 14, 1944
Zinovy Grigorevich Ostrovsky, field post office 48828

GARF 8114, op. 1, d. 963, ll. 95–96. A typewritten manuscript with corrections.

25. Tanks were crushing people
ATROCITIES AGAINST THE JEWS, THE CIVILIAN POPULATION, AND PRISONERS OF WAR IN THE CITY OF DEBALTSEVO [57]
THE STORIES OF M. YU. KATZ AND NIKULIN
RECORDED BY A. MUROVSKY [58]
[1944]

The Nazis went to the limits of inhumanity in their cruelties. They are savagely doing away with the peoples of the temporarily occupied Soviet lands.

There is an air of horror in the stories of individuals who chanced to break out of the fascist hell. It was not without trembling and irrepressible anger toward the fascist monsters that I listened to the story of the Soviet citizen, M. Yu. Katz, who escaped from the German-occupied Ukrainian city of Debaltsevo.

"After entering the city," he said, "this band of thieves robbed the population like the criminals that they are. They grabbed everything that came to hand. They didn't even turn their noses up at children's toys or old rags.

"The entire Jewish population was registered and, under threat of being shot, was forced to wear white armbands on their left sleeves. Bloody atrocities against defenseless old people, children, and women—all Jews—soon followed. One night, a drunken band of Germans carried out a terrible pogrom in Jewish homes. They burst into the houses of civilians and beat and killed them. Their moans and death cries hung in the air that night for a long while.

"They loaded the Jews who had survived these horrors into trucks and, as it later turned out, shot them outside the city.

"Another time, after their latest pogrom, the Germans loaded up a truck with a group of Jews and drove them to an anti-tank ditch, where they began dealing with

---
57. Debaltsevo, in the Voroshilovgrad (now Lugansk) Region.
58. The surname of A. Murovsky appears above the text, while his address is written in beneath the text in the hand of A. Ivanov, who edited the text.

them savagely. They stripped men, women, and children naked, beat them, and then threw them half alive into the ditch, piled straw on them and set it alight.

"Infant children were taken from their mothers and thrown alive into the fire. Young people were subjected to slow torture. First their noses, fingers, arms, and legs were cut off.

"Another large group of Jews was herded into a barbed wire enclosure with the apparent idea of imprisoning them in a concentration camp. These people, not realizing what was going to be done to them, watched the bloody preparations of the butchers with horror. With the dull composure of killers, the Germans let loose tanks into this crowd of people who were mad with fear. The tanks were crushing people with their treads and firing their cannons and machine guns."

Comrade Nikulin, another Soviet citizen who had been in German captivity and who was a witness to their bestial acts, told me the following:

"The Nazi guards practice unheard-of humiliations on Red Army captives. As a rule, they separate Jewish soldiers from the others. The hard labor regime of gradual death that they had established for prisoners was meted out to Jews with full force.

"I had occasion to witness a horrific scene of bestial conduct toward Jewish soldiers. One day, for their own amusement, some drunken Nazi prison guards led out two Jewish prisoners and forced them at gunpoint to crawl on all fours and to bark like dogs or meow like cats. The Germans were standing right there, laughing sadistically, and forcing other prisoners to watch this inhuman scene.

"The next day, they forced two exhausted Jews half dead from their sufferings to fight each other, and when they began to resist, the butchers beat them up and then shot them."

This was how the Nazi executioners savagely abused the Jewish population.

GARF 8114, op. 1, d. 953, ll. 318–320. A typewritten manuscript with corrections and the signature of A. Ivanov.

26. Local Petlura[59] supporters slaughtered all the Jews in the shtetl of Medvedino [Medvin], Kiev Region
LETTER FROM A. M. KARMAYAN TO ILYA EHRENBURG
NOVEMBER [1944]

---

59. Simon Petlura (1879–1926) was a famous Ukrainian nationalist and leader of the separatist Ukrainian republic in 1919, a time when tens of thousands of Jews were killed by White, other anti-Soviet, and even occasionally Red forces. Petlura was assassinated in Paris on May 26, 1926, by Shlomo [Samuel] Schwartzbard, who claimed that he was driven to kill Petlura as revenge for these massacres. A jury in Paris acquitted him of murder. The writer of this letter, A. M. Karmayan, is referring to extreme Ukrainian antisemites by calling them followers of Petlura; they were local inhabitants of the town, but in order to show they could not be normal people, it was necessary to call them followers of Petlura and therefore ideological enemies of the Soviet state.

Dear Comrade Ehrenburg!

I have heard that you are writing a book about the murder of Jews during the occupation of our territory by the Germans. I would like to inform you of one incident involving the killing of the Jews that my father described to me in a letter.

In the shtetl of Medvedino in the Kiev Region (thirty-five kilometers from Korsun-Shevchensky), several Jewish families remained. A few days before the arrival of the Germans, local Petlura supporters slaughtered all the Jews to the last one, after abusing them beforehand and, naturally, stealing all their property. When the Germans arrived and learned of this, they shot the ringleaders of the massacre (obviously for having dared to do it in an "unorganized" way, and because they had taken everything for themselves and not left any for them), while the rest took to their heels. I am afraid that these very bandits, who were forced, quite unexpectedly to themselves, to run away from the Germans, whom they probably had been waiting for and greeted joyfully, will now be considered fighters for the motherland. Petlura's people in Medvedino had a solid record of attacking Jews. In 1918, nearly the first pogrom in Ukraine took place there. In 1920, an uprising against Soviet power also took place there, and my sister, who happened to be visiting the town, was killed. It would not be a bad thing to pass on the above information to the appropriate place.

Forgive me if I have taken you away from your work, but I wanted to share my story with a person who would take human suffering close to his heart, and I consider you such a person.

All the best. I wish you health and strength.

A. Karmayan

Field post office 33457. A. M. Karmayan

GARF 8114, op. 1, d. 960, l. 100–100ob. This is the original copy.

27. In the shtetl of Pyatigory, Kiev Region
THE RECOLLECTIONS OF RAISA ZELENKOVA[60]

The weather was sunny. As I did every day, I was at work sorting books in alphabetical order in the library. Suddenly I heard the frightened voice of a young reader, Vanya Klebansky. "Haven't you heard? They're bombing Kiev! Everyone has to show up at the meeting!" His words came out in a trembling, frightened voice. It seemed incredible to me somehow. Still, I closed the library. Ten minutes later I was in Zagrebyonka Street where the meeting was taking place. Afterward, the young people went to a club. It was our last time going out; it was already forbidden to walk the streets in the evening. A week later, the evacuation of other towns in the region began. Day and night, hundreds, thousands of people were on the move, but everyone was reassuring us that the Front was still very far away. I decided to ask the

---

60. There is a notation on the typewritten manuscript of *The Black Book*: "Material rejected by Efros. Not to be used."

director of the collective farm to see to our evacuation. The director helped all of us. I, like the other families, received a pair of bulls. Another ten people came with them. We began to prepare for our departure. I had four meters of cloth; I sold them all and began getting ready to take to the road. Everyone wanted to bring something essential. For us, the adults, it was small children. And that meant that there would be nothing to feed the bulls with for a trip of such a distance. My father refused to go on the journey altogether.

"I'm sixty-seven," he said. "I've been working since I was eleven. What have I got to be afraid of? You," my father said, turning to me, "you're in the Komsomol. You save your life. I've got nothing to be afraid of."

But I decided to stay with my father. My brother, Zalya, had become well-off; he had a pair of bulls as well. But a fight broke out between my brother and the neighbors. They decided to forget about the train as well. Times turned very hard. Every day we were expecting something serious to happen. And while people were being evacuated in cars and horse-drawn carriages, they all kept on reassuring us that the Front was still far away.

The wait for our "guest," however, was not long. On July 16, 1941, two light German tanks appeared. They quickly drove through the center of the shtetl to shouts of "*Befreit die Ukraine!*" (Free Ukraine!) Everything came to a stop, as though there were not a living soul in the shtetl.

A few minutes later, both of the light tanks came back. And then on July 19, the German advance began. The Germans were met by the wives and children of the members of the 1918 gang. For example: Matryona Tasevich, the wife of a bandit; Maria Kravchenko, the wife of an enemy of the people; Gordy Ishchenko, who was shouting at the top of her lungs: "I've been waiting for you for twenty-three years, brothers!" There were other German toadies like this as well. The Gestapo appeared a few days after that. They introduced a new internal order in the village. They posted a decree to surrender all weapons. Zakotynsky, the manager of the mill, who had not surrendered some weapons, went into hiding. The commandant issued an order: any Jews seen on the street would be arrested. They arrested: Avram Strizhevsky, Bunya Klotzman, and Zakotynsky's wife. They were shot as hostages on July 31, except for Zakotynsky's wife, who escaped.

After this, the village elder, Mazurak, announced that all Jews would have to immediately put on armbands bearing six-pointed stars, on a visible place on the right sleeve. With tears in our eyes, we took up our handiwork—sewing on the stars. I decided that I would rather die than wear the despised armband. Since my husband was Russian, I appealed to the village elder. The mayor gave me a certificate releasing me from wearing the star. I was happy to have this document. Later, the entire Jewish community was pressed into forced labor on the collective farm to bring in the harvest. The monthly wage was six kilograms. They worked in fear, not knowing a day of rest. On the right arm, a ribbon could be seen from a kilometer away that it was Jews who were working. While the work was going on, the Tetyev District police would come and rob us. I was working in the fields at the time. I worked up the nerve to quit work and go directly to the town. I went up to the car, and a tall blonde man—the bastard—was standing there: the commandant. I showed him my document. He slapped me on the shoulder and said: "Get something for yourself." I said: "*Danke schön*" [thank you]. At the door, he ordered me to make a cross over the notation "*Befreit von Betraubung*" [released from requisition]. I thanked him and continued to look at this tragedy: They were carrying absolutely everything out of the apartments. The vehicle moved off. I went to work.

After a hard day's work, I went home to bare walls. There was nothing to put on and nothing to cover myself with. And instead of letting us rest, they made us peel potatoes and wash the floors of the officers' quarters.

On August 28, coming home from work, we received an order from the village council: All men fourteen and older were to appear for a meeting at the school at 9:00 AM. I tried to convince my father to go into hiding because there seemed to be some kind of deception going on. We did not sleep the whole night. We talked of only one thing—whether it was necessary to leave for somewhere. Papa did not agree with me. Early the next morning, there was a heavy fog outside. Papa got up, prayed to God, and said: "All right, Raya, give me some clean underwear. If we're to be sentenced to death, then I want to be clean for the next world."

I also started getting myself and my child ready for a trip.

"Where are you going? At least tell me where you'll be!"

I felt my heart tighten out of pity for my father, and I answered:

"I have two options. And, by the way, if anyone takes me in, I will stay there until tonight. Maybe by then we'll know what's going on."

I took a step forward and was just about to leave when Papa opened a cupboard and said:

"Come back. Here in this black sock are seven hundred rubles that I earned with these old hands. If you come back alive with the child, take them for yourself."

I burst into tears and left the apartment. I walked and then began to feel so sad. Why had I not kissed my father? But going back now was out of the question. Dawn was breaking. I went away. It was on that foggy morning that I saw my old gray-haired father for the last time.

On that day, seventeen souls were killed, including my beloved father. It was difficult to think that this hardworking shoemaker had gone off to such an awful death.

Hard months raced by. We carried on working. The depths of autumn were approaching. The sun was warming these unfortunate, ragged, naked people less and less. We began preparing for winter. Several families were living in each apartment. At the time, there were two girls in my apartment who had escaped the Germans in Cherkassy. Sonya Ostrovskaya was registered as Nadya Ivanchenko, and Tanya as Ilenko. They were working alongside Ukrainians and gave no sign that they were Jews. After work, we would get together and speak as usual in Yiddish. But the enemy does not sleep. One evening we were at my brother Zala's place. Nadya and Tanya were there. A village policeman named Fanas learned our secret. That night he knocked at our door. Before I could open the door, he had already ripped it off its hinges and kept on shouting: "You're hiding yourself under the cross and now you're hiding kikes!" He set about smashing dishes and furniture. It was a cold, wintry night. We took off, without clothes or shoes, and ran to my brother's place.

The next morning I made a statement to the chief of police. Fanas was sent to the gendarmerie for his hooligan antics. There they gave him a good twenty-five lashes, and he had to pay a fine of another hundred rubles for tiring out Gokhman, the chief. But this was not enough for Fanas and he carried on with his work. We decided, all three of us, to get out of town. The talk around us was very bad. We were all expecting something serious to happen. To leave with a child, however, was impossible. I decided to have my daughter baptized since my husband was Russian, and to leave the child with her godmother. My plan was adopted by the girls. Tanya, Nadya, and I were doing housework. All at once, a good friend named Ivan Pavlovich Grechany came to see me.

"Raechka, you have to go into hiding these days because they're going to kill everyone. That's what they are saying."

We quit our jobs, gathered some junk together and traded it for provisions, and then began making the preparations for the baptism at top speed. I took some grain and went to the Hitlerite mill. In the evening, the three of us began to think about who the godfather and godmother would be.

"To my way of thinking," I said, "the godfather ought to be the mayor of the village since he has a German seal, and the godmother should be the doctor's wife since she has no children. So then, dear friends, you can congratulate me. I have a baptized daughter. She wears a big cross that the village priest gave her himself. Now the only thing we have to do is get ourselves some good papers."

We were waiting for a long time until our guest arrived, the godfather. Tanya poured the vodka, Nadya prepared the appetizers.

I embraced the godfather and discreetly took out the seal. And then the godfather passed out and snored so that the whole apartment could hear it. We locked the door and got to work. Tanya was writing the certificates while I stamped them. We wrote out six certificates plus copies, providing place and year of birth, and nationality. Obviously, we put Ukrainian as the nationality. The godfather woke up when everything had been finished.

On April 25, 1942, the police surrounded the village. They herded all the Jews into the village council building. The girls were at work and managed to escape. I also hid with my child. I went to see the godmother to leave the child, and decided for myself to go out into the world.

In the evening, I found out that the childless and the young were taken to a concentration camp in the shtetl of Buka. I did not have time to rest at home before V. Sheputa, the chief of police, dropped by to see me. "Why did you take off?" he shouted. "You have to report at the police station without fail at eight this evening." That night, I was arrested along with my child. In the morning, the chief of police came and began to interrogate me about where I had sent Nadya and Tanya, and what road they had taken. I indicated another road, one that they would not have taken. The chief called round to everyone in the police, so that any such people on foot would be arrested. He kept after me for a long time: "You're lucky," he said, "that you've got a kid. Otherwise I'd send you to Buka."

So there I was, free again, continuing to work on the collective farm. My life was very uneasy. I had a vague premonition of some great sadness, but I could not bring myself to abandon my child and go into hiding. I kept on consoling myself with the thought that I would still be able to go wandering through the world. The talk was very bad; they were saying that Jews were being wiped out everywhere. But no one made their mind up to leave because things would have been even worse in a strange village.

On November 14, 1942, the politsai arrived. They spent the night in the school. Alarm spread throughout the shtetl. I thought very seriously about things. In the evening, I went to see my brother; all the neighbors had already gathered there, everyone was frightened. We all went to our homes. But really, who could sleep on a night like that? I pressed myself closer and closer to my child and thought: "Is this really the end of our lives? Do they really need sixty policemen to shoot us? It seems to me that twelve dogs would do." Tired, I fell into a deep sleep. "Mama!" I heard the voice of my child say, "Someone's knocking!" And it was true. Someone was quietly knocking. I opened the door. Before me stood Vanya Pravuk, a policeman. "All right, Raya, get your little girl and come with me." "What, it's all over, then? (That was what I guessed straight away.) "There's no one, it's just a summons." "Vanyechka, be a pal, go tell them that I wasn't home and that I took off for the wide world." "No!" he said. "They sent me, and I have to bring you!" I managed to say:

On a Sunday, very early
The bells are all ringing
And they're already taking
Me and my daughter out to death!

"What makes you think that?" the policeman asked. I wasn't thinking anything, I was just anticipating. Before we reached the police station, I opened up my satchel and tore up the document. I went into the station. The whole gendarmerie was sitting there, and they opened the cell where all the Jews were. My best friend, Manya Aletka, was as overjoyed to see me as I was to see her. We would perish together! "Yes," Manya replied. "Only together." I took out my poems and began to read aloud. Suddenly the cell door opened—they were calling us by surname and sending us somewhere.

"Zelenkova" I heard called. I took my daughter and walked out. Policemen were leading me somewhere. They took us to the big Grebenyuk house. I came upon several families there. It was a quiet, freezing, but sunny day. It happened to be a market day. I was sitting by a little window and watching: They are taking everything out of my apartment and dragging stuff to the market.

Jews were added to our number. Around four in the afternoon, the door opened and they brought in Jung, the interpreter, who had been working for Shefer. Jung stood out from all of us. His boots shone like mirrors. He was wearing a splendid overcoat and had a watch on his left wrist. He did not say anything, but paced around the cell looking down frequently and smoking aromatic cigarettes. Slowly walking around the room, he grabbed his black forelock and softly whispered: "That's it!" We understood him. A wail rose in the room, as in the synagogue on Yom Kippur. The police opened the door and called Jung out into the corridor. They made him suffer there for some time. We could hear Jung's conversation in the cell: "I won't give you my overcoat! I'll give it away where it's needed!" With these words he came into the cell.

"Yes," Jung said to us there, "tomorrow they're taking us out to be shot! Come on, girls, let's go to be shot together! We ought to die a heroic death! No waiting!" We agreed. It was a moonlit night. The moon shone down on all these poor suffering people. All around was quiet, and they were afraid to disturb it. Everyone kept silent as though under a spell. This beautiful weather was not for us. For us there were only a few last minutes of enjoyment. And there, there was the damp grave. The night seemed very long, there was no way to sleep, the only sound to be heard was the wailing of a child asking for water. She cried the entire night. The parasites did not pay her cries any attention.

"Officer," the mother would cry, "please give us a bit of snow, the heat's unbearable." Her words sounded in vain. The bandits had no sympathy for the heart of a poor mother.

Now dawn was breaking. Gokhman gave the policemen the order: Form two ranks. They opened the cell, we found ourselves surrounded. Manya Aletka was holding me and my daughter by the hand. Manya kept on pushing my little daughter so that at least she could be saved. But no sooner had my daughter managed to make a leap than one of the bastards brought her back. I heard my little girl's voice: "Mama! Wait for me! Where's my mama?" Again, the three of us walked on. And in front of us, my brother with his family and Manya's mother with her four brothers. They brought us to the park, to the machine-tractor station, a long barn, where the order was given: "Strip down to your underwear!" Jung winked at us, Manya gave me a nudge as if to say "Time to go." "There's still time, Manya. Every minute counts." "No!" Manya shouted, "If a little flower like Jung leaves us, we ought to go together! How can you look at your brother's blood, after all?" I wouldn't agree to it. Jung took out his papers and photo, took off his overcoat, produced a comb and combed his fringe. He gave the order: "One, two, three" and put one leg forward, yelling: "Shoot, I'm ready!" Gokhman fired five shots and that was the end of Jung. Manya cried: "Raya! My mother's gone!" Her brothers joined hands, went up to Manya, kissed her, and, after saying "Goodbye" left.

Next to me stood my six-year-old daughter asking me to take her hand. I took her hand, but just as soon let it go; I had no strength left. Our turn came. I stood in front of [. . .][61] I had five hundred rubles in my pocket. I threw them at the police and yelled: "Drink our blood!" Then I took off my dress and stood there in just a black shirt. My little daughter was standing a few meters from me shouting: "Mr. Gokhman, I'm not a Jew, I don't know how to talk in Jew language!"

"Let's go, now, daughter, let's die together!" I began to kick off my shoes. Just then, a thought flashed through my mind: I ought to beg! I can't believe that I'm to die. I'm still young, after all, and there's so much in front of me. I began to plead: "*Ich will leben. Ich bin jung. Mein Vater ist Ukrainer und ich bin keine Jüdin.*" [I want to live, I'm young, my father is Ukrainian, and I'm not a Jew].

"Who've you got here?" asked Gokhman. I pointed to my poor little girl, who was crying without stop. He ordered that we be taken to the police. I took the child and everything went black before my eyes. I asked for a bit of snow. Then Gokhman shouted: "*Zurück!*" [Back!] I was very frightened. "Take your coat!" he ordered. I thanked him and was led away to the police. On the way, I could only think of one thing: Who could I bring as a witness? Who would step forward for such a lie!

After all, everybody knows that I did not speak the truth. That's all right, I said to myself to calm my heart. I will live another twenty minutes until they get me to the police station, and there, until the interrogation begins, I will live at least a bit longer in this world. I will breathe the fresh winter air a bit longer, I will at least hear the voice of this little one who has pressed herself to her mother's breast and is sleeping soundly, sobbing all the while.

Do you hear the shots? That's it for Manya. There were two little girls sitting in the police station. Both blondes. They were looking at me with their little blue eyes as though they were looking for their own dead mothers. They had also been spared because their fathers were Russians. That is where she would be sitting helpless, then; no one has any use for my daughter, was the thought that came to mind. Then the door opened and they brought in Manya.

"Manya, you mean you're still alive? Is it really you? You were there altogether naked!"

"Hold on, Raya, it's not over yet. If it weren't for our local scoundrels, we might have wriggled out of it, but there's no way like this. We're still breathing fresh air, though, while our brothers and sisters are being finished off!"

"On your feet!" a policeman shouted. "The gendarmes are coming!"

---

61. There is a gap in the text.

Gokhman appeared. His coat was spattered with blood and bits of flesh. The policemen's boots were red with blood, as though they were red leather. Taratsansky, the Oberleutnant; Pobyl, a gendarme; and Kuravsky, the district chief of police, were sitting behind a table.

I behaved calmly, carried myself freely, and smiled from time to time at my small daughter, who had awakened from all the noise. My plan had long since been sketched out in my mind. The Oberleutnant called me over to the table, on which there was a typewriter, and said to me: "If you're three-quarters Jewish and one quarter Ukrainian, then you're *kaput* here and now. If it's the other way round, you'll live."

The interrogation began: "How can you prove to us that your father's Ukrainian?"

"I am Raisa Zelenkova, born 1912. My mother was a kike. Her husband was also a kike, but he went to America in 1907. There was a cobbler's shop in our apartment where Ukrainians worked. At the time when Mama's husband was in America, she was living with a Ukrainian worker from the shop. When Mama's husband, Leyba Kleter, found out that Mama had betrayed him and had a child—that is, me—by a Ukrainian, he did not even want to come home. My mother told me about this when I was already a grownup. Leyba Kleter brought me up very badly. My mother tried to marry me off to a Ukrainian, and I was doing my best to get married myself. In 1934, I married a Ukrainian, but my husband, Vasily Ivanovich Zelenkov, died from a severe illness and left me with a daughter."

The Oberleutnant said: "You have witnesses to this?"

"There will be witnesses," I said.

They summon Manya Aletka. She started trying to twist her way out of it. The Germans took a break and went outside to have a smoke. Someone had betrayed Manya. Gokhman ordered her outside into the courtyard. A cart was waiting there. He seated her in it, laid aside a shovel, and came for me. "Right," he said to the child, "You—*zurück* [back], and you—*komm* [come]!" Lida began to scream. I managed to beg another half hour from them to summon witnesses. Gokhman agreed to it.

When they brought Manya up to a freshly dug grave, which was indeed still fresh—it was scarcely covered over—blood was seeping up to the surface, and the soil was rising in places from those who had been buried alive. They made a shallow pit for Manya on the top of this grave. Lying in this pit, Manya appealed to Gokhman to let her live another five minutes. Gokhman took out his watch and said: "Eh, you've already lived long enough!" Then Manya began to ask for another ten minutes, but when Gohkman heard that, he went into a rage and reached for his pocket. Manya cried out: "Long live comrade Stalin!"

Gokhman fired an explosive round and Manya's skull flew into bits. Like a beast, Gokhman came back to me and asked whether or not I had a witness. "I'll have one soon," I said. My God, I thought, why didn't they just kill me straight away? Why should I have to bear so much sorrow? But who will go to their death just for me? If it hadn't been for our own scoundrels, I could have thought of something.

"Fine," said Gokhman. "We'll go to lunch and you call a witness!"

I was still thinking—maybe I'll live yet! The Germans went off to lunch. I stayed behind with Lida. Galya Mikhaylova, a clerk for the local village council, a Komsomol member and a teacher, came over to me. "Galya!" I appealed to her. "You've got to do something so that at least I will be saved!" Galya agreed.

We needed to act fast, and discreetly as well. I had Ivan Pavlovich Grechany summoned; I needed to talk to him properly so that our stories would coincide. They hitched up the horses. A young policeman set off for Grechany. "We've got to save one person. You know her. You work in their apartment, in the workshop."

"Raechka!" Ivan Pavlovich cried. "I'm ready. I'll go whether it means life or death!" The horses rushed along briskly. Galya was coming toward me, and she asked Grechany into her office. She explained everything to him. When Grechany appeared in the doors of my room, I was kneeling over my sleeping daughter and crying bitterly. Grechany winked at me, but a tear was rolling down his wrinkled face. He went out. I quickly assumed a happy look on my face. The gendarmerie came in.

"Well, got a witness?" he asked. "I'll have one soon! Ivan Petrovich will get here in about twenty minutes." I was not looking at him. Grechany repeated my story and added something that was very valuable to me: "I worked in America in the same factory with Leyba Kliner, and when I asked him to come home with me, he said to me: "How am I supposed to go home when my wife's expecting a *baystryuk* [bastard] from some Ukrainian." Everyone there burst out laughing. I did the same. The Oberleutnant who was taking down these words looked serious, not understanding the word. Galya tried to explain it to him. Grechany left the room. They summoned Z. I. Sitinok, a clerk to the village council. He said: "I didn't know her father at all." They called in F. K. Slobodyanik, who worked for the council as well. He repeated the same words. Then they asked me what school I had attended, a Ukrainian one or a Jewish one? I called a witness, Odarka Bachinskaya, who confirmed that we had gone to a Ukrainian school together. They called in the chief of police. The commandant also confirmed that he did not know my father at all. The only thing that he knew for sure was that I had been married to a Ukrainian.

It was only then that I felt that I would live. "Well," Gokhman said, "Let's go to your place." Pobyl and Gokhman went with me. There was nothing in my apartment. The gendarmes and the police had taken everything. Gokhman ordered me to come to the police station at 2:30. I began weighing what to do. Should I try to escape or should I go? I began to consult with my neighbors, and then I decided to go. I arrived there. Gokhman told me that I was an hour late: "We wanted to give you your things back. You'll have to go to the gendarmerie." I went to the gendarmerie. "Well come on, follow me, only be quick about it, march like a German!" the policeman shouted. That's it, I thought, I'm done for. My legs would not move at all. He led me into a storeroom where all the Jewish things were. If I had not been so frightened, I could have picked out my belongings, but I asked him to give me back only my bed. I took it home.

It was very difficult to adjust to this new life: I had no one close to me, while enemies were abusing me all around. Just one conversation of theirs was enough to make it impossible for me to live with peace of mind: "They left her so she could live an extra week." More than once I had occasion to curse my life. It would have been better for me to go through that terrible moment of being led out to be shot than to suffer now, to endure cold, hunger, and fear. It had been ten days since the death of all the Jews. I decided to take a woman with a child into my apartment, so that I wouldn't be so afraid; her name was Maria Poganenko. At twelve o'clock on November 28, Fanas Korobkov and B. Sheputa, the chief of police, came to see me. They checked our papers and arrested us both along with our children. Fanas led me along, shouting: "You're not going to beg in German anymore. Today I'm going to kill you myself. I found a kike woman at your place at twelve o'clock." We went to the council building and they put us in a cell. Sheputa was summoned to the gendarmerie. Fanas came into the cell and asked us how we were feeling, congratulating himself all the while on how he would get to shoot me himself that day.

Sheputa turned up in the evening, opened the cell and told me to go home. I decided not to sleep at home that night. I went to sleep at a friend's place. I got up in the morning, and, passing by the commandant's headquarters where my friend worked, knocked at the door.

"Raya, go wherever you want, they've been looking for you all night! They even went to places where you set foot a year ago. They searched my cellar and my attic, and they were saying: 'When we find her, we'll shoot her on the spot,'" Grisha Shulyak told me. Where to go, what to do! I went to the collective farm. I saw the director, Kondrat Ivanovich Dyachenko, standing there. I told him everything. He took me to his office and rang up Sheputa. I stood there trembling. All the workers were hurrying to their jobs.

"Yes, yes, it's me, Kondrat Ivanovich. Listen Sheputa, they tell me that they're looking for Raya again. No, I don't know where she is. I'm just wondering who wants her. The gendarmerie? For when? The twelfth? All right, Sheputa, all the best." And Kondrat Ivanovich put the phone down.

"See here, Raya, don't be in a hurry to go to other villages. Save yourself here." I shook his hand and went to the lady of the same house where I had spent the previous night. She received me and told me to lie down on the stove.[62] I stayed with this woman for two weeks. It was impossible to stay with her for a longer time because she was very poor. I decided to write to a friend who worked in the commandant's office.

---

62. In Ukrainian and Russian peasant houses, the stove was a large structure whose top, as the warmest spot in the house, served as a bed.

I was very glad indeed when Nina brought me some supplies. In the evening, Nina asked me to come back to her place, since Herman was away. I went. "Do you want to see Lyusya Beznalenko?" Nina said. "She's here at my place; they're taking her to Germany tonight, so she came to stay with me." Seeing Lyusya, I was overjoyed. "So this is where the farmhands get together!" I said. Nina went out somewhere at that point. "Get out of here, quick!" a coachman opened the door and said. "The police are coming!" We did not have time to run out of the apartment before shots rang out. And when we wound up back in the apartment, the lady of the house could not find out anything from us. I fell onto the bed where my poor little girl lay and covered her with bitter tears. Lyusya stood there as motionless as death. We realized it was all Nina's doing. There were no police. The fear, hunger, and filth were impossible to bear. I would go to the gendarmerie the next day and say: "Do whatever you want."

"I'm leaving my daughter with you. If I don't come back, give her to the farmers!" I said to the lady of the house. We lay there together for a long time, shivering.

In the morning at dawn, Lyusya accompanied me to the district gendarmerie. I came into the outer yard and stood there thinking, should I go or not? How awful! No, I'll go, I can't suffer like this anymore! I knocked on the door. "Whom do you want?" a little girl asked me. "Pobyl." "Wait here." Ten minutes later, Pobyl called me into his office.

"Mr. Pobyl, I was visiting someone in a village near here. I came home in the evening and they told me that the gendarmerie wanted to see me. So, here I am."

"We don't need you now. We had your lodger brought in and we found out that she's not a kike." I said: "*Auf Wiedersehen* [Goodbye]" and left the commandant's headquarters. Walking quickly and boldly, I went home. Who was I to fear now, after all? I have fooled the gendarmerie itself, I thought to myself. It was with joy that I met my daughter, who was still hiding over the stove. I went home and my lodger would not let me into the building. It was late autumn outside. It was cold and raining. I was standing there with my daughter and trembling all over. My neighbor called me over to her place. Before I had time to warm up, my "friend" Fanas Korobkov turned up. "What are you doing sitting here? All right, then, come with me. I'll show you where your apartment is." And with these words, he loaded his rifle. I heard the cry of my neighbor: "Fanas, my friend, don't shoot her here!" He took me into my apartment and said: "You'll spend the night here for now. Tomorrow, we'll see about everything." He was still trying to frighten me. I found nothing at all in my apartment. What the gendarmerie had given back to me, Nina had already taken away.

Winter came on. There was nothing to burn to keep warm. There was nowhere to take shelter. There was nothing to eat. By day I went to other people's apartments to get warm. I would go to one apartment and Lida to another. There were good people who would give us something to eat; there were some who would not even let us into their apartments. In the evening I would go to find my daughter and we would go back to our cold apartment where the walls were sprinkled with diamond-like clusters of ice. We suffered a great deal that cold winter.

In those unfortunate days, I had occasion to meet up with my neighbors: Khannah Shvarts; the young woman Khaye Kagan; and the daughter of Shura at the home of my rescuer, Ivan Pavlovich Grechany. It was not a meeting, but a farewell, for at that moment I could have fallen into the hands of the fascist bandits. So, I saw the Jews for the last time.

Spring came. The snow melted. The sun rose higher in the sky so we felt more cheerful. On Sunday, April 5, at three in the afternoon, the policeman, Ivan Yaremich, came to see me and congratulated me on still being alive. I thanked him. He sat a while and then went away. An hour later he came back in a drunken state and arrested me, telling me that I could expect a new interrogation: "The gendarmes will be summoning you." "Vanya, my dear man, go and tell them that you didn't find me in, and I'll just go wherever the wind carries me. Oh my God! Do I really have to say goodbye to the world? Can this really be the last day I'll see the sun? Only God and man know how I survived this cold and hungry winter, and now another interrogation. Mr. Yaremich! Aren't you a father to your children? How can you stand the screams of this suffering little girl?"

He loaded a round in his gun and shouted: "Two steps forward!"

He took me to the police, locked me in a cell and rang the gendarmerie himself. Five minutes later, he opened the cell: "All right, get your daughter, come outside with me. Just know that if you run, I'll shoot!" I passed out and did not hear anything more. When I came around, I saw my poor little girl next to me, crying loudly: "Mama, Mama!"

The chief of police arrived and began asking about who had made the arrest. I pointed to Yaremich. Yaremich took my place in the cell. "So, just for a bit of varnish you wanted to snuff out my life?" I said to Yaremich.[63] I went home.

The next day, Yaremich was summoned to the gendarmerie, where he was kicked off the police force and given twenty-five lashes for having arrested me on his own initiative. I could not regain my composure for a long time after this arrest.

On April 15, I went to work at the state farm, pulling weeds. The foreman was standing there with some unknown person who was smoking and looking at me. Somewhere far off was the sound of singing, and the work was humming along. I was trying to pull up as many weeds as possible, and kept on looking at this young man, who was not taking his eyes off me. There was the bell; work was over. The young stranger came up to me and said: "If you want, go slowly, I'll catch up with you." "Fine," I said, "I'll wait for you." I started to think: Could the foreman really have told him who I am? He might turn out to be some fascist who will turn me in. But I decided to wait for him anyway. He caught up with me in short order. He held out

---

63. Russians were known to drink bottles of commercial varnish for their alcohol content.

his hand and said: "My name's Petya Boguslav." "Nice to meet you! My name's Raya," I answered him. He did not say anything serious along the way. He only asked where I was from and if he could come round in the evening.

"Have you got a family?" I asked. "Yes," Petya said, "I have a wife who lives here." What sort of candor is this? I wondered. After all, men are usually bachelors when they meet young women. I thought very seriously about this. He did not say anything else. Our paths separated. He had to [. . .][64] "So I can come round in the evening, then?" "Please do!"

I was already wanting to go. He continued to hold my hand and say: "You and I, Raya, have one path in life. We'll talk about it when we meet."

I walked along thinking that I cannot understand him at all. He dropped by in the evening, but not for long as he was hurrying to get somewhere. He told me that he was working on a farm and that he had things to do.

"We'll get together tomorrow!" We met the next day. He came to see me after work. I started to tell him how I had saved my own life, but I was still on my guard with him.

"Yes," he said, "You've been through a lot. I've already heard a bit about you. But don't hold yourself back around me, speak openly. As I already told you, we have one common path in life." With these words, he kissed me. "Raya! I need a secretary!" Everything became clear to me. "Fine," I said, "Since I don't write very nicely, I'll introduce you to my girlfriend. She used to be a Pioneer leader at the school. Her name is Fanya Kursanivska."

"Fine, we'll get together at your place after work."

This friend, Pyotr Volkov, was actually the commander of a partisan detachment. They wrote their first proclamations at my place under the title "An Appeal." They were posted on the farm and along the Tetiev Road. In the morning we went off to work. Everyone realized that there was some news, and when we got near the farm, we saw that Pyotr Boguslav was standing there and reading a leaflet aloud. They continued to work at my place; they were making flyers for three villages: Pyatigory, Ralayki, Nenadykha. And when Volkov's wife, Boguslava, began keeping an eye on him, we decided to transfer the work to the woods beyond the Azarovets state farm. The work continued there.

On August 1, a round-up of all the remaining Jews began throughout the region. They took every last one, even those who had been baptized. It was the start of a difficult time for me, but I continued to comfort myself with the thought that I would still be able to hide. I was arrested on August 1 by Yaremich and sent to the Pyatigory police station. They put me in a dark room. I groped about in the darkness and came upon a box. I sat there, took my child in my arms, and bitterly, bitterly wept: "On this dark night, I'm saying goodbye to you, my little daughter. I won't see you anymore.

---

64. There is a gap in the text.

They'll kill me. I will no longer be among the living. I'm hearing your voice for the last time. You're calling me. They're coming. Do you hear them, dear, they're coming! Goodbye, goodbye, I'm no longer here! Oh, it's scary how we want to go on living." The footsteps stopped. Exhausted, I bent over my child and fell sound asleep. "Oh, Mama, is that you?" "Dearest! It's so good that you're with me! I had a dream. I'm behind bars again, waiting to be executed." "So why do you look so happy, Mama?" "Today, dear, is a great day of celebration, don't you know that? Give me your hand, I'll give you a kiss. Don't cry, don't cry, I'm coming! I won't forget you, no, I won't!"

"Wake up! The kid's crying and you're sleeping."

I opened my eyes. There was a soldier in front of me. "Oh, what a lovely dream, to see your own mother." "And where's your mother?" asked the soldier. I told him about the conversation. "Soldier! Look over there. That cat walks the streets freely, no one despises it, and I'm sitting here waiting for the cart to take me to Gokhman. Oh, if only I could be a cat." "Right, then." The policeman Chernenko opened the cell. "Get yourself ready. The cart's here!"

The trip to the gendarmerie went very quickly. And just as quickly, I found myself in a cell.

"Officer!" I said to Chernenko. "Tell the interpreter that I'm here and that I want to do the interrogation." "You'll spend the night here, and then they'll know!" the scum answered.

The day was very long and the night even longer. All the prisoners were saying that there was a car waiting to take me to Belaya Tserkov. There had been cases where Jews were sent there to be shot. The next morning a policeman opened the cell, and behind him came the interpreter, Rita Litke.

"What are you doing here, Raya? What's the matter with you?" "Once again," I said. "Do the interrogation! I'll call a witness, perhaps I'll save myself?!" "What interrogation? Tell me, how did you get here?" "The gendarmerie called: What's that? Me? I'll go to Gokhman right now!"

Twenty minutes or so later, she came back alone: "Take your child and go home!"

Could it really be true? I went home.

And there I was again, calm, cleared by the gendarmes.

On August 20, Fanas Korobkov came to my apartment along with two Germans; they had been sent by Volkov's wife in connection with the search for him, Pyotr, who was now in hiding. Volkov's wife had sent the police and the Germans round to my place saying that I was a Jew who was connected to him. "Well, all right, if we need to, we'll come back." Difficult times had come again. I decided not to leave the village. On August 25, I went to see Nina at the commandant's headquarters so as to find out any sort of news about myself. The commandant suddenly came in. "Okay, *komm mit mir* [come with me]," he said, and pointed to a spot on the floor to tell me to wait for him. Twenty minutes later I was at home. My little daughter just happened to be there. "Come on, darling, get ready. We've got to get out of here. They mean to shoot us. We'll run wherever the wind blows us!" I quickly opened my hiding place, shoved all my poems and flyers into it, and set off for Byednovka. The sun was sitting on the horizon. The weather was very gloomy. Darkness was gathering and it was drizzling. In that weather, I set out on the road without knowing what to expect in the next village. The road was unfamiliar. I began to get very anxious. Thanks to the barking of a dog I knew that the village was not far off. It was already quite dark by the time I came to the village. I spent the night with a woman I knew. "Tell me," I said to her, "do you know where Vasily Kravets the blacksmith works?" "He works here, on collective farm number 2. I'll show you first thing tomorrow."

In the morning, when dawn was just breaking, I set off to see Vasya. Vasya was a good friend of mine. When Vasya and I got together, we exchanged opinions. Vasya had told me more than once that there was danger hanging over me and that I needed to get out of our village. That was why I decided to see him. When my child and I turned up on Vasya's doorstep, he realized what was going on. "Today, after lunch, you and I will take off. We'll go as one family. I'll deal with anyone we meet along the way." We took a long detour and came to the village of Klyuchki as it was getting dark. We could not go any farther.

We asked a woman if we could come in. "Sure, come on in," she said. "We're not allowed to have guests in the evening." I was thinking that it was forbidden by the police and that I was in for it again. But the woman went on: "They work during the day. At night they walk along the streets with their accordions and then drive off on some mission, and in the morning they rest." Vasya, sitting beside me, gave me a nudge. It became clear to me that this was a partisan village. I felt as though I had been born into the world all over again, that I was only beginning to live. What luck one has to have to land in a partisan village. In the morning we moved on to the next town. Vasya knew where to take poor Raya.

My life changed. If you have ever happened to jump out of a scalding bath, then I jumped out of danger. Here, on the small Balka state farm where Vasya and I stopped, lived partisan families and prisoners, while the rest were exclusively Jews. How do you like a community like that?[65]

Vasya introduced me to his friend Semyonov. The latter looked me over and it was obvious that he was figuring everything out: "Everything's okay here. A man can live well here on our little farm." "Sure," Vasya said, "but I still need your recommendation for getting set up."

"Right. It just so happens that we need a blacksmith." "And where are the rest of our lads?" Vasya asked. "Out there, in the woods. They're working hard, these guys. They come to our place almost every day. And they should be here today." Vasya glanced at

---

65. It is not clear what she means by "prisoners." Perhaps they were escaped Soviet prisoners of war.

me. I was bright red as I sat there. "Yes. We'll have to go and see your director." Vasya and Semyonov went off, and I felt right at home. I could rest here.

Vasya put all of us on the books. I, as the wife of Kravets the blacksmith, became the shopkeeper's assistant. My daughter went to nursery school. In the evening, the young people coming from work would gather in the street to have a good time. Our daughter also sang and danced. Vasya and I looked with great pleasure at our daughter. "Oh, what a lovely little girl. She doesn't take after you at all: a dark dad and mother." "It's because the neighbor was a redhead." Everyone laughed and was satisfied with my answer. "They're coming, they're coming," a little boy cried, and everyone ran to the dormitory. And it was true. You could hear the clatter of wheels, the sound of the accordion, and then a song rang out: "A man walks along like the master." I stood there without moving, listening to the words of the song as they drew closer. The cart stopped. I continued to stand there. A small, swarthy, armed partisan in a long leather coat passed by me. He didn't say anything. When he came back out of the dormitory, I said quietly: "Ah, our own brave soldiers." He stopped: "Why don't you come by the apartment? And why are you crying? Did I hurt your feelings somehow?" Leaning against a fence, I burst into sobs: "Call Volkov out here, boys," the short one shouted: "Ah, Volkov is here!" I cried even harder. "What's wrong with her? Take her to the apartment. There's nothing to see here." And when Volkov took me to the apartment, he held me in his arms for a long time and kissed me. "Raya. Is it really you? Are you really alive?" "Yes, Petya, friends meet up again." Volkov introduced me to his men, whom I did not know yet. His comrade Fedya gave me a black shirt as a gift. I thanked him and felt a bit better. "You'll be okay now, Raya. We'll be coming here quite often. We'll take care of you and stay in contact with you." An accordion began to play. The men began moving off from the farm on their missions. After three days at the forge, Vasya said to me: "Well, Raya, it's time for me to go do my own work now. I've saved you. The men will be dropping by, and you and the child will be looked after. Everything's going well at the Front. Our people have already crossed the Dniepr, and things are getting better."

Vasya arranged for the written permission he needed to go somewhere, to get some stuff, and then left. It was hard for me to say goodbye to as good a friend as Vasya. This was how my new life began. Gursky, the director of the state farm, did not behave badly toward the workers. Comrade Gursky hid about forty-four Jews from the German fascist bandits, along with many prisoners and partisan families. When we were threatened with any danger, he always let us know about it beforehand. And when hard times came for the enemy, Gursky said to us: "My dear friends, if you and I have managed to save ourselves from the hands of the German fascists, that doesn't mean that we can't suffer in the last minutes of the German retreat. We need to spread out to the villages." Gursky provided help to everyone. He paid particular attention to those who had suffered, seeing to it that they had food and fuel for heating, and I was one of those. I traveled to Khmelevka, where the partisans usually came by during the day. On November 25, the partisan Danko Dudnik invited me to the funeral of another partisan in Belobonivka. I left my daughter with my landlady. I went with him alone. And before the arrival of our troops, I was in the detachment. In Khmelyovka, I had the good fortune to see the first Red Army patrol, which was stopped beside a church. "Hello!" I said in a trembling voice, and shook hands with each of them. "Tell me, is it true that there are Reds in Dengofovka? Has my region really been liberated?"

"If you want to see for yourself," said the Kirghiz in command of the patrol, "come with us." Even though I had not seen my daughter for a long time, I decided to go with them. My heart filled with happiness when I saw the red flag fluttering over the sugar factory. They brought me to army headquarters, and there I told the story of what I had been through and asked to volunteer for the army. The commander of the headquarters shook my hand and said: "You need to get back to your daughter and to her upbringing, as the Motherland expects of you. You should work and live with your daughter." So I went back with the scouting party to Khmelyovka. Because of foul weather, I stayed there until February 9. And on February 9, I went home on a Stalin tractor.

GARF f. 8114, op.1, d. 944, ll. 61–83. A typewritten text with manuscript insertions.

28. In the city of Shpola and its environs [66]
STORIES OF LOCAL INHABITANTS RECORDED BY A TEACHER NAMED KRUGLYAK
[1944]

Between September 3 and 9, 1941, the Gestapo took 160 people on their list away from Shpola and shot them. They were doctors, jurists, the most skilled workers. Then they herded the Jews into a ghetto and closed off those blocks with barbed wire. The Germans mockingly referred to the ghetto as "Palestine." They put armbands on the Jews. They would not let them out to go to the market. They gave them no bread, while the population outside the ghetto was getting two hundred grams per person per day. People were paying two hundred rubles for two hundred grams of bread. A famine began in the ghetto; ten or twelve people were dying every day. They were given no electricity. In this way they tortured everyone in the ghetto until April 15, 1942. After that date, there remained thirteen Jewish tradesmen (a cooper, several tailors, and a few blacksmiths), who were left by force of circumstance and at the request of the population. They were shot in 1943. The rest were put in concentration camps.

Four kilometers from Shpola, in the depths of Darevsky Forest, there was a concentration camp where they kept people for a month. On May 15, 1942, 760 women, children, and elderly people were shot in a pit there. Before they were shot, they were mocked and abused in every way imaginable. The shootings were carried out by Ukrainian police under German command.

---

66. Shpola is located in the Cherkassy (then Kiev) Region.

Before being shot, the daughter of Dr. Goldberg raised the hands of her two children and said that the blood of innocent children would not be forgiven the Germans.

A group of Jews capable of working were driven out to construct the Kirovograd-Odessa highway. In the Zvenigorodka District, there were several camps for the construction of roads.

A group of 225 Jews capable of working were herded into the Bradetsky concentration camp; they worked there for several months and then were shot on December 15, 1942. On December 15, 1942, they shot 105 people working in the Shostakov camp. After December 15, 1942, they brought 250 Romanian Jews here and shot them.

A German came to see a thirty-five-year-old woman named Manya Glayzer and ordered her to make him something to eat. He came again that night with a friend. They intended to rape her. The woman resisted. For this, they stabbed her to death, stabbed her aging mother, and cut off the head of her fourteen-year-old little brother. (This story was told by the sixteen-year-old niece of Manya Glayzer, a girl who hid behind a Ukrainian passport. Manya's husband is at the Front.)

If a person's temperature went over 38°, he or she was shot. Four girls and a twenty-year-old boy were shot for this. The temperature was checked by a Ukrainian doctor and a German commandant. Sick girls and boys said that they were well and ready to work. "Shut up, no one's asking you," the doctor said to them. Those who were ill were told that they were being taken to the Zvenigorod Hospital, but they were taken to a pit instead that had already been dug. While the commandant smoked a cigarette, the police shot three girls.

When they took away the sick, an eighteen-year-old named Kucher (the son of a lathe turner, he had completed the eighth grade) noticed that someone had taken his mess tin, and that if he did not have a mess tin, he would not receive any food. He took off after them. For this "crime," the commandant forced Kucher's father to dig a hole for his son. The father cried, and begged that they kill him instead of his son, but nothing helped. They made the father bury his son alive. A few days later the father died of a broken heart.

Dr. Kaufmann was in the camp with his fourteen-year-old son. The son's temperature went up to 38°. His mother realized that they would shoot him and told the doctor that her son would go out to work the next day. But they took away mother and son. Before her death, she lifted her son and said to the doctor: "Hitler and a thousand of his men will pay for this innocent blood."

GARF f. 8114, op. 1, d. 965, ll. 51–52. A typewritten manuscript with corrections.

29. In Uman
THE RECOLLECTIONS OF MANYA FEYNGOLD
[1944]

On August 1, 1941, the Germans captured Uman. After mobilization and evacuation, there were still more than fifteen thousand Jews in the city. A black cloud hung over the heads of the inhabitants. Most of all, the Jews were frightened by the fact that there were signs reading "No entry to kikes!" hanging everywhere. The Jewish children, unable to understand this, asked more than once: "What are kikes? How can you see them?" Their parents, however, had to own up and tell them that we are the kikes, and that we are the ones being referred to.

At that time, the order was given for the Jewish intelligentsia to appear at City Hall to clear up certain questions. On the August 13, 1941, a group of around eighty people appeared at City Hall. The fascist barbarians dealt with them savagely, forcing them to do calisthenics while chopping off hands and feet with every movement, before torturing them to death. There were numerous individual acts of killing, while Jewish apartments were systematically raided, where the Jews were robbed, spat on, and killed. Then the registration of the whole Jewish population was announced. They registered every Jew with a club, a gun butt, and a whip. Those going through registration were all beaten and bloodied. In order to distinguish the Jews from everyone else, all of them, regardless of age, had to wear white armbands with six-pointed stars on their right arms; without such signs, they were beaten and fined an unlimited amount of money. Not only German police took part in the murder and abuse of Jews. The Ukrainian police took great pleasure in helping them, with an eye to robbing people and gaining authority with the Germans.

On the morning of September 21, 1941, all the Jews were taken and put to work, and in the process they found out that some of these people had been driven off to dig a pit. They threw more than a thousand people into the grave and by morning all had suffocated. Other Jews who landed in jail stayed there until evening. A crowd came to see these pathetic people and they were forced to dance and sing. Of course the Jews did not willingly dance: they were forced to do it, and were beaten while doing it, beaten even to death. When people begged for a bullet, they did not want to give them that pleasure; the most entertaining thing to do was to kill them with a rifle butt. An order came toward morning to release women with children and to kill the men. The pogrom went on for several days in a row, and they killed mostly men. All Jews had to resettle in the old market by October 1, that is, live on the same street so that it would be easier to gather them up and kill them. In spite of the fact that the deadline for resettlement had been established, the Ukrainian police made a raid and would not allow belongings to be taken, demanding that they clear out of the apartment immediately. More than 50 percent of the Ukrainians of Uman took an active part in this pogrom in order to rob the Jews. I was met by an ordinary-looking woman who was undressing people and collecting clothing, and while she was doing it said: "Here's one more kike-woman. Take her away, or it'll be impossible to live because of them." I was hiding in a Ukrainian house, and a neighbor boy, the son of a policeman, came round and talked about how successful his mother had been, how many things she had collected, and as he was leaving said: "Mama only got herself a winter coat, but she says that as soon as they start beating the kikes again, she'll get a summer one, too."

There was nowhere for the Jews to hide and it was impossible for them to flee; the German fascists were all around and the Ukrainian police as well. Many Uman officials helped the Germans to find and exterminate Jews. Ukrainians who tried to hide Jews were killed. The resettlement was finished. They hounded Jews out to work. Above all, they herded them to the police station, where the police mercilessly beat and murdered men, women, and children. This was where they displayed their courage, by beating and mistreating poor helpless people. The fiends wallowed in pleasure from it, since they were sending abused people off to work, after all. After this "concert," they drove the Jews off in herds to the hardest labor. Quite often they would pick up young girls and force them to clean latrines with their bare hands, and there were other tasks like this one.

They did not have to work for long. On October 8, 1941, at four in the morning, another pogrom began. So that they would not have to yell their heads off, the gendarmerie took the Ukrainian police and others who wished to take part. It was still dark outside when three men burst into our home with shots, pounding, and yelling. We decided that they had come to loot us. Before we had time to turn on the light and get out of bed, the three came in. Two of them were like rabid tigers with awful eyes that filled you with fear as soon as you looked at them. They were the usual SS barbarians, while the third, a civilian, was hitting the door and windows with a club and shouting: "Let's go. Let's go!" It was obvious that he was a Ukrainian and not even a policeman. We did not know what to give him, and it was impossible to ask him about anything. There were thirty-four of us in the building, including children. The frightened children began to cry, and we were all confused, not knowing what would happen. Finally, the civilian with a club shouted: "Everybody out!"

Not understanding what was going on, everyone began to go outside. Behind them came two bandits with rifles in their hands, showing where to go. We knew what it was all about, but there was nothing to defend ourselves with. Ten minutes later, this little group was herded onto the market square, which was ringed on all sides with guards, and the number of people increased with each passing minute. By 7:00 AM, more than ten thousand Jews could be counted on the square. Five heavy trucks were parked there as well, into which small children and old people were thrown; all the rest were driven along on foot. An old Jew took his wife by the arm—they had lived together for fifty years—and said goodbye with tears in his eyes, knowing that in half an hour they would be killed and that they would never see each other again. Their last words were addressed to their sons, who were fighting the accursed Germans and defending their motherland: "Goodbye, my dear children! You will never see your parents again. We are poor victims. Take revenge on our behalf!"

Little Sarochka hugged her mother and kissed her firmly; this little girl of six understood everything that was happening. She asked her mama for another drink, but Mama told her that she would soon drink enough to last forever. The previous year, Sarochka had gotten sick but had not died; it was her fate, as it was for thousands of others, to perish at the miserable hands of the fascist bandits. Sarochka's blue eyes, brimming with tears, looked on sadly, but the bandits had no pity: they were beating people, firing into the crowd in order to scare people even more. Sending women off, they tore children out of the arms of their parents, and beat old people with clubs and rifle butts. The bandits forced those who remained to move in the direction of the prison. They did not keep these people in jail for long. They stripped them, took all their money and valuables, and then drove them all out of town. People who had collapsed and lost the strength to go on further were killed on the spot; all the rest went to the pit. Invalids were thrown out of second story windows into trucks; in this way they "cleansed" the orphanages and the sick from hospitals. While these people were being driven to the pit, the entire town was piled high with the bodies of people killed with clubs and of those who had tried to escape.

The Jews then saw three deep pits, and it was only then that they understood that they had been brought there to be shot. The frightened Sarochka was looking into her mother's face as though she were asking her for help. Mama embraced her, kissed her for the last time; she was not crying and was unable to say any more. She was helpless and could do nothing to help her little daughter. She walked along with her firstborn daughter, stood over the pit, and begged for immediate execution. They granted her wish. Some dreadful bandit ran Sarochka through with a bayonet and threw her into the pit; a minute or two later, a gun barked, and the poor mother tumbled into the pit where her Sarochka was already lying. They were at rest forever now, things were already easier for them than for the people who were standing fifty meters from the pit. They came up five at a time, took their places over the pit and received their bullets. Jews who were still alive lay at the bottom of the pit—old people, cripples. They did not want to waste bullets on them. Dead and wounded Jews were falling on top of them, and thanks to this the old people and cripples suffocated to death. The number of Jews was growing smaller and smaller. They were coming up in groups of five, but each one in the group was trying to bring up the rear so as to live another few minutes. Others could not stand it at all and ran forward ahead of their turn. The Germans were standing there laughing and taking pictures of the scene.

There was no small number of Sarochkas. Ten-year-old Mayechka even consoled her mother; she tried to explain to her that they were not killing them, that they would live. Mama, naturally, felt sorry for her daughter and for her own life, and even asked her to try to escape, but the little girl refused. Mayechka said: "I don't want to leave. Even if they let me go, Mummy, I'd be where you are. I'll never leave you. If they kill you, then let them kill me along with you, but don't cry, Mummy. They won't kill us!" With these words, Mayechka comforted her mother, even though she herself understood perfectly well that nothing could comfort them. Nothing would be of any help, it was all up for them. They killed Maya along with her mother. Her last words were: "Mummy! I'm glad that I'll be lying next to you. Daddy will get even for our blood. Daddy! This is the last time I'll remember your name. Don't forget us, and kill the horrid fascists!"

At first the children appealed to the barbarians and asked: "Uncle, where's your heart? How can you kill little kids like us?" In reply, the bandits showed them that they had no hearts, pointing to their rifles. The adolescents had the presence of mind to realize that pleading would do no good, and that nothing would help them. Some wept, saying goodbye to their families and friends; others walked along heads held high, singing the *Internationale* one last time. Boys of twelve looked death boldly in the face and cried out: "There will be vengeance! Blood will flow for blood!" The last woman whom they killed went off her head and laughed as she approached the pit. Before she had time to utter her last words, she staggered and fell on top of the ten thousand corpses of those who had just been killed.

The blood was still warm and some were still raising their hands or their legs; it was obvious that many were only seriously wounded. They quickly began burying them with earth, but for three days after that, the ground was still moving. No one could help these people, and they rapidly died.

However insulted she may have been, one Ukrainian woman found herself among them. She turned to a German officer and showed him her papers saying that she was Ukrainian. The officer had a three-word reply for her: "I don't care." He shot her and she fell, just like all the Jews. The German officer turned with a laugh to his friend: "Let's not let the Ukrainians think that we love them. They're *kaput* too. What does this Ukrainian care if I kill her now or later? It's all the same to me." It was only little Volodya who managed to get out of the hands of the fascists this time and to hide, thanks to the fact that he looked like a Ukrainian, spoke the language fluently, and that neither the German gendarmerie nor the Ukrainian police, who were making every effort to seek out Jews, could spot him. For two days in a row, the police searched possible and impossible places alike. A policeman named Polamarchuk hauled an old man out of the grave in which he had lain for a full day—the frightened old man pitifully begged Polamarchuk to let him go. The policeman demanded a thousand rubles and the old man handed them over. He let him go and then went straight off to find a friend of his on the force and told him where the old man was and to pick him up. Polamarchuk's friend decided that he did not want to have anything to do with the old man, but he asked him for money just the same. The old man did not have any more money. The policeman killed him on the spot, then went round to the neighbors to look for loot.

Twelve-year-old Volodka, standing on the mouth of the pit, contrived to throw himself into the pit alive when they fired on his group of five. Half an hour later, the "performance" was finished. The contemptible bandits finished their work and went away. Volodka then slowly crawled out of the pit, looked around, and quickly hid himself. He did not go looking for his parents. He would never find them; they had been killed in front of him. With his own eyes he had seen them kill his mother, his older sister, and two younger brothers. Volodka had said goodbye to them. He had not expected to live through a pogrom like that one, but it was his fate to live on a bit longer. It is difficult to imagine or to describe a scene like this one. It is difficult to describe Volodka's thoughts when he walked off alone, without a family, never again to find his relatives or even his close friends. The poor boy was not crying; he was trying to find a reason for everything that was happening, and so he walked along through the city, lost in his thoughts.

He saw the police running around like mad dogs, still leading isolated Jews that they had only just found. The police were exulting! Volodka walked past them and went on, getting closer to his own street, where Ukrainian boys and girls as well as adults were dragging everything imaginable in sacks from the apartments of Jews. All the windows and doors of the buildings were smashed in, and the apartments were empty. People were carrying all manner of pots and pans. Volodka also picked up a sack, gathered some useless rags and tried to get closer to his own apartment. The sack full of rags weighing two kilos or so felt to him more like three poods. He was so horrified that his legs would not support him, but he still carried the sack so that he would not be recognized. Volodka went into his family's apartment and saw a dreadful sight: his grandmother lying dead on the floor. She had been badly beaten, probably killed because she had been unable to go with all the rest since she was old and blind. Volodka quickly turned around and went out, holding the tears back with all his might because they could have recognized him and killed him on the spot. He picked up his bagful of rags and quickly walked away from his family home. A young Ukrainian woman came toward him and asked him where he had gotten the things and asked him to show her the apartment where he had found them. "Maybe there's some more left. I'll take some too." Volodka was unable to speak. He could only point, in what direction he himself did not know. He went to see a friend of his whom he had gone to school with for five years. The friend, a Ukrainian and a pioneer named Senka, gave him a friendly welcome and offered him a place to hide until the next morning. "Tomorrow, we'll see," he said. Volodka was crying. Senka consoled him. In the evening, the two friends lay down together to sleep, but did not drop off until it was almost morning; the whole time, they were talking, discussing what to do. Senka tried as best he could to help his friend.

On the morning of October 9, the police were still on the streets, still looking for Jews, and no one thought that any Jew found on that day would not be killed. And yet, not all of those found on the second day of the pogrom (there were around eight hundred of them) were killed. And just before evening on October 9, they were all released and ordered to occupy dwellings indicated by the police. An announcement was made that everyone should report to work on the tenth, and they promised that no one else would be killed. People who were suffering, hungry and cold after being hunted for two days, came to apartments in which only traces remained that others had lived in them, other people who were no more. They were sleeping the eternal sleep, they were better off than the living, who still existed in order to be abused further. There was not a single family left intact. There were children without relatives, families without children. Every human being was broken, shattered, and envious of the dead.

People somehow got through that night—they were expecting to be killed the next day. No, they were not killed the next day. They lived until April 22, 1942. But how they lived! They were right, of course, to envy the dead. How they were abused and tortured, no pen could describe, and no fairy tale could relate. There are no words that could describe their life. There were even more people after the word got round that there would be no more killings: many crawled out of cellars and attics, or arrived from villages. Two weeks after the pogrom, there were already around fifteen hundred people in the ghetto (the street in which the Jews lived), including children. They had killed more than ten thousand Jews in the second pogrom. They were mourned for a long time by their families and friends who remained alive, but at the same time they envied the dead because they would no longer be tortured, as the survivors still were while waiting for a third pogrom.

Life moved on as before. Once again there were isolated incidents of arrests and shootings, again there were raids by the Germans and the police on Jewish apartments, again there were robberies and acts of persecution. On January 1 three people were arrested, among them an attractive Jewish woman named Yatsus. The police investigator wanted to sleep with her but she refused, so they decided to hang all three of them. On January 5, 1942, they hanged them before a crowd. Yatsus went up to the gallows, threw off her headscarf and put the noose around her neck herself. The executioner Voropaev dragged her by the legs and the police secretary Tonkoshkur made a speech in which he pointed out that Soviet power had trampled and tortured Ukrainians for twenty-three years, and that it was the Jews who were to blame for it. On January 8, they announced that all Jews would henceforth have to wear yellow patches on their chests and on their backs, patches seven centimeters in diameter. Now there was a reason to spit on them if there was not one before! One person would be beaten for having a patch larger than specified, a second for having a patch that was too small or too dark a shade of yellow, and still another for a patch that was bright yellow. It was impossible to walk through the city. There were police all around, chasing people with clubs like mad dogs and mercilessly beating anyone within reach. At the same time, it was ordered that every Jew would have to remove his hat in the presence of Germans and policemen, and for this, too, more than one person was set upon. Taking off his hat, a Jew would have to be very lucky indeed to pass by untouched. Usually, the city was full of all kinds of fiends; it was impossible to take one's hat off before each one. In the event that you did not take it off fast enough, you received such a blow that your head flew off along with your hat. Five-year-old Mishka said to his grandfather: "Grandpa, so what if it's cold. You should just walk along without a hat, or else your arm will hurt from taking it off all the time." The grandfather took more than one beating, and no small number of clubbings from the police, but he never said anything about it at home. He endured all of this quite calmly, knowing that no one would help him in any way.

There were eighteen hundred Jews still in the ghetto after the second pogrom. All of them were driven out to work. Meanwhile, people were being herded every day into the hands of the police, who stood there with clubs in their hands to meet the Jews who were assembling for work. They gave every Jew a good thrashing with the clubs, and then they sent them off to shovel snow or move stones. They hounded the Jews out to their jobs in herds, and every group was escorted by police. One day as we were being taken out to work, we ran into a school teacher from Uman. She said to the police with a smile:[67] [. . .] you take us, ha, ha, ha!" After working a full day, people returned home hungry, cold, and unpaid. No one even wanted to eat; they wanted only to rest until morning because tomorrow they would again be in the hands of the police, again on the receiving end of the clubs, again the same thing. In the evening, everyone thought about rest. But here, God himself intervened and thought: "Why should the Jews rest? After all, I can find work for them at night as well." And from ten or even nine in the evening, another comedy was played out. A fire. Some house is on fire from overheating. The whole police force is already on their feet, driving all the Jews outside, men, women and children, to put out the fire. Everyone, agitated, runs to the stream with buckets in their hands. The dark. . . .[68]

Approaching the stream, the policemen threw these people into the water and at the same time forced them to crawl out, gather water, and put out the fire. The people who crawled out of the stream took several blows from rifle butts, and then ran with the buckets to the fire; they made them all stand on the roof and shot at them at the same time. People immediately began falling to the ground. The police stood there and laughed. The night passed in this way. In the morning, one could see ten or fifteen people who had been hanged for doing a bad job of putting out the fire. Everyone else returned home bloodied and tortured, humiliated by both God and man. Then came morning, and it was yesterday again, and the same thing. In addition to this, a tax was imposed on the Jews after every fire. After the first fire, they levied a tax of 80,000 rubles, after the second 170,000, and the third time it was 360,000. All the Jews were threatened with shooting for non-payment of the tax. But when there was nothing more to pay with, they confiscated property and furniture, and dismantled homes.

---

67. The next few words are illegible in the original text.
68. This phrase is not legible in the original text.

That was not all. People, as we have seen, could not take any more. One evening, the old man Fridman, beaten and in rags, came home from work. He walked along and thought that the day had gone by and that a dreadful night was approaching. How was he to get through the night? Just then, a policeman came toward him, the notorious butcher Voropaev. Fridman took off his hat and went on past, but Voropaev would not let the Jew go. He called him back and asked: "Make a rude gesture at me, will you?" Fridman did not have time to answer the question before Voropaev began beating him with the butt of his gun. He sent the badly beaten Fridman to the police station, where they tossed him into a cell. Half an hour later, Tonkoshur, the secretary, summoned him to be interrogated. They did not ask him anything, but a "merry band" of policemen surrounded him. They all began beating him with clubs and gun butts, and forced him to dance and sing. While all this was going on, blood was streaming down Fridman's face, and he could no longer stay on his feet. Tonkoshur shouted at him that he must not soil the floor with blood, and made him protect the wound with his hat. After they had thrown Fridman in a cell dead to the world, some man brought him round. Opening his eyes, Fridman got angry with the man and said: "It would be better to let me die. What did you do that for? I don't want anymore of this cursed life!" The man tried to console him, explaining to him that he was no better off. His . . .[69]

GARF, f. 8114, op. 1, d. 965, ll. 135–147. The original manuscript.

30. What I went through in fascist captivity
A LETTER FROM NINE-YEAR-OLD BORIS GERSHENZON FROM UMAN TO THE JEWISH ANTI-FASCIST COMMITTEE
[1944]

Dear sirs:

I will describe for you once again how I suffered at the hands of the fascist monsters. As soon as the Germans reached us in Uman, they drove us all into the ghetto. Old people, women, and children, as well as the sick, were with us. They took everyone straight into the woods to shoot them. That was where they shot my grandmother and my Aunt Zina and her children, but I managed to escape. I concealed myself in the Sofievka woods for a long time, and then they caught me again and locked me up in the House of Pioneers. Many of us were kept there. They beat us up, choked us, stripped us naked, and threw us in the cellar. Many could not stand the torture and perished right there. Then they sent the ones who were still alive to a camp. I was the smallest one in the group, but they made me do hard labor just the same. Besides that, they stripped us and started beating us unconscious. They starved us. They took away our clothes. They only gave us some grain husks and fifty grams of bread to eat. We slept in crumbling stables.

---

69. Just where the text breaks off, this final phrase is not legible.

Snow fell right on us, and to keep warm we lay there one boy on top of another. I spent about eight months in that camp, and then I ran off to my father in the woods, to his partisan unit. Together with Papa, I helped distribute leaflets in the villages. But a little while after that they caught me again and sent me to a Romanian camp in the city of Bershad. The Romanians made us suffer as much as the Germans did. Every Sunday they took hundreds of Soviet people out of the camp. They hanged some and shot the others. They caught my father as well. They shot him along with a group of partisans not long before the Red Army came.

As soon as they liberated Uman, I went straight there. But I did not stay for long. Aunt Riva, who is in the Red Army and who works as a doctor in a hospital, learned about me and took me in. I live in the hospital with Aunt Riva now. I am learning to be a projectionist here. I am nine years old. I am thinking about going to the Suvorov school. When I grow up, I want to be an officer in the Red Army. If you would like to write to me, write to the address: Field Post Office No. 23336-A, Borya Gershenzon.

GARF f. 8114, op. 1, d. 966, ll. 27–28. A typewritten manuscript.

31. The story of the partisan Raisa Dudnik, who escaped from Uman
Recorded by Miriam Zheleznova [70]
[1944]

A few days ago, a young partisan, Raisa Dudnik, visited the Jewish Anti-Fascist Committee. She had fled Uman. Here is what she told us.

When the Germans entered Uman on August 1, 1941, my father, Leyb Dudnik, told me and my sister, Khaya, to flee the city. But we refused to leave our parents alone.

The Germans organized their first pogrom in Uman on September 23. On that day, I left at dawn for a neighboring village. When I got back, I found no one at home. The apartment had been turned upside down. I rushed to the town jail. From the other side of the fence I heard cries of "*Shma Yisroel,*" the sobbing of women, the crying of children. All at once the prison gates opened wide. The Germans brought some Jewish men out into the street. Each had a shovel in his hands. I saw my father and ran toward him.

"Goodbye, Raya!" my father said. "Mother and Khaya are in the jail. They're taking us to be shot."

The Germans threw me aside and herded the men into the cemetery.

The women and children—as many as three thousand of them—were driven into the heated cellar, where every door and opening was tightly sealed. Many were suffocated.

---

70. Miriam Zheleznova was a journalist associated with the Yiddish-language newspaper *Eynikayt* (Unity), which was published by the Jewish Anti-Fascist Committee. She was arrested in 1950 and subsequently executed because of her connection to the JAC.

The corpses gave off an awful stench. And it was only when the smell began to spread throughout the prison that the Germans opened the door. During those several days I did not go away from the fence. I saw wagons loaded down with naked bodies coming out of the prison. These were the women and children who had suffocated to death. The Germans shamelessly brought out these corpses in their disorderly heaps in broad daylight. I saw among them the curly heads of three of my little first cousins.

When there were about three hundred people left in the cellars of the jail, the Germans hounded them out onto the street stark naked. Among these frightened people, who saw no one and who did not understand anything, I found my mother, my sister, and my Aunt Sonya with her surviving son. Two days later, a ghetto was created in Rakovka. Every night, drunken bandits burst into our little homes. They raped girls. They beat up the old women and took their last belongings. On October 7, ominous rumors circulated in the ghetto. It was said that a new punitive unit had arrived in Uman. In order to verify this, my little sister and I made for Sofievka and our Russian friends. The bookkeeper Larzhevsky gave us a warm welcome and let us stay the night. I woke up in the morning with fear for my mother lying heavily upon me. I went out into the street and saw a neighbor sobbing:

"Oh my little girl, get going! They've taken the Jews from the ghetto to kill them!"

I decided to leave my little sister with the Larzhevskys, who promised to save her, and I myself went off to look for our mother.

On the way to the ghetto, I was stopped by a policeman who said to me: "Before you die, go wash the floors of the police station." I saw two other Jewish girls there. We spent the whole day cleaning up the place, and in the evening the three of us managed to hide ourselves without being noticed.

On that day, the Germans shot ten thousand Jews in Uman. Among them was my mother.

Having fled the police, I turned to Nikolai Vasilevich Rudkevich, who gave me a passport in the name of Lukia Korotenko, a Ukrainian. With this document I headed off for points unknown.

I covered more than two thousand kilometers. I was in Kirovograd, Kremenchug, Kharkov, Poltava, and Dnepropetrovsk Regions. And nowhere did I come across any Jews. I would come into villages. I worked in vegetable gardens, I worked as a nanny and a scrubwoman. Good people gave me food. Many knew that I was a Jew, and, risking their lives, gave me shelter and their last crust of bread. I looked for partisans. I often saw small bridges that they had blown up, crippled rail lines, the houses of bürgermeisters that they had burned down. I reached Belorussia. Along the way, I met a seventeen-year-old Belorussian girl named Maria Chik who had fled the Donbass. She was making her way toward her homeland in the Kostyukovichi Region. This region was a center of partisan resistance. In helpless rage, the Germans burned down nineteen villages, but still never found our national avengers. Maria's father, Sylvester Chik, showed me how to reach the partisans.

Vasily Kostyukov, the commander of the unit, greeted me as though I were a member of his family. For the first time in two and a half years, I felt like a full-fledged human being.

I found an old Jewish woman named Fanka Gibkhina in the detachment. She had been with them from the very first day. She became a second mother to me. The Germans had shot her daughter and her husband. Fanya, who by some miracle survived, had gone off to the partisans with her sixteen-year-old son Baruch. There were several Jews in the unit. I met an old shoemaker named Khaim Lezner and a nurse named Basya Pivchenko.

I was dying to get into the fight. The commander assigned me to a diversionary unit and provided me with a captured rifle. During my time in the frontlines, all sorts of things happened. Most often we attacked the Germans while they were crossing the Bezet river. We would kill all the Nazis, take their horses and, after resting a bit, set off for new missions. Our unit controlled the Unecha-Krichev railway. We attacked the guards posted along the railway roadbed, wiped out the Germans, and then, unhindered, blew up the railway line.

The Front began to get closer to us in the autumn of 1943. On September 22, 1943, the first Red Army scouts reached our unit. That evening, there was a great celebration in the village.

The majority of the partisans joined regular units of the Red Army and proceeded farther west. At the insistence of the unit commander, women and children were sent to the rear to rest.

Raisa Dudnik has just left for Uman in the hope of finding her sister, Khaya.

GARF f. 8114, op. 1, d. 958, ll. 1–3. Typewritten manuscript with additional material by Miriam Zheleznova.

32. Do not consider me a stranger
A LETTER FROM OLGA SUPRUN OF ZOLOTONOSHA[71] TO THE FAMILY OF HER HUSBAND, BORIS YUDKOVSKY
JANUARY 12, 1944

Hello, Yudkovskys![72]

I received your letter and I am very grateful that you responded. I am writing you a letter, and although it might not make you happy to receive it, there is nothing to be done about that. It is difficult to remember such things.

---

71. Town of Zolotonosha in the Poltava (now Cherkassy) Region. Olga Suprun was living at the time in the village of Gladovshchina, Gelmyazov Region. (Her return address was indicated on the envelope.)
72. The letter was addressed to David I. Yudkovsky in Baku.

I left with my children and with the Krainsky family, but I stayed in Gadyach, where Borya told me to wait for him. He would not allow me to go any farther without him.

That was on August 25, 1941. On August 30, Srulik came to me and passed on Borya's message that "he would be there any day now," but after that I waited until I could not wait any longer. A few days later I learned that we were already surrounded. There was nowhere for me to go, so I went back home. After I arrived, Borya turned up the next day. When they left Zolotonosha, they fell into an encirclement and were taken prisoner.[73] They starved and beat him, and he tried to escape. He came home, but it was impossible to live there; he had to live in the woods. I would go to see him and bring him food, but he could not stay there long because winter was already starting. He decided to come home. After he came home, he stayed in the hut for a month, not going out and not knowing anything except what I told him about the fact that all [of the Jews] in the city had been singled out and marked, and that they were being hunted. It was difficult to live; they were shooting several people every day after forcing them to dig their own graves. Borya suffered through all this, knowing that it was his fate; he asked only that I take care of the children, but I was not able to take care of them.

And that day came, November 22, 1941. On Saturday morning, the police stood on guard over the whole city and began bringing everyone in. They took us and locked us up at the military registration office. On Sunday morning, they took everyone out of town and began shooting, but after that I could not know what had happened. They took me out of there because they thought I was not Jewish, and had fainted. Ginda stayed there with her children, along with Borya, Isya, Zhenya, Srulik and all the others; there were more than two thousand people so that I do not know who was there, since it was no joy to look at, and I had things to think about and look at. To this day, I still cannot think about it. You ask me to write down where I was and what I was doing all that time. But my heart is not in the work. For two and a half years I have been in constant pain. It was getting to the point where I was asking them to shoot me. I cannot live in Zolotonosha just now. As soon as I set foot in Zolotonosha, all the memories come back to me, and it is difficult for me to bear.

The hut is still standing, but I cannot be happy about it. The Krainsky's hut is still standing; all of them are except for the old ones, which were pulled down for firewood, and the Germans burned down all the government buildings, so that everything in the city is muffled and sad, and I have got no one to see there anyway, and

---

73. The German advance was so unrelenting in the summer and fall of 1941 that the Wehrmacht succeeded in overrunning Soviet defense lines, cutting off Red Army troops from routes of retreat. Caught behind enemy lines, hundreds of thousands were captured in battle after battle. Those who succeeded in making their way back to Red Army positions were looked on with suspicion because they had been behind enemy lines. They even faced the possibility of execution.

no one to tell stories to or ask about anything because while the Germans were there, everyone looked at me like a beast, and they jeered at me. If anyone will come back and help me, though, then we will have our revenge on them, we will try to pay them back for everything. Some have already returned to their dwellings, those about whom you write so that I will recognize whether or not the hut is still standing and whether or not Boyarsky is still living; I don't know exactly about whom, then, but if it is the Manin hut, then it is still intact.

And those who had seemed nice changed while the Germans were there, and now it's easy to ask them.

Tusya and Frida, I wish you happiness and joy in life, and not to know what I have known because the parasites took my whole life so let them live to see everything come down on their own children and after their children, on themselves. Borya ran into Gitya when he was coming home from captivity. She was on her way to Lubny and after that wanted to cross the frontlines, but she was already only half-dressed, beaten, and exhausted. She was going along naked and barefoot, though it was already cold and there was nowhere and nothing to return to. She and Borya went their separate ways, and after that nothing more is known about her, which means that she probably perished. She had a goal: to get through to Baku, but since no one knows where she is, and since the horrors that went on here happened everywhere, it would have been difficult for her to survive.

You wanted to get a letter from Isa, but he will not be writing to anyone anymore; the damned German took away his soul. They would not allow the poor unfortunate to live in the world.

I have written to you, but it is not a source of happiness for you. It was not easy for me to write to you either, but there is nothing to be done about it. I have lived through no small number of things for them, and in the future I will try not to forget; nothing else is needed. Write to me about how your life is going, whether or not the Germans have bombed you. I do not know anything about Grisha Rakhkovsky.

More than 2,000 Jews were shot in Zolotonosha, and 12,700 people altogether.[74] Some were dug up and then buried in common graves in the park, but it would be impossible to recognize them. I would write more, but I cannot see anything, and my head could not stand it. Yet it seems to me that no one will believe me.

I want to visit them, but they are not answering me. They are sleeping their peaceful sleep.

Read and do not worry. I survived alongside them for everyone. They took everything away from me. I do not even have a change of clothes anymore. So, I will stop writing. I was in Zolotonosha recently and after my arrival, I fell ill. I am not going anywhere. If I survive, all will be well. But it seems they will not have much longer to wait for me.

---

74. There was a camp for Soviet prisoners of war in Zolotonosha.

Greetings to everyone from me.

Olga

Do not consider me a stranger or useless, as I seemed to you before. None of this happened because of me. If it had not been me, it would have been another. Still, it seems that Borya and Isa did not have such a bad life, no worse than others. Which I now bear for them, but I am not counting on anything.

Archive of Ilya Ehrenburg (vol. 1, pp. 153–155). The original is in Ukrainian. The translation is abridged and edited.

GARF f. 8114, op. 1, d. 952, ll. 139. A typewritten manuscript.

33. He is my husband
LETTERS FROM NADEZHDA TERESHCHENKO OF KIROVOGRAD TO MAJOR A. A. ROZEN

[1944]

I am sending you[75] the letters of a Ukrainian girl named Nadya Tereshchenko about how she saved the life of my brother, David Rozenfeld, during the German occupation.

Before the war, my brother was an engineer in an air force unit. After July 1941, I lost track of him, and in March 1944, this letter which I received in Kirovograd from a girl whom I did not know, but who knew of my address, helped me to find him again.

A few days ago, I received a second letter from her in which she told me of my brother's death at the Front. I am enclosing an excerpt from the second letter. Nadya Tereshchenko works as a veterinarian in the Kirovograd regional agricultural office.

Regards,

Major A. Rozen

Field post office 47763

First letter

I will tell you briefly, Abram Anatolevich, about your brother, because one cannot write about everything all at once. David was in a camp in Kirovograd in 1941. The Germans released him from the camp only because he did not look at all like a Jew. He walked to the village of Bolshaya Mamayka and could not go any farther; he had dysentery and was generally exhausted. In Bolshaya Mamayka he ran into a friend of his, and this fellow was a friend of mine as well. One day, his comrade came to the Zagotskot farm, which I was managing, and asked me: "Do you think you could find a job for a comrade of mine?"

This man who had come to see me warned me to behave cautiously toward this friend of his, to treat him with care because he was a Jew.

---

75. The letter was addressed to Ilya Ehrenburg.

I took him on as a herdsman and then obtained papers for him in the name of Daniil Antonovich Rudenko. Later on, I brought him into the office as a bookkeeper. In 1942, I took the cattle out to pasture. David went with me.

He worked on the farm the entire time. From December 10, 1943, until January 11, 1944, I hid him on the steppe during a roundup of men that the Germans were carrying out before shipping them out of Kirovograd. Walking around was permitted only between 6:00 AM and 7:00 PM. But I would go out into the steppe after 7:00 PM or between three and six in the morning to take him food and water.

It had to be done every day in such a way as to cover up the hole in which he was staying on the steppe. I would camouflage myself as well when I took him food, covering myself with a white blanket, and taking along a sack full of snow as well to throw around his hole, which was in a patch of tall weeds, in such a place that even the best scout standing on the spot would not have seen where your brother was hiding.

I would spread sagebrush neatly around the hole and level the snow. The entrance was from the side and was covered from above by the brush.

We went through the most dreadful things.

From the very beginning of getting to know David, no one except for me knew that he was a Jew. I have a very good brother. David will tell you something about him someday. He is a candidate for the Party, with an exemption from military service. When our army entered Western Ukraine in 1939, the Komsomol Central Committee sent him there as a worker. He worked in Drogobych as the director of a factory. I believed in him and also hid him from the Germans. SD teams came for him twice, and we gave them an address in another district. And even so, I could not tell my brother that David was a Jew so that he would not happen to let it slip out.

When we were liberated from the German occupiers, David immediately left for the Front.

Please do not tell my mother and my sister about this. He was always worried when he thought about my mother. I am not writing about this in great detail. Maybe someday when we meet, I will tell you about it. Just now it is better not to remember the past.

Please do not send this letter on to his mother. I will write her another one. She has obviously suffered a lot. I consider David a member of the family, someone very close, and I am sure that he feels the same way about me. We were brought together by a great sorrow. Until we were freed from the bloodthirsty Nazis, we both risked our lives more than once. He is my husband. We never actually got the piece of paper, but we trust each other more than many of those who are legally married.

Take care, and regards to all my family.

N. Tereshchenko

Second letter

I received your letter. Danyusha is no longer with us. He died outside of the village of Novaya Ivanovka on the Rovno Road. His field postal number was 44623. There has still been no official notice. A wounded soldier, a comrade of David's came by here. I saw them both off to the Front.

I am cried out from grief and now I am writing this letter to you. Here is something that I want to say: For the sake of everything that is dear and holy to you, please see to it that this news does not reach his mother or his sister. This is the last thing I will ask of you. I will write to them and tell them that David left for the Front and that I have heard nothing more from him. He wrote me a letter on March 13, 1944, and already on March 24 I received word from a soldier that David had been killed. I have not yet written anything to your brother, Boris, either. He got word to me that he was wounded, and I do not want to upset him with this letter. I received two letters from Iosif Borisovich in Omsk, but I won't say anything to him about it either. It would have been better if all of you had not known that David had been rescued. You would have gradually forgotten, and now this new grief has come down on us. He asked me then to write a letter to all the family saying that he was alive. At first I would not send it, but he insisted, so I wrote it.

It is so hard, so hard. If only someone knew what he went through, how long he waited for the liberation, and how little time he survived it! If you come to Kirovograd, I will tell you everything.

If it were possible for his mother to come to stay with me, I would look after her as though I were her own daughter.

That is all. Take care.

Yours,

N. Tereshchenko.

City of Kirovograd, 17 Balkovsky Lane

GARF f. 8114, op. 1, d. 962, ll. 105–108. A typewritten manuscript.

34. Fate
THE RECOLLECTIONS OF THE WIFE OF THE ENGINEER P. KREPAK OF DNEPROPETROVSK
1944

I am the wife of P. I. Krepak, a factory worker in Dnepropetrovsk for more than twenty years. At the time of the evacuation, my husband was sent to the Andreyev plant in Taganrog. My husband suffered from a stomach ulcer; in Taganrog, he began vomiting blood, which kept him bedridden. I could not leave him. On October 17, 1941, the Germans occupied Taganrog. Three days later, the order came down: Jews are to wear an armband with a six-pointed star and could not leave the city under penalty of death by firing squad.

We decided to leave Taganrog. Outside the city, we were stopped by gendarmes: "*Jude?*" We managed to get past. I know how to sew, so I was a seamstress in the villages, and they gave us food. We walked thirty-five kilometers per day. The rains began in October and our feet got stuck in the mud. In the village of Fyodorovka, we were given a warm welcome by a Cossack family. Then we came to a German village; the leader there was a German who had been born in Russia. They took our clothes, beat up my husband, and spat in his face. My husband is a Ukrainian and he was made to endure the lot of a Jew. We passed through many villages and the villagers alerted us how to avoid the Germans. In Karan (a Greek village), it rained the entire day. An old Greek woman gave us shelter and dried our clothes. On the way to Pologi, we had to make a long detour: there was a punitive unit in Orekhov. The peasants were terrified and we had to spend the night under the stars. Our young son was running a temperature—he was only eleven—and I thought at the time: "Thank God, he's going to die a natural death!"

In Pologi, we were given a place to stay and a pair of felt boots for our son. There are lots of good people in the world. We walked through Sinelnikovo and made it to Igren. A puny German with red eyes stopped us there. He was turning the bags of people passing by upside down and taking whatever he wanted. If he did not like someone, he would yell "*Jude!*" and kill them on the spot. Again we were lucky; we slipped through. In Igren, after waiting for darkness to fall, we made it to my husband's family. They hid me right away, and told the neighbors that my husband and son had arrived. There were still Jews in Igren, but three days later they were taken away to a mental hospital. I left on foot for the place of my aunt's husband in Amur, where they gave us a warm welcome. A few days later, though, they started looking for Jews there as well. My husband carried me in a bag by night across the Dniepr to the edge of Dnepropetrovsk, to my relatives. I did not find anyone there, and if anyone were to come, I would hide in the cellar or under the bed. There were rumors that our boys were coming. Then my husband took me in secret to Amur. After that, we went to Igren. The Germans had taken over the house of my husband's parents. I lived alongside them, I heard their laughter, the tread of their boots, and waited to die. Spring came, but I did not see it. Finally, the Germans left the house. I put on my son's suit—it fit me perfectly—and went out into the garden. But after my long imprisonment, I could not stand it. I could not feel anything.

Sometimes my husband would say to me, after putting his ear to the ground, that he could hear the firing of long-range artillery, and then hope would spring forth. And in Igrenevka, we found Jews who had been saved from the firing squad. We came to my husband's parents' place. They hid me in the bed, under the feather mattress. Once again, there was a knock on the door at night. We decided that it was the Germans. My husband covered me with the featherbed. He lay down on top of it and said that they would only take him dead. But it turned out that it was someone coming to seek medical assistance from my husband's sister; she's a doctor. The Germans began to carry out a thorough search. They announced that the penalty for hiding Jews would be death. It was then that I decided to kill myself. I asked my sister-in-law for some morphine, telling her that it was for only in case I fell into the hands of the Germans. Then I took the poison. But I took too small a dose, so I only became deathly ill and stayed alive.

My husband's mother took me into town again. There was little chance of rescue; the frontline was near Stalingrad. My husband's aunt greeted me warmly—she is a very good person who, besides me, saved the daughter of Goldshteyn, the engineer, and one other Jew. I spent several months in her attic. Then my husband arrived and took me away to the Dolgintsevo station. I worked there as a seamstress, and passed for a Pole.

Hatred for the Germans grew among the peasants; they were taking many of them away to Germany. There were rumors that our boys were getting closer. And now I could really hear the firing of the long-range artillery. Never in my life had I heard such beautiful music! The Germans were rounding up men and herding them off to the west. My husband dug a hole in a field for himself. We would remove the soil by night. He spent two and half months in this pit. On February 22, the Red Army liberated Dolgintsevo. I cannot describe what I felt when I saw my first Red Army soldier!

The next day we drove to Dnepropetrovsk. There I learned that the fascists had killed my entire family. My husband died two days after that. He had so looked forward to the liberation, and he lived all of two days on Soviet soil. I was left with my small son.

F. Krepak
1944

GARF f. 8114, op. 1, d. 950, ll. 295–297. A typewritten manuscript.

35. The rescue of Jews by local inhabitants of Starozhinets, Chernovitsy Region
Accounts of survivors recorded by N. G. Kon
Translated by D. Manevich
[1944]

In Starozhinets, Chernovitsy Region, there were more than 300 Jewish families before the war. For the most part, they were artisans, laborers, and employees of local enterprises. Having seized the city, the Germano-Romanian fascists began resettling Jews in Transnistria, where special ghettos had been created.

In the third week of their rule, the occupiers issued a decree giving the entire Jewish population a specific time at which they were to report to Vokzalnaya Square, bringing what they considered necessary with themselves. Death was threatened for any violations.

By this time, many refugees from Germany, Czechoslovakia, Austria, and other places had massed in Bukovina. They knew what these "special ghettos" meant. The

Bukovina Jews knew it as well, but there was no way out for them. The Romanian *Siguranţa* (secret police), under the command of Gestapo instructors, surrounded the Jewish neighborhoods and drove all the Jewish inhabitants from their homes. All the building superintendents received a summons from the Gestapo. They warned them that if any Jew were found hiding in any building, the superintendent would be shot along with them.

The Jews filled Vokzalnaya Square. For three weeks they were kept there, out in the open, waiting to be shipped off. Fifteen hundred souls—women with children at their breasts, the elderly, and children lay on the damp ground. Many died right there on the square from the cold and damp and from hunger. Some managed to escape, and they ran into the forest.

The forest ranger Stepan Burlecu and his two daughters-in-law, who lived beside the railway station, saved a large group of Jews with the help of the agronomist Pascaranu. They hid them for a time in the woods, and finally, after dressing them in peasant outfits, sent them out to work in the fields and in the forest.

Burlecu and Pascaranu saved a music teacher named Gecht along with his wife and son; Gayzer, the tailor, with his wife and two daughters; Gottlib, the director of a soap factory, and his young daughter (his wife died on Vokzalnaya Square); Bekhler the engineer, whose wife had been shot trying to escape from Vokzalnaya Square; Finder, the teacher, and his two boys; workers in the tannery and the soap factory: Solomon Neyman, David Rubinger, Moisey Rozner, Yakov Zinger, and Ariel Kurtzman.

In addition to these, individual Jewish families survived who had dared, at pain of death, not to show themselves on Vokzalnaya Square and to hide with their Moldavian neighbors. Building superintendents Geccu Lupescu, Nikolai Peranu, and Jan Brugia saved a lawyer named Bislinger and his family; Dr. Velt, the headmaster of the Realschule; the pharmacist Ribayzen; and Kantarovich, a bookkeeper at the city bank.

GARF f. 8114, op. 1, d. 950, l. 280–280ob. A typewritten manuscript.

36. The rescue of a Jewish family in the Novo-Zlatopol District, Zaporozhe Region
An account by Leah Tsviling
Recorded by Dmitry Stonov[76]
1944

---

76. Dmitry Stonov (1898–1962) was a Russian-Jewish writer and journalist. He suffered shell-shock at the Front in 1944 and returned home that summer. He was a member of the Jewish Anti-Fascist Committee and wrote for the Sovinformburo. He was arrested during the wave of repression directed against Jewish cultural figures in 1949 and sentenced to ten years. After Stalin's death he was able to return to Moscow in 1954. His stories about his time in the labor camps were published in Russia only after Gorbachev loosened censorship; see Dmitry Stonov, *In the Past Night: The Siberian Stories* (Lubbock, Texas, 1995).

The Tsviling family is one of the very few that survived in the Novo-Zlatopol Jewish District.[77] We went through many Jewish villages, or rather towns in which there were Jewish villages, and everywhere there were witnesses to one and the same scene. Houses had been burned down—only chimneys still stood erect—vineyards trampled, weeds were growing in the fields. Two or three kilometers from the burned-out ruins, one could see a long, deep trench that looked like an anti-tank ditch. All the inhabitants of the village were buried here, from doddering old people to infant children. Only a few had managed to escape, and one of them was Leah Tsviling, a resident of the village of Friling, with three of her children.

On February 6, 1942, she was supposed to appear along with her children at the assembly point, bringing with her a small shovel and a bundle with her valuables; this was what the commandant's order had said.

On February 5, an enormous cart loaded with vegetables rolled into the Tsvilings' yard, and a few moments later Nikifor Cheredenko, an old farmer from the village of Prishib, came into the house.

Until his marriage, Moisey Tsviling, Leah's husband, had lived in Prishib. The house that he was born and raised in was next door to Nikifor Cheredenko's. The Tsviling family had been friends with the Cheredenkos for many years. Their sons, Moisey Tsviling and Semyon Cheredenko, were the best of friends from childhood. The friendship had not been broken off in the years that followed, right up to the war, when Moisey Tsviling and Semyon Cheredenko had gone to the Front to defend the motherland.

It is forty-five kilometers from Prishib to Friling. In order to reach the Jewish village by evening, Nikifor Cheredenko had left at dawn. He was stopped many times by German patrols, and Cheredenko had shown them certificates confirming that he was transporting vegetables to town.

"Pack up and come visit us," the old farmer said to Leah, not wasting words. "And please don't be long. I've got to get going in half an hour!"

Leah, weakened from sorrow, could hardly have suspected anything. She was about to start talking about the unhappiness that awaited her. It turned out, though, that old Cheredenko already knew all about it. It was this trouble that had brought him to her house.

"Nikifor covered me and the children with cabbage," she tells me now. "All night long we jolted over the potholes, made our way out into the snowy steppe, even though, to tell you the truth, I didn't see the snow or the ground or the sky. Nothing. It was hard for me to breathe, all around was darkness and stuffy air. We traveled for a long time, and no matter how shaken I was, I still managed to think that my flight would do hardly anything to change my fate. Nikifor said that we were going to

---

77. The Novo-Zlatopol Jewish District in the Zaporozhe Region was one of three Jewish districts in southern Ukraine.

Prishib. I'd been in Prishib several times and knew that it was a big village, about five times larger than our Friling. Could someone hide in a village like this, and for that matter, could anyone survive where the Germans were? But a person always hopes; a vague hope still gleamed in my soul."

Hope did not deceive Tsviling. The removal of the family had been carefully thought through by Nikifor Cheredenko, and not by him alone. The outrages of the Germans had deeply affected many of the peasants of Prishib, and they had firmly made up their minds to save the family that they knew. A detailed rescue plan had been worked out: someone obtained a passport in the name of a citizen of Melitopol named Maria Chernysheva, while someone started a rumor in the village that a distant relative of Cheredenko was supposed to come. The entire village—a few hundred people—knew that Chernysheva's real name was Tsviling, and the entire village kept the secret.

The next day, the commandant of Friling discovered the family's escape. They looked for Leah and her children in the nearby villages, bulletins were sent all over the region, and more than once, making the rounds of the village, the commandant of Prishib looked into the Cheredenko house and interrogated Nikifor, his wife, his children, and the neighbors. But each time, they confirmed that they personally knew Maria Chernysheva and her children. The woman remained in Prishib, and she and her children were saved.

GARF f. 8114, op. 1, d. 952, ll. 132–133. A typewritten manuscript.

37. The fraternal grave of ten orphans in the steppe
RECORDED BY N. G. KON
TRANSLATED BY D. MANEVICH
[1944]

Just by the railway station of Kupyansk, on the way from Kharkov to the Donbass, there is a small burial mound. Beneath it rest the remains of ten Jewish orphans who died by Germano-fascist shells two and a half years ago during the evacuation of the Poltava orphange. During the entire time of their stay here, the local inhabitants lied to the Germans, telling them that the "burial mound" had been there from time immemorial. For that reason, the occupiers did not dig up the low hill. When the Red Army liberated Kharkov and the Donbass, a delegation of staff and children from the orphanage arrived from far off Alma-Ata, where the institution had been evacuated to, and with the help of the authorities of reestablished Soviet power, erected a splendid monument bearing the names of the dead children on the fraternal grave. Here are their names: Yosl Lerner, 12, born in Lublin; Riva Riderman, 10, born in Lublin; Velvl Morgenshteyn, 12, born in Khrubishov; Motl Khaykin, 9, born in Warsaw; Moyshe Vaynbern, 10, born in Keltsy; Gershel Fishbeyn, 12, born in Keltsy; Monek Gershman, 12, born in Warsaw; Malka Tipovitskaya, 9, born in Kholm; Moyshe Grossman, 11, born in Krakow; Isaak Ayzikson, 10, born in Krakow.

They were all children of Polish Jews. At the end of 1939, their parents were fleeing from ravaged Poland to the east. Their parents died along the way, and the children were taken in by the Soviet state. They were sent along with the children of hundreds of other refugees to a well-organized orphanage in Poltava. But even here, the bloodthirsty enemy, German fascism, caught up with them. The orphanage was evacuated to the east in good order by a special train. On the way, at the Kupyansk station, the train was attacked by Hitler's airplanes, which dove and rained a death-dealing fire down on the train with the children. Ten children fell dead;[78] many were wounded. The dead were hastily buried beside the station. Children's hands sprinkled earth over the grave and formed a "burial mound." The train went on with a special escort of Soviet warplanes. The Poltava orphanage found refuge in Alma-Ata. In the delegation that came to Kupyansk from far-off Kazakhstan were two orphans who had been wounded during the attack: twelve-year-old Riva Bernshteyn from Brisk and thirteen-year-old Motele Zaltsman from Warsaw. On behalf of their hundreds of comrades who are now being raised in Alma-Ata, Riva Bernshteyn and Motele Zaltsman paid their respects at the fraternal grave and laid a wreath upon it.

On the edge of the steppe, just beside the Kupyansk station, rises a grave in the form of a burial mound. It will be an eternal reminder of the savagery of the Nazi bandits, the Germano-fascist child killers.

GARF, f. 8114, op. 1, d. 950, l. 281–281ob. A typewritten manuscript with corrections by the translator.

38. The shooting of Hungarian Jews in Sumy
THE RECOLLECTIONS OF THE STUDENT TATYANA TARANOVA [79]
[1944]

The town of Sumy. February 1943. A severe winter. Magyars were coming from the Gryazi Station. The Magyars were not accustomed to the cold. Almost all of them were wrapped in pilfered blankets and shawls, beginning with Gypsy headscarves and ending with children's diapers.

Behind the Hungarian units came a labor battalion attached to them. The labor battalion consisted of Hungarian Jews.[80] Early in the mobilization, they were taking everyone into the Hungarian army. But the Germans were already sifting out the Jews. They did not give the Jews uniforms. There were broad yellow armbands on their left arms. The unit was used for the heaviest and dirtiest jobs. When it came to our town, the Jews were dressed in tattered summer clothes. (It was more than a year, after all, since they had received a change of underwear or clothing; noth-

---

78. In the original text, the number "eleven" is written here by mistake.
79. She was a third-year student in the philology department of Kiev University.
80. After Hungary entered the war as an ally of Germany in June 1941, "more than 14,000 young Jews [were] drafted into the Labor Service." Early in 1942, 50,000 were sent to the Eastern Front; *The Holocaust Encyclopedia* (New Haven, 2001), p. 316.

ing had been washed and the work was hard.) The majority had hands and feet that were black from frostbite. They were not fed, and had to feed themselves as best they could. All of them were profoundly miserable. They had a beaten-down look about them. They were afraid of everyone and everything.

Two days later, the Magyars moved on, and the Jews were herded to the other side of Sumy, where they were shot—some six hundred people.

One Jew fell ill and stayed with collective farm workers at a sugar refinery. After a day or two he felt better, but there were no longer any Magyars or Jews around. He decided to ask the German commandant for help because he did not believe that they had shot the Jews. The commandant smiled and called over a soldier with a submachine gun, and the naïve Jew was shot right there.

GARF, f. 8114, op. 1, d. 965, l. 50. A typewritten manuscript with handwritten corrections.

39. Liquidation of the Tarnopol ghetto
TESTIMONY OF THE GERMAN NON-COMMISSIONED OFFICER P. TRAUGOT
[1942]

It was at the end of September or the beginning of October 1942 that the liquidation of the Tarnopol ghetto began. As the forage commander of the 2nd battalion of a unit on the Belorussian Front, I traveled that day to the battalion. It was there that I heard the first news of the "Aktions" that had begun that morning. How involved the commanders of the battalion were in this matter and how much they knew about it, I do not know. Captain Kazar or Podzian could give more detailed information about this, as could the adjutant, 1st Senior Lieutenant Dzhan or Sergeant Gruber, chief clerk of the battalion. This has to do first and foremost with the attitude of the regiment that was under the command of the field headquarters of the city of Lvov, where it was stationed. It is clear that individual units of the battalion took part in this. A rifle company that was garrisoned in the Franz Josef Barracks in Tarnopol at the time, as well as units of an armored train regiment, were also present.

Early in the morning the alarm was sounded in these units, and they encircled the ghetto. The Aktion was directed by the security chief stationed in Tarnopol. In addition, Ukrainian gendarmes and camp guards took part in the Aktion.[81] They were supposed to help drag their compatriots out of various secret hiding places. The latter were, as I learned, the last to be shot that same day. Furthermore, the so-called "store managers" were supposed to carry out their functions until the security chief took over the shop from them. I also want to point out that people were working in the bakery and in the kitchen until evening, until they had, as it were, finished feeding their executioners. The Aktion was divided into stages: to seek out

---

81. "Camp guards" refers to the Jewish police in the ghetto.

the unarmed victims and to gather them in one place. The last ones were hiding in the most impossible corners and refuges.

The scene was approximately as follows: in front of the ghetto stood a large crowd of people made up of inhabitants and visitors from the city, and of soldiers, too. Guards were posted along the fence that surrounded the ghetto. There were even machine guns set up here and there. The Ukrainian police looked for victims and dragged them out of the crowd and their hiding places. I myself witnessed the following: several people were hiding in the cellar of one house that stood to the left of the hospital. The Ukrainian police and the soldiers looked for the entrance to the cellar. It was clear that one resident of a nearby house knew the way into this hiding place and showed it to them. They proceeded with great care because, as I later found out, several shots had rung out in the neighborhood. Several hand grenades had even been tossed from an opening. When the victims came out, they were led to the assembly point under guard. I want to mention here that I was posted in the ghetto that day, and that I saw for myself part of what I related above. Until that time I had been unable to imagine that such things could happen. That dreadful reality gave me the ability that day to live through all the horrors.

During my time in the ghetto, I visited a hospital and one apartment. Everything was smashed, scattered about and lying in dreadful disorder. Beneath the building (the hospital, that is) there was supposedly a bunker. More detailed information revealed that approximately sixty to one hundred people were walled up in there. These were more substantial people, including doctors. As I later learned, this bunker was discovered a few days later (the Aktion continued for several days), as such secret refuges had not yet been uncovered. I know that the security chief even took pictures of this bunker. A junior officer from the armored train was stabbed sometime later; it was said that he had taken part in the search for concealed hide-outs without a corresponding order. Before I go on, I also want to tell you about rumors that were circulating concerning the commandant of the camp. A day before all of this, he got in a motorcycle sidecar, left the camp and never returned again.

The victims who went to the assembly point had to pass by the dead who were already lying there. Their bodies had been lying there for many days. The victims herded together to the assembly point were supposed to surrender all their valuables as well as everything that they were carrying on their persons. They had to get undressed; their clothes formed an entire mountain. Several victims burrowed their way into this heap of clothing, but they were found afterward and shot then and there. Groups that numbered between two and three hundred were led off to the place of execution. Heavily armed soldiers escorted the transport so that none of the innocents could get away. The victims had to make their last journey to the place of execution on foot. They came out from the lower or back gates past the slaughterhouse.

A large group of inhabitants thronged the streets. The route continued on across the bridge over the Seret River at Petoykovo. Here, some jumped off the bridge into the stream and were, from all appearances, shot by the guards escorting them. During one of my trips in a boat, I saw a body in the water.

The place of execution was located in one of the hollows between Petoykovo and Zagrobelye. People from the Ukrainian Labor Front had dug large pits there. The last act of this terrible crime was played out in approximately this way: the victims had to undress almost completely at an appointed place as they arrived and to sit beside each other. The first ones stood single file in front of the pit and had to strip entirely. Eight to ten people would go up to the pit and would sit on the edge facing inward. The security chief's "erasers" did their work. One of them was walking among the victims with a pistol and shooting each of them in the back of the head. He pushed those who did not fall by themselves down into the pit with a kick. There were three men who were carrying out this process. While one kept up constant fire, a second loaded a pistol and passed the loaded weapon to him. The third man helped out with a machine gun. They say that this team had carried out this horrid work not only in this instance, but also earlier, in various places. While they were fulfilling this dreadful duty, it would seem that they were always under the influence of alcohol. And yet the process of execution was always carried out in the manner indicated above.

In the course of all of this, there were heartrending scenes. Yet the thing that struck everyone was the calm with which the victims went to their death. Whole families were led to their executions. Just before, they kissed each other goodbye. Couples in love walked to their deaths with their arms wrapped tightly round each other. The shootings went on that day until evening. Almost everyone was exterminated. In the days that followed, as I have already mentioned, searches were made for those who had gone into hiding.

Non-commissioned officer Paotukha Traugot, Forage Director, 2nd Headquarters Battalion, Belorussian Front, Unit FPN 57158

Headquarters established as district battalion, 755th State Court G.G. on second day of Whitsuntide.

Codicil: Obersturmführer Schneider of the Tarnopol Security Office ruled over the ghetto.

GARF, f. 8114, op. 1, d. 963, ll. 100–102. A typewritten copy.

40. The destruction of the Jews of Mariupol
THE DIARY OF THE STUDENT SARA GLEYKH [82]
[1941]

---

82. Sara Gleykh was a Kharkov student who was evacuated to Mariupol at the beginning of the war. She sent the original pages of her diary to Ilya Ehrenburg during the war. (Ehrenburg refers to them in his memoirs; *Lyudi, gody, zhizn*, vol. 2, pp. 430–431. After the war, Sara Gleykh lived near Moscow. Entries from her diary covering October 8–23, 1941, were published in *The Black Book*, pp. 50–55.

September 17. Finally, a month after my arrival from Kharkov, I am starting to work at the Mariupol Communications Office. At home, the talk is about nothing but leaving. The old people do not want to go. Fanya has signed us up for the factory convoy, but there is no guarantee that they will take the entire family. The most important thing is finding a place for the old people. I can go with the office, which will no doubt be evacuated.

September 23. Everything is quiet in Mariupol, no bombing, people are calming down. This makes many people think that it will not be necessary to leave, all the more since the appearance of the people from Odessa who were evacuated to Mariupol and who have nowhere to stay leads one to think that it would be better to stay put than to go somewhere to be hungry and to sit out in the cold. The Kazhdans are hesitating whether or not to go to Novosibirsk. Manichka is against the trip, Gdanya is insisting on it. They want to send Katyusha along with Ganochka and M. F., and to stay in Mariupol themselves.

October 1. Fanya, Raya, and Fira—military wives—went to the army registration office, where they were told that there was no evacuation planned, that they could issue a ticket without an executive order, and that, in general, it was their opinion that there was no need to go, and that there would be no evacuation of Mariupol before spring.

October 6. Today at 11:00 AM the Kazhdans left for Novosibirsk. Masha cried at their departure. She is sure that they will not make it, that they will be killed along the way since trains are being bombed.

October 7. Last night there was a German air raid, bombs were dropped on the port. The alarm did not last long. In the morning there was another raid. They took the troops and the wounded out of the hospital. There were many refugees from the bombings of Berdyansk and Melitopol.

In the evening, Fira Shternshteyn got the news that her husband had died in the fighting near Osipenko.[83] Tomorrow morning the Shternshteyns are leaving with the Azovstal Factory convoy. The convoy of the Ilych Factory is leaving tomorrow as well. But Fanya says that we will get in the next one.

October 8. The night was quiet. Everyone has gone to work, the shops are open for business, but there is a certain tension in the air in town. Melnikov, the head of the Communications Office, called me in and told me that we would be evacuated on October 10, that it would be necessary to get our documents ready, and that it would be possible to take the family. So, one way or another, the departure would be taken care of. At ten in the morning, random shooting began. Someone came in and said that the Germans had reached the city. Everyone took off running. I ran home. A low-flying plane was strafing the city, the bullets landed right at my feet. A crowd of draftees with rucksacks over their backs scattered for their homes.

---

83. The city of Osipenko is today called Berdyansk; they are the same city.

At twelve o'clock on October 8, the Germans were in the city. Everyone was at home except for Fanya, who was at the factory where she went to work this morning. Is she alive? And if she is, how will she get here, since the trams are not running? Basya is with Ganya, who has typhoid. At six in the evening, Fanya came home from the factory on foot. The Germans arrived at the factory at two in the afternoon, but the workers and administrators were in the bomb shelter; they had taken the firing of the artillery for anti-aircraft guns. Someone happened to find out about the arrival of the Germans. The director of the factory tried to organize a detachment, arms were distributed, but nothing came of it. They say that Gerber, the secretary of the Molotov District Soviet, was killed by the Germans in his office. Ushkatz, the chairman of the city soviet, managed to get away.

October 9. Absolutely nothing to eat in the house. The bakeries in the town are wrecked, there is neither water nor lights. The bakery in the port is still working, but the bread is for the German army only. Yesterday the Germans posted announcements saying that all Jews are obliged to wear identifying marks: a white Star of David on the left arm. It is strictly forbidden to go out without it. Jews are not allowed to move from apartment to apartment. Fanya and her colleague Tanya move their things from their rooms at the factory to Mama's place all the same. She gave a part of her things away to Royanova, Vasya's mother. Fanya has moved in with us, although Papa thinks that she should stay with the Royanovs.

October 11. The arrival of the Germans has torn away the masks. Handwritten announcements are posted around town calling for pogroms. The Black Hundreds have come back to life.[84]

October 12. By decree, the Jewish community has to select a group of thirty people: the group will be answerable with their lives for "the good conduct of the Jewish population," as the order says. The head of the group is Dr. Erber. Apart from Fayn, I do not know any of the members.

In addition, the Jewish community has to register at community points (nine thousand Jews are registered in all). Every point covers several streets. Our point is 64 Pushkin Street; Boru, the bookkeeper, Zegelman, the lawyer, and Tomshinsky are in charge of it. Fanya has to make a special trip to the factory to register; the chairman of the factory group is Dr. Belopolsky, and Spivakov is a member. Demchenko has been appointed city head. They say that he worked in the city's office for communal apartments. Budnyevich is the head of the factory; he lives next door to the Royanovs.

Fanya was at their place—Shura and Leva (Ana's husband) and their neighbor Kayuda left town on October 10. For the time being, there have not been any mass

---

84. The Black Hundreds was a populist, xenophobic, and violent anti-Semitic movement that emerged in Russia at the beginning of the twentieth century. During World War II, the name signified "reactionary" or "fascist."

repressions. Our neighbor Traevsky says that the Gestapo has not gotten here yet, and that later, things will be different.

October 13. The Germans were at our place during the night. At nine in the evening, anti-aircraft fire began. We were all dressed. Vladya was sleeping. Papa went outside to see if there was anyone in the bomb shelter and happened on three Germans; they were in the yard looking for Jews. The neighbors were standing there in a state of indecision, not knowing what to do—to point out our apartment or not. Papa's turning up decided the question. He brought the Germans to our apartment. Sticking a gun in his face, they asked where the butter and sugar were, then they began breaking the doors of the wardrobe even though the wardrobe was open. They took all of Basya's things; she was at Ganya's place. Ganya is alone, Basya is there day and night. Then they came to our things. By twelve o'clock we were literally left with what we were wearing. Two were looting without stopping, they took everything right down to the meat-grinder. After gathering everything up in a tablecloth, they left.

Everything in the apartment was thrown around and scattered about, smashed. We decided not to tidy up. If any more come, let them see that there is nothing for them to do in our place. In the morning we will find out that there has been mass looting in town. The stealing goes on, and during the day they grab up everything: pillows, blankets, food, and clothing. They do not go about alone, but in groups of three or four. You can hear the tread of their boots from a long way off.

There is an order for everyone to report to their place of work, and not showing up is considered sabotage. I was at the office. Melnikov had fled, old man Vernigora was announced as the new boss, with Mikhaylov as his assistant. People are afraid not only to talk to me, but even to stand next to me—I am a Jew, after all. Fanya did not go to the factory. Basya was at the bank, and Karavay, her boss, did not give her a very warm reception and advised her to go home—Jews will not be working.

Papa went to the store. Everything was intact. On the way, a German stopped him and ordered him to carry a big plate glass window. But seeing that he was not up to the task, he called over a younger man and let Papa go home. We went with Fanya to the Kondatskys. It turns out that they had attempted to leave on a barge on October 8, but did not manage to escape.

Tanya went down to the port and got some bread. Now there is something to give to Vladik since the Germans had sprinkled the bread that we had saved for Vladik with camphor. After the Germans left, Mama was crying. She was saying: "They don't consider us people, we're done for."

October 14. In the night, the marauders came again. Tanya, who works with Fanya, saved the rest of the things by pretending that they were hers; the Germans left empty-handed. They went to the Schwartzes and took their blankets and pillows. The Gestapo is already in town, local people are working for the police. Arikhbaev is in the Gestapo. They say that he had been the secretary of the city executive committee.

An order has been given to the council: within two hours collect two kilograms of pepper, 2,500 tins of black shoe polish, and seventy kilograms of sugar from the Jewish population. They go round to the houses collecting things. Everyone gives what they have; after all, the council answers for the "good conduct of the Jewish population."

October 15. The looting continues. Soviet air raids every day. The Germans are afraid to go into Ganya's place. They will not go beyond the threshold now that they have learned that someone in the house is sick with typhoid.

Basya says that a certain Ivan Dimitrovich Kulpe, who works in the supply office of the Azovstal Factory, has begun spending time at her place. He is offering her his help; just what that help is supposed to consist of I do not know.

While Fayn was occupied with council business, the Germans opened up his place in broad daylight and settled in. When he came home in the evening, they would not let him in or give him any of his things. He had nothing but the clothes on his back. Rumors have begun to circulate in town that they are shooting communists who stayed behind in the city.

They pick them up by night. The registration of Party and Komsomol members has been announced as an obligatory measure. Nine thousand Jews have been registered at specific locations points. The remainder of the Jewish population has left town or gone into hiding.

October 16. Fanya was at the Royanovs with Tanya. Kayuda has come back. He says that there is nowhere to go, that the Germans are wiping out everything and everyone on the roads. Shura and Leva did not want to return, though, and had carried on. Kayuda thinks that they went to their deaths. I do not think that the Royanovs will invite Fanya to move to their place. And she herself does not want to ask them. Do they really not understand how serious the situation is? Ulyana came by to see if we were still alive.

October 17. It was announced today that all those who registered must report to assembly points tomorrow with their valuables.

The Germans have put up notices that the bodies of twenty-six people savagely tortured by the Jews were found in the cellars of the NKVD. The burial is scheduled for today. The Jews were forced to dig graves in the Jewish cemetery and to bury the corpses there. The whole population has to appear at the burial. They are being called to identify the bodies. Ulyana says that she went to look, but of course it was impossible to identify anyone. The Black Hundreds are thirsting for a pogrom.

October 18. Today we went to the assembly point—Mama, Papa, Basya, and I. We handed over three silver serving spoons and a ring, after which they would not let us out of the yard. When the entire population of the district had surrendered what they had, it was announced that we had two hours to leave town and that they would resettle us on the nearest collective farm. We would be going on foot, taking warm things and enough food for four days. Everyone was to present themselves here with their things in two hours. There would be vehicles for the elderly and for women with children.

The Jewish women who had Russian or Ukrainian husbands can stay in the city if their husbands are with them. If the husband is in the army or absent for any other reason, the wife and children have to leave the city. If a Russian woman is married to a Jew, she has the right to choose: she can either stay alone or go with her husband. Her children may remain with her.

The Royanovs came to ask Fanya to give them back their grandson. Papa insisted that Fanya and Vladya go to the Royanovs. Fanya categorically refused, wept, and begged Papa not to send her to the Royanovs because "Either way, without you I'll hurt myself. I won't live anyway, I'll go with you." She would not give up Vladya, and decided to take him with her.

The neighbors waited like vultures for us to leave the apartment. In fact, they were not even shy in our presence. Masha opened the doors and told them to take whatever they wanted. They all rushed into the apartment. Mama, Papa, and Fanya with her child immediately kept going, they could not bear to watch it. The neighbors quarrelled over things before my eyes, snatching things out of each others' hands and dragging off pillows, pots and pans, quilts. I waved my hand and left. Basya was the last to remain in the apartment. It was almost empty when she locked the door. Tanya, Fanya's cleaning lady, kept on following us, asking us to leave Vladya with the Royanovs and promising to look after him. Fanya did not even want to hear about it.

We reached the regimental building, where we stood outside until evening. At nightfall they herded everyone into the building. We were given a place in the cellar. It was dark, cold, filthy.

October 19. It has been announced that we will be moving on tomorrow, but today is Sunday and the Gestapo is resting. Tanya, Fedya Belousov, and Ulyana have come, bringing a packet of food. Yesterday, in the commotion, Fanya left her watch on the table. We gave Tanya the spare key to the apartment since everyone had handed over their keys at the assembly point the day before. The Gestapo posted specially printed signs on the doors of all the Jewish apartments: "No entry for unauthorized persons." So Tanya had to sneak into the apartment and, if none of the neighbors had taken the watch, bring it to us the next day.

Friends and acquaintances are bringing everyone parcels, many have received permission to get more things from their homes; people are still coming and coming.

The police have allowed the council to organize the preparation of hot food. They have allowed anyone who is willing and able to bring horses and carts, with the following arrangement: they must write the family name clearly on all bags and bundles in Russian and in German; one family member will ride with the things, while the rest will go on foot.

Vladya has gotten bored here, he is asking to go home. Papa, Schwartz, and Nyusya Kaprilova's stepfather have gotten together and bought a horse and a wagon.

They will not let us go beyond the gate. Fedya Belousov made the purchase, Nyusya managed to get past the gate, and came back upset. She thinks that we should not have come here. She says that lots of people have stayed in the city and that she even met them on the street.

Tomorrow at 7:00 AM we have to abandon our last refuge in the city.

October 20. It rained all night. The morning is gloomy, damp, but not cold.

The entire council left at 7:00 AM, then the trucks with the elderly and women with children moved off. We have to go nine or ten kilometers on foot, and it will be a dreadful journey, judging by the way that the Germans are treating those who have come to say goodbye and to bring parcels. The journey promises nothing good. The Germans club all those who come and drive them out of the regimental building into the quarter. The question has come up as to whether or not Mama, Papa, Fanya, and Vladya should get in a truck. Mama and Papa left at 9:00 AM. Fanya and Vladya stayed behind; they will go in the next truck. The organizers are standing by the truck: V. Osovets and Usiya Reyzins. There are fewer and fewer people in the yard. The only ones left are those who, as the Germans explain it, will follow with the belongings. Shmukler, Vayner, and R. and L. Koldobsky came to see us. I told them that I was afraid for the elderly. There were nasty rumors: some said that the trucks would fall off the road. Someone else said that they are going to take us out of town and kill us there.

Vayner looks awful. It turns out that the Gestapo let him go only yesterday; someone had turned him in for working in the Torgsin.[85] Several Germans came into the yard and began driving people into the street with clubs. The cries of those being beaten could be heard from inside the building; Basya and I came out. Fanya and Vladya were beside a truck. V. Osovets helped her into it and she rode off. We walked along. The road was dreadful. The rain had washed much of it away, it was impassable. It was difficult to lift one's feet. If you stopped, you got hit by a club. They beat people regardless of age.

Raykhelson was walking alongside me and then disappeared somewhere. Next to us now were Shmerok, F. Gurevich and his father, and L. Polunova. It was two o'clock when we arrived at the Petrovsky Agricultural Base. There were lots of people there. I rushed off to look for Fanya and our parents. Fanya called to me. She had been looking for our parents before we got there and had not found them. They were probably already in the barns, where people had been taken in groups of forty or fifty.

Vladya was hungry. It was a good thing that I had taken apples and sugar in my coat pocket. It was enough for Vladik for a day. We had nothing more anyway. It had been impossible to bring anything to eat since the Germans had confiscated everything when we came out of the regimental building, including food.

Our turn came, and the whole scene of senseless horror—senseless to the point of savagery—and uncomplaining death appeared before our eyes when we made our

---

85. Torgsin was the Soviet agency that ran special hard currency shops.

way past the barns. The bodies of Mama and Papa were already lying there somewhere. By sending them off in the truck, I had shortened their lives by several hours. They herded us into trenches that had been dug for civil defense. Nine thousand people from the Jewish community went to their deaths in these trenches. They were no longer of any use to the Germans. They ordered us to strip down to our underwear, and then they searched for money and papers and confiscated them. They drove us along the edge of the trench, but there was no longer any edge. The trenches were filled with corpses for a distance of half a kilometer, while those dying from wounds pleaded for one more bullet, if one had not sufficed to bring death.

We walked on the bodies. It seemed to me that I could see Mama in every gray-haired woman. I threw myself at the bodies, and Basya followed, but the blows of the clubs returned us to our places. Once it seemed to me that an old man with an exposed brain was Papa, but I could not get any closer. We began to say our goodbyes, all of us trying to kiss each other. We remembered Dora. Fanya did not believe that it was the end: "You mean I'll never see the sun and the sky again?" she was saying, her face bluish-gray, and Vladya kept on asking: "Are we going to have a bath? How come we're taking our clothes off? Let's go home, Mama, it's not nice here." Fanya was taking him by the hand. It was difficult for him to walk along the slippery clay. Basya would not stop wringing her hands and whispering: "Vladya, Vladya, why you? No one will even know what they did to us." Fanya turned around and said: "I can die peacefully with him. I know I'm not leaving an orphan." Those were Fanya's last words. I could not stand it any more. I clutched at my head and began screaming wildly. I thought that Fanya would turn around and say: "Quiet, Sara, quiet!" And then everything went black.

When I came to, it was dusk. The bodies lying on top of me were twitching: it was the Germans shooting them again as they left, just in case, to make sure that none of the wounded would get away by night. I gathered this from the Germans' conversation; they were afraid there were quite a few who had not been finished off. They were not wrong. There were many of them. They had been buried alive. No one could give them any help, though they were crying and pleading. Children were crying somewhere underneath the corpses. Most of them, especially infants whom their mothers had been carrying (they had shot us in the back), fell from their mothers' arms unharmed and been covered by corpses—buried alive beneath them.

B. Samoylovich, who had reached the place of execution before his mother (she had been with him, while his wife, who was Greek, did not have to die that very day) asked for permission to wait for his mother. He undressed, and they took him off to one side.

I began making my way out from under the corpses. I tore off my toenails, but discovered this only later, when I got to the Royanovs on October 24. I reached the surface and glanced back; the wounded were floundering about, moaning, trying to stand up and then falling again. I started calling Fanya's name in the hope that she could hear me. A man next to me ordered me to be quiet. It was Grodzinsky; they had killed his mother. He was afraid that my cries would attract the attention of the Germans. A small group of people who had figured out what was going on and who had leapt into the trenches at the first volleys turned up unhurt: Vera Kulman, Major Shmaevsky, Tsilya (I do not remember her surname). They kept asking me to be quiet. I began asking everyone who was leaving to help me look for Fanya.

No one turned back, everybody was going. Grodzinsky, who had been wounded in the leg and could not walk, advised me to leave. I tried to help him, but was in no condition to do so by myself. After two steps he fell down and refused to go any farther. He advised me to catch up with those who had left. I sat down and listened intently. Some old-timer was singing: "*Leite Nacht, Leite Nacht*" [Yiddish for bright night, bright night]—there was so much horror in those endlessly repeated words. Somewhere down in the depths, someone was crying out: "Lord, don't kill me." I happened to catch up with V. Kulman. She had wandered off into the darkness from the group that she had left with, and the two of us, naked except for our underwear, covered with blood from head to toe, set about looking for a place for the night by following the barking of some dogs. We knocked at the door of one hut; no one answered. We went to another and were chased off. At a third they gave us some rags to cover ourselves with and advised us to head off into the steppe, which we did. At twilight, we reached a haystack and sat there until daybreak. In the morning we went back to the farmstead. Its name turned out to be Shevchenko. It was not far from the trenches, only on the other side. The cries of women and children were still reaching us at the end of the day.

October 23. We have already been on the steppe for two days now. We do not know any of the roads. Today, by chance, as she was going from haystack to haystack, V. Kulman discovered a group of men, one of whom was Shmaevsky. Naked and bloodied, they have been sitting here the whole time. We decided to make for the Ilych Factory by day because we would not find the road by night. On the way to the factory, we came upon a group of young men, collective farm workers, from the looks of them. One of them advised us to stay on the steppe until nightfall. A second warned us that the sooner we got away, the better, because his friend had deceived us with his advice; he would bring the Germans. We got away as fast as we could. On the morning of October 24, we knocked at the Royanovs' door. They let me in. When they found out that everyone was dead, they were horrified. They helped me to clean myself up, fed me, and gave me a bed.

October 25. Zina has come. She is living with her mother on the left bank. When she found out what had happened, she burst into tears and said: "If they'd give us permission, we'd find Vladik and give him a proper burial." Not a word of condolence for Fanya.

October 26. It is not possible to stay with the Royanovs any longer. Their neighbor, Kayuda, advises us to leave. Zina brought me my coat and Mama's. I got dressed and decided to go into the city. I walked through the whole town and no one stopped me. Who knows me, though, except for the neighbors? No one. I quickly walked across the courtyard and went up to the Stetsenkos' apartment. A. I. was home by herself. When she saw me, she was amazed and became flustered. I asked her to call Tanya.

I had to change my clothes. My old dress and underwear had remained in our apartment, but Tanya told me that there was nothing left. L. Leymunskaya came and brought me Basya's old dresses. It was then that I remembered that she had my things and that my dresses were there, and that she had probably used them. I could not stay here. I decided to stay in the bomb shelter until dusk. I sat in the bomb shelter until 11:00 PM. At 11:00 PM, F. Belousov came and took me to his place. I spent the night with them, and at daybreak went to the barn to see L. Leymunskaya; it is just near our building. A cat was locked in the house. It ran from the terrace into the kitchen, overturning everything in its path, and it seemed to me all the while that at any moment I would hear someone's voice, that all at once there would be someone there, but no, it did not happen. During the day, Tanya, Vera, and Lyusya gave me food, cautiously, so as not to reveal my presence. Lyusya, at my request, went to see Ganya and told her where I was. In the evening I was supposed to go to her place.

From the barn I could see the entire courtyard: Travsky was strutting around warning everyone not to hide Jews, that Jews had to be wiped out. V. Shwartz told me that he had gone to see her yesterday and asked for her father's fur coat. "It makes no difference," he said. "He doesn't need it any longer."

October 27. Yesterday evening I was lucky to make it to Ganya's. Fedya and Tanya (Fanya's cleaning lady) came with me. Kulpe was very attentive and caring. They promise to give me a place to hide, since it would be dangerous at Ganya's; the Germans do not believe either of them, but disease frightens them, and this saves her for the time being. Even so, they have already been here once and they threatened them both.

October 29. Kulpe brought his father, and I went with him on a worker's train to the left bank where Kulpe has a room, but I only spent two days there before I had to come back to Ganya's. Kulpe's sister is frightened by my presence.

November 2. I am in hiding at Ganya's again. I am sitting in the second room. I must not talk loudly so that the neighbors on the other side of the door will not detect the presence of a third person in the apartment. Still, every ring and knock at the door sets everyone to trembling. Where can I find a safer place to stay? This question never leaves my mind. Ganya's former cleaning lady, Vasilisa Popova, happened to come by. She lives on the right bank. Her husband left with the Azovstal Factory convoy, leaving her with two children. After long negotiations, we decided that she would come back in the late afternoon, and that I would go to the right bank with her for a few days, and then we will see what happens. Ganya resists all my attempts to convince her that I need to leave and try to cross the frontline. She thinks that it makes no sense to go without money and papers. Besides, it is very cold, and I am almost completely undressed. Her things are still hidden at the home of one of her co-workers from the canning factory. She is intending to dispatch Kulpe to him in a few days, and offers me her own fur coat. For the time being I have to stay with V. Popova.

November 3. I am in a new apartment. It is an uncompleted shack, so inconspicuous that the Germans will not even look this way. Vasya Popova goes to town regularly and visits Ganya, but for the moment all Ganya's efforts to get her things returned have been unsuccessful. They have agreed that on November 8, Vasya Popova and Kulpe will go together to the engineer's place and bring back what he gives them. Judging by what Vasya says, Ganya's colleague will not be too happy to part with her suitcases.

November 8. In the morning, V. Popova went over to see Ganya, but soon came back and told me that Ganya and Kulpe had been taken to the Gestapo during the night. It was the neighbors who told her. I have got to leave, there is no other solution. I got my things together quickly, said goodbye to Vasya, and left. I do not know the roads. I am walking and I do not even know where.

November 9. I came to some settlement. It turned out that it was a Greek village called Stary Krym. That means that I am heading into the German rear; I have got to go back. Decided to go along the coast to Budennovka, Taganrog, Rostov. It is hard going, particularly at night. It is cold even in the haystacks, the grain doesn't warm you at all, but asking for a place to stay in the villages is dangerous. Sometimes I cannot even walk by day. My feet are swollen, I sit in the hay for three days, but still get up. I go on again. I meet up with travelers, city folk on their way to the villages to exchange their belongings for bread, or people escaping from captivity. To judge by their conversations, the Germans are advancing rapidly, Taganrog has been taken and fighting is going on near Rostov.

November 22. I am in Taganrog. The streets are empty, met a group of people on the outskirts. They (as a talkative old woman said to me) were on their way to the Petrushkin Ravine, where the Jewish population of Taganrog had been shot.

November 25. Approaching Rostov. Very tired. Reached Olimpiadovka. It is not far from Rostov. They say that there is even a tram line here. Decided to ask the first person I meet for a place for the night.

November 26. Spent the night in Olimpiadovka. Snow fell in the night. There is a frost. Asked the way and I am going to Rostov.

Signs in town of recent fighting. Here and there on the edges of town the bodies of Red Army soldiers are lying about. Decided to go to Novocherkassk. I approach Nakhichevan; asked at one of the houses to be able to stay a while, get warm and rest. My feet are hurting terribly, they are swollen, I have irritated them with uncomfortable shoes. Every step is torture for me.

November 27. Spent the night in Nakhichevan. In the morning decided to go on. No sooner had I gone outside than shooting started; firing from Bataysk at Rostov.

Reached Bolshoy Log, a hamlet beside a station. I follow the railway line. Strong wind, snow.

It was already getting dark. I learn that Russian forces are 5 kilometers away. German patrols all around are guarding the railroad line. Asked to be let in at the hut of a woman living in the village, she has two children. Decided to go on tomorrow morning. It was not necessary to leave in the morning, though. At dawn on November 28, fighting began that lasted day and night. On November 29, no sooner had I left Bolshoy Log than I met a Russian scouting party.

GARF, f. 8114, op. 1, d. 961, ll. 65–80. A typewritten manuscript.

41. An execution in Mariupol
A LETTER FROM SAMUIL ARONOVICH BELOUS
PREPARED BY S. GOLOVANIVSKY

The Germans stormed into Mariupol on October 8, [1941], and began hunting for Jews. At nightfall, there was robbing and killing. Shots were ringing out all over town: it was the Germans breaking into apartments, robbing people, beating them, and shooting Jews. The inhabitants, full of fear, hid in corners as they waited for the terrifying visitors. The next morning, announcements were posted in town with orders to immediately organize a Jewish council. Under threat of execution, the Jews were forced to select their representatives, among whom were the very best people—doctors and engineers. These people were the first to taste all the loathsome cruelty of the German butchers: the most repulsive and unrealizable demands were made of them, and they were subject to merciless beatings for failing to meet them. Every day, representatives of the Jewish council were summoned by the Gestapo or by the city commandant. Through them, the Germans demanded certain amounts of flour, sugar, honey, shoe polish, soap, and so on. The Jewish population, living in great fear and feeling that something dreadful was hanging over their heads, rushed about giving away everything they had left, everything they had in their homes, in the hope that any day the Red Army would return and free them from all this horror.

A few days passed like that. There was more and more looting of the population. The conquerors drove up to apartment buildings in broad daylight and took away anything they pleased. They would load it all onto trucks and drive away. Any protest or resistance on the part of the inhabitants brought with it the harshest reactions, right up to murder. Every morning, new groups of shooting victims turned up. If the family of a victim tried to take the body away or bury it, they were subjected to inhuman beatings. Days passed, and the bodies were not picked up. The demands of the Germans on the Jews became greater and greater. Another order followed, saying that Jews would have to wear six-pointed stars made from white material on their left sleeves. The penalty for violation of this rule, or any rule, for that matter, was shooting. The life of the Jewish community was complicated even further by the onset of hunger. Supplies were either confiscated by the Germans or used up altogether. It was dangerous to go out on the street because the Germans were seizing every Jew they came upon, beating him, then taking him off to work. Almost no one managed to make it home from work; they were finishing them off right there. Hunger grew greater. There was nowhere to buy anything, all the shops had been looted.

Eight days later, on October 16, all the Jews had to go for registration. Avoiding registration meant death. Then came the next order: all valuables that the Jews possessed were to be turned in within two hours. This was followed by an order for the "evacuation" of the Jewish inhabitants. You could bring anything you wanted. Two assembly points were designated for the entire population of Jewish nationality. Everyone was bustling about in great alarm. Everyone was searching, running back and forth, packing and wrapping up their best things. Anxious eyes full of alarm and despair would ask you: "Where are they taking us?" Mute silence served as an answer.

With our best things, my son and I went to the assembly point. Groups of people carrying heavy suitcases and sacks were moving in from all directions. With downcast faces, puffing from the weight of their belongings, men, women, and children went along full of fear and doubt, not knowing where they were being taken or why. There were even some who brought their possessions in a cart hitched to a cow or horse. Two hours later, the Germans moved the whole enormous crowd (exceeding three thousand people) in the direction of the mill. They halted us on a square beside a large, four-story building. Movie cameras appeared and began filming these unfortunate people in order to show "great" Germany how the conquerors were dealing with the conquered. They quickly herded us into the building, where they kept us for two days and nights without food and water. At brief intervals, the Gestapo would storm into the building and the next round of looting would begin. They demanded money, watches, and other valuables. When they had stuffed their pockets and wallets with their plunder, the officers would leave with a smile, only to return an hour or two later. In this difficult, nerve-wracking atmosphere, exhausted from hunger, I endured these two days along with my son. Tension and unease were heightened further by each rumor that was circulating in the crowd. Nevertheless, no one would suppose that this huge mass of people would be taken out for execution.

On the morning of October 18, the Germans chased away all those who were outside next to their wagons and carts. These people went off in an unknown direction, leaving their possessions behind. Seeing this, our hearts sank even more. Nightmarish thoughts went through our brains: the hope that we would come out of this alive grew weaker. Everyone was restless, running back and forth to each other, looking for family members, friends, telling stories, asking questions. Lips trembled, faces were pale as death. Again the Germans burst in, and again they shouted and demanded watches, money, and the like. After half an hour the wave of looting passed, and the Germans moved off. The people waited for the next raid, followed by the removal of the crowd to an unknown destination. Two hours later they took out those on the second floor, also without their things. If anyone grabbed hold of anything, they were savagely beaten. They formed people into ranks and drove them off. More and more clearly we began to realize that something dreadful awaited us. Yet at the same time we did not believe that our hours were numbered. My son began trying to persuade me to escape. The guard detail was too strong, and any attempt at escape would have meant a premature bullet. I tried to calm my son, but he would have none of it. Finally, he got my permission to go himself. Knowing there was no escape, I allowed my son to flee. For the first time in my life, I saw my son's eyes fill with tears as he said goodbye.

From a window on third floor I watched him go. The Germans stopped him, but he told them that he was a Russian, and they let him go. And I never saw my son again. I myself stayed in the enormous crowd. Noise, shouting, and wailing filled the entire hall in which I found myself. Sitting beside me were my eighteen-year-old nephew (my brother's son) and his aunt and uncle. We were all in a desperate state. An hour later, they chased us all out into the street, formed us into ranks, and beat us with sticks. My female relative took the first hard blow to the head. A fine autumn rain was lashing us the whole way. People went along in a suffering, weakened state from hunger; any sort of mud makes movement even more difficult. Germans with submachine guns stood by the side of the road. We came out onto the road leading to the *Krasnaya zvezda* [Red Star] state farm. We ran into cars full of Germans along the way. Officers would jump out of the vehicles with cameras in their hands. The crowd kept on moving.

Finally, we drew near the collective farm. A small bridge separated us from its barns. As soon as we set foot on the bridge, it became clear to everyone what awaited us: on the ground wet from the rain lay belongings, shoes, overcoats, pillows, watches, and money. A dreadful feeling seizes me. My head is spinning, everything is flickering before my eyes. And the farther on we go, the more we become convinced that we will not come back from here alive. Thoughts lose their natural course. We want to shout, to tell the whole living world what the "cultured and civilized" Germans are doing with people in the twentieth century. A woman doctor named Goltsman makes her way through the crowd toward me with a friend of hers. Fear and horror are reflected on their beautiful, delicate faces. Both of them, tripping over each other's words, say to me: "You see what's going on here. Let's get away. It'll be dark soon. Let's slow down, maybe we'll manage to get out of here."

The three of us are no longer hurrying forward, but are slowly making our way through the crowd as we move in the opposite direction. The Germans, who are standing in lines, grab their rifles with a shout when they notice our movements. I receive a powerful blow from a gun butt. I lose sight of my traveling companions and move on with the whole crowd as though drunk. The officers are carefully watching those passing by. In front of me is a gracefully built young woman wearing an expensive fur coat. A German clubs her over the head and orders her to take off the fur coat. The bewildered and helpless girl obeys the order. I am approaching the doors to the barn. Several people run in different directions, detaching themselves from the crowd. Bullets catch up with them, and they fall dead. It is dark and frightening in the barn, filled with people. I call out to my nephew, to my relatives, but no one responds.

I understood that they there were in a different stable. The constant noise and yelling kept up all night: children were wailing, asking for bread, for water. This was one of the most terrifying nights of my life. I realized that it was all over, but the urge to live with all its power comes over me. The brain works feverishly. A single question is before me: how to save your life and tell the world about everything that you have seen. Isolated shots ring out here and there, bullets pierce the thin walls and wound several women. The men try to calm and give encouragement to the women and children, trying to persuade them to be strong and await the break of day with courage.

Finally, dawn begins to gleam faintly. There is movement outside. Everyone is waiting in great alarm. Soon after, the heavy doors open. The Germans burst into the barn with clubs and chase out several dozen people, form them up and lead them off. Through a narrow opening, I see them take a group up to the edge of an antitank ditch and shoot them with submachine guns. The bodies of people who had just been living and thinking fall dead into the ditch. Then they bring up a second group, then a third, and the same process is carried out. Shouts, roars rose up in the barn. A young, beautiful girl (a neighbor from my apartment building) was running from corner to corner clutching at her head, shouting and crying: "What are they doing this for? I'm young, I want to live!" But her turn comes soon.

The brain does not stop working, you see death. And the thirst for life is still greater. A sharp thought goes through my brain. Following it, I grab my passport and tear it into small bits. And when the doors open for the fifth time, I run out ahead of the rest and announce to a German: "I'm a Russian!" His evil, bloodthirsty eyes go right through me. And to the question of how I had ended up in the middle of these Jews, I reply that I am a Russian but that my wife is a Jew. My trick works; the German leads me off to one side. Another woman is standing next to me; her passport says that she is Ukrainian. We both stand there petrified while group after group is led past us to the slaughter. The bodies cut down by the submachine guns fall on one another. Everyone is mixed together in this grave: the wounded, the dead, women, men, and children. People are falling on one another, gradually filling the ditch. Here comes my nephew. His face paler than pale, his eyes looking dully at his feet. Now his aunt comes hurrying, almost running, her face flushed. And a minute later her husband comes running, yelling inhumanly, like an animal's roar. The heart breaks to pieces.

GARF f. 8114, op. 1, d. 961, ll. 30–36. A typewritten manuscript.

Portrait of a Jewish man holding the hand of his young son at an assembly point in Ukraine, July 1941. USHMM, courtesy of Bildarchiv Preussischer Kulturbesitz.

A group of Jewish men, rounded up by German troops for allegedly betraying five German soldiers to the Red Army, are marched to a killing site, June 28, 1941. USHMM, courtesy of Bundesarchiv.

Jews from Lubny at an assembly point before their murder, probably in October or November 1941 or April 1942. USHMM, courtesy of Hamburger Institut fuer Sozialforschung.

German police and auxiliaries in civilian clothing prepare to murder naked Jewish men and boys who are being lined up at the edge of a mass grave, Snyatyn, May 11, 1943. USHMM, courtesy of Bildarchiv Preussischer Kulturbesitz.

Ukrainian auxiliaries prepare to murder Jewish prisoners, Chernigov, 1942. USHMM, courtesy of A Magyar Nemzeti Múzeum Történeti Fényképtára.

A German policeman shoots a Jewish woman sitting on the edge of a mass grave, June 1941–1943. USHMM, courtesy of Lydia Chagoll.

Lithuanian auxiliary police herd a column of Jews to be murdered at a previous Soviet construction site in the Ponary Forest, Lithuania, summer 1941. USHMM, courtesy of Yad Vashem Photo Archives.

Men with an unidentified unit murder a group of Soviet civilians kneeling by the side of a mass grave, June 22–September 1941. USHMM, courtesy of National Archives and Records Administration, College Park.

II
BELORUSSIA

Cities throughout Belorussia, most notably Minsk, Volozhin, Vitebsk, Mogilev, Gomel, Orsha, and Bobruysk, among many others, had long been centers of Jewish life and learning. Before 1939, the Jewish population of the republic was 405,000. As happened in Ukraine, the Hitler-Stalin Pact created a shift in the western border of Belorussia, bringing hitherto Polish cities such as Grodno, Belostok (Bialystok), Mir, and Brest within its borders. It also vastly increased the Jewish population by as many as 670,000, including Jews who had fled the German-occupied part of Poland.

The German advance into Belorussia was so quick and devastating that the entire republic was captured by the end of August 1941. Nonetheless, about 120,000 Jews from within the pre-1939 border (including an insignificant number of fugitives from the West) managed to flee into the Soviet interior. Einsatzgruppe B followed closely behind the Wehrmacht and carried out systematic massacres. By summer 1944, when the Red Army succeeded in liberating Belorussia (the capital, Minsk, was freed on July 3, 1944, having been occupied for three full years), as many as 800,000 Belorussian and former Polish Jews had been killed.

Belorussia also served the Germans as a killing center for Jews from Western Europe, "a dumping ground for undesirables" as Alexander Dallin put it.[1] In November 1941, and then from May to October 1942, the Germans transported tens of thousands of Jews from Hamburg, Germany, from Austria, and from parts of Czechoslovakia (what the Germans called the Protectorate of Bohemia and Moravia). Most were killed immediately in Maly Trostyanets outside of Minsk,

---

1. Alexander Dallin, *German Rule in Russia 1941–1945; A Study of Occupation Politics*, 2nd ed. (London, 1981), p. 201.

where an estimated 65,000 Jews were murdered during the German occupation; other groups of Jews from Western Europe were kept for a time in the Minsk ghetto, where they were not supposed to have contact with Soviet Jews. There was even a plan to construct a full-scale extermination camp in Mogilev, in eastern Belorussia, in which Jews from Western and Central Europe could be killed. But under wartime conditions, it seemed unlikely they could transport hundreds of thousands, if not millions, by rail into Belorussia; sending them by boat via the Western Bug, Pripet, and Dnieper proved similarly unworkable as the rivers were vulnerable to attack by the growing partisan movement.[2]

Indeed, within Belorussia, the partisan movement was particularly large and widespread. Much of the territory was forest and swamp, providing favorable concealment for partisan groups. As many as 30,000 Jews joined an estimated 340,000 other partisans in units that operated against the Germans, in spite of the fact that non-Jewish partisans were not always willing to accept Jews into their units and the central staff of the partisan movement resisted the creation of independent Jewish partisan detachments. Surprisingly, given these unbearable conditions, Jewish partisans were able to organize camps for Jewish families in several heavily wooded areas. In these family camps, saving Jews was as important a goal as fighting the Germans, so women and children were protected along with the elderly and the infirm. According to the Israeli specialist on Belorussian Jewry Leonid Smilovitsky, as many as 5,000 people managed to survive the Final Solution in Jewish family camps in Belorussia.[3]

Minsk

42. In the Minsk ghetto
FROM THE NOTES OF THE PARTISAN MIKHAIL GRICHANIK [4]
PREPARED BY A. MARGULIS
[1944]

When the German occupiers entered Minsk, they published a decree calling for the mandatory registration of all men aged eighteen to fifty. As it turned out, no registration was carried out; all those who reported to the place indicated for "registration" were marched out of town in formation by the Germans to an open field.

---

2. See Christian Gerlach, "Failure of Plans for an SS Extermination Camp in Mogilev, Belorussia," *Holocaust and Genocide Studies* 11, no. 1 (Spring, 1997), pp. 60–78.
3. See Leonid Smilovitsky, "Righteous Gentiles, the Partisans, and Jewish Survival in Belorussia, 1941–1944," *Holocaust and Genocide Studies* 11, no. 3 (1997), p. 317.
4. Mikhail Grichanik, a Jewish tailor and resident of Minsk, worked for several months in a garment factory during the German occupation. His entire family of eight people was killed by the Germans. As a tailor, his life was temporarily spared. Grichanik escaped and joined the partisans. During one combat operation, both of his legs were frostbitten and he was transported to a hospital in the rear, where his recollections were noted down.

Sentries were posted around the field. The people arrived, one group after another. It was cold at night in an open field, and the people kept warm by lying against each other.

The first night was spent this way, followed by a bright, clear day. Many people were hungry, but no food was distributed. It was very hot, people were thirsty. They asked for water, but they were not given that, either. You no sooner went up to ask for water than soldiers shot you point blank with explosive rounds. More than ten people were killed on the second day because they asked for water. The Germans forced others to dig a hole and to bury them. Anyone who was still breathing they finished off with a shot. So ended *the second day*.

The second night came on. People were lying there cold and hungry. Some were dressed, and some were only in short-sleeved shirts. They had not gone out to be tortured, but "to be counted." Daylight came on. People kept arriving. A German appeared with a bucket and began distributing water. People surrounded him and nearly crushed him. Again the bastards fired on the crowd!

The eighth night was coming on. People were lying in the field. They were warned not to get up in the night or they would be shot. So the night passed. There was often machine gun fire. Suddenly I heard a shout: "They've killed him!" People would get up to take care of their needs, and they were shooting them!

For example, one man was lying there. A bullet hit him in the small of the back and went out by his stomach. His innards were torn out. Still alive, he asked someone to take down his address and to write to his wife and children to tell them how he perished. A German came up to him and asked him who "split his belly open with a knife."

The thirteenth day. Ten o'clock in the morning. A car drives up. There is an announcement that all Poles should go to the left, all Russians to the right, and that all criminals should keep themselves separate; an area beside the stream will be set aside for the Jews. It is cordoned off with thick ropes. The crowd begins to divide itself as ordered. Criminals seize the moment: from one Jew they steal food, from another a raincoat, from another a jacket or shoes. Things reach the point where people are standing in nothing but their underwear. The Germans stand off to one side and laugh.

Germans stand around the field with rubber truncheons. Some of them drive the Jews toward the ropes and beat them with clubs. Criminals help the Germans to persecute the Jews. Anyone who resists is beaten to death or shot. Suddenly, an announcement comes from the car that all the Poles can go home. Then another announcement: the Russians can go home, while nothing is said about the Jews. They begin to let some of the Poles go home.

The seventeenth day in the morning. Toward ten o'clock, a car with an interpreter arrives. There is an announcement that all Jews who are engineers, doctors, technicians, bookkeepers, teachers, and other intellectual professions must register themselves. They are releasing them from the camp and sending them to work. The registration begins. They sign up all the intelligentsia, form them up and lead them away from the workers. It gets dark. Beside the Jews and the POWs, there is no one else in the field.

The nineteenth day, before dawn. It is still dark. The roar of vehicles can be heard. Trucks drive up to the intelligentsia, load them and take them off "to work." About twenty minutes go by after the departure of the trucks, then a burst of machine gun fire is heard. Fifteen minutes later, the trucks return and again take people away. In this way they take away all the intelligentsia, leaving only the workers. An officer appeared, selected two hundred or so working men and led them off on foot "to work." He announced that the next day they would be taking us out of here to another place; it would be warm there, and the rain would not be pouring down.

The twentieth day, in the morning. Only Jews were left in the field. A Gestapo unit turned up. They formed all of us into rows and led us through the city. Anyone who tried to approach us was shot on the spot. Sentries stood all along the route to the prison. We were put in small cells on the second floor. The cells were full to bursting. It was very hot. There was an iron bucket in each cell. The stink made it impossible to breathe. People took turns standing "in two stories" (climbing on top of each other) beside the bars, in order to breathe. They distributed very little water and nothing at all to eat.

The Gestapo agents would show up, surround the cells, and drive everyone out into the main yard. Down below, beside the doors, Gestapo men stood with birch rods and would let no one go out without a blow from his stick. But now they began beating people up above on the staircase as well, and those rushing downstairs raced past the Gestapo agents standing down below by the doors. Everyone was already outside. The order was given: "Make fours." Everyone formed up. The interpreter said that the lists of all those arrested, along with a towel and a bar of soap, had been taken from the desk of one of the officers, and that the person who had done it should confess. Anyone who knew who had done it should point the person out. No one would be released from the prison until they had found the thief, but as soon as he was discovered, then we would all be released in two days' time. The rods went to work. They grabbed one fellow and broke a rod over his head. He fell down. It was said that they found a piece of a towel on him. They herded us all back into the prison. At the entrance to the corridor they beat us with the rods again.

Two days later, an interpreter appeared and said they were letting us go home that day. They distributed paper among the cells, and the interpreter proposed that we make lists of those arrested by cell in Russian and German and to give them to him. At two o'clock in the afternoon, the Gestapo turned up and drove everyone out into the yard. We formed up as we sat—by cell. When everyone was assembled, the interpreter began to call some out by their surnames, ordering them to form up separately. Some did not answer or step forward. Thanks to this, they stayed alive this time.

For example, Botvinnik, a Party member and a worker in the Oktyabr Factory, and Kagan, who was an office worker in a bread factory, saved themselves in this way.

So the interpreter chose two hundred men and announced that they would be staying in the jail to clean things up. No one has so much as looked them in the eye since then. The remaining prisoners were ordered by the interpreter to go the "Jewish Council." (While we were in jail, the Germans had organized a "Jewish Council.")

And so, they opened the gates and let us out. We went to the "Council." Our wives and children ran toward us; there was kissing and crying.

At the "Jewish Council," they announced to all those who had been freed from the jail that they were ordered to live in the ghetto, to wear yellow marks on their chests and backs, not to walk on the sidewalks, and to report daily to the "Council," from where they would be sent to work, and so on.

Signs in German and in Russian were posted on the corners and in the alleyways of the ghetto: "Ghetto. Entry forbidden to all but kikes."

Coming upon Jews without the yellow mark, the Germans would give them a beating and demand that they wear it. The Jews were forbidden to use the sidewalks; they had to walk in the middle of the street. Jews were obliged to take off their hats when they passed Germans; if they did not, any German could beat them to death.

Suddenly the Gestapo swoop down on the ghetto in trucks and begin seizing men. They go into apartments, beat people with rubber truncheons and lead them out under the guise of sending them off to work: to the peat bogs and such places. No one ever saw any of those taken away alive again.

At night, almost every night, in one street or another, armed men attack, rob, and kill.

Now the Gestapo agents surround the ghetto again; again they catch men. Some of them manage to conceal themselves in attics, others conceal themselves by digging tunnels. When the Gestapo catch people, they take them away. Some end up in the camp on Shirokaya Street. They work there and are not allowed to go home. There are many POWs in the camp. The Germans send Russians and other people there who are guilty in their eyes. People in the camp are shot for the smallest trifle. Many are sick. They often catch new people for this camp and for others. People drop out of the ranks quickly there.

The Germans begin breaking down apartment doors at night, and taking away things that they like.

The Germans often surround entire streets of the ghetto and check papers, search homes, and haul away young people.

At night, the Germans show up in the ghetto and, on the pretext of having discovered weapons, kill people—one hundred every night.

On November 7, 1941, open persecution of other people began, not only of Jews. Gallows appeared throughout the city—on streets, on corners, in open air markets, on the outskirts. Around one hundred people were hanged that day. Small plywood boards reading "Partisan," "For contact with partisans," "Communist," and so on, were hung around their necks.

On November 7, at five in the morning, the Gestapo and the local scoundrels who had sold out to the Germans formed a tight ring around the ghetto, each three paces from the other. This was the first open operation of mass slaughter of the Jewish population by the German bandits. They smashed windows and doors, went into apartments, ordered people to put on their best clothes and to dress their children, making them take even nursing infants. Some tried to run away, but there were sentries everywhere, and they shot those who were trying to escape.

On one of the streets, they formed up the Jews into ranks of four and led them under guard down Novokrasnaya Street. A machine gun began blazing away, cutting down the whole formation. They photographed the slaughter from a car that was parked beside the square.

A former worker of the Oktyabr Factory told me about this atrocity; he had observed it from his hiding place in an attic. They said that those who were shot were supposed to represent a group of Soviet citizens demonstrating in honor of the October Revolution.

I was working at the Oktyabr Garment Factory. All told, there were 300 to 350 Jews, men and women, working at the factory. The Jewish workers hear the shooting and realize that an outright pogrom has begun in the ghetto. They run crying to the bosses. It is only toward midday that certificates are issued for their family members so that they would not be killed. The workers grab the certificates and run to the ghetto. Each man hurries to his own apartment, but many of them no longer find anyone at home. From the appearance of the apartments, it seems that people were dragged straight from their beds.

What a thunderbolt strikes me! Out of eight people—my wife, three children, my elderly mother, my sister, and her two children—not a soul left! The apartment is dead, empty.

A few find some members of their families, those who had managed to hide.

Others approach the trucks in which they are putting people and show their certificates; those who are still alive are released by an officer.

Not finding their family members, several workers ask for permission to go with the trucks to look for them; perhaps they can manage to save them. The officer gives them a straightforward answer: those who had been taken away are no longer alive. If you want to go, I won't stop you, but whether or not you'll come back, I don't know. It is all very clear.

The trucks do not manage to take everyone away. They gather up many on Khlebnaya Street at a big courtyard. They take them away in a truck from there. People run there with their certificates. Many workers do not find their families there. Many on the truck plead with the workers to rescue them, and, pretending that they are their relatives, take away other doomed people according to the number marked on their certificates. No small number of those saved in this way do not leave their rescuers and still live with them as family.

Then there comes word that even on Tankovaya Street, on the other side of the railroad tracks, many victims are languishing in the former Red Army barracks; they have not managed to slaughter them all yet. The workers set off in that direction. When they are not far from the barracks, they hear bursts of machine gun fire, and trucks carrying people come through the gates. Trucks carrying clothing—coats, shoes, boots, and so on—are making the return trip. The trucks are open, and some of the clothes have fresh blood on them. The sentry does not let the workers through and summons an officer. The officer does not recognize any certificates and chases everyone away: "Off to the ghetto." People go back with nothing.

In this way, the mass slaughter of Jews continues through November 7, 8, and 9 of 1941.

On November 20, a Gestapo unit raids Rakovaya Street. Local police surround the street and drive everyone out of their apartments. They leave no one.

Some of the workers have not yet left for their jobs. The Gestapo demands their papers. And then they tear them up before their eyes. Some try to run away, but they are shot with explosive rounds. Many lie dead in the street and at the entrances to courtyards.

One of the workers succeeded in saving himself. He ran to the factory and told everyone that another massacre was underway in the ghetto. The management gave them a truck and an armed escort; some ten men headed for the ghetto. But they were not allowed in. Among the victims were highly skilled workers whom the Germans needed, so an officer drove out, but he did not find them there when he arrived. Learning where they had been taken, he headed out of town to the field where they were killing Jews. Many of his workers turned out to have been killed already. He recognized several of the survivors, though, and negotiated for their release. One of them was a furrier by the name of Alperovich. Another one, named Levin, was a barber who had shaved the officers. Alperovich's wife and daughter were with the barber. The "boss" of the killings agreed to release only Alperovich and the barber, along with one of the other two—either Levin's wife or daughter. Levin took his daughter. When the workers were brought to the factory, they were as white as paper and could not say anything. Alperovich was ill for a long time afterward.

This was only one of the episodes of the second mass slaughter of the Jews on November 20, 1941, committed two weeks after the first.

The labor office asked for lists showing which Jew was working where, and in what job. When the lists had been issued, skilled workers began to receive cards. Unskilled workers did not receive any cards. Skilled workers had to live in a certain section of the ghetto; all the others who lived in the area were ordered to leave. A new resettlement began. And something else started to happen: women looked for workers "with cards" and young women got married to old men. People condemned to death by the Germans were going mad.

When everyone had been settled according to regulations, the Germans began giving out small wooden boards with names on them for the doors. Skilled workers had to hang up the board over the front door indicating the workplace of the man of the house and the name of his dependents. When this had been done, an order was issued that every worker would receive from the "Council" the number of the house in which he lives, and would have to sew it beneath the yellow mark on his chest and back. The number was printed on a piece of white canvas. I was living in the ghetto at no. 12 on [. . .][5] Street and wore the number 12 in front and in back.

Now everyone is wearing numbers. The Germans announce that if anyone from any household violates German law, all those bearing the number of that household will be shot.

New regulations are introduced. Workers do not have the right to freely go to work from the ghetto: they will be escorted to and from the job. The workers are required to form up beside the labor office. They build gates for us. At the gates is a policeman. Germans who come for Jewish workers have to fill out forms saying how many people they are taking, and those bringing them from work fill in forms saying how many they brought. Upon departure through the gates, the police check the number of people. If there turn out to be more than are listed, the policeman does not allow one person more outside the ghetto walls. After work, they march everyone to the labor office. They are counted again there, and it is only then that they are allowed to go to their homes.

At the former Oktyabr Factory, the Jewish workers were separated from the Gentiles. The Jews worked on one half of the shop floor, walled off from the other half of the shop. Even the toilets were divided—for Jews and for non-Jews.

The following event occurred at the factory: twelve Jewish women were working to clean up the yard. The Germans did not like the way they were working. They took away their work papers and told them not to show up anymore. The women, however, decided to ask to be allowed to stay on the job. Then a report was sent to the Gestapo claiming that the women were being careless about their work. The next day, Gestapo agents showed up and took them off to jail. They kept the women there for two weeks. Then they put them in a truck and took them to the ghetto on Yubileynaya Square. The women were overjoyed. They thought that they were being allowed to go home. But this is what happened: the Germans chased everyone out of their homes and onto the square. When the square had filled with people, a man from the Gestapo got on the truck and said: "Before you are twelve women. For malingering and refusal to work, they will be shot immediately before your eyes." One of the Jews was forced to blindfold them. They shot them, firing explosive rounds into their

---

5. The name of the street is not legible in the original text.

heads. The bodies lay on the square for two days. Signs around their necks said that they had been shot for refusing to work.

Once, in the winter, when the Germans were marching us from work, we were surrounded by the Gestapo not far from the ghetto. Drunken local policemen turned up in a truck to help them; they still had traces of fresh blood on their overcoats and boots. They shot any worker who tried to slip under the wire in order to hide in the ghetto. Bodies were lying in every street. Pots, bones, potato peelings—everything that people were taking with them to work—was lying there, too.

Some groups consisting of skilled workers were taken off to one side. I was in one of these groups and in this way I escaped. They made the workers kneel, then beat them with rubber truncheons and finally led them away in entire columns.

Now a light truck pulled up. An old, thin general got out. It was Kube, the general commissar for Belorussia.[6] He went up to an officer and said something to him. Then he shouted at the column of skilled workers: "*Juden, schnell zu Hause!*" [Jews, get to your homes quickly!] Anyone who did not run fast enough was beaten by Kube with clubs; he also fired warning shots with his pistol. People broke from the ranks, running in different directions. The rest remained on their knees. A check of papers began. Anyone who had a skilled worker card was released. The pogrom went on in this way until seven in the evening.

Many of those killed were lying in the ditches around the wallpaper factory. The workers who had been taken away were led to the station, loaded into boxcars, and taken by night in the direction of Molodechno. Along the route by which they were being transported, the German guards would come into the cars packed with people and select young, beautiful girls, take them away and rape them. Not far from Molodechno, ditches had been dug. The Germans beasts opened the boxcars, fired on the people with machine guns, threw them into the ditches, and tossed in hand grenades.

It was still dark when the killing began, said a Jew who had been working in a German jail as a blacksmith. Approaching Moldechno, the train slowed down. It was still dark, and the boxcar doors were shut. The blacksmith opened a window in the car that he and his daughter were in. He jumped out of the window, grabbed his daughter, and ran.

One day the Germans announced that all Jews would have to report to the square at ten o'clock the next morning to receive green armbands. The workers went off to their jobs in the morning. The rest stayed behind on the square. Suddenly, the Gestapo attacked them, along with local police and men with all kinds of weapons. The Germans surrounded the ghetto, loaded all those assembled onto trucks, and took them away. Some ran away, and they were fired on. Corpses lay in the streets.

---

6. Wilhelm Kube was assassinated by partisans in September 1943.

When the Jewish workers (from the former Oktyabr Factory) heard the shots coming from the ghetto, they became very agitated. An officer drove out to them. Upon arrival, he announced that people were being taken out of the ghetto for labor in the fields, and that the Jewish workers would not be allowed to go home for the next three days. Over those three days, the German butchers saw to the liquidation of the ghetto. People were even dragged out from cellars. Wherever they suspected that Jews were hiding, they would bombard that house or structure with grenades.

The Tsibel family hid in an underground passage on Shornaya Street. They heard footsteps over their heads; the Gestapo was searching for them in their apartment. Suddenly, their baby began to cry, and the parents, fearing that the crying would attract the attention of the Gestapo men, smothered him. The Germans killed many German Jews in this cellar.[7]

Russian and Poles would come up to the barbed wire at the entrance to the ghetto, carrying food in exchange for clothing.

The people adapted to the situation. When they left the ghetto, they would take off the yellow patches or throw large kerchiefs over themselves, then go to Gentiles of their acquaintance and exchange belongings for food. Some would make it back successfully. Others paid with their lives.

One time, they were herding some "strange people" into the Minsk ghetto. They wore fish-skin capes, pink, dark blue, or light blue in color, capes that have hoods on top. On the right side of their chests were Stars of David with the word "*Jude*" on them. They spoke German.

The Gestapo chased out the residents of several streets and housed these people in their place. They brought poles and barbed wire and forced the new inhabitants to dig ditches. They put in the poles and strung the barbed wire. The Germans made an announcement that anyone who approached to talk to them would be shot. At first, sentries patrolled the barriers. People would go up to the fences and strike up conversations with the "strange people." They were easy to talk to. They said that they were German Jews. The Germans had robbed them of everything and had mockingly announced that they were being sent to America. They were not letting them go anywhere. They begged for bread. They assumed that Russian Jews could freely go anywhere they please and freely buy whatever struck their fancy. The Germans found work for them: at night they made them cart the bodies of murdered Jews to the cemetery.

Every Sunday, everyone was required to report to the square at midday for a "meeting." There the commandant of the Minsk ghetto, the high-ranking Gestapo officer [. . .],[8] would speak. He demanded that anyone who knew a partisan or was

---

7. This incident is referring to Jews from Germany and Czechoslovakia who were taken to Minsk and held in a separate ghetto.
8. His name is illegible in the text.

in contact with one should speak up. The penalty for not appearing at the meeting was prison. In fact, they hounded everyone onto the square every free day. Once they even brought German Jews with horns and violins and made them play on the square.

One time, they were taking us from work down Novomyasnitskaya Street. A young fellow stepped out of the formation and went toward a kiosk to buy a newspaper. Suddenly, a policeman appeared from somewhere and shot him for trying buy a paper. The formation moved off. The young worker remained there dead.

GARF f. 8114, op. 1, d. 961, ll. 85–87, 100–116. A typewritten manuscript.

43. Five pogroms in Minsk
ACCOUNTS OF PERLA AGINSKAYA, MALKA KOFMAN, DARYA LYUSIK, AND RAISA GELFOND
RECORDED BY MAJOR A. KRASOV
[1944]

I will not add any artist's colors. They are unnecessary here. I am passing on the stories of people who lived in Minsk for three years, who saw with their own eyes what the Germans did in the captive city. These are the stories of the martyrs Perla Aginskaya, Malka Kofman, Darya Losik [sic] and Raisa Gelfond. These are the stories of five pogroms in Minsk.

In the first days of the occupation, the German authorities ordered the entire Jewish population to move to the ghetto within three days. Outlying streets and lanes were set aside for the ghetto: Zamkovaya, Zavalnaya, Vyzvolenia, Khlebnaya, Podzamkovaya, Staromyasnitskaya, Ratomskaya, Nemichsky, Shpalernaya, Glukhoy, and others.

Before their removal to the ghetto, the Germans carried out a registration of the Jewish population. They registered some 85,000 people. Then the requisitions began. At first fifty rubles from each person, then thirty, then twenty. In connection with such demands, harsh decrees were issued, and ninety hostages were thrown in jail. The population was severely warned that new hostages would be taken if the required amount was not paid before the deadline.

The ghetto quarter was soon fenced off from the rest of the world with barbed wire. And it was from that time that nights of St. Bartholomew began in Minsk.[9] By order of the occupying authorities, Jews were issued special symbols—round, yellow patches ten centimeters in diameter. They were to wear these patches on the right side of the chest and on the right side of the back. Later on, white squares bearing a serial number were added to these. Leaving the ghetto was strictly prohibited.

Woe to anyone who dared to go near the barbed wire to exchange belongings for food. Such people were shot on the spot.

---

9. "Nights of St. Bartholomew" refers to a massacre of French protestants in 1572.

The Germans put a part of the population of the ghetto to work. They would be marched away under guard. Those who worked received 250 grams of bread and a liter of a watery swill made from green, buckwheat chaff, and horsemeat.

Soldiers and local police burst into the buildings almost every night, looting and killing entire Jewish families.

One day in the autumn, Perla Aginskaya went to see what was happening in one of the houses on Zeleny Lane. The following scene met her eyes like a mirage: a little room, a table, a bed. An oil lamp flickering. A girl of about eighteen was lying by the table. She was completely naked. Blood was streaming down the girl's body from deep, blackish wounds in her chest. It was quite clear that the girl had been raped and killed. There were gunshot wounds around her genitals.

Not far from the girl lay a man who had been strangled. Behind him was a bed. In the bed was a woman who had been stabbed, and beside her lay the small bodies of children, shot to death.

The Kovarsky family had met with an agonizing death. They were done away with in the third month of the city's occupation. The father and one son survived. The father had managed to hide in the attic and the son beneath a bed. They told the story of how this savagery had taken place. Late one autumn night, the police burst into the house. They got the unfortunates out of bed. They stripped their grown daughter naked. They put her up on the table and forced her to dance, then killed her. The grandmother and grandson were killed in their beds. Two children, a boy and a girl, who had been killed in their beds lay with their arms around each other. Malka, a little girl, was badly wounded. She died the next day.

That terrible night, all the inhabitants of that house were killed.

On the fifty-third day of the occupation, the first roundup of Jewish men was carried out. The Germans took several hundred away in trucks. The Nazis said that they were gathering men for work. But those who were taken out of the ghetto never returned to their loved ones. Two weeks later, the roundup was repeated. They grabbed several thousand men and a certain number of women. This time, they formed them up into columns and marched them off to a prison. It was a procession of the doomed to their death.

A week later, there was a third roundup. They grabbed up many men and women, including the infirm. They were all shot.

Black clouds continued to gather over the ghetto. On November 6, when memories of the triumphant holiday celebrations in years past were in the heart of every Soviet citizen, people suddenly learned that there would be a pogrom the next day.

That morning, the city rose unusually early. SS troopers and local police were prowling the streets. A part of the ghetto—encompassing Nemich, Bashkovaya, Khlebnaya, Rakovskaya, Ostrovskaya, and other streets—was surrounded. They smashed open doors, along with trunks, cupboards, and wardrobes, while window glass showered down into the street. Trucks rolled up to the houses and took away clothing, pots and pans, furniture. Beaten and bleeding, people were driven into the streets. The column of people gradually grew. Young and old women, and small children were standing there. Many mothers held infants in their arms. Moaning and heartrending cries could be heard everywhere.

They threw thirty thousand people out into the street in this way. For a whole day, columns of martyrs driven along by storm troopers walked toward the village of Tuchinka. In order to justify their crime, the Germans staged a "revolutionary demonstration." They took the first man that came along, thrust a red banner into his hands, and put him in front of the crowd. The Nazis forced people to sing revolutionary songs at gunpoint. Then the mass shootings began. They laid living people single file in a huge trench. From above, they sprayed them with automatic fire as from a hose. Then they laid a new group atop the killed and wounded and shot them in the same way.

Three days after the first pogrom, Jews from Hamburg, Berlin, and Frankfurt were brought into the ghetto. They were housed separately on Respublikanskaya, Obuvnaya, Sukhaya, and Opanasskaya Streets. Around eighteen thousand people lived there, among them engineers, doctors, and office and factory workers.

There was another pogrom before another two weeks had gone by. Just like the first time, they took those they seized to Tuchinka. There they shot them as well. One woman was hit in the leg during the shooting and thrown into the pit, but the pit was not filled in, and she crawled out of the grave and returned to the ghetto.

They killed children by throwing them against rocks or the ground, or they threw them into the pit alive.

During the third pogrom, which took place on March 2, 1942, the Germans seized people not only from the ghetto, but also from those who worked outside the ghetto. This was how sixteen-year-old Moisey Pekar fell into the Germans' hands. As the shootings were going on, while still on the road to Tuchinka, he fell down and played dead. One or two hours later, trucks came along behind the columns and picked up the bodies of those who had been shot. The bloodied body of Pekar was thrown out near the ditch in Zeleny Lane along with the corpses.

After the third pogrom, the raids in the night grew more frequent. By night, the Germans liquidated families of Jews suspected of partisan connections. From dusk until dawn, covered black trucks prowled the streets of the ghetto. These were the mobile gas vans. They put the Jews they seized into these vehicles. The motor ran, and a loud knocking was heard in the truck, but no more sounds were heard from it after two or three minutes. Every night except Saturdays and Sundays, the mobile gas van rolled up to the gates of the ghetto.

Near the end of summer, 1942, orders were posted along the streets of the ghetto. Those Jews who were left alive were to assemble on Twenty-Fifth of October Square to receive new patches. When the people had gathered, police ringed the square. Those same covered black trucks that had been working for four straight days drove up.

The bodies of those martyred by the Germans were transported to the small town of Trostyanets [i.e., Maly Trostyanets], where they were dumped into a pit.

After the fourth pogrom, things became quieter by comparison. Nevertheless, the extermination of the Jews continued. At the beginning there had been a home for orphans and invalids in the ghetto. Soon after, however, all of its residents as well were taken away in the mobile gas vans.

The inhabitants of Minsk remember how the German bandits killed children with daggers, they remember the pleas of the children to the Germans: "Please, sirs, don't hit us, we can get to the trucks on our own."

In February 1942, a German officer was killed on Kirov Street. On that same day, several hundred people—Jews, Russians, and Belorussians—were taken into the torture chambers of the Gestapo as hostages. A few days after that, the people of Minsk saw their friends motionless on the gallows. Small wooden placards with the inscription "For contact with partisans" fluttered on their chests.

The fifth and final pogrom took place in the autumn of last year, 1943. There were the same tears, tortures, and sufferings, and thousands of new innocent victims.

GARF f. 8114, op. 1, d. 958, ll. 187–191. A typewritten manuscript, with corrections and the signature of A. Krasov.

44. An account by Professor Prilezhaev about the fate of the Jews in the Minsk ghetto
Recorded by M. Grubian

The seventy-five-year-old professor and member of the Belorussian Academy of Sciences Nikolay Prilezhaev made his way out of occupied Minsk with the help of the partisans. In a conversation with our correspondent,[10] Professor Prilezhaev told of the mind-boggling cruelties committed against Jews in Minsk, Belorussia.

The Germans immediately began the systematic extermination of the Jewish population on the very first day of their occupation, June 29, 1941. They began with a diabolical game: throwing Jewish babies out of windows. After a short time, they created a ghetto that took in the area from the fish pond to the Jewish and Polish cemetery (Kalvaria). The first to fall victim to the fascist terror were the best representatives of the Jewish intelligentsia. Among the professors killed early on was the Russian scientist Professor Markov. He was killed because his wife had given refuge to a Jew.

The German butchers intended to surround the ghetto with a high brick wall, but their voracious appetite for Jewish blood outstripped their plans. Even before the wall was built, large trucks loaded with people were beginning to head off in an unknown direction, day and night.

At the same time, a never-ending pogrom broke out. Professor Prilezhaev was himself a witness to how the Nazis threw live Jewish children into open graves.

---

10. This refers to a correspondent of the Yiddish-language newspaper *Eynikayt*, which was published by the Jewish Anti-Fascist Committee.

Furthermore, Professor Prilezhaev says that not a trace remained of Minsk's native Jews, and that a certain number of Jews from Lodz[11] and Hamburg are still languishing in the ghetto, dying from hunger and disease. Although there are no Jews left in occupied Belorussian cities, the Nazi authorities are still carrying out a bestial antisemitic campaign day after day. Whatever misfortune happens to the subjugated Belorussian population, the fascist authorities and fascist press in Minsk always blame it on the Jews. But these empty acts of intimidation have no effect on anyone. The sympathies of the Belorussian population are on the side of the persecuted Jews. The local residents speak with sadness and indignation of the nightmarish cruelties visited on their Jewish fellow citizens.

GARF f. 8114, op. 1, d. 961, ll. 337–337ob. A typewritten manuscript.

45. The liquidation of the Minsk ghetto
An account by Abram Mashkeleyson
Recorded by A. Idin
Translated by D. Manevich
[1944]

Abram Mashkeleyson, the director of a food processing factory, recently returned from a tour of liberated Belorussian cities. His assignment was to organize food processing plants in those cities.

When the war began, Mashkeleyson's father-in-law, Ber Perelman, a seventy-year-old man, and his brother-in-law, Yekhiel Perelman, and his family remained in Minsk. They, along with tens of thousands of other Minsk Jews, were shot in Trostyanets, thirteen kilometers from Minsk.

Former Jewish partisans from Minsk, who are now working in various Soviet institutions, told Mashkeleyson stories about the fate of Minsk Jews and of Jews brought there by the Germans from Hamburg.

More than fifteen thousand Jews were in the Minsk ghetto. Around one thousand of them who left to join partisan units survived, along with twenty or so who made it to various hideouts.

As is well known, the Minsk ghetto was located in the area of Rakovka, Tarasovka, and Osvobozhdenie Streets. One bakery with three ovens worked in the ghetto. Beneath one of these stoves the Jews dug a tunnel approximately 180 meters long, with its exit outside the ghetto boundaries. The exit was camouflaged with a large rubbish bin. Hundreds of Jews escaped and made their way to the partisans through this tunnel.

A butcher from Minsk named Lunin also managed to escape from the ghetto. In exchange for a tidy sum, he obtained a pistol from a German policeman and went off to the partisans. The old butcher took part in numerous diversionary actions

---

11. This is a mistake in the text; Jews from various German cities were brought to Minsk.

organized by the partisans. For the heroism that he displayed, Lunin was awarded the Partisan Medal, 1st Class, and the Order of the Red Star.

Based on what we know from the partisans and the surviving inhabitants of Minsk, the liquidation of the Minsk ghetto was organized in the following way:

In accordance with the plan drawn up by the Gestapo ahead of time, they first moved the Jews from one residential district. This area, which was now "liberated," was excluded from the ghetto. Then they moved the barbed wire barriers to the next district. In this way, they removed block after block from the ghetto, which became smaller and smaller.

They took the Jews away to Trostyanets and Khasonovshchina, not far from Minsk. These two places were also the site of mass killings of Jews. They brought them there in enormous groups of five or six thousand people, stripped them naked, and drove them into a ditch, after which motorcyclists with machine pistols would drive up and down the ditch shooting these unfortunates. They covered the dead and wounded with a thin layer of earth, whereupon they smoothed the burial site over with tractors.

Not long before their retreat from Minsk, the Germans began driving Soviet POWs to Trostyanets and Khasonovshchina, making them drag out the bodies of the slaughtered Jews and burn the remains.

The advance of the Red Army was so rapid that the German mobile gas vans did not have time to complete their diabolical work, and several thousand bodies remained in stacks in the uncovered ditches.

GARF f. 8114, op. 1, d. 958, ll. 15–15ob. A typewritten manuscript.

46. They were dealing in children
ACCOUNTS OF MARIA GOTOVTSEVA, MARFA ORLOVA, AND FENYA LEPESHKO RECORDED BY A. VERBITSKY

When the war broke out, hundreds of Minsk's Jewish children were in summer camps, kindergartens, and nurseries. On the very first day of the war, many children were evacuated from Minsk to surrounding villages, where the threat of bombing and strafing did not seem as great as in the city. Many of the Jewish children stayed in the camps and nurseries, too, along with Belorussian, Ukrainian, and Russian children.

After taking Minsk, the Nazis paid no attention for a long time to the children who were wasting away, concealed in hiding places and orphanages. In the summer of 1942, it came to the attention of the local fascist authorities that there were many Jews among the unsupervised, orphaned mass of youngsters. So they decided to go about liquidating thousands of young Soviet citizens.

The gassing buses or mobile gas vans fished Jewish children out of the streets, courtyards, hospitals, and orphanages. Children filled the enormous vehicles. The Germans tossed piles of small bodies into ditches in the village of Bolshoy Trostyanets.

Some were alive, still breathing. Several were crying out, but the plans for fascist banditry included the burying or burning not only of the dead, but of the living as well; this was how they dealt with the children, too.

The extermination of Jewish children went on for many months. They drove small children away to Trostyanets—to their deaths—on the slightest suspicion or denunciation. In the spring of 1943, an entire barracks full of children was discovered in one of the ruined collective farms in the Minsk region. They had been left to fend for themselves. The peasants had been bringing them things; seven-year-olds had been looking after three-year-olds. Many of them had perished from cold and hunger.

The Germans burst into the barracks and made it their first order of business to find out from the children which of them were Jewish. The children were so small that they were unable to say anything in reply. Unable to sort the matter out, the Gestapo decided to kill [all] the children. They loaded them onto freight cars and sent them to the Minsk train station. There the children suffered without food and water for two days. Three of them tried to escape into the city, but the Germans shot them down. What the German fiends were waiting for, no one knew.

They decided to make use of the crying mass of youngsters by holding a sale. News that the Germans were selling children at the train station quickly spread through the city. Heartsick women made their way toward the station. It was an unbelievable auction. The Germans disposed of the children for twenty-five or thirty marks apiece. The women would select a youngster, put their money down on a German overcoat, then take the child. Belorussian women rushed to save innocent children from the clutches of the Nazis.

Here is what was told to us by Maria Gotovtseva, who now works at the Minsk radio factory:

"I was at the train station by chance. The Germans were beckoning people in, appraising the children, haggling. I saw one old woman, weeping and sighing, take away two little girls. When most of the children had been sold, the Germans began letting the orphans go for ten marks. The children were crying, holding out their little hands, as though saying: 'Buy us, otherwise they'll kill us.'"

Minsk native Marfa Orlova, who lives at 42 Gorky Street, showed us a four-year-old boy whom she had bought at the station that morning for twenty marks. Orlova is looking after the child and hopes that little Yuri's parents will return soon and collect their son.

At 26 Torgovaya Street, we saw a Jewish girl of six and a boy of five or six who had been bought from the Germans for fifty marks. The children are being looked after by Fenya Lepeshko, the mother of two sons at the Front.

"You see this child?" says Fenya Lepeshko. "He's already smiling now, he's blossomed. But when I took him in, he was almost dead. He didn't speak, all he did was moan and call out for someone. I thought he'd die, and here he's survived, the little trooper. I couldn't even tell you what his name is or how old he is. Ignatenko, the lady just next door, bought a four-year-old girl from these scoundrels. She was very sick. The poor little thing didn't pull through. She died."

GARF f. 8114, op. 1, d. 959, ll. 197–199. A typewritten manuscript with handwritten corrections.

47. Minsk Hell
THE RECOLLECTIONS OF THE TEACHER SOFIA OZERSKAYA

At the end of June, when the fascists landed their troops in Minsk, I was in the country with the children on their summer holidays at camp. Along with the rest of the camp staff, I was concerned most of all that the children be returned to their parents. I myself was unable to get out of Minsk before the Germans arrived.

In the first days of their occupation of Minsk, the Germans set aside twelve small streets as the Jewish ghetto and herded Minsk's Jewish population of 75,000 into it. And that was not all. They also brought in Jews from every small town and collective farm in the Minsk region. In unimaginably cramped quarters, amid the ruins of bombed-out city blocks, on the ashes of burned-out houses with collapsed roofs and gaping holes where once there had been windows, thousands of unfortunate, hungry creatures trembled with fear.

At first, the fascist barbarians had the idea of erecting a high wall around the Jewish ghetto, and had already begun hauling in the bricks, but then they gave up on the idea and limited themselves to running barbed wire around the Jewish quarter.

It was forbidden for Jews to leave the ghetto. When, on rare occasions, a Jew received permission to go into the city, he was forced to wear a special patch on his chest, a yellow circle no smaller than ten centimeters in diameter. Any Jew who showed himself outside the ghetto without this mark was subject to death on the spot. Any Nazi could kill any person who looked to him like a Jew violating this rule. And no small number of Russians, Poles, and Belorussians perished because the fascists had taken them for Jews coming out into the city without the yellow patch on their chests. But even this badge did not always save a Jew from death. On the contrary, it often served as a target for the foul bullet of a fascist.

To mock their unfortunate victims, the fascists offered them "self-government" in the form of a "Jewish Council." The ghetto, in fact, was outside the rule of law, and the "Council" was given only one right: to count the number of Jews killed, the number who had fallen at the hands of the crazed enemy. Sometimes the "Council" was granted one additional "right"—that of organizing the looting of the poor, destitute Jewish population. From people who had lost all of their property in air raids, fires, and endless rounds of robbery, they demanded that they bring several thousand knives, forks, and spoons, then several thousand articles of warm underwear and clothing, then dishes, pots, and pans. And all of it by the thousands, and all of it under the threat of death!

Alongside the organized looting, unorganized looting flourished as well. No more than a few hours each day would pass before this or that Nazi unit would burst into the ghetto and, making the rounds of these pathetic quarters, snatch everything that came to hand.

No one even thought about protest or resistance. People were happy if they stayed alive during these endless plagues of locusts. Submissiveness did not help anyone much, though. Not a single bandit raid passed without a blood sacrifice. Irritated by the fact that there was nothing to steal from the impoverished residents, the Nazi youths let all their bile flow out in murders and bloody acts of violence.

One of the forms of organized mass murder of Jews was the system of special concentration camps for Jewish men. The Nazis created dungeons in the form of labor camps, where in systematic fashion they killed scores of innocent people on a daily basis. It was known in the ghetto that to be sent to the so-called concentration camps was tantamount to inevitable death.

The fascist beast knew no bounds in his striving to exterminate the Jewish people. Not confining themselves to the systematic, day-in, day-out extermination of Jews, the fascist barbarians organized particularly grandiose massacres on Soviet holidays.

On November 7, 1941, on the anniversary of the great October Socialist Revolution, large armed units of fascists broke into the Jewish ghetto at 5:00 AM, surrounded five of its twelve blocks, and herded everyone into the street—men and women, the elderly, and children. The howls of mortal fear and horror, the cries of desperation, the weeping of children, and the sobbing of women filled the surrounding areas and could be heard throughout the city. The fascists chased the crowd in its many thousands onto a nearby square, where they formed them into columns and then, after loading them onto trucks, transported them out of town. There, by the old German cemetery, outside of Kalvaria, long deep trenches had been excavated ahead of time with the help of dynamite. Several days before that, rumors had been going about in the city that these trenches had not been dug for no reason at all, that the fascists were preparing mass murder. But the human brain refused to believe in the possibility of such an atrocity. However, the foray of the Nazi bands into the Jewish ghetto and, most important of all, the dispatch of many thousands of people in the direction of the trenches, unsettled the whole of Minsk. Many Russians and Belorussians who had friends and relatives in the ghetto rushed there to see for themselves if the rumors that had reached them were true, and became witnesses to the savage treatment meted out to a defenseless people. Many—and I was included in their number—followed the trucks on foot right up to the place of slaughter. What we saw there makes us tremble from horror to this day.

When the enormous crowd of Jews condemned to death by the Nazis had been assembled beside the trenches, the German soldiers began throwing them in while they were still alive. The children first (suckling infants pulled from their mothers' arms were torn in two by the fascists and flung into the ditches); then the women on top of the children; and finally the men. Then they began blazing away with machine guns into this half-dead human mass writhing in the convulsions preceding death. Sunset was already approaching when the chatter of the machine guns ceased. The fascists soon covered the common graves with a thin layer of earth, so thin that the earth rose and fell slightly for a long time afterward from the pressure of those who were only wounded or who by chance were left untouched by the bullets. Tatars living not far from the place of execution reported that some of those thrown into the trenches had succeeded in scraping away the earth at night and crawling out of the awful graves. They hid out in the Tatars' gardens; the Tatars did not hand them over, and after keeping them at their homes for several days, helped them to escape from the fascist hell.

On November 7, 1941, my mother died as well, along with her entire family of nine people. My father was a Belorussian, and I was listed as a Belorussian in my passport. This allowed me to live in Minsk for a year or so under Hitler's occupation regime. My mother, though, was a Jew; the Hitlerites hounded her into the ghetto after their arrival, and on November 7, killed her along with the rest.

On that day alone, November 7, 1941, approximately 35,000 Jews perished in Minsk at the hands of the Hitlerites.

The fascists committed the same sort of atrocity on Red Army Day, February 23, 1942. On that day, the same methods of bestial abuse of a defenseless population as those of November 7 were repeated. The only difference was that due to a shortage of trucks for the unfortunate people formed up in columns, they herded them on foot to the place of slaughter. On that day, some 18,000 Jewish martyrs fell at the blood-stained hands of the Hitlerites.

On March 8, the German occupiers killed more than 5,000 people, principally women, who were loaded into freight cars and taken out of town. After perpetrating various outrages against them, the Germans hacked and shot them to death near Smolovichi.[12]

The March slaughter did not seem like enough to the German monsters, so on April 29, just before the proletarian holiday of May 1, they organized another slaughter on a grand scale, during which they killed around 11,000 Jews.

On May 6, 1942, one of my neighbors called me off to one side.

"Sonya!" she whispered in my ear. "I just happened to find out that the building superintendent has received two letters denouncing you as a Jew. You know what that smells of, don't you? Well, try to get away from here as soon as possible."

I knew what such a denunciation could lead to. Every resident of occupied Minsk knew it. Seventy-five gallows erected by the Germans stand in the capital of Soviet

---

12. March 8 is commemorated as International Women's Day.

Belorussia to this day. Not a day passed without dozens of innocent victims of the Nazi beasts dying on them. The bodies of those executed were not taken away for several days. The very look of these gallows called forth horror in the half burned-out, hungry city, and strengthened in the hearts of these people deprived of any civil rights whatsoever an unquenchable hatred for their tormentors.

The population of the city was for all intents and purposes placed outside the law. At any moment, the drunken Nazi troops could open fire at random on the street without rhyme or reason, killing anyone at hand, without regard to sex, age, or nationality. Day and night, the fascist youths would burst into the apartments of the people of Minsk and rob, rape, and murder. No passer-by had any guarantee that he would not be shot or cut to pieces by some enraged German bandit who did not like his nose or admired the look of his watch. It was all the same, Belorussian or Pole, Russian or Jew. But the Jews received the worst of it.

Having disappeared from Minsk along with my friend and fellow Komsomol member Maria Kuleshova from Dnepropetrovsk, we made our way from Minsk to Borisov and Orsha in three days and did not come across any Germans or local police. We only saw a German outpost when we approached a large town. They interrogated us for an entire day, but then let us go without having obtained anything. We were so glad to get out of there that we ran straight into the fields. We met an old shepherd near a small forest and asked him for advice. We told him straight out that we were on the run from the Germans and that we were heading through the frontlines to the Soviet Union. When he found out that we had nearly fallen into the clutches of the Nazis, he scolded us like a father:

"You foolish women! You shouldn't show your faces in cities and towns. Get yourselves to forests, little paths, trails, and back roads through villages, then you'll make it. There aren't any Germans in the villages."

We listened to the wise advice of the shepherd. We avoided the cities and towns, bypassing Borisov, Orsha, Smolyany, Bogushevsk, and other sizeable population centers. We made our way calmly through the villages right up to the very frontline without meeting a German or a policeman. It was only in one place, not having found a place to ford a river and forced to cross a bridge, that we came upon a German sentry post.

All along the way, the inhabitants, upon learning that we were making our way to Soviet Russia, helped us any way they could, giving us a place to stay, indicating the shortest and safest route. Even when we were quite near Vitebsk, some nine kilometers from the city, a woman showed us a place where there was a secret way over the Western Dvina River.

A bright lad of about fifteen, along with four of his friends who were on the run from Vitebsk, took us across the river in a boat. On the opposite bank we immediately found ourselves in a Soviet partisan zone, the center of which at the time was the village of Verkhove.

This was so unexpected that for a long time we could not believe our good fortune. And it was only when the partisans, having taken us in like family, fed us, let us rest up with them for three days and, after putting us into carts, sent us deep into the Soviet Union that we felt that we had actually broken out of the Nazi hell.

GARF f. 8114, op. 1, d. 963, ll. 59–68. The Russian translation and the original Yiddish text were both typewritten. The Yiddish text can be found in the same archival file, d. 963, ll. 75–81.

48. The recollections of Dr. Tsetsilia Mikhaylovna Shapiro
Recorded by A. V. Veysbrod
September 20, 1944

Tsetsilia Mikhaylovna Shapiro, born in 1915, a doctor, resident of Minsk until the war, recounts the following story.

The war found her in a maternity home immediately after giving birth. With her five-year-old son, a newborn, and her aging mother, she tried to get out of Minsk in the first days of the war, when Minsk had not yet been occupied, and to make her way for Borisov. They walked some 50 kilometers under constant aerial bombardment. Post-partum fatigue and a high temperature made it impossible for her to continue. They stopped at a road where advancing Germans caught up with them. They had to return to Minsk.

An order for the registration of all Jews was issued in the first days of the German presence in Minsk. The registration was done by Jews who had been appointed by the Germans. Registration involved taking down last name, first name and patronymic, age, and address. At the same time, "branding" was done. "Branding" consisted of sewing distinguishing patches on clothing: yellow scraps of cloth without any inscriptions, and white pieces of material on which numbers were stamped in black ink.

An order was issued forbidding Jews to walk in the main streets; they were permitted to walk along the remaining streets only out on the roadway, not on the sidewalks. It was also forbidden for Jews to greet Gentiles of their acquaintance whom they might encounter.

There were very few instances of failure to comply with registration or "branding," and there were very few violations of regulations, either. Violations of the rules were punished by death.

The next measure taken was the setting up of a ghetto. An order was issued requiring all inhabitants of Jewish nationality living in Minsk to move to buildings prepared for them in designated streets set apart for them especially. The overcrowding in the apartments and rooms was tremendous. By the orders of the Germans, local inhabitants had taken over the Jews' former apartments. A German named Gottenbach was named assistant to the ghetto commandant, and as deputy a German named Mendel. By his orders, a certain Mushkin was designated as the "head of the Jewish Council."

The head of the ghetto would be killed in the next "pogrom," and in his place they would appoint someone else.

They cordoned off the ghetto with barbed wire. A small number of German gendarmes were kept on the spot, but for the most part, the police were from the Russian and Belorussian population. The Jews were forbidden to leave the ghetto, except for those Jews (up to a certain age) who went to work. Most of the jobs were with the railroad, in the loading and unloading of heavy goods (lumber, iron beams, and the like), with working hours every day from six in the morning until eight in the evening. They went to and from work under armed guard: German gendarmes were at the head and rear of the columns, while local police cordoned them off along the sides. One hundred grams of bread per day were distributed on the job. At first they issued the entire bread ration once a month. Later on, it became possible to arrange the distribution of bread on a daily basis—in exchange for a bribe—which was considered a great achievement.

Entry into the ghetto was forbidden to all Gentiles except for the police. Sometimes, one managed to have contact with the local population through the barbed wire. For a bribe of vodka, the police occasionally allowed inhabitants of the ghetto to pass belongings through the barbed wire in exchange for potatoes (at a rate of exchange that was laughable, naturally). There were rare cases of escape through the wire, but very few Jews fled to the city and concealed themselves, since they were afraid of being betrayed by the local inhabitants. After that, the barbed wire was electrified. This made escape through the wire much more difficult, if not impossible. The children of mixed marriages went with their fathers: if the father was a Jew, the children stayed with him in the ghetto, while the Aryan mother lived in town. If the father was an Aryan, the children lived with him in town, while the mother stayed in the ghetto. We heard of a case in which a Professor Afonsky, a Russian who was married to a Jewish woman, gained her release from the German command by paying a ransom. She was allowed to live with her husband and daughter in town (outside of the ghetto) on the condition that she be sterilized. The corresponding operation was performed by Professor Klumov under German observation. This case was an exception. The professor had stored away a sizeable quantity of gold coins, which he paid to the Germans as a ransom along with paper money obtained from the sale of everything he owned. Curiously, this ransom was entered into the official books.

As a rule, the Jews were used for manual labor. Skilled laborers were the exception: tailors, seamstresses, shoemakers, carpenters, and others were used by the Germans in workshops according to their trade. These people were issued special identity cards, and in the gradual extermination of the Jews, their killings were the last to be carried out.

Jews who were doctors, engineers, and specialized scientific workers were not used; they were subjected to hard labor and extermination along with the rest of the ghetto population. On the day that the ghetto was set up, Professor Siterman, a popular doctor, a distinguished scientist, and a Jew, was taken by the Germans out into the main square of the ghetto, made to get down on all fours and photographed in this position with a soccer ball on his back. After that, the Germans led him away "for a consultation," as his family was told, though in fact he was shot.

How did the population of the ghetto feed itself? Some people had small amounts of provisions stored away, which, by the way, quickly ran out. A few inhabitants had modest vegetable gardens. Some managed to exchange their belongings for next to nothing in the manner indicated earlier, passing them through the barbed wire which surrounded the ghetto. The daily ration of one hundred grams for those who worked was an insignificant help. The basic diet was potato peels and other refuse picked up in town, on the way to and from work, and outside the kitchens. Serious fights broke out between starving people over these scraps. It goes without saying that there were many deaths from hunger and inadequate nutrition.

There was no economic activity, much less any attempt on the part of the inhabitants of the ghetto to organize themselves. The time passed in the agonizing expectation of death, in conversations about the fate that awaited everyone. Incidents of buying and selling in the ghetto were broken off by the execution of both the buyer and the seller.

The extermination of the population began shortly after the ghetto was established and assumed a gradual character. The means of extermination varied from occasion to occasion. It was announced for a start that thirty-six Jews would be publicly executed by firing squad on the main square for having contact with partisans (there had been no such contacts). A short while later, it was announced that a certain number of Jews would be hanged for going about the city and greeting Gentiles. Thereafter, the killings were carried out without a pretext. For several days, then, crowds of Jews would be led out of the ghetto into the city and forced to dig foundation pits. When the pits had been dug, the Jews would be ordered to lie down in them. Then the Germans fired machine guns at those lying down and covered up the dead, the wounded, and those who were not even wounded with a thin layer of earth; on top of them they laid a new row of people, shot them, again threw earth over them, and so on until the foundation pits were full, whereupon they were covered over completely.

The most finely perfected instruments of extermination were the notorious mobile gas vans, which soon began to be used on a large scale.

After every "pogrom"—as the inhabitants of the ghetto called each new slaughter—the area of the ghetto grew smaller, as more and more streets were freed of Jews and resettled by the local Gentile population. They shifted the barbed wire, taking in less and less of the neighborhood. The slaughter itself was carried out for the most part street by street: such and such a number of residents of such and such streets of the ghetto were wiped out, after which they moved the boundary of the ghetto, excluding the streets newly freed of Jews. After a certain time, the residents of other streets were subjected to extermination, and so on.

The extermination of a significant number of Jews was set for November 7, 1942. Several days before this, Shapiro escaped from Minsk with a false passport. Some time before, she had managed, thanks to the help of Russian friends, to get her five-year-old son out of the ghetto and to place him, under a Russian surname, in an orphanage set up by the local population with the permission of the Germans. Anna Maximovna Izraelit, the storyteller's mother, had her skull fractured by a local policeman, but she survived. A short time later, she was killed in a mobile gas van. Before the boy was placed in an orphanage, a policeman threw him down a sewer during one of the regular raids on the ghetto, but he survived.

In addition to the local Jewish population, Jews from other countries—France, Germany, and elsewhere—were transported to the Minsk ghetto. The Jews of each country were settled in the ghetto separately. Barbed wire separated these different "associations of compatriots" one from the other. They were forbidden to have contact with each other or with the local Jews. All of them shared the fate of the Jews of Minsk, that is, gradually they were all murdered.[13]

If anyone managed to escape and was caught, they would be put through a public "preparation" on the main square, that is, they would be cut into pieces until death took them. The "preparation" began with the cutting of the eyeballs from their sockets.

In the course of exterminations by the mobile gas vans, young women had their braids tied to the axles of the vehicles in such a way that they were dragged alive through the city until death overtook them. Meanwhile, the killing by gas of those who were inside the mobile vans was being carried out. Polizeimeister Gottenbach more than once, in his walks around the ghetto, for reasons of his own, killed Jews that crossed his path, including children, with his revolver.

In addition to the separate incidents of killing known to the woman telling this story, there were four major pogroms: the first was on November 11, 1941; the second (a very large one) on March 2, 1942; the third, in April 1942; and the fourth, on November 7, 1942. The storyteller believes that the fourth pogrom completed the extermination of all the Jews in Minsk, but she is not sure of this, since in early November, 1942, several days before the fourth pogrom, she succeeded in fleeing Minsk. According to other sources, the extermination of all the Jews in Minsk was completed in April 1944. Even before that, seeking to be saved, Shapiro had turned to Professor Onishchenko, whom she had known in the past through her medical work, asking him to arrange work for her as a doctor in one of the nearby villages where it was not known that she was a Jew. Onishchenko, who had been a member

---

13. The narrator is mistaken on two points: No French Jews are known to have been among them, and the foreign Jews were not cordoned off from each other.

of the Communist Party under the Soviets and who had occupied an important post in the health care system, was working under the Germans as the assistant director of the Minsk health administration. In response to her request, he said: "We don't send kikes to work. We exterminate them if they don't understand that they're supposed to drop dead from hunger." Soon after, Onishchenko went on a "scientific research trip" to Paris, which at the time was also occupied by the Germans. Nothing is known of his subsequent fate.

Regarding other separate incidents of killings, the storyteller recalls that one day, Jews who had been deported from Germany to Minsk were summoned to the ghetto's main square, supposedly for a meeting. No meeting took place, and they loaded all those who reported into the mobile gas vans and took them away to their deaths.

During the intervals between the mass exterminations, there were many occasions when the German commandant demanded tribute from the population of the ghetto: money, fabric, shoes, various things like this. And they threatened to shoot hostages for non-compliance. The tribute was usually raised in the required amounts and within the required timeframe.

After her escape from Minsk with a false passport in the name of a Russian woman, Shapiro made it to Gomel. There, while registering her passport, Chief of Police Kardakov (a former Red Army colonel, a former member of the Communist Party, and a traitor), dispatched her, in light of doubts that had arisen, to a German professor named Weber to determine her racial origins. The professor, in taking measurements of her skull, nose, mouth, and other such details, made a mistake, pronouncing her "undoubtedly of Aryan descent," which saved her life.

Shapiro's son, Edouard (born in 1936), whom Shapiro, thanks to the help of a Russian friend, had managed to get out of the ghetto and to place in an orphanage, recalled that a commission for the verification of racial origins of children operated in the city's orphanages. The goal of the commission was to discover which of the children in the orphanages were Jews. In addition to interrogating the children, there was also a physical examination of skulls, noses, mouths, and jaws, and a check to see if any were circumcised. Any Jewish children who were discovered were done away with—shot or put in mobile gas vans. According to the boy, he personally witnessed the shootings of children. He himself escaped death by passing himself off as a Russian, since he had not been circumcised. The orphanage was maintained by the charitable donations of the local population. Still, the children were practically starving. If there were doubts about whether any children had been baptized, they were christened in the church. The boy was baptized and christened Kolya. The children had to attend church and participate in the prayers and the singing.[14]

Recorded by A. V. Veysbrod, 11 Markhlevskogo Street, apartment 101, Moscow.

GARF f. 8114, op. 1, d. 955, ll. 64–72. This is a handwritten manuscript by A. V. Veysbrod.

---

14. There is a handwritten note in the text at this point: "Very valuable material."

49. A meeting in Minsk
Accounts of Tamara Gershakovich, Captain Lifshitz, and Sofia Disner
Recorded by L. Katzovich

The story that I want to tell took place in Minsk during the bloody occupation.

One has to remember that Belorussians and Russians were threatened with execution for going into the ghetto or even for exchanging a word with a Jew through the fence.

Jews were threatened with death for leaving the ghetto without a yellow patch. In any case, entry into the ghetto was allowed only in the column that headed to work in the morning and returned in the evening. If they caught a Jew outside the ghetto talking with a Russian, they shot both of them on the spot.

It was no accident that the Jews of Minsk, as soon as they were imprisoned in the ghetto, understood the word "ghetto" in this way: "a divorce from the local population." Nevertheless, no small number of Jews were in constant contact with Russians and Belorussians. And if everyone in the ghetto did not die of hunger before the last day of its existence (when the Germans liquidated the ghetto once and for all), then it was only thanks to the fact that the Jews had maintained relations with the local inhabitants.

And, in spite of all the Germans' threats, many Russians and Belorussians, risking not only their own lives but the lives of their families, hid Jewish children in their homes.

My niece, Tamara Gershakovich, was afraid to leave her six-year-old child at home after the terrible pogrom in the summer, which had lasted for four days. The Germans killed children, the elderly, and women first of all, and then men who for any reason did not turn up for work. For this reason, Tamara, when she went out to work in the mornings, would carry her little girl in a sack to the home of a Russian woman friend, and in the evening, returning from work, would take the child back home in the ghetto.

Many children who were left without parents went to the Russian neighborhoods on their own. Good people took them to their apartments and would not let them out again. In this way, the children of Dr. Levin, of the artist Sladek, and of Dr. Lipets remained alive, along with the son of Alter, a military man, and scores of other children.

Many Jewish children left for Russian orphanages. The teachers knew they were Jewish and that by giving them refuge in the orphanages they were risking their own lives. In spite of this, the teachers took the Jewish children in, gave them Russian or Belorussian names, and kept them safe until the day of liberation.

In Minsk, I met several fortunate parents who had found their children in the best of health. Captain Lifshitz found his children—a thirteen-year-old boy and a six-year-old girl—in one of Minsk's orphanages. The boy told the story of how he had been rescued:

"After the Germans killed Mama, I didn't want to stay in the ghetto anymore. My sister and I left for a nearby village. We stayed there for a little while, but I felt drawn to the city. Then we thought up Russian first and last names for ourselves and left for the city. There, we were taken in at a Russian orphanage. The teachers realized that we were Jews, but they didn't give the game away."

There were such Jewish children in every orphanage in Minsk. These children were so well instructed and cautious that even a month and a half after the liberation of Minsk, I frequently met Jewish children who, in conversations with their teachers, made up stories about their fathers and mothers, while a little Jewish girl in an orphanage replied fearfully to my question "What's your name?" by saying "Vierka Ivanovna."

There were 31 Jewish children among the 60 children in Minsk Orphanage No. 2, and 11 Jewish children among more than 100 children in Orphanage No. 3. In Orphanage No. 7, there were 8 Jewish children and one Negro child named Jim, whom the teachers hid from the German cannibals, as they did the Jewish children.

As was mentioned earlier, the Germans killed anyone who concealed Jews with the greatest barbarity. They wiped out the entire village of Skirmuntovo in the Kaydanov Region, where they found ten Jews living with peasants. There was a transshipping point in the village of Skirmuntovo through which one passed to get to the partisans. They hid Jews here in large barns. Every night, scores of Jews would come here from the ghetto. The Germans learned of this and surrounded the ghetto. Ten Jews whom they found in a barn they killed right away. Then they herded all the inhabitants of the village, upward of 280 people, into that barn and set it on fire from all sides.

But this did not put a stop to the willingness of many people to save Jews. Thirteen Jews who were concealed for three months in the Jewish cemetery of Minsk remained alive only because a Belorussian worker named Manya Kantsevich helped them. Had it not been for her and a few other Russian friends, these Jews would have starved to death.

Two peasants from Western Belorussia—Kostyush Kozlovsky and Matvey Boyarov—played a genuinely important role in lending aid to the Jewish partisan unit commanded by Tuvia Bielski by giving timely warnings of German raids.[15]

Sonya Disner worked at the Telman Shoe Factory in Minsk. Before the war, she and Maria Ignatevna Avgustovich worked at the Kaganovich Shoe Factory.

When the Germans fenced off the ghetto, Disner found herself trapped and nearly perished during the first pogrom. Maria, her sister Natalya, and their seventy-six-year-old mother Yelizaveta Avgustovich concealed Sonya Disner in their home for three years. In order to do this, they moved to an unfinished cellar, where it would

---

15. Tuvia Bielski and his brothers, Asrael and Zus, led a partisan unit in Belorussia. See Peter Duffy, *The Bielski Brothers: The True Story of Three Men Who Defied the Nazis, Built a Village in the Forest, and Saved 1,200 Jews* (New York, 2003); and Nehama Tec, *Defiance: The Bielski Partisans* (New York, 1993).

be easier to hide Sonya. They were on guard every night. Finally, the police figured out that there was an outsider at their place. They arrested Maria and held her for six weeks. But the police learned nothing from her.

Meanwhile, the Jews were doing everything possible to help their Russian and Belorussian comrades in the partisan movement. Once, injured Belorussian and Russian comrades from partisan units were brought to a hospital in the ghetto. (There was a hospital in the Minsk ghetto which was famous for the quality of its staff.) They were given yellow patches before being taken into the ghetto. While recovering in this hospital, they were called by Jewish names: Stepan became Khaim; Andrei was called Yankel; Taras was known as Leybe. When they got better, they were helped to return to their partisan units. In addition, the Jews began to use every possibility to rescue Soviet POWs from fascist concentration [actually POW] camps, where they were dying from torture, hunger, and cold.

In this way, a Minsk Jew named Gedalye, who was a metalworker, saved 1st Lieutenant Semyon Gunzenko from a POW camp. Gedalye brought him out of the camp in a trashcan. He took him into the ghetto and gave him the chance to escape into the forest, where he soon became the commander of a partisan detachment and then the commander of the Ponomarenko Partisan Brigade.

GARF f. 8114, op. 1, d. 958, ll. 203–208. *A typewritten manuscript translated from Yiddish.*

50. The camp and ghetto in Minsk
A LETTER FROM THE FRONTLINE SOLDIER M. LOKSHIN TO ILYA EHRENBURG [FEBRUARY 1945]

[. . .][16] It was July 6, 1941. I met a writer from Birobidzhan named Dobin in the concentration camp on the edge of town. Many thousands of civilians had been herded together there. Several thousand POWs had been gathered there as well. They had not yet separated out the Jews. As Dobin and I walked around the camp, we saw the Germans beating people with rifle butts and firing into crowds that were throwing themselves on rusks tossed from vehicles. They would shoot people who stepped out of line to draw water from a swampy stream.

On July 10, 1941, the Germans began to implement their Nazi racial policies by laying out the camp according to nationality. The Jews were cordoned off on four sides with ropes, then watched by a reinforced guard. The inauguration of the transformed camp was marked by the shooting of a Jew for not having run quickly enough to the area set aside for the Jews. They shot him anyway according to standard fascist procedures. That is, they beat him, mocked him, forced him to run and crawl, and then, when he was exhausted, finished him off with a bullet and forced someone to bury him inside the camp. It was on that day that massive violence began. They formed up

---

16. The opening of the letter is missing from the archives of the Jewish Anti-Fascist Committee.

3,000 Jews in an area of no more than 1,500 or 2,000 square meters. Those fenced in between the POWs and the former prisoners were pinned to the ground from evening onward by machine-gun fire, accused of doing business with the POWs and not sharing their food with the former prisoners. Dobin and I tried to calm those who were agitated in order to ease their grief. I myself learned from Dobin to go begging, to keep up my health, and to feed myself somehow.

They broke us up into nine columns. Each day they would take a few men from each column and herd them away in trucks. A burst of submachine gun fire was heard coming from somewhere, and that was all.

Around July 15, they selected individuals from a group of three thousand intellectuals and also took them away to some unknown destination.

For the time being, they were leaving the civilian women alone, and even allowed them to bring in parcels. Each day, however, less and less food reached the prisoners, since the Germans were organizing the looting first of the prisoners and then of those who were bringing parcels.

On July 18, they marched around two thousand Jews who had been left in the camp to jail. On the way, there were shootings and instances of abuse organized as a kind of spectacle. At first, they led them into the stone courtyard of the prison. They locked the gates and forced this two-thousand-strong mass to curl up in a ball in one corner of the yard. Bursts of submachine gun fire were let off methodically. Outside the prison gates, women and children were crying. The Gestapo did its dirty work with surprising calm. Then they herded us up to the second floor of the prison. Two solidly built fascists with clubs stood by the door, while men with submachine guns stayed behind our backs. Some were shouting "*Schnell! Schnell!*" [Faster! Faster!]; those who were by the doors were delivering blows to the head. Prisoners who had slipped through the prison corridor entered the cells almost mechanically. Dusk was falling and we could hear the steady din of running feet. Fascists burst into the cells and began beating and then shooting everyone. Again they chased us outside and demanded that we give up the thief who had stolen a bar of soap, a towel, and something else besides from the commandant. There had not been any theft, of course. But there was a state of great alarm all night long. They let us out on July 20 and took us to the so-called *Judenrat*. One of the "representatives" of the "Jewish Council" stood before us and made an announcement about the amount of gold, silver, and cash that the Jewish population of the city had forty-eight hours to bring to the German authorities. Meanwhile, he rather clearly hinted that what had happened so far was no comparison with what was to come.

They opened the ghetto on August 1. By that time, the Germans had already laid the foundations of hostility on the part of the Belorussian population toward the Jews, who were blamed for the fact that it was supposedly necessary for many Belorussians to abandon their houses and gardens, since the land set aside for the ghetto was a considerable distance from the city center.

The forcible drives to work began on that day, and until the middle of August, almost everything was done without any shootings. But beginning on August 14–15, there were instances of beatings; attitudes toward women changed and there were rumors of Jews being castrated. But at the same time, a collection was being taken for the building of a Jewish hospital. And we tried to form an underground group of young people with one of the doctors. We attempted to set up a radio receiver and hand out flyers. They forced me out to work on August 19. That same day a concentration camp opened on Shirokaya Street. The camp was under the authority of the military field police. Brought there under force of arms, 120 Jews had to dismantle several structures near the cavalry barracks with their bare hands and clear a space for the camp within two hours. They had to carry the first beams, logs, or boards that fell into their hands for 200 meters at a run and to lay them down sorted by type and size.

At approximately the halfway point, the Germans would greet the martyrs with a dog. And they would seize and begin to beat any fellow that the dog rushed at. And so work went on.

My dear friend! I do not have the strength to describe these horrors. But if hell, in our understanding, is terrible, then August 19, 1941, was a day spent in hell.

On that day, they beat me twice and dunked me in a well when I was in a state of semi-consciousness, as if they were trying to revive me, and then they put me up against a wall and made ready to shoot me. But when they realized that I was happy about it, they ordered me off to one side. I lay on the ground, burning up, greedily breathing in the damp smell of the untrampled grass. The SS men with skull insignias on their service caps and sleeves were coming up to me and kicking me in the face, covering my body with bruises, and taunting me all the while with "Stalin, Stalin."

Dusk was falling. I had been beaten up and picked clean. I was without trousers or underpants. They put a hundred unfortunates in front of me and forced me to lead them in singing.

Dear God! We sang. It seems that only heaven itself heard this sorrow. When evening came on they drove us into the horse stables and told us that the Judenrat knew where we were, and that our liberation depended on us and on no one else. That is, the sooner we finished our work, the sooner they would let us go home.

On August 20, they broke us up into columns. They appointed Kolonnenführers (column leaders) from among us and armed them with clubs. From that time onward, more and more new groups of people began arriving. The camp grew to hold two thousand unfortunates. Only those who escaped gained their liberation from that hell.

Comrade Ehrenburg! Our dear, beloved friend! I was born in 1916. I was raised in the Komsomol, and now, during the war, I, like a sponge, have drunk my fill of grief, and there has formed in me a feeling that has, truth be told, not entirely taken shape yet. However, as I would wish it, the long-suffering Jewish people should be not only a people with equal rights, but a heroic people. Here I am on the soil of accursed Germany, and yet I have no thirst to slaughter and wipe out German elderly, children, or women. But I rejoice with all my heart at the sound of artillery fire on the German armed forces. I am glad that there will never be another German night in Russia. I am glad that you, my dear Ehrenburg, can work peacefully for the sake of the peoples of our native country. But I also ask you to pay attention to the mistakes committed by the Jews between 1940 and 1945.

Excuse me for having written so much. I am imposing on you. But what is to be done when it is so painful, and anyway, this is only the smallest part of what I wanted to tell you. It could be that the war will end soon, and that someday I will write down as best I can what I went through and what I saw. For now at least, perhaps what I have shared with you can be of some use in your work.

By the way, our unit took part in the storming of the town of Schneidemuechl.[17] We wiped out a small group of encircled Germans, and at dawn on the morning of February 15 we left that town near the border of barbaric Germany. The glow of burning Hitlerite Germany was visible a long way off.

The other day in Landsberg,[18] I happened to chat with a German medic. Our conversation was on the subject of the defeat of Germany. He put to me two basic questions. The first was: How will Germany be treated after the war? The second was: How could Russia have grown so strong in such a short period of time? The first question I answered according to the resolutions of the Crimean conference of the three leaders of the Allied powers, and the second we answered collectively. Then they told us, or, more accurately, tried to persuade us, that the Hitlerites made up no more than 25 percent of the German people. They talked about the conclusions drawn by Bismarck.

I want to point out that the Germans who did not get away in time put on white armbands and tried to be hospitable. Many of them are becoming human. The more educated Germans were more welcoming in appearance than the less educated ones.

On the whole, it is difficult just now to reach any conclusions, not to mention the fact that one cannot manage to get down all the impressions received in the twelve pages written by me.

With a military salute and deep love for you,
M. Lokshin

GARF f. 8114, op. 1, 960, ll. 293–298. Signed.

51. A prisoner in the Minsk camp
THE RECOLLECTIONS OF RED ARMY SOLDIER YEFIM LEYNOV
MARCH 14, 1943

---

17. Schneidemuechl is today the Polish city of Pila.
18. Landsberg is today the Polish city of Gorzow Wielkopolski.

Our unit was captured in an encirclement in the Chernigov Region. I spent time in four prison camps: in Novgorod-Seversky, Gomel, Bobruysk, and Minsk. It would be impossible to describe all the horrors. I will focus on the last camp, Minsk.

The camp was in Komarovka, on the Moscow Highway. It was an unfinished, five-story building in which more than five thousand POWs were held. When we arrived—there were around a thousand of us—they put us in a barn. They fed us a swill made from scorched flour and gave us no bread. We built a fire to keep warm; it was October. Then came shouts of "Soup!" Everyone ran out, they did not extinguish the fire, and the shed caught on fire. They formed us up. The commandant counted off one hundred men; they were shot on the spot.

Everyone wanted to go out to work, since the locals would give us pieces of bread. There were too many who wanted to. The sentries beat men with rubber truncheons and shot them. Each day they killed thirty or forty men. People came down with dysentery. When they went out to relieve themselves, the Germans shot at them. We found the bodies of those who had been killed each morning.

They killed us when they took us out to work, for talking to someone, or for stopping for a minute when one was exhausted. One could see the bodies of prisoners from as far away as the Komarovka Station.

One day they took some prisoners from the camp to Novgorod-Seversky. Of 2,000 men, 300 made it there—the rest died along the way. Many died on arrival. It took us two days to bury them.

A typhus epidemic began. Around 200 prisoners were dying every day. Everyone who could still walk hauled the corpses to the park. We could not bury them—the ground was frozen—so we stacked them in piles. With the coming of spring, the bodies began to decompose. Then the general commissar of Belorussia gave the order to douse the bodies with gasoline and burn them.

I survived by chance; I do not look like a Jew. The Jews in the camp were stripped naked, flogged, and then tossed into a cellar where the water was above their knees. After three days, they were dragged out of there and finished off.

There were many Jews, old people and women with children who had not managed to be evacuated, left in Minsk. There were those who had fled Western Belorussia. They were put in the ghetto. Ten thousand Jews from Hamburg were brought there. There were people of various professions in the ghetto: professors, craftsmen, doctors, workers, musicians. The killings were carried out with ceremony. The condemned dug their own graves. The musicians had to play arias from "The Jewess" and "Kol Nidre."[19] They walked in columns, old women and mothers with children. The Germans opened fire with machine guns and submachine guns. The dead,

---

19. The opera *La Juive* (The Jewess) was written by Jacques Fromental Halévy in 1835. "Kol Nidre" is the opening prayer of the Yom Kippur service; Max Bruch composed a piece for cello and orchestra under that title in 1881.

wounded, and half-dead tumbled into the ditches. Afterward, the ditches were filled in with earth. These slaughters were carried out once a week, without fail, on Saturdays.

They collected children who had survived their parents, more than two hundred of them. They took them by the legs and slammed their heads into stones or pillars.

The whole city was horrified, in deep gloom from these unheard-of atrocities.

Throughout the summer of 1942, the Germans were bringing Jews from Western Europe to Minsk. They were supposedly bringing them to work. The Jews arrived with suitcases and handbags. On the Mogilev Highway, eight kilometers from Minsk, there is an abandoned military base. That was where they took the Jews from Western Europe. They dug ditches, and the Germans, so as not to waste cartridges, gassed them. They drove them up to the ditches in hermetically sealed vehicles and tipped out the corpses of those who had been asphyxiated. They sent us there to pick up pieces of lumber, and I struck up a conversation with one of the Jews working there. He said that he had been brought from Czechoslovakia.

In August, 1942, I managed to escape.

Yefim Leynov

March 14, 1943

GARF f. 8114, op. 1, d. 956, ll. 184–185. A typewritten manuscript. Ehrenburg archive, vol. 2, ll. 139–142. Signed.

52. The gassing of inhabitants of Minsk in mobile gas vans and the shooting of Minsk Jews

STENOGRAM OF THE INTERROGATION OF A GERMAN OFFICER NAMED JULIUS RAIHOF

JULY 21, 1944

FROM THE DOCUMENTS OF THE EXTRAORDINARY STATE COMMISSION

Interrogation begun in Minsk at 1:00 PM, on July 21, 1944.

Q: What do you know about the truck known as the mobile gas van, its construction, and how it was used?

A: While stationed in the village of Menyatino, Spassk-Demensk district in Smolensk Region,[20] I had occasion more than once to meet the commander of the field gendarmerie of the German 267th Infantry Division, Oberleutnant Evald Homaier. In a conversation with him at the officers' mess of the division in September 1942—I do not recall the exact date—Homaier told me that a special vehicle called a mobile gas van was being used by operatives of the SD in Minsk for the extermination of Soviet citizens. He did not give me their names. The mobile gas vans were constructed as follows: they were in the form of a heavy truck with a sealed frame. A pipe was run from the engine of the vehicle into the bed into which

---

20. In Kaluga Region today.

the Germans loaded Soviet citizens with the intention of gassing them. The vehicle was hermetically sealed, and the people in it were poisoned within several minutes by the emitted gasses. As for the length of time that the mobile gas vans operated in Minsk and the number of Soviet citizens that were killed by that method, I do not know.

Q: Do you know precisely which of those SD operatives took part in the poisoning of Soviet citizens with the help of the mobile gas vans?

A: I had no occasion personally to see a so-called mobile gas van, by means of which the mass poisoning of Soviet citizens was carried out. I heard of it for the first time from Oberleutnant Evald Homaier and subsequently from inhabitants of the city of Minsk with whom I was acquainted. Which of the SD operatives operated the mobile gas van in Minsk and poisoned Soviet citizens with the aid of these vehicles, I do not know, and am unable to provide any material information on the matter in question.

Q: On whose orders was the poisoning of Soviet citizens by means of the mobile gas vans carried out?

A: All of these atrocities and the extermination of Soviet citizens with the mobile gas vans were carried out in accordance with the orders and decrees of the German government, of which I spoke earlier in a previous interrogation.

Q: Who is Oberleutnant Evald Homaier?

A: Evald Homaier, rank Oberleutnant, was the commander of the field gendarmerie of the German 267th Infantry Division, in the field tribunal of which I served as the presiding magistrate. Several months before the arrival of the Red Army, I left for Germany and did not subsequently return to the 267th Infantry Division. I can further say with regard to Evald Homaier that he personally executed approximately fifty Soviet citizens by shooting, but as to when these crimes were committed by him, I am unable to say.

Q: What else do you know concerning the bestial actions committed by the Germans against Soviet citizens in the city of Minsk?

A: Following the occupation of the city of Minsk by the Germans in the early days of July 1941, the entire Jewish population of Minsk was assembled by punitive units of the SS on the pretext of sending them to work in Germany. Once having assembled the Jews in one place, on the outskirts of Minsk, the SS divided them up into groups, threw large tarpaulins over them, and shot them with machine guns that they had deployed ahead of time. All told, several thousand members of the Jewish population of Minsk were shot that day. Who in the SS was the direct organizer of the atrocities committed against the Jews in Minsk, I do not know, since the facts in question were recounted to me by an NCO named Büchel, who was serving in the 268th Infantry Division at the time as the commander of a signals group, and who in November 1943 was transferred to the Italian Front along with the 268th Division. Where he is at present, I do not know.

Interrogator: Senior investigator, investigative section NKGB BSSR Senior Lt. State Security (Myagkov)

Stenographer: Sergushkina

GARF f. 8114, op. 1, d. 940, ll. 105–106. A typewritten, notarized copy.

Cities and Shtetls of Belorussia

53. Shootings, gallows, human torches

ACCOUNTS OF THE INHABITANTS OF THE TOWN OF STARYE DOROGI
RECORDED BY M. GRUBIAN
TRANSLATED BY D. MANEVICH

The Jewish Anti-Fascist Committee has received a series of new documents and depositions concerning the bestial cruelties perpetrated by the Germans against the Jews in Belorussia. Shchorbatov, a Belorussian and inhabitant of the town of Starye Dorogi who escaped from the German hell to the Soviet side, tells of the mass shooting of Jewish families in his town: in one day the SS killed 363 families. Shchorbatov tells of the terrible acts of vengeance directed at those Russian and Belorussian people whom the Germans suspected of concealing Jews. An old doctor named Shapelko lived in Starye Dorogi. In one of the sections of the hospital in which he worked, two ill Jewish women were concealed in great secrecy. In the end, the Gestapo learned of this "crime." They dragged the sick women from their beds and shot them, then hanged the doctor.

The same fate befell the agronomist Kunbin and Anna Koroleva, both Belorussians. The Germans accused them of collaborating with the partisans and hiding Jews in their homes. A Russian resident named Sipnov, who was captured by the Germans and escaped, tells the following story:

"When I was captured, they sent me and several others like me to a camp for prisoners on the banks of the Druch River. One day, through the barbed wire fence, we saw the German guards chase several dozen completely naked Jewish women and children into the river, yelling at them 'Wash up, you dirty kikes!' When the poor unfortunates tried to swim, the Germans opened fire on them. Not one of them came back from the river."

The Belorussian partisan Mikola B., recently returned from the Polotsk District, reports:

"In the village of Zaborye in the Polotsk District, the Germans herded together eighty Jewish men and twenty women, the wives of Belorussian partisans, locked them in a small local blacksmith's shop, doused the shop with kerosene, and put a match to it. They forbid anyone to put out the fire. One hundred people died in the flames in awful suffering."

The list of German atrocities grows longer every day. Anyone arriving from an area occupied by the Germans can tell dreadful stories of the evil acts of the bloodthirsty occupiers.

GARF f. 8114, op. 1, d. 961, ll. 328–328ob. A typewritten manuscript with handwritten corrections.

54. Extermination of the Jews in Western Belorussia
An account by L. Shaus
Translated by D. Manevich

The Jewish Anti-Fascist Committee has received a number of new materials concerning the physical extermination of the Jews in Western Belorussia. The extermination began on the first day of the Germano-fascist occupation, but the liquidation of the Jewish population took on its cruelest form in 1943.

In Grodno, there were some twenty thousand Jews at the time of the Hitlerite invasion, including several thousand driven there from nearby towns. In the spring of 1943, eleven Jews were left in the entire city all of whom were being forced to work on the construction of a new garage for the Gestapo.

The majority of Grodno's Jews were sent to the nearby shtetl of Kolbasenka (Kolbasin), where the Hitlerite scoundrels shot many of them, while the rest died from hunger and epidemic diseases. Those left alive were sent to the terrible death camp of Treblinka. There, the remainder of the Jewish population of Grodno perished in mobile gas vans.[21]

The Jews in Baranovichi numbered 12,000. They were shot in three different stages: 2,400 Jews were killed on March 4, 1942; 5,000 were killed on September 22, 1942; and 3,000 were shot in 1943. The rest were taken to various torture camps. Some managed to escape, and they joined partisan units.

There were 6,700 Jews in Lida before the war. They were all shot in the vicinity of the town of Kotorovo. The Hitlerites dug an enormous mass grave there, herded living men, women, and children into it, and opened fire on them all with machine guns. After the extermination of the Jewish population of Lida, they gathered the Jews from shtetls surrounding Lida—Voronovo, Skidel, Dzhentsol, and others—then shot them in groups.

At the beginning of the war there were more than 1,600 Jews in Smorgon. The Hitlerites locked them away in a ghetto consisting of several half-destroyed shacks. At the beginning of 1943, the entire population of the ghetto was wiped out.

There were more than 700 Jews in Nemenchina. They were driven into a local school. For several days they were given no food or water, and then they were taken to a nearby forest. One hundred people managed to escape. The remaining 600 were shot.

In Rodoshkovichi the Hitlerite bandits shot every last one of the Jews.

In Molodechno 2,000 Jews were exterminated. A sign posted at the station read: "No Jews here—clean."

---

21. Mobile gas vans were not used at Treblinka.

In the shtetl of Rakov they herded 900 Jews into the school and burned them to death. Anyone who tried to escape from the fire was shot with submachine guns.

In Volozhin the Jewish population was wiped out in three stages: on December 1, 1941, the first group of 300 was shot; on May 2, 1942, 1,500–1,800 people were killed. The bodies were stacked into a pile and a fire lit beneath it.

The final remnants of the Jewish population were murdered in the summer of 1943.

There had been Jewish villages in the Smorgon District for centuries: Korko, Leypuny, Zhidovnya, and others. In the autumn of 1942, the inhabitants of these villages were exterminated to the last person. The Hitlerites settled German colonists in place of the Jewish villagers.

The cities and shtetls of all of Western Belorussia were transformed into mass graves for tens of thousands of Jews who perished at the hands of the Germano-fascist criminals.

The blood of our murdered brothers and sisters cries out for vengeance. It calls us to a terrible revenge that knows no pity!

GARF f. 8114, op. 1, d. 955, ll. 107–108. A typewritten manuscript.

55. Reports by partisans from the town of Slutsk
Recorded by M. Grubian
Translated by D. Manevich

The Jewish population of the Belorussian town of Slutsk was annihilated in two stages.

A short time after the Germans occupied the town, they exterminated 2,800 Jews. The killing took two days. They took the Jews to the village of Makrita, several kilometers from Slutsk. There they shot them in groups, with submachine guns. Those who resisted or tried to escape the Hitlerites were doused with gasoline and set alight.

From the time of this first slaughter until the summer of 1942, things were comparatively calm in Slutsk. The surviving Jews were locked away in the ghetto. They were joined by the Jews of the surrounding district.

According to the partisans, until the summer of 1942, there were more than 2,000 Jewish households in the Slutsk ghetto. In July 1942, all the inhabitants of the Slutsk ghetto were taken to that same village of Makrita and shot. Among those killed were 700 small children.

Yet even after that, Slutsk was not entirely cleansed of Jews. Even though they had destroyed the ghetto, a certain number of Jews remained in the Slutsk jail. According to the reports of those same partisans, it was not a jail, in fact, but a torture chamber. During the time of the German rule of Slutsk, 47,000 people passed through that torture chamber—Jews, Russians, and Belorussians. No fewer than 14,000 people were tortured to death there. The rest were crippled for life.

GARF f. 8114, op. 1, d. 961, l. 332. A typewritten manuscript.

56. In the shtetl of Lyubavichi [22]
RECORDED BY M. GRUBIAN
TRANSLATED BY M. BREGMAN
[1944]

Who does not remember the sweet Jewish folk song "From Lyubavich to Khislavich"? [23] The Jewish people glorified the little Belorussian town of Lyubavich, which has such deep connection with Jewish traditions.

This celebrated small town is now no longer the subject of happy folk songs. Lyubavich, over the last two and a half years, during the time of the German occupation, was transformed into a vale of tears, into a place of sorrow for hundreds of Jewish families. Lyubavich has been reunited with the Soviet Union. The Red Army liberated the little town a short time ago. And it is only now that the crimes committed there by the Nazi criminals are being discovered.

The Nazis took particular sadistic delight in abusing some one hundred Jewish families who had not managed to be evacuated in time. The German press wrote that Lyubavich was a holy city for the Jews: "A holy city for Jehovah, rabbis, and ritual killings" (this was just what the *Minsk Gazette* reported). The commandant of Lyubavich declared that Lyubavich should be punished with particular severity. He formed two groups of Jews—one younger and one elderly. The first group was shot right on the spot; the second group of Jews, whom the Germans called the rabbis, was thrown into a terrible torture camp just outside the village of Rudnya. Here, for several weeks and with the most refined methods, the fascist monsters tortured old men (there were several dozen of them), yanked hair from their beards with tongs, organized daily public floggings, forced them to dance on Torah parchments, and so on. All of those who were in a condition to withstand these torments were shot in the end. Some time later, the rest of the Jews who were still in Lyubavich were murdered.

The Hitlerite masters of the martyred town paid dearly for their crimes, however. Even before the Red Army liberated Lyubavich, a group of Belorussian partisans stormed the village of Rudnya and captured it. After that, four stout young men led by Ts., a Jewish youth from Novograd-Volynsky, laid an ambush outside of Lyubavich, and seized the town commandant, whose trip they had found out about ahead of time. The Hitlerite scum got what was coming to him. At the same time, another group of partisans stormed Lyubavich, tossed grenades into the German barracks, destroyed them, and killed several dozen Germans in the process.

GARF, f. 8114, op. 1, d. 961, l. 331-331ob. A typewritten manuscript.

---

22. Lyubavichi is located in the Smolensk Region of Russia.
23. Lyubavich and Khislavich are Yiddish names for Lyubavichi and Khislavichi.

57. In Chausy
An account by the local resident Larisa Grigorevna Gmenko
Recorded by S. Bank

The bestial acts of the Hitlerites do not surprise anyone nowadays. They drowned the towns and villages of Belorussia in rivers of blood. Now, when the Red Army is swiftly and triumphantly moving west, we are learning of new acts of savagery on the part of the German occupiers, who wiped out hundreds of thousands of Jews and Belorussians.

Chausy is a small town in the Mogilev Region. Before the war it teemed with gardens and berry bushes. Life there was quiet, prosperous, thoroughly provincial. Now it is a heap of ruins. There is not so much as one surviving stone house in the town, and for that matter, there are very few of the wooden ones left either. The orchards have been chopped down, the berry bushes trampled.

As many as five thousand Jews lived in this small town. In August 1941, they were herded into a ghetto in Kozinka District, a suburb of Chausy. A few days later, these unfortunate people were forced to load their belongings onto carts. The Germans said that they were taking the Jews to a former Jewish collective farm (five kilometers from Chausy). It was all a lie. The Hitlerites robbed them, then took all the inhabitants of the ghetto out of town, to the bank of the Pronya River. Women, children, the elderly—they stood them on the edge of a ditch and prepared machine guns.

A local resident named Larisa Grigorevna Gmenko, an unwilling witness to this appalling mass killing, told me how it all happened.

As the unfortunates were standing on the edge of the ditch, one of the doomed, a schoolteacher named Dora Ruvimovna Kagan, turned to the butchers and cried:

"We're defenseless and can't fight you. But you can't kill us all. Millions of Soviet people are left, they'll avenge us. Our innocent blood will be on their banners."

A burst of automatic fire cut her speech short.

Then the Hitlerites opened fire with their heavy machine guns. The dead and wounded fell into the ditch. People who were entirely unharmed fell in as well. The Germans filled in the ditch any which way. They posted sentries. It was August 16, 1941. The moans of people buried alive could be heard from under the earth until late that night.

After the mass murder of all the Jews, the Germans began killing the second and third generations, that is, those whose mothers were Jews and whose fathers were Russians, or vice versa (anyone who had a Jewish parent). They began killing those whose parents were Russians, but whose grandfather or grandmother had been Jewish.

In Chausy, that small provincial town, eighteen-year-old Ira Gubnykh was well-known for her beauty; she was a slender blonde with big eyes that were always smiling. Her mother worked before the war as a pharmacist, her father was a doctor. Her grandfather was a Jew. All the residents of Chausy who were still alive came out to watch Ira on her final, sad journey. The girl walked down the middle of the road surrounded by dozens of young people whose only crime was that their fathers or mothers had been Jews. The youngsters were crying, and the blonde beauty was consoling them: "Don't cry! Don't let the butchers see that we're afraid of them. We'll be avenged in the end all the same."

Ira Gubnykh was shot along with that group of youngsters on a green bank of the Pronya on a bright, sunny August day in 1941.

GARF f. 8114, op. 1, d. 959, l. 100–100ob. A typewritten manuscript with handwritten corrections.

58. The death of a heroic schoolteacher in Chausy
RECORDED BY M. GRUBIAN

A Jewish woman died a hero's death. She was a high school teacher at the time of the horrifying pogrom mounted by the Germans against the remainder of the Jewish population in the Belorussian town of Chausy. It has not been possible to establish the name of the teacher to this day.[24] She perished in the circumstances described here.

The Hitlerites forcibly assembled the nine hundred Jewish families left among the living in the town of Chausy and herded them in the direction of the village of Dranukha; at the same time, the fascist bandits drove the handful of Jews remaining in Dranukha toward Chausy. At the halfway point, when the two groups of Jews met, the Hitlerites, with the assistance of the fascist police,[25] began firing on the unfortunates from all sides. The organization of this mass murder was directed by Danilov, the chief of the German police. When the shooting started, the above-mentioned schoolteacher, leaping out of the seething mass of people, spat in Danilov's face.

The police immediately seized this courageous daughter of the Jewish people and dragged her to the pit that was to become her living grave. At the last moment before her death, the teacher managed to cry out to the Jews who were falling: "Dear brothers and sisters! Spit in the faces of these scoundrels! The Red Army will get here and settle accounts with the German dogs for our blood!"

She did not have time to finish before a burst of fire from a heavy machine gun cut short her young life.

More than one thousand Jewish families were killed on the road between Chausy and Dranukha.

GARF, f. 8114, op. 1, d. 961, l. 330. A typewritten manuscript.

59. The Germans in Mozyr
RECORDED BY M. GRUBIAN
TRANSLATED BY M. BREGMAN

---

24. We know from the previous document that her name was Dora Ruvimovna Kagan.
25. This phrase refers to the local police drawn from the Belorussian population.

In the town of Mozyr (the center of Belorussian Polesye) a German newspaper called *Mozyr News* is published. In the issue of December 20, 1943, this insolent rag published a long article on the "Jewish Question." It would be superfluous to dwell on the various "brilliant" thoughts expressed on the "Jewish danger," and so on. The author concludes the article with the contention that the Germans have settled the "Jewish Question" once and for all in Belorussia as a whole and in the Mozyr District in particular. At the same time he considers it necessary to brag that the Germans had solved the "Jewish Question" along with all the other problems that they faced in the Mozyr district, particularly that of "Bolshevik influence."

One can judge how the Germans "solved the Jewish Question" and how they solved all their problems from the following statistic: In Mozyr alone, the Germans wiped out 1,155 Jews during their occupation. They were not successful in catching any more in that city. Over the same period of time, they killed more than 10,000 people of other nationalities—Russians, Belorussians, and Ukrainians. Among those killed were women, children, the elderly, and the sick.

As for how the Germans "solved" problems in the Mozyr district on the whole, the following facts tell us a great deal:

When the Jews were taken from their apartments to be shot, Liza Lozinskaya, a schoolteacher, was hiding somewhere. The next day, after the mass shootings, the Gestapo cutthroats caught her. The bandits dragged her onto the market square, tied her to a telegraph pole, and began throwing sharp daggers at her. The monsters hung a placard around her neck with the inscription "I impeded German officials from carrying out laws and regulations." The same nightmarish scene was repeated sometime later on the market square in Mozyr when Sh., a female partisan, was subjected to the same punishment.

The same issue of the *Mozyr News* carried an article on page two in fine print that a local commissar had been attacked on one of the suburban highways by "unknown bandits." Had it not been for the intervention of the security forces that hurried to the scene, the commissar would have had to say goodbye to this world.

That is how the Germans solved all their problems in the Mozyr District, and the problem of the "Bolshevik" danger in particular.

GARF f. 8114, op. 1, d. 961, ll. 329–329ob. A typewritten manuscript.

60. Liquidation of the Jews in Mstislavl
RECORDED BY F. KRASOTKIN
JANUARY 2, 1944

The triumphant Red Army, purging the territory of Belorussia of the Germano-fascist bandits, liberated the town of Mstislavl not long ago. It is only just now, after the liberation of the town, that they have managed to document all the bestial crimes that were committed there by the Hitlerite fiends. Outside of town, in the so-called Kagalny ditch, some twenty pits containing the corpses of citizens of the towns killed by the Nazis were discovered. The pits were filled with the bodies of men, women, and children.

The testimony of witnesses has established that immediately after the capture of the town by the Germans, Major Krupp, the German commandant, forced all Jews to wear a white armband with a Star of David on their left arms and a yellow circle on their right. The entire Jewish population was driven out each day to do forced labor.

On October 15, 1941, a German punitive unit arrived in Mstislavl. By order of Feldwebel Krauze, the unit commander, the entire Jewish population was gathered on the market square. They formed up men and women separately. Then they rounded up some thirty elderly Jewish men, loaded them into a truck and drove them off to the Leshensky ditch, where they were shot and their bodies left unburied. From the assembled women the Germans selected the young ones, herded them into a shop, stripped them naked and subjected them to rape and torture. Anyone who resisted was shot on the public square.

Then, all the remaining Jews were driven into the courtyard of the teacher training school. From there they led them out onto the street, formed them up in rows of ten, and took them forcibly to the Kagalny ditch. The fascist cannibals led the Jews in groups of ten up to pits dug ahead of time, took their clothes and jewelry, then shot them. They killed the men in this way first, followed by the women with older children. The small children were thrown into the pit alive. The schoolteacher, Minkina-Orlovskaya, pleaded with them to spare her six-year-old son, whose father was Russian. In reply, the butchers raised the infant on their bayonets and flung him into the ditch.

This nightmare lasted from 11:00 AM until 4:00 PM All in all, the Hitlerites killed 1,300 Jews that day.

After this savagery committed against the Jews, they began doing away with other residents of the town. People were shot on the slightest pretext or for no reason at all. The executions were carried out, as a rule, on Fridays at four in the morning. Between 25 and 70 people were shot at a time. In addition, the police and gendarmes shot their own victims each day.

According to incomplete figures, the Hitlerites killed more than 3,000 citizens of Mstislavl during their occupation. January 2, 1944.

GARF f. 8114, op. 1, d. 960, l. 282–282ob. A typewritten manuscript with handwritten corrections.

61. Hitlerite atrocities in the shtetl of Cherikov
RECORDED BY M. TSUNTS
NOVEMBER 25, 1943

The Hitlerites arrived in the shtetl of Cherikov, Mogilev Region of Belorussia, on July 16, 1941. After beginning with isolated shootings of unarmed civilians, the Germans then proceeded to mass killings and shootings. In October 1941, the Hitlerites announced the "resettlement of the entire Jewish population to another locality." Approximately five hundred Jews were herded into the House of the People.[26] At the time, the population still did not know what bloodthirsty animals they were dealing with. The Jews walked to the place where they were being led under German guard. At Mostovoe, by the mill, they were ordered to stop. Suddenly the command was given:

"Fire!"

The soldiers opened fire with submachine guns on the defenseless crowd that was speechless with fear. The Germans did not leave until they had wiped out every last one of the five hundred Jews. The wounded were finished off with a shot at point-blank range, while some of those still barely alive were thrown into a ditch, then covered with earth and new heaps of dead bodies.

It would be impossible to number all the crimes committed by the Hitlerites in this small town. They used peaceful civilians to clear minefields. Attaching people to each other with chains, the Germans, armed with submachine guns, would push them into the minefields. Dozens of men and women died from these mines.

In the winter of 1941, the Hitlerites gathered more than four hundred people to build a bridge over the Sozh River. It seemed to a German officer that the work was going too slowly. So he ordered all the men and women working to take off all their clothes and to lie down in the snow. All of those who had been working were subjected to a whipping in the terrible cold.

The fascists cruelly abused women and girls. Residents tell of witnessing how a group of German soldiers seized two girls in broad daylight and raped them right on the main square.

The Germans went on their worst rampage just before their retreat from the town. Of the 893 houses, they blew up or burned down 870. Three schools went up in the flames, along with the House of the People, the veterinary college, the sawmill, two cement factories, a bakery, two hospitals, the post office, and the public baths. Those whom the Germans did not manage to take away with them, they shot. Two lonely old people, Pimen Ivashkov, seventy, and Marfa Dynova, sixty-three, begged the Germans on their knees and with tears in their eyes to have pity on their age and not to touch their dwellings. The old people's tears made the Germans laugh. They set fire to their huts and threw the owners into the flames. November 25, 1943.

GARF f. 8114, op. 1, d. 955, l. 9–9ob. A typewritten manuscript.

---

26. An official meeting hall common to virtually every city or town.

III
LITHUANIA

Lithuania was once the home of a proud tradition of Jewish life and scholarship, renowned for rabbinical academies in Telz (Telshyay, Telsiai), Slobodka (Viliampol, Viljampole), and Kelme. Vilna (Vilno, Vilnius), its historic capital, was called "The Jerusalem of Lithuania." Following the German and Soviet invasions of Poland in 1939, the city of Vilna and its environs were transferred from Poland (to which it had been assigned in 1920) to Lithuania. The Soviet Union formally annexed Lithuania in the summer of 1940. By the spring of 1941, Lithuania's Jewish population reached 250,000, including 15,000 who had fled German-occupied Poland. Some 6,000 of these succeeded in emigrating to Palestine, the Far East, and elsewhere; several thousand more were deported by Soviet officials to remote parts of the Soviet Union.

The Germans actually began their campaign of mass murder in Lithuania, killing over five hundred Jews in three small border towns—Gargsdai, Kretinge, and Palanga—at the end of June 1941.[1] At the same time, SS commanders observed the enthusiastic willingness of many local people to kill their Jewish neighbors. The Balts, the Romanians, and others, blamed the Jews for Sovietization, and this attitude hardened their hostility toward them. On June 30, 1941, Einsatzgruppe A reported from Kovno (Kovna, Kaunas) that "during the last three days Lithuanian partisan groups have killed several thousand Jews."[2] By July, another communiqué reported

---

1. Yitzhak Arad, Shmuel Krakowski, and Shmuel Spector, eds., *The Einsatzgruppen Reports: Selections from the Dispatches of the Nazi Death Squads' Campaign Against the Jews in Occupied Territories of the Soviet Union July 1941–January 1943* (New York, 1989), p. 10. See also Konrad Kweit, "Rehearsing for Murder: The Beginning of the Final Solution in Lithuania in June 1941," *Holocaust and Genocide Studies* 12, no. 1 (1998), pp. 3–26.
2. Ibid., p. 1.

that "In Kaunas, up to now, a total of 7,800 Jews have been liquidated, partly through pogroms and partly through shooting by Lithuanian kommandos."[3] Such murderous cooperation helped the Germans kill 80 percent of Lithuanian Jewry by the close of 1941 and over 95 percent by the end of the war.

Near Vilna, where the pre-war Jewish population had reached 57,000—one-fourth of the total population—the city's Jews were killed in the Ponary Forest. In Kovno, whose Jewish population was 40,000, the Germans used a network of fortifications dating back to tsarist times, and in particular the "Ninth Fort," as massacre sites. By 1942, after the initial waves of killing, the Germans established ghettos, principally in Vilna, Kovno, and Shavli (Shaulyay, Siauliai), in order to employ the Jews in the service of the German war effort. As in all the wartime ghettos, the Jews were confined, permitted only starvation rations, and forced to perform slave labor until they either perished of disease or were murdered when they were no longer strong enough to work.

It was in Vilna that Jewish leaders first understood that there was a comprehensive German plan to kill all the Jews. On New Year's Eve 1942, three weeks before the Wannsee Conference and even longer before the main killing centers became fully operational, the poet and leftist youth leader Abba Kovner issued an exhortation to his fellow Jews: "Let us not go like sheep to the slaughter."[4] Kovner warned his listeners that the Germans were planning to kill every Jew they could find, beginning with the Jews of Lithuania. Such calls led to the creation of an underground movement that united various ideological groups in a common struggle. It also helped hundreds of Jews to escape the ghetto and join anti-German partisan units.

Jews who remained in the ghettos documented the drama of their steady destruction. In Kovno, they collected photographs, drawings, music, memoirs, statistical graphs, and theological essays. The material was concealed from the Germans and after the war survivors were able to retrieve at least some of this precious archive. The surviving ghettos, nonetheless, were liquidated in the autumn of 1943. When the Red Army reached Lithuania in the summer of 1944, they found very few Jews alive: about 2,500 survivors in and around Vilna, and another 5,500 elsewhere in the republic.

62. The truth about the terror against the Jews in Lithuania during the German occupation of 1941
AN APPEAL TO THE NATIONS OF THE WORLD
FROM THE DIARY OF DR. VIKTOR KUTORGA [5]
TRANSLATED FROM THE GERMAN BY K. GERSHATER

---

3. Ibid., p. 17.
4. For the full text of the proclamation, see Arad, Gutman, and Margalit, eds., *Documents on the Holocaust*, pp. 433–434.
5. The oncologist Viktor Kutorga lived in Vilnius and died in 1992. He was a participant in the Lithuanian underground movement and a nephew of Dr. Elena Kutorgiene-Buivydaité, who was

Let the whole world know of the dreadful terror which the Germans inflicted on the Jews! We ask that you publish this document in the free press of the entire world so that all freedom-loving nations will know what befell us. We ask that the leaders of all free countries take steps to distribute news of these evil deeds to the entire world and thereby to force the mad leaders of Germany to cease these crimes. It is necessary to show their true face to the whole world and to bring them to justice for their bestial deeds, which are aimed at the extermination of the Jewish people as a whole. We ask that everything possible be done so that the entire world, and the German people in particular, should be told of these crimes. Do everything possible to put an end to these vile actions.

The present document concerns the mass murder of approximately one hundred thousand people for the sole reason that they were of Jewish descent. This document deals with the indescribable violence perpetrated against them and constitutes the most terrible of accusations against National Socialism. It demonstrates the true face and methods of the builders of the "New Europe" to the entire world. We will recount here unheard-of events that might seem improbable and fantastic, but we nonetheless categorically affirm that all the descriptions presented are based on harsh reality, and that all the facts presented are known to everyone in Lithuania. These bloody crimes against mankind and God must enter into history as a monstrous insanity contradicting any concepts of culture and humanity. We once again ask that everything possible and conceivable be done to circulate the testimonies presented here as widely as possible, and in this way to assist those who are not yet beyond the reach of help.

All free countries are morally obliged to demand of Germany, clearly and openly: To hand over all the Jews in their occupied territories. I recognize the difficulties involved in such a demand, but it represents the only possible way to save millions of human lives. We demand decisive action: thousands of people are perishing daily.

The facts in chronological order

June 22, [1941]. The beginning of the war. Toward evening, many of the Jews of Kovno flee the city—by rail, in carts and carriages and on bicycles, on horseback and on foot, along with the departing Communists and family members of Red Army soldiers. They head east, for Vilnius and Dvinsk [Daugavpils]. Throughout the night,

---

awarded the title of Righteous Among the Nations by Yad Vashem in 1982; parts of her diary from the years 1941–1943 have appeared in the following publications: in the Soviet journal *Druzhba narodov* (Friendship of the Peoples), Moscow, no. 8 (1968), pp. 198–226; in Hebrew in the journal *Yalkut moreshet* (Anthology of our Heritage), Tel Aviv, no. 17 (January, 1974), pp. 31–72; and in Yiddish in *The Black Book*, I. Ehrenburg and V. Grossman, eds. (Jerusalem, 1984), pp. 472–490. This "Appeal" is clearly based on the above-mentioned diary, in which Viktor Kutorga is mentioned several times. No information concerning the publication of the Appeal in the West has been found. It was probably written at the end of 1941.

thousands of people were abandoning the city in which they had spent their entire lives, people whose ancestors had lived on this land for many centuries. They were fleeing for the borders of the Soviet Union with their children, with hand luggage, with as much as they could take with them.

June 23. Beginning in the early morning, trains (around ten in all) with 20 to 35 open platforms and freight cars overflowing with Jewish refugees, have been departing in the direction of Vilnius. Masses of Jews are hurrying to the station with their hastily packed suitcases. There are scenes of desperation, the crying of children (several orphanages are being evacuated), the screams of the insane. Around seven thousand people are leaving from Kaunas by train. The last train bound for the border of the USSR did not cross it: the Kovno-Vilno line was the target of bombing and destruction. Some of the passengers were killed.

When all the jails were opened, all manner of political prisoners came out into freedom. In a burst of anger at Soviet power, they joined ranks with various shady characters who had been armed ahead of time by German secret agents and spies. At this point so-called "partisans" emerged who hurled themselves in a frenzy on every Red Army straggler.[6] That very evening, these bands began terrorizing the Jews. It was a fact that Jews had participated actively in Party, soviet, and administrative work, and so the unenlightened masses, dissatisfied with Soviet power, were given the possibility of taking revenge against the unarmed Jewish population. In addition, secret German propaganda made thorough use of the excited mood of the local population, which had been aroused by the deportation of 25,000 Lithuanian citizens to the interior of the Soviet Union between June 14 and 21.

These "partisans" burst into Jewish apartments, killed men, women, and children, and looted the property of those murdered. Subsequently, a battalion wearing the former Lithuanian uniform of the Smetona[7] era was formed from these "partisan" elements. Under German leadership, this battalion earned a reputation for harsh cruelty when it voluntarily carried out executions of masses of Jews in provincial cities. As a reward for their zeal these bandits were granted permission to take the clothing of their victims for themselves and sometimes even their valuables as well.

The scenes of the executions of Jews were filmed with great care.[8] They made an effort to avoid including in the film a single German among the leaders and accomplices in these killings. In this way, the Germans painstakingly prepared falsified records for future historians which would show the Lithuanian people responsible for all the vile actions committed in Lithuania upon the arrival of the Germans.

---

6. The word "partisan" usually refers to Soviet fighters, either Red Army soldiers or Soviet civilians, who fought the Germans behind enemy lines. However, in this document, Dr. Kutorga is referring to Lithuanian civilians who joined the Nazis in terrorizing Jews and Soviet POWs.
7. Antonas Smetona was president of Lithuania from 1926 until 1940, when he fled the country following the occupation by Soviet forces in the wake of the Hitler-Stalin non-aggression pact.
8. The atrocities were recorded either on film or by still photography.

Throughout the night of June 24, the wild orgy of killings and looting continued without interruption. Entire families were put to death. Synagogues and schools were looted. The terror was in full swing.

June 24. Persecuted and hounded Jews were escorted en masse to jails on the charge of having fired at "partisans" or German forces which toward evening on that same day had occupied the city. The prisons filled up again. There were many cases in which "partisans" broke into Jewish homes, terrorized those living there or took them all to jail (on Kant Street, they led away a man, a woman, and two children) and then looted their houses and apartments.

From the moment the Germans reached many provincial towns, the Jews were partly, and sometimes entirely, wiped out (for example, in Zarasay—two thousand; in Kretinge, Zhezhmary, Zhosli, Baltishkis—three thousand people).

June 25. The hunt for isolated Jews continues. They assault old people—men and women. Jews who are ill are transported in carts to the prisons. "Partisans" hound children and women with infants in their arms, beating and kicking them. The Jews cannot make up their minds to leave their apartments, since they are arrested immediately on the street and sent to jail or formed up into work parties and sent off to do the dirtiest and heaviest jobs, such as, for example, burying the bodies of the slain, digging ditches, carting away rubbish and animal carcasses, and so on.

June 26. An epidemic of suicides among the arrested Jews. The newspaper *Ilaisve* (what cynicism, it is called Toward Freedom) is mounting a desperate campaign of persecution against the Jews, giving sanction to the widespread insinuation that the Jews have supposedly been agitating for the enslavement of Germany.

June 28. On Vitauskas Avenue, in the open yard of the Letukis garages at 4:00 PM, the Lithuanian "partisans" and the Germans gathered around forty Jews and, after spraying them with water from fire hoses, beat the unfortunates to death with clubs. This scene took place in the presence of many German officers and a large crowd of people made up of men, women, and children who avidly observed the terrifying picture. No one tried to intervene; the victims (communists, they were sure) died in front of everyone after two hours of suffering. After that, the bodies were finally taken away.

June 30. In the Seventh Fort (of the old central archives), around five thousand Jews, most of them intellectuals who had been picked up over the previous few days, were exterminated. This mass killing was carried out with machine guns. The executioners in this case were Lithuanians, supplied by the Germans for the task. They forced the Jews to undress and lie down on the ground, and then wiped them out with machine guns. Large heaps of corpses were intermingled with still living victims who had not yet been finished off. The sufferings and horrors of these unfortunates were indescribable. They said at the time that they were getting even with the Jews for the killing of a German officer that had supposedly been carried out by a Jew. "A hundred Jews for one German." It was very doubtful that any such thing happened at all; in any case, it was only a pretext for the carrying out of the German plan to exterminate all the Jews of occupied Lithuania.

July 5. Jews have been treated contemptuously at every turn. They have been receiving food via their ration cards much later than the rest of the population, and in quantities below the norm. They divided the Jews into groups and sent them out to do hard manual labor. German soldiers often took over their apartments. Radios and bicycles were confiscated from the Jews.

July 10. The commandant of the city of Kaunas issues a special order to the effect that Jews who abandon their apartments for any reason whatsoever lose any right to return to them. All Jews are obliged to wear a yellow identifying mark in the form of the "Shield of David" on their chests (later, they will be obliged to wear the same sort of mark on their backs). By August 15, the Jews must relocate to the ghetto in the suburb of Viliampol (on the right bank of the Vilia River), which consists of old wooden houses without running water or indoor plumbing.[9]

August 1. Carts carrying the belongings of Jews are heading in the direction of the ghetto. For the most part, the Jews have left their property in their old apartments. After all, each person will be given only two square meters of living space. German soldiers and Lithuanian "partisans" often burst into the Jews' new apartments in the ghetto and take whatever they please.

A ghetto–concentration camp has also been set up in other Lithuanian cities. They have brought Jews from small towns to the ghettos of the larger cities. At the same time, they are exterminating groups of Jews and also entire families. Families that have lost fathers go hungry. The food rations for Jews are being sharply reduced. Every day they have to stand for hours in long lines in front of stores designated especially for them in order to receive their two hundred grams of bread.

August 15. The ghetto–concentration camp is being closed off and surrounded with a barbed wire fence. They allow Jews to leave the ghetto only in groups to go to work. Not long before that they were forbidden to walk on the sidewalks. These groups always walk with German soldiers, police, or Lithuanian sentries escorting them. These are the "gentlemen" who kill the Jews en masse whenever it suits them. In order to get themselves watches or other valuables, for example, they have been going into the ghetto and grabbing more or less anything of value that comes to hand. And if anyone dares to offer even a word of objection, it is death on the spot. From August 15 to 20, 1941, ten people were killed in this way. For entire days, the terrorized and cowed population stands in lines outside the food shops. The normal ration consists of 200 grams of bread per day and 250 grams of flour, 150 grams of groats, and 50 grams of salt for an entire week. There has been not a trace of fat or meat for some time now. Those who work in brigades in the city bring greens and potatoes with them when they return from work.

---

9. This area was also infamous under the name Slobodka.

The commandant of the Kaunas ghetto is a German named Kazlauskas, and his adjutants are Welle and Krause. The Oberkommandant over all the Jews in Kaunas is Jordan, a terrible and cruel "judge." One day, in the marketplace, in full view of everyone, he shot a Jew who in spite of the restrictions had bought some vegetables. The entire quantity of greens that had been purchased by the victim (all of four peasant cartfuls) was divided partly among the witnesses present, while the rest was sent to the hospital. After every such killing, he would assure the Jews that that execution had been the last one, and the poor people believed his words, like drowning people clutching at straws.

August 18. The Germans announced that they needed five hundred well-dressed men who speak German. They began to choose them from among the intelligentsia, of course. The Germans picked up these people and took them away, but no one saw them come back. It became clear that they had all been shot. This was the first large execution (action) in the Kaunas ghetto.

August 25. An order has been issued stating that the Jews have to give up all their money so that none of them have more than one hundred rubles, along with any pots, pans, and electrical appliances, and all valuables, including silver and gold. The German police, together with the "partisans," have repeatedly searched and ransacked every Jewish apartment, in the process shooting more than twenty people whom they had caught with concealed goods. In these searches, they took everything that there was to take from the Jews.

September 1. The mass extermination of Jews in the provinces by members of Lithuanian "partisan" units under the leadership and control of the Germans has begun. According to a systematically worked out plan, the action moves from one town to another. The Jews have been made to dig their own graves. Then they have to bring their sick and their children and remove their outer clothes. After that, they are shot in groups. Those still alive have to bury the bodies of their loved ones, wives, and children, and then they themselves are shot. All of this has been happening in broad daylight, often in front of thousands of witnesses. It would be quite impossible to describe the horror of these scenes, just as it is impossible to find an example of similar crimes in the history of the last thousand years (centuries). In some places they have asked for Jewish engineers, announcing that they are needed to work on the water supply system. When the wells were dug, these engineers were shot, tossed into the wells, and then buried (Mariampol). Each time, care was taken to have chemicals (calcium chloride) on hand to cover the bodies. The slightly wounded were finished off with bayonets or else buried alive; the small children were treated the same way. Often, the "partisans" simply killed children with shovels. This has been going on throughout September in all the small towns of Lithuania: Mariampol, Vilkavishky, Rumnishky, Zhezhmary, Ariogal, Keydany (3,000 people), Simny, Alitus, Vilki (500 people), Zapishki (150 people).

The peasants were very frightened. The intelligentsia, lawyers, and the Catholic church tried to intervene, but the Germans were implacable. They refused to engage in any discussions or explanation on the subject. Many half-Jews and Jews of the Catholic confession and the Protestant church were killed as well.

In many cases, the Germans filmed these massacres, all the while taking great care to insure that only Lithuanian executioners appeared before the camera lens.

Jewish homes have been confiscated, and all the personal property in them divided up among the killers in the guise of a reward.

And in the newspapers, not a word about any of this. The German regime could not reveal these awful secrets to its own people. Many German soldiers have unambiguously spoken out against these bloody and horrifying killings.

September 15. [This entry and the following one are reversed in the original.] It is absolutely impossible to describe the cruelties that have begun. The "partisans" have demanded that all the Jews in every provincial town and village be wiped out by the end of September. Only in Kaunas, Vilnius, Shaulyay, and Shumelishkis are there any remaining.

September 14. Five thousand Jews in Kaunas received tradesman's licenses (including seven doctors). They were organized into brigades and worked in different parts of town. They have been paid quite sporadically for their work, or not at all. These people believed that the tradesman's licenses would save them from death. As it later turned out, these hopes were in vain.

A council of elders directed all the affairs of the ghetto. The head of the Kaunas ghetto was the well-known doctor [Elkhanan] Elkes. The Jewish police saw to internal order. There was a hospital in the ghetto with wards for surgery and infectious diseases, but the doctors were forced to perform operations in the most primitive conditions, without the necessary preparations or medicines.

September 16. Jordan is taking all the available funds from the coffers of the ghetto commune, the food cooperative, and the infectious disease section of the hospital.

At the Ninth Fort, approximately two kilometers southwest of the ghetto, Russian POWs are digging ditches.

September 17. At 7:00 AM, Lithuanian patrols chased all the inhabitants out of their apartments in the direction of the hospital square. They loaded the elderly, women in the late months of pregnancy, and the sick onto carts. The square is surrounded by German police under the command of Tornbaum. Machine guns were posted all around. There was no time to get dressed. Many people were in their pajamas. Children were driven out of the orphanage and onto the square. Transfer to the Ninth Fort, the place of execution, was already underway. Just then, a German officer appeared from his automobile brandishing some piece of paper, then announced for all to hear that thanks to the military authorities (the Wehrmacht) the projected mass action had been cancelled, and that the Jews were obliged to the Wehrmacht for this. All of this was captured on film, and gave the impression that what was happening was a skillful mise en scène aimed at confusing the facts in such a way as to convince everyone that it was the Lithuanians who were supposedly demanding these executions, while the Germans were opposing them. After this, all the Jews, including those who had already been sent to the fort, were released to their homes. Once again, the Jews believed, and Jordan was convincing them of this, that there would be no more such actions.

This incident coincided with the beginning of work by the Jews on the airfield. Some 1,200 men and 500 women were going out to this project every day. At first, two shifts were established, then later three. At first they took the Jews to the airfield in trucks, but starting in October, they marched them there on foot. Work on the airfield went on day and night without let-up. The guards on duty at the airfield, German soldiers (including many who were unhappy with the Nazi regime), displayed a sympathetic attitude toward the Jews. The police and soldiers of the SA, however, behaved with utmost cruelty and savagery toward the Jews. Almost every night the inhabitants of the ghetto were frightened by all manner of attacks by the sentries, who would try to intimidate the Jews with their frequent shooting, and then break into their apartments. One night a woman was killed in her bed during one of these assaults.

The inhabitants of Kaunas were forbidden to sell anything to the Jews, to give them anything, or even to talk to them. In fact, they were forbidden to have any sort of contact with the Jews.

There were cases in which Christians who, in defiance of the ban, had had some dealings with the Jews, were taken off to jail. After that, they led the "criminal" along the streets of the city with a sign on his chest reading "Friend of the Jews." There were many instances in which Jews were shot on the spot for having tried to receive goods or food through the barbed wire barrier (the official ration, after all, was not enough). Many of the elderly and children who had not received enough milk died from exhaustion.

When the Jews of the Kaunas ghetto learned of the terrible killings of Jews in the provinces, they began to expect the same fate any day. On the night of September 26, they could hear a large number of shootings.

September 26. From four in the morning until sunrise, Lithuanian patrols (now in the uniform of the old Lithuanian army), as well as German police and units of the SA, herded all the inhabitants of the blocks on the left side of Paneriu Street (the so-called "little ghetto") onto a square, formed them all into ranks, and marched them off to the Ninth Fort. They loaded children onto carts and told them that they were being taken to some other ghetto. They took those who were unable to walk in trucks. Around four hundred people were taken to the Ninth Fort and murdered with machine guns. As usual, they were made to take their clothes off before they were shot, then the clothing was taken in trucks to a disinfection point.

October 2. Jordan and several men of his command searched the entire ghetto and found twelve people near the infectious disease ward of the hospital.

On the night of October 4, horrific shooting was heard in the area of the ghetto.

October 4. Beginning at 3:00 AM, all traffic was halted across the bridge above

Paneriu Street that connects the "big" and "little" ghettos. German and "partisan" patrols ringed the entire small ghetto, and in particular the hospital building for infectious disease. Jews were forced to dig ditches around the hospital. There were forty-five patients in the hospital (with typhus, scarlet fever, tuberculosis, and appendicitis), Dr. Davidavichus, and one nurse. While the Jews were digging ditches, the Germans, under Tornbaum's command, chased everyone onto the square. They brought children (including 145 from the orphanage) and the sick here from their apartments. The order was given to divide the people up into ten groups. They transported one woman to the Ninth Fort. Around twelve o'clock, they doused the infectious disease building with fuel. Dr. Davidavichus and the nurse, who had tried to get off the hospital premises, were shot in the courtyard, while all forty-five patients were burned alive. All that remained of the entire hospital were blackened smokestacks! One X-ray and ten EKG machines in the hospital building were lost in the fire. The Germans explained their appalling action—the burning of people alive—by saying that in this way they had cut short the spread of the terrible disease of leprosy. A barefaced lie!

They sent two thousand people to the Ninth Fort and shot them there (including 145 children from the orphanage). All of those left in the little ghetto were transferred to the big ghetto. The residential block on the left side of Paneriu Street was left empty, while the apartments remained open.

They took all the patients in the surgical ward away and exterminated them. Only seven women in the maternity ward were left alive. And again they gave assurances that this was "the last time."

October 16. They did away with 900 Jews in Semelishki. There, in the ghetto, the "partisans" and the Germans particularly distinguished themselves by their savagery—they robbed, killed, and raped women. The Jews worked every day in three shifts, day and night, at the airfield—1,200 men and 800 women from the ages of 17 to 55. When on any day these numbers did not reach their preliminary levels, the Germans would go through the apartments in the ghetto and drag men and women out of their beds to work.

The same thing was happening in Vilno. They killed Jews there en masse. Everyone lives there under constant threat of terror, in a state of mortal fear. There were cases in which the Germans wiped out entire Polish families for keeping Jews hidden in their homes.

October 27. It has been announced in the Kovno ghetto that all Jews—a number amounting to approximately 28,000—must report to the main square with their families by six the next morning, where they will be formed into brigades.

October 28. On the square, Jews were surrounded by a cordon of "partisans" and Germans. Jordan and Tornbaum divided them into two groups. The Jews had to march past them, and each one was told whether to go to the right or to the left. Old people were sent to the right first of all. When the Germans finally grew tired of this job, they simply divided the entire group into two sections: for the most part, the children were placed on the side opposite their parents. The Germans said that they would be sending them off to a new job on the night of October 28–29. All those "rightists" (that is, those put on the right side) were led to the vacant apartments in the little ghetto and, the next morning at 5:00 AM, all of them, ten thousand people, were sent to the Ninth Fort. The sick, as always, were taken in carts. All of them were exterminated on that very day. The entire city was stunned by these horrific events. The intelligentsia was extremely indignant about it. The slaughter took place in the trenches of the fort. All those passing by saw the execution and the clothes left on the ground, which were then collected and sent to the disinfection chamber.

Behavior like this cries out to the heavens!

November 2. The ghetto and the remainder of its population are a dreadful sight today. The apartments of the murdered, located among those of the still living, stand empty, looted; all the household items have been thrown together in a heap. Poor, homeless people overcome with grief move around behind the barbed wire. They try to exchange clothing for bread, shoes, and other items. The "partisans" often allow these operations, receiving a corresponding bribe in exchange. Many times they forbid such an exchange and even kill people for making them.

The soul is torn in two at the sight of the pathetic state that men, women, and children are in as they walk along the streets of the ghetto, separated from the rest of the world by barbed wire. These people have lost all hope and any urge to live. The only thing they now live for is that the world should know of their sufferings. They hope that not all the Jews in the world will perish in this way and that it is only they themselves who have fallen under such a curse. The situation is hopeless. Small Jewish children run around without supervision, little boys play across the barbed wire fence with their former friends. Death is reflected in the eyes of their mothers. The faces of these women, visible across the barbed wire fence, are testimony to their aimlessness and indifference. Their smiles seem to come from another world, as though they are issuing a challenge to the world's conscience.

Help them! Tell everyone the real truth, let the whole world know about it, all the Germans. Publish this throughout Africa and North and South America.

Help, oh help as soon as possible!

Dr. Viktor Kutorga.

GARF f. 8114, op. 1, d. 958, ll. 143–157. A typewritten manuscript with handwritten corrections.

63. Kaunas during the occupation
ACCOUNTS OF LOCAL RESIDENTS AND THE PARTISAN ARON VILENCHUK
RECORDED BY MAJOR Z. G. OSTROVSKY
[1944]

We are on the streets of Kaunas, which has just been liberated from the German occupation.

Three women, residents of Kaunas, come toward us. They say to us, in Russian with a heavy Lithuanian accent:

"We waited a long time for the coming of the Red Army, and we lived to see it. Thank you!"

The inhabitants of the city tell of lootings and killings. The Germans intended to turn Kaunas into a purely German city. They wiped out the Jews, deported some of the Lithuanians to Germany, and resettled some in Belorussia and even the Smolensk Region. They plundered the property of the murdered Jews and the displaced Lithuanians. The Germans took over local enterprises, the state-owned ones as well as those privately owned.

The stories of local residents entirely confirm the horrors that I had occasion to hear of several days ago from a group of Jewish partisans who had emerged from behind enemy lines. The majority of them were from Kaunas. And here is what they told me.

The Germans captured Kaunas in the first days of the war. Around thirty thousand Jews remained in the city when the Germans reached it.

The Jews did not have to wait long for their fate. Pogroms and mass shootings began in the very first days. As early as the end of June 1941, passers-by could read the inscription "*Yiden, nemt nekome far mir*" [Jews, avenge me] written in blood on the wall of a house on Linkuvos Street. It was written by a woman who had been fatally wounded in the chest with a dagger by a fascist bandit who had robbed a Jewish family.

There was looting everywhere. German occupation authorities took an active part in this pillaging. An announcement was posted: "Any robberies are be to reported to such and such a telephone number." Anyone who actually dared to resort to this usually paid for it with his life. German police would turn up at the address of the victim, seize him, then take him away; such a person never came back.

Three weeks after the Germans took Kaunas, the first announcement concerning the Jews appeared on the walls of buildings, signed by a well-known butcher who had a great deal of experience in the mass extermination of the Lodz Jews, namely Brigadenführer Kramer. The decree contained fifteen points. Jews were forbidden to

> walk on the sidewalks
> ride in cars, in buses, or on bicycles
> trade in shops and outdoor markets
> speak with local residents
> go to and from the city
> go to restaurants, theaters, or movie houses
> attend schools and universities.

Jews appearing on the street without the yellow Star of David on their chest and back were subject to execution.

Finally, it was announced that all Jews were required to move to Slobodka, on the edge of town, on the other side of the Neman River, by August 15.[10]

As of August 16, 1941, they closed the gates to the ghetto. From that moment on, not one Jew had the right to appear on the streets of the city. The move into the ghetto was accompanied by mass looting. People were not allowed to take even underwear with them; they had to leave for the ghetto in what they were wearing, and clothes were often taken from the unfortunates if the robbers—German officers and soldiers—liked them. In those days, one could see on the streets of Kaunas revolting scenes of fighting between German bastards who could not divide the property of the Jews among themselves.

On August 16, 1941, the first "action" against the doomed Jews began. It started with the intelligentsia. The advisor to the local commissar on Jewish affairs, the butcher Jordan, announced that the commissariat needed five hundred well-dressed Jewish intellectuals with a command of foreign languages, supposedly for work in the archives. The ghetto provided the five hundred. None of them returned. Soon, traces of the shootings of this first group of Jewish victims were discovered in the Kaunas forts.[11]

After that, it was quiet for two weeks. The Jews were not touched. By decree of the Lithuanian ambassador to Berlin under the former bourgeois government, Dr. Elkes was appointed head of the ghetto. The Germans summoned him to help resolve organizational questions, or more accurately, every time they wanted to extort valuables from the Jewish prisoners in the ghetto.

In mid-September, the German police surrounded part of the ghetto. By order of a butcher commanding this latest action, they drove all the Jews onto the square. Here, according to lists drawn up ahead of time, all those capable of work or trained in some profession were separated from the rest. The others—two thousand people—were sent to the forts and shot there. Two weeks later, the other three thousand were executed in the same way.

The next large "action" took place on October 27, 1941. The day before came this announcement: "Everyone to assemble on Democrats Square by 6:00 AM." There was an autumn frost. Trembling from cold and fear, the innocent people condemned to death began to assemble on the square. Children, the ill, the elderly were on the move. They were ordered to report to the square without any belongings. The looting began as soon as people left the places where their remaining things were. The rowdy German swine rummaged through every corner in search of anything that they could profit from.

---

10. There is a mistake in the text. Slobodka is located on the other side of the Vilia River.
11. Not counting the mass killings in the first days of the occupation.

They began to sort people into groups. Large families were taken off to one side, single people to another. Around ten thousand people were selected for the next act of savagery. As before, the shootings were carried out in the area of the forts.

After that, Dr. Elkes, the head of the ghetto, was summoned to the office of the local commissariat. They assured him that there would be no more shootings in the ghetto. "Now," they told him, "the ghetto has been purified of all undesirable elements. You can reassure everyone that they may go about their own business. We won't touch you anymore." At the same time, they demanded of Dr. Elkes that the Jews contribute money for "the maintenance of the Jewish affairs system."

The well-known Rabbi Shapiro from Kovno lived in the ghetto. They came for him one day. It turned out, however, that Rabbi Shapiro was no longer among the living; he had died, not having been able to withstand the hardships of the ghetto. So they began seeking out his relatives. Rabbi Shapiro's son, a professor of Jewish literature, was taken away, and did not come back.[12]

In September 1942, it became known that Sturmbannführer Goecke, who was famous for his bestial treatment of Jews in Riga and Warsaw, had been put in charge of Jewish affairs. No one spoke of him as anything other than "the Butcher of Riga and Warsaw." This out-and-out hangman came to Kaunas with new powers given by Berlin. He did not have to answer to local military authorities, but only to Berlin.

The first measure that he took was a new mass "action." He demanded that two thousand people be moved out of the ghetto, supposedly to work at peat processing. On October 24, Dr. Elkes went to see the butcher in order to see for himself that all these people would in fact be sent to work. The butcher Goecke received the mayor and calmed him down, assuring him that not a single person would be shot. Two days later, however, the police began to surround the ghetto again. Fifty trucks rolled up to the gates. In a few hours, the trucks were loaded with 1,700 people. The number of healthy people capable of working at peat processing in the ghetto was insufficient. Then two companies of police began seizing anyone they could get their hands on, one after the other. In this way, they took another 1,900. They brought all these people to the airfield and loaded them into cattle cars. All their belongings were taken from them. They took the entire group off in the direction of the frontier. The women and children remaining at the airfield were exterminated on the spot.

So it continued until April 1944. The population of the ghetto grew smaller and smaller. One of the last large-scale actions took place in April 1944, when 1,200 women and children were transported to the forts and shot there in bestial fashion.

I was speaking to a Jewish partisan, a young student named Aron Vilenchuk. He was mobilized along with other Jews in the ghetto for the disinterment of the bodies of those who had been shot. In order to conceal their crimes, the butchers decided to

---

12. American relatives tried to gain Rabbi Shapiro's release in exchange for a large number of German prisoners, but without success.

dig up all the corpses and burn them. It is easy to imagine what it was like for those still alive to unearth the bodies of their loved ones, family, and friends, and take part in burning them. "Many of them," Vilenchuk tells the story, "could not bear it and committed suicide then and there." Vilenchuk himself and several of his friends fled the fort while they were working and joined a partisan unit.

After the Red Army liberated Vilno, the fascists decided to liquidate the Kaunas ghetto. Seven thousand Jews left in the ghetto were loaded onto convoys and driven in the direction of the German border. They all shared the same fate. The only ones who survived were those who managed to escape.[13]

No matter how hard conditions were under the regime of the butchers, there always existed two underground organizations in the ghetto: the "Union of Activists" and a self-defense group. Unfortunately, they were almost entirely unarmed. Their activities consisted of organizing escapes from the ghetto and mutual assistance. From time to time the underground organizations would contact the partisans, and, with great care, smuggle small groups of Jews out of the ghetto to partisan units.

One day, one of these groups, numbering sixty, was coming out of the ghetto with the intention of making their way to the partisan detachments operating in the Avgustov Forests. The group was provided with weapons that had been gradually collected by the underground over a long time. On the way to the Avgustov Forest, a German punitive unit wiped the group out almost to the last man. Another group of 130 made it safely to the Rudnya Forest, where they were taken in by the "Death to the Occupiers" partisan detachment, in whose ranks they successfully operated until the coming of the Red Army.

GARF f. 8114, op. 1, d. 963, ll. 103–108. A typewritten manuscript with handwritten corrections.

64. The Kaunas ghetto
THE RECOLLECTIONS OF VIKTOR LAZERSON
[1944]

The nightmare began on a beautiful sunny morning, June 22, 1941, which would later be cursed by so many thousands of people. The streets of my native city ran red with blood. I lost my brother on the fourth day of the slaughter. The introduction of a distinguishing mark, the ban on using the sidewalks and means of transport followed the pogrom. From June 24 until August 15, abundant streams of Jewish blood flowed at the Sixth, Seventh, and Ninth Forts. The butchers demanded new victims.

On August 15, the gates of the barbed wire barriers of the village of death called Viliampol (a ghetto) closed behind 28,000 people.

Several weeks later, a demand was issued to gather five hundred young people for work in the fields. Mothers let their sons go, hoping that the work would save them.

---

13. Several hundred of those deported to the camp survived.

It was the earth at the Fourth Fort, however, that gave them shelter. They learned of this only in 1944.

This "action" was followed by a strict order to hand over all money, valuables, and clothing. Silently, people gave up their property, hoping that once they were naked and barefoot, the Nazi bandits would leave them in peace.

The director of this measure, Hauptsturmführer SA Jordan, a fiend with blood on his hands, drove away trucks loaded to the top with gold, silver, and other riches.

After this came the searches, the so-called *Stichproben*. The Nazis would go house-to-house with packs of dogs, beating people, looting what was left, mixing up stocks of provisions: salt with sugar, with flour, and so on. Jordan delighted in beating naked women into unconsciousness. Before my eyes a German killed an old man who had left some money in a book. The earth received the maimed victims.

On September 17, 1941, there was, so to speak, a dress rehearsal. The ghetto area was cut off from the city; people were brought out onto the main square, then trucks arrived. All at once, though, they were allowed to go home. The Jews could not fathom what miracle had saved them.

But soon, on September 22 and October 4, the bloody feast began to play out for real. The hospital, with its patients, doctors, and nurses, was burned down, and whole blocks were made *judenrein* [rid of Jews]. The inhabitants of these blocks breathed their last at the Ninth Fort.

The ghetto was growing smaller and smaller. Going to and from work under armed guard, forced labor, the whole bag of sadistic, fascist tricks used on the prisoners of the ghetto, starvation, and so on—all of these were mere insignificant chords in this symphony of death.

On October 28, they herded all of us out onto the square in the middle of the ghetto and stood us in ranks of four families each. The "lottery of life" began there. Families were divided arbitrarily in half, and the "halves" were led off in opposite directions. Toward evening, one side was released, and the ten thousand on the other were led off to the Ninth Fort, where they were put to death the very next night. Wild howls and sobs resounded through the half-empty ghetto.

This operation was headed by a Gestapo agent named Rauke. After such experiences, Jews could relax for a day or two, or so Jordan considered. Soon after the "large action" that has been described, convoys of Jews from Western Europe went to their rest at the Ninth Fort. We had to load their belongings, filling up Jordan's warehouses.

Dreadful days of terror against individuals and shipments to the camps continued until the autumn of 1943.

The police battalion guarding the ghetto was replaced by the so-called 4th NSKK company.[14] The black-shirted NSKK band headed by the young sadist Widemann,

---

14. *National Sozialistische Kraftfahrer-Korps* (National Socialist Driving Corps).

Jordan's successor, took up our case in earnest. They turned up in the ghetto in order to observe everything that was going on there. New humiliating laws, the obligatory removal of one's hat in the presence of Germans, back-breaking work, new acts of mockery and abuse filled this period of grief and stabilization. After the return from work, they organized searches: they undressed people, beat them, took away everything that they were trying to bring into the ghetto so as somehow to feed themselves and keep their wretched families warm—food, firewood, and so on. The heroes of these "humane" tortures, NSKK members Ross, Baro, and Levrenu were masters of their craft.

It was around this time that news reached us of Jordan's death at the Front. This event was celebrated in the ghetto.

Labor deportations began in March 1942. The Riga deportation, deportations to hard labor in the camps of Ionava, Palemonas, Kaisiadorys, and Mariampol created new torture points and gave rise to new acts of savagery. When the work was completed, the camps were liquidated.

The colossal number of victims of the Gestapo agent Stitze, the organization's adviser on Jewish matters; public hangings for "educational" purposes; executions for failure to take off one's hat, for buying a newspaper during working hours, for a patch (or a "target" as it was called) not sewn on; the execution of an entire family for the transgression of one of its members; sadistic displays like the shooting of bottles on our heads—such were the conditions they made us live in during this period of "stabilization."

Moreover, we fed on the dreadful rumors reaching us from Majdanek, Vilnius, and other camps, and on the replies given us by the German bosses.

We managed to learn during this time who our executioners were. Kramer, the commissar for the city of Kaunas, believed that Jews should not use doors, and made the Jews who worked for him come in through the windows. Jordan considered a conversation with a Jew *Rassenschande* [a racial disgrace]; General Vysoki claimed that he lost his appetite at the sight of a Jew; Rosenberg, like the legendary dragon, could not stand the smell of Jews; district commissar Lenzen regaled Jews with bouillon made from a dead cat.

In the autumn of 1943, we were taken over by a band of savage Hungarian SS commanded by the head blood drinker, Obersturmbannführer SS Goecke, who had wiped out the Jews of Warsaw.[15] This individual—one look at him made your hair stand on end—started out by acting diplomatically. His assignment was to finish off the Jews. He made everyone work, from the ages of thirteen to sixty-five. He increased our rations, but we knew that they were fattening the cattle for slaughter.

---

15. Earlier in this account, Wilhelm Goecke is referred to as Sturmbannführer (major). Obersturmbannführer is the equivalent of a lieutenant colonel. It seems more likely that he was a Standartenführer, the equivalent of a colonel, as of 1942.

On October 26, 1943, the Estonian deportation took place, which reduced the population of the ghetto by three thousand people. It would be impossible to describe the horrors of this deportation. People began trying to escape from the ghetto. The authorities took severe measures; spying was increased. Earlier, work outside of the ghetto had offered the possibility of obtaining some sort of food or fuel there, and, albeit at a risk, of bringing it into the ghetto. Now that possibility was taken away; dealings with the outside world were strictly forbidden. The ghetto was under the command of Kittel, who had arrived after the liquidation of the Vilensky ghetto.

The Unterscharführers of the SS—Pilgram, Fiffinger; Oberscharführers Ridel, Pich, Auf; Hauptsturmführer Ring; Bemichen, the commandant of the central concentration camp; Walther, the doctor who was practicing medical extermination; all of the these Ober and Unter bandits had decided to put an end to our existence. In Kaunas, they opened another two forced labor camps, in Aleksoty and Shantsy. The area of the camp was surrounded by two rows of barbed wire, with machine gun towers at the corners and barracks with three tiers of bunks—in all, the camps of the new system held another 2,500 people. The variety of sadistic devices was significantly enriched by Unterscharführer Mie, the former commandant of the Aleksoty POW camp, who considered that wholesale beatings would have a good effect on his "inventory." He would send Jews to swim in the swamps after a rain, dragging them from the bunks at night, and so on.

Meanwhile, there was a smell of burning bones in the air in the ghetto. Goecke was covering his tracks. After the death of Shmitz, who was killed by the partisans, Kittel took care to see that the fire at the Ninth Fort did not go out. Eight thousand Jews were waiting for their sentence.

On March 27, 1944, bands of butchers surrounded the ghetto and began catching children, the old, and the infirm. I saw a German shepherd tear a baby from its mother's breast. I saw the eyes of a mother after a German had taken her child and smashed it against the side of a truck. That image haunts me even now, making me forget that I am free. I saw a German officer who had ripped a child away from its mother roar: "You wanted a war, well, here it is!" Mothers pleaded to be shot, and the Germans eagerly did them this favor. The Jewish police of the ghetto, lured to the fort under the threat of death, gave away the hiding places where mothers were concealing themselves and their children.

And the day ended like all of the others—the heavens did not open and the earth did not turn red. The little bodies were buried, the eyes of their mothers dried.

We were expecting new tortures. The days of individualized terror began again. They counted us every day, escape became impossible. In the camps, they dressed people in Sing-Sing pajamas,[16] shaved their heads and herded them out to work like zebras. They separated me from my parents and sent me to the camp at Shantsy.

---

16. The clothing of the prisoners in the concentration camp.

But the end was approaching. On July 9 [1944], we were stunned to see suspicious troop movement, and we realized that our moment had come. One Feldwebel, seeing us riding along in a convoy, stared at us wide-eyed and yelled: "*So was lebt Noch?*" [Something like this is still alive?]. This phrase contained the answer to the question of our fate.

And after that? Boxcars packed with people, with the words of a German officer in our ears: "We won't hand you over to the Red barbarians." So I jumped through a window from the train while it was traveling at full speed; the prospect of seeing the "New Europe" did not appeal to me.

Three weeks in the rye fields. The sweetness of liberation! I woke up. I am without a yellow star, I am no longer a dog or a slave. I am standing in the middle of the ruins of the ghetto and I do not recognize this place.

Vengeance!

GARF f. 8114, op. 1, d. 953, ll. 3–8. A typewritten manuscript with handwritten corrections.

65. Extermination of the Jewish children in Kaunas
Account of Maria Ilinichna Yarmovskaya

The Germans built a ghetto that turned into a death camp in Slobodka, beyond the Vilia River. Periodically, executioners would show up there and exterminate several thousand inhabitants. This was called the "cleansing" of the ghetto. So, on December 17, 1941, more than 10,000 people were removed from the ghetto and shot. In August 1943, a certain Goecke came to Kaunas; he was already known in Poland as "the butcher in white gloves." He had just carried out the liquidation of the Warsaw and Vilnius ghettos. Once in Kaunas, what interested this German beast most of all was whether or not there were many children left in the ghetto. On October 27, [1943], the Germans collected 3,500 women and children and herded them to the station. There they separated the children from their mothers and poisoned them. The children were dying before their mothers' eyes. But some of the children were left with their families. Goecke issued a special order for the immediate handing over of all children. It was announced that severe punishment awaited those who evaded carrying out this order. A couple named Zeller was publicly executed for failing to hand over their child to the butchers. The unfortunate parents were beaten, forced to sit on a red hot stove, and had needles shoved under their fingernails. When they lost consciousness, they were carried to the gallows. Holding their victims in the nooses in a way that was calculated not to kill them, the Germans took them down and put off completing the execution until the next day. Then they lashed the father to a stake and lit a fire beneath his feet. They stripped the mother naked and continued to torture her.

"That's how it will go with anyone who puts up resistance to us," Goecke announced through a megaphone.

GARF f. 8114, op. 1, d. 953, ll. 109–109ob. A typewritten manuscript.

66. Killing the Jews in the shtetl of Stoklishki
ACCOUNTS OF MARIA YARMOLINSKAYA AND SARA EPSHTEYN
RECORDED BY MAJOR Z. G. OSTROVSKY
[1944]

I met several Jewish women in the Lithuanian shtetl of Stoklishki. They were walking along, trembling and looking around with every step. The town had already been in the hands of the Red Army for several days. These women had seen with their own eyes how the Red Army, sweeping the enemy before them, was liberating their country. They had seen the Germans running, throwing away their weapons, equipment, clothing, and booty as they went. Even so, the horrors that they had lived through over the previous three years had left such deep sadness in their faces that they would not easily be able to free themselves from it.

They had seen the brown-shirted plague destroy Jewish towns and shtetls. These women had been witnesses to shootings and mass *auto-da-fé* that the Germans had organized in Kaunas. Near the Ninth Fort, there is a place that the Jews called "the Altar" (*Mizbeakh* in Hebrew). Masha Yarmolinskaya was a witness to how five respected Jewish families of Kaunas were burned alive. She saw with her own eyes how the butchers armed with submachine guns escorted several hundred Jewish children through the streets of the Kaunas ghetto. Among them were three- and four-year-old toddlers. The children had been torn from the arms of their parents. Mothers rushed to save their little ones, so the Germans released the dogs from their leashes. They hurled themselves on the women, sank fangs into their arms, tried to bite at their throats. The mothers jumped back, howling, and their unfortunate children were led away to be shot.

The Germans snatched the sick mother of Khaya Shuster of the shtetl of Stoklishki. For five years, she had been lying in bed without moving. The entire family, exhausting itself, had tried to prolong the life of their mother, to ease her sufferings. It would have been better for her to have died from her illness without living to see the day when these repulsive enemies of humanity showed their faces in her house. They grabbed her from her bed and dragged her off like a sheep to be slaughtered.

Khaya Efron gave birth to a child. The next day, they snatched her along with her newborn, threw them into a cart, and hauled them away to Butrimantsy, a shtetl where mass "actions" had been carried out against the Jews. Another woman, the pregnant Feyga Miller, was seized by the butchers on the day when she was supposed to give birth. They dragged her to a car. She was struggling and moaning; her Lithuanian neighbors saw how the innocent woman was struggling. One dared to say: "What are you doing? Can't you see that she's just about to give birth?" The Germans then grabbed this Lithuanian as well and took him off to be executed along with the Jews.

As Sara Epshteyn tells the story, her mother, not wanting to wait to be executed, took poison along with the Rabinoviches (a married couple and both of them doctors), and died by her own hand. There were many other cases of suicides, but one can hardly remember or name them all.

There were hundreds of reported cases of Lithuanian peasants hiding Jews who had fled the ghetto in their own homes. The very same Epshteyn family—eight people—hid out for more than three years with thirty Lithuanian peasants in various villages and homesteads. These were complete strangers who had not known this Jewish family before the war. In the village of Romashishki they were hidden by the Lithuanian Vevioras Antonevich; in the village of Vashtatany by Khmelevsky and Gavinovsky; in the village of Yaromlishki, by Tarasevich and Milevich. A Roman Catholic priest from the village of Vysoky Dvor concealed Vilna Jews in his home. And to this day, Jewish women, girls, and children who were saved from the Nazis live with Lithuanian peasants as though they were family. Lithuanians adopted many Jewish orphans, whom they are raising with redoubled tenderness, taking into account their tragedy. I saw such families in Troki and in Keydanyay, Zhizhmory, Preny, Yevno, and Stoklishki, as well as in Vilna and Kaunas themselves.

The bestial German behavior toward Jews in Lithuania demands a thorough investigation. The criminals must answer for everything with blood. As these lines are being written, the Red Army is not making a bad job of seeing to this already, even as it is approaching Germany's very borders.

Now, peace has come to Kaunas and Vilna. A few isolated families that miraculously survived the fascist terror are returning. Soviet organizations have already begun excavating in the area of the Kaunas forts where the mass "actions" against the Jews were committed. Shocking new accounts of the inhumane tortures and sufferings to which Jewish people guilty of nothing at all were subjected in these cities have already been found and will soon be given a public hearing.

GARF f. 8114, op. 1, d. 963, ll. 97–99. A typewritten manuscript with handwritten corrections.

67. The shtetl of Stoklishki
The recollections of Rasha Shuster
[1944]

On June 22, 1941, our little town of Stoklishki heard the sad news that the barbarian murderer, who maligns our people, had burst into Lithuanian territory along with his fascist gang of hooligans. This sad news struck like thunder and penetrated the heart of every Jew from young to old. Every Jew felt and knew that Hitler meant evil for us. Yet we somehow did not want to believe that the end of our young days of innocence had come. We felt it right away. The sky of our lives immediately filled with gray clouds. A savage, Lithuanian, fascist band of hooligans started to chase after us. The scoundrel Hitler had untied their bestial paws, and the savages immediately began to dig their dirty claws into our pure, innocent Jewish hearts. They tore, tortured, and clawed our hearts until they ripped them out; they spilled pure, innocent blood on all the fields and sowed them with corpses. In our towns there was a sign hanging over every Jewish door saying that Jews lived there, and they put yellow patches on our arms. I, however, decided, that I would not put on such a thing, even if it meant being shot. But they soon gave the order to tear them off and to sew the Jewish symbol—two triangles—in their place: one on the chest and one on the back. All Communists and propagandists were supposed to appear at six o'clock. If anyone delayed, he was immediately shot or hauled off to jail. Jewish doors and windows had to be shut by eight o'clock. Anyone who did not have shutters was made to hang black curtains, and no Jew was to appear either on the street or in the courtyard of his building before 6:00 AM.

No sooner would someone appear than he was arrested. One case is worth remarking on. A ninety-year-old man came into the synagogue to pray, and, after finding no one there, sat down on a log to wait for other worshippers. A Lithuanian bandit came up to him, began to beat him, and took him off to prison. The old, ill, and nearly blind Jew, named Shmerl-Leyb, barely dragging his feet, went to jail escorted by this hooligan. Similar tragedies occurred daily. At night, they would deliberately open fire so that Jews would come running outside and they could shoot them. We would run to the cellar every night and carry our mother, Khaya-Riva by name, who had been ill with her nerves for five years. But this was only fear, after all. After that, they got down to practical work. A month after the invasion by these bloodthirsty beasts, they led forty of the sturdiest young men and women out of our little town. They told them that they were taking them out to work; this was only a pretext, however, and two weeks later the police ordered more people to report. And those who went there were rarely released. Barbarians were standing at the police station with rifles, and immediately in front of them were the worst bandits and criminals. And still they seized another seventy people and took them to another small town twenty-eight kilometers from ours and shot them there. Just before their deaths they were ordered to write letters saying that they were alive and working. But this was only a ruse so that the rest would not be frightened and think about fighting back. Quietly, like sheep, calmly and without resistance they went to the slaughter, not knowing where they were being led.

We were a family of ten. I had three sisters: one was named Dvoyra, the second Ester, and the third, married and younger than I, Lyusya. I also had two brothers: a married brother named Isaak and an older brother named Zeylik. There were my sisters-in-law, a brother-in-law, and my ailing mother. My father had vanished without a trace; where he went I myself do not know. Perhaps he took off for Russia. I have not had any news of him; perhaps he is still alive somewhere. No one from our house was taken out those two times, supposedly to be led to work. We had a small plot of land, you see, and worked it ourselves, and so they could not take us away.

But when for the second time they began taking people away, we began to clear out of the house and hide in the fields. Our sick mother stayed in her bed alone. At night we would run home to see her. She lay there pale and weak, unable to believe that she was seeing us, just as we considered ourselves lucky that we could still come and see her for whom we were suffering so much. To kiss her pale, thin hands and to be racked with quiet, heartrending sobs. We could not allow ourselves to cry loudly; the local bandits were standing watch over every Jewish home at night.

I remember that when I came into the house, I was afraid even of the walls. A deathly silence reigned there. It was dark in every corner and it seemed to me that no one could be more unhappy than I was. Unfortunately, however, I was wrong; these were the happiest days of my unhappy life to come, when I was forced to go into hiding. For three weeks our entire family would assemble in this way, until one sad day, we learned that the next day, August 9, they would be taking away all the remaining Jews. We all took off from the house that night under the great, tragic impression that we were leaving our mother for the last time. I wanted to stay with my ill mother, but my mother sobbed that she would die if I stayed.

We took off, and the next day they took everyone to the nearby shtetl of Butrtsymani, twelve kilometers away. They stood twelve thousand Jews beside open pits and stripped them. Anyone who did not want to undress was savagely beaten, and children were thrown alive into the pit. This was how they exterminated Jews in Lithuania, and it happened in this way everywhere the German barbarians went to work. I escaped along with my two sisters, and the others went individually. My sisters made for the home of a Russian, while I ran into a friend, and he took me with him. The next evening, I went to look for my sisters. I was walking along on a dark night, wandering alone, and suddenly I heard a familiar voice: "Rashka, is that you?" I recognized the voices of my unfortunate sisters. We were walking along through a field crying as though our hearts would break, not knowing where to go. We went to the nearest Russian bathhouse.

We stayed there for three weeks; a peasant would bring us food. His name was Vintsis Yaskutelis, and he took me into his home for a month where I stayed in the attic. My sisters stayed for weeks on end in the dilapidated barn of one of the neighbors, suffering from cold and hunger. This was in September. The neighbor knew nothing about this, and from time to time they would come to me at night to get warm. So it went until the final night. Toward morning, they went back to the farmer's place, and while they were giving their daughters something to eat, the father managed to go for the police. My sisters were shot on the spot. I stayed in the attic during all of this. I heard the shots which pierced the hearts of my young sisters and spilled their pure, innocent blood on the fields. I lay there quietly, entirely frozen, feeling neither alive nor dead. When the peasant came up and called to me, it seemed that I woke up. He told me that he could no longer harbor me and that that night he would take me into the village. No one there was taking anyone in either, and I was forced to come back. My brother was hiding not far from here, and I went to him. I told him the sad news about our sisters and stayed with him for two weeks.

After that, they chased me out again. I went to another peasant's place where I stayed for only one day. I was lying low in the barn, when suddenly they called me to the house. I sat at the window and listened to the awful barking of a dog. I looked and saw a dreadful sight: a policeman standing out in the yard with a rifle in his hands, with another pacing by at the window. I did not know how I was going to escape but when they went to look for me in the barn, I jumped out of the window, crawled across the road on all fours and then went into the forest. I was in the forest for the first time. I came out onto the road, but I did not know where to go. A cold, autumn wind hit my face, along with a light snow. I remembered that a Russian woman, an acquaintance named Malanya Griboy, lived somewhere on the edge of the forest. I found a small grayish-black hut, knocked at the window, and they let me in. I lived there for two and a half months. In January I learned that my brother Isaak had been shot. They chased me out of there, too, because the police were on the hunt for Jews again.

This was in January 1942. There was a minus-forty-degree frost, tall snow drifts covered the fields, there was nowhere to go, so I left for the Jewish cemetery. I hid there for a day before the police came to look for me. The peasants had seen me and I heard the police questioning them. So I turned my back and thought: "Let them shoot me, so that I won't have to see the criminals." By chance, they did not find me. The next day I went back into the forest, where I lived for a week in the winter snow. It was clear that if the peasants found out about me, I would have to get out of there. My feet swelled up, I could barely walk, my hands became terribly swollen as well. Streaks like icicles appeared on all of my fingers. From the forest I go out again into the cemetery and lie there for two days without food, and feel that I no longer have the strength to stand the cold and hunger. I would get up in the night. There is a fierce frost, not even the dog is barking; he lies there in his house. And I am alone, hungry, walking on my own. I do not know where the wind is coming from and the frost is hitting me in the face, and I fall. I return to the cemetery and sit down in a corner where the day before they had shot two Jews. I slip in and sit down in Jewish blood because that spot had been shielded from the wind. I sit there for a third day, and at night walk through the fields, barely dragging my feet through the snow. I come to a peasant's place; he gives me bread, but does not allow me to warm myself and chases me away. I go off to the place of a peasant woman who lives next door, and stay there for a day. The police turn up in the evening, informed by the peasants. I leap from the roof and run off into the fields. Upon returning to the peasants when the police had gone, I come upon a Russian[17] who agrees to take me in for a day. I lie down in his sled, he covers me with hay, and takes me toward his place.

---

17. The author misspeaks here; the rescuer's name below is clearly Lithuanian.

On the way there, he tells me that I will not be able to stay with him after all. With great difficulty I prevail upon him and he takes me home. But I felt awful from all that I had been through.

A tumbledown, smoky little house, all white inside from snow, a half-ruined stove without a pipe, and dirt everywhere. I climbed onto the stove and warmed myself a bit. I stayed with him and lived there for two and a half years. The poor peasant, a forty-five-year old plowman by the name of Yuzus Yaskutelis, lived alone. He would buy bread and give me some of it. And when I asked him why he was doing this and risking his life—if the police had caught me at his place they would have shot us both, after all—he answered that it was because I was not guilty of anything. When the German search teams were operating, he would take me everywhere, digging holes in other people's granaries and hiding me. He would take me out into the forest, where I stayed for a week at a time and more. There were times when German spies would tell him that they knew that I was at his place, and then I was forced to take off for anywhere that I could. To lie beneath the burning sun in the summer and to claw at the earth with my fingernails in order to give myself cover. I would go for two or three days without food. I would take bread and water with me; the water I would drink straight away, but I could not swallow the bread afterward. I lived with this peasant in this way for two and a half years. And on July 14, 1944, the Red Army came and liberated us.

I forgot the most important thing. I am the sole survivor of the village of Stoklishki.[18] All of my brothers and sisters were shot.

GARF f. 8114, op. 1, d. 955, ll. 56–63. A manuscript.

68. What happened in Telshyay to the entire Jewish population of Zhmud[19]
ACCOUNTS OF LOCAL INHABITANTS NESYA MISELEVICH, VEKSLER, AND YAZHGUR
RECORDED BY L. YERUSALIMSKY[20]

Nesya Miselevich:
When the war broke out, I was in Taurogen. I fled to Roseynay [Rossiyeni]. In Roseynay the Germans and local fascists had already been wreaking havoc. They were arresting men and women and herding them out to work. While they were working, the women were subjected to all sorts of humiliations. The arrested men were first sent to do forced labor in the forests; there they were abused and tortured.

---

18. Compare with the previous testimony.
19. Zhmud (Zemaitija) is a region located in northwestern Lithuania. Telshyay is considered to be the capital of the region.
20. Lazar (Eliezer) Yerusalimsky kept a diary of the Siauliai ghetto, which was published in Hebrew in Tel Aviv in 1959. In 1944–1945, at the request of Ilya Ehrenburg, he assembled eyewitness accounts of massacres of Jews and sent them to the Literary Commission of *The Black Book*.

On July 15, [1941], I left Roseynay for Plunge (Plungyany). There were no more Jews in Plunge; they had already been liquidated on July 7 and 8. I went to the hamlet of Laukovo. I spent one night in Laukovo. In the morning, our house was surrounded by the local white bandits.[21] They came into the house, supposedly to make a search, but in fact grabbed everything of value that they found. After that, they herded all the Jews into the synagogue; these were almost entirely women and children, since the men had already been deported to Germany a week earlier to do forced labor (we in Shavli received letters from Germany from some of them—the Kaganov brothers who ran a flour mill in Laukuvo, and Smelyansky from Smaleninkesh—at first from the camp at Lauksergen, later from camps in Silesia with the stamp *Reichsvereinigung der Juden in Deutschland, Berlin* [Reich Association of Jews in Germany, Berlin]). They told me in the synagogue that the Germans were raiding the homes of Jewish inhabitants at night and stealing everything of value. They were torturing the men. They had beaten up a rabbi, shaved off half of his beard; they made threats to the women, saying that they would shoot them all. They took two young girls and a boy, members of the Komsomol, to the Jewish cemetery, made them dig a hole, then shot them. It was crowded in the synagogue. They would not allow food to be brought in, they would not allow anyone to go outside. Every so often, the bandits would burst into the synagogue, jeer at the prisoners, and threaten to shoot them all.

Then the Germans began spreading rumors that they were all to be taken to Lublin or to the firing range.

On July 23, when it was raining terribly hard, heavy trucks rolled up to the synagogue and the Germans herded some of their prisoners into them. The next day, the twenty-fourth, another group was driven away, including me. They let us out in a large enclosure in which there were horse stables with dirt floors and with two tiers of bunks. It was filthy in the stables and in the bunks. Even so, those who arrived later were given even worse places to stay, in barns knocked together from thin boards with big holes in them, or in storerooms without walls. This was in Vishvyany near Telshyay. Life there was awful. They gave us 150 grams of bread per day. They would not allow us to go out to buy food. Anyone who went out fell into the hands of the guards and was beaten in the cruelest way imaginable.

The commandant of the camp, Alexandrovicius Platakis, and the Anzilevicius brothers particularly distinguished themselves by their cruelty. Dirt and lice increased the sufferings of the people even more. The bandits would burst into the camp by night, drag young women out, then have their way with them.

To avoid these night raids, the women themselves organized duty shifts, and the women on duty would not even let the guards in at night. These nocturnal scandals came to an end then. Upon entering the camp, everyone was picked clean by the

---

21. Lithuanian collaborators who wore white armbands.

guards. What did the women tell me about what was happening in the Reynyay and Vishvyany camps?

In the Vishvyany camps, where I myself was, and in the nearby Gerulyay camp there were only women and children. There were no longer any men. They had been done away with in the Reynyay camp.

They had the following story to tell about what happened in Reynyay:

On June 26, the Germans gathered the entire Jewish population of the town of Telshyay around the lake; they posted machine guns around them and announced: "We're going to try the force of machinery on you, and may your God help you." The rabbi of Telshyay replied to this with: "It won't do you any good to laugh at our God. He's the same for us and for you." (He later paid for this insolence.)

They kept the Jews under the threat of death for a long time and then let them go to their homes. On June 27, they released the women, but they kept the men behind.

On June 27, that is, the next day, all those who were still free were herded onto the estate of the well-known singer Kipras Petrauskas—the Reynyay camp. The men who had been arrested a day earlier were taken there as well. Along with the Reynyay camp, another camp, Vishvyany, was opened for the Jews of the shtetls in the environs of Telshyay.

The resettlement of the Jews of Telshyay and the surrounding shtetls was carried out in the course of an hour, meaning that those displaced had the chance to take only their vital necessities with them. The property remaining in their homes, of course, was looted.

Upon entering the camp, everyone had to hand over their valuables to the guards and the Germans on pain of death. They began abusing and humiliating everyone living in the camps, particularly the men, who were driven to desperation. One torture stands out most clearly—the so-called "devil's dance."

Around July 18, 1941, two Gestapo agents came to the Reynyay camp along with an entire detachment of local bandits. They called out several men and forced them to dig several large pits, the purpose of which these unfortunates did not even guess.

The next day, the Gestapo again called out all the men. They locked the women in the barracks, with the exception of those who happened just then to be collecting valuables to be handed over to their butchers. They encircled them with armed guards, and then one of the Gestapo men made a speech to the following effect: "You, the Jews, have mounted a conspiracy against the entire cultured world. You, along with the Bolsheviks, have ignited a worldwide conflagration, and because of that, the hour of retribution has arrived. You will pay for the evil that you have done." When he had finished, he gave an order, and the ring of guards around those assembled grew tighter, and a dreadful torture began.

The Gestapo officer gave an order and all the prisoners formed a circle. Then he "explained" to them the meaning of different commands: "Run! Fall down! Run fast, turn right, turn left" and so on, and the "gymnastics" started. The executioners put sticks in between everyone's legs, then they had to run, turn, fall down, bend, jump, and so on like this. Local fascist bandits followed behind them, beating them with clubs and rifle butts. Anyone who fell was finished off on the spot with gun butts. Many of the old and weak left the formation and were tortured where they fell. Some of the younger ones picked up the weakened and the fallen and took them on their shoulders and ran along with them, but the butchers would beat them all together. The commands came faster and faster with every passing moment, the pace was picking up, so that those running were gasping for breath and becoming even more tired. The butchers would hit them even harder. The number of those who had fallen out of the formation was steadily increasing, and those left in the ranks were using up their last strength, while the executioners kept on beating and torturing them more and more.

Women, sisters, and mothers were looking out from the barracks through wide chinks and wringing their hands, pleading, fainting, while the butchers laughed. One of the women caught up among the guards could not stand it anymore and collapsed half dead. Just then, another one, who was carrying valuables collected for the butchers, pleaded with the guards to let her go, so that she could bring some water to save the exhausted woman, but the guards would not allow it. "Let that kike woman croak," Commandant Platakis said and refused permission. Then one of the women in the barracks broke out, burst through the chain of guards, and brought water. This dance went on for three whole hours. Only when all were absolutely exhausted and could no longer stand on their feet, were beaten and bloodied, did they let them go.

The tortured, beaten men, faces twisted in pain from suffering and abuse, returned to their home, the barracks. With no more strength, humiliated, they did not say a word—they were scarcely even breathing—and climbed directly into the bunks (in the words of Veksler, the wife of the director of the Telshyay national bank). At that moment they had been stripped of all will of their own. Nothing mattered to them, just so long as it would all be over as soon as possible.

The end did come very soon. That same night (approximately July 20–21), thirty-three men, for the most part between the ages of twenty and twenty-five, one of them the Yeshivah teacher Rabbi Avner, were taken away from the barracks and did not come back. Their cries and moans could be heard throughout the night. As people who were in the barracks close to the place of execution tell the story, and as the butchers themselves boasted, including the Inzulevich brothers, they were tortured the entire night. They bound them and lowered their heads into the waters of the lake, pulling them out half drowned; then they would revive them and plunge them in again. The butchers took turns beating them about the head with gun butts, and tortured them until they breathed their last. Their bodies were the first to fill the pits.

Early the next morning, the butchers burst into the barracks and shouted: "Rabbis and half-rabbis (Telshyay was a center of rabbinical seminaries) come out!" Then they called all the men out of the barracks and formed them up outside. They led them out in groups of fifteen to twenty to a nearby grove in which pits had already been dug; bursts of submachine gunfire were heard from there. This slaughter went on all day Tuesday until four o'clock. All at once a storm blew up, and the butchers wanted to go home. They were so unashamed of themselves that they sent the last group back from the edge of the pit to the barracks. Those same victims were chosen the next day, Wednesday. They knew it already and went out to sure death. There was a lawyer named Abramovich whose wife and mother-in-law wanted to save him and could have saved him, but he did nothing about it, saying that he desired to be where the other Jews would be. (I asked those questioned how they explained such passivity on the part of the Reynyay victims, and they told me that the tragedy had come upon everyone so unexpectedly that there was no time to make any preparations. Furthermore, no one imagined that the Germans, even Nazis, would be capable of killing women and children, and they cherished the hope that the women and children would be spared death. In the event of resistance or mass escape, they would have feared for the lives of their women and children.—L.Y.)

There were isolated cases of resistance. When they took Dr. Zaks from Retovo to be shot, his wife would not allow him to go alone, and went with him along with her infant. The butchers drove her back, but she would not give in, struggling, cursing the executioners with the harshest language she knew. The butchers finally grew tired of dealing with the unhappy woman, and they did her the service of shooting her and her child.

Itskhak Blok asked for permission to say a few words before his death. His executioners allowed it. He stood up and said: "Now you are shedding our innocent blood. The time will come when your damn blood will spray the pavement." They beat him to death with their rifle butts.

Each group of those shot was covered with a thin layer of sand, then another group was shot on top of them. There were many cases of wounded people who were still alive being covered over. The following story is told of one such example. Leybzon from Laukovo was taken up to a pit along with others and there was made to cover those who had just been shot. When he began sprinkling them with sand, he burst into loud sobs; he had heard from the pit the voices of his own children, who had been taken out with the previous party. "Father! Don't cover us over! We're still alive!"

This slaughter continued on Tuesday, Wednesday, and Thursday. Approximately five thousand men from Telshyay and its surrounding shtetls were exterminated. The earth on top of the pits was heaving the entire time, since many had been buried alive. For an entire week after this, blood burst from the pits like a fountain.

For several days after this massacre, life in the camp came to a virtual standstill. The women and even the children lost interest in life. No one would go out of the camp for food, no one would even accept any food from the hands of the butchers. They even stopped taking care of their small children. The only desire of each one was to somehow break out of the camp and to steal up to that awful place where their loved ones had perished, to follow the fountain of blood with horror, to find among the clothes and shoes left behind something belonging to a loved one and to feel the earth heaving beneath their feet (in Veksler's words).

Seven days after the slaughter, all those still alive were transferred to the new camp at Gerulyay. At Gerulyay, everything was even dirtier than at Reynyay. The lice problem was unbearable. Lice were everywhere: in one's clothes, on the walls, even in the bushes by the river. The food there was terrible. The assigned work in the forests and fields was too much for them.

The nights were awful. The exhausted women would hallucinate: the entire barracks appeared full of the ghosts of the dead before their suffering eyes. The horror of what they were suffering was made even greater by the abuse of the guards who threatened and shot them. To make the terror greater, the butchers spread rumors that the entire camp was to be liquidated soon, that the date for this liquidation had even been set. They would talk about the separation of children from their mothers, about new acts of extermination. And each time the terrified women would send delegations to town to ask for help. They went to see Staugautis, the local bishop of the Roman Catholic church; Romanauskas, the district governor; and other close acquaintances. No one, however, could offer any help. The bishop spoke out against the butchers several times in the cathedral. Others expressed sympathy, but, of course, nothing came of any of this. Others, like Romanauskas, scared off the delegations. There would be no more hope of rescue.

Rumors of the liquidation of the camp were becoming more and more persistent. On top of all that, various epidemics were raging in the camp: typhus, diphtheria, and others. The majority of the small children died in them, since there were neither doctors nor medicines, and those children who were sent to the local hospital also died as a result of poor care. Some seven weeks after the establishment of the camp, two trucks full of armed bandits pulled up to the gates and surrounded the camp with armed guards. Commandant Platakis and his bandits feasted throughout the night. That night, he invited the representatives of the camp—Yazhgur, Blokh, and Fridman—to come and see him, and demanded the last remaining valuables in the camp as a bribe for stopping the planned "action." The frightened women made the rounds of the barracks and gathered what was left from the whole camp, saying that in this way they would buy their way out of the slaughter that was being prepared. At 2:00 AM, the representatives brought their final cash installment to the commandant, and found him and his accomplices in a state of complete drunkenness. The commandant deigned to accept the money and valuables—around thirty thousand rubles and several dozen wedding rings—and promised to spare the camp.

Early in the morning, however, the bandits burst into the camp, awakened everyone, and ordered them to come out into the yard, saying that the camp had to be prepared for evacuation. They advised everyone to take only good things with them and to bring them out into the yard. And indeed, carts belonging to peasants who had been ordered to come were standing there. Everyone got dressed, took their last remaining belongings, and went out into the yard. They were immediately hemmed in by a closely packed formation of bandits and ordered to sit down on the ground. They began separating them into groups: young women and girls up to around the age of thirty were placed on the right; the others—old women and boys regardless of age—on the left.

At first, the disconcerted women did not understand the significance of the two sides, but afterward, when they guessed that those standing on the left were marked for death, they began to jostle each other to get to the right. But the bandits were no longer allowing anyone to pass from one formation to another. On the right were about four hundred people; on the left, several thousand. Those on the right were sent on foot and by cart to the ghetto at Telshyay, while those on the other side remained where they were. There were cases in which the bandits themselves wanted to move someone or other to the right, but the victims themselves preferred death to leaving their loved ones to die alone.

Yazhgur received a special "favor" from Commandant Platakis, and he took her and her daughters (who died in the summer of 1944 in action with the partisans) under his personal protection, installing them in his own room. Yazhgur, however, also had a son, who was unusually gifted (in 1941 he had been sent to art school), and he ended up going to the left. All her pleas to have him brought over to the right were of no help. The mother, then, went to die with her son of her own free will. One of the bandits wanted to bring the girl Ioselevich over to the right, but she insisted on bringing her aging mother with her; to this the bandit refused. Three times he offered to take her over to the other side, but she would not go without her mother, and with her mother she went to be shot.

There were many similar cases.

The slaughter began—women were taken out of the ranks in groups of fifteen or twenty to the nearest grove, where pits had already been dug. They were ordered to undress and were shot. They did not want to waste bullets on children, so they took them by the legs and smashed their little heads against trees, then threw them into the pit.

Mira Shlemovich, who escaped from the pit, saw for herself how one of the bandits took a seven-year-old child out of his bed, and before the eyes of his mother (Dveyre Levi from Laukovo) smashed his head against the side of the bed. Yet there were also cases in which mothers themselves asked the executioners to shoot their own naked young daughters before their eyes, so that they would not be raped.

The massacre went on for an entire day, and about four thousand women and children died in it.

The butchers looted belongings and divided them up among themselves or sold them to peasants who had gathered around. In the evening, after this "job" had been accomplished, the bandits drove two heavy trucks to the next town. Along the way they were howling and laughing. Madame Veksler was a witness to this. On that day of slaughter, she was working at a peasant's place, and on the advice of the man (who in all probability knew what was happening) stayed with him. She saw the butchers returning from their glorious "work"; they were singing songs in high spirits.

A new life began for the four hundred women who were still alive. They were lodged in several small houses. There was no furniture, bedding, or pillows. They had to sleep on the floor. The inhabitants of the ghetto received next to no rations, and they had to feed themselves by begging.

Some of them escaped to the Shavli ghetto. The rest lived until Christmas, 1941. On Christmas Day, 1941, the bandits gathered everyone still left in the ghetto and dispatched them to be shot. A small number of them ran off; they were caught, held in jail without food or water, and in the cold, and, half-dressed and barefoot, were then taken out to be shot. The Jews of Zhmud, of the shtetls of Rietovo, Alseday, Akmyane, Telshyay, and other towns died in this way. Only three ghettos remained in the whole of Lithuania—Vilnius (about 22,000), Kaunas (about 17,000) and Shavli (4,000).

The Jews of Alseday suffered the most bitter fate of all. They were protected there by the town's Roman Catholic priest and prelate. He stood among the Jews and said to the bandits: "You'll go to your bloody work over my dead body." The bandits held back. At the demand of the priest, the bandits allowed the Jews to be evacuated, taking provisions and belongings with them, even farm implements and livestock—horses, cows, goats, and chickens.

In Telshyay, however, they were made to do convict labor, and in the end were killed. On the last day, they were harnessed to carts full of stones and made to drag the load through the town. Along the way, the bandits beat them with their gun butts. Some were beaten to death, while those remaining were taken out of the camp and shot.

The last four hundred women living in the ghetto were liquidated on Christmas Day, 1941. Some ran away and were caught. They were held in prison for four or five days in rags and barefoot, and then, half-naked, were taken out and shot.

Several dozen managed to survive until September 1944. They lived in dugouts until they were discovered and executed. The man who had been keeping them, a Lithuanian named Bladis, was tied to the tails of two horses and dismembered.

L. Yerusalimsky

GARF f. 8114, op. 1, d. 960, ll. 101–125. The original manuscript.

69. Slaughter in the shtetl of Utyan
THE RECOLLECTIONS OF TSODIK YAKOVLEVICH BLEYMAN
[1945]

As the sole living witness, I am able to share the following.

I arrived in Utyan on July 25, 1941. My father was Rabbi Yakov Bleyman, the former rabbi of Karasubazar in the Crimea; he had recently been a rabbi in Utyan. I also had a brother-in-law, Efraim Yudelovich, who lived there with his family. I was in Kovna when the war broke out. I decided to go to my parents' place and to be evacuated along with them if necessary. But that was no longer possible: the Germans entered the town on the day of my arrival. Our fate was determined in advance; we were destined to die.

Thursday. The first day of the German regime. Dozens of Jews are herded out to work. They are taken to the Germans and to their assistants, the Lithuanian fascists. The work is entirely unnecessary, useless, good only for abusing Jews: to chase them around for days on end with brooms, shovels, and other tools. They are given nothing to eat. Only isolated groups manage to beg for a bit of bread. When they return home from work, the condition of the Jews is even worse. German units, along with Lithuanian scum, are killing them and stealing their goods and property. This state of affairs continues uninterrupted for a week. Over this period, not a single Jewish building remains intact. Dozens of Jews are killed. Fear of death grows stronger and stronger. In the morning, they waited for the evening, and in the evening they waited for the morning. "Order" was established in the town.

The first step toward "order" was the humiliation of the Jews. The scoundrels came along with Lithuanian bandits and tossed out all the Torah scrolls, books, and other things from three synagogues. They brought my father, an old man, to the place where all the books had been thrown out, and ordered him to tear them up and burn them. He refused. So the murderers set fire to his beard, while one of them shot him.

They brought my father back in very serious condition. His brother-in-law operated on him. The operation was a success and he could have recovered. New misfortunes begin, however. Jews are forbidden to show themselves on the main streets unaccompanied, and on every Jewish house appears the inscription "Jew." Jews are made to sew two yellow patches on their clothes—one in front and one in back. Gentiles are forbidden to have any dealings with Jews, and yet they are arrested for that reason without any basis in fact. All the synagogues are turned into prisons, and in addition to these there is still the old, large, and spacious prison. They also arrested two Jewish doctors and their families: my brother-in-law Yudelovich and Dr. Aks. They left one Jewish doctor alone for the time being, but later on they lured him in and killed him as well. In addition to the large number of those arrested, they took another forty-one hostages, among them Zurata, the Jewish vice-bürgermeister [22] of Utyan, and other prominent citizens of the town. More than a month went by. Everyone was living in the shadow of death. The terror against the Jews did not diminish. The struggle for a crust of bread became more and more difficult.

---

22. Essentially, the deputy mayor of the town.

On July 14, 1941, at 6:00 AM, the following decree was posted on walls: All Jews in Utyan would have to leave the town by twelve noon. Anyone found after that time would be shot. One has to walk two versts through the forest from the town, along the road to Malat.[23] At 7:00 AM, though, armed Lithuanians chased many Jews from their homes and arrested them as well. A terrible state of anxiety arose. The Jews wanted to escape into the forest as quickly as possible. Everything looked awful. The population of several thousand Jews was forced to leave the places in which they had always lived, where they had spent their entire lives, to go into the forest with their possessions in little knotted bags, not realizing what was waiting for them there.

Lithuanian police and Germans were posted near the forest and examined the bags. They confiscated money, gold, silver, and all valuable items. The forest was under guard. They were strictly forbidden to spread out over long distances. Building a fire was not allowed either. It was possible to fetch a bit of cold water if escorted by one of the sentries. They were told that they would be held for only three days and that during that time they would enclose a ghetto in town for the Jews. They believed that things would turn out this way, but it took longer than three days.

The situation in the forest was becoming worse and worse: more people were sick and there was no medical care. All those in the synagogues and in the main prison were shot. Some of the hostages were taken into the forest in order to show them that no more Jews would be killed. Everyone dreamed of finally being let into the ghetto. On August 1, 1941, the police came into the forest and registered all men and women between the ages of seventeen and sixty. They thought that this was for work. I registered, too.

After that, they took me and ten other Jews to work, and the rest remained in the forest. They took us to the job: we worked late into the night cleaning up a ruined house. Just before evening, they led a group of around four or five hundred Jews out of the forest past us. Among them was the young Utyan rabbi Nakhman Girshovich, and Zurata with both of his sons. They were taking them in the direction of the prison. We thought that they would take us there as well, but they marched us back to the forest. In the forest, we found all the men ready to return to the town. At the last minute, though, a policeman turned up and whispered something to the other agents. After that, they dismissed everyone and gave the order to go back into the forest. Another week passed this way. The Russians secretly communicated that the group that had been led away had been shot.

But they did not believe these rumors, and they did not spread them in the forest; this would have deeply affected the women whose husbands had been taken away. On Thursday, August 7, they drove us all out to work at dawn. Just as before, we did not notice anything in particular at the time. I kissed my father and mother goodbye, certain that I would come back after work. Unfortunately, this was the last time. I never

---

23. A verst is equal to about 3,500 feet, about two-thirds of a mile.

saw the deep, kind-hearted eyes of my father again, and would no longer touch the trembling hands of my mother. I was saying goodbye to them forever. They told us that they were taking us out to work. There were three hundred of us; three sentries escorted us. They took us to the jail, searched us carefully, confiscated everything, and left us there to wait for the boss. There were more Jews in the prison yard brought from Lelig, Malat, Aniksht, and other shtetls near Utyan. We were forbidden to talk to them. At midday a German from the Gestapo arrived. He formed us all into rows of four. The warden of the prison appeared and ordered those who were wearing outer clothing to take it off, explaining, "Now you're going to go work a bit." We walked out of the prison. Before us was the following scene: a group of Jewish women standing in ranks four deep, with columns of armed Lithuanians facing them on two sides. They began leading us off; as soon as we were outside of town, they began beating and chasing us. They chased us in this way for some distance. Anyone who fell along the way was shot, while the rest were beaten and chased. We asked to die, as we were in no condition to take any more.

All at once they ordered the men to lie face down on the ground and the women to continue walking. We heard gunshots and women's cries. When they had finished off the women—this went on for around twenty minutes—they ordered the men to keep on going. And once more the same: shooting, cries, then silence. My turn came next. We were all young, strong men, and we quietly agreed to defend ourselves as best as we possibly could. The place of slaughter had the following appearance: a hillock enclosed on three sides by woods, with a swampy landscape stretching out below it, overgrown with dense grass, shrubs, and low trees. Trenches three to four meters deep and up to ten meters long had been dug in the hillock. A Lithuanian in uniform stood not far from the trenches. He was wearing a special mask that made him look like a scarecrow. He held a long whip in his hands with which he hit each man so as to make him jump into the trench as quickly as possible. A German with a light machine gun, shirtless, just like a butcher, stood off to one side from the trenches on our left, and was shooting the Jews as they approached the trenches. Not far away were several Germans and Lithuanians, including the bürgermeister and others whose names I did not know. The German with the machine gun ordered us to come up to the trench. We rushed him. I grabbed him by the legs and he fell. Bullets came down on us like hail from all sides.

I heard the moans of my other three friends, who had been killed beside me. Playing dead, I rolled down the hillock. Thanks to the high grass and the bog, crawling on my stomach, I managed to reach a watery pit, which was also full of dense overgrowth, several hundred meters from the place of execution. I lay there for an entire day in the water and breathed through a reed until nightfall. During this time I heard them bringing up new groups and shooting them. A heavy rain was falling and it was getting quite dark. I was nearly frozen, and decided to crawl out of the pit. I was warmed a bit by the walk and made for the forest. I did not find anyone there.

Not knowing where to go, I walked down the road in the direction of Kovna. For six weeks or so I wandered through the forests, barely dressed and hungry, until I reached a camp in Kovna. There I found other Jews, and a life of suffering, privation, and fear started again. The year 1944 arrived. The Red Army was approaching the borders of Lithuania. We believed that they would free us, and our hope did not disappoint us.

I escaped from the camp in the spring, lying low in various places, and waited for liberation.

GARF f. 8114, op. 1, d. 959, ll. 141–144ob. Handwritten by the translator.

70. Killing the Jews of Sventsyany
A LETTER FROM A LOCAL RESIDENT NAMED GURYAN TO ILYA EHRENBURG
NOVEMBER 20, 1944

Dear Comrade Ehrenburg!

I received your letter of February 17 and am now replying. Excuse me for not writing in Russian. It is very difficult. I lived in Poland for 20 years.

Comrade Ehrenburg! You have given me a very difficult task. It is very hard to describe for you what we went through during the German-Lithuanian occupation; my nerves are too weak to describe everything. No matter how much I write, I will not be able to relate everything that I saw with my own eyes. I decided not to write to you. I hope that I will manage to come to Moscow, then I will tell you everything face to face. Comrade Ehrenburg, you probably know that toward the end of 1943, some Jews were taken away to Estonia. I was in Vilna just recently and spoke personally with a Jewish girl who survived the dreadful Estonian pogrom. They took them off on steamboats, telling them that they were being taken to East Prussia, but this was a lie. They threw them alive into the sea, some of the Jews were burned alive, while the rest were shot. This was how they liquidated the Jews of Estonia. Only forty people were saved. This is how they survived: they dug a forty-meter-long tunnel with their bare hands. They kept the earth beneath the bunks that they slept on.

Comrade Ehrenburg! October 9, 1944, was the third anniversary of the pogrom in Sventsyany. There is a common grave fourteen kilometers from Sventsyany. A few of us Jews gathered by this grave. The grave is five hundred meters long and seven meters wide. As soon as the Germans entered Sventsyany, on the very first day, they shot forty people. The White Lithuanian partisans did the shooting because the Germans did not yet know which Jew was a communist.

On July 30, 1941, they shot another one hundred people, among them the well-known Dr. Kovarsky. They made him suffer for a long time, holding him by the legs and lowering his head into a bog before shooting him.

After the pogrom, we were no longer allowed to walk on the sidewalks; we had to wear yellow stars on our chests and clean latrines with our bare hands. The Germans would sit in carts and make Jews take them places. I myself was forced to lie down and stand up twenty times because I was walking on the sidewalk. On September 27, 1944, all the Jews in Sventsyany and the area around it were gathered in a camp two kilometers from the town of Novye Sventsyany. We had no water or food. There was no place to lie down or to stand up. They were killing us at every step. One day, Comrade Murashkin, a barber from Sventsyany, made a speech to the Jews. He predicted that they would all be killed, and said that they should prepare to defend themselves. To the Lithuanians he said that they were killing us today, but that there would come a time when they would be killed, when the Red Army would come. Then they tortured him to death.

You must have heard the weeping of mothers and children in Moscow. On October 9, 1941, they were all led to the pit in groups of thirty to forty, stripped naked, and shot; some were thrown into the pit alive, children were grabbed by the legs, their heads smashed against stones. Over a period of two days, they killed seven thousand Jews.

In the shtetl of Ionishki, they harnessed a Jew to a cart. Many Germans and Lithuanians got in and forced the Jew to pull the cart while they beat him with whips.

At the Lubany estate, seventeen Jews were cut up with a saw, each of them into three sections. In the small town of Duknin, POWs were bound to train cars with barbed wire in such a way that their knees touched the ties, then the train was run at full throttle, torturing the prisoners. In Novye Sventsyany, one Lithuanian led a POW on a chain like a dog.

That is enough for today. In the next letter, I will tell you about everything that you asked about. [24]

Regards,

Guryan

GARF f. 8114, op. 1, d. 960, ll. 318–319. A typewritten manuscript.

71. A camp in Kotsynishki [Kochenishki]
A LETTER FROM THE WORKER ITSIK YUKHNIKOV [25]

I am lying down but cannot sleep. Suddenly I hear a knock at the door. I look at my watch—two in the morning. "Open the door, it's the police." I open the door. Two policemen come in. They arrest me and take me to the station house. At the police station they tell me that they are sending me to Riga. They lead me to jail, where I find another eight comrades. Not far from the Kochenishki estate, they unload us and drive us along on foot: "Faster, faster, come on, faster." We fall behind. They hit us about the head.

---

24. No other letters from this individual have been located in the archives of the JAC or among Ehrenburg's papers.
25. On the first page of the document, there is a notation in the right margin that Itsik Yukhnikov was a worker from Kovno made to do forced labor on the Waffen SS estate at Kotsyunishki (Lithuanian SSR).

Finally we reached the estate. First order: "If anyone tries to escape, we'll shoot all of you." They order us to take off our six-pointed stars. And then the second order: If we strike up a conversation with anyone, Lithuanian or Jewish, they will shoot us.

They give us a job. When we have not managed to finish it in two hours, we hear them yelling: "All Jews, over here." We present ourselves, then there is a new order. "Lie down! Get up! Lie down! Run!" We run to the Nevyazha River. Again comes an order: "Into the water!" We go in. The water is up to our knees. We are ordered to keep going. But there is no way to go on; it is twelve or fifteen meters deep. A German sees that we cannot walk any farther and gives the command: "Lie down!" We lie down. For a whole hour they keep us in the water. Suddenly, another shout: "Crawl out!" We jump out of the river. "To work!" We set to work, but things are not going well. We are trembling, our teeth are chattering. We wait for night to come. They order us into our quarters. We get one hundred grams of bread and water. We head off to sleep.

We hear a drunken voice at three in the morning. "Everybody up!" We get up. "Jews, everyone here?" "Everyone." Immediately comes an order: "Everyone take turns lying down on the bench." I step out first. I take thirty lashes on my naked body. And then everyone else, one after another. In the morning we turn up for work. I see a truck going by a long way off; there are Jews in it. I yell: "Give my regards to the ghetto!" The Germans hear me, so I endure a few slaps. They take me to some sort of barn, order me to strip, and I receive thirty lashes. Because I am so weak, I am in no condition to move. They beat me again until I crawl out on my hands and knees.

Once, the Germans show up at two in the morning. They order everyone to get up and show whether or not their feet are clean. Obviously, in the sty that we were kept in along with the pigs, we could not have clean feet. The Germans look at our feet and every one of us—we are nine—suffers ten lashes. The Germans leave. Half an hour later, they turn up again and ask one of the fellows a question: "Was it a good meal?" "*Jawohl,* boss, it was a good meal." They order us to lie down on the bench again and we each receive five lashes. The Germans leave.

They reach the door, come back, and one of them barks: "Who sabotaged my motorcycle?" Everyone keeps their mouth shut, no one could say anything, no one had set eyes on the motorcycle. We each receive another fifteen lashes.

A couple of days go by. They leave us alone. Sunday comes. We go out to work. Toward ten o'clock or so, our boss runs up to me with the look of an animal on his face, drags me to the stove, and asks me a question about the Talmud. Before I can answer, he says: "It says in the Talmud that a Jew is allowed to violate a three-year-old Christian girl and then to kill her." I did not know what to say to him. The German begins to beat my head against the stove and hit me over the head with his revolver until I collapse. Then he throws himself on another worker, striking him hard in the face and putting a hole right through his cheek. The guy falls over. Then the German throws a third worker down the stairs and begins beating him. This last one breaks free from his tormentor and begins to run. The Germans run after him and wound him in the leg with a shot from a submachine gun. The fellow stops and puts his hands up. The Germans approach him and shoot our comrade Girsh Zaydberg. Then, thirsting for blood, they order us to form up two to a rank, and put shovels in our hands in order to bury our comrade.

All of this happened between February 5 and April 20, 1943.

GARF f. 8114, op. 1, d. 944, ll. 196–198. A typewritten manuscript translated from Yiddish.

IV
LATVIA

Latvia was home to 94,000 Jews in 1935. Like the other Baltic states, it had been an independent republic beginning in 1918. Jews enjoyed full and equal citizenship as individuals and also benefited from a constitution that granted ethnic minorities considerable cultural autonomy. Even after President Kārlis Ulmanis, the leader of the Farmers Union Party, carried out a military coup against the country's parliament in 1934, Jews and Jewish institutions were not specifically targeted or compromised by the new authoritarian regime, leaving the country's rich network of Jewish schools and other cultural institutions intact.

But with the annexation of Latvia in July 1940, the Kremlin embarked on a program of Sovietization. This process encompassed the destruction of Latvia's governing political and social institutions, and the deportation of 19,000 of its citizens, including 5,000 Jews. (Another 5,000 Jews had succeeded in emigrating before the war.) This repression affected Jewish institutions as well, all of which were abolished. Despite the impact of Sovietization in the Jewish community, many Latvians blamed the Jews as a pro-Soviet element.[1]

Once the Germans invaded in June 1941, they were able to gain control of Latvia within days; Riga was captured on July 1. Still, as many as 15,000 Jews had managed to flee the Germans eastward into the Soviet interior and thereby saved themselves. This left between 66,000 and 70,000 under German control. Just three days after reaching Riga, the Germans carried out a horrific massacre, herding 300 Jews, most of them refugees from Lithuania, into the basement of the Great Choral Synagogue.

---

1. Andrew Ezergailis, "Latvia," in David Wyman, ed., *The World Reacts to the Holocaust* (Baltimore, 1996), p. 365, and *The Holocaust in Latvia 1941–1944* (Riga and Washington, 1996).

German soldiers hurled grenades into the windows to burn down the building and murder all these Jews. Einsatzgruppe A, under the command of General Walter Stahlecker, recruited special Latvian units to help carry out further massacres. Later that fall, much of Einsatzgruppe A was transferred to the Leningrad region, after which SS-Brigadeführer Friedrich Jeckeln took over. Most of Latvia's Jews were murdered in two series of massacres: from July to October 1941, when 30,000 were killed in Latvia's small towns, along with 4,000 from Riga; and then in November and December, when the great majority of Jews in Riga, Daugavpils (Dvinsk), and Liepaja were murdered. The Germans were assisted by an extreme Latvian nationalist group, the Arajs Kommando, led by Viktor Arajs.[2] Arajs's men later also participated in massacres in Ukraine, Belorussia, and Russia.

The Rumbula Forest outside Riga was the site of one of the largest massacres on Soviet territory. On November 30 and December 8, a total of 24,000 Jews were slaughtered at Rumbula. The renowned Jewish historian Simon Dubnow was among them. By the beginning of 1942, only 6,000 Jews remained alive, working as slave laborers near Riga, Daugavpils, and Liepaja.

For a while, the Germans considered using Latvia as a killing center for Europe's Jews. About 21,000 Jews were shipped to Latvia and imprisoned in the Riga ghetto and in various labor camps. About half these "foreign" Jews were killed in the early months of 1942. The Kaiserwald concentration camp, located near Riga, housed 2,000 Jews when the Red Army began to liberate Latvia in the late summer of 1944. The Germans sent 10,000 Jews who were still alive in Latvian ghettos and camps to Germany, where the majority were housed in the Stutthof concentration camp.

Around 1,000 Latvian Jews returned from camps in Germany after the war. Only a handful, about 150, survived the war by hiding with the help of non-Jewish Latvians.

72. Our situation is hopeless and yet
THE FATE OF THE JEWS OF LIBAVA[3] ACCORDING TO THE DIARIES OF KALMAN LINKIMER[4]
PREPARED BY SH. GOMAN
TRANSLATED BY M. SHAMBADAL
JUNE 11, [1944]

The diaries of Kalman Linkimer describe the destruction of the Jews of Libava in detail.

As early as June 30—one week after the outbreak of the war—the fate of the Jews of Libava, in Linkimer's words, "was already sealed." Never, however, did these scoun-

---

2. Viktor Arajs was prosecuted by German authorities in Hamburg, sentenced to life in prison in 1971, and died there in 1988.
3. Present-day Liepaja.
4. The text of Kalman Linkimer's diaries is not among the documents of *The Black Book* collection; only his photographs and those of his friends have been preserved.

drels dare to announce openly that they intended to carry out extermination. Every time they would find a new way to deceive people: "You're going to work." "You need to be re-registered." "We're sending you to a camp."

The result, however, was always the same; no one ever came back.

Chapter after chapter, Linkimer's diaries tell how the Germans, with the help of traitors from among the Latvians, did their bloody work. Every day, small groups of Jews, or large ones, would vanish. Those left still did not believe that such a fate awaited them. They were still hoping for something. Running through Linkimer's diaries like a red thread is the thought: "We'll think our way out of this, we'll get by, we'll be rescued!" Of course, though, there could be no question of the Jews' helping or collaborating with cannibals.

Revulsion, hatred, horror—this is what every Jew felt toward these villains. And if, naturally, there were very few Latvians who helped or concealed Red Army soldiers or Communists in their homes, there was on the other hand more than enough scum among the Latvian people whom the Germans armed and who helped the Germans any way that they could. It will be difficult for the Latvian people to cleanse themselves of this dark, humanity-hating *Aizsargi* work![5]

It is not true that all the Jews of Libava went to their deaths like sheep. Unfortunately, however, the times when the saying "An eye for an eye" was put into practice were rare.

The barber Bene Brant escaped from the scoundrels. He was shot making his escape. He, as Linkimer puts it, "did not have to strip himself naked and go through the whole ceremony by the open grave on the square."

Yet how many of the bloody German and Latvian beasts would have paid with their heads if only Bene Brant and those like him had been united.

And there were many courageous and daring people in Libava. Before the remaining Libava Jews were locked up in the ghetto, healthy young people were perishing every day. Everyone was thinking: "Perhaps I'll be saved." They would run to register at the labor exchange, then would be delighted to receive the piece of paper which, basically, would only delay the dreadful end. How many Jews could have been saved! How many bloody dogs could have been put down if there had been organizers in Libava the way there were in Warsaw.

But Libava did not know anything about Warsaw, and because of that, people who in other places and in other circumstances would have been heroes, in Libava died, at best, like people and not like sheep.

A Russian officer, who had escaped from the Germans and was hiding outside, met Kabi. And though Kabi, like every Jew, expected to die every day, he hid the officer and supported him as best he could. However, when the officer fell into the

---

5. The Aizsargi were a pre-war civil defense group. With the start of the war, many Aizsargi became collaborators and actively participated in the persecution and murder of Latvia's Jews.

villains' hands one day, and they learned that Kabi had been hiding him, he was arrested along with the other Jews living in the building. Jews from whom Kabi had obtained food or money for the officer on more than one occasion were trembling from fear. Yet no matter how they tortured Kabi, he did not utter a word. Kabi was shot. That day, the Jewish workers disabled their electric motors and "out of solidarity with Kabi, a courageous and conscientious citizen, did not work," as Linkimer tells the story. What contribution to society could Kabi have made in more appropriate conditions?

There were many instances of genuine heroism, fearlessness, and disregard for death. Nonetheless, only about eight hundred of the nine thousand Jews of Libava went into the ghetto!

It would be impossible to pause and describe in detail every example of genuine heroism and bravery in this cursory review of Linkimer's diaries. Impossible because it would require dozens of pages. It would also be difficult to speak of Linkimer's work in ordinary words, since the very lines of the diary are written in brain matter and blood!

Each chapter begins with Linkimer's words: "Our fate has been determined in advance. Our situation is hopeless. And yet. . . ." And yet the lines go on. And again people go to their deaths, including mothers with children and with infants in their arms.

Jews—young people working for the Schutzpolizei—clean blood and bits of human remains from automobiles. They clean their boots, seeing perfectly well what has soiled them.

How could one have enough spirit and patience to make a note of a theft from a ghetto shop?

Yet Linkimer had patience enough. He describes in detail the lives of the eight hundred Jews left in the ghetto, if one could call it a life at all.

There cannot be dishonorable people among the Jews in the ghetto! This is why the community deals so severely with the case of theft from a shop. That Jews should steal! And from other Jews besides! And where? In the ghetto!

This event occupies an entire chapter. Then again, workers, honest people doing the hardest and dirtiest work in the ghetto, are described in just as much detail.

Khaim Levinson is a building superintendent. His domain is "vast," he is constantly attending to something since it is winter outside and the pipes are freezing. People from other buildings come to him for water. The pipes in Levinson's building work without interruption. He does not sleep at night, heating the pipes any way he can. And when neighbors ask him to clean some kind of toilet, he jokes: "It's good when, whatever you do, it sticks to your hands."

There is no small number of lines of genuine native wisdom, humor, and good cheer in the diaries. It was not Linkimer who thought up the words of Tsimmerman, the tailor. He heard them and wrote them down. The seventy-year-old Tsimmerman is a remarkable master of his craft. Every time he gives the scoundrels finished work, they promise him: "Well, we're going to shoot you like a dog soon. One more suit and it's all over! No more work for you!"

The council advises Tsimmerman not to go to work anymore. But Tsimmerman promises with a smile: "I'm not scared of them. No matter how hard they try, they won't shoot me while I'm still young!"

The old woman Fridman would not put on patches or get off the sidewalk when she met Germans. On Yom Kippur, 1941, she was sitting at home and praying. And the Aizsargi broke down her front door and were already about to set their hands to the inner doors as well, but the old lady did not utter a sound. The criminals decided that there was no one there and went away. Fridman remained alive. "I should interrupt my prayers because of them?" she said. "They should live so long!"

These facts, which have not been forgotten because Linkimer was able to see them, remember them, and conscientiously take them down, are genuine sources of folk wisdom which should be recorded so as to last forever.

Fleischman, who was a member of the Maccabi, the Jewish athletic club, escaped from the firing squad and ran six kilometers half naked and bloody. The armed beasts went after her, firing as they ran. One of them later admitted that he had never seen such a brave and gallant woman in his life.

A certain fellow named David, who worked for the SD man Sabek, happened to see photos in the laboratory of the awful places where the bandits had carried out their "actions." He told Linkimer about this. And when Sabek went out, David went into his room, locked the door, and reproduced copies of the photos, wearing gloves and keeping his feet wrapped in rags as he worked, so as to leave no traces, and worked with no regard for the mortal danger that he was in. And there they are, he has the photographs! Now they must be preserved, so that they can be presented as evidence when the day of judgment comes. This episode takes up almost five pages in the diary. Another ten pages carry a description of each photograph individually, since Linkimer wants to preserve a precise description of each of them in the event that they should be lost.

It is understandable that David, who copied each one of these photographs in Sabek's room—that is, in the very jaws of the wolf—in other circumstances could really have done damage to the German bandits.

It is also worth marveling at the endurance shown by the women who had the hardest jobs: cold and half-naked, they hauled bricks and raised pillars in the rain and snow, in the heaviest frosts. Yet not a single one of them ever went to the council with a complaint. All of them hoped for a miracle, for the coming of the Red Army. This hope gave them strength and courage, patience and confidence.

Linkimer also tells the story of how they inhumanely and sadistically tortured Red Army POWs. Here is one example: A number of German SD men are savagely beating a Red Army POW for having brought a small sack of bread to his hungry comrades.

Each time he is asked where he got the bread, the Red Army soldier replies with a different location. The scoundrels torment him, break his arms, but he cries out: "You dogs, there are dozens of you, and only one of me. But the day will come when ten of your beasts will be judged by one of us!" With these words, he falls, and lies there crushed, trampled in the snow.

The drunken, gluttonous, sated beasts in human form tracked down their innocent and unarmed victims in order to torture, humiliate, and only then to kill them by a method devised by the Aryan dogs.

For forced labor they gave neither money nor food. For a week's work, Linkimer received a rusty thimble. "This is a present for your mother, so that she doesn't prick her finger when she's sewing," said one SD member. Another time they gave him two or three cigarettes for having sawed and chopped up a whole shed full of uprooted stumps.

The system remained unchanged: to suck the marrow from the victim's bones, and then to kill him.

However, if the inhabitants of the ghetto were incapable of an outright uprising, then they at least kept a fierce hatred in their hearts for the foul enemies and for the indignities, unknown until then, that they inflicted.

Some boys were living in a ditch behind a shed, hungry, cold, exhausted to the limits of endurance. They did not want to come out of their ditch and go into the ghetto. "The Red Army will come! Let the Red Army see how we lived under the 'Aryans,'" the boys would say when people from the ghetto came for them.

Of nine thousand Jews, twenty-two survived! They remained only because the Red Army chased away the scoundrels. Linkimer was among these twenty-two.

I happen to know that Linkimer has other materials in his possession. The editorial board of *The Black Book* is undoubtedly in touch with him. The materials that have been in my report take up about three hundred pages. What one reads produces a tremendous impression. The extermination of infants, women, the destruction of the Libava almshouse, of thousands of tormented, innocent people—all of this is concrete fact. But it is difficult for a person with a normal psyche to take it in.

People committed acts of sabotage, listened to the radio in secret, knew about the fighting in Stalingrad. The scoundrels met with no resistance in the Libava ghetto. In Libava, out of nine thousand Jews, twenty-two survived.

And many of those who did the killing are walking about free. Innocent blood cries out for vengeance. Tell the story and remember that only fascism is responsible for the people's great misfortune!

June 11, [1944]

GARF f. 8114, op. 1, d. 961, ll. 1–6. A typewritten manuscript with handwritten corrections.

73. The voice of Sheyna Gram
THE DIARY OF A FIFTEEN-YEAR-OLD GIRL FROM THE SHTETL OF PREYLI
FOREWORD AND TRANSLATION FROM YIDDISH BY B. GERTSBAKH [6]
JUNE 22–AUGUST 8, 1941

In addition to the six Jews who survived in the small Latvian town of Preyli, one document survived that, better than any other, gives an account of the bestial nature of the German fascists. This document is the small notebook-diary of a fifteen-year-old Jewish girl named Sheyna Gram, who was killed along with the rest of her family and 1,500 other Jews at the hands of the German fascists in this little town in Soviet Latvia.

This modest diary was handed over by a Russian woman, a neighbor of the Gram family, after the dead girl's brother, Gutman Gram, a soldier in a Latvian rifle division, entered Preyli along with units of the Red Army.

The Khagi family from Preyli, who survived, offer the following details concerning the diary's author, Sheyna Gram:

When the war broke out, the Gram family was made up of six people: the father, Itzik, 60, a tailor by profession; his 52-year-old wife; their older daughter Freyda, 20; their son Gutman, 18; their daughter Sheyna, 15; and their son Leyba, 12. Out of the entire family, only Gutman survived; he was evacuated to the Soviet Union and is now in the ranks of the Red Army.

The Gram's daughter, fifteen-year-old Sheyna, had just finished the sixth grade when the war broke out. She was an intelligent girl of good spiritual development. She was a model student.

Sheyna Gram kept her diary in Yiddish. Only the heading, "The Diary of Sheyna Gram," was in Latvian.

According to the Khagi family, Sheyna Gram and all of her family were killed on August 9, 1941. Her older sister, Freyda, who is mentioned in the diary, was kept back after work that day by the commandant, who, when he had had his fill of her, had her killed on August 16. Sheyna's diary begins on June 22, 1941, the day the war broke out.

B. Gertsbakh.

***

June 22. At twelve o'clock, the radio announced: "Germany has declared war on the USSR. At four o'clock this morning, German aircraft bombed several Russian cities."

Toward evening, I went to Ribenishki (seven kilometers from the shtetl of Preyli—B.G.) I sit by the radio all the time until midnight. They tell you how to protect yourself from an air raid.

---

6. The original text of the diary is absent from *The Black Book* collection. Using Gram's diary and B. Gertsbakh's foreword, V. Gerasimova (one of the contributors to *The Black Book*) wrote an essay entitled "Sheyna's Voice," which was not included in the final version. An abridged and edited version of the diary is included here. GARF f. 8114, op. 1, d. 962, ll. 10–15.

June 23. In the morning we find out that they have bombed Dvinsk. I find myself a cart and make my way home. A state of siege has been declared, and we are allowed to be on the streets only until 8:00 PM. We talk at home until eleven. At night the noise of lots of airplanes can be heard. Tanks go along the streets. There is a great deal of noise everywhere. Everyone at home stays awake throughout the night.

June 24. I got up very early. Outside, everything is quiet. There is no news at all. A first aid group is set up, and I sign up right away. The first lecture was at four o'clock. The doctor explains how one ought to give first aid. After the lesson, we all wait for the bus. New people are coming into town all the time. Each person has something new to report. The Germans are successfully advancing. Everyone in town is growing anxious. It begins to rain toward evening. We have to cover the windows. I lie in bed fully dressed. My sister wakes me up at one in the morning. Airplanes can be heard flying overhead. I listen to the noise for a long time, but then fall asleep.

Wednesday, June 25. I go out into the street early in the morning. There is no news from the Front. Everyone is waiting for the bus. Radios are being confiscated from everyone. Airplanes are flying over head every minute. The outdoor bazaar has been broken up. Assembling in groups is forbidden. The bus comes only toward evening. I go to the Red Cross at 6:00 PM. They teach us how to bandage people. They have divided the group into two shifts: one from eight in the evening until one in the morning, and another from one in the morning until 5:00 AM. They assign me to the second group. It is quiet until 2:00 AM. From two until sunrise, one can hear muffled explosions. They are bombing the railroad beds. They release us from duty at five o'clock.

Thursday, June 26. There is tremendous agitation in town. The Germans are advancing. Soviet cars are hurrying back and forth. Everyone is stocking up on things. Many are heading in the direction of the border. My brother and two of his comrades are heading off on bicycles. I get myself a bicycle and also leave with one other girl. We reach Ribenishki in the evening and spend the night there.

Friday, June 27. We go no farther. We spend the entire day at my aunt's place. Soldiers ride by. Many of them are on the move, running from Poland and Lithuania. In the evening, my friend's uncle comes over. She leaves with him. I go with them as well. Later, though, I thought better of it, and toward morning I return home.

Thursday, July 3. We are living with the Germans for the second day already. No one goes into the streets. A huge German formation with lots of equipment passed through Preyli.

The first day went by quietly. On the second day, the Germans smashed the shops and looted everything. They broke into the synagogue, hauled out the Torah scrolls, and trampled on them. In other streets, they go on various sorts of rampages. All the time, German troop carriers and tanks keep going by. We do not know anything about the situation at the Front. We are all living in a state of great fear. Many German soldiers have stopped in our town. There are some proper gentlemen among them as well. They keep on reassuring us that they are not going to touch the workers. A decree is published that Jews and Russians do not have the right to fly their national flags. Walking on the street is permitted until 10:00 PM, but no one dares poke their head out the door. We can only sit in the apartment.

There are new acts of repression every day. They send people out to work: weeding gardens, washing floors, and so on. The local peasant population has been ordered not to sell anything to Jews.

Saturday, July 19. An order has been issued that Jews must wear a yellow distinguishing mark. It consists of a five-pointed yellow star,[7] twelve centimeters wide and long. Men are to wear it on their backs, their chests, and their legs, just above the knee. Women will wear them on their chests and on their backs. Many are arrested and put in prison.

Monday, July 21. A group of fifty Jews is sent to work on peat processing. Each one of them has to work fifteen *ster* (five cubic meters—B.G.). They work for four days and then go home. No one has been taken from our apartment.

Thursday, July 24. A new group has been driven out to do the peat work. I am fed up with sitting at home and would like to work myself. They register me along with my sister. In the evening, they inform me that on Friday at five in the morning we will need to go to work.

Friday, July 25. At five in the morning, we gather on the market square around the fire tower. There is a roll call, then we move off. It is ten kilometers to the peat works. By eight-thirty, they are already dividing us up into work parties. We work in groups of ten: eight girls and two boys. Our job is to turn over the cut turf. It is heavy work. Every minute, a forest ranger comes running up and urges us on. Work stops at 7:00 PM. A barn has been allotted us as our place to stay for the night. At 2:00 AM we are surrounded by a group of strangers, partisans as it seems.[8] One of them calls for all the Jews to come out, but when none of us answers, they open fire. The scene in the barn was dreadful. Everyone gathered in one corner, and everyone was praying to God. Fortunately, they were only making fun of us. After the shooting, when no one answered, the men surrounding the barn went away. But we did not sleep the whole night. We went back out to work at 5:00 AM.

Saturday, July 26. At six o'clock we go off to work. They give us one hour for lunch. After lunch, they take away several people in our group. Seven of us are left. We meet our quota before three o'clock, however, and go into the forest, where our things are. After a while, the rest come together, and we head for home. Coming out of the forest, we suddenly realize that one of our group is missing. We start looking, but without any result. Greatly worried about the fate of this one man who disappeared, we make for home. Arriving home, we find him in the room. It turned out that he took

---

7. This is a mistake in the text; the Jewish star, the *Magen David*, is six-pointed.
8. This is a reference to an organization of Latvian "partisans" who collaborated with the Nazis.

another route. There is a stir in our small town. They are picking up horses, and that night several Jews are taken off to Malta.

Sunday, July 27. This is a bloody Sunday for the Latvian Jewish people.

Morning. All the Jews in Dvinskaya Street are ordered to put on their best clothes, take some provisions with them, and go out into the street. Searches of the homes are carried out. At twelve o'clock, all the Jews are herded into the synagogue. One group of young Jews is sent to dig graves behind the cemetery. Then the Jews of two more streets are driven in to the synagogue.

It is 3:30 in the afternoon. All the Jews are chased out beyond the cemetery and shot there. All 250 Jews: men, women, and children.

This is terrible. We did not expect things to end this way. The handful of survivors expects death at any moment.

Monday, July 28. A nightmare of a day. We learn the details of the awful and tragic end. In the afternoon, a new group of surviving Jews is herded out to do the peat work.

Tuesday, July 29. They leave early in the morning. The word goes around that they have also been taken away to dig graves. Girls are picked up to clean the streets. We look at one another and are amazed that we are still alive. Each person desires their own death. The position of the Jews is dreadful. How long will we suffer? The rumor gets around that they will pick people up again toward evening. We decide not to spend the night at home. A peasant allows us to spend the night in his bathhouse. Late evening, one by one, we go to the baths to sleep. There are six of us, and the bath is small. Only three can sleep there. No one sleeps, however. Dogs are barking the whole night. I sit with my eyes closed. Before me appear the faces of those who have been shot. It seems to me that they are crying through closed eyelids.

Wednesday, July 30. In the morning we return to the apartment. The rooms are untouched. Everything is calm. I stretch out on the bed and immediately fall asleep. There is fresh news every hour. Someone says that they are going to take some more, someone else says that they won't. Whom to believe? For the moment, things are awful. Everyone is sitting and waiting for death.

We learn that an even more horrible death is being prepared for the Jews who are still alive. They will burn us. It makes no difference to me. I don't want to live, I don't want to die. Only one thing amazes me: How is it that we are in any condition to endure all of this? My sister and I decide to conceal ourselves in the baths. We hear good news. They are not going to touch the Jews again. They are satisfied with the 250. They take my sister to work to wash the floors. I was sleeping at the time. Today we sleep at home. It is eight 8 o'clock. It is forbidden to go out on the street. Such amazing weather. Can it really be all up for the young Jews? Will better times really never come again? As for what is going on at the Front, we do not know. There are rumors that the Germans have taken a tremendous blow and that they are being forced back. It is not known how much of this is true. It is quiet at night. I can't sleep for a long time and look out of the window. It is quiet all around. Only far away in the fields are there some dogs barking.

Thursday, July 31. It is quiet today. We receive greetings from Ribenishki. No one has been touched there. In the morning, they send us out to work. My sister and I go into the fields. We sit there until two in the afternoon. A Jewish ghetto is being set up. Three men are going around taking down the names of those able to work. Every day, some forty of the Jews have to go to the peat works and to sweep the streets. Every day there are new persecutions, and there is no end in sight. We have lived this long, but we do not know whether or not we will manage to survive. They send Jewish girls to clean freed-up Jewish apartments for those who have been killing them. They do not take me. But when they clean out the apartment of my murdered friend Mery Plagova, which they are preparing for a police officer, I go. I gather up her photos and keep them with me. I cannot believe that my friends the Plagovas are already dead.[9]

Friday, August 1. For the moment, all is quiet. We still do not know whether or not we should leave our street. During the night my sister thinks she hears yelling from somewhere. Today she is sleeping with me. I open the window. I let myself out into the street and listen. No one in sight, though. It is quiet all around.

At 6:30, my sister and I have to go and sweep the streets. There are fifteen people in our group. We are cleaning Dvinskaya Street. Then they send us to sweep up the market. After this job, a police officer gives the order to gather two hundred Jews into a group. We stand with our brooms in the market for a long time. Every passerby runs to get a look at us. But then they let us go. I go home and lie down to sleep. When I get up, my sister and I look around the apartment in case they throw us out. We decide to go to see my friend, Damba. Her father was arrested and no one knows what happened to him. There is fresh news. They come and tell us that the ones who were doing the shootings here are leaving for Ribenishki. We want to warn them, but we do not know how. Again, panic. My heart tells me, however, that nothing is going to happen. At 8:30 we have our dinner. Last night, there were footsteps going past our window. I go to the window. A German soldier is walking. Not more than a few minutes go by before a whole group of soldiers appears. We are terribly frightened. I stand by the window the entire time and watch. The soldiers go by and come right back. I sit at the window for a long time, but my eyes close and I go to sleep on my things.

Saturday, August 2. In the morning, they call me and my sister out to work right away. There are six of us girls, and we are cleaning the same policeman's apartment. This is again in the home of my murdered friend, Mery Plagova. Everything in my heart is so heavy and painful. In addition to everything else, a police spy has been assigned to us as an observer, and this means nothing good. We clean until two

---

9. V. Gerasimova mentions the school photograph of Sheyna Gram and Mery Plagova that she had when she was writing her essay. This photograph has not been found in the JAC archives.

o'clock, and when the only thing left to do is to hang the curtains, they let us go to lunch. We have to be back in an hour. So the whole day goes. Late in the evening, the policeman meets with us and lets us go home. The night is quiet.

Sunday, August 3. Today is Tisha B'Av.[10] I have never fasted on this day or ever fasted at all. Today, however, a week after the great catastrophe, after that bloody Sunday, when so many innocent victims fell, I have decided, keeping it a secret from the authorities, of course, to fast the entire day. At 1:30, they come to see me and register me for the peat work. Mama orders me to eat something, otherwise I will not be able to work. I obey her. Then they change the list and send my little brother instead of me. He has to leave at 5:00 AM. I go to sweep out the market. Coming back from work, I sit at home. There are rumors that the Germans have been thrown back to the border. Everything is so quiet. People are moving into the ghetto. Our street has been ordered to stay where it is for the moment. The night passes quietly.

Monday, August 4. In the morning, I am ordered to sweep the market. After that, I do various household chores. There is a rumor going around that all those who have left their homes and moved to the Jewish street will have to go back. I do not know whether or not it is true. At one o'clock, there is more news. Our police officer is a dreadfully evil man. He announced to three Jewish representatives, whom he had designated himself, that if the streets were not clean enough, he would have them shot. They decided, then, that five girls would work every hour. For the moment, three girls go out to work, and we are sweeping all of Rezhitskaya Street. Russian peasants live there. No news of any kind from the Front. Then I do a few chores. There is nothing to read.

Tuesday, August 5. I get up late. The others in the house are out working. I study my Russian a bit, then go up into the attic and stack issues of the journal *Yidishe bilder* [Pictures of Jewish Life].[11] At four, I go to sweep the market. They come to our place and tell us that we have to clear out of the apartment.

In the evening, the policeman comes to look at the building. We have to get out. Our neighbors are ordered to stay. We do not know quite what to do, then. The policeman comes into our apartment and examines the furniture. They are probably going to give our apartment to someone else, as they did with the Plagovas. We are ready for it. He allows us to take everything with us. For the time being, we can stay until morning.

---

10. The ninth day of the month of Av in the Jewish calendar commemorates the destruction of both the First and Second Temples in Jerusalem; observant Jews conduct a full-day fast as an expression of mourning.
11. *Yidishe bilder* was published in Riga, Latvia from May 28, 1937, to September 22, 1939. It was a heavily illustrated weekly journal in Yiddish about Jewish life, replete with short stories, crossword puzzles, and political and cultural reporting. It was directed toward secular Jewish families. I am grateful to Lyudmila Sholokhova of the YIVO Institute for Jewish Research in New York for her assistance in locating copies of this journal.

Wednesday, August 6. The night was quiet. Excitement again in the morning. A commission comes. One man gives the order to stay, another to clear out. There are no apartments to move to. It is as though we are living up in the air. No one knows when our suffering will end! Yet another commission comes and decides that we can stay where we are. So far, so good. At four o'clock, I leave to sweep the streets. It was market day so the streets are full of litter. At seven-thirty, I come home tired and dusty. I have a wash and go to bed by eight-thirty.

Thursday, August 7. Early in the morning they call us out to scrub floors for the policeman at the station house. The policeman treats us very well. We clean in groups of four, and he orders us to come every day to do this work. There are new rumors today that they will be burning or shooting the Jews. Everyone who comes around brings news.

Friday, August 8. The peasants say that lots of airplanes flew over during the night. At seven o'clock we go to wash the floors at the police station. The boss is in a bad mood today. It rains the entire time. At twelve o'clock, they arrest the three Jewish representatives. They demand that they send thirty people out to work. Twenty-one turn up, leaving nine short. The commandant demands the nine; otherwise things will go badly. The nine have hidden themselves. We are all dreadfully worried.

Rain the entire day. They want to select nine other Jews, but he insists only on the ones from before. For the moment, the representatives are under arrest. No one knows when our sufferings will end. I feel as though the next awful thing is getting closer and closer to me.

✴✴✴

Indeed, the diary ends here. The next day, Sheyna Gram was killed along with her family.

GARF 8114, op. 1, d. 966, ll. 8–24, 26. A typewritten manuscript with handwritten corrections.

74. The death of 5,000 Jews in Rezekne (Rezhitsa)
AN ACCOUNT BY KHAIM AND YAKOV IZRAELIT
RECORDED BY B. GERTSBAKH
[1944]

More than 6,000 Jews lived in the city of Rezhitsa before the war within a total population of 25,000. The city grew rapidly before the war, with a great deal of new construction being completed. Now Rezhitsa is unrecognizable. The German bandits burned and blew up 70 percent of the stone dwellings four days before units of the Red Army arrived. The main streets are nothing but heaps of rubble.

Out of a total number of five thousand Jews remaining in Rezhitsa at the moment of the city's capture by the Germans, only three Jews survived and now live there: Motya Tager, the five-year-old son of K. Tager; fifty-seven-year-old Khaim Izraelit; and his sixteen-year-old nephew, Yakov Izraelit.

The Tager child was saved by their domestic, O. Varushkina. When Tager's father and mother were killed, she concealed him and looked after him during the three years of the fascist regime.

Khaim Izraelit and his nephew, Yakov, were saved by a Polish family in Rezhitsa by the name of Matusevich, who hid them in their attic. For almost three years they concealed the Izraelits in their home, exposing themselves to the risk of being shot. In spite of this, though, they took good care of their unwilling prisoners and brought food to the attic every day.

For the first three months following the arrival of the Germans, the Izraelits wandered from yard to yard and shed to shed in the city itself and in nearby villages, subjecting themselves hourly to the risk that they might be recognized by someone. It was only later that they were taken in by the Matusevich family and their vagabond life came to an end.

Izraelit and his nephew relate the nightmarish details of the martyring of the Jewish community of Rezhitsa, five thousand strong.

The Germans entered Rezhitsa on July 3, and the atrocities against the Jews began the very next day. On July 4, the city was blanketed with posters announcing that all Jewish men between the ages of eighteen and sixty were to assemble on the city's market square. Some 1,400 made their way there. Police surrounded the square. All those assembled were sent to prison. The next day, the butchers selected the healthiest men and shot them in the courtyard of the building where the NKVD had kept their offices in 1940–1941. Among those executed were Boris Veksler, 35, and Mitya Manteyfel, 30. Mordukh Gassel, 30, the owner of a pharmacy, poisoned himself before he could be shot. Iosel Silno, 18, ran, jumped a fence, and tried to swim across the river. But the bullets of the German fascists caught up with him, and he went to the bottom. The rest were tortured dreadfully before they were executed: they were skinned and beaten with clubs. When the turn of dental technician Kh. Izraelit came, an order from the German command to hold off on his execution intervened. He was set free, but subsequently shot as well.

The fascists were not satisfied with this. Every day, dozens of Jews were beaten to death in the prison. They were buried in the Jewish cemetery, and Jews themselves had to bury them. Often, the victims of the fascist terror were those Jews who had buried those killed before them.

So, for example, after Khaim Lotz was tortured to death in prison, a group of Jews was summoned to bury him in the cemetery. Among those wishing to take part were the father of Izraelit's nephew, Khanon Izraelit, Bash, Zuterman (who had escaped from Riga), and a butcher from Malta (the man telling the story does not remember his name). When they buried Lotz, the fascists present dealt savagely with the volunteer gravediggers. It was only after the third shot at point-blank range that Khanon Izraelit fell. Then they killed the butcher. The survivors, Bash and Zuterman, had to dig another grave and bury them.

All of July and August were marked by bloody outrages and acts of violence against Jews both in the prison and in the apartments where the Jewish women and children had been allowed to live temporarily. All the apartments were searched daily, and the fascists grabbed whatever they found of value.

In David Kukl's apartment, three German fascists raped a seventeen-year-old girl named Dora before her mother's eyes. She died the next day.

GARF f. 8114, op. 1, d. 966, l. 200–200ob. A typewritten manuscript with handwritten corrections.

V
ESTONIA

Estonia is the smallest of the three Baltic states. Situated along the southern coast of the Baltic Sea and the Gulf of Finland, Estonia had a modest Jewish population of only 4,500 on the eve of World War II. Following the Soviet takeover in August 1940, about 500 Jewish communal leaders and their families, among the 10,000 Estonian civilians targeted by the Kremlin as "class enemies," were dispatched to remote internal frontiers of the Soviet Union.

After the German invasion, the Wehrmacht met fierce resistance in the North of Estonia, permitting most of the republic's Jews to escape. The capital, Tallinn, was not occupied until September 3, 1941. By then, about a thousand Jews remained in the country. They were targeted by Einsatzkommando 1a under SS-Sturmbannführer Dr. Martin Sandberger. The Germans were assisted by men from the Estonian nationalist group Omakaitse. The killings were carried out in and around the capital, Tallinn, where half of the country's Jews lived, and in smaller towns throughout the country. Estonia was the first country to be proclaimed *judenfrei* [free of Jews], a triumph discussed at the Wannsee Conference on January 20, 1942.

The Germans used Estonia as a site for slave labor. They established twenty separate labor camps there, the largest being at Vaivara. As many as twenty thousand Jews were taken to Estonia from Theresienstadt outside Prague, from the ghettos of Vilna and Kovno in Lithuania, from Transylvania, and from Latvia. The Jews were forced to mine oil shale for the production of synthetic fuel, to dig antitank ditches (later in the war), to construct bunkers, and to perform other defense-related work.

In the fall of 1944, when the Red Army drew near to Estonia, the Germans transferred thousands of Jews to the Stutthof concentration camp just east of Danzig in northern Poland. This camp, in turn, was largely evacuated in January 1945, and its still surviving inmates (who at one time had included Jewish women from Auschwitz and many thousands of Poles) were forced to endure a death march westward. Almost all of these perished. Nearly three thousand other Jews who had been kept in the Klooga and Lagedi camps in Estonia were simply murdered.

75. In the camps of Estonia
STENOGRAPHIC RECORD OF A CONVERSATION WITH NISIM ANOLIK[1]

They took me away to Estonia on September 3, 1943. At first, we came to the Vaivara camp. The directorate for all the camps was located there. Vaivara was the main one. It was surrounded by a double barbed wire fence. Towers were stationed on each side of the camp where soldiers armed with machine guns stood guard. The Fifikon camp was eight kilometers away. The place was quite swampy; the bog came up to one's knees. They would put old men in the bog entirely naked, then beat them to death.

We were working there, clearing the forest and building a railroad. The rations were these: coffee in the morning, some watery soup during the day, and three hundred grams of bread and twenty-five grams of margarine in the evening. The camp soon came under the administration of the SS, and the work was carried out by the Todt organization.[2] Todt members would beat us while we were doing our work. Then the roll calls—the *Appele*—were set up. An Appel would go on for three or four hours, and for up to eight hours on Sundays. We worked on Sundays, and if once a month we did not work, then things got even worse. They immediately took away all our belongings and left each of us with only a shirt and a towel. Inspections were carried out daily. If contraband were found on anyone, he would be beaten. The punishment was to be left for a whole day without food. They would bind a man without a coat to a column and leave him there for several hours. There were special benches on which the man being punished was placed, bound hand and foot. One German would sit on his neck, while another would beat him, sometimes delivering 20, 50, or even 75 strokes, with a special whip fashioned from the skin of an ox and wrapped round with steel wire.

When we went out to work and someone fell one or two meters behind the rest of the group, they shot him. If they noticed anyone talking to a civilian or taking a piece of bread from him, they also shot him.

There was an incident when one of the prisoners took a shirt from one of his comrades in order to sell it to an Estonian or exchange it for bread. One German spotted this, all the bread was taken from him, and since the prisoner now had nothing

---

1. The interview with Anolik evidently took place on the premises of the JAC in Moscow, where records of conversations with witnesses to the Holocaust were kept. Another version of the conversation with Nisim Anolik appears in *The Black Book*, pp. 459–460.
2. German military construction organization named after its leader Franz Todt.

to return to the owner of the shirt, he threw himself under a train. The German laughed and said that that was what every prisoner should do. At the beginning of December, an epidemic of typhus broke out. For once the Germans met us halfway and allowed us to heat water to bathe in instead of to make soup with. Men and women had to wash together in the baths. After the bath one had to stand outside completely naked in -18 degrees centigrade. Between typhus and malnutrition, the mortality rate rose to 40 percent. During the epidemic, I lay in the so-called camp infirmary for two weeks with a temperature of 40 degrees centigrade, without food (since I could not eat bread and they gave no other nourishment). Since there was little water there, I could drink tea in only limited quantities.

Immediately after my illness I was sent out to work; many, of course, did not come back from work. On February 4, when the advance of the Red Army around Narva began, all the camps of eastern Estonia were evacuated westward, to the camps of Kiviõli and Ereda. Since the main road was occupied by the retreating armies, we were ordered to go along the seacoast. Anyone who was weak or lagging behind was thrown into the sea.

The men and women lived in separate barracks. As a rule, there were no children in the camp. All the children and elderly had been exterminated. There were two cases of children being born in the camp. They were thrown alive into a boiler before their mothers' eyes. In the Kurema camp, a German doctor named Gent summoned twenty-three old men to his office, including the well-known Warsaw gynecologist Fingergut and the Vilnius radiologist Ivanter. He ordered them to kneel, then took an axe and cut them in half, and ordered us to throw the body parts of the dead men into the fire. Upon the arrival in the camp of Dr. Botman, the chief physician for all the camps, all the patients, whenever he came into a hospital and yelled "*Achtung!*" had to fold their hands on top of their blanket. Anyone who did not manage to get their hands out in time was struck by the doctor's stick. He injected all those lying ill for more than a week with evipan, which, according to him, was supposed to cure them quickly. It was an anesthetic from which the patient, of course, died.

In Kiviõli and Ereda, they worked on shale. A second large camp was built in Ereda for the ill and weak. They were taken there from all the camps. There they were either destroyed or taken to Riga or even to Vilnius to be shot. Of course, those who were taken away were told that they were being taken to a sanitorium.

In principle, it was forbidden to bow to the Germans, yet if one did not bow to them one was beaten, and if one did, then one was also beaten. Work went on from dawn to dusk. Most people in the camp came from Kaunas and Vilno. There were also people from Prague, Berlin, Hamburg, Vienna, Riga, Brussels, and Paris. They lived separately from us, but we found out about them, since we would receive clothes with their names on them after they had been exterminated. All the prisoners wore numbers on the left side of their chests and on the right leg near the knee. If anyone wandered away during work and went a little farther, they attached a special red star on his back. He was already under suspicion. One woman left the camp and came back after two days. They hung two large boards on her with the inscription: "Hurrah, hurrah, I've come back again."

In spite of the severity of the regimen, we received German newspapers, and many had the opportunity to listen to broadcasts from Moscow while repairing the Germans' radios.

In May, a large shipment of boards arrived from the town of Klooga, and on them were written the names of Vilnius Jews. This was how we learned of the existence of a large camp. It was how I learned about my father's stay in Klooga. In May, they marked off two hundred people during roll call, including, as it happened, me and my little brother.[3] We were sent to the Klooga camp. When I arrived at the camp, my father and other friends were literally unrecognizable, they had grown so thin. It was very hard in that camp, although the everyday living conditions were a bit better than those we had experienced in the building at the former military base. There was no chance of coming into contact with the local population and in that way of obtaining some sort of food. Work was done within the camp itself. We were building concrete reinforcements, women as well as men. Women would haul fifty-kilogram sacks of cement all day long.

In June, the camps of central Estonia (Kiviõli, Ereda) were evacuated to Klooga, in the western region.

During the evacuation, some of the prisoners were shot at Ereda, some were shipped to Danzig,[4] while some made it to Klooga. In August, they selected five hundred people, loaded them into two large trucks, and sent them to another camp, Lagedi. During the journey, the Germans walked on our heads. There, we built reinforcements. On September 18, the commandant-in-chief came and said that he could not bear to see the conditions in which we were living. He decided to improve them. He said that he would transfer us to a new camp, where we would be given blankets, clothing, and decent rooms. He gave the order to issue us two kilos of bread, fat, sugar, and so on. This surprised us greatly; we did not yet understand what was going on. They loaded us into buses in groups of fifty. My father left in one of these. My brother and I were the last to go. Along the way the bus broke down, and it was only at eight-thirty in the evening that we arrived at the place where the new camp was supposed to be. I heard some Germans saying that it was already late, and that we were too late as well, since the camp was already overfilled, and that they would send us to Tallinn to spend the night in a hotel; from there they would send us back to Klooga in the morning. They brought us to Tallinn. They drove us to the "hotel," which turned out to be the Tallinn prison. We spent the night there, and in the morning they took us

---

3. For the recollections of Nisim Anolik's brother, Benyamin, see *The Black Book*, p. 462. He was interviewed by the Moscow journalist Ovady Savich, who was Ilya Ehrenburg's closest friend.
4. This refers to the Stutthof camp.

back to Klooga. Fifty Germans rode along with us from a special Sonderkommando unit of the SD. In the prison we learned that they had been keeping Jews from Paris there for a month before we arrived. After Liberation, when I was at the spot where five hundred people from Lagedi had been shot, an Estonian woman told me that a month earlier there had been another execution. It was obvious that the Parisian Jews had been shot. When we arrived at Klooga, we saw that everyone was lined up for roll call by the hundreds, and not by workplace, as was always the case with roll calls. Some of the people were squatting. They selected three hundred men from this group of people, supposedly to unload logs from a train. Orders were given in the kitchen to prepare a good lunch for the men who had been chosen. Meanwhile, the men went into the forest and erected a structure out of the logs for a bonfire. Those on the structure were the first to be shot. At 2:00 PM they took another thirty men. Five minutes later, we heard a burst of machine gun fire, and the Germans came for others. At that moment, I realized that they were shooting people out there, and wanted to get out to the bonfires as soon as possible, but my younger brother said to me that they should just shoot him where he was. Then we went down to the ground floor and hid under the first bed that we saw. Many people came after us. Then came the Germans, who shot everyone on the bunks and under them at random.

A little while later, they brought in ninety Russian women, along with a three-month-old child who was with them. They shot them all in the aisles between the bunks, and we found ourselves with corpses piled all around us. We lay there like that for two full days, and on the third day we crawled out and went up to the attic, where there were still some Jews hiding. Through a window, we saw something burning in the woods. On the fifth day, September 24, we saw our first [Soviet] officer from the Baltic fleet. Then we all went out and walked in the direction in which our comrades had been taken five days before. We saw that an eight-room house had burned down; the bones of the people who had perished were there. One of our comrades had escaped from the house. This is what he told us: when they led him out with the first party of three hundred, they made use of the logs for a bonfire a short distance into the forest. After that, a part of the group had to lie down on the structure, while thirty men were herded toward the little house. In front of the house, they lay face down on the ground, then the Germans took each man by the scruff of the neck and took him into a room. When they came into the room, it was full of bodies. They put him down on these bodies, and an SS soldier said: "Relax, kid, you're not going to live long anyway." He shot him three times and he fell, covered with blood, yet without losing consciousness. When the German left, he tried to lie down on top of the corpses. There were many women crying in the room. Many were only wounded; the wounded were trying to crawl out from under the bodies, but they could not manage it. Just before they left, the Germans began pouring gasoline into the room. He managed to jump out of a window and run into the forest, where he lived for several days. His name is Abram Moiseevich Vakhnik.

Three hundred meters from the camp, we found more bonfires assembled which had not been used at all.

Three bonfires turned up with their centers consumed but with the edges untouched. Items were scattered around them. First a layer of wood had formed, then a layer of people; they were shot in the back of the head as they were lying there. For a hundred meters around there were the bodies of people who had not died right away and who had tried to flee.

On that day, 3,000 people died in the camp, and 102 saved themselves. They shaved the heads of the women in the camp, and took a strip five centimeters wide from the men, from the forehead to the nape of the neck.

One day, a single man escaped from the camp. As a reprisal for this escape, sixty prisoners from the camp were shot.

One of the guards in the camp was called "six-legs" because he always walked about with a dog. If he saw anyone sit down to rest, he would set the dog on him, and the animal would bring the "guilty party" to him. He would beat him and take his number down to give to the camp commandant; the camp commandant would punish the "criminal" with fifty lashes.

GARF f. 8114, op. 1, d. 940, ll. 16–21. A typewritten manuscript with handwritten corrections.

VI
THE CRIMEA

At the outset of the war, the Crimea was a territorial unit of the Russian Soviet Federated Socialist Republic.[1] A large proportion of the peninsula's Jews, who numbered over 40,000, were able to escape before the Germans reached the Crimea in October and November 1941. Simferopol had a Jewish population of 20,000, but although most of the city's Jews escaped, Jewish refugees from the Ukrainian cities of Kherson and Dnepropetrovsk, and from collective farms in the Larindorf and Fraydorf Jewish National Districts,[2] had sought refuge there, bringing the Jewish population of Simferopol to 13,000 by the time it was occupied by the Germans on November 1. They were all quickly singled out for murder by Einsatzgruppen D under the leadership of Otto Ohlendorf.

But in the Crimea the Germans faced an unexpected challenge to their racial and ethnic assumptions. The Crimea was the historic home to two small Jewish ethnic groups, the Karaites and the Krimchaks. When Ohlendorf happened upon their communities, he duly inquired to his superiors in Berlin about their status as Jews. He needed to know if they should be killed.

---

1. In 1954 Nikita Khrushchev transferred control of the Crimea to Ukraine.
2. As far back as 1795, under Catherine the Great, Jews had been encouraged to establish farms in the Crimea. Throughout the nineteenth century as well, there were attempts to organize Jewish agricultural colonies there. The Bolsheviks also tried to turn parts of Northern Crimea into a Jewish agrarian region in the 1920s and 1930s, with the assistance of the American Jewish Joint Distribution Committee in New York; at the height of this project, as many as 20,000 Jews inhabited these colonies. See Yehuda Bauer, *My Brother's Keeper: A History of the American Jewish Joint Distribution Committee, 1929-1939* (Philadelphia, 1974), pp. 57-104 for a history of the Agro-Joint project. In 1944 all places with Yiddish names received new names, so Larindorf became Pervomayskoe and Fraydorf became Novosyolovskoe.

The Karaites were descended from a group who first emerged in the eighth century. One principal doctrine of their faith is the denial of the oral tradition, of the body of Jewish law associated with the Talmud, and of rabbinical authority. But they do accept earlier aspects of Jewish law and tradition. By the twentieth century, small Karaite communities resided in the Crimea, Turkey, Poland, Lithuania, and Palestine. Following the promulgation of the Nuremberg Laws in 1935, Karaites living in Berlin appealed to the German authorities to be exempt from their onerous restrictions on Jewish participation in civic life. The German Ministry of the Interior ruled in January 1939 that the Karaites "did not belong to the Jewish religious community" and that their "racial psychology" was not Jewish.[3] This ruling was extended to the Crimea, sparing the Karaites, who numbered no more than ten thousand in all of the Soviet Union, although two hundred had already been murdered at Babi Yar.[4]

The Krimchaks were not so fortunate. They could date their emergence as a distinct sect within the Jewish community to the second century BCE when Jews first settled in the Crimean peninsula. Over the years they adopted customs of their Crimean Tatar neighbors and developed a recognizable Crimean Tatar dialect. The Germans found about 7,000 Krimchaks in the Crimea, residing primarily in Simferopol, Karasubazar (Belogorsk), Bakhchisaray, Yevpatoria, Feodosia, and Kerch. Most were rounded up and killed along with the other Jews. By April 1942, the Germans confidently declared the Crimea *judenrein* [rid of Jews]. In all, they murdered about 25,000 Ashkenazi Jews and Krimchaks there. Of the Krimchaks, about 1,500 managed to elude the Germans and their supporters, but the other 5,500 perished.

76. Stenographic record of a conversation with Simferopol resident Yevsei Yefimovich Gopshteyn[5]
RECORDED BY D. BRICHINSKY
AUGUST 16–17, 1944

The Germans entered Simferopol on the morning of November 2, 1941. They took over the medical school building on Vokzalnaya Street for their headquarters, while the population of the city center learned about it from people who lived on the outskirts and who, for one reason or another, began to appear in various parts of town. Around nine or ten in the morning on November 2, the first Germans began appearing in the city.

The first thing that the inhabitants paid attention to was how overly dressed they were: they were all closely shaven, smartly dressed in clean new uniforms, as though they had come out on parade and had not just arrived from Perekop.[6] It turned out

---

3. *Encyclopedia Judaica*, vol. 10 (Jerusalem, 1971), p. 775.
4. See *Encyclopedia of the Holocaust*, vol. 2 (New York, 1990), p. 786.
5. An abridged and altered version of this document appeared in *The Black Book*, pp. 324–327.
6. Perekop Isthmus links the Crimean Peninsula with the mainland.

that units from the rear had been dispatched, so that the inhabitants of the city would get a particular impression. This was talked about in town for a long time. They said: "They've been fighting and fighting, and just look how clean and neat they are." So in the first few hours of November 2, they spread out over the city, began racing about on motorcycles because of some orders or other; one felt that they were the masters of the place. Road signs began to appear in the central districts. The day was a sunny one, the weather not yet really autumn-like. It was merely cool, and the part of the population that was not working was scattered along the streets. There were groups of people on street corners. People who understood German struck up conversations with the soldiers. The Jewish community began to talk.

I came out of my building around noon, walked down the city's main streets, and glanced down Pushkin Street. I came upon a crowd outside the theater, and when I got closer, I could see that the first public order had been posted in three languages: Russian, Ukrainian, and German.

A decree hung on a wall; it had three parallel columns, framed by a bright red border. It was quite obvious that several dozen people in the crowd could not read the order at all, so someone began to read it aloud in a booming voice, and if I did not get everything, I grasped the gist of it straight away. It must be said that the decree was fairly long and that it immediately made a frightful, disheartening impression. One felt that the life of Simferopol (until then, one did not have this feeling) had been severed with an axe. The whole tone of life, how people of different nationalities got along with each other, the whole atmosphere, had been friendly. Simferopol was a multiethnic city. According to the census, fifty different nationalities were represented in the Crimea, among only 1,126,800 inhabitants; an enormous number of nationalities for a comparatively small number of people. People lived together like a family, always friendly; ethnic tension was entirely absent. This decree, however, changed the atmosphere entirely. The word "Jew" was not used in the decree, but rather "kikes."

The first decree said that the German army had entered the territory of the Crimea. As best I can recall, it said that the German army had come not as conquerors, not to seize territory, but to fight against kikes and Bolsheviks. Half of the decree was given over to the "kikes"; The word "kike," in fact, was declined in every possible form: "the kikes," "to the kikes," "about the kikes."[7]

Throughout the decree, one got the feeling that something new was happening. I had a sick feeling about it. I felt this as a Jew, and others felt that the life of Simferopol was beginning to move in an unhealthy direction. When the contents of the decree became clear, hardly anyone said anything; the majority preferred to keep silent. The order mentioned prisoners of war: one was not to give them shelter. Anyone concealing a POW would answer for it before the law. I stopped listening to the

---

7. In Russian, the word *zhid,* or kike, would decline into *zhidy; zhidam; zhidakh;* etc.

decree and began to look at the faces in the crowd. They formed a motley group: Armenians, Tatars, Jews, and Russians. I was wondering how the crowd would react, how it would take this order, the basic idea of it. I wanted to see if one would meet with any signs of acceptance, if it would be possible to see it on the faces of the inhabitants, and I must say that I believed it then and believe it now when I tell you that the mood was not favorable to the decree. People stood with bowed heads, intent faces, furrowed brows. It was evident, as far as I could see around me, that there was no acceptance. Publishing this decree, they had counted on animal instincts, on finding the old leaven, and I have to say that in the first moments I did not see this. The crowd was huge, silent, not exchanging any impressions. That was my first impression of the Germans' arrival in the city. That was the first decree.

I remember something that drew attention to itself in this first decree: the fact that kikes were to be brought in to do physical labor—filling in foundation pits, picking up rubbish, taking away corpses, both German and ours alike—this is what the Jews were supposed to be used for. The responsibility for bringing in the Jews was laid on the city fathers, who were appointed by the German command and partly chosen by the local inhabitants. Kikes were to be brought in for all physical jobs.

Around November 8, huge posters announcing the creation of a Jewish Committee were placed in the streets: "By order of the German commander, a Jewish Committee [sic, *judenrat*] of 13 people has been created." As for the functions of this committee, what it was supposed to do, whether or not it would represent the interests of the Jewish people—nothing was said about either its tasks or its functions. It was announced that such-and-such people had been selected to make up the committee, and that so-and-so had been elected chairman. None of them survived, since they perished along with everyone else.

Several days after this committee was set up, an order appeared. The order was written by hand and, it must be said, by a large number of Jewish volunteers who surrounded the Jewish Committee, including members of the intelligentsia—lawyers and engineers. One had the feeling that they had united around the Jewish Committee as a center that they could hold on to. They had joined the Jewish Committee in order to help with the work.

The makeup of the Jewish Committee was rather simple and colorless. I will say a few words about how it was recruited. There was a man in Simferopol who lacked a definite profession. His name was Zeltser. Now he was working in a housing cooperative. Zeltser was given the task of forming the Jewish Committee by the German command. What led him to do it? I think that Zeltser had had some contact with the German command, and that was why they chose him.

Either the Germans arrived with a large number of addresses from émigrés, or they obtained them from the native population. However it was, the political apparatus that came along with the command had the addresses of the necessary people.

Maybe that was how they found Zeltser and handed him the task of organizing the Jewish Committee. Maybe they found him in another way; a man would go to the headquarters for all sorts of reasons.

There were many among the Germans who spoke fluent Russian. Maybe Zeltser was the first to get in touch with them, as he came from the little world of small-time speculators and bookkeepers. I have already said that the makeup of the committee was simple and colorless, and by its level of culture not up to the role for which it had been put forward. This was what prompted the Jewish intelligentsia to join in with them, so as to be able to help if need be. This intelligentsia rewrote the announcements, in spite of the demand for them to be distributed in huge quantities. Whenever it was necessary, they would write out announcements, and Jewish youngsters would go throughout the city with pots of glue to post them. Within a few hours, the German orders were displayed all over town. For example, the decree concerning cattle. It was written: "The entire Jewish population, by order of the German command, is to deliver information concerning all cows and sheep." Or: "The entire Jewish population is required to place Persian rugs at the disposal of the German command. Jewish inhabitants are required to deliver three thousand blankets, mattresses, and sets of linen"; these were gathered for the hospital. These demands began to be accompanied by verbal orders, as well. I, like a large portion of the intelligentsia, stopped by the Jewish Committee. There was nothing to do, it was not functioning, but we needed to be clear about the situation. I wanted to know what was in the air. I, like many others, went around, chatted with people, and was witness to or else learned from members of the committee about the demands that were being made and the outrages of the German command.

There were demands such as these: to deliver nine lengths of blue woolen fabric to the German command. A polizeimeister came by while I was there and said that forty place settings and as many tablecloths and napkins would have to be delivered to such and such an address by that evening. It turned out that General [Erich von] Manstein, who had just taken the Crimea, was giving a banquet for the senior officers, and that they needed a dining room service. Where was the Jewish Committee supposed to find forty place settings that had to be identical as well? They turned to Balaban, the director of the local mental hospital; he was a Jew with a large quantity of pots and pans. In my presence they wrote a note asking him to come to the committee's aid and dispatched it with two men. The envoys left, I left as well, and the next day (one was allowed to be out on the street only until 5:00 PM) I learned that the service and the linen had been turned over by Dr. Balaban.

And there were orders to the effect that the Jewish population would have to hand over sweaters, jerseys, scarves, and mittens. It was getting to be winter, and they were beginning to feel it necessary to get ready. They began to take mittens off the hands of passersby in the streets, and if underneath a mitten there turned out to be a watch, then they would quite calmly take the watch as well. I was told of an incident where they took an engineer's gloves and watch at the very beginning of winter, when he was already working in the service of some German organization. After they took his gloves, he showed them his identity card with a swastika on it, and they immediately returned the gloves and the watch.

On November 12, they began inspecting apartments: they would come into the courtyards and ask where the Jews were living. This was the first order of business. They would go from building to building, from apartment to apartment, and begin their first experiments in looting.

Initially it was announced that civilians would be allowed to move about on the streets until 5:00 PM, and then that all movement would be halted.

So the Germans would go from apartment to apartment, and if there were Jews in one, then they would go up to things without the slightest inhibition and begin rummaging through everything: wardrobes, trunks, buffets, cupboards. They arrive, the family is sitting at tea. Sugar was rationed at the time. The sugar bowl is sitting there with its finely cut cubes and a German comes up and pours the contents into his pocket. If he finds a small jar of jam or butter—neither one an article that was particularly easy to find—he takes it, just as they always took potatoes whenever they could. These initial steps taken during the first week were part of the general policy of proceeding from robbery to robbery. At the same time, orders were posted in the name of the German command that looting was forbidden. On the one hand, it was forbidden, and on the other, it was being carried out officially. The Germans were committing the lowest acts of banditry: they began with potatoes, sugar and small provisions, and then moved on to women's blouses, dresses, and undergarments, and shipped all of it to Germany. Shoes and women's clothing all went to Germany. I will not even mention children's things; they took everything.

Beginning on November 12, the Jewish inhabitants were made to wear armbands with a star on both arms. I wore them myself. I wore them for the first few days, and then stopped. The occupation authorities noticed that people were no longer wearing the armbands and demanded absolute obedience to the order.

I am walking down Soviet Street. German soldiers are walking along, cracking sunflower seeds, laughing among themselves, and talking. (I was wearing a decent winter coat.) As they go by, they say: "It would be good to take that coat off him." It was daylight. Once they came to my home around one in the afternoon; I would go out so as not to wreck my nerves waiting around for my fate and to avoid any scenes. If they came into the apartment, then they began rifling through things. I had nothing that would be of value to them: my library contained only scholarly books and could not be of any attraction to them. There was no food in the place and my family had left in August.

I was working as an economist in the NKKKh (People's Commissariat of Communal Services). In addition to that I was a researcher, and working in literature as a compiler of bibliographies.

I had almost no provisions. There was a pood [thirty-six pounds] or so of flour, a pood and a half of potatoes, and one bottle of sunflower oil.

I was at home one Sunday. There was a knock at the door and I opened it to find two soldiers. I said in German: "What do you want?" (I am not a coward, it might have been that there was serious danger to deal with.) When he made as if to enter, I pushed his arm aside and asked him severely: "What do you want in my apartment?" "We want to take a look." What was there to look at? Nothing. One of them was young and clearly inexperienced; he had not been hardened yet. The other was a bit older. The young man said: "We're looking for a room." Even though it was forbidden to live in apartments, they were looking to set themselves up in a family home. I said: "I live alone. If that doesn't suit you, then you need to talk to your headquarters. If you need an apartment, there's a vacant one, and it's furnished besides, where the State Bank inspector lived. Apart from that, I want to remind you that there are orders posted from the commandant saying that looting is forbidden. One should talk to me like an educated man, otherwise I'll grab you by the collar." They apologized, clicked their heels, and went out. Just for show, they looked through the room at the empty apartment, excused themselves, and left. A few days later, when it was dark, I hung a blanket over the window because my lamp was burning. I heard the characteristic rap of knuckles on the door. "What do you want?" "Open up." I open up, and there is a Gestapo agent standing there. "Any Jews living here?" He goes into the first, then into the second room. "Bring up the light." I climbed up to take down the shutters and began to remove the blanket, and made the light brighter. He looked around the first room; the first thing that he paid attention to was the abundance of books. Books on the tables, on the couch, on the chairs. "Your profession?" I say: "Economist. I work in literature as well." "You wrote all this?" The question seemed strange, since, judging by the look of him, he ought to have been educated. I was inwardly surprised, and said with a smile: "No, that would be too much for one person." I said that I work in printing. He puttered about for a few minutes, touching books protected by dust jackets, shrugged, and left.

Approximately a week later, on the eighteenth, the Jewish Committee issued a decree which, making reference to orders from the German command, announced the registration of the Jewish population. It was explained that the adults would appear alone, and that they would provide information about the children. The committee was located on Fountain Square, opposite the city laboratory. There was a line of Jewish people there to register, and I went, too.

This was the information required for registration: name, patronymic, surname, address, age, and profession. I do not remember whether or not there was anything else. A special mark was made by hand on our passports. No one knew the purpose of this registration—neither the Jewish community nor the Jewish Committee.

The fact that they asked us for our professions made us think that they wanted to rebuild the work force. The Jewish population lived under this impression until December 8.

Demands for more manpower came to the committee every day. An endless number of people came around. Soldiers and officers would come demanding young, healthy women for cleaning offices and buildings, or to assign so many dozens of men for manual labor. There was always a crowd of people pushing and shoving there. Besides that, I recall that the Jewish population made obligatory appearances at the committee office. Approximately twelve thousand people were registered and there was always an enormous crowd around the committee building.

There came a demand to hand over a dozen and half or two dozen women. Someone would go out and choose: "You, you, come with me." He would bring them into the office and say: "Here are your fifteen or twenty." They took people to do cleaning, to do kitchen work, to clear obstructions from the streets. All of Sevastopolskaya Street looked like one enormous dump. As a result of air raids, the streets were filled with stones for three or four days. I did not see any bodies because they had all been cleared away, but there was a huge number of horses scattered about.

I was walking down Rosa Luxemburg Street, where the German headquarters were. A German was standing there, and as I walked by, he said: "Go on in." I looked at him in confusion and asked: "What for?" "They'll tell you inside." I go inside. I meet one of them (a local German) who had hidden from deportation in his time, as many had managed to do, and who had now turned up in the role of one of those in charge. It turns out that they needed to move some furniture from one room to another, so I had to help out.

When they saw that the Jewish community was poor—they had come from Warsaw, where the Jewish population was wealthy—they asked where the rich Jews were. They told them: "There aren't any here." Show us, they would say in different languages. The Germans did not believe the Jewish Committee, while the Jews were surprised at what a false image the Germans had of the Jewish population. Some time passed, and they said: "We'll find them ourselves." They ordered Gurvich to go with them and point out those who were the most affluent. They planned to rob them. They put him in a car, and he remembered thinking where he should take them when he thought of a lawyer—they always make a good living. His name was Dovgalevsky. So he took them to his place.

So Jewish life proceeded. Little by little, the Germans acquired a taste for the looting of the Jewish community. They went to see Dr. Kazas and saw a pair of Zeiss binoculars and just took them.

Fidlon the bookkeeper lived here. On November 12, two Germans came and asked where the Jew lived. When they turned up at his place and proposed that he hand over things, he protested. They said: "You've got some gold here." They pulled out a dagger and threatened him. Whether he handed the things over himself or whether they took them themselves, who can say.

Life went more or less like this until the first days of December.

After the registration process, which went on for two to four days, the German command demanded that the Jewish Committee work up a summary of the materials, and gave them several days to do it. I was in charge of the UNKhU (National Economy Accounting Directorate) section of the city administration, with nine years of experience. In fact, I worked in the field of city management, not demographics. I wanted to help the committee, but they beat me to it, as it were, and did the work for me.

There was a man working at Gosplan [the State Plan Bureau], a half-bookkeeper, half-economist named Nisselovich. He wanted to help the committee and worked a great deal for it. He never let a job go by and was significantly younger, and this Nisselovich took on materials for processing. He was consulted on several questions. For this reason, he had to deal with the auxiliary labor pool, with people who, though educated, did not know anything about statistics. The compilation of the summary dragged on, and every day someone was coming from the command to demand this summary. The compilation of the summary continued to be delayed, and it was demanded with threats.

I wrote out the results for myself. The results were these: the whole Jewish population numbered fourteen thousand, including fifteen hundred or so from the Krimchak population. This was not the previous Jewish population of Simferopol, because a part of it had been evacuated from Simferopol and other cities during the period of military action, and also because refugees from Kherson and Dnepropetrovsk had settled here; naturally, they had settled for the most part in Simferopol. The populations of the Jewish villages of the Fraydorf and Larindorf districts and of Yevpatoria flooded into Simferopol; they all remained in Simferopol because their situation was so uncertain. They thought that here they would be in their element, in the thick of a Jewish community, so as a result of this process, we reached a population of about fourteen thousand.

I do not know how many there were according to the census of 1939 because that data had not yet been published. Part of the local population was here, along with some from adjoining districts.

On December 7, a Krimchak neighbor, an old woman whose son was in the Red Army and whose daughter-in-law worked in a cooperative came by. This woman, who was barely literate, got along well with me and in moments of crisis would come to ask for advice. Here is what was on her mind: It turned out that an order had come down from the Jewish Committee, on the basis of a decree from the German command, stating that on December 8, and no later than the ninth, the whole Krimchak population was to gather at an assembly point that had been designated on Gelvig Square, where the Pedagogical Institute dormitories were located. The old lady was crying and said: "It'll be the death of us all, no two ways about it." I tried to console her. No one had been discussing this. I did not believe in the possibility of mass extermination.

Professor Karasik of the University of Vienna, a specialist in ethnic studies, had come here along with the German army. I knew of his presence from my connections with the library. The librarians were good friends of mine, and I learned from them that a certain job was being done for him in the Central Library of the Pedagogical Institute. I went to see them and found out that they were doing the work in the three libraries. They were working on finding literature. I did not know what the substance of his research was, but I knew what the purpose of the library was; his mission, however, was obviously not to become familiar with the population in the given region. When the rumor went around, I explained to her that there could not possibly be any extermination in the offing, that he was perhaps doing some scientific research. I thought that he was taking measurements of skulls. The Krimchaks were undoubtedly Jews, but they spoke a different language, kept Tatar and mixed customs, and prayed in synagogues in ancient Hebrew. Their everyday speech was Tatar. The Krimchak savant Lekhnu had lived in Karasubazar in the seventeenth century.

The Karaites also spoke the Tatar language. The Karaite language is the language of the Crimean Tatars.

Persian, Turkish, or Arabic were accepted in the Khan's court in 1883[8] as everyday languages. The courtiers spoke them, and this could not have failed to have an impact on the milieu of Bakhchisaray.

In the south there were a large number of Greeks and Armenians. The language of the Karaites used to be much purer; in its phonetics, phraseology, and other elements, it was close to the Nogay language. The Karaites are a mixture of Khazars and Jews, but they are not Jews.[9]

I listened to these rumors and considered for my part that the extermination of a national group of one and a half thousand people could not happen. Exterminate them? What for? I could not get my mind around it.

The next day, my neighbor comes by and says: "There's been an order to take warm things, warm clothing, and food for eight days and meet at an assembly point." The old lady continued: "This is the end. We won't see each other again."

A kind of shadow began to fall over me as well. I began to reflect on things, to connect one thing with another. There was cannibalism in the air, aimed at the kikes.

My neighbor said goodbye and left. This was on the evening of December 8.

Then it turned out that a similar order was directed at the entire Jewish population: to appear on December 9 and 10 at the student dormitory on Hospital Square, at the medical institute dormitory across from Lenin Park, or the district Party offices on Gogol Street (no. 14); these were the assembly points. We had until December 10 or 11 to present ourselves.

---

8. The Crimean Khanate existed until 1783.
9. The Karaites, in fact, are regarded as a sect within the Jewish people; a sizable community resides in Israel.

But there had been no printed or posted announcements at all for the Karaite or the Jewish population. They knew each other well. I went to the Jewish Committee. I could find out what others could not. We had many sore points, and there were any number of people in the committee offices who had stories to tell about looting. I learned that the order to appear at the assembly points with warm clothing and food was authentic. On December 9, I went along to find out, and they told me that it was true, that such an order had been received from the German commandant, and that it was necessary to appear. A whole series of rumors had already made its way around the city.

As of December 10 there were five variations, and they could be summed up as follows:

1) that the Jewish community was to be sent out in front of the German army advancing on Sevastopol to act as a shield;
2) that they were being sent to work in Bessarabia;
3) that they were to be sent to farms in the Fraydorf and Larindorf Districts, since the winter crops had not yet been sown—in a word, they would be sent to work;
4) that every Jew in the USSR would be sent to the Front;
5) and finally, that they would all be exterminated.

These five options fermented in the minds of the Jewish and Russian populations alike.

The Russians lived on the outskirts and had close connections with POWs, or else they were people who were looking for work: railroad or factory workers. (Some factories had survived and the railroad depot was still functioning.) The people's whole way of life was drawn into the process of Germanization. Which way was the right way, who could tell?

I did not believe that there would be a mass slaughter.

On the morning of December 10, a rumor went about that the need to assemble had been cancelled. My sister lived apart from us. She was a chemist in the city laboratory, had a college education, and spoke German. We had agreed to go together. I waited for her on the morning of December 10, but she was late in arriving. She turned up around eleven or twelve and said that there were rumors in town that the order had been cancelled, and that she had heard them from her neighbor and from someone else besides. She decided that she would have to get the information first-hand, and went to the Gestapo post on Hospital Square. She went there to find out whether or not it would be necessary to appear, and they jumped on her shouting (she was not entirely fluent in German) that the order had not yet been cancelled. She said that there ought to be an order, that there had not yet been one, and that the proposal that everyone should appear was only a rumor. It was with this that she came to my place.

We decided that we would lose nothing if we went the next day; perhaps things really would change. So, the tenth went by, the eleventh—the last day for appearing—was upon us.

The night before the eleventh was a very difficult one; our nerves were stretched to the breaking point, some sort of catastrophe was in the air, a feeling that nothing good was in the offing, not even being sent to work, at best to the Fraydorf District (Crimean ASSR),[10] at worst to Bessarabia. One could not even conceive that they would send us to the Front ahead of their own forces or deport us from the USSR. I banished from my mind all thought of being shot. People gathered with children and the elderly. Everyone who was healthy had gone into the army; everyone who was honorable and of good conscience had left for the army.

I say that when I read the newspaper *Red Crimea* in the summer, it had always reported very little, and the central newspapers reached us very rarely, because they were so hard to obtain. If light was thrown on something, then it was in *Pravda* or *Izvestia*; in *Red Crimea*, the light was only a dim one. The central papers were, however, rarely accessible. So little was known about what the Germans, who had already occupied our territory, were doing.

As I saw it, it was undoubtedly true that exaggeration was politically necessary to create a certain mood in the masses, but that some colors had been laid on a bit thick.

It seemed clear that the outlying areas knew more from their contact with the Germans, or through work. Whichever of the five variants one took, all of them threatened catastrophe. I was almost sixty at the time, my sister around forty-five; she was not fit for physical labor. I was almost sixty; what sort of a worker would I make in the absence of warm clothing in the midst of an agricultural steppe area? We had no warm things at all, so we would not last long.

I knew the situation in our districts, particularly those in the steppe, and I had been in the villages in 1931. As an economist and planner, I had had occasion to give reports at meetings to the District Executive Committee, and knew that there would be nothing better there than a heap of straw on a dirt floor. I made up my mind not to go, and to not let my sister go, either. For myself, I had noted the possibility of staying with a friend. In the past, I had done this man a great favor and had done him a number of smaller favors, as well, and felt justified in thinking that he would not refuse to help.

The ethnic makeup of our building was quite varied: Russians, Jews, Tatars in its twenty apartments. I had lived in the building for twenty-eight years, and everyone got on well with me. I went to see this man on December 11, and told him my plans and hopes. "All right, come along." I said: "Today at two o'clock, I'll come to your place with a bed. You'll have to put me up for a while. For how long, I don't know."

---

10. The Crimean Autonomous Soviet Socialist Republic (ASSR) became the Crimean Region in 1944.

We agreed on it. Now I had to think about my sister. She had a separate group of friends from among the chemists. I decided that when she came, I would tell her about my proposal, and after that would go to the secure apartment.

My wife had left with our son's family. He is a pilot, three times decorated. His wife is a young professor, a Russian; they have a mixed marriage. My wife was a doctor practicing on the south coast. In August, everyone received an order to leave Simeiz, and so my wife, our daughter-in-law, and our two granddaughters left. Our daughter-in-law had some document from the army giving her the right to expect a welcome in the town of Turtkul, since our son was based there. He had been in the army before the mobilization, and then received his orders on August 19; my wife, my daughter-in-law, and the two grandchildren left.

I decided that I would leave the apartment. There was no furniture, none of our belongings. We had good neighbors, though, who were kind to us at a difficult time. Leaving my home, I made an official request that it be handed over to this close friend, a specialist, a Russian. I wrote that the apartment belonged to a Russian.

The mayor came to say goodbye and to remind me about the order, because someone from the police was going around the neighborhood giving orders to keep track of whether or not people had left. This was around midday. My sister was not there. I was already beginning to feel the need to move quickly because it would be necessary to go and collect her in order to not to violate the deadline. The mayor came by. I explained to him what I had in mind. He countersigned, saying that the apartment belonged to a Russian. I gave him a farewell kiss and went to my sister's place, but did not find her at home. When I asked after her, it turned out that the Russian auxiliary police had gone from house to house, apartment to apartment on Arkhivnaya Street on the tenth and eleventh and had rounded up the entire Jewish population. That meant that she had been detained, that was why she had not come. I could not wait, I had to hurry. I went out with a small suitcase containing two changes of underwear and a bar of soap. I took a pillow and blankets, locked the apartment, and put the key in my pocket. I intended to hand the key over to the man who would be living there next.

It was around one in the afternoon. I no longer had the time to go in search of my sister, and was forced to go where I was intending to go: to hide from the Germans. I could not take anything on that day. The next day, at my request, the individual who was hiding me made the rounds of the assembly points with the intention of making contact with my sister, but these attempts came to nothing because he did not manage to find her.

During the final hours designated for assembling, there were lines of Jews heading for the assembly points with suitcases in their hands, and, in rare cases, on carts. A group of residents took a cart from our building and loaded it with bundles, suitcases, and bedrolls until it would accept no more, and off they went. There were youngsters and small children, and elderly people moving along. It was difficult to watch. I remember the faces. I was looking at the Russian people as well, the impression was a painful one.

On the twelfth, after the last attempts to find my sister had been made at my request, I was told by people that they had been to Gogol Street (where the Regional Party Committee offices were) and to the Medical Institute building, but that they had not come upon my sister.

There were seven or eight bodies hanging here and there in the city. In the neighborhood of the city garden on Leninskaya Street, the body of an old man was hanging with a sign around his neck—"For not appearing on time."

I did not find my sister on the twelfth. On the thirteenth, the same. But on the thirteenth, someone passed along a note from her which had been delivered through a Jewish woman who had been released by the Germans; they had made a curious notation on her passport: "*Wird nicht umgebracht*" (Not to be killed, or something to that effect).

There was a professor Klepinin, who had made a number of soil maps, and who was married to one of the daughters in the Frig family. There were five sisters in the Frig family and all of them were married to Russians. One sister was married to Bobrovsky, another to Klepinin. Two or three went to the assembly points and appeared on time. They said that they were married to Russians, and someone made notations in their passports as well: "Not to be killed."

Through her, my sister passed on a note to my friends in which she asked about me. I still have this note. It was the last one that I received from her. It was along with this information, by the way, that I received the news of the bodies hanging in the streets. I also heard that Dr. Rusinov had tried to hang himself on the hospital grounds, not wishing to make his wife a witness to this act. They took him out of the noose, and his medical colleagues wrote a declaration on the spot, in the name of the German commander, that he was not to be arrested. They brought him around, but then the Germans came for him and took him away.

After that, my connection with the outside world was broken. I began to sit waiting to see what to do.

In the first days following the assembly, one of the Germans living in this building—who had contact with the people living in it and with the individual with whom I was staying—told how he had witnessed a mass execution of Jews in Bucharest and that he had a friend there, a doctor in the Romanian army, whom he had taken away either from his home or from the place of execution. He said all of this under the influence of the mood that the city was in, which naturally had an indirect effect on everyone else. This German was in charge of the automobile section of a garage, and his driver, who was also a friend of his, was a fascist. He made him hand over the car, loaded a Jewish doctor and his family into it, then drove them, where I do not remember, but saved them from execution. The thought occurred to me that something of this sort could happen here. I am talking about what was happening in town.

It would not suffice to say that the atmosphere was heavy. I felt as though I would go out of my mind, there was such a great weight on me. One could not even get one's mind around it, to understand the monstrous intentions of the German command concerning the extermination of twelve thousand Jews. The town, the population, were being terrorized. People were simply afraid to go out on the street, including Russians. It seemed as though even the air had changed and was now saturated with horror and blood. In a word, all of this produced a painful impression on all the nationalities.

In the first days after the order to assemble, many tried to evade coming and so were hanged for it.

After this, roundups were carried out only in the streets. At first, the field gendarmerie went into action, stopping pedestrians in the streets and demanding that they show their passports. It goes without saying that many were stopped, and not only Jews. These were the first attempts at combing through the population on the streets of the town. They were carried out fairly often, at short intervals, in separate neighborhoods and streets, at different times of the day. So it went throughout December of 1941. But at the beginning of January 1942, after the fifth, they carried out the first mass roundup among the town's population as a whole. The city was surrounded block by block, neighborhood by neighborhood; everywhere there were sentries directing the inhabitants to designated points. Starting at the break of day, they made the rounds from building to building, from apartment to apartment. There was a complete, massive, simultaneous check of the population and a search for weapons. This was the first check of the whole population, and there would be five more to endure. It was all very painful.

The individual who was hiding me would leave the building. Trying to remain unnoticed, I shut the window to my room. The window looked out onto the street, and the common door from the room led into a corridor. The door was an old-fashioned one, strong, massive, with a good American lock. I tried to block up the keyhole.

Every time that my landlord went out, I closed the keyhole with the latch so that it would be impossible for anyone to look into the room. There was a table by the window where I read or wrote. So that if I were to look out from there, I would be in the background of the window. The lower window was covered over with plywood.

I already knew that a roundup was underway in the city, and that the Germans could well come here. We did not know what was happening or what was being done, whether they were checking everyone or simply taking people at random. I was on the lookout; there was no way out. Precautionary measures were called for. I could not think about it because any movement had been made difficult. There was no possibility of going up into the attic or down into the cellar. I had no idea of where they might search. I collected all my strength of will to maintain my equilibrium because keeping my head depended on it.

Around nine o'clock, I knew from the unusual steps that the Germans had arrived. I am used to sorting out all kinds of sounds and all sorts of footsteps. There was no doubt that the Germans had entered the building. The local inhabitants spoke a bit of German. It was a large building, there were lots of rooms in it, and I could tell from the steps that they were coming to our room. They came into the adjoining room, then up to my door. There was a furious knocking. I did not react at all. The knocking was repeated. I decided to keep silent. What would happen next? I heard the voice of a German asking, "Who lives in this room?" A Russian woman, a lonely schoolteacher, answered that no one lived there. The residents of the building who had a command of German explained the situation, and then the German who lived in our building joined in the conversation. Obviously, he was not a bad person. He was an innkeeper by profession from a town on the Rhine, and this Willi was a good-hearted sort. The officer was satisfied with his answer, but still wanted to get into the room. They made an attempt to open the door, but the door was massive, strong, with an American lock; they pushed hard against the door, but it did not give way. And suddenly, I heard the most awful thing of all, a dog alongside them scratching. The officer, as it turned out, had come with a German shepherd. You understand, of course, that a dog can smell things through a door, and one way or another the officer realized that there was someone behind the door. What happened here I can only call a miracle. One of the residents of the building had a dog, an enormous, young, joyful purebred. Healthy and strong, she would run up and down the street all day long, playing with children and passersby, and would come home only in the evening. At the last moment, when the decisive knock on the door came, the neighbor's dog was by some miracle in the apartment—perhaps she had been nearby, perhaps someone had called her—either way, there began such a commotion between the two dogs that the German feared for the safety of his own animal. Willi and the officer rushed to separate the two dogs. The officer was afraid to let his dog out of his hands, while the soldier could not drag the other one away. In the end, though, he did manage to pull her a certain distance away.

After this room, there was only one more left on this side, and that was the room in which German anti-aircraft gunners took their meals. We knew that groups of Germans stopped there. A few moments passed, they left, and everything calmed down. That was the first roundup.

The Germans did not discuss the fate of the Jews with the local inhabitants. At first they had little contact with the population; there were obstacles. Of course, the inhabitants could not be uninterested, and rumors about what had happened began to get about in the town, at first on the outskirts, then in the center. They reached me as well. Something vague, the idea of a catastrophe or mass extermination, began to penetrate into people's minds and to become fixed there.

There was a rumor of how a group of women that was being led out of the building at 14 Gogol Street had come out with their hands up, and that the sentries had taken their purses away from them at the door. It was also said that another group was let go with suitcases in their hands, and that still another had been wiped out; that they had been led out empty-handed, with their arms above their heads.

Mass shootings were taking place near Kurman. They said that POWs were digging the mass graves. The shootings were being done with submachine guns. Then the story was that the shooting was happening eight kilometers away, but I did not manage to find out in which direction. Just by connecting separate sources in this way, I think that it was on the Feodosia highway, by the anti-tank ditch. Such is the scanty information that came from the residents of the town.

In March, rumors began reaching us that individuals in mixed marriages who had been set free, like the widow Klepinina and others, would also be summoned to the assembly points. Individuals were going about town establishing which marriages were mixed and identifying the children of these marriages.

Mikhaylov, a young professor, was here with his Jewish wife; when they came for his wife, he did not want to let her go alone, so he went along with her. His fate is unknown. I did manage to find out that he failed to return home.

I heard the grandson of the engineer Shchirovsky had perished; his mother was a Jew who had divorced her husband, and the child was being brought up by his grandparents. They came and took the child.

I heard of one case where the husband was Armenian and his wife a Jew. He did not let her go alone but went along with her.

Several months later, I heard of the case of a daughter who had been separated from her family when they left for the assembly point. She remained behind on the street and was taken in by some Karaites of her acquaintance, who kept her for several months. Then they took the little girl to Saki. There was a Russian woman there whom they knew well; they let her in on the secret and asked her to take care of the girl because they were afraid to keep her in Simferopol. It must be said that the Russian woman who took this little girl into her home—I do not know what she put down on her papers—even found a job not far from where she lived. The little girl survived. I was interested in knowing what would become of her, and I asked a friend to bring me news of her fate while she was living with this Karaite family.

After a long interval, when she had had no contact at all with the authorities, and everything was as it should be, the girl, helping to keep up the household, was walking somewhere in the street and met someone she knew from Simferopol. She said hello as children do, and the other was very surprised and asked, naturally, how she came to be there. She told him, and she was gone by that evening. What spiritual urges were within that man? It is hard to say.

Apparently, people who tried to conceal themselves from the outset with friends or relatives were gradually discovered. My wife's sister was supposed to go to a friend's place two days before the assembly date. An old lady came by to ask for advice about what to do. I asked: "What do you think?" "I don't want to go," she responded. I asked:

"And who's putting you up?" She said: "I've decided to go to the settlement near the workers' village. My son-in-law's mother lives there. A Russian woman. She'll help me. I want to go to her place to dig some potatoes." From all appearances, however, she perished during one of the roundups that took place from time to time. All the roundups were happening right over my head.

During the second roundup—it must have been in March of 1942—I had to get out of the room. There were many rooms in the building with a lot of dark, secluded corners. There was a small storeroom where entry was forbidden. During the first roundup, the Germans had walked right by without noticing this room. My landlady had the key to the storeroom. It contained a large library of medical books and collections of medical instruments, geographical maps, and all manner of junk as well, including boards and beds. I thought of hiding in the storeroom. But it would be difficult to do because there was constant traffic in all the corridors. I would have to find the right moment in order to enter the storeroom.

We performed this operation soon after the roundup began. The roundup was at daybreak. Around five o'clock, there was a report that a roundup was underway in town, and we decided that I would have to move from the room to the storeroom. I moved to the storeroom. There was not much movement in the house. My friend stood guard in the corridor, then signaled me that it was all right, then she moved farther inside and stood on the threshold. I entered the storeroom wearing my overcoat and fur hat and hid behind the bookshelf, since we had agreed that I would hide there in the event of a raid on the house, behind a board. My friend had the key to the storeroom. She closed the door behind me and put the key in her pocket. The Germans came into the building. She walked up to the storeroom and coughed. I went behind the cupboard and shifted some of the books. I made myself a small seat out of the books; above me, all was blocked, jammed with all sorts of things. I could tell from their footsteps that the Germans were getting closer. I heard them approaching this part of the apartment and stopping near this door. They did not notice it the first time, but the second time they asked in German what was in the room. The neighbor said: "A little storeroom, all jammed with books." "Where's the key?" they asked. "I'll bring it just now," she said. They opened the storeroom. He was interested in this collection of books, instruments, and suitcases, and began taking books at random and to move about the storeroom, even though there was literally no place to walk. He moved back to the opening that had been closed off, moved the wall aside, took hold of the board and, in spite of how dim the light was in the storeroom, must have seen my outline, and suddenly, and quite clearly, said "Ah."

I decided that this time it looked that I would not be able to escape. It took all my strength not to give anything away and not to let them think that kikes were clinging so desperately to life that they did not know how to die.

At the last second, though, something happened; there must have been scales over his eyes. All the books got in the way of seeing everything in the room. With perfectly calm movements, he put the board back in its place and announced to my friend that a soldier would arrive in a quarter of an hour to gather up the books, instruments, and so on. He went out of the storeroom, locked the door, put the key in his pocket, and left. Fifteen or twenty minutes later, five or six soldiers came in, but I was no longer in the storeroom. Imagine the risk. It was difficult to do, because a thousand eyes could have been watching me. I needed to get out of the storeroom in such a way that none of the neighbors or German anti-aircraft gunners would see me, and I had to do it within fifteen minutes. In a word, no one saw me. I left the room confidently, calmly, then went into my room, the door to which had been left open just in case, and locked myself in. My friend closed up the storeroom and returned to the room. The soldiers came with the key and wanted to have my neighbor with them as an interpreter. These six soldiers went about their work in the most painstaking way because they were collecting an entire library. They sent the medical books to their infirmary, while the rest they placed in a library for servicing hospitals.

I remember what I had to go through. I was astonished not by the fact that I had left for a second time. I was astonished by the intervention of some power from above into my modest existence. There were five such times. On one occasion, I had to hide in the cellar; on the fourth in the attic; and once in another apartment, where my landlady had moved during the mass deportations from Lugovaya Street to Krestyanskaya. We had to make the move in such a way that neither the old neighbors nor the new ones would notice, that they would not see me nor would they see those who would carry away all our things. We had to consider every minor detail. I had to go to the attic on the very day when my landlady had decided to move. It was two o'clock in the afternoon. There were no more German anti-aircraft gunners in the building. I would have to move to the attic at daybreak, with the idea that my friend would return in the evening; the door would be wide open, anyone would be able to look into the room, and she would have to come in the evening (movement was permitted until seven in the evening). This was at the end of September or the beginning of October [1942]. Everyone saw that she had moved to another apartment. She was the only tenant of the landlords, a married couple. The door was a separate one, meaning that we could come and go without worry.

I had to endure the visits of the Germans in the second apartment on Krestyanskaya Street as well. They took a liking to apartments in the sunny spring days of 1942. The Germans would make the rounds of apartment buildings, and they stopped by this one too. The landlords were elderly people. They tried all sorts of tricks to keep the Germans away. They told us when the Germans were coming; the stoves had broken down, and this was bad and that was bad. It was after 4:00 PM, already near dark. They came into the corridor and there was a knock at the door. A German asked if there was a room there that would suit him. My friend was not there. I was afraid to approach him myself. They came up to the door, and a German asked that someone open it. The landlords said: "What can we do about it? The door's locked and we've no key. We can't open it." An officer came up to the door and began to knock. The landlady said: "Perhaps we could try to open it with our key." Her husband replied: "Go ahead." So the landlady went for the key. I had to decide what to do. Our options were these: my landlady had two cupboards, one a wardrobe and the second a buffet. These cupboards stood near each other, with enough space in between so that it was possible to stand between them. The room was small, jammed with a couch, a bed, tables, chairs and cupboards, and the cupboards were at the other end of the room. When the landlady went for the key, I was standing a short distance away. I went to one of the cupboards and hid behind it. If the German had taken it into this head to come closer, he would have found me, but this time everything turned out well. The landlady felt badly about opening a room with my friend away. When they opened it, everyone stood at the entrance. The room, truth be told, was not presentable. The couple said a schoolteacher lived in it. They shut the door. The landlady felt awkward. I am saying this because she had not even told my friend hiding me that the Germans had come by. This was my last alarm.

I was engaged with books, reading, and writing. I compiled bibliographic works. I have a reputation as a bibliographer, I also wrote about library science. Whole card catalogues have been compiled on various questions that held great interest for me and had genuine scholarly value. I managed to take out some of the library material. This gave me the chance to hold on and work calmly.

The general mood was very heavy, particularly when Kerch was taken on May 15, 1942, along with Sevastopol on July 1. This was the first great feeling of alarm after those December days. It was difficult after Kerch fell, and even more distressing after the fall of Sevastopol. As long as Kerch and Sevastopol remained in Soviet hands, the hope that liberation was just around the corner could be kept alive. When the Germans took Kerch and Sevastopol, they converted the railroad and changed the street names to German-sounding ones; I felt as though I had been buried.

Of course the taking of Kerch was not the end of the war. In war, all sorts of turn-arounds are possible. The Germans perhaps knew that they would have to give the Crimea back. The Soviet people were certain that the Crimea would be liberated, but that it would take some time to find the mental strength to bring themselves to a certain equilibrium.

Everyone was hungry and cold, the populace as whole and my friend in particular, even though we had our scanty provisions: a pood of flour, a pood and a half of potatoes, a bottle of vegetable oil, and a container of fatback that a Russian friend who was a carpenter had brought me. I had met him somewhere near the Feodosia bridge. He asked: "How are you keeping?" This was on December 3 or 4. I said: "Everyone is hungry. Things are hard all over." He said: "I can help you out a bit. I butchered a hog and I'll bring you some of the bacon." And he actually did. What happened, in fact, was that he did not find me in and gave it to my friends, the Kenifests, and asked them to pass it on to me. When I returned in the evening, they brought the fatback and a few other things. In addition, I had about twelve kilograms of groats. We lived on this for about three months. We ate once a day. We would cook the potatoes in their skins; we made dumplings from the flour, adding some groats and a spoonful of oil, which yielded a sort of edible slop. Then came the efforts to get the pedagogical institute back on its feet, and my friend was hired as a librarian. She put the library in order and received a bread ration, so we divided up the bread into two 150-gram portions. She also gave private lessons in exchange for food. We went hungry, it is difficult to tell the story. We cooked only in the evening. The stove did not have "warm" settings. We would finish cooking, then all the warmth would fly away. I was afraid to move lest I make any noise. We had to sit in the dark in the evenings so that there would be no flickers of light.

So life went for two and a half years. I read newspapers regularly, not only *Golos Kryma* [Voice of the Crimea], but also the German-language *Deutsche Krim Zeitung* [German Crimean Times]. In the German newspaper, which was aimed at a broad audience, there were an insignificant number of antisemitic attacks; the propaganda, evidently, was aimed in other directions. As for the Russian-language *Golos Kryma*, this is something else! I have read numerous antisemitic publications. I had occasion to read *Novoe vremya* [New Times] and Illiodor's *Pochaevskie izvestia* [Pochaev News].[11] Illiodor was a cruel monk and, as it turned out, a swindler who had terrorized the Russian Tsarist government. I knew the antisemitic literature of the pre-revolutionary period, but it could hardly compare with *Golos Kryma*. The latter was truly horrifying. If you read that paper from issue to issue, you saw what sort of a publication it was; one article after another of an antisemitic nature. It is difficult to imagine how expert they were at it, how concentrated their pronouncements were under the direction of the German representative Maurach, who was the head of the local propaganda bureau. His father had been a good ophthalmologist. In 1920, he had gone to Germany and his son had been raised in Berlin. The boy arrived in Germany in 1920. Now he came back as an activist in the propaganda bureau. In 1920, Hitler had only begun to take his first steps. Dr. Maurach died, and the family found itself in difficult circumstances; his wife joined the ranks of the fascist movement, and it was against this backdrop that Maurach's son was raised in Germany and turned up here as the representative of the bureau of propaganda.

The son threw himself into this concentrated antisemitic production in a way that was difficult to imagine. Every line expressed an antisemitism that was from the gutter—crude, vulgar, calculated to appeal to the most base instincts. This was the leitmotif that showed through all the material, in the news articles and in the opinion columns as well. One sensed that the group of people who made up that paper

---

11. The *Pochaevsky Sheet* began to appear in 1887, published by Pochaev Monastery in Western Ukraine. In 1906, a monk named Illiodor became the editor. He conducted ferocious antisemitic propaganda in its pages. He also founded the Black Hundreds organization Union of Russian People in the Volyn Region.

had set their sights on a perfectly clear goal: to throw a psychological shadow over what the Germans were doing in the Crimea. It was a cover-up of sorts, Jew-baiting, it was a screen that was held up by a whole array of coordinated efforts. Every channel of life was subject to this newspaper. A young lady, a technical worker, sat in the office of the assistant director. She would sit and attentively copy antisemitic passages from Dostoevsky's diaries, and then do the same from the pages of Suvorin, Rozanov, Shmakov.[12] These were hefty tomes, and the young lady would spend days copying these materials for the articles of Bykovich and others.

Hitlerism attacked not only the economic life of the people, but their psyche as well. It was a laboratory in which poison was being manufactured. The poison did not pass away without leaving a trace. This antisemitism poisoned the population. It was not that they believed all the lies, but they inhaled the printed words.

The destruction of buildings in the city of Simferopol, explosions, and fires, had begun long before and would go on for a long time.

In January 1942, after the Soviet landings had taken place, the mood among the Germans was so tense that the German command was sitting on its suitcases. If the high command of the Soviet army had been more energetic about making a leap into the Crimea, the peninsula would have been liberated. In Simferopol they were ready to flee by January 7, but they allowed the pressure to dissipate. The Germans brought reinforcements from Leningrad. If this thrust into the Crimea had been carried out more energetically by our high command, the Crimea would have been liberated much earlier.

The second time our troops approached Perekop, the fires and the destruction of buildings began. But they went about it with particular vigor just before the fall of the Crimea, and finally, quite extraordinarily, was what happened in Simferopol on April 12 [1944], when some four hundred major buildings burned. The whole horizon was a solid sea of fire; archives were also burning. Warehouses were burning in various parts of the city, and as a crowning touch, soldiers with submachine guns began to drive round the city in the evening and toss grenades into residential buildings. They seemed to be in some sort of fevered state.

On April 13 there were partisans who fought briefly, for perhaps an hour.

In the Archive Bridge District, the partisans set up a covering detachment, and on the evening of the thirteenth, I emerged from my twenty-eight months of imprisonment for the first time. I walked around the city, met several Russians whom I knew—they greeted me with tears, embraces, handshakes—and on the fourteenth I went back to my old apartment. I found a generally good mood in

---

12. Dostoevsky was famous for his antipathy toward the Jews. Alexei Suvorin (1834–1912) was an important publisher in St. Petersburg, who was also well known for his Jew-baiting. Vasily Rozanov (1856–1919) was a controversial writer and philosopher; he too expressed hostility to the Jews. Alexey Shmakov was a lawyer who warned against intermarriage with Jews.

the city. Russian people were embracing, crying, marveling, greeting each other with kisses and hugs. I found a Tatar family in my apartment. The Germans had broken in, destroyed books that were on the tables, carted off the chairs. Some of the books had been sold to a second-hand shop, while those in the cupboards had been saved. At first they had made a casino in my apartment for a small number of people. The casino operated for six months. All the furniture was moved out by the housing department, and the books given away to the central library. Now I am getting them back. There are identifying marks on my books. At the central library, they were selecting books for the pedagogical institute and the Party office, and had chosen mine, putting them off to one side. My library had been made up of two thousand volumes; it represented forty years of work. Many books had been lost, along with a portion of my manuscripts and a collection of maps of the city of Simferopol, which I had assembled over a long period of time. All of that, unfortunately, has been lost.

August 17, 1944

GARF 8114, op. 1, d. 961, ll. 48–64; d. 959, ll. 160–175. A typewritten manuscript.

77. An account of the bookkeeper Lev Yurovsky (Simferopol)
RECORDED BY LEV KVITKO
[1944]

Here is the story of Lev Yurovsky, the bookkeeper of a sporting goods store in Simferopol.

There remained fourteen thousand Jews in Simferopol who had not been evacuated. On November 10, 1941, the Germans "organized" the Jewish Committee. They appointed a respected elder named Beylinson chairman and warned all the Jews that they would be subject to the orders of the committee.

With the help of the leadership of the committee, the Germans extorted everything that they wanted. The commandant of the city would make an order and the committee would be obliged to supply everything exactly on time—furniture, clothing, gold, and carpets.

The following incident took place: a certain general "ordered" some boots, but the committee did not manage to deliver the required number on time. For this, the aging chairman received a slap in the face.

When there was nothing more to get through the committee, the fascists began looting with their own hands.

The Germans gave orders through the committee that everyone must register at the labor exchange. They commanded that everyone should put on armbands with the *Mogen dovid* (the Jewish six-pointed star), and then sent them out to do the hardest jobs: digging earth, hauling stones. They herded them along with whips. I did not register and did not put on an armband since I wanted to get out of the city.

One day, though, I went out to work. We were covering trucks with plywood, while others were dragging along piles of spades. We did not know then what all these preparations were for. Then they used the trucks to take people off to their deaths, while the spades were used to throw earth on top of the bodies. We, the group who had been working here, were ordered to go home, then come back the next day, on the condition that each of us bring back with him a Jew who was either a cabinetmaker or a locksmith. It was an impossible condition; all the skilled workers had already been grabbed up. In desperation we turned to the chairman of the committee: "What's to be done?" He waved his hand and replied: "There's nothing to be done anymore." Obviously, he could see how things stood.

On the way home, we met people with suitcases and bundles over their shoulders. These were the old-time residents of the city: Jews, Krimchaks. They had been summoned for "evacuation" on November 9.[13]

The Germans designated three assembly points. They were the finest multistoried buildings in the very center of the city and were occupied by the Gestapo: the pedagogical institute, the medical institute, and the Regional Party Committee building. On the next day, the tenth, in accordance with the order, the "evacuation" of the Simferopol Jews began. People took their most valuable possessions and made for the assembly points. It is impossible to convey this tragic picture. The weeping, the howling! Thousands of people were trudging along in broad daylight, not knowing where they were going or why. The Germans were behaving calmly and politely, not arousing any suspicion. "They're evacuating you to Ukraine," they would say, "to colonies."

On the eleventh, my wife and I made a decision: we would go as well. Our minds could not take any more of the tension of the previous few days. Come what may, just so there is an end to it as soon as possible.

On the way to the assembly point, we met a Russian woman whom we knew. She said: "Whatever you do, don't go there! You're going to your deaths. I met a Gypsy in disguise who by some miracle escaped being shot."

The Germans had "evacuated" the Gypsies several days earlier. We went back. My wife went to hide in one place, and I in another. I went to the place of a friend of my parents' named Mateyka. Vasilisa Mitrofanovna Mateyka would help me a great deal. I spent six days and nights with them; they fed me, concealed me, and kept me informed of everything that was happening in the city. Jews were being shot on December 11, 12, and 13. Bodies were hanging in the streets bearings signs: "For not obeying the decree." These were the people who had not come to the assembly points in time. I realized that I had no right to put my friends in danger any longer, and left town.

Several days before that, my wife had received papers confirming that she had been baptized. They hauled her to the Gestapo anyway, and when she was taken out to be shot, she went out of her mind. Only on the sixteenth, just before my departure

---

13. This is a mistake in the text; the "evacuation" began on December 9.

from the city, Vasilisa gave me a letter from her. She was saying goodbye to me, to life. She was being summoned by the Gestapo.

A Russian woman offered me the passport of her husband who was at the Front. The passport had to be put in order. Vasilisa's grandson, a fourteen-year old boy, got hold of some ink, and we made changes to the document. Mateyka's father accompanied me to the station, and I walked through some villages, in the direction of Melitopol. Along the way, I met several people who were in the same position as I was, as well as German patrols. The passport did not let me down. In this way, I arrived in Melitopol on December 31. I was allowed to spend the night and to greet the New Year at the house of a bookkeeper on the edge of town. You can imagine what sort of a "holiday" it was for me.

Along the way I had occasion to pass through the Crimean Jewish settlements. They still knew nothing of what was going on, but they had a premonition and were terribly worried. I could not bring myself to tell them about everything that had happened in Simferopol and what awaited them, and I left.

In Melitopol, they did not want to register me. I went to another town, but they did not want to do it there, either. What was to be done? I decided to go back to the Crimea. I went to the police for safe passage papers back. The chief of police wondered why I had left the Crimea. I explained that I had wanted to find work in these parts, but had not been able to.

It was in those very days that our forces made a landing in Kerch. The Germans were scared to death. Having spotted a Krimchak, they surrounded and examined me for a long time. Then they took me to a separate room and began to interrogate me. From there, I was taken to a higher authority, the Ortkommandantura (the local commandant's office of the German army).

The commandant, two other Germans, and an interpreter subjected me to further interrogation. It seemed as though everything was going smoothly. Suddenly, the commandant leapt up from his seat, slammed his fist down on the table, and yelled: "There's a Jewish head hiding here!" And they threw me into a Gestapo cell.

The Gestapo prison yard was served by two Jewish boys. They would bring prisoners food on the sly. One day the Gestapo found out about this and beat the two boys so badly that I could no longer recognize them. Nevertheless, they kept on bringing us food. I was sure that they were going to shoot me, so I decided to hang myself. I wanted to give the two thousand rubles that I had with me to the boys. But they absolutely refused to take money, and said to me: "No, they're not going to shoot you."

After that, I began to believe in various omens. A drowning man clutching at straws.

Later, I lived in a village, in a house that had formerly belonged to a Jew. There was a pile of papers, letters, and documents lying in the attic. One day, when I was in a particularly depressed mood, some sort of letter fell directly on me from the attic. The attic was swarming with chickens. I opened the letter and read:

"Dear Leyb (my name was also Leyb), don't be sad, everything will be all right." And this calmed me.

Meanwhile, they moved me from a cell at the Melitopol Gestapo precinct to a barn with a cement floor. It would have been easier to sit outside in the freezing cold than in this barn. They gave me nothing to eat. It got to the point where my own breath was barely warm. In a word, I was finished!

But at this time, I was unexpectedly freed. I could return to the Crimea. I remembered that I had a letter with me which Vasilisa Mitrofanovna had given me for her sister who was living on the former Jewish collective farm Vozrozhdenie [Revival]. The name of the farm seemed significant, so I set out for it.

Vasilisa's sister and her husband gave me a warm welcome, and I remained in the village as the collective's groom. It was then that I learned that the majority of Jews who had been living in the village had managed to be evacuated in time, and that the Germans had taken the remaining forty people away to Dzhankoy.

They checked my papers several times, but everything turned out well. Then, all at once, a new misfortune: Why wasn't I married? Everyone here is married. So, there must be some reason.

However, my guardian angel Vasilisa Mitrofanovna soon turned up to help me. She came to visit her sister. A light gleamed in my eyes when I saw the old woman. Loneliness and the constant need to pretend were oppressing me. I told her what was happening with me. She proposed telling her sister as a secret that my wife, whom I dearly loved, had run off with a German, and for this reason, I could not be satisfied with anyone. A "secret" like this, of course, went round the village quickly, so they left me alone. That is what happened.

In the meantime, I got acquainted with all the farmers, and also with the teacher, a Korean named Tochey, and his wife.[14] I no longer felt so alone. He would come to see me at the stables, chat with me, and then invite me to his home. One day, Tochey said to me: "I see that you're a reliable man. You hate the Germans. You have to get involved with people."

That was a happy day for me. When we next met, Tochey told me that he had an assignment from a certain communist to create a group around himself, and offered me the chance to help him. At night, Tochey would go to Karasan, where there was a radio receiver. We were able to hear the latest news and established contact with the partisans. Tochey's wife was a wonderful person: she inspired us to the boldest undertakings against the Germans. She had a small child, and she was expecting a second any day. She would say: "I don't want my children to see those monsters. And if, in spite of everything, the Germans managed to hold on here for a short while, I will bring up children who will be sick at the sight of them!"

---

14. The author is probably confused about Tochey's national origins. In 1937 the Soviet regime had sent all Koreans to Central Asia.

I stayed on the Vozrozhdenie Collective Farm until the arrival of the Red Army.

GARF f. 8114, op. 1, d. 950, ll. 196–201. A typewritten manuscript.

78. The story of the Simferopol tailor Maks Solomin
RECORDED BY LEV KVITKO
[1944]

In a tailor's shop connected to the army, I found a Simferopol tailor named Solomin who had survived. He was thin, of medium height, with an intelligent, wizened face, and looked to be about fifty years old. There was nowhere for us to sit down and talk in the crowded noisy shop. He led us outside into a narrow iron gallery running around the large multi-story building from within. We leaned against the railing, and he began:

"Four days before the Germans arrived in Simferopol, I came home from a business trip. I'm a ladies' tailor. I come and find an empty house: my wife had managed to be evacuated in time with the children. Our Jewish neighbors as well. I felt uncomfortable puttering around in an empty apartment. I went to my sister's place and found her there. She threw her arms around me crying: her child is sick and so she cannot be evacuated.

"I come home, and some Germans have already set themselves up for the night. They left at dawn, though.

"Meanwhile, the order was given—all Jews would have to register.

"This is what happened during the first days of the occupation: two Germans came into a house on Tolstoy Street where Pekerman the bookkeeper lived. When they saw an infant in the arms of its mother, one of them grabbed it and stuck it in the stove. The mother rushed at the German, but the second shot her. The father threw himself at these two bandits, but they overpowered him, hauled him outside, beat him on the legs, and began dragging him down the street.

"I invited over fifty or so people whom I knew and told them about this misfortune. I proposed that one or two thousand of our people get together and attack the Germans. Many will be killed doing it, but several hundred people will get weapons for themselves and will make it to the forests, to the mountains. They argued with me, though, saying that it would be impossible to wipe out a population of fifteen or twenty thousand. The best proof of this was the fact that the Germans were behaving decently: they weren't beating anyone on the street, they were polite.

"But then that day came. They began hauling Jews away and killing them. One day went by, two, three. Something dreadful is going on. I do not go out of the house. They are hanging people in the street for not registering. I do not go. But when the roundup started, I could not stay at home alone any longer. I found the nerve and went to hand myself over to the butchers. It was daylight. On my way to the Gestapo, I suddenly hear someone calling me. I turn around and see Maria Ivanovna, a customer of mine from some time back. I told her what was happening, and she says:

'That's madness! Go to the Gestapo yourself? Even I'm afraid to stay in this city. I'm going to the country. Come along with me. I'll register you as my husband.'"

"At the same time she gave me the name of a man who could make me a passport. To make a long story short, we both left Simferopol the next day. We walked for three days until we reached a village whose mayor was a relative of Maria Ivanovna's. She introduced me.

"'When did you get married?' the mayor asks, looking at me.

"'Three years ago!' she answers.

"'So that means he's got the name of your first husband, then?'

"We were thunderstruck. We had not even considered this. We had not managed to squirm our way out of this difficulty when another one turned up.

"'Well, all right,' says the mayor. 'This hasn't gone anywhere yet. But how can you stay here with your husband, when all he has to do is open his mouth for anyone to know who he is.[15] No, it's better if you leave here. I can't let you stay here.'

"He did let us stay the night, though. And there I am lying awake, suffering. What to do? My Jewish accent will be the end of me! I toss and turn, I feel as though I'm lying on needles. And then, a thought suddenly strikes me. Here's an idea! I'm ready to wake up Maria Ivanovna right now. I can't wait until morning!

"In the morning, I told her about my plan. She liked it. We went to the mayor and announced that I would become a deaf-mute!

"He burst out laughing.

"'Think you can keep it up?' he asks.

"'I can!' I say.

"So the mayor took my passport and wrote 'deaf-mute' on it. But he still did not want to let us stay in the village, and gave us a document: 'So-and-so and her deaf-mute husband named such-and-such are going to this place to look for work.'

"We set out on the road, our hopes set on my 'deaf-mute' condition. We came to the village of Onufrievka. It was dark. One had to get permission from the mayor to stay the night.

"He looks at my documents, and then says, 'I won't let you go any farther. I need a tailor. I have a big family, they all need new clothes.'

"Maria Ivanovna pretended that there was no way that we could stay, and she showed me by gestures what was going on. I also indicated with my head and my hands that it was impossible. Within myself, though, I was rejoicing at the fact that we had a roof over our heads, that I had a job! True, it was dangerous that we would be staying with the mayor himself, in the jaws of the beast, as they say. By the way, he had grey, shaggy hair like a wild man. He gave us permission to spend the night

---

15. There is a widely held assumption in Russian culture that Jews have a peculiar accent when they speak Russian—that they "swallow" the letter "r." Jews whose native language was Yiddish often had difficulty trilling their "r"s as native Russian speakers do.

and the next morning refused to let us go. His wife set the table and a young girl brought her mother fabric and a sewing machine. They got the table ready and Maria Ivanovna—my tongue and my ears—showed me through gestures what they wanted me to do. So we stayed there and set to work. We sewed things for the house and for the entire family, and the mayor refuses to let us go. It is a good deal for him: he is not paying us for our work. And I, they say, am a deaf-mute who is a quick learner, and each of them boasts about the fact that I understand their signs. A day goes by, then another, then a week, then a second week, and I remain deaf and dumb. There are people around constantly, so I cannot even manage to exchange a single word with Maria Ivanovna. Do you see how I even have wrinkles round my mouth? It's because I was keeping my mouth shut tight the entire time. You're around women and children constantly. Sometimes you hear something that makes you have to be stronger than iron to keep from bursting out laughing, or, on the other hand, to keep from clenching your fists in rage. But once you've started, you've got to stay silent.

"But here's what happened one day: Our bombers attacked the village by night; they were hitting German trains at the station. I woke up when everyone in the house was already out of bed. I became flustered and suddenly called out, 'Where're my trousers?'

"Just then, the room became bright as day from an incendiary bomb, and I saw the mayor standing beside me.

"'Blast you!' Maria Ivanovna spat in my direction.

"The mayor is standing over me, looking confused and seething with rage, and I'm feeling that I'm done for. The air raid is over, the German trains are burning, and I can't even be glad about it: I've put a noose around my own neck.

"Maria Ivanovna and I are sitting in the room in the light of the fires and not saying anything. What could you think of to say? The mayor, of course, is going to tell us to get out, perhaps he'll even have us shot. We decided to leave quietly, not waiting until morning, and to head off in no particular direction. That was what we did.

"When the Red Army liberated us, Maria Ivanovna went her way, and I went mine."

GARF f. 8114, op. 1, d. 950, ll. 205–208. A typewritten manuscript.

79. The death and rescue of Jewish children in Simferopol
THE STORIES OF LYUSYA RABIN AND MIRIAM PAVER
RECORDED BY LEV KVITKO
[1944]

In the neat little apartment of Lyusya Rabin, we sat and listened to her sorrowful story of the Simferopol Jews, and of her friends and family who hid in the attic of this very house for two months after the mass exterminations.

We listen to her indignation at people, to her bitter conclusions: the fruits of three years of persecution. I try to console her, but my words do not reach her. I gather facts and episodes from what she tells me and offer them as examples that contradict her lack of faith in people and in the friendship of those around her. Her young heart is too embittered, though. She has too strong a sense of the loneliness that took hold of her after she lost her joyous and talented family. The pain expressed on this beautiful and noble young face is not the sort that passes or is healed, even when the face is only twenty-six years old.

"No one who didn't live through it can understand," she says again and again. "Only someone who is as lonely as I am can understand."

"You're very dear to all of us!" they tell her. "You're not alone. The people have given you all the love and concern that they owe to the millions who perished, on you, the few who survived. You're among us like orphans. Out of seventeen thousand, how many Jews are still in Simferopol?"

"Thirteen or fourteen out of seventeen thousand. It's almost six months now since the Crimea was liberated, and no more than that have appeared. We know all the survivors: Auntie Paver; Lev Ilych Yurovsky, who worked at the Dinamo Factory; the tailor Maks Yefimovich Solomin, who played a deaf-mute for two years; the wife of Pukaylo, the engineer; and myself."

A powerfully built middle-aged woman comes into the room. They introduce her to us—Maria Isaakovna Pavner. She immediately brings a great deal of new information.

"And you've forgotten about the more than fifty Jewish boys?" she says. "The whole town is talking about Prus, the director of the orphanage. She saved Jewish children, found homes for them in safe places. The relatives or parents of these children come to see her now and don't know how to thank her. How many times did director Prus risk her life, how many times was she on the verge of destruction! But she was a clever one. She fooled the Germans and took the children right from under their noses. She sought out Russian people that she could rely on to save a Jewish child. They would come to her and she would take care of everything. A priest in the city asked her about raising a Jewish boy. Many Gentiles took in children in order to save them from the German butchers.

"Pukaylo the engineer worked at the People's Commissariat of Agriculture. His Jewish wife and daughter were taken away by the Germans. They managed to break away, though, and fled to the cemetery at night. An agronomist that they knew lived not far from him. They went to his place. The agronomist installed them in his cellar and concealed them there until the arrival of the Red Army. Pukaylo was sure that his wife and daughter had perished. He let himself go, became indifferent to everything, unshaven, crushed, and silent. When the Red Army came, it was as though he'd been born again. The agronomist brought his wife and daughter to him, safe and sound.

"When the Germans shot the Krimchaks, my husband and I and our fourteen-year-old son were in the attic. Soon they began searching the houses. My husband said:

'Leave, save the boy, you don't look Jewish. And I'll stay here.' A certain Alexandra Trofimovna Shlyakhova came to see the old lady who lived next door to us. She saw how dejected I was and gave me her ID card, and she was a total stranger to me. The neighbor, a devout old lady, put a cross around my son's neck. From that day on, he was called Vasya. I said goodbye to my other neighbor, Yekaterina Andreevna Stolyar, and her children, then we left town."

"We went from village to village—where we spent a day and did not spend the night—until we reached the village of Kentugay. Here we had an address. We exchanged some of our clothes for food and began to live any way we could. They called us in for interrogations dozens of times. Day and night, all we did was to look for ways to allay suspicions that were following our every step."

"Little by little we settled in. My 'Vasya' became a shepherd. I would come to see him in the fields. He would play a fife, and the kids from the village were always all around him. He would make up games with them in which one had to say prayers and make the sign of the Cross. In this way, we learned this bit of wisdom from the kids. A Russian family by the name of Danilin, whom we became friendly with, had been evacuated to Kentugay from Perekop. A few days after their arrival, though, the Germans and the police came around to their place. They took the Danilins away and shot them.

"One day our neighbor invited me over for the dinner following a funeral. It was in the evening. In the middle of the prayers, the Germans and the police descended on us and took everyone away. I slipped out in the confusion and ran off. That night, the Germans seized and dragged away about sixty families. They also picked up my Vasya and led him off to the gendarmerie. There I am, standing by the doors and hearing them beat up my son."

"From my hiding place, I see a truck pull up, full of people from the area, from Nayzan or Funduklea, old Russian people. Lots of children. I remember a little girl whom someone was clutching to himself. It was cold. They did not unload anyone from the truck. They brought shovels out of the police station, deposited them in the cab, and ordered the driver to move off. I realized that it was their last trip.

"My son was left half dead. He had to be treated, he was wounded all over and it was impossible to keep him at home. Bad luck was coming down on my head: a relative of the man whose house we were staying in came from Simferopol. She knows us. And my boy has to go off with the herd before she gets up, then come back late at night when she's already asleep. She hasn't been here in twenty-five years and now she turns up! And I have to hide the whole time and pretend to be ill so that, God forbid, she doesn't spot me."

"Suddenly, a dear guest shows up: Yekaterina Andreevna, my neighbor from Simferopol. This is the second time that the woman has made the ninety-kilometer trip to see me and to bring me some things to exchange for provisions. She also brought some of the food that she and the children had managed to set aside from their meager ration for 'Auntie Manya.' I learn that her oldest boy has gone off to the partisans, to the Yampolsky detachment. Her two younger sons live with her. They're getting along somehow. I know that even before the war she was having a hard time of it—her husband has been ill for a long time and she's the sole support of the family. My eyes fill up with tears from gratitude to her for her friendship and attention. 'What's all this, then,' I say to her, 'You set out on a trip at a time like this, when you're barely holding up yourself, when you yourself need help.'

"I'm crying, and looking at me, she's crying as well. After staying in the village for two or three days, she returned home. In the two years that I spent in Kentugay, Yekaterina Andreevna came to see me four times, and the help and comfort that she gave me made it possible for me and my son to stay alive. This is the kind of people that exist. When I sat locked up for six days at the gendarmerie, someone gave me food. To this day, I don't know who that kind soul was.

"A German unit was based in the village. Five POWs, all of them still boys, worked in their kitchen. Our children got to know them. My Vasya brought one of them, named Grishka, to see me. The young man was terribly depressed from his work in the Germans' kitchen. He came by to see us several more times, and I could see that something was deeply troubling my son. In the end, the boys let me in on their plan: five of them, together with my Vasya, were about ready to run off to the partisans. But since Vasya's leaving here could do harm to me, his mother, they came up with the idea that Vasya should also go to work in the German field kitchen, then leave Kentugay along with it. Later, he could take off from some other village or from the road.

"I looked at Vasya and his comrades and saw that there was no other way out. That was what they did. Several days later, they left our village, and somewhere on the road left the German kitchen and set off for the Taman Peninsula. To this day I don't know what happened to my son."

GARF f. 8114, op. 1, d. 941, ll. 31–35. A typewritten manuscript.

80. In the attic, in the Gestapo's courtyard (in the city of Feodosia)
A SKETCH BY LAZAR LAGIN
[1945]

I could tell you about the thousands of corpses of women, old people, and children who had been shot, and whom we unearthed in an anti-tank ditch; about looted apartments, and houses burned down and blown up. All of that has been written about, though.

I want to tell you about a little clapboard structure on the grounds of the Feodosia Gestapo post. It is already more than a year now since I was in it, but isolation from Moscow and days of fighting filled with thousands of troubles have made it impossible until now for me to find the time needed to write this brief bit of correspondence. To tell the truth, it would have been difficult to write it when the impressions were fresh.

At the very beginning of January of last year [1944], I managed to enter Feodosia, which had just been taken by our forces. It was the first city that we had liberated from the Germans that I had occasion to visit. I had been there more than once before the war, but even so, I had to ask for directions every minute to such-and-such a street. It was almost impossible to get one's bearings in the chaos of destruction that had once been the charming resort city of Feodosia. There remained on the boulevard of luxurious sanatoria on the seafront only blackened and collapsing walls, while the lovely little train station located on the same boulevard had also been so completely razed to the ground that I managed to find its remains only after consulting with one of the local inhabitants.

Legitimate curiosity led me, finally, to a three-story brick building in which until just a few days before the local Gestapo had had its offices. I walked through the gloomy rooms, in which every paper on the floor seemed to be a small clot of human misery and monstrous, criminal injustice, every innocent photograph "material evidence" sufficient for the destruction of a human life. Neat little cards were preserved on the doors with the names of people written in careful Gothic script; compared to these people, Jack the Ripper was an angel.

After surveying all the rooms of this department of murder, I went outside and then mounted the creaky, shaking steps leading to the attic with its weather-beaten veranda characteristic of these parts. And it was here that my eyes met with what was perhaps the most terrible thing that I saw in this cursed place.

I saw several rooms crammed to the ceiling with clothing: men's, women's, and children's overcoats; jackets and stoles. An emblem was sewn on every one of them: the six-pointed star, the *Magen-David*. I knew that all Jews, under threat of the severest punishment, had been required to wear this star as a sign of their outcast status, that they belonged to those very people who lived outside the law in the Third Reich.

Not long before the landing of our troops, a decree was posted in the streets of Feodosia: All Jews are required to assemble at designated points for "resettlement." One was permitted to bring only the most necessary things and enough provisions for two days. But when the Jews appeared at these "designated points," their coats were taken from them with the efficiency of butchers, their clothes and food gathered up. Then they were taken out of town and machine gunned. Not all of them, though. They did not shoot the children. They rubbed the children's lips with some sort of poison, perhaps with potassium cyanide.

I was told by a Russian woman (there are no more Jews in Feodosia) how the Jews, shivering from the cold and from fear for their lives, were led through the streets of the city on their last journey, and how a young woman, her face frozen in fear, walked along holding the hand of her five-year-old daughter, who, fortunately for her, did not realize what was going on. The little girl was in high spirits, hopping on one foot from time to time and quite unable to understand why her mama did not praise her agility and skill.

And now I began to dig through these mountains of clothes.

In one coat with an old-fashioned cut, I found four lumps of sugar wrapped up in a piece of paper, a piece of bread sprinkled with salt, and a little velvet *tefillin* bag.[16]

In the pocket of a child's coat, I found rolled in a tube an oilcloth-covered school notebook; its pages were covered with postage stamps. This, obviously, was the most important thing that a nameless Jewish youngster had taken with him as he was sent off for "resettlement."

Someday, when the war is over and memories of the nightmare of fascism have been obscured by the smoke of time, I will send this album, which I saved, to the first international philatelic convention, so that no one will ever be able or even dare to forget the Hitlerite killers.

In a woman's jacket I found photographs of a young woman with a dark-eyed child in her arms. On the other side of it was the inscription: "To our dear mother and grandmother from her loving daughter and grandson. Yalta. April 12, 1931."

Perhaps this jacket belonged to none other than the grandmother of our young philatelist. In any case, his little coat lay right alongside her jacket.

In an attractive fur coat belonging to a little girl of seven or so, I found nothing except a perfectly clean, never used handkerchief. I took a small cardboard six-pointed star from this little coat as a keepsake. I always carry it with me in my field pouch.

And in an old housecoat, I found a statement written on a piece of graph paper torn from a notebook. I permit myself to offer it in its entirety.

> To the commander of the German police
> From citizen Margoly Izraelevna Katz,
> residing at 87 Karl Liebknecht Street
> A statement
> In view of the fact that I have a mentally ill husband, age fifty-one, and a boy, age twelve, who is incapable of physical labor, I ask that we be left in the city of Feodosia. I hereby notify you that our family worked in the tobacco factory for ten years. Recently, I have worked as a shop assistant at a refreshment stand and have not been a member of any party. I beg you to take this into consideration and to leave us alone.
> Petitioner (signature)
> December 2, 1941
> Feodosia

This statement had been written hurriedly, at the last minute before having to leave for the ill-fated "assembly point." The writing was askew and at an angle. Of course

---

16. Tefillin, commonly called phylacteries in English, are a Jewish religious article worn on the left arm and the forehead of male worshipers during morning prayers. They consist of leather straps and two black leather boxes, each of which contains a piece of parchment with a quotation from the Torah.

she knew perfectly well what sort of "resettlement" had been prepared for her by the German authorities, but she needed, for herself and her unfortunate family, to create some sort of pathetic illusion that all was not lost.

I do not know why Margoly Katz's statement stayed in the pocket of her housecoat and did not reach the hands of the chief of police. It is possible that she was ordered to undress so unexpectedly that she did not have time to remember it. And maybe she, upon reaching the "assembly point," realized that now there was no chance for her to be saved.

And so, I keep with me the stamp album, the little cardboard Star of David, and the statement of Margoly Katz, who "worked as a shop assistant at a refreshment stand and have not been a member of any party," a plea that is horrifying in its hopelessness and tragic helplessness.

GARF f. 8114, op. 1, d. 953, ll. 9–11. A typewritten manuscript with handwritten corrections.

81. A girl from Feodosia, Alla-Roza Brazgol
RECORDED BY LEV KVITKO

Anna Stepanovna Sklyarenko lived with her husband, a mechanic, in the village of Saragol, three kilometers from Feodosia.

She received a stern summons from the Gestapo to appear and pay a tax on her dog. Anna Stepanovna hurries into Feodosia to answer the summons; she knows better than to get involved with "them."

In the city, a crying little girl runs up to her at an intersection. Anna Stepanovna takes her by the hand: "What is it?" Then a woman comes running up. The little girl presses herself up against Anna Stepanovna, holds on to her, and screams: "This lady wants to hand me over to the Gestapo!"

"Why's that, then?"

The woman explains that the child had been left with her by the child's mother, who was then killed. Now the Germans are shooting anyone who hides Jewish children in their home. So, she was on her way to hand the child over to the Gestapo, but the little imp broke free.

Anna Stepanovna was indignant.

"What's all this, then. Is nothing sacred anymore?" she said, rebuking the woman.

And she took the little girl by the hand and hurried back to Saragol.

Once out of the city, and having calmed down, she stopped and began to examine the child. She was an emaciated, exhausted creature with dark, intelligent eyes. The little girl appeared to be around four years old, although she maintained that she was actually six. She spoke and carried herself like a grownup.

The little girl also felt more like herself, and said that her name was Roza, and that her grandfather, a Krimchak named Abram Brazgol, lived in Feodosia with her grandmother Stera and with her and her mother, who was named Riva. The Germans had shot them all and chopped down her grandfather's garden.

Anna Stepanovna embraced the child:

"My children aren't with me, and you've no family, so we'll live together."

She took the girl home with her. They arranged a warm little place for the night for her in an air raid trench, dressed her warmly, and made sure she had food. At night, Anna Stepanovna would go and sleep with Roza. At dusk, her husband would bring Roza out into the fresh air. Caring for this child became the principal concern in the lives of these lonely people. They would chat with Roza (they called her Alla for some reason) as if she were an adult, tell her about their two sons who were at the Front, and pour their hearts out to her.

Roza lived in the trench for a month. She never saw the light of day. Suddenly, the word went around: our forces had landed in Feodosia! And sure enough, soon after, our troops established a headquarters in the little house. The army staff and the soldiers fussed over her.

A new life began. Roza/Alla moved from the trench to the house. By day she would stroll down the street to her heart's content.

Then the landing party decided to pull out. One of the first things our soldiers did, however, was to ship the Sklyarenkos and the child to the mainland.

While they were crossing the water, a misfortune occurred: the Germans fired on them and killed Sklyarenko the father.

Anna Stepanovna left for Tashkent with the child and settled there. One day a letter arrived from her younger son at the Front. He wrote that he had been wounded and was coming to Tashkent to recuperate.

At the moment, Roza/Alla is with her second mother, Anna Stepanovna, in Moscow, at her son's place. He is now a student at the Art Institute. The three of them live together quite amicably. They do not want to give Alla away to anyone, and moreover, Alla/Roza does not want to go anywhere either.

GARF f. 8114, op. 1, d. 950, ll. 218–219. A typewritten manuscript.

82. The destruction of the Jewish colonies in the Crimea
FROM THE REPORTS OF THE EXTRAORDINARY STATE COMMISSON
PREPARED BY LEV KVITKO

I am presenting several reports about the massacres that took place in the Jewish colonies of the Yevpatoria District. The majority of the victims were children, women, the infirm, and the elderly. The stronger and healthier ones were taken away to regional centers and killed there.

The village of Ikor (from a report)

On the very first day of the occupation of the Ikor Rural Soviet, the butchers began their bloody work: the extermination of Soviet civilians, sparing no one, from old people to nursing infants.

The entire Jewish population was strictly registered and suffered tortures, expecting death to come at any minute, since all the Jews in the city had already been killed by then.

Knowing that they were doomed to destruction, the people still kept on working, and after work they were taken out to be shot.

The extermination of the Jews was taking place two kilometers from a village where the bodies of those who had already been shot were thrown down a deep well. Some were thrown in alive. Thirty-one people perished: the elderly, the sick, pregnant women, and children.

The commission emphasizes the bestial acts committed against the wife and children of Senior Lieutenant Savchenko. This woman, a Jew, remained in Ikor for a month and a half after the extermination of the Jews in this village. She was not Jewish in appearance. One day, a German unit passed through the village. The Germans shot her, along with a four-year-old girl and a two-week-old boy, ninety meters from her home.

Not only Jews were victims of German atrocities. After the landing in Yevpatoria, when several Red Army soldiers and sailors managed to disperse and hide themselves, there were traitors who turned them in. After dreadful torture, twenty-one people were shot, along with seven of our people's finest sons.

The district commission granted the request of First Lieutenant Savchenko and placed a monument on the main square in Ikor, which was dedicated to martyred Soviet citizens and the heroes of the landing.

Chairman of the Commission Knyazev
Major Marchenko
Senior Lieutenant Savchenko
Chairman of the Ikor Collective Farm Muratov

In the village of Ikor, we stopped in at the home of Raya Feldman, who had already returned from evacuation in the Urals. Raya Feldman's house was clean, cool, and neatly laid out, as though she had never left. The walls were painted white, with decorative trimming all around. The floor was painted and covered by a small rug. There was a row of bottles of homemade pickles and liqueurs on the shelf beside the stove, just as in the best days before the war.

She took some cantaloupes and watermelons from a large box in the loft, sliced them, and generously treated us. She also served fresh, fragrant country bread.

"Why didn't they tell me that you were supposed to come? I would have prepared a rabbit," she said to us.

"Where do you get rabbits?"

"My son catches them."

Her son comes in. He is a shy boy of about ten. The first thing that comes to mind upon seeing him is to rebuild the school the Germans blew up as soon as possible and put this young boy behind a desk!

Raya Feldman tells her story: She has already been at home for three months, and she has managed to put in one hundred working days. Three of her brothers are at the Front, while another was killed.

Not far from Perekop, during the retreat of our forces, many of her relatives were killed. And the twelve-year-old son of her brother was left here in Ikor after the Germans wiped out all the Jews. The boy managed to escape and conceal himself, but some time later, he fell into the butchers' hands anyway.

Her cousin Tsilya Savchenko and her two children had been here in the village. Her husband, Lieutenant Savchenko, a Ukrainian, brought her here thinking that it would be a safe place, but the Germans reached her anyway.

After the Red Army liberated the Crimea, Lieutenant Savchenko and his unit entered the village and learned the awful truth about his family. He convened a large meeting, disinterred the dead, and gave them a proper burial. They raised a monument to them in the very center of the village.

When they dug up the pit in which the Germans had buried Tsilya Savchenko, everyone saw that the murdered mother was on her knees clutching her children to herself. She was covering them with her coat, so that they would not see the butchers who were slaughtering them.

On the Kolkhoznik Collective Farm (report)

On the Kolkhoznik Collective Farm, in the village of Alchan, Bagay Rural Soviet, Yevpatoria District, the Germans wiped out three Jewish families, including two elderly people, three children ages three to eleven, and three adults, eight people in all.

Commission: Kamber, V. Sagets, Plokhovoy

Molotov Collective Farm, Dobrushino Rural District (report)

In December, 1941, vehicles appeared in the village. They stopped outside the mayor's house and remained there for two hours. Then two more vehicles carrying gendarmes arrived, followed by another automobile. The entire village was then immediately surrounded and they began to round up the Jews who had run off in different directions. The automobile would catch up with them and the Germans would shoot them on the spot. When they had finished with this, the Germans drove away, leaving several gendarmes in the village, who, with the help of the local police, searched homes and killed people throughout the night. Twenty-one people hid out on the steppe in a pit which they dug themselves. They lived there for several months, coming into the village for bread. The mayor and his staff made their way to the hideout in order to follow people who were going for bread on the collective farm at the house of a woman named Berezhuk. They seized those who came and locked them in an office under police guard. In the morning, the mayor summoned some Romanians. The Romanians beat the prisoners half to death, then tortured them to force them to say where their families were hiding. After that, they went there with a cart and took them all to the village of Bagay, where they tortured them all to death. This happened in February of 1942.

Commission Chairman Nizelnik (chairman of the collective farm)
Sidorenko, Kuznetsov (farmers and witnesses)

List of the Jews shot by the Germans on the Molotov Collective Farm, Dobrushin Rural Soviet, Yevpatoria District

1. Reyzberg, Nakhman, 45
2. Reyzberg, Khaya, 40; his wife
3. Reyzberg, Fira, 17; daughter
4. Reyzberg, Tanya, 10; daughter
5. Reyzberg, 7; son
6. Frumson, Leyb, 50
7. Frumson, Basheva, 49; his wife
8. Frumson, Khana, 27; daughter
9. Polyakov, 3; daughter's son
10. Frumson, Kalman, 20; son
11. Perkus, David, 50
12. Keselman, Esther, 55
13. Keselman, Sheva, 25; daughter
14. Keselman, Basheva, 33; daughter
15. Polyakov, Meyer, 60
16. Polyakova, 55; his wife
17. Polyakova, Zina, 18; daughter
18. Polyakov, Pinya, 20; son
19. Polyakov, Yasha, 37; son
20. Polyakov, Leva, 15; Yasha's son
21. Polyakov, David, 6; Yasha's son
22. Polyakov, 1; Yasha's son
23. Gonchar, Dina, 60
24. Gonchar, Freyda, 20; daughter
25. Zarina, Sata, 22
26. Troyanovsky, Abram, 57
27. Troyanovskaya, Sosl, 53; his wife
28. Polyakova, Sonya, 30
29. Polyakov, 12; her son
30. Polyakov, 8; her son
31. Cherkasskaya, 45
32. Cherkasskaya, Lia, 19; her daughter, killed in the city
33. Cherkassky, 15; son
34. Cherkassky, 12; son
35. Troyanovskaya, Manya, 16
36. Reyzberg, Grisha, 5
37. Polyakov, David, 17
38. Polyakova, Celia, 25
39. Shturko, Lyusya, 3
40. Puritson, Boris, 48
41. Koimon, Yakov, 52
42. Vichinsky, David, 30
43. Vichinskaya, Manya, 30
44. Vichinsky, Izya, 6
45. Vichinskaya, 4

Kalinin Collective Farm (report)
German atrocities on the Kalinin Collective Farm, Yevpatoria District.

We, the witnesses, as a commission—Ivan Knysh, Yefim Postny, and Natalia Pasechnik—have compiled the present document. In December 1941, the Germans arrived in vehicles at the home of the mayor of our village. The mayor ordered that all the Jews be gathered in the school. From the school, they were taken to a ditch and shot.

A list of those shot on the Kalinin collective farm

1. Zeyger, Ruvim, 60
2. Zeyger, Sofia, 50; his wife
3. Lifshitz, Samuel, 55
4. Lifshitz, Khaya, 46; his wife
5. Lifshitz, Mikhail, 10; son
6. Lifshitz, Tulya, 16; son
7. Gerchikov, Benjamin, 50
8. Gerchikova, Vera, 50; his wife
9. Rakita, Feodosia, 40
10. Rakita, Yakov, 18
11. Rakita, Tula, 12
12. Rakita, Khana, 4
13. Rakita, Lyubov, 6
14. Segal, Naum, 70
15. Segal, 65; his wife
16. Segal, Simon, 38; his son
17. Segal, Olga, 35; daughter-in-law
18. Segal, Anna, 14; Simon's wife (?)
19. Shmelkin, Khaim, 23

Neydorf (report)

On December 16, 1941, a group of Germans in two vehicles arrived in our village of Neydorf, Yevpatoria District, at around twelve noon. They took up positions at both ends of the village. With the aid of the mayor and the local police, the Germans chased Jewish families out of their homes and, after loading them into their trucks, drove them four hundred meters from the village, formed them up beside an old ditch, and shot them with submachine guns.

Ten families were shot, 41 people in all, including 10 elderly people and 13 children.

The chairman of the commission is the director of the Kaganovich Collective Farm, Stepan Ivanovich Luchno.

Members of the commission: Velikorodny, Chuprenko.

GARF f. 8114, op. 1, d. 950, ll. 224–230. A typewritten manuscript.

Ilya Ehrenburg speaks with Soviet peasants near the Front during an investigation of German war crimes, 1944. USHMM, courtesy of Irina Ehrenburg.

Soviet soldiers and local residents view in 1944 or 1945 an opened mass grave in Ivye, which may have been the site of the May 12, 1942, mass shooting of 2,500 Jews by German units. USHMM, courtesy of Beit Lohamei Haghettaot.

Postwar inspection of Auschwitz by Soviet civilians and military personnel. The camp had been liberated on January 27, 1945. USHMM, courtesy of Beit Lohamei Haghettaot.

Soviet investigators in the Klooga concentration camp in Estonia examine corpses stacked for burning, August–September, 1944. USHMM, courtesy of Esther Ancoli-Barbasch.

Three members of the Polish-Soviet Extraordinary Commission, outside a warehouse in Majdanek, view a pile of shoes that belonged to prisoners killed there. Pictured from left to right are: V. Prozorovsky, A. Witos, and D. Kudryavtsev, July 24(?), 1944. USHMM, courtesy of Martin Smith.

Soviet women mourn the death of children killed in a German action. USHMM, courtesy of Lydia Chagoll.

VII
RUSSIA

The Russian Soviet Federated Socialist Republic (hereafter Russia) was the largest and most populous constituent republic of the Soviet Union. Historically Jews had not lived in Russia in great numbers, but once the Pale of Settlement was abolished after the abdication of the tsar in February 1917, followed by the Bolshevik Revolution in October, Jews flocked to Russia's cities and within a decade were a significant part of its urban population. On the eve of World War II, its two largest cities, Moscow and Leningrad, had sizable Jewish populations of 400,000 and 175,000 respectively, within a total Jewish population of nearly 1,000,000.

The Wehrmacht advanced along three separate invasion routes into Russia. The Germans reached Leningrad in September 1941 but failed to capture the city, even after laying siege to it for nine hundred days. Other divisions converged on Moscow and directly threatened the Soviet capital; on October 15 there was a massive and hasty evacuation of government, diplomatic, and cultural offices. But Moscow withstood the German attack, permitting the Red Army to mount a successful counterattack in December and liberate a good deal of territory in the northwest portion of Russia. The Germans' failure to capture Moscow and Leningrad spared the cities' Jews from mass murder at the hands of the Einsatzgruppen and other German units. Nonetheless, massacres of Jews took place in districts near Leningrad, including in the city of Pushkin, which marked the northernmost point of the Final Solution.[1]

Ghettos were also established in Russia in the summer and fall of 1941. With a few exceptions, they were almost all in the western portion of the republic near the

---

1. See Ilya Altman, *Zhertvy nenavisti: kholokost v SSSR, 1941–1945* (Victims of Hatred: The Holocaust in the USSR, 1941–1945), (Moscow, 2002), p. 252.

border with Belorussia, where there had been Jewish communities dating from tsarist times. Most of these ghettos were established as a means to confine Jews before Einsatzgruppe B found the time to murder them. With the exception of the largest, which was located in Smolensk and held over two thousand Jews, ghettos in Russia existed for fewer than six months and were not the sites of long-term forced labor. The Smolensk ghetto remained in existence for eleven months, until July 15, 1942. Other ghettos were established in cities such as Kaluga, Orel, and Pskov.[2]

The failure to capture Moscow did not stop the German offensive. The Wehrmacht continued to drive deep into the country, occupying Ukraine and an enormous swath of southeastern Russia and the North Caucasus, until the advance was halted at Stalingrad on the banks of the Volga in late 1942. By that time, the Germans had captured a line from Novgorod to Tver, Bryansk, Kursk, Rostov-on-Don, Voroshilovsk (Stavropol), and Krasnodar, and on from there into the North Caucasus. And though many Jews were alerted to the Germans' plans and succeeded in escaping, the Germans still managed to murder between 120,000 to 140,000 on the territory of Russia.[3]

83. The Germans in Yessentuki
A LETTER FROM THE PAINTER L. N. TARABUKIN AND HIS WIFE, D. R. GOLDSHTEYN, TO THE WRITER YU. KALUGIN[4]
[1943]

You ask how we survived? How the miracle came about? Had the Germans stayed in Yessentuki any longer, we would have perished in a torturous way. Our turn would have come. But let me begin at the beginning.

As soon as the Germans entered Yessentuki, a fierce antisemitic campaign began; there were flyers, posters, and caricatures. A few days after that, they began giving bread to the population: two hundred grams per person per day. They did not give bread to the Jews. Signs appeared in the bakeries: "No bread for Jews." When receiving bread, one had to present a passport as proof that its holder was not a Jew. Then came an order: to create a Jewish Council, which would have to register the entire Jewish population. A local Jew, a jurist, was appointed as the head of the council. The registration showed that there were five hundred Jews left in Yessentuki. Two or

---

2. See Vadim Dubson, "Getto na okkupirovannoi territorii rossiskoi federatsii (1941–1942)" (Ghettos in the occupied territory of the Russian Federation [1941–1942]), *Vestnik yevreiskogo universiteta* (Herald of the Jewish University), no. 3 (21) 2000, pp. 157–184. This journal is published by the Vyshaya gumanitarnaya shkola imeni S. Dubnova (The S. Dubnow Higher Liberal Arts School).
3. Altman, *Zhertvy nenavisti*, p. 286, for Altman's tabulation of victims according to administrative districts in Russia.
4. The letter from L. N. Tarabukin and his wife, D. R. Goldshteyn—who was Jewish and a professor at the Kishinev conservatory—was sent from Yessentuki, where they were evacuated following their stay in Kishinev. It was addressed to the writer Yu. A. Kalugin in Tashkent.

three days later another order appeared: "Forced labor in the cleaning of the military hospitals is hereby instituted for all Jews between the ages of 15 and 75." The work went on for two weeks. When it was finished, there came the following order:

"Due to the fact that the necessity of transporting all Jews to sparsely populated areas has arisen, all registered Jews in Yessentuki are required to assemble in the school on such-and-such a date at such-and-such a time. Up to thirty kilograms of baggage may be brought. Jews in mixed marriages are excused from having to appear."

It turned out that there were fifteen such mixed marriages in Yessentuki, and these fifteen people survived. In the final days, though, when the Red Army began to approach Yessentuki, the fascists started making advances in our direction as well, and we had to go into hiding. (Later we learned that the Hitlerite scoundrels shot all the Jews in Pyatigorsk and Kislovodsk without exception on the eve of their retreat.)

A month before the Germans' arrival, we met your relatives Polina Yefrussi and Zinaida Michnik. We saw each other rather frequently, and then we moved in with Yefrussi. And she, like her sister Zinaida Michnik, is a researcher at the Leningrad medical institute.

In spite of their venerable age (both of them were over sixty), they too were driven out to do forced labor. When, on September 9, the order appeared sending the Jews to "sparsely populated places," the sisters Yefrussi and Michnik poisoned themselves, taking an overdose of morphine. Unfortunately, the morphine did not work; they survived. I write "unfortunately" because it was the fate of these unfortunate women to die a more terrible death than one by morphine.

The sisters had many fine and valuable things. Before their suicide, they gave them all away to their colleagues. When they survived and, after a time, it turned out that the Gestapo was leaving them alone, their colleagues began to return the things they had received. As it turned out, that was all the Gestapo was waiting for. When all the things had been returned to their owners, the local head of the Gestapo appeared at the sisters' place with two adjutants. (I was at Yefrussi's at the time.) I do not remember the Gestapo agent's name just now, but I will never forget his icy, translucent eyes, his abrupt way of speaking that sounded like a dog barking, or his enormous height and long, ape-like arms. The adjutants took the unfortunate women from the house, put them in their car, and drove away. The Gestapo commander remained in the apartment, gathered up the belongings, even the pail for rags to mop the floor, and, having cleaned the place out, took off with everything.

The fascist scoundrels shot Polina Yefrussi and Zinaida Michnik in the forest. It was October 29. That day, another 483 Jews were shot: all the Jews who remained in Yessentuki had been herded together into the school a month and a half earlier for dispatch to "sparsely populated areas." Among those shot were very old men and women and nursing infants. The fascist barbarians spared no one!

GARF f. 8114, op. 1, 963, ll. 116–118. A typewritten manuscript.

84. The rescue of a Jewish family from the shtetl of Khislavichi, Smolensk Region
A LETTER FROM B. M. SORINA TO ILYA EHRENBURG

Dear Comrade Ilya Ehrenburg!

I read your book *War*.[5] I have no comment to make about it, but will only say that it made me relive the awful things that I had already endured. I wrote about the book to my husband at the Front. He answered that not only had he read your book, but that he had met you personally in Vilno,[6] and that you were interested in the story of how I was rescued. I want to tell you the story, and if it can contribute even a useful little grain to the overall struggle against fascism, I will be happy. If, however, my material turns out to be of no use to you for whatever reason, then I apologize. Perhaps it will not be my fault then, but my intentions are only the best. I am not a writer, and it is hard for me to set things out the way they should be, but that can be fixed. There are people who specialize in this and I will turn to them. I also ask you to forgive me for my handwriting; I do not know how to write well and there is nowhere to type. Not a single typewriter is left in the entire region. And I urgently ask you to grant me one last request. Whether my story is useful or not to you, please respond to me. Let it be the bitter reality, but that is still better than waiting and uncertainty. I know that you are overburdened with work, but I am waiting for a reply. I wish you health and long life.

I have left a great deal out of my story. All of this is very difficult to describe. It would easier to tell it out loud. And it is not possible anyway to write everything down that one could pass on orally. It is difficult for me to describe in writing the mood, the things I went through which would be important for you. Maybe some things will not be clear to you; in that case, write to me, and I will try to explain and fill out my story. Maybe my brother can be of some help to you.

The awful war with the cannibals began in the summer of 1941. They bombed Smolensk five or six times a day. Fires burned everywhere. They poured fire over the city from above; days and nights were spent in fear. After June 28, I had no roof over my head. The house is burning. The first blow has been dealt by the enemy. Where to find a refuge and temporary peace and quiet? The old, remote shtetl of Zakharino in the Khislavichi District comes to mind. Rasya Mirkovich, my husband's sister, lives

---

5. Ehrenburg was able to publish three collections of wartime columns in separate volumes while the conflict was still unfolding. But in 1945, following Georgy Alexandrov's denunciation of Ehrenburg in *Pravda* on April 14, a fourth collection failed to appear although galleys of the book had already been prepared.
6. Ehrenburg was in Vilna in July 1944, when the city was liberated. He met a unit of Jewish partisans who had been assisting Red Army troops. Ehrenburg kept a picture of their meeting on display in his study.

there. I go there with my children. My husband stays in Smolensk and promises to take me away in case anything happens. But things did not turn out that way at all. On July 10, I received a telegram from my husband; he had been drafted into the Red Army. Six days later, that is, on July 16, the German forces reached Khislavichi. People were leaving, running from the hurricane of death. I looked at them with sadness. I had three children, ages one to eight, and three hundred rubles. I tried to convince my sister-in-law and her husband Moisey (their children were both grown-up: a daughter, Liza, who was twenty, and a boy of fifteen) to leave, but Moisey said to me: "I'm not going to leave the place I've lived all my life, and I won't let anyone go. You can leave. There can't be a situation where the Germans just shoot all the Jews indiscriminately." He was rich and commanded authority in the town. Looking at him, no one in Zakharino set off. I made ready to go several times, but I immediately imagined myself losing my kids one by one at each train station. There I am, boarding the train, and before I can get all the kids in with me, the train starts off, and a child is left on the platform. He is crying and the train is taking me away. I lost my strength and will at this thought and decided to die, but to die along with my children. I knew very well that if I stayed I would die, since I am a Jew and my husband a communist.

The Germans did not enter Zakharino until August 1. Then the black night began. I realized that very day what a German lash meant. A huge German came up to me and demanded: "Eggs." I answered that there weren't any, so his animal face flushed and he struck me with his whip. Anger boiled up inside me, but I was powerless. I was a small woman with a child in her arms standing in front of an armed soldier-beast, so I kept silent.

The Germans were resting. There were chickens, ducks, and geese—they took everything that caught their fancy, but they did not lay a hand on the inhabitants. They only enjoyed themselves. They would find the oldest, weakest Jews and force them to haul water from the well, and then would pour the water out right there. The fun would go on for hours, and the Fritzes had a fine time. What was more, they would shout "*Jude kaput! Alles kaput!*" [Jews are finished! Everybody is finished!] in a way that was no longer even human. A month later, the unit went up to the Desna Front at the Desna River, and things became quiet in Zakharino, but it was a dreadful calm that comes before a storm. Germans would often come from Khislavichi; they, too, would have a good time, walking down the streets and firing into windows, at doors, people, children, anyone that crossed their sights. So, one day they killed a girl of eighteen, a little girl of eight, and two men (we are talking about Jews). Having eaten their fill, satisfied with their "work," they would go away, then come back again, always inventing new amusements. Once they harnessed a decrepit old man to a cart. Two fat Germans got in and began to drive him, beating him with whips. They drove him through town. The poor man was pulling with all his might, his eyes became bloodshot, the veins stood out on his forehead and looked as if they were about to burst. But the Germans love human blood, so they drove him to the other end of town. There was an old broom tree standing there. The "fun" ended when they hanged this unfortunate man from the broom tree and his sufferings came to an end.

It was difficult to live, but one did not want to die. I decided to try my luck. I had a nanny named Katya. She had been living with me for eight years. She was from the Khislavichi District. Her old mother and sister lived twenty kilometers from Zakharino, in the village of Pykovka. Katya went to see them. She came back and said that she would not leave me in this difficult hour, so I decided to set out for her place. My friends gave me a "ticket" to start my life again: they wrote out a birth certificate and attached a stamped seal from the Zakharino village soviet, then backdated it by several years, to 1939. I became Vera Sokolova of the Orthodox faith. With this document and with my children, I set off for Katya's place in Pykovka.

The village began to indulge in rumors and idle talk: where's she from, what's she like. I listened, kept my mouth shut, and worked hard. The potato harvest was underway at the time. The situation was tense; punitive squads were making the rounds, coming to every hut in search of Jews and Red Army soldiers. Every time, we were afraid that one of our neighbors would point a finger at us and it would be death for everyone. But the village only talked and did not hand over anyone. The days went by, the work in the fields was long since finished. I waited for the arrival of the Red Army, but it did not come. Winter was coming on. Unfortunately for me, Katya's brother joined the local police (he was married and lived elsewhere). He began to take cattle, furs, and woolens from the inhabitants. The indignant locals began saying that they would not put up with him for long and would hand him over to the German authorities since he was hiding a kike woman. (The villagers did not know exactly who I was, but they were presuming and guessing.) This idle talk reached me and I decided to go into hiding for a time. I went to Zakharino and took my two little girls with me and left my son Dima with Katya. This was at the beginning of February 1942.

I rode into the shtetl. All the Jews were in the streets with shovels clearing the road. When they saw me, they came up to me and burst into tears; they were no longer people, but human shadows. There were newcomers among them, people who had fled Belorussia (Vitebsk, Minsk, and Mstislavl). They had managed to get out from under the bullet. They had witnessed the mass shootings of old people, women, and children. As they told it, children had not even been shot in Mstislavl, but rather had been buried alive. The fresh burial mound heaved, and moans could be heard coming from it. Death hovered over the shtetl, but had not yet arrived. The Zakharinites were waiting, but their turn had not yet come. The Germans killed according to a calculated plan. The gendarmes and their henchmen would come, carry out searches, rape girls, look for goods, beat people, and cart men away in groups to points and purposes unknown. Several weeks after my arrival in Zakharino, a large punitive squad turned up one February morning. They herded all the Jews into one place and ordered them to move all their belongings from their own homes into several huts set aside for them especially. They had already drawn up a column of vehicles, and they loaded on everything from the Jewish homes: featherbeds, pillows, clothing, shoes, pots and pans. They loaded on everything that was not nailed down.

I crawled up into the attic of my house and observed everything that was going on. I wondered how to get away and where to go. After they had taken away everything from our house and the column had moved off, I leaped down into the house, grabbed my girls, and left. I wanted to get to a village a kilometer and a half from Zakharino, but I lost my way. There was a snowstorm and freezing weather. I tramped through the snow and went into a cemetery. I am carrying little Innochka in my arms, and Klarochka, who is older, is following after me. Her coat is thin, the sleeves are torn and short for her, and she is clutching a loaf of bread in her slender little hands. We sink into the snowbanks. I drop my child, pick her up again and go on, as though I am going to find safety in a cemetery. Bereft of strength, we find a tree stump and sit down. I look at Klarochka. Large tears are freezing on her cheeks, she is crying, she is cold, her hands have turned blue. She wants to throw the bread away, but I will not let her. I look around; death surrounds us. Where should we go?

The idea of staying there and sleeping the eternal sleep flashed into my mind. I heard the crying of the children, pulled myself together, and went to the village. I came down the hill and saw a small bathhouse. How glad I was to see it! I went in. It was damp, but not yet freezing. It had obviously been heated not long before. I sat Klarochka down, put Inna in her arms, and ran to the village myself to beg someone who might warm these poor children. I went to five huts, but no one was letting us in, while evening was already coming on. Desperation took hold of me. I was dashing from hut to hut like a hunted animal. Finally I found a woman who had four children; she took pity on me and allowed me to bring mine. I did not walk to the bathhouse; I was carried there by some force. The children warmed up and slept peacefully. I could not calm down at all, the thought of "what to do next?" would not leave me.

Two days went by this way. The stove had a screen around it, so we were hidden from the eyes of other people. Meanwhile, my sister-in-law had found out where I was and came to see me. She said to me: "Let's go into a camp. Whatever God gives will happen." I said nothing. My heart was squeezed by pain. I remembered my child whom I had abandoned with strangers. I imagined how he would suffer; he would cry out for his mama, but I had abandoned him. What kind of a mother was I? So I answered: "I'll have time enough to die. I'm going to fight for my life and try to save my children." And I decided to go back to Pykovka. I hired Fillipp, an alcoholic barely on his feet. There was a snowstorm, the frost was cracking beneath us, but we left anyway. The horse soon ran out of strength and stopped altogether. My cart driver cursed the whole world and me. Then he stopped in the middle of the field and said roughly: "Get out, kike woman, I'm not taking you any farther. Stay here and freeze with your kike pups." I begged him, pleaded with him. My urgent pleas must have touched his heart because we moved off again.

Late in the evening, frozen to the bone, we arrived in the village. Katya's sister Praskovya and their mother, who were expecting me, were very unhappy. Katya said nothing; she sensed the hopelessness of my situation and felt sorry for me and the children. I was an uninvited guest. I paid no mind to anyone and tolerated everything. The old woman nagged at me: "Don't put that there. Don't sit down. Don't eat. Don't make noise." In a word, she felt crowded. "Leave my hut, you kikes." Life began to feel unbearable. We would have to go searching again, to think of something else.

So I took my birth certificate and went to see the mayor of the village. He was an old man of sixty or so, gray-haired, but still strong. Children and grownups alike called him Uncle Rivon (his real name was Illarion). I did not expect to achieve anything, but what did I have to lose? I made the following speech to him: "You're an Orthodox Christian and you can't let four innocent souls perish. My husband's a Jew, I'm a Russian myself, but all my papers are in his name. It's impossible for me to live by these documents, so I destroyed them. I kept only my birth certificate, and now I'm asking you to give me papers saying that I'm a refugee from Smolensk. My life's in your hands now. You can have me killed, or you can save me." The old man kept promising to write what I wanted, but couldn't make up his mind to do it. He was afraid. He had a son named Yegor, born 1913, who was a bookkeeper. One day I went to see them and found them both in. I repeated my request. Yegor heard me out and said: "We've got to write them." This decided the matter. I received papers saying that I was a refugee. They were given to me for the purpose of presenting myself to the school department. These papers made it possible for me to hide my birth certificate, which had the shortcoming of bearing a seal from Zakharino, and *that* could have given me away; everyone there knew me, after all, and they could have betrayed my disguised identity.

The head of the school department was a former secondary school German teacher from the town of Khislavichi named Rzhetsky. He was a man of around fifty, tall and trim; judging by his appearance, he looked around forty. He was from a clerical family, was educated, and knew languages: German, English, and Yiddish. Before the war he had been persecuted by the NKVD. It was clear that he hated the Soviet regime but was able to effectively conceal his contempt and enjoyed substantial authority among the village residents. But when the Germans came, he breathed freely, immediately became an interpreter for the commandant, and later was put in charge of school instruction. He opened schools in the area and compelled all the teachers to work. The teachers were all registered.

Meanwhile, I was being forced out of the hut where I was staying, so I decided to go see Rzhetsky. I had once known him well, and he had known me, but I was not about to open up to him. I wanted only to receive an apartment and some bread with my new papers. At the beginning of March 1942 I went to the school department in

Khislavichi. I did not look like myself. I was wearing bast sandals, a long fur coat, and a large dress, and was so wrapped up that only my eyes were visible. The March sun was shining, the snow was sparkling, a range of different forms and flowers were appearing before my eyes. There was a frost, but spring was already in the air. I did not want to part with life, but I had no guarantee that I would not have to. I told Rzhetsky that I was a teacher and a refugee, that I had no place to live, and that I had no means of existence. In telling him this I showed him the papers that I had received not long before from the mayor. He believed my words, and wrote me out a permit to move into the school building.

The school was in the village of Pykovka, on a hill slightly removed from the village itself. It was a fine new building constructed in 1938. It contained ten rooms and a broad corridor. The accommodations for the teachers were there as well. The Germans lorded it over everyone: they burned books, maps, valuable teaching materials. All the windows were broken. All that was left were the walls and partitions. There were snowdrifts knee-deep in the classrooms and corridors. There was a smell of desolation in the air, but to me it was a welcoming spot. I chose a room, covered the windows, fashioned bunks and a desk out of boards, brought my children there, and breathed freely.

I gained a great deal by moving to the school. First of all, I lived at a distance from people and gave them no reminder of my existence. Second, I made life easier for Katya and her family, relieving them of the responsibility for hiding such "dangerous people" as me and my children. And third, I was spared my daily dose of curses and reproaches from the old woman, who could have sucked the last strength out of me by her grumbling. No one came around to my room and I was rarely to be seen in the village. We suffered terribly from the cold. Winter was raging, snow was piling up higher than the windows, wind blew through the room, and every crack filled up with snow. There was no firewood, there was nothing to warm oneself with and nowhere to do it, and the children were crying. I would set them down close together, and then lie down beside them myself and try to warm them with the heat of my body. I spent the days in fear, afraid that someone would denounce me. I would often look through the window to see whether or not anyone was coming. When night fell, I became bolder. The children fell asleep. Outside is a snowstorm, a howling blizzard. The wind is rushing through the classrooms and corridors, torn-away frames and boards are knocking, as though an entire band of witches and demons are celebrating a wedding. I am not sleeping, but I am also not afraid. I was only afraid of people, and at night they could not come for me. At night I would think of all the plans and variations for my future rescue. Under the cover of darkness, I was calm.

On March 21, a teacher came from Khislavichi. I asked him what was new, and he replied: "New? They shot every Jew in the village yesterday." My head began to spin, things went dark before my eyes, tears rose in my throat, I was ready to burst into sobs. The teacher looked at me attentively, and it seemed to me that he was trying to read something on my face. The thought flickered in my mind that my behavior had given me away. I made myself calm down. Our conversation was not a long one, and he went away. A few days later I went to Khislavichi. I will never be able to forget what I heard and saw there. I will not forget, and a curse on anyone who forgives the enemy this blood! There was a heavy frost on March 20. The unfortunate people lived on the edge of the village above a broad ravine. The ghetto was fenced in with barbed wire. No one had the right to enter or leave. Germans and local police would often drive up and rummage through the household belongings again, looking for anything of value. Then they turned their attentions to young girls and even children. These fiends were not afraid to torture twin girls in front of their parents, girls who were barely fifteen. And then one day they herded all the teenagers into a barn and whipped them, beating them until their bodies were covered with reddish-blue welts.

The men were all taken out and shot. Women, children, and elderly, decrepit people were left. At dawn on March 20, the local police surrounded the camp on the orders of Shavanda, the commandant and the prefect of the district. They had strict orders not let anyone out of the camp and to shoot those who ran. They, these monsters, stood with weapons at the ready facing defenseless women and children. Another group of police went to drive out the doomed people. They did not give them the chance to get dressed. They herded them up to the ravine barefoot and naked. Mothers were carrying their infants, clutching them to their breasts and sobbing loudly. Footprints of children of various ages were left in the snow. They were driven along, shoved, then finally shots rang out. Women hugged their children and fell. Children were crying over their dying mothers and falling as well. Here is a mother who has lost her son; she has quite forgotten that they are about to shoot her. She looks around for him, finds him, embraces and kisses him, and at that moment a policeman comes galloping up, thrusts a bayonet into the child and lifts him into the air. The mother flings herself at the bayonet and shares the fate of her son.

After a few hours, there is quiet on the street and in the ravine. There are puddles of blood in the snow, bodies lying everywhere. The ill and the bedridden were shot where they lay. The "work" finished, every corner was searched to see whether or not anyone was still alive. Then they began bringing up wagons to cart off the remainder of the household goods: mattresses, pillows, clothes, and utensils. The bosses and the police selected the best things for themselves and took them home. Anything in poorer condition or bloodstained went into the warehouse. Then came the relatives and in-laws of the police. Accompanied by fistfights and loud arguments, they divided up the remaining rags. The corpses were still lying around; they were left there to be contemplated. Some five days later, the bodies of around a thousand women and children were taken to the ravine and buried just below the surface. A few individuals managed to get away under cover of darkness; they fled to

Zakharino and took the news there. Precisely a month and a half later, another five hundred or so people were wiped out in Zakharino.

There were still some more Jews hiding in the villages and forests. The hunt for them began. Killing a Jew became a profitable business. For every one found and killed, the policeman received the victim's rags and several packets of tobacco from the commandant. So they worked diligently. They searched attics, bathhouses, and cellars. They found them and led them off to show them to the commandant before taking them to the ravine. A policeman named Kundelev told of his findings and successes face-to-face with a Soviet judge. He spoke with perfect calm: "One day, I managed to catch two women, one young and one old. The young one had two children, one not yet weaned and the other ten years old or so. I ordered them to sit in the sled. They took their seats, and I drove the horse straight to the ravine. The ten-year-old boy was begging: 'Mister, don't shoot me. I'll polish your boots, look after your horse, weave baskets. I can weave good baskets, mister, don't kill me.' I didn't say anything. The old woman was crying, and the young one kept her mouth shut. I stopped the horse and ordered them to get out and walk. The young one got up and said: 'Just shoot us right away. You've already learned to shoot straight.' They all walked off and I killed them." This was how this murderer of innocent women and children ended his story. I wanted to throw myself on him and strangle him. It was disgusting even to look at him. They were all like this.

My relations in Zakharino were still alive. They were in hiding. The police were looking for them everywhere. They kept Liza hidden for a long time; she could not be found at all. One day, the police searched all the huts. Liza was buried under a pile of straw in a cart, then taken to a barnyard in the nearest collective farm. There, however, someone turned her in. The police rushed into the barnyard. They searched the whole pile of straw with their bayonets, but did not find Liza. So they left empty-handed. On top of all that, Liza suffered a personal tragedy. She joined her life to that of a man, reckoning that marriage would save her from death. His relatives and sisters lived in Zakharino. He himself had lived in the Donbas until the war, and had a wife and son. He was called up, threw down his weapon, and came back to his native region. His name was Matvey, and he swore that he would not leave her. Liza's parents did not say anything; they sensed that this marriage would not save her. When Liza got pregnant, her mother made her get an abortion. The operation was done in the home of some woman in the filthiest conditions imaginable. Liza suffered terribly and bled profusely, but she was young and survived. She recovered and suggested to Matvey that he join a partisan band, but he refused.

So, Liza took off for God-knows-where, and Matvey got married to the mayor's daughter and moved into Liza's house. They found the goods that been hidden there and lived peacefully. A short time later, Moisey and Rasya (Liza's parents) were seized. Moisey was shot straight away, but Rasya was bound hand and foot and locked in the barn. The police wanted to torture her, but Rasya did not wait for them; she freed herself, and when they opened the barn in the morning, they found a body hanging from a beam. The boy Gilya was still at large. He did not wait to be found. He came to the police himself and said: "Well, you've killed my mother and father, so kill me too. Bury me beside my parents." The beasts did not even grant him this last request. They sent him to another village, and some time later, some peasants who knew him found his body. He was lying there completely naked, with the bones of his skull and his brains strewn around. He had been hit in the head by an exploding bullet.

I do not know what happened to Liza after that. No one knows where she went or what became of her. Only one thing is clear to me: if she were alive, she would come back to her native ground.

Meanwhile, life in the area seemed to be flowing along in its normal course. The process of issuing passports was continuing. Many exchanged their Soviet passports for German ones without the slightest pang of conscience. Others, who gave no cause for doubt or suspicion, received their passports easily and simply. For me, though, it was a difficult question to resolve. Everyone had to have a passport, and I could get one through the prefect of the rural district. I thought the plan through and put my hopes on the gold lid of the watch that had been left me. It was all that I had left after ten years of marriage. I "made a gift" of this lid to the prefect and explained my request to him. My calculations were correct. The man was unable to resist the gleam of the noble metal. I received my passport, or rather, the mayor himself received it and brought it to me. I often laughed to myself at the "vigilant" servants of the red-headed Fritzes. These papers served most of all as a guarantee for my life, but to a lesser degree for the lives of my children, since they looked like Jewish children, especially my son, Dima.

He was the image of his father, swarthy complexion, big, dark, expressive eyes, a slightly protruding lower lip, and curly hair. He was chatty, entering easily into conversations and answering questions willingly. It was easy for him to find out the whole truth about something. I took various measures of prevention against all sorts of possibilities. I devised a special system of upbringing and conduct for this period. "Lessons" would begin in the evening. I would say: "Remember, children, we're Jews, and for that they have to shoot us. If the police take us in, then they'll question us. They'll tell you that you're Jews, that Mama has already confessed. At first they'll try to persuade you, then they'll beat you, beat you badly, but you'll keep on claiming that you're Russians. If you confess, they'll shoot you all." How hard it was for me, their mother, to play this kind of "teacher." The children would listen to me, their faces showed the strain on their little minds and their sufferings. Finally, they would fall asleep, and dreadful thoughts would come into my mind. If they come for them suddenly one day, what's to be done then? Then, I would think: The girls hardly look like Jews. We'd have to save them at least, but Dima? To give my son up, to give him up to be shot because his father was a Jew! To sanction the killing of one child and to save the others by explaining that their father is Russian! I was close to madness at the thought and wept. My heart was breaking in two. I was thinking about it. Would I be able to live afterward? And I decided that these sufferings were too great, that the price was too high. If we were going to die, then we would do it all together.

For a little more than two years, the children did not know what laughter was. Klarochka, the older girl (she was born in January 1934) understood the tragedy. She spoke very little and carried herself like an adult, but at night her nerves gave out. She would leap out of bed, run to the window, and from the window to me. She would say, trembling all over, "Oh, Mama, the police are coming on bicycles. Hide me, Mama, now they're already near the school! They're shooting, they're shooting!" The little girl could not sit still. I hold her tightly in my arms and try to bring her around. With great effort, she becomes more herself. Drenched with sweat and pale, she lies down on her bed and falls asleep. She was never able to tell what she dreamed. Curious women tried to find out anything they could from the children. In my absence, they put questions to Klarochka, such as: "And what was your little brother's name before the war? And what was your papa's name in Smolensk?" Klarochka always came up with the needed answer. For two years, the children did not take their kerchiefs off their heads. They knew that they must not show their curly hair. Dima knew his place when suspicious strangers turned up. He would lie facing the wall, "ill." He could not show his "suspicious face." And he knew it very well.

A typhus epidemic was raging in the village. They would summon me to be with the sick, and I would help however I could: applying cupping glasses and administering enemas, taking temperatures, and so on. Women would call on me to be with their children. I helped them with advice, I helped everyone I could. Their suspicious, hostile attitude toward me changed to one of sympathy and they began to respect me. The local people spoke of me as a hard-working, good, and useful woman. Their opinion was important to me because my life was in their hands. All they needed to do was say aloud what they presumed and the game would be up.

I became friends with a woman whom I met in a rather odd way. One day, an old woman came to see me and introduced herself as a teacher in the school where I was living. She said to me straight out: "I came to find out who you are, since there are rumors going around that you're a Jew." She astonished me, but I liked her for her directness. She had a kind face which helped me to trust her. I answered that there was a grain of truth in these rumors, but that I myself was a genuine Russian (I showed her my birth certificate as I said this). My husband, though, was a Jew. I also told her that I was entrusting her with the most precious thing to me: the lives of my children. She reassured me, and a little while later left me (her name was Ksenia Fyodorovna) with the complete certainty that I was Russian, which was important for me. She subsequently dispelled the rumors going about among the local people that I was Jewish. She reported to everyone that she had seen my papers for herself. Moreover, Ksenia Fyodorovna always told me what people were saying about me, and who felt what toward me. These rumors would spoil my mood, but on the other hand I knew how each person felt about me, and knew how to talk to each one. She was the link connecting me to the outside world.

September and October of 1942 came on. There came an order to open the school. I was faced with the choice of either working or dying. For the sake of saving the children, I decided to work. The teaching staff was drawn almost solely from refugees, young people disposed to do only a semblance of work, so long as it meant being able to hide from Germany and the police. They worked from the Soviet curriculum with Soviet textbooks. Several months later, the education department ordered the teachers to remove all political content from the curriculum and to paste over all portraits of Soviet leaders in the textbooks. Ksenia Fyodorovna, two other teachers who were Komsomol members, and I did not carry out the order. Fortunately, no one checked up on us, and all turned out well. The school was open for the sake of appearances. My room was a kind of staff lounge. The teachers would often gather in my room after the lessons to sing their Soviet songs and to read leaflets. Ksenia Fyodorovna would often spend the night with us. Together we dreamed and hoped. We looked forward impatiently to the coming of the Red Army.

Sometimes we would also read German lies. A newspaper came out in Smolensk, and from its contradictory reports we would judge the real situation; we learned to read between the lines. I remember an article under the headline "Sixth Army Reborn." It said that the German army was invincible, but to us it became clear that this same Sixth Army had been smashed at Stalingrad. What was more, rumors reached us that the Red Army was winning victories.

Time passed. The spring was spent in farm work and in dreaming. Autumn came on. The Red Army was getting nearer to us. In September 1943, German troops were on all the roads. They were retreating. Vlasov's army went by, along with people who had collaborated with the Germans, driving cattle and hauling the goods that they had looted.[7] Some of the German soldiers pitched camp in Pykovka; they drove all the inhabitants out of their huts and settled in them themselves. They committed atrocities. The young people went into hiding; the very old and the very young were in ditches and behind bushes. I left the school and went into a ditch. The Germans were not hiding, they were retreating. We knew that our soldiers would reach us in a few days. I was afraid of only one thing: that our boys would come but we would no longer be here, that we would be driven into slavery.

Fortunately, the Germans did not have time to drive out all the inhabitants. On September 26, the German soldiers became very agitated. Toward evening, they took almost all the horses and cows and were preparing to withdraw. The ditch

---

7. General Andrey Vlasov had been a hero in the defense of Moscow in late 1941. But after his capture by the Germans outside of Leningrad, he began recruiting Soviet POWs to fight alongside Hitler's armies. In 1945, Vlasov's troops turned on the Germans and participated in the liberation of Prague. Vlasov was handed over to the Kremlin after the war, and was executed.

was a convenient place from which to observe what was going on. The school soon caught fire, along with huts at every end of the village. I looked around, fire was everywhere. They did their work, the scoundrels, and then left. At 1:00 AM, I heard the last order of a German officer, and then all was quiet. It seemed to me that the earth was breathing freely, that the air had become so clean and pleasant, that everything all around was so festive and Russian. At five o'clock in the morning of September 27, I met the first sapper of our own army. I was crying for joy, it seemed like a dream to me. I was running like a madwoman, talking with the soldiers, offering them milk, fatback, and eggs. I stood in the road and gazed in admiration at our Russian army, my very own and well-loved.

I was reborn.

(I managed to find a typist and have this material typed out. It is true that the typist was not very literate. It is even difficult to correct the mistakes. I ask you to forgive her and to pay no attention to these errors.)

Sorina

GARF f. 8114, op. 1, d. 960, ll. 228–232ob. A typewritten manuscript.

85. Town of Novozybkov—eight hundred victims in one day

A LETTER FROM ANASTASIA MIKHEYLETS TO KALMAN AYZENSHTEYN CONCERNING THE FATE OF HER FAMILY

PREPARED BY A. KAGAN.

TRANSLATED BY M. BREGMAN.

I, your neighbor Anastasia Mikheylets, who lived on Tsvetnaya Street with you in Novozybkov, am answering your written inquiry about the fate of your sister, Ginda Tirkltoyd.

On February 17, 1942, she left for the market in order to buy something for herself and her ailing mother. A German punitive unit surrounded the market and rounded up the Jews. More than eight hundred people were seized and herded into the club at the Revolutionary Wave Match Factory. They were locked in there, then shot the next day. Among these unfortunates were also the dentist Barkman, the medic Shrayber, the entire Altshuler family (he was a dentist), and many others.

Your mother, Risya Ayzenshteyn, was bedridden. During the roundup of the Jews, the police locked her in her room, where she soon died of hunger and of all that she had gone through.

After the police tossed her body into the street, they looted her apartment and took all her things away.

Your cousin Makhlya Markina perished along with Ginda.

Please forgive me for sending you this sad news. This is all that I can say.

Your neighbor, Anastasia Mikheylets.

GARF f. 8114, op. 1, d. 950, l. 293. A typewritten manuscript with handwritten corrections.

86. Nazi cannibals
AN ACCOUNT BY YEVA PILETSKAYA, A RESIDENT OF KURSK
PREPARED BY F. KRASOTKIN
JANUARY 28, 1944

When the Germans entered Kursk, they immediately began exterminating the Jewish population down to the last man. Over several days, around five hundred Jews were shot in the city—children, women, and the elderly. They took out the adults in groups of ten to fifteen and shot them on the spot, while they poisoned the children.

On the morning of November 2, 1941, the Gestapo knocked on my door. My heart sank, my hands began to tremble. I realized that the end had come. I quickly snatched up my little Liza and ran out into the corridor. I knocked on the door of my neighbor Nastya:

"My dear," I said, as my heart was pounding, "let my Liza stay with you. I've got to dash out for a minute."

I do not know if Nastya realized how much grief I was in, only that she gladly took Liza, while I slipped down the corridor to the Yamskaya quarter, where I had friends. It was only the next day that I sent a friend for Liza. They wrapped her in rags and brought her to me in a sleigh. The Gestapo drove all my family and all those close to me into prison: my husband, Ilya Pinkhasovich Piletsky; my mother, Mekhlya Tevelevna; and other relatives: Mikhail Borisovich Shpitzenburg, his wife—Vera Osipovna—and his sisters, Khaya and Sonya.

Three days later, I met my neighbor, and she said to me: "Yeva, don't go to Dzerzhinsky Street." But I went, and saw ten bodies lying there. Among them I found my husband. My heart bled, but it was impossible for me to cry—they would find me out and kill me. For two straight weeks I went to this street every day, and each time I was ready to burst out sobbing. I do not know where I found the strength to conceal my endless grief from these monsters, to hold back the tears.

It was impossible for me to stay in the Yamskaya quarter. Death awaited not only me, but my protectors as well. So I left. But where was a Jewish woman supposed to go? All over the region, the Germans were seizing Jews and shooting them on the spot. I went from village to village, just following my nose. I made my way through the snowdrifts to the village of Sapogovo—over a whole day without food. Quite exhausted, I began to freeze along with Liza. An old man came walking along, he helped me to make it to the village.

"Good people," I said, turning to the first house I came to, "let us spend the night." But they answered: "There are strict orders, only the mayor can give permission to spend the night to people passing through." "Well, here comes death, then," I thought. "I have to remain outside in the freezing cold."

An old woman turned up, and she kept me warm until morning. And in the morning she said: "You can't stay any more, the mayor will find out." I went to another village. And so, day after day, for many long months my daughter and I roamed from village to village, changing lodgings. How many times did the police catch me, and only by a miracle I walked away from death? Wanting to save my little daughter Liza, I told everyone that she was not my daughter, but my granddaughter, that her mother was Russian. My daughter heard this many times and came to believe it herself.

One day, when night found us in a field, Liza asked me: "Mama, where's my real mother?"

"Daughter, I'm your mother," I said to her. "There's no life for us among the Germans, though. We've died."

And she answered me "Don't cry, Mama. The Reds will get here soon, don't cry."

And in the morning, on the road again. Near Lgov a man met me and said: "Who are you?" I said: "To tell you the truth, I'm a Jew." He said: "Don't be afraid. I'm a Jew as well." We sat a while, cried a few tears, then went our separate ways. On that day, the Germans were organizing a roundup of Jews. I made a detour across a lake and almost drowned along with my daughter. From a distance, I saw the police seize this man and shoot him right there.

It is impossible for me to tell how much torment and grief I went through. For ten months I wandered in this way, like an outcast, with death lying in wait for me at every step. It sometimes happened that I would change villages thirty times in a month. It was only my passionate love for my daughter and hope in the Red Army that gave me strength, and I would move on again for parts unknown.

I came into the village of Arbolino to spend the night in the home of the collective farmer Yegor Besedin. He said to me: "I share your pain. You can stay with me as a visiting friend." I began to live at Besedin's place. The old man knew, of course, that I was a Jew, but never asked about it. Only once, seeing how carefully I hid my nationality, he said to me jokingly:

"So, Marusya (that was the name I went by), you don't believe in God?"

"I do," I hurriedly replied. "But I'm a Baptist."

I liked this little lie myself. That evening, I went to the Baptist church. This was the scene that I saw there: the Baptists were on their knees and kept on repeating one prayer: "Lord, help our Red Army to smash the foe." I liked this, and I began to go to their church almost every day to pray.

I tried with all my strength to protect my Liza, but hunger consumed her. She fell ill with tuberculosis. My Liza died two months before the liberation of the Kursk Region. The Germans killed her. I buried her out of sight of anyone so as not to give myself away.

And now I'm alone, I have no one. I'm forty, yet I'm an old woman. This is all that I have left after the Hitlerites.

Thus Piletskaya ended her story.

GARF f. 8114, op. 950, ll. 284-286. A typewritten manuscript with handwritten corrections.

87. The death of my father
THE STORY OF YEVGENIA SHENDELS, LECTURER, MOSCOW INSTITUTE OF FOREIGN LANGUAGES

It was February 9, 1943. I was sitting in the teachers' room of our institute. It was twelve o'clock. The radio announced the time. I checked my watch and saw it was correct. Then all of us, the teachers who had gathered in the room, prepared to listen to the daily bulletin of the Information Bureau.[8]

I listened intently to the announcer's words. At the time, the radio was covering the taking of Kursk, my hometown. My father had remained there; he was an old man, a doctor specializing in pulmonary diseases who was known to everyone. I had heard nothing of him since the occupation of Kursk.

The announcer proceeded to read about military events. The military correspondent of *Pravda* described his impressions upon entering Kursk. I listened with sadness to the words about the destroyed houses, squares, and streets of the devastated city. After all, I knew every tree and stone there. Then the announcer told of how many members of the intelligentsia had been shot by the Germans. My heart shrank. Suddenly, I heard the words "the well-known Dr. Shendels died a hero's death." Perhaps I cried out. Perhaps I only imagined that I did. Rings of fire danced before my eyes and I lost consciousness.

Three days later, my husband accompanied me to Kursk. His friend, a pilot in the civil air fleet, was taking medicines to the liberated city. He agreed to take me with him.

Here I was in my hometown. Sometimes in the summer, when they would let the students go for vacation, I would travel to Kursk. My father would meet me at the station. I loved him very much; for that matter, everyone loved Dr. Shendels. He was the most popular man in town, intelligent, sincere, humane, everything that a doctor ought to be.

Now I walked through the city alone. Ruined buildings, broken windows, scraps of wallpaper hanging from the beams of scorched facades of houses—the last sign of the haven of the past. How it hurt my eyes, how sick I felt at heart!

Friends told me my father's story. About his life and death. When the Germans were approaching the city, he was offered the chance to be evacuated. "I won't leave my patients," said my father, who was the director of a tuberculosis sanatorium. "It's impossible for them to move. Moreover, any agitation would be fraught with consequences for them. I'm staying with them."

And he stayed. The Germans came into the city. They began committing atrocities. All the patients were expelled from the well-lighted, spacious sanatorium by the Germans, whose officers billeted themselves there. My father was at home when they told him of this. Beside himself with indignation, he rushed to the sanatorium.

---

8. The Soviet Information Bureau, or Sovinformburo as it was called.

His patients were lying on the ground around the sanatorium. "Oh," was all my father could say, full of rage. "On the ground, that's deadly for their lungs." He hurried into the building. The sentries would not let him pass—he had worked there for forty years and had given so much attention and love to treating people. An officer came out attracted by the noise.

My father was a hot-tempered man. He rushed at the officer, he demanded the return of the patients to the wards. Perhaps he even wanted to strike the officer, who had replied with a cynical laugh and a volley of curses at the patients.

"Shoot him!" shouted the officer, disappearing through the doorway. They killed my father right away. He lay on the city's central square, and the inhabitants who had known him well looked sorrowfully at the body of the old doctor. It was not until a week later that the Germans gave permission to take the corpse away. My father was buried quietly outside the city.

I sat by his grave. A small mound of earth covered the remains of my father. I had no tears. I was cried out. I looked silently at the earth, thinking of my father and knowing that I would never see him again.

GARF f. 8114, op. 1, 955, l. 114–114ob. A typewritten manuscript.

88. The petition
A SKETCH BY ROZA BASS OF KURSK

The people of Kursk will never forget Dr. Gelman, who was killed by the fascists. Dr. Gelman worked in the Kursk city hospital for many years. A sensitive man and first-rate doctor, a man greatly schooled in his work, he had saved many people from the brink of death. The people of Kursk valued and loved their doctor. When the Red Army retreated from Kursk, Dr. Gelman did not want to leave his patients and remained in town. He greeted the arrival of the Germans fearlessly and was as always at his post, beside his patients. But the old man did not go on working for long. One day, at an early hour when he was making his rounds, the bandits with their swastikas burst into the hospital and arrested Gelman. The patients pleaded in vain with the butchers to spare their doctor. Gelman was taken away. The hospital was orphaned. Dr. Gelman, along with his wife and their sixteen-year-old daughter, was tossed into the cellar at German headquarters. The city became agitated. A petition, drawn up by an unknown person, appeared among the local population and passed from hand to hand, from house to house. Thousands of people appealed to the city authorities and the commandant's office to try to save the life of a man who had dedicated all his years to saving people. But it did not help. On the contrary, the more excitement and bother people raised over Gelman, the more furious the Germans became, indignant at the idea that Russians dared to stand up for a Jew.

For ten days, Dr. Gelman and his family lay helpless in the cellar. No one will ever know the tortures these people endured during this time. On the eleventh day, when a woman who had been saved from death by Gelman brought the prisoners bread as always, the guards cynically announced to her:

"Enough coddling of these kikes! They don't need anything anymore."

Dr. Gelman's family had been shot that day. But vivid memories of him will remain in the hearts of the local residents for a long time to come. To this day, people in Kursk remember with tears in their eyes their kindly old doctor who was brutally tortured by the fascists.

> GARF f. 8114, op. 1, d. 959, l. 102–102ob. A typewritten manuscript with handwritten corrections.

89. They suffered through this themselves
ACCOUNTS OF HUNGARIAN JEWS
RECORDED BY P. BALASHOV
DECEMBER 20, 1942

Miklos Levy, who served in the 109/13 labor battalion of the Hungarian army, and who surrendered on the Voronezh Front, saw everything with his own eyes and experienced for himself the full measure of the human degradation spoken of in the note of the Allied governments and in the statement of the Sovinformburo.[9]

Miklos Levy is 32 years old. He graduated from the High Rabbinical School of Bratislava. Until 1941 he was a private English and German teacher. After that, owing to unemployment, he worked in a leather goods factory in Budapest. In March 1942 Miklos Levy was drafted into a labor battalion of the Hungarian army.

On the way to Russia, he witnessed the dreadful poverty and the absence of rights of the inhabitants of the countries occupied by Germany, particularly in Poland. The Jewish communities were subjected to indescribable abuse. The train was surrounded at the station by crowds of absolutely exhausted women and children with tears in their eyes. They were begging for bits of bread. They were feeble human shadows. One's heart was squeezed with pain to look at them.

During the entire length of the journey to the Front, Miklos Levy saw the charred ruins of towns and villages and dreadful poverty. He saw many Russian women, children, and elderly people working on the roads under the supervision of German soldiers. "These people looked so hungry and pathetic," Miklos Levy says, "that even we, the half-starved, shared crumbs from our paltry bread ration with them."

As Levy walked though the streets of Orel, which had been turned into ruins, it was as though he was walking through a dead city. The inhabitants were almost invisible, while drunken German soldiers and officers, singing fascist songs at the top of their lungs, appeared here and there.

---

9. Two days earlier, on December 18, *Pravda* had carried the Allied declaration on the front page, which condemned the persecution and murder of the Jews in all territory occupied by the Germans, and declared that "such events can only reinforce the determination of freedom-loving peoples to overthrow Hitler's barbaric tyranny."

Miklos Levy was utterly exhausted, like a workhorse with no rights. "After all," he says, "they had always given us Jews very little to eat, and of late they'd been starving us outright. Most of us were overcome by hunger and unbearable work."

During our advance, Miklos Levy surrendered. "The Russians," he says, "opened a withering fire. Hungarians were literally falling around me by the dozen. Those still alive were running away, loudly cursing the officers who had sent them to a sure death. Taking advantage of this flight, I crawled off to one side and hid in a foxhole. Several Red Army soldiers soon showed up, and it was then that I got to my feet, put up my hands and said: "Don't shoot, I'm a Jew." They did not touch me. They gave me some tobacco and a good meal. During all the months I had been at the Front this was the first time that I ate so much and so well."

Ferenc Hedvis, a worker in the 442nd Special Labor Company who gave himself up on the Voronezh Front, witnessed scenes no less tragic. He is thirty-two, an electrical engineer by training. His company was formed in May 1942 in the Hungarian town of Szigetvar. The Third Platoon was made up entirely of Jews, while others had been taken directly from prison. These last were Jehovah's Witnesses who because of their religious convictions had refused to enter the fascist army. The company constructed pillboxes, dug trenches and anti-tank ditches, laid mine fields and anti-tank obstacles.

The fascist officers vied with each other in abusing the Jews any way they could. "When our company arrived in Kursk," Ferenc Hedvis recalls, "the gendarmes carried out a search and took all money, valuables, tins of food, and soap from the Jews. They fed us very badly, and what was more, the officers and soldiers in the guard units stole what little food we had. The company commander, Lt. Tot Shander, forbade us to cook potatoes or corn, and Miklos Miller, Karl Kravets, Gergel Bondar, Laszlo Trifon, and Matiash Lunsha were punished for violating this regulation by being tied up for two hours. We were strictly forbidden to talk to Russians or to ask them for food. The officers tried to set the soldiers against us. I heard Lt. Tot Shander talking to the junior officers: 'Thrash them properly. Let them die, that's not so bad. The fewer of them that return, the better.' The junior officers and soldiers from among the guards carried out his order: they beat us with sticks, rifle butts, or just with their fists."

Ferenc Hedvis saw six Jehovah's Witnesses hanged for refusing to load munitions, while others were shot. Talatzi Shandor, the company commander, ordered them to choose graves for themselves, then shot two of them with his own pistol.

Under guard by German soldiers, with identifying marks on their left sleeves, the Jews worked day and night like slaves in the so-called labor battalions. Many of them died from cold, disease, unbearable forced labor, and sadistic beatings. They were blown up by mines when the Hitlerite monsters sent them ahead of their troops, clearing the way for the army. All these facts are a manifestation of one and the same thing, all of it speaks to the Hitlerites' plan for the destruction of the Jewish population in the occupied territories of Europe.

Everyone who values freedom and the existence of freedom-loving people will lend all their strength to the struggle against the bloody Nazis and their pogroms.

GARF f. 8114, op. 1, d. 959, ll. 92–93. A typewritten manuscript with handwritten corrections and the signature of P. Balashov.

90. Murder of the Jews in the Kalinin Region
FROM THE NOTEBOOK OF THE WOMAN PARTISAN KLAVDIA I.[10]

I had occasion to spend an extended amount of time as the leader of a small band of partisans on the territory of Belorussia, in the Smolensk Region, and in several districts of the Kalinin Region[11] where the Germans still rule. I saw thousands of orphaned children, whose parents had been shot by the Germans or taken away to perform forced labor.

In my partisan's notebook there are many passages about fascist atrocities. It is a reckoning for vengeance. We will repay the Germans for these atrocities. Here are some facts from my notebook.

Recently, in the Oshevsk District of the Kalinin Region, the Germans seized an elderly Jewish schoolteacher named Druzhevskaya. Comrade Druzhevskaya was martyred by Nazi soldiers before the eyes of her three children.

In the village of Bezhanitsy, Bezhanitsy District, Kalinin Region, the Germans arrested 120 Jews. These were people of widely varying professions and ages. All those arrested were placed in one room of an unheated house whose windows had been smashed. They did not receive a drop of water or a piece of bread for many days. If one of the elderly people or the very young pleaded with a soldier for a sip of water, he was immediately beaten. The Nazis declared a virtual St. Bartholomew's Day massacre. Fascists in villages of the Bezhanitsy District exterminated hundreds of Jewish families in the course of that night. The turn of those under arrest also arrived. An officer entered the room containing these 120 people and chose ten. He led them out into the yard and ordered them to dig two graves. When the pits had been dug, they were taken up to the edge of a grave and shot. Then another ten prisoners were taken outside. They threw dirt on the graves in which lay those who had already been shot, then dug a new pit, after which they were shot as well. So it went throughout the night. All 120 of those under arrest were executed.

In Vitebsk, the German barbarians shot the family of Abramsky. There were two children in the family in addition to the mother and father. After breaking into their home during the night, the Hitlerites shot the Abramsky couple and cut off the hands of their two sons, Moisey, 8, and Aron, 7. They locked them in the apartment and went away. The children died.

In the village of Chikhachevo, Kalinin Region, the Germans organized a system of forced labor for the Jewish population. Not so long ago, a train containing

---

10. The author of these notes is a friend of the famous partisan Liza Chaykina.
11. This is the Tver Region today.

three hundred Jews was taken there. They were forced to do the most difficult jobs, hauling stones and logs. People lived in the unheated cars. They did not receive any food for several days. Later, they began to give them one bowl of watery soup per day. Weakened from hunger, emaciation, and overwork, the captives were dying by the dozens. After ten days, only forty of the three hundred Jews who had come to Chikhachevo were still alive, but they were doomed as well. Soon not one of them could move. Then the Germans loaded them into one of the wagons and took them to an unknown destination.

In Novosokolniki, the fascist scoundrels took eleven Jewish women and put them in the same house. The Germans humiliated and abused their victims, and then doused the building with kerosene and set it on fire. All eleven women perished in the fire.

During my time behind the fascist lines, I met many people from Minsk. They told me how the Germans had made their intentions very clear: the elimination of the growing Jewish male children. They are carrying out this program with savage cruelty. It is common for the Gestapo to burst into a block of buildings located in the Jewish ghetto and take away all the young and adolescent boys, who then disappear without a trace.

GARF f. 8114, op. 1, d. 963, ll. 111–112. A typewritten manuscript.

VIII
PRISONERS OF WAR

Jews fought against Germany in all of the Allied armies, and approximately 200,000 were captured. With some exceptions, Jewish POWs from the armies of the Western countries—including Jews from Palestine who fought under the British flag—were treated in the same way as their non-Jewish comrades-in-arms. In these cases, the Germans honored their obligations under the Geneva Convention, if not out of altruistic or legal motives, then out of fear that their captured soldiers would face reprisals.

But Polish Jewish POWs who were captured by the Germans during the fighting in September 1939 were systematically killed. This policy was applied even more deliberately to Soviet Jewish POWs.

A staggering 5.7 million Red Army personnel were captured by German and allied forces over the course of World War II. As many as 3.3 million were murdered or forced to live under such harsh conditions that survival proved impossible, even though they were young men. Only 500,000 were liberated or succeeded in escaping. Another 1 million were released in order to serve as auxiliaries in the German armies. And still another 930,000 remained in German camps as of January 1945.

Germany's indifference to the lives and well-being of Soviet POWs was made easier by the lack of clarity in the reciprocal obligations of the two countries under international law. Under the Bolsheviks, the Soviet Union refused to ratify the 1929 Geneva Convention on Prisoners of War, nor had it declared its commitment to the 1907 Hague Convention on the Rules of War. Germany, therefore, claimed it had no obligation to protect the lives of Soviet POWs, provide humane treatment, or supply them with a minimal degree of food or shelter. So Soviet POWs, particularly in 1941, succumbed to starvation, disease, and exposure after being transported in open freight cars, forced to endure long marches, or made to live in open fields, in dugouts, or without shelter of any kind.

Moreover, six hundred Soviet POWs were subjected to a gruesome and ominous experiment. In September 1941, the deputy commander of Auschwitz, Karl Fritsch, placed them in a sealed room and subjected them to the effects of Zyklon B pesticide. Evidently the Germans were pleased with the results; they adopted this method of murder in Auschwitz-Birkenau and other camps under the authority of the SS Inspectorate of concentration camps. But by 1942, the Germans began to improve conditions somewhat for Soviet POWs in general; policymakers understood that the war would take time and require a supply of forced labor.

Nonetheless, Soviet Jewish POWs fared the worst. Weeks before the German invasion, Wehrmacht commanders issued the so-called "Commissar Order," on June 6, 1941, mandating "ruthless and energetic measures against Bolshevist instigators, partisans, saboteurs, and Jews, and the total eradication of any active or passive resistance."[1] Upon capture, Soviet Jewish POWs were identified and immediately shot. Between seventy-five and eighty thousand met this fate. Even the Soviet press, which rarely highlighted Jewish suffering, did not ignore it. No less a figure than the Soviet writer Mikhail Sholokohov, notorious for his antisemitism, wrote a sympathetic description of how captured Jewish soldiers were singled out by the Germans. His article, entitled "The Science of Hatred," appeared in *Pravda* on June 22, 1942, on the first anniversary of the German invasion. It told of a Siberian lieutenant who fell into German captivity. After he and his comrades were captured, they were lined up and confronted by an enemy officer.

> A German lieutenant asked in poor Russian if there were any commissars and commanders among us. Everyone was silent. Then he said again, "Commissars and officers, two steps forward." No one left the line. Walking by slowly, the lieutenant picked out about sixteen people who looked like Jews. He asked each one, "*Jude?*" and without waiting for a response, ordered them out of line. Among those selected were Jews, Armenians, and simply Russians with a dark complexion and black hair. Before our very eyes, all of them were taken aside and shot with submachine guns.[2]

91. Glukhov camp
THE RECOLLECTIONS OF M. YU. KOFMAN
JANUARY 20, 1945[3]

---

1. Cited in Christopher R. Browning, *The Origins of the Final Solution: The Evolution of Nazi Jewish Policy, September 1939–March 1942* (Lincoln, Neb., 2004), pp. 250–251.
2. This translation is from Karel C. Berkhoff, "The Mass Murder of Soviet Prisoners of War and the Holocaust—How Were They Related?" *Kritika: Explorations in Russian and Eurasian History* 4 (Fall 2005), p. 789.
3. These recollections were sent to Ilya Ehrenburg from Odessa on January 20, 1945.

On the eve

On the morning of November 7, 1941, we woke up as usual when the sky-blue dawn of the approaching day showed itself in the window of the ward. There were eleven of us in the third ward. I remember my comrades: Rusalkin, Kravchenko, Captain Cherchenko, Dudaev, Gavrilov, Sbitnev, Rustakov, Semibratov, and two others whose names I have forgotten. Some got up to see to their personal needs, others lit cigarettes, while still others stretched, cracking their joints and groaning from sleep.

Comrade Cherchenko, stretching himself sleepily as he sat down on the edge of his bed, announced to everyone: "Comrades, I salute you on the occasion of the anniversary of the Great October Revolution. I hope that you will meet its next anniversary with your nearest and dearest in a Russia free from the fascist occupiers." Several voices, answering with gratitude and greetings in return, brought a lively atmosphere into the ward. Coming to see us a short while later from the neighboring ward was Comrade Viktor Mikhaylovich Rassadin, an air force navigator who had been wounded in both legs when his plane was shot down, but who had recovered and now walked on his own. With him were Lt. Vinokurov of Gorky, the highway engineer Alexander Popandopulo of Tbilisi, and Dr. Kochetkov, who had been wounded in the eye. Comrades with patriotic Soviet sentiments gravitated toward our ward because of the presence of Captain Cherchenko, who was senior in rank, and of myself, to whom the majority of our comrades turned when they wondered about various questions in all domains of science, politics, and literature. I was the first to ask the nurses and other medical personnel to provide us with chess sets and different kinds of literature. Both were provided thanks to the warm and sympathetic attitude of the nurses toward the wounded and the POWs. We alternated reading with playing chess. When we needed a break from playing and reading, we sat down to discuss everything connected to the war and our captivity.

There were anti-Soviet types among us, in particular, Alexey Gavrilov (born in 1908) of Voroshilovgrad, who distinguished himself with his vile and slanderous attacks. Cherchenko and Kochetkov answered him impressively and, to the unanimous approval of the entire ward, put him in his place. This squabbling continued for several days after we were transferred out of the villages to the hospital at Krolevets. Finding no supporters in the remaining group of wounded, Gavrilov quieted down and began to give in to the general mood prevailing among his other comrades.

On the morning of November 8, I was the first to wake up, and, after getting out of bed, I saw a German soldier in the window; he was armed and wearing a steel helmet while he marched back and forth in front of the hospital exit. I immediately let my comrades know about this, since I quickly sensed that something ominous was going on. They were just waking up and began to keep an eye out through the window. The nurses who came in explained that some Germans had come from the commandant's office and would be taking recovered and ambulatory prisoners to the camps. Commotion and panic broke out among the wounded. The doctor, Comrade Lev Nikolaevich Nezhebitsky of Pyatigorsk, who was also a POW, came in and ordered everyone to get dressed and ready. Indeed, half an hour later, the Germans turned up.

The group of five or so officers (one of whom spoke fluent Russian) accompanied by several armed soldiers, came into our ward. Comrade Nezhebitsky accompanied them, took down biographical data, and determined diagnoses for the wounded, as well as their general state of health. In his determinations, one could tell he wanted to protect the wounded from being transferred to the camps. Over the course of our stay in the hospital (beginning on September 15, 1941), we had heard from the citizens and peasants who had visited us of the horrors raging in the environs of the Konotop camp near Krolevets. Women who had visited the camp hoping to find family members and friends recounted with horror the scenes that they had witnessed: of prisoners of war perishing from torture, hunger, and the firing squad.

I was registered on the hospital books as a Russian. Just in case it was discovered that I was not a Christian (because of the rite of circumcision), I put myself down as a native of Feodosia, so that in case the question arose, I could claim that my father was a Crimean Tatar and my mother of Italian descent. But neither my father nor my mother had brought me up. They had given me to a Russian woman, in whose home I had been raised and educated. From 1921 to 1924, after being demobilized from the Red Army following the civil war, I worked as a customs agent in a port. In the course of my duties I had occasion to be on all the foreign ships, where I spent most of my time, right up to accompanying these steamships along our inner Black Sea coast. This gave me the opportunity to study the daily life and terminology of sailors. In the space for "occupation," I would casually reply to the question with: "Write ship's watchman, or harbor pilot, or even just a sailor." During hours of idleness, lying on cots, each wounded man would distract the others with stories of his own life, usually ones having to do with his job before the war.

When it was my turn to divert my comrades with conversation, I would engage their attention with stories of life on boats and of fantastic voyages from one foreign port of call to another. I would tell them about Istanbul, Marseille, and Liverpool, where in fact I had never been in my life. All of these stories about ports and sailing, known to me only through literature, stood me in good stead. Thanks to my clear diction, for which I am genuinely indebted to my nanny, Avdotya Timofeevna Laukhina, who had lived with us from the day I was born until I was twenty-two, and whom I had even helped to bury, no one would have guessed that I was a Jew by nationality. I was able to use archaic Russian words and expressions, which dispelled any doubts about my roots. The sum total of all of these facts—a profession in which one hardly ever found a Jew, pure Russian speech, and an appearance radically changed by wounds and weight loss—made it possible for me to conceal my nationality, in particular from less educated people. I would often notice the long drawn-out looks that the more curious gave me, as they wondered whether or not it was a Russian standing before them. In those instances I would, as they say, get right to work. I would not turn away and hide, but would immediately turn casually to such a person and stubbornly ply them with requests for tobacco, books, paper, and so on. At the same time, I would try to engage the man in conversation until I became convinced that I had dispelled all of his doubts. This was unquestionably the right approach, since I subsequently witnessed the end of many Jewish POWs as a result of their having betrayed themselves by their diffidence at the first curious glance. This happened many times in the Slavuta camp in particular, where the famous butcher Mitrofansky, known throughout the camp as "the Father of the Jews," wrought his havoc. But more of that later.

When Dr. Nezhebitsky, accompanied by the Germans, came up to me I already knew that it would be impossible for him to protect me, since other wounded men in a state of health equal to mine, who had preceded me into the examination, had ended up on the lists of those to be removed to the camp. In the process of being entered on the list, I felt the blood pounding in my head and my heart beating faster at the question of "nationality." I instantly pulled myself together, though. Drawing every nerve taut, I answered with seeming nonchalance: "Russian." I do not know whether or not my momentary agitation betrayed itself in some way that I was unaware of, but unexpectedly, in the absolutely silent ward, one of the SS said to me in perfect Russian: "Are you telling the truth when you say that you're Russian?" For a moment I had the feeling that I was done for. In the next instant I tried to grin. With a smile on my face, I answered: "I'm not lying, ask my comrades." The SS trooper, without taking his eyes off me, said, as though he were giving me a moral lesson: "It's not nice to deceive people." Unexpectedly, Comrade Nezhebitsky, holding his list and his pencil, turned to the soldier: "He was born to a Tatar father and an Italian mother, but he was brought up by Russians." Over the three or four minutes in which this conversation took place, I was the center of attention in our ward: for the Germans, the wounded, and the staff. The Germans were curious why the SS soldier was focusing on me, and from his reply I understood that he was answering them concerning my half-Italian ancestry. They smiled with self-satisfaction, as if to say, why, he's almost a comrade-in-arms. They entered my name on the list of those to be sent to the camp.

The commission moved on. In the next ward was Abram Markovich Beker, forty-three, a Jew from Odessa who had lived with his wife's family and their two children on Sverdlov Street. He had been wounded in the right shoulder, and his arm dangled lifelessly by his side. With the exception of two or three people, including the previously described Gavrilov, everyone treated him with particular attention because they sensed that he was doomed. He himself was the most inoffensive of creatures. A machinist by profession, he worked in a trade school. Thanks to a vividly expressive face and accent, he could not hide his nationality. He was always alone, spent time with no one, and only rarely spoke to me or to Captain Leonty Kuzmich Cherchenko of Melitopol (born in 1902), who had been wounded in both legs. He would request salt, bread, and onions from us, or ask us to prevail upon the barber (who was also among the wounded) to give him a shave and a haircut since the fellow did not want to shave everyone, much less a Jew. Our barber was David Yakovlevich Dunaev, from Dagestan. He was not a bad fellow, but he managed to become infected with the poison of hostility toward Jews. I remember Comrade Cherchenko saying to him: "David, be a Soviet man—give Beker a shave." Dunaev came back with some meaningless answer; half an hour later, though, Beker was clean-shaven and trimmed.

For their part, the medical staff, particularly Drs. Viktor Fyodorovich Zelinsky, L. N. Nezhebitsky, Varvara Nikiforovna Pivovarova; the nurses Maria Alexandrovna and Maria Alexeevna; and the orderly Klava, behaved with particular warmth and sensitivity toward Beker. It is possible that what was happening here was pity for a doomed man, whose execution was expected any day. Rumors of the horrors of the extermination in Kiev of perhaps forty or even sixty thousand Jews in a single day reached the hospital.

One day, as I was taking a walk through the streets of Krolevets with Comrades Cherchenko and Naumenko, I read some announcements posted on fences on which there appeared, over the signature of police chief Seredinin, the order that all Jews needed to register by October 15. On the street, I happened to see three Jews coming toward me wearing armbands. Passers-by were watching them with curious looks, and many had smiles and joking remarks for them. At a busy intersection, a group of two or three young drunks with rifles and wearing "P" (for *polizei*) armbands stopped one of the Jews. He looked to be forty-five to forty-eight years old, a tailor or a cobbler. They surrounded him, and, to the sound of laughter and hollering, began to play with him as if he were a volleyball. He found himself inside a circle, where the policeman closest to him in this peculiar game would simply shove him. The unfortunate Jew was terrified. Hatless, his jacket unbuttoned, holding his head in his hands, he fell to the ground several times, often hitting a rock. They made him get up again with kicks, and the "game" went on.

With a grimace of disgust at this scene, Cherchenko took me by the arm and we went to the hospital. What we had seen troubled us all day. I tried not to show any outward signs of my suffering. Cherchenko, on the other hand, twitched with horror at every mention of what we had witnessed, and his deep sighs told me clearly how bitter his sufferings were from our temporary humiliation as a result of the war's initial reverses. He was a career army man. He began his service as a private and was then promoted to the rank of captain just before the war and was responsible for technical supplies to the 10th Tank Division. We were friends from the very start, as soon as we met in the ward. In the course of our conversations, we were joined by other comrades who felt among ourselves that they were still living the Soviet life, in spite of the fact that we were living on territory occupied by the German fascists. All of our discussions and conversations, in the limited circle of those comrades standing by us with whom we could confide our thoughts, turned on the options for future action that would present themselves. None of us doubted that the misfortune that had overtaken us was a temporary phenomenon, and the words of Comrade Molotov: "Our cause is just, the enemy will be crushed," were repeated in every discussion. We were all firmly convinced of the ultimate victory over fascism. Our ultimate aim was to make our way back to the ranks of the Red Army, or into a partisan detachment. However, the nature of our wounds and our varying states of health made for differences in the timetable for carrying out these intentions.

The first to go were two without serious wounds. I do not remember their surnames. They would see Comrade Cherchenko every day with maps, and we would sit on his cot tracing the routes to follow. On one of these days, they did not appear. Someone informed the police that they had been associating with partisans and had escaped into the forest, and that another mass escape was being planned from the hospital. Two or three days later, Seredinin, the chief of police (prior to the occupation he had been a bookkeeper in some kind of enterprise), turned up at the hospital. He made the rounds of all of the wards and announced to the wounded (and in our ward to Captain Cherchenko personally) that patients absent from the hospital would be arrested and remanded by the German commandant's office to a military field tribunal for attempting to defect to the partisans. Simultaneously, a police post was set up in the hospital and given the job of not allowing any prisoner of war to leave. These measures, of course, could not put a stop to our plans.

A few days later, Comrades Mangutov and Rassadin escaped. But when they reached the eighteen kilometer point, their festering wounds compelled them to come back to the hospital in peasant carts and resume treatment. One of the first who escaped and managed to make it to the partisans contacted Dr. Kochetkov. One day he went out to the village of Gruzskoye, fifteen kilometers from the hospital, to visit a patient, taking with him a variety of medicines for dressing wounds. The local inhabitants, as well as the nurses and orderlies who came to see us, would bring us daily reports from the town and the surrounding areas. They told us about a bridge that had been blown up by the partisans at Baturin; that the Germans were afraid to go out alone; that the fascists were robbing and raping in town and in the villages. The radio spoke two or three times a day of the imminent fall of Moscow and Leningrad, and the end of the blitzkrieg.

This was our situation on November 8, when, upon waking in the morning, we discovered that the entire hospital was under SS guard. This day turned out to be the last in the lives of Kochetkov and Beker and fateful for many others who ended it in the POW camp at Glukhov.

The death of Kochetkov, Beker, and an unknown soldier

Death. I grew accustomed in my life to perceiving all abstract feelings as something physical, material. Life, joy, and love have always presented themselves to me as a sort of bright, sunny, warm day, with greenery and smiling, happy people all around. Everything is living, moving, thoughts are peaceful, and, most important of all, thought is constantly producing, like birth, one and the same product: consciousness. Life, life, life—the brain gives off the concept endlessly, and you see everything around yourself through this tangible, seemingly material mass: the sun, warmth, light. In other words, what you are accustomed to feeling and calling "life."

Today, November 8, through some sixth sense that science did not foresee, I recognized and felt death. From that day forward my consciousness did not see the sun, did not feel warmth, did not know life. It might have been daylight, with the sun shining, but I saw and sensed darkness and cold. Something dark, gloomy, and cold stood before me from that morning on. Later on, I got used to the idea that I was suffering from a fear of light. Like it or not, I became less nervous when it was dark. I would wait for daybreak with horror. Night, wind, darkness. What a time to be thankful for; no one sees me, no one comes for me, no one begins to look at me intently. I can lie and sit in my bunk without throwing an overcoat over my head first. No one looks at me when I spend the night thinking, thinking, thinking. How much distress and suffering the first light of the breaking dawn in the east brought me.

I was not sleeping. I say this again with full awareness! Glukhov, Krolevets, Slavuta, Vladimir-Volynsky, Konotop, Sedlets, villages, forests, farms. I was not sleeping. I was departing into death, into non-being. I saw Beker, Kochetkov, Anatoly Pavlov, a crowd of faces, whole rows of Jews standing by the pit at Glukhov, Slavuta, and Konotop. There they are, national minorities running by me single file, chased along by SS clubs toward the pit to be shot. I see them torturing women and the elderly in Konotop. They beat 344 peasants there, men and women, for three days. On the fourth day, they shot them by the brick factory. They left 22 dead in their bunks from beatings. In our block in Slavuta, 8 to 10 Jews were taken out to be shot every two or three days. Then they brought the legless Katz in a wagon, with a man from the Abwehr following behind on a motorcycle with a submachine gun to shoot him.[4] More and more pictures rise up in my memory: I see all the faces, I remember the smallest details of their bodies, the way they walked, their underwear down to the smallest fold. I committed their faces to memory forever. I feel them! I was in "death," you see, and I, paradoxically, lived with them not in life, but in death. I felt the blows of the clubs that rained down on Beker. I felt the icy cold felt by the Jewish POWs herded out into the November frost in their underwear at the Kremenchug camp; I froze at the telling of the story of the Jewish doctors taken naked out of the Lutsk bathhouse in January and loaded into a truck to be shot.

---

4. Abwehr refers to German military intelligence.

There turned out to be thirteen of us chosen for transfer to the camp. Among us, as I recall, there were: Cherchenko, Dudaev, Vinokurov, Mangutov, Kochetkov and Beker. Kochetkov for some reason had not been included on the general list. They chased all of us into the main building. They did a roll call there, then drove us back outside. They brought up a heavy truck. The nurses helped us in. SS soldiers occupied the outside places on the back of the truck, and we moved off. They drove us to the commandant's office. Before we were even near the place, we noticed, from some distance off, a group of POWs waiting there for us, around sixty men stopped at different times on the roads and assembled at the commandant's headquarters for transfer to the camp. They got us out of the truck, counted us again, and formed us up in ranks of five in the rear of the group. One of the Germans, who had been in the hospital during our selection, called over the senior guard and said something to him, pointing to Beker and Kochetkov as he did so. A German came out of the commandant's building with a piece of paper and shouted: "Kochetkov!" The latter replied: "That's me!" He beckoned with a finger: "*Komm hier!*" [Come over here!] and, turning around, went back into the building. Kochetkov followed him.

Not far from the commandant's headquarters, which was in a school building, there was a small but dense garden. We continued to stand outside the commandant's office surrounded by steel-helmeted SS men tucking camouflaged raincoats into their belts. The POWs brought from the hospital were relatively well-dressed. All were wearing overcoats and boots. Some were wearing fur hats, though most had cloth caps on. The group of sixty or so POWs that had been detained by the local police stood out brightly in motley rags into which they had changed in the homes of peasants for purposes of disguising themselves as they tried to escape through the villages. Before the war, the clothes on their backs would have been good only for the ragman. There were quilted jackets full of holes, homespun peasant sweaters, old sheepskin coats with patches, while most had bast sandals on their feet. An hour or so passed. Many began trying to warm themselves, jumping up and down in place. There was a mild frost. The water in the puddles was covered with a glassy crust.

It was around ten o'clock. Some women, children, and old people were gathered not far away on the opposite side of the yard. One of the prisoners began making signs to them to show that we needed food. A woman produced half a loaf of bread from a bag and gave it to one of the children to take to us. One of the Germans guarding us, however, let us know with a shout and the click of the bolt on his rifle that the slightest attempt at fraternization would bring instant death. The crowd that was observing us expressed its sympathy in gestures. Many women were wiping away tears with their handkerchiefs. But they could not give us any substantial help.

We were chilled to the bone by the time we heard the voices and the tread of the Germans coming out of the commandant's headquarters. An officer was in the front, followed by two soldiers with submachine guns. After them came Dr. Kochetkov, who was being prodded in the back by two soldiers with bayonets. Not everyone recognized him immediately. He was wearing only his underwear. He was barefoot, without a hat, his hair dishevelled, his shirt in tatters in the back. He was carrying his clothes, overcoat, and boots. The Germans were taking him in the direction of the garden. Coming up to the fence from the right, the officer showed him where to stand, indicating to him with gestures that he should place his clothes and shoes on the ground off to one side. A group of four soldiers with rifles and submachine guns came to a halt approximately fifteen feet from him. The officer moved aside. Kochetkov was looking around in bewilderment. To an outsider it would have seemed that he was making a fuss about something or looking for someone. There was a feeling that he was worried about something off to the side and not about the danger that was threatening his life. The volley that rang out caught him in the middle of these cares. He was not even looking in the direction of his executioners, did not even see them preparing to shoot, or hear the order. He fell, hit by four bullets. His head was shattered entirely. His face was no longer visible. There was some sort of dark red stain on the earth, bright against a fine layer of snow.

I remembered: "I graduated from medical school. I'm the son of a peasant. There is no other country where the children of peasants and workers can become doctors, engineers, agronomists, professors, and other sorts of great and important people."

This was something that Kochetkov had said during an argument with that scoundrel Gavrilov, not heeding the danger of being overheard by one of those few hardened enemies of the Soviet system who were with us in the hospital. This excessive disregard for the danger of being denounced for devotion to Soviet Russia led to his premature death. He spoke out openly against the fascists, suggested in the presence of everyone that they leave the hospital as soon as possible, and incited others to do it, ignoring as he did it any caution or conspiratorial secrecy. He was, of course, sold out by the hospital staff. None of the wounded would have done such a thing, if only out of a feeling of gratitude to him for his care, since in the early going there had not been a single doctor in the hospital except for him, and in spite of the fact that he himself had been wounded in the eye by mine fragments, he still tended to the injured. I was standing alongside Comrades Cherchenko and Vinokurov. When the command to shoot was given, Cherchenko turned away, moaned, and grabbed my good arm, leaning with all his weight on his cane. "Oh, Misha, I can't look. I'll never forget this." No one else said anything.

A crowd of local peasants standing not far off began to stir. A woman shrieked. Someone made the sign of the cross. The officer called for two men from the crowd, showing the number with fingers spread apart. An elderly man and a teenage boy of fifteen or sixteen came out of the crowd. The German made gestures telling them to bring up shovels, dig a hole, and bury Kochetkov's body. After that he pointed the clothes out to them, saying that after the work was done the clothing would be theirs. Both of those summoned, nodding their heads as a sign that all was clear and that they understood everything that was being asked of them, quickly took off after the shovels.

An order was given, and the prisoners, surrounded by an SS escort, formed up in ranks of five. The senior guard among the junior officers took some papers from an officer, after which both of them looked in the direction of our group of wounded. Speaking quickly to one another, they approached, looking for someone. All of the wounded sensed intuitively that Beker was the object of their words and looks. The guards standing near us, overhearing the discussion of their superiors, also looked us over, and everyone's attention was fixed on Beker. The officer gave the senior guard his final orders, looking at Beker as he did so. The officer, nodding as a sign of obedience and looking at Beker, answered in a staccato voice: "*Jawohl, jawohl*" [Yes, yes!]. The officer's last shout was "*Marsch!*" [March!] and, surrounded by ten or so SS, we moved off through the outlying streets and out of town.

We marched down the middle of the road, stepping on the clods churned up by wheels and horses' hooves. Somewhere on the way, we sank into a puddle of muck from horse urine and dung. The guards walked alongside on the edges, holding on to fences while they tried to walk on the trodden, dry paths. Whenever one of the prisoners tried to go around a puddle or some of the muck, the nearest guard prodded him in the buttocks with a bayonet. For more than half a kilometer, I went into filth and water several times, the icy liquid pouring over the tops of my boots. Upon leaving the city, we noticed three peasant carts with one guard beside them standing by the last hut waiting for us. A light machine gun lay in one of the carts. When we had drawn even with the carts, the junior officer halted us, chose six men who were limping or leaning on canes, and had them seated in two of the carts. Cherchenko and I wound up in the same cart. We moved along immediately behind the crowd of prisoners, who were surrounded by guards. Bringing up the rear of the procession was the third cart with the machine gun and the German along with it. A field was already in sight. Several soldiers had pulled long, heavy poles out of the last fence in an outlying village and were walking along waving them in the air or using them as walking sticks.

Beker was in the last row of those walking in front of our cart. All of a sudden, two soldiers separated themselves from the escort and immediately began to follow behind Beker's back. Each one of them had a pole in his hands. One of the Germans went ahead of him and, looking right in his face, asked him: "*Du bist ein Jude?*" [Are you a Jew?] I did not hear Beker's reply. The second soldier, though, having drawn back his pole, brought it down on Beker's back. The pole must have struck him on his injured shoulder, because Beker jumped and clutched the wound with his good hand. The German who was questioning him fell back and, finding himself behind him, followed the example of the first man. Beker jumped again. From behind, his leaps seemed comical, like those of a man dancing.

Yes, it was a dance of death. It made the Germans laugh. They began raining blows down on his shoulders to the accompaniment of some song that an SS soldier of twenty-one or twenty-two was humming, accompanying each beat of the song with a blow from his pole to the man's shoulder. Beker was "dancing." There were already eight or so guards following him. His "dance" amused them all. They were singing in chorus, five or six voices could be heard. Beker tried in vain to squeeze himself into the ranks of prisoners marching in front of him. The last ones, so as not to serve as targets for the Germans, gave way so that the ranks to their rear would not close on them, and Beker's back continued to act as a drum for the meter of some merry little tune. The "dance" took peculiar forms: now he would give little leaps, or, picking up the pace, would rock from side to side, and now would sit down and then get back to his feet. I did not see his face. Not a moan or complaint could be heard. Horror overcame everyone. The prisoners were glancing at each other, as though looking for the answer to the questions: "Am I guilty of something?" and "Will it be my turn after Beker?" Although everyone knew perfectly well why he was being tortured, the absence of any such reason in their case was no guarantee of their safety, given the enthusiasm and passion the Germans lent to the business of tormenting their victim.

We were coming up to a gully. The road was going downhill. There was a shallow ditch on one side, sloping farther down into a precipice that formed a sort of ravine. Reaching the halfway point on the hill, the officer halted the whole team. They led Beker away from the crowd of POWs, then chose a man wearing bast sandals and ordered him to remove Beker's boots. The prisoner quickly went up to Beker and took off Beker's boots. He immediately threw off his own sandals and slid his feet into the boots. One of the Germans unbuttoned Beker's overcoat, took it by the sides and pulled it from his arms. The unfortunate man was standing barefoot, in his trousers and a lilac knitted shirt.

I saw a dark, unshaven face. I could not make out any separate features, since there was only one thing coming from his eyes and it impressed itself on me for life. Two suffering eyes full of melancholy and sadness. I had seen eyes like that only in paintings showing Jesus Christ crucified on the cross. Or more accurately, not the eyes, but the lids. He lowered them with such hopelessness and kept them so motionless that all of his sufferings and torments were concentrated in those two small parts of his body. The officer took his pistol from its holster. Two guards led Beker back along the road to the precipice. All four passed by us. Prisoners, Germans, and the peasant cart drivers were standing there motionless and seeing Beker off on his final journey. Beker was departing life. He was walking calmly, businesslike. He was no longer "dancing," no longer asking his butchers for anything. Had he realized the uselessness of it all, or did he realize anything at all in these last minutes?

GARF f. 8114, op. 1, d. 960, ll. 92–97ob. The original manuscript.

92. In German captivity, escape, and wandering through Ukraine
A LETTER FROM RED ARMY SOLDIER ALEXANDER SHAPIRO
NOVEMBER 19, 1942

On the morning of October 21, 1941, while crossing the Sula River, I found myself in an encirclement and was taken prisoner. The Germans immediately sent us out onto the steppe. There, they picked out the Jews and officers. Everyone was silent, but the Germans who had lived in the USSR betrayed them. They led away thirty men, mocked them as they undressed, confiscated their money, watches, and all sorts of odds and ends. They marched us to a village, where we were beaten and forced to dig a ditch. They made us kneel, shouting "*Judische Schweine!*" [Jewish pig!]. I refused to dig the ditch because I knew that it was for me. They beat me badly. They began shooting, taking men by the legs and throwing them into the ditch.

I told the interpreter that I was an Uzbek but that I lived in Azerbaijan. I was dark-skinned, long-haired, with a black beard and a black moustache. They beat me about the head with sticks and took me to a barn. A woman whom I did not know came up to me and handed me a torn forage cap and a fur hat. She had nothing else. She called the Germans bandits, and said to them: "What are you shooting them for? They're defending their country." They beat her up, and she went away.

They fed us millet and beat us daily. I suffered through eighteen days of this. The commandant came and said that they were going take us to Lvov, and from there to Norway. I turned to the other fellows and told them that I was born in Ukraine and that I would die there. I said that we had to make a run for it. That night, a hundred men ran away, but I did not manage to go with them. They ordered us to line up. A few of us hid out in a pig shed; it was warm there and they did not find us. The Germans were shouting [in broken Russian]: "*Russ, vykhodi!*" [Russian, come out!], but we kept our mouths shut. I made it to the next farm. They said that there were no Germans there, gave me something to eat, then showed me the road. I decided to go to Kharkov.

I passed through occupied towns and villages. I saw the abuse and acts of violence committed against our brothers. I saw the gallows and the brothels, and a great deal of plundering. I passed through Dnepropetrovsk, where I was born and had lived. I learned that my brother and his family had been shot. On October 15, 1941, the Germans shot thirty thousand peaceful civilians in my hometown, and I was in Dnepropetrovsk on October 24. I kept going, was in Sinelnikovo, saw my first cousin in secret along with his wife and children. The Germans had robbed and beaten them, but the Gestapo had not yet been in Sinelnikovo, and so my cousin and his family were still alive. I passed through Pavlograd, and found out there that another cousin had been killed along with four thousand residents of the city. I saw and read the dull bulletins of the Germans in which nothing was said about murders and plundering. I saw the Germans gathering wheat and sending it westward, and how they confiscated clothing, beds, and cattle.

As I walked along an embankment, I saw Germans, Italians, Romanians, and Hungarians on their way to pillage. The Italians were on donkeys and heading for Lozovaya, the Hungarians with them, while the Romanians were going south. I walked along with a pitchfork, a bucket, and a whip. I was unkempt and looked like an old man. In this way, I reached the Front and crossed it.

Red Army soldier Alexander Shapiro
November 14, 1942

GARF f. 8114, op. 1, d. 955, ll. 109–110. A typewritten manuscript.

93. Rescue from a POW camp in the village of Latonovo, Rostov Region
A SURVIVOR'S ACCOUNT [5]

In this letter, I want to talk about the friendship of our multiethnic people, since I, a Jew by nationality who spent more time on the territory temporarily occupied by the Germans than almost anyone else, have experienced the mutual assistance of our people for each other. I spent one year and nineteen days on temporarily occupied territory. I will tell things in their proper order. I was in a German camp in the village of Latonovo, Rostov Region. Among the prisoners of war, the majority of whom were wounded, there were representatives of almost all the nations of our Union. The Germans who were guarding us did everything they could through their interpreter, a German colonist, to incite nationalistic enmity among the prisoners. They promised freedom or a promotion to the post of guard for the handing over of a Jew. In spite of all that, during my entire stay in the camp, it never happened once. In the camp, I met a Georgian named Georgy Sakhnoshvili who, knowing that I was a Jew, exposed himself to colossal danger by always staying near me. He shared his ration with me, and when there was the chance to leave for Taganrog in order to enter the local hospital, he dragged me forty kilometers, virtually carrying me in his arms. (I was seriously wounded and ill with typhus.)

In the city of Taganrog, in the Third Soviet Hospital, there were wounded soldiers in one of the wings. The inhabitants of the city of Taganrog, in spite of harassment by the Germans, helped the wounded soldiers as best they could. In the hospital, I got to know Tamara Zozulenko and Nadya Nagornaya. Following my recovery, these two Russian girls went to the military police and signed me out of the hospital as their cousin. They knew the risk they were taking very well. I lived in the city of Taganrog for five months in the home of the Russian citizen Klavdia Ivanovna Kravchenko. She put me back on my feet after treating my wounds, and helped me to return to my family. For having concealed me, since she was betrayed by her neighbors, she suffered greatly.

Here is an excerpt from a letter of hers that I received: "When I saw you out of Taganrog on September 2, 1942, our building was surrounded that very night and searched by armed men. Of course, they took me to the police. They charged me with concealing a Jew. They beat me, and I sat in the police station for a long time. But I kept on saying that you were a Russian. They asked Tatyana Ivanovna (an old

---

5. This letter does not carry a signature or the name of the correspondent.

lady in the building) whether or not you were a Jew, and she answered that she had not been at your baptism. When they finally let me go, I don't know what I looked like."

I was treated in the hospital by Dr. Upryamtsev (a POW). He was shot by the Germans. Knowing that I was Jew, he had obtained for me the papers of a civilian patient named Morozov who had died. All of these facts confirm that our people have been educated in such a way that no German campaign to sow dissension and enmity among nationalities will produce any fruitful results.

GARF f. 8114, op. 1, d. 956, ll. 176–177. A typewritten manuscript.

Detailed Table of Contents

Contents   v

Preface   vii

Acknowledgments   ix

The Destruction of the Jews in German-Occupied
   Territories of the Soviet Union   xiii
YITZHAK ARAD

The History and Fate of *The Black Book* and *The Unknown Black Book*   xix
ILYA ALTMAN

Note on Translation   xl

The War and the Final Solution on the Russian Front   3
JOSHUA RUBENSTEIN

I. UKRAINE   51
Kiev

1. Life in occupied Kiev: The recollections of Ida S. Belozovskaya   53

2. A list of members of the Jewish intelligentsia, with their families, who perished at Babi Yar. Compiled by A. Kagan, January 15, 1945   59

3. Nineteen months in a coffin: The story of the midwife Sofia Borisovna Ayzenshteyn-Dolgusheva   60

4. A stranger from the other world: The story of the artist Felix Zinovevich Giterman   62

5. How I was saved from Hitler: The recollections of the teacher Emilia Borisovna Kotlova. From letters to Ilya Ehrenburg, 1945   67

Lvov

6. A forced labor camp: The recollections of Stepan Yakimovich Shenfeld [1943]   89

Kharkov

7. The story of one individual who was saved from the Kharkov ghetto: The recollections of the engineer S. S. Krivoruchko   99

8. Pages from Dante: From the diary of Kharkov resident N. F. Belonozhko. Prepared by Vladimir Lidin [1941–1942]   103

9. The destruction of the Jews of Kharkov: The recollections of Nina Mogilevskaya, wife of a welder. Recorded by S. Golovanivsky   105

Odessa and Transnistria

10. Why did it happen to us? The recollections of Dr. Lidia Maximovna Slipchenko (Kozman) [1944]   109

11. The story of Anna Morgulis from Odessa. Recorded by R. A. Davis. Translated by M. Bregman [1944]   115

12. In prison for concealing Jews: The testimony of nurse Alexandra Yakovlevna Volovtseva, May 10, 1944. From the files of the Extraordinary State Commission for the Investigation of Atrocities Committed on Soviet Territory by the German-Fascist Invaders and Their Accomplices   119

13. To avenge my children: A letter from Tatyana Rekochinskaya to her brother, Abram, on active duty in the army [1944]   120

14. My life in a fascist prison: The recollections and verses of the schoolboy Lev Rozhetsky, April 4–August 16, 1944   121

15. In occupied Odessa and Transnistria: The recollections of Dr. Israel Borisovich Adesman and the list he compiled of Odessa doctors who perished. Recorded by his wife, Rakhil Iosifovna Goldental [1944]   132

16. The camp at Bogdanovka: The testimony of Filipp Borisovich Klinov, Pavel Ivanovich Stonoga, Karp Korneevich Sheremet, and Vera Pavlovna Kabanets, May 1–2, 1944. From the archives of the Extraordinary State Commission   138

17. Resistance: A report on the activities of an underground group in Odessa [1944]   141

18. The escape of twenty-five Jewish girls from the Tulchin ghetto: Reminiscences of the partisan fighter Golda Vasserman [1944]   149

19. Mama, save me! A letter from Blyuma Isaakovna Bronfin, Khmelnik, Vinnitsa Region, to Ilya Ehrenburg [1944]   151

Cities and Shtetls of Ukraine

20. Avenge us! Farewell inscriptions on the walls of the synagogue in Kovel, Volyn Region. Letter from Sergeant S. N. Grutman to Ilya Ehrenburg, December 2, 1944   154

21. The fate of the Jews of the shtetl of Yedintsy, Khotin District, Chernovitsy Region. From a letter by Rakhil Fradis-Milner to Rakhil Kovnator, September 25, 1944   157

22. The boy from Berdichev: The story of Khaim Roytman   161

23. At the family grave: The fate of the Jews of the shtetl of Chudnov, Zhitomir Region. Recorded by P. Zozulya, February 15–16, 1944   161

24. Tragedy in the shtetl of Slavuta, Kamenets-Podolsky Region: The stories of Dr. Voitseshchuk, the Catholic priest Milevsky, the teacher Vysotskaya, the worker Fyodorova, and the metalworker Yenin. Recorded by Major Z. G. Ostrovsky, February 14, 1944   165

25. Tanks were crushing people: Atrocities against the Jews, the civilian population, and

prisoners of war in the city of Debaltsevo. The stories of M. Yu. Katz and Nikulin. Recorded by A. Murovsky [1944]   167
26. Local Petlura supporters slaughtered all the Jews in the shtetl of Medvedino [Medvin], Kiev Region. Letter from A. M. Karmayan to Ilya Ehrenburg, November [1944]   168
27. In the shtetl of Pyatigory, Kiev Region: The recollections of Raisa Zelenkova   169
28. In the city of Shpola and its environs: Stories of local inhabitants recorded by a teacher named Kruglyak [1944]   185
29. In Uman: The recollections of Manya Feyngold [1944]   186
30. What I went through in fascist captivity: A letter from nine-year-old Boris Gershenzon from Uman to the Jewish Anti-Fascist Committee [1944]   194
31. The story of the partisan Raisa Dudnik, who escaped from Uman. Recorded by Miriam Zheleznova [1944]   195
32. Do not consider me a stranger: A letter from Olga Suprun of Zolotonosha to the family of her husband, Boris Yudkovsky, January 12, 1944   197
33. He is my husband: Letters from Nadezhda Tereshchenko of Kirovograd to Major A. A. Rozen [1944]   200
34. Fate: The recollections of the wife of the engineer P. Krepak of Dnepropetrovsk, 1944   202
35. The rescue of Jews by local inhabitants of Starozhinets, Chernovitsy Region: Accounts of survivors recorded by N. G. Kon. Translated by D. Manevich [1944]   204
36. The rescue of a Jewish family in the Novo-Zlatopol District, Zaporozhe Region: An account by Leah Tsviling. Recorded by Dmitry Stonov, 1944   205
37. The fraternal grave of ten orphans in the steppe. Recorded by N. G. Kon. Translated by D. Manevich [1944]   207
38. The shooting of Hungarian Jews in Sumy: The recollections of the student Tatyana Taranova [1944]   208
39. Liquidation of the Tarnopol ghetto: Testimony of the German non-commissioned officer P. Traugot [1942]   209
40. The destruction of the Jews of Mariupol: The diary of the student Sara Gleykh [1941]   211
41. An execution in Mariupol: A letter from Samuil Aronovich Belous. Prepared by S. Golovanivsky   222

II. BELORUSSIA   233
Minsk
42. In the Minsk ghetto: From the notes of the partisan Mikhail Grichanik. Prepared by A. Margulis [1944]   234
43. Five pogroms in Minsk: Accounts of Perla Aginskaya, Malka Kofman, Darya Lyusik, and Raisa Gelfond. Recorded by Major A. Krasov [1944]   243

44. An account by Professor Prilezhaev about the fate of the Jews in the Minsk ghetto. Recorded by M. Grubian   246
45. The liquidation of the Minsk ghetto: An account by Abram Mashkeleyson. Recorded by A. Idin. Translated by D. Manevich [1944]   247
46. They were dealing in children: Accounts of Maria Gotovtseva, Marfa Orlova, and Fenya Lepeshko. Recorded by A. Verbitsky   248
47. Minsk Hell: The recollections of the teacher Sofia Ozerskaya   250
48. The recollections of Dr. Tsetsilia Mikhaylovna Shapiro. Recorded by A. V. Veysbrod, September 20, 1944   254
49. A meeting in Minsk: Accounts of Tamara Gershakovich, Captain Lifshitz, and Sofia Disner. Recorded by L. Katzovich   259
50. The camp and ghetto in Minsk: A letter from the frontline soldier M. Lokshin to Ilya Ehrenburg [February 1945]   261
51. A prisoner in the Minsk camp: The recollections of Red Army soldier Yefim Leynov, March 14, 1943   264
52. The gassing of inhabitants of Minsk in mobile gas vans and the shooting of Minsk Jews. Stenogram of the interrogation of a German officer named Julius Raihof, July 21, 1944. From the documents of the Extraordinary State Commission   266

Cities and Shtetls of Belorussia

53. Shootings, gallows, human torches: Accounts of the inhabitants of the town of Starye Dorogi. Recorded by M. Grubian. Translated by D. Manevich   268
54. Extermination of the Jews in Western Belorussia: An account by L. Shaus. Translated by D. Manevich   269
55. Reports by partisans from the town of Slutsk. Recorded by M. Grubian. Translated by D. Manevich   270
56. In the shtetl of Lyubavichi. Recorded by M. Grubian. Translated by M. Bregman [1944]   271
57. In Chausy: An account by the local resident Larisa Grigorevna Gmenko. Recorded by S. Bank   272
58. The death of a heroic schoolteacher in Chausy. Recorded by M. Grubian   273
59. The Germans in Mozyr. Recorded by M. Grubian. Translated by M. Bregman   273
60. Liquidation of the Jews in Mstislavl. Recorded by F. Krasotkin, January 2, 1944   274
61. Hitlerite atrocities in the shtetl of Cherikov. Recorded by M. Tsunts, November 25, 1943   275

III. LITHUANIA   277

62. The truth about the terror against the Jews in Lithuania during the German occupation of 1941: An appeal to the nations of the world. From the diary of Dr. Viktor Kutorga. Translated from the German by K. Gershater   278
63. Kaunas during the occupation: Accounts of local residents and the partisan Aron Vilenchuk. Recorded by Major Z. G. Ostrovsky [1944]   287

64. The Kaunas ghetto: The recollections of Viktor Lazerson [1944]   291
65. Extermination of the Jewish children in Kaunas: Account of Maria Ilinichna Yarmovskaya   295
66. Killing the Jews in the shtetl of Stoklishki: Accounts of Maria Yarmolinskaya and Sara Epshteyn. Recorded by Major Z. G. Ostrovsky [1944]   296
67. The shtetl of Stoklishki: The recollections of Rasha Shuster [1944]   297
68. What happened in Telshyay to the entire Jewish population of Zhmud: Accounts of local inhabitants Nesya Miselevich, Veksler, and Yazhgur. Recorded by L. Yerusalimsky   301
69. Slaughter in the shtetl of Utyan: The recollections of Tsodik Yakovlevich Bleyman [1945]   308
70. Killing the Jews of Sventsyany: A letter from a local resident named Guryan to Ilya Ehrenburg, November 20, 1944   312
71. A camp in Kotsynishki [Kochenishki]: A letter from the worker Itsik Yukhnikov   313

IV. LATVIA   316

72. Our situation is hopeless and yet: The fate of the Jews of Libava according to the diaries of Kalman Linkimer. Prepared by Sh. Goman. Translated by M. Shambadal, June 11 [1944]   317
73. The voice of Sheyna Gram: The diary of a fifteen-year-old girl from the shtetl of Preyli. Foreword and translation from Yiddish by B. Gertsbakh, June 22–August 8, 1941   322
74. The death of 5,000 Jews in Rezekne (Rezhitsa): An account by Khaim and Yakov Izraelit. Recorded by B. Gertsbakh [1944]   328

V. ESTONIA   331

75. In the camps of Estonia: Stenographic record of a conversation with Nisim Anolik   332

VI. THE CRIMEA   337

76. Stenographic record of a conversation with Simferopol resident Yevsei Yefimovich Gopshteyn. Recorded by D. Brichinsky, August 16–17, 1944   338
77. An account of the bookkeeper Lev Yurovsky (Simferopol). Recorded by Lev Kvitko [1944]   359
78. The story of the Simferopol tailor Maks Solomin. Recorded by Lev Kvitko [1944]   363
79. The death and rescue of Jewish children in Simferopol: The stories of Lyusya Rabin and Miriam Paver. Recorded by Lev Kvitko [1944]   365
80. In the attic, in the Gestapo's courtyard (in the city of Feodosia). A sketch by Lazar Lagin [1945]   368
81. A girl from Feodosia, Alla-Roza Brazgol. Recorded by Lev Kvtiko   371

82. The destruction of the Jewish colonies in the Crimea. From the reports of the Extraordinary State Commission. Prepared by Lev Kvitko   372

VII. RUSSIA   383

83. The Germans in Yessentuki: A letter from the painter L. N. Tarabukin and his wife, D. R. Goldshteyn, to the writer Yu. Kalugin [1943]   384
84. The rescue of a Jewish family from the shtetl of Khislavichi, Smolensk Region: A letter from B. M. Sorina to Ilya Ehrenburg   386
85. Town of Novozybkov—eight hundred victims in one day: A letter from Anastasia Mikheylets to Kalman Ayzenshteyn concerning the fate of her family. Prepared by A. Kagan. Translated by M. Bregman   397
86. Nazi cannibals: An account by Yeva Piletskaya, a resident of Kursk. Prepared by F. Krasotkin, January 28, 1944   398
87. The death of my father: The story of Yevgenia Shendels, lecturer, Moscow Institute of Foreign Languages   400
88. The petition: A sketch by Roza Bass of Kursk   401
89. They suffered through this themselves: Accounts of Hungarian Jews. Recorded by P. Balashov, December 20, 1942   402
90. Murder of the Jews in the Kalinin region: From the notebook of the woman partisan Klavdia I.   404

VIII. PRISONERS OF WAR   406

91. Glukhov camp: The recollections of M. Yu. Kofman, January 20, 1945   407
92. In German captivity, escape, and wandering through Ukraine: A letter from Red Army soldier Alexander Shapiro, November 19, 1942   417
93. Rescue from a POW camp in the village of Latonovo, Rostov Region: A survivor's account   419

Detailed Table of Contents   421

Index   427

Index

Page numbers in italics indicate illustrations.

Abramsky family (victims in Bezhanitsy), 404
Accidental Justice (Earl), 35
Adenauer, Konrad, 39, 41
Adesman, Israel Borisovich, 132–37
Aginskaya, Perla, 243, 244
air raids, 212, 215, 250, 322, 344, 365
Akmechetka, *xlii*, 14, 53, 129, 135
Aks, Dr. (victim in Utyan), 309
Aktion 1005, 12
Aktionen, xvi, 160, 161, 209–11
Aleichem, Sholem, xxii
Aleksianu (governor of Transnistria), 138
Aletka, Manya, 173, 174–75, 176
Alexandrov, Georgy, xxviii, xxxii, 386n5
Aliger, Margarita, xxv
Alperovich (survivor in Belorussia), 239
Altman, Ilya, xl, 28
Altshuler family (victims in Novozybkov), 397
American Committee of Jewish Writers, Artists, and Scientists, xxii, xxiii, xxvii
American Jewish Joint Distribution Committee, 337n2
Anatomy of the Nuremberg Trials, The (Taylor), 7
Ancel, Jean, 14–15, 16
Andronov, Nikolai, 141
Anolik, Nisim, 332–36
antisemitism, xvi, xxxvi, 6, 357–58; condemned by Soviet leaders, 19; in Romania, 13; in Soviet Union, xxiii, 26, 28, 407; in western Ukraine, 51
Antonescu, Gen. Ion, 13, 14, 15, 149, 150
Antonevich, Vevioras, 297
Anzilevicius brothers (Lithuanian collaborators), 302
apartments, neighbors' takeover of, 13, 74–75, 254
Arad, Yitzhak, xl
Arajs, Viktor, 317
archives, Soviet, 28, 29
Arikbaev (Ukrainian in Gestapo), 214
Armenians, 340, 346, 353, 407
Artemenko, Kristina Stepanova, 74, 75, 76
artisans, 11, 204
Asch, Sholem, xxii
Auschwitz death camp, *xlii*, 15, 332; judgment of history and, 44; liberated by Red Army troops, xxxix, *379*; Nuremberg trial testimony on, 32; slave labor factories at, 40; Soviet POWs murdered in, 407
Austria, 204, 233
Avgustovich, Maria Ignatevna, 260–61
Avgustovich, Yelena, 260
Aysin, Sigizmund, 59
Ayzenshteyn, Kalman, 397
Ayzenshteyn, Risya, 397
Ayzenshteyn-Dolgusheva, Sofia Borisovna, 60–62
Ayzikson, Isaak, 207

Babat (Babi Yar victim), 60
Babel, Isaac, 25
Babi Yar (Kuznetsov novel), 52–53
Babi Yar massacre, xv, xx, *xlii*, 27; Blobel in command at, 12; conflicting passions and memory of, 52–53; Einsatzgruppen Trial and, 33, 35; as emblematic atrocity, 52; eyewitness accounts, 73, 74; Jewish intelligentsia as victims, 59–60; Karaites as victims of, 338; number of Jews killed at, 7; survivors of, *47*
"Babi Yar" (Yevtushenko poem), 28, 52
Bach-Zelewski, Gen. Erich von dem, 8–9, 31
Bachinskaya, Odarka, 177
Bakhchisaray, 338, 346
Balashov, P., 402–4
Baltic states, xiv, xvi, 12, 20, 30. *See also* Estonia; Latvia; Lithuania
Baltishkis, 281
Bank, S., 272
Bantysheva, Alexandra, 148
Baptists, Russian, 399
Baranovichi, *xlii*, 269
Barkman (victim in Novozybkov), 397
Barshtman, Pupa, 164–65
Barshtman, Yankel, 163
Bartkevich, Ivan Alexandrovich, 153
Bash (victim in Latvia), 329
Bass, Roza, 401–2
Becker, August, 10
Beilis, Mendel, 99n19

Beker, Abram Markovich, 410–17
Beker, Khannah, 151
Bekhler (Bukovina survivor), 205
Belaya Tserkov, 182
Belgium, 27
Belgorod, *xliii*
Belmak (Odessa resistance), 143
Belonozhko, N. F., 103–5
Belorussia, 12, 30, 196; border shift from Hitler-Stalin Pact, 233; cities and shtetls of, 268–76; Einsatzgruppen in, xiv; liberated by Red Army, 233, 274; map, *xlii*; partisans in, xvii, 18, 234; prewar Jewish population of, 233; refugees from, 388; in Reichskommissariat Ostland, xv; western part annexed by Soviet Union, 20. *See also specific places in* Belorussians, 247, 253, 272, 274; as German collaborators, xv, xxix, 238, 241, 257–58; held by Gestapo as hostages, 246; Jewish children saved by, 249–50, 259; Jews rescued or aided by, xvi–xvii, xxv, xxix, 260–61; killed for hiding Jews, 246, 268; mistaken for Jews, 250; partisans, 196–97, 261, 268; Soviet military decorations awarded to, 18; witnesses to slaughter, 251, 268
Belostok (Bialystok), *xlii*, 233
Belousov, Fedya, 216, 217, 220
Belozovskaya, Ida, xxxviii, 53–59
Belzec death camp, xvi, *xlii*
Benyash, Moisey, 59
Berdichev, x, *xlii*, 23–24, 51, 80–81, 161
Berenbaum, Michael, 16
Berenshteyn, Sofia, 60
Berenshteyn (Babi Yar victim), 59
Bergelson, David, xix, xxiii
Bernshteyn, Riva, 208
Beryozovka, *xlii*, 113, 124, 125, 134
Besedin, Yegor, 399
Bessarabia, 14, 158; annexed by Soviet Union, 13, 20, 51; Crimean Jews and, 347, 348; Einsatzgruppen in, xiv; map, *xlii*; returned to Romania, xv
Bezhanitsy, *xlii*, 404
Beznalenko, Lyusya, 179
Biberstein, Ernst, 5, 34, 41–42
Bielski, Tuvia, 260
Bikhman, E. M., 136
Bingel, Lt. Erwin, 7, 9
Birbraf (Odessa doctor), 137
Bird, Kai, 41
Birobidzhan, 261
Birobidzhaner shtern [Birobidzhan Star] (newspaper), 26

Bislinger family (Bukovina survivors), 205
The Black Book, xix, 321; Ehrenburg's role in, 27–28; evolution of idea for, xx–xxiii; eyewitness accounts in, xxvii, xxviii; first steps in production of, xxiii–xxiv; new editorial board for, xxix; Nuremberg trial and, xxxv; production delayed by Soviet politics, xxxii–xxxvii, 28; two versions planned, xxvii–xxx
The Black Book: The Nazi Crime Against the Jewish People, xxxi
The Black Book Project (memorandum), xxv
Black Hundreds, 213, 215
black market, 127
Bladis (Lithuanian killed for hiding Jews), 308
Blank, L. P., 136
Bleyman, Tsodik Yakovlevich, 308–12
Bleyman, Rabbi Yakov, 309
Blobel, Paul, 5, 12, 34, 35–36, 41, 42
Block, Itskhak, 305
Blokh (Gerulyay camp representative), 306
Bludy, Itsik, 163
Blume, Walter, 42
Bobrovskaya, Jadwiga, 146
Bobruysk, 233, 265
Bochkovsky, Misha, 145, 146
Bodayev-Molodetsky, Volodya, 143
Bogdanovka, xv, *xlii*, 14, 53, 121, 133; Jews burned alive in, 116, 123, 138; mass killings at, 128–29, 138–39; number of Jews killed at, 136
Boguslav, Petya, 181
Bolsheviks, 25, 383, 406
Bondar, Gergel, 403
Borispol, 23, 74
Borodin, Mikhail, xxix
Borovsky (Odessa resistance), 145
Boskis (Babi Yar victim), 59
Botman (Nazi doctor), 333
Boyarov, Matvey, 260
Boyarsky, Semyon, 59
Bradetsky concentration camp, 186
Braham, Randolph, 15, 16
"branding," 254
Brant, Bene, 318
Braune, Werner, 10, 37, 41, 42
Brazgol, Abram, 371–72
Brazgol, Alla-Roza, 371–72
Bregman, M., 271, 273, 397
Bregman, Solomon, xxii, xxvii, xxviii
Brest, *xlii*, 233
Brichinsky, D., 338
Britain (England), xxi, xxiii, xxviii; Einsatzgruppen Trial and, 38–39;

Jews of, 20; Nazi expectation of defeating, 4; Nuremberg trial and, 31; surrender of Germany and, 34, 35
Britan, Nusya, 163
Brodskaya (Odessa doctor), 137
Brodsky (Odessa doctor), 136
Bromberg, Garry, 115
Bronfin, Blyuma Isaakovna, 151–54
Bronfman (Odessa doctor), 137
Bronshteyn, Pesya, 158
Bronshteyn (Odessa doctor), 137
Brugia, Jan, 205
Bruskina, Masha, 18
Bryansk, *xlii,* 384
Bucharest, *xlii,* 13, 15, 16, 350
Büchel (German soldier), 267
Budnik, Viktor, 142
Bukovina, xv, xvi, 14, 204; annexed by Soviet Union, 13, 20, 51; Jews saved in, 205
Bulgaria, xix
burial alive, 166, 272, 276, 283, 313
Burlecu, Stepan, 205
Burman (Odessa doctor), 137
burning alive: in Belorussia, 260, 268, 270, 276, 286, 296, 312; in Russia, 405
Burshteyn, Lidia, 60
Butrtsymani, 299
Buzanov, Georgy, 142

castration, 263
Catherine the Great, 337n2
Catholic church/priests (Lithuania), 283, 284, 297, 306, 308
Caucasus Mountains, xv
Ceaușescu, Nicolae, 15
censorship, Soviet, xxxiii, xxxvii
Charenin, Jack, 115
Chatskin (Odessa doctor), 136
Chausy, *xlii,* 272–73
Chaykina, Liza, 404n10
Chelmno, *xlii*
Cherchenko, Capt. Leonty Kuzmich, 408, 411, 412, 414, 415
Cheredenko, Nikifor, 206–7
Cheredenko, Semyon, 206
Cherikov, 275–76
Cherkassy, *xlii,* 171
Cherkassy (Babi Yar victim), 60
Cherkassy family (victims in Crimea), 375
Chernigov, *xlii, 229,* 265
Chernomorskaya kommuna [Black Sea Commune] (newspaper), 136
Chernovitsy, *xlii,* 157–61, 204–5

Chernyavker, E. L., 137
Chernyavker, M. L., 137
Chernysheva, Maria, 207
Chibiryak, Vera, 88
Chik, Maria, 196–97
Chik, Sylvester, 197
Chikhachevo, *xlii,* 404–5
children and infants, 10, 16, 30, 73, 79–80; born into death, 162–63, 333; buried alive, 166, 186, 218, 246, 249, 252; burned alive, 168; in death camps, 129; in forest family camps, 234; in hiding, 160, 173, 259–61; in Kaunas ghetto, 294; in Kiev under occupation, 55–56, 72, 86–87; killed by Lithuanian "partisans," 283, 307; life on the run, 394–95; lost and found, 153; in Minsk ghetto, 246, 248–50; of mixed marriages, 255; mourners over dead children, *382;* mutilation of, 404; orphans, 207–8; parents' killing of, 102; poisoned, 369; prospect of death and, 189–90
Christian Aid Committee, 41
Christianity, conversion to, 116, 117, 284
Chudnov, *xlii,* 162–65
Chudnovsky (Odessa doctor), 137
Churchill, Winston, 37, 38
Clay, Gen. Lucius, 39
Cohen, Arthur A., 16
cold, exposure to, 71, 112, 178; death from, 106, 158–59, 406–7; in hiding, 299; in sealed railroad boxcars, 113; winter in Ukraine, 125, 161, 179–80
Cold War, xxxii, 38, 40
collaborators, local, 12–13, 114; camp guards, 129; children killed by, 115; robbery and looting by, 106, 126, 128, 135; Soviet reaction to *Black Book* and, 28; Soviet trials of, 29, 30. *See also* collaborators by nationality
"Commissar decree/order," xiv, 407
communism/Sovietization, Jews associated with, xiii, 245; in Baltic countries, 13, 277, 280, 316; in Nazi propaganda, 20, 38; in Ukraine, 107, 192
Communist Party, Soviet, xx, xxi, 87; Central Committee, xxvi, xxxii, xxxiii, xxxiv, 28; communists turned collaborators, 257–58; members registered by Nazis, 215; position on "Jewish Question," xxiii; Propaganda Department, xxxiii–xxxiv
communists, xiv, 5, 70, 298, 387; executed by Germans, 215, 238; in Odessa resistance, 141–49

The Complete Black Book of Russian Jewry (Ehrenburg and Grossman), xl
concentration camps, 40, 99, 127; in Belorussia, 251; liberation of, 21, 38; in Ukraine, 63, 185, 186
corpses, disposal of, 110, 114, 150, 340; burning, 139; incineration on Himmler's orders, 12; Jews forced to work at, 131, 242; in POW camps, 265; tossed in heaps, 127–28
Crimea, xiv, xxviii, xxxi, 337–38; destruction of Jewish colonies in, 372–76; Einsatzgruppe D in, 31, 37; liberated by Red Army, 363, 365, 366, 369, 372; political status in Soviet Union, 348n10
Czechoslovakia, 204, 233, 266

Dachau concentration camp, 37
Dallin, Alexander, 233
Dancu, Vasile, 15
Dante Alighieri, 103
Danzig, *xlii*, 334
Darevsky Forest, 185
Davis, R. A., xxxviii
death camps, 121, 126, 129–30, 295. *See also* Auschwitz; Majdanek; Treblinka
Debaltsevo, *xliii*, 167–68
Deonchenko, Andrey and Mikhail, 148
Desbois, Father Patrick, 29
Deutsche Krim Zeitung [German Crimean Times] (newspaper), 357
Deutscher, Isaac, 44
Deych, Yakov, 60
disease epidemics, 127, 128, 269, 395; in concentration camps, 306; forced labor and, 333, 403; lack of sanitation and, 101, 159; in POW camps, 265, 406; in Stavki, 129, 130; venereal diseases, 150
Disner, Sonya, 260
Disraeli, Benjamin, 26
Dnepropetrovsk, 51, 196, 202–4, 418; Jewish refugees from, 337, 345; on map, *xliii*
Dniepr River, xv, 184
Dniestr River, 14
Dobin (Minsk ghetto inhabitant), 261–62
Dobrov, Pyotr, 143, 145, 146, 147, 148
Dobrovolsky (Odessa resistance), 148
doctors, fascist, 9, 32, 40, 186, 333
doctors, Jewish, 210, 245, 306; Babi Yar victims, 59–60; killing of, 255–56, 265, 284, 292, 309, 413; lack of medicines and supplies, 284; Odessa victims, 132–37; registration of, 235–36; in resistance groups, 263; suicides, 297

documents, false, xvii, xxxviii, 65, 77, 85; baptism certificates, 172, 360; birth certificates, 388, 390; deaf-mute status, 364–65; in Odessa resistance, 144, 148; passports, 186, 196, 207, 257, 258, 361
Dodds, Joe, 36
Dolberg (Babi Yar victim), 60
Dolgushev, Grigory, 60, 61, 62
Domanyovka, *xlii*, 14, 53, 126–27, 135
Dostoevsky, Fyodor, 358
Dovbnya, Ivan, 142
Dragunsky, Col. David, xx, 28
Drang nach Osten, xiii
Dranukha, 273
Drobitsky Yar, xv, *xliii*
Druzhevskaya (victim in Bezhanitsy), 404
Dubno, *xlii*, 7
Dubnow, Simon, 317
Dudaev (Soviet POW), 408, 414
Dudnik, Danko, 185
Dudnik, Khaya (Valentina), xxxix
Dudnik, Leyb, 195
Dudnik, Raisa, xxxix, 195–97
Dukelsky, Vladimir, 59
Dunaev, David Yakovlevich, 411
Dvinsk (Daugavpils), *xlii*, 279, 317, 323
Dyachenko, Kondrat Ivanovich, 178
Dynova, Marfa, 276
Dzhentsol, 269
Dzyuba, Ivan, 52

Earl, Hilary, 34, 35
East Prussia, 27, 312
Eforn, Khaya, 296
Ehrenburg, Ilya, xxi, xxiii, 157n46; calls for revenge against Germans, xxviii, 157n46; campaign to publicize Jewish suffering, 21–22; contribution to Soviet war effort, 25–27; critics of, xxvii–xxix; eyewitnesses' letters to, 67–89, 122, 151–57, 168–69, 200–202, 261–64, 312–13, 386–97; JAC and, xix, xxxiv, 20; on Kharkov trial, 29–30; memoir, xxiv, xxxv, xxxix; Nuremberg trials and, 32nn101–2; *100 Letters,* 25, 26; in photographs, *48, 377*; role in production of *Black Book,* xxiv–xxvi, xxxvi; *The Storm,* 52; "Triumph of a Man," 22
Ehrenburg, Irina, xxxiii, xxxvi
Eichmann, Adolf, 16, 44
Einsatzgruppe A (Baltic states), xiv, 6; in Estonia, 12, 331; in Latvia, 317; in Lithuania, 277–78; map of executions, xli
Einsatzgruppe B (Belorussia), xiv, 8, 233, 384

Einsatzgruppe C (Ukraine), xiv, 5, 6–7, 52
Einsatzgruppe D (Bessarabia/southern Ukraine), xiv, 5, 52; in Crimea, 337; Nuremberg trial and, 34; Ohlendorf in command, 31; Wehrmacht and, 37
Einsatzgruppen, xiv, 11, 383; commanding officers of, 5; Nuremberg trials and, 7, 31, 32, 33–36, 39, 41–43; Soviet trials of war criminals and, 29; Wehrmacht and, 37
Einstein, Albert, xxii, xxxi
Elis, Yankel, 164
Elista, *xliii*
Elkes, Elkhanan, 284, 289, 290
Elzon (Odessa doctor), 137
England. *See* Britain (England)
Epshteyn, Sara, 296–97, 297
Epshteyn, Shakhno, xxii, xxiii, xxvii, xxix
Ereda, *xlii*, 333, 334
escapes, xxv, 102–3, 335; collective punishment for, 336; of communist resistance fighters, 147; in Eastern Ukraine, 51; evasion as most effective resistance, 18; from Minsk ghetto, 255; into Soviet interior, 316; of Soviet POWs, 412, 417–19; from Tulchin ghetto, 149–51
Estonia, 312, 331–32; annexed by Soviet Union, 331; Einsatzgruppe A in, 12; Jewish population of, 331; map, *xlii*; Omakaitse collaborators in, 331; police auxiliaries in, xv; in Reichskommissariat Ostland, xv; Soviet rule associated with Jews, 13. *See also specific places in*
Europe, Eastern: German colonization plans for, xiii; ghettos of, 4
Europe, Western, 233–34, 266, 292
Extraordinary State Commission for the Investigation of Atrocities Committed on Soviet Territory by the German-Fascist Invaders and their Accomplices, xxx, xxxviii, 119, 138, 372–76
Eynikayt (JAC newspaper), xxiii, xxiv, xxxi, xxxviii, 195n70; Ehrenburg's articles in, 26; Grossman's writing in, 23

Falkenhorst, Col.-Gen. Nikolaus von, 37, 38
families, killing of, 163, 211, 244, 293, 296, 375–76; burning alive, 296; for hiding Jews, 286; survivors and, 191
fascism, xxii, xxiii, xxxi; antisemitism and, 19, 26; German allies, 13; rise of, 25; Russians credited with defeat of, 52
Fayngersh (Odessa doctor), 137
Fayngold, M., 136

Federal Republic of Germany (West Germany), 38–40, 41, 43–44
Fefer, Itsik, xix, xxiii, xxvii; indictment against, xxxi, xxxiv, xxxv; on origins of *Black Book*, xxii; plea to Propaganda Department, xxxiv; travels of, xx, xxii, xxiii
Feldman, Naum, 46
Feldman, Raya, 373–74
Felyuva, Natasha, 145
Fendler, Lothar, 42
Feodosia, *xliii*, 338, 368–72
Ferencz, Benjamin, 32–33, 39, 40, 42
Feygelman, K., 46
Feyngold, Manya, 186–94
Fifikon camp, 332
Filler (Odessa doctor), 136
"Final Solution of the Jewish Question," xxiii, xxiv, 6; in Belorussia, 234, 274; Ehrenburg's understanding of, 27; evidence gathered on, 27–28; eyewitness accounts, xxx; Pushkin at northernmost point of, 383; stages of, xiii
Finder (Bukovina survivor), 205
Fingergut, Dr. (victim in Estonia), 333
Fishberg (Odessa doctor), 137
Fishbeyn, Gershel, 207
Fleischman (woman in Libava), 320
forests: as execution sites, 155, 194; hiding in, 64, 80, 150, 311–12, 393; Jewish family camps in, xvii, 234; partisans in, 18, 80, 150, 291; POWs driven through, 413
Fradis, Shmil, 159
Fradis, Tseytel, 158
Fradis-Milner, Rakhil, 157
Frak (Odessa doctor), 137
France, 4, 25, 27; French Jews in Minsk ghetto, 257; Nuremberg trial and, 31; trials of Nazis in, 43
Fraydorf Jewish National District, 337, 345, 347, 348
"French Jews and the War" (Ehrenburg), 26n79
French language, 25, 26
Frenkel, Dr. (Chudnov victim), 164
Frenkel (Babi Yar victim), 59
Frenkel (Odessa doctor), 137
Freydl, Yankel, 163
Fridman (Gerulyay camp representative), 306
Fridman (old lady in Libava), 320
Friedman, Polya, 156
Friedman, Zelig, 156
Fritsch, Karl, 407
Frumson family (victims in Crimea), 375
Fuks, Sonya, 151
Fuks, Zhenya, 150

Furman, P. M., 137
Furman, Ruzya, 164–65
Fyodorova (dairy worker in Slavuta), 165–66

Gabrilian, Mikhail, 146
Galbershtadt (Odessa doctor), 137
Galicia, East, xv, 51
GARF (State Archive of the Russian Federation), xxxvii, xl
Gargsdai, 277
gas vans, mobile, 10, 34, 245, 269; in Belorussia, 256, 257, 258; children killed in, 248, 258; testimony of German officer about, 266–67
Gassel, Mordukh, 329
Gaukhman (Odessa doctor), 137
Gauzenberg (Odessa doctor), 137
Gavinovsky (Lithuanian rescuer), 297
Gavrilov, Alexey, 408, 410, 415
Gaynevich, Nikolay, 142
Gayzer (Bukovina survivor), 205
Gecht family (Bukovina survivors), 205
Gelfond, Raisa, 243
Gelman, Dr. (victim in Kursk), 401–2
General Government, of Poland, xv
Geneva Convention, 406
Genig (German police commander), 160
genocide, 31, 33, 35
Gent (Nazi doctor), 333
Gerasimova, V., 322n6
Gerchikov, Benjamin, 376
Gerchikova, Vera, 376
German colonists (Ukraine), 114, 135, 140
German Democratic Republic (East Germany), 37
German High Command, 34
German language, 72, 95, 104, 339, 343, 352; begging for life in, 175, 178; ghetto signs in, 237
German Order Police, xiv, 5
Germany, West. *See* Federal Republic of Germany (West Germany)
Gershakovich, Tamara, 259
Gershater, K., 278
Gershenzon, Boris, 194–95
Gershman, Monek, 207
Gertsbakh, B., 322, 328
Gerulyay camp, 306
Gestapo, 64, 65, 68–71, 79, 82, 84–86; Babi Yar massacre and, 73; Einsatzgruppen and, 33; in Feodosia, 368–71, 371; Jewish resistance and, 142; in Kaunas, 292, 293; in Kiev, 75, 170; in Kursk, 398; in Mariupol, 214, 216, 217, 221, 222, 223; mass shootings

and, 162; in Minsk, 236–42, 248, 249, 262; Romanian secret police and, 205; in Russia, 385, 405; in Shpola, 185; in Simferopol, 343, 347, 360, 361, 363–64; Soviet POWs and, 418; tortures carried out by, 303–4
ghettos, xvi, 4, 52, 130–31; in areas under Wehrmacht control, xv; Jewish police in, 294; Kaunas (Kovno), xvi, 11, 16–17, 282–83, 291–95, 308, 331; Kharkov, 99–103; in Latvia, 326; liquidation of, xvi, 209–11, 242, 247–48, 295; in Lithuania, 278; local collaborators as guards, 13; Odessa, 109, 110–11; as "Palestine," 185; Rakovka (Uman), 196; in Russia, 383–84, 392; skilled workers in, 11; Tarnopol, 209–11; in Transnistria, 204; Tulchin, 17–18, 149–51; underground organizations in, xxv. *See also* Minsk ghetto
Gibb, Lady Dorothy, 157
Gibkhina, Fanka, 197
Gilshteyn, Uka, 165
Gimelfarb, Isaak, 59
Gimelfarb (Babi Yar victim), 60
Girshovich, Rabbi Nakhman, 310
Giselevich, Arnold, 117
Gitelman, Zvi, 19
Giterman, Felix (Yefim) Zinovevich, 62–67
Glavlit (Main Administration for Literary and Publishing Affairs), xxxiii
Glayzer, Manya, 186
Gleykh, Sara, xxiv, xxxix, 13, 211–22
Glovatskaya, Yevgenia, 148
Glukhov POW camp, *xlii*, 407–17
Gmenko, Larisa Grigorevna, 272–73
Gnip, Liza, 162
Goecke, Wilhelm, 16, 17, 290, 293, 294, 295
Goering, Hermann, 30, 31
Gokhman (Ukrainian police chief), 172, 174–77, 182
Goldberg, B. Z., xxii, xxvi, xxx
Goldberg (Odessa doctor), 137
Goldenberg, A. F., 136
Goldenberg, N. A., 136
Goldensohn, Leon, 35n120
Goldental, Rakhil Iosifovna, 132
Goldman, Nahum, xxvi
Goldshteyn, D. R., 384–85
Golos Kryma [Voice of the Crimea] (newspaper), 357
Golovanivsky, Savva, xxxviii, 105
Goman, Sh., 317
Gomel, *xlii*, 233, 265
Gonchar, Dina, 375

Gonchar, Freyda, 375
Gopshteyn, Yevsei Yefimovich, 338–59
Gorbachev, Mikhail, xxxvii, 205n76
Gorenshteyn (Babi Yar victim), 60
Gorka, 126, 127–28
Gorn (Odessa doctor), 137
Gorovitz (Odessa doctor), 137
Gotovtseva, Maria, 248, 249
Gottlib (Bukovina survivor), 205
Graebe, Hermann Friedrich, 7–8, 17
Graf, Matthias, 42
Gram, Freyda, 322
Gram, Gutman, 322
Gram, Sheyna, 322–28
graves, mass: in Belorussia, 269, *378;* in Crimea, 353; at Dachau, 37; Nazis' attempts at secrecy of crimes and, 11–12; photographs of executions, *228, 230, 232;* postwar looting of, 28; in Ukraine, 29, 128
Grawitz, Ernst, 9
Great Britain. *See* Britain (England)
Grechany, Ivan Pavlovich, 172, 177, 180
Greeks, 203, 218, 221, 346
Griboy, Malanya, 300
Grichanik, Mikhail, 234–43
Grinberg, Roza, 151
Grodno, *xlii,* 6, 233, 269
Grodzinsky (Mariupol survivor), 219
Gromyko, Andrei, xxvii
Grossman, Moyshe, 207
Grossman, Vasily, xix, xx, xxv; campaign to publicize Jewish suffering, 21–22; Ehrenburg's eulogy of, 24–25; on eyewitness accounts, xxvii, xxx; as head of *Black Book* project, 28; "The Hell of Treblinka," 24; introduction to *Black Book* and, xxx; JAC trial and, xxxiv; mother as victim of Nazis, 23–24; "Murder of the Jews of Berdichev," 24, 161n53; in photograph, *48;* "Ukraine Without Jews," 23; as war correspondent, 23–24
Grubian, Matvey, xxxviii, 268, 270, 271, 273
Grutman, S. N., 154–57
Gubnykh, Ira, 272–73
Gunzenko, Lt. Semyon, 261
Gurevich, F., 217
Gurfinkel (Odessa doctor), 137
Gursky (partisan), 184
Guryan (eyewitness in Lithuania), 312–13
Gusak, Lyudmila Filippovna, 63
Guz (Odessa doctor), 137
Gypsies, 5, 161, 360

Haensch, Walter, 35, 42
Hague Convention on the Rules of War, 406
Hedvis, Ferenc, 403
Heine, Heinrich, 26
"The Hell of Treblinka" (Grossman), 24
Henderson, J. L., 36
Hero of the Soviet Union, Order of, xvii, 18
Hess, Rudolf, 30
Heydrich, Reinhard, 3
Himmler, Heinrich, xiv, 5, 30; Final Solution and, 3; incineration of corpses ordered by, 12; liquidation of ghettos and labor camps ordered by, 52; Minsk massacre witnessed by, 8–9; SS leaders' obedience to, 35
Hitler, Adolf, xiii, 21, 99, 150, 297; aim to destroy Jewish people, xxi; beginnings of fascist movement and, 357; on Ehrenburg, 27; Einsatzgruppen and, 33; Final Solution and, 3; judgment of history and, 44; Madagascar option and, 4; *Mein Kampf,* 5; rise to power, 19; SS leaders' obedience to, 35
Hitler-Stalin Pact, 6, 13, 20, 51, 53, 233
Hofshteyn, David, xix, xx
Holocaust: commemorated in Moscow, xxxix; moral exhaustion of World War II victors and, 42; Romanian reluctance to acknowledge, 15–16; in Ukraine, 53
Homaier, Oberleutnant Evald, 266, 267
hostages, 110, 170, 243, 246, 258, 309
hot weather, exposure to, 235, 236
humanity, crimes against, xiv, 31
Hungarian fascists, 150, 208, 402–3, 418
Hungary, 13, 27, 52
hunger, 81, 88, 178, 235, 405; black marketers and, 127; death by starvation, xvii, 158, 256, 406; denial of food as punishment, 332; food situation in ghettos, 89, 100, 101, 149, 255, 282; German confiscation of food, 106, 215, 217, 222–23; hiding in forests and, 151; in hiding with peasants, 299; in labor camps, 98; obtaining of food, xvi, 104, 105, 256, 356–57

Idin, A., 247
Ikhelzon (Babi Yar victim), 60
Ikor village (Crimea), 372–74
Ilaisve [Toward Freedom] (fascist newspaper), 281
Iliescu, Ion, 15, 16
Illiodor (antisemitic Russian monk), 357
"In Exile" (Rozhetsky), 122, 131–32
In the Days of Simon Stern (Cohen), 16
Inferno (Dante), 103

intelligentsia, Jewish, 236, 246, 289, 400; executions of, 283, 289, 400; Jewish Committee of Simferopol and, 340, 341; Stalin's campaign against, xxxv
International Military Tribunal. *See* Nuremberg trials
Inzulevich brothers (Lithuanian collaborators), 304
Ioanid, Radu, 16
Ionescu, Lt. Col. Modest, 138
Ioselevich, David, 59
Iron Guard, 13
Ishchenko, Gordy, 170
Israel, 43, 157n48, 346n9
Italian fascists, 150, 418
Ivanov, Vsevolod, xxvi
Ivanter, Dr. (victim in Estonia), 333
Ivashkov, Pimen, 276
Ivye, *378*
Izraelit, Anna Maximovna, 257
Izraelit, Khaim and Yakov, 328–30
Izraelit, Khanon, 329
Izvestia (Soviet newspaper), 21, 25, 103n26, 348

Jackson, Justice Robert, 31
Jeckeln, SS-Brigadeführer Friedrich, 30, *49*, 317
Jehovah's Witnesses, 403
Jewish Anti-Fascist Committee (JAC), xxvi, xxxvii, xxxviii, 23; arrests and trials of members of, 195n70, 205n76; crackdown on, xxxiv–xxxv; creation of, xxi, 20; Ehrenburg's role and, xxix, 27; eyewitnesses' letters to, 194–95; *Eynikayt* newspaper, xxiii; gathering of evidence on Nazi crimes, xxii–xxiii, 268; Literary Commission, xxv, xxvii, xxviii; members of, xix; trial of fifteen members (1952), xxxi, xxxiv–xxxv
Jewish National Council of Palestine, xxvi–xxvii
Jewish stars *(Magen David)* and armbands, as identifying marks, 202, 208, 213, 243, 275, 309, 312; in Crimea, 359; exemption from, 170; Hungarian Jews, 403; in Latvia, 324; as license for violent abuse, 111; in Minsk ghetto, 250, 254; outcast status, 369; punishment for refusal or "improper" wearing of, 187, 192, 222, 293, 298; "Shield of David," 282
Jewish Telegraphic Agency, 19
Jews: apparent passivity of victims, 298, 305, 321; of Crimea, 340; German Jews, 242–43, 245, 247, 257, 265; Nazi program to exterminate, xiii; non-Jewish spouses of (*See* marriages, mixed); in partisan units, 18, *46*, 234, 247–48, 278; as POWs held by Germans, xvii, 406–7, 409–10, 413, 418; purged from Soviet cultural institutions, 26; in Red Army, xvii, xxiii, 18–19, 22, *45*, 115, 195; refugees from German-occupied Poland, xiii, 208, 233; relatives in America, 115, 117, 176; resistance in ghettos, xvi, xvii; as soldiers in Allied armies, 406; Soviet accusations of "bourgeois nationalism," xxxiv, xxxv; Soviet military decorations awarded to, 18; victims referred to as Soviet citizens/civilians, xxiii, xxx, 21, 30, 123, *232*, 266–67; war blamed on, 294, 303. *See also* communism/Sovietization, Jews associated with; property of Jews, looting of; registration, of Jews
Joint Declaration by the Allied Powers Concerning Nazi Crimes against the Jews, xxii
Jordan (German officer), 283, 285, 286, 292, 293
Jost, Heinz, 43
journalists, Western, 13, 24
Judenräte (Jewish councils): in Belorussia (Minsk), 237, 240, 250, 254, 262, 263; in Lithuania, xxxviii, 284; in Simferopol (Crimea), 340; in Ukraine, 213, 215, 217, 222; in Yessentuki (Russia), 384

Kabanets, Vera Pavlovna, 138, 141
Kabi (resisting victim in Latvia), 318–19
Kagan, A., 59, 60, 397
Kagan, Dora Ruvimovna, 272
Kagan, Khaye, 180
Kaiserwald concentration camp, 317
Kalashnikova, Nina, 145
Kalika, Lyusya, xxxix, 144
Kalinin Collective Farm (Crimea), 375–76
Kalinin (Tver) Region, 404–5
Kalmin, *xlii*
Kaltenbrunner, Ernst, 30
Kaluga, 384
Kalugin, Yu., 384
Kamenets-Podolsky, *xlii*, 6–7, 52, 165–67
Kamenetskaya (Odessa doctor), 137
Kamenetsky (Odessa doctor), 137
Kan (Odessa doctor), 137
Kanevsky, Lev, 60
Kantarovich, Olga, xxxviii, xxxix, 142, 144–49
Kantarovich, Robert, 144
Kantarovich, Yelena, xxxviii, xxxix, 142, 143, 144–49
Kantarovich (Bukovina survivor), 205
Kantsevich, Manya, 260

Kaplinskaya, Yekaterina, 60
Kaprilova, Nyusya, 216, 217
Kaptelov, Boris, xl
Karaites, 337–38, 346–47, 353
Karasik (Nazi professor), 346
Karasubazar (Belogorsk), *xliii,* 338
Kardakov (Belorussian collaborator), 258
Karicher, Robert, 41–42
Karmayan, A. M., 168–69
Katrich, Ivan, 147
Katz, M. Yu., 167–68
Katz, Margoly Izraelevna, 370–71
Katz, Sroul, 156
Kaunas (Kovno, Kovna), xv, xvii, 284; children exterminated in, 295; Einsatzgruppe A in, 277–78; ghettos and labor camps, xvi, 11, 16–17, 291–95, 308, 331; liberated by Red Army, 288; life under German occupation, 287–91; on map, *xlii;* prewar Jewish population of, 278; refugees from, 280
Kaverin, Veniamin, xxv
Kazakhstan, 208
Kazlauskas (German officer), 283
Keimach, David, 18
Keitel, Gen. Wilhelm, 30
Kerch, *xliii,* 338, 356, 361
Keselman family (victims in Crimea), 375
Kesselring, Field Marshal Albert, 37, 38
KGB (Soviet secret police), xxxvii
Khabad, Sima, 151
Khanys, Moshko, 164
Kharitonovich, Lazar, 162
Kharkov, xiv, xv, *xliii,* 29, 196; absence of survivors in, 23; destruction of Jews of, 105–8; diary from, 103–5; German capture of, 99–100; liberated by Red Army, xxxviii, 103, 207; prewar Jewish population of, 51; survival in ghetto of, 99–103
Khasnovshchina, 248
Khaykin, Motl, 207
Khaymovich, B., 46
Khazan, Riva, 73
Khazars, 346
Kherson, *xlii,* 337, 345
Khislavichi, *xlii,* 386–97
Khmelevsky (Lithuanian rescuer), 297
Khmelnik, *xlii,* 51, 151–54, 153, 154
Khrushchev, Nikita, 67
Khuvo (Odessa doctor), 137
Kiev, xiv, *xlii,* 21, 30, 411; Babi Yar killing site near, 28, 52, 59–60; "blood libel" trial (1913), 88n19; German capture of, 6, 53–54, 72; liberated by Red Army, 62, 67, 68; life under German occupation, 53–59, 75, 83; prewar Jewish population of, 51; region of, 168–85; survival stories from, 60–62, 62–67; war crimes trial in, *47, 50*
Kilup, Aron, 163
Kimelman, Berta, 151
Kirbis (Odessa doctor), 137
Kirovograd, xxxix, *xlii,* 196, 200–202
Kishinev, *xlii,* 151
Kislovodsk, 385
Kivioli, 333
Klaipedia, 43
Klebansky, Vanya, 169
Kliner, Leyba, 177
Klinglhofer, Waldemar, 43
Klinov, Filipp Borisovich, 138–39
Klooga, *xlii,* 332, 334–35, *380*
Klotzman, Bunya, 170
Knysh, Ivan, 375
Kochetkov, Dr. (Soviet POW), 408, 412–15
Kochuk, Anatoly, 148
Kodinsky (Babi Yar victim), 59
Koenigsberg, *xlii*
Kofman, M. Yu., 407–17
Kofman, Malka, 243
Kogan, Ya., 60
Kogan, Ye., 60
Koimon, Yakov, 375
"Kol Nidre" (Sutzkever poem), 22
Kolbasenka (Kolbasin), 269
Koldobsky, R. and L., 217
Komsomol (Communist youth organization), 170, 177, 201, 215, 253, 263, 302, 396
Kon, N. G., 204–5
Konotop POW camp, 409, 413
Kopyl, Shoykhet, 138
Korean conflict (1950s), 40
Koreans, 362
Korko, 270
Korobkov, Fanas, 178, 179, 182
Koroleva, Anna, 268
Kostovetsky, Abrasha, 71
Kostyukov, Vasily, 197
Kotesman, Regina, 151
Kotlova, Emilia Borisovna, 67–89
Kotsyunishki (Kochenishki), *xlii,* 313–15
Kovarsky, Dr. (victim in Lithuania), 312
Kovarsky family (Minsk victims), 244
Kovel, *xlii,* 154–57
Kovnator, Raisa, xxiv
Kovnator, Rakhil, 157, 158
Kovner, Abba, 278
Kozlovsky, Kostyush, 260

Krachinsky, Y., *46*
Kraevskaya, Stanislawa, 117
Krakow, *xlii*
Krakowski, Shmuel, xl
Kramer (German officer), 288
Krasnaya zvezda [Red Star] (Soviet army newspaper), 22, 23, 25, 29–30, 157n46
Krasnodar, *xliii*, 29, 384
Krasotkin, F., 398
Krasov, Major A., 243
Krauze, Feldwebel (German officer), 275
Kravchenko, Klavdia Ivanovna, 419
Kravchenko, Maria, 170
Kravchenko (Soviet POW), 408
Kravets, Karl, 403
Kravets, Vasily, 183, 184
Kravets (Ukrainian policeman), 128
Kremenchug, 23, 196, 413
Kremenets, 12
Krepak, F., 202–4
Krepak, P. I., 202
Kretinge, 277, 281
Kreyser, Gen. Yakov, xxiii
Krieger, Blyuma, 150
Krimchaks, 337–38, 345–46, 360, 361, 366, 371
Kristallnacht, 3, 19
Krivoruchko, S. S., 99–103
Krolevets, 408, 411, 413
Kruglyak (teacher in Shpola), 185–86
Krupp, Alfried, 40, 41
Krupp, Major (German officer), 275
Kube, Wilhelm, 10, 11n24, 18, 241
Kuchuk, Klavdia, 145
Kudryavtsev, D., *381*
Kukl, David, 330
Kuleshova, Maria, 253
Kulman, Vera, 219
Kulpe, Ivan Dimitrovich, 215
Kunbin (Belorussian), 268
Kuperman, Leah, 151
Kurema, 333
Kursanivska, Fanya, 181
Kursk, *xliii*, 23, 29, 384, 398–402
Kurtz, Sonya, 151
Kurtzman, Ariel, 205
Kushch, Alexander, 142
Kutorga, Viktor, 278–87
Kutorgiene-Buivydaité, Elena, 278–79n5
Kuznetsov, Anatoly, 52–53
Kvitko, Leyb (Lev), xix, xxiii, xxxi, xxxii, xxxviii; Extraordinary State Commission reports and, 372; eyewitness accounts recorded by, 359, 365, 371; indicted in JAC trial, xxxiv

La Guardia, Fiorello, xx
labor camps, Nazi, xvi, 52, 153, 251, 317; "Cossack" guards, 90–91, 93, 97, 98, 99; eyewitness accounts of, 90–99; liquidation of, xvi; local collaborators as guards, 13; skilled workers in, 11
labor camps, Soviet, 205n76
Lagedi, *xlii*, 332, 334, 335
Lagin, Lazar, xxxviii, 368–71
Langer, Lawrence, 44
Larindorf, *xlii*, 345, 347
Latonovo, *xliii*, 419–20
Latvia, 30, 316–17; annexed by Soviet Union, 316; Einsatzgruppe A in, 6, 12; Jewish population of, 316; liberated by Red Army, 317; map, *xlii*; in Reichskommissariat Ostland, xv; Rezekne (Rezhitsa), 328–30; Soviet rule associated with Jews, 13. See also specific places in
Latvian language, 322
Latvians: collaborators, xv, 317, 318, 320, 324; Jews rescued or aided by, xvi–xvii, 317
Laukhina, Avdotya Timofeevna, 409
Lazerson, Viktor, 291–95
Leningrad, xiv, xv, xvii, *xlii*, 358; Jewish population of, 383; siege of, 6, 383, 412
Lepeshko, Fenya, 248, 249–50
Lerner, David, 160
Lerner, Yosl, 207
Levchenko, Sofia Antonovna, 120
Levi, Dveyre, 307
Levi (Odessa doctor), 137
Levin (Babi Yar victim), 60
Levin (survivor in Belorussia), 239
Levinson, Khaim, 319
Levit (Babi Yar victim), 60
Levy, Miklos, 402–3
Leymunskaya, L., 220
Leynov, Yefim, 264–66
Leypuny, 270
Leytman (Babi Yar victim), 60
Leyzer, Tserun, 156
Lezner, Khaim, 197
Libava (Liepaja), *xlii*, 317–21
Libov, Dr. (Chudnov victim), 164
lice (insect) infestations, 91, 93, 124, 129, 130, 302, 306
Lida, *xlii*, 6, 269
Lidin, Vladimir, xxxviii, 103
Lifshitz family (victims in Crimea), 376
Lincoln, Abraham, 39
Linkimer, Kalman, 317–21
Literaturnaya gazeta (newspaper), 52

Lithuania: annexed by Soviet Union, 277; Einsatzgruppe A in, 12; Jewish life and scholarship in, 277; Karaites in, 338; Kutorga's appeal to nations of the world, 278–87; liberated by Red Army, 278; map, *xlii*; mass killings in, 43; partisans in, xvii; in Reichskommissariat Ostland, xv; Soviet rule associated with Jews, 13. *See also specific places in*

Lithuanian collaborators, 6, 12, 28, 285, 309–11, 313; *Black Book* criticized for overemphasizing, xxviii; eagerness of, 277–78; as "partisans," 280, 281, 282, 283; police auxiliaries, xv, *231*; Red Army stragglers attacked by, 280; "white bandits," 302, 312

Lithuanians: Jews rescued or aided by, xvi–xvii, 297, 299–301; punished for contact with Jews, 285

Lodz, *xlii*, 4, 288

Logan, Andy, 33, 36, 37

Lokshin, M., 261–64

Lozinskaya, Liza, 274

Lozovsky, Solomon, xxi, xxii, xxiii, xxvii; indicted in JAC trial, xxxi, xxxiv; introduction to *Black Book* and, xxx; Sovinformburo and, 142n39; on "two versions" of *Black Book*, xxviii

Lublin, *xlii*, 3

Luchno, Stepan Ivanovich, 376

Lunin (partisan in Minsk), 247–48

Lunsha, Matiash, 403

Lupescu, Geccu, 205

Lutsk, *xlii*

Lvov (Lviv), xv, *xlii*; ghettos and labor camps, xvi, 89–99; prewar Jewish population of, 51; Ukrainian collaborators in, 12; Yanovsky camp, xxviii

Lyubavich, *xlii*, 271

Lyusik, Darya, 243

McCloy, John J., 40–43

Madagascar, 3, 4

Magen David. *See* Jewish stars *(Magen David)* and armbands, as identifying marks

Majdanek death camp, xxvi, *xlii*, 27, 44, 155, *381*

Malaparte, Curzio, 14n32

Maly Trostyanets, xv, *xlii*, 233–34, 246

Manevich, D., 204, 207, 247, 268, 269, 270

Mangutov (Soviet POW), 412, 414

Manstein, Field Marshal Erich von, 37, 38–39, 341

Manteyfel, Mitya, 329

Marauch (German propaganda chief in Crimea), 357–58

Margulis, A., 234

Mariupol, *xliii*, 211–25

Markina, Makhlya, 397

Markish, Peretz, xix, xxiii, xxxiv

Markovich (Babi Yar victim), 59

marriages, mixed: in Belorussia, 255, 275; in Crimea, 350, 353; in Russia, 385; in Ukraine, 76, 172, 175, 176, 177, 203, 216

Marrus, Michael, 31

Marshak, Samuil, 122

Marx, Karl, 19

Mashkeleyson, Abram, 247–48

Mashkovskaya, Lida, 148

Mashtaler, Maria, 88

Mateyka, Vasilisa Mitrofanovna, 360–61, 362

Matthäus, Jürgen, 3n

Matusevich family (rescuers in Latvia), 329

Maydan (Babi Yar victim), 59

Mazurak (shtetl elder, Pyatigory), 170

Medvin (Medvedino), *xlii*, 168–69

Mein Kampf (Hitler), 5

Meiser, Bishop Hans, 39

Memorial Day for Victims of the Holocaust in Russia, xxxix

Merder fun felker (Murder of Peoples), xxvi

Meydler, Klara, 150

Meyer, Jack, 115

Michnik, Zinaida, 385

Mikhaylova, Galya, 177

Mikheylets, Anastasia, 397

Mikhoels, Solomon, xix, xxiii, xxxviii; death of, xxxiv, 28; eyewitnesses' letters to, 149; as leading voice of JAC, 20; letters to Zhdanov, xxxii, xxxiii; travels of, xx, xxii, xxiii; warning about mass murder of Jews, xx–xxi

Mikman (Odessa doctor), 137

Milevich (Lithuanian rescuer), 297

Milevsky (Catholic priest in Slavuta), 165–66

Miller, Feyga, 296

Miller, Miklos, 403

Milner, Reyza, 158

Minkin, Adolf, 19

Minsk, xv, 30, 233; German capture of, 6; Himmler in, 8–9; Jewish refugees from, 388; liberated by Red Army, 233; on map, *xlii*; POW camp near, 264–66

Minsk ghetto, xvii, 18, 46, 254–58; concentration camp in, 261–64; life in, 234–43; liquidation of, 247–48; as a Nazi-made hell, 250–54; outside contacts with local inhabitants, 259–61; pogroms in, 243–46; Prilezhaev account of massacre in, 246–47; testimony of German officer, 266–68

Mir, 233
Mirkovich, Rasya, 386–87
Mironenko, V. F., 146
Miselevich, Nesya, 301
Mitinsky, David, 59
Mitrofansky (POW camp collaborator), 410
Mogila (Odessa resistance), 143
Mogilev, *xlii*, 233, 234, 272
Mogilevskaya, Nina, 105–8
Mogilyansky (Babi Yar victim), 59
Moldavia, xv, xvi, 13, 157n47
Moldavians, 205
Molodechno, 269
Molotov, Vyacheslav, 11, 19, 21, 412
Molotov Collective Farm (Crimea), 374–75
Molva [Common Talk] (newspaper), 135
Morgenshteyn, Velvl, 207
Morgulis, Anna Yakovlevna, 115–18
Morozov, M., xxxiii
Morris, Christopher, xl
Moscow, xx, *xliii*, 20; German advance on, 6, 21, 383, 384, 412; Holocaust Center, xxxix; Jewish population of, 383; Soviet archives in, 28
Moscow State Jewish Theater, xix, xx
Moshkovich, N. M., 137
Mosuk, Iosif Yakovlevich, 162
Moyshe-Meyer, Vyest, 163
Mozyr, *xlii*, 273–74
Mstislavl, *xlii*, 274–75, 388
Müller, Heinrich, 33
"The Murder of the Jews of Berdichev" (Grossman), 24, 161n53
musicians, 96, 265
Musmanno, Michael, 35–36
Mussolini, Benito, 4

Nagornaya, Nadya, 419
Nalchik, *xliii*
nationalism: Estonian, 331; in Federal Republic of Germany, 41; JAC accused of Jewish "bourgeois nationalism," xxxi, xxxiv, xxxv; Latvian, 317; Ukrainian, 51, 168n59
NATO (North Atlantic Treaty Organization), 38
Naumann, Erich, 41, 43
Naumenko (Soviet POW), 411
Nazi Germany (Third Reich): allies of, 13; concentration camps, xvi; deportation to, 99, 204; extermination of "enemies" of, xiv; foundations of Nazi ideology, xiii; invasion of Soviet Union (Operation Barbarossa), xiii, xiv, 4, 322–23; military defeat of, 264, 297; Nuremberg laws, 3, 19, 338; pact with Soviet Union, 6, 13, 20, 51, 53, 233
Nazis, 3, 26; dependence on Jewish labor, 11, 37, 239, 255; dissatisfaction with Romanian allies, 14–15; documents kept by, 32–33; dogs used to attack people, 263, 296, 336; intelligence-gathering practices, 34; postwar leniency toward, 39–42; psychological toll on killers, 9–10, 34; reprisals for acts of resistance, 281; sadism of, 16, 35, 294; searches and roundups conducted by, 12, 66, 283, 292–93, 351–55, 388; Soviet holidays chosen for massacres, 251–52; Soviet trials of, 29–30. *See also* Gestapo; Hitler, Adolf; Nuremberg trials; SS *(Schutzstaffel)*, Nazi
Nebe, Arthur, 8
Nefedova, Valya, 117
Nemenchina, 269
Netherlands, 27
New York, city of, xx, 19, 21, 115
New York Times, 42
Neydorf village (Crimea), 376
Neyman, Solomon, 205
Nezhebitsky, Lev Nikolaevich, 409, 410, 411
Nezhin, 74
Nikandrov, Mikhail, 142
Nikolaev, *xlii*
Nikolenko, Pyotr, 143, 146, 147, 148
Nikulin (survivor of Debaltsevo), 167, 168
Ninth Fort, xv, 278, 285, 287, 291; on map, *xlii*; Russian POWs at, 284
NKVD (Soviet secret police), 67, 74, 143, 144, 390; Jews identified with, 215; in Latvia, 329; Odessa headquarters used by Romanians, 110, 116
North Caucasus, xiv, 384
Nosske, Gustav, 35, 43
Novgorod, *xlii*, 384
Novgorod-Seversky, 265
Novo-Zlatopol, *xliii*, 205–7
Novoe vremya [New Times] (newspaper), 357
Novorossiysk, *xliii*, 121
Novosokolniki, *xlii*, 405
Novosti Press Agency, xxxvi
Novozybkov, *xlii*, 397
Nuremberg laws, 3, 19, 338
Nuremberg trials, xxxv, xli; Einsatzgruppen Trial, 32, 33–36, 39, 41–43; International Military Tribunal (IMT), 30–32, 34, 36; legacy of uneven justice, 30–31; Soviet trials and, 29; statements of Nazis at, 10

Obodzinskaya, Maria, 146
Odessa, xv, *xlii;* doctors who perished in, 132–37; ghetto, 110–11, 133–34; letter to Red Army soldier from, 120–21; liberated by Red Army, 118, 148; as part of Transnistria, xvi; prewar Jewish population of, 51; Romanian capture of, 115–18, 123, 132, 142; under Romanian control, 14, 15, 109–19, 123–24; Slobodka ghetto, 111–13, 117–18, 125; underground activities, xxxviii, xxxix
Ohlendorf, SS Gen. Otto, 5, 33, 39, 41, 337; execution of, 41, 43; testimony at trial, 31, 34–35
Omakaitse (Estonian nationalist group), 331
100 Letters (Ehrenburg), 25, 26
Onishchenko (Belorussian collaborator), 257–58
Operation Barbarossa, xiii, xiv, 4
Orel, *xliii*, 384, 402
Orlova, Marfa, 248, 249
Orlova, Olga, 117
Orlyuk (Odessa doctor), 137
orphanages: in Belorussia, 247, 258, 259–60; in Crimea, 366; in Lithuania, 284, 286; in Ukraine, 79–81, 87, 207–8
Orsha, 233, 253
ORT (Society for Rehabilitation and Training), xxxviii
Ortenberg, David, 23
Orthodox Christianity, 81–82, 85, 388
Osovets, V., 217
Ostapchuk, Gerasim Profofevich, 161
Ostrovskaya, Sonya, 171
Ostrovsky, Major Z. G., xxxviii, 165–67, 287
Ott, Adolf, 42, 43
"Our Place" (Ehrenburg), 26
Ozerskaya, Sofia, 250–54

Palanga, 277
Pale of Settlement, 26n79, 383
Palestine, xxiii, xxxi, 156; emigration to, 277; independent Jewish state in, xxxiv; Jews in British army from, 406; Karaites in, 338
partisans, xiv, xvii, xxv; in Belorussia, 196–97, 234, 247, 253–54, 270; in Crimea, 358; executed by Nazis, 238; fascist "partisans" in Baltic countries, 280, 281, 282, 283, 324; in forests, 18, 80, 150, 291; Jews killed for suspected contact with, 245–46, 256; in Lithuania, 278, 291, 386n6; in Minsk ghetto, 46, 261; recollections of, 149–51; in Ukraine, 67, 143, 145, 150, 181, 184–85, 195–97, 412; in Vilna ghetto, 32
Pascaranu (Moldavian rescuer of Jews), 205

Pasechnik, Natalia, 375
Pasternak (Odessa doctor), 137
Patterson, David, xl
Paver, Miriam, 365–68
Pavlov, Anatoly, 413
Pavlova, Tatyana, xl
Pechora, *xlii*, 160
Peck, David W., 40
Peck Commission, 40
Pekar, Moisey, 245
People, Years, Life (Ehrenburg), xxiv, xxxvii
Peranu, Nikolai, 205
Perepecheva, Anna, 88
Peretiatko, Yevgenia Golovataya, 45
Pereyaslav, 74
Perkus, David, 375
Petlura, Simon, 168n59
Petrauskas, Kipras, 303
Petrushkin (Odessa doctor), 136
Pikman, Basya, xxiv
Piletskaya, Yeva, 398–99
Piletsky, Ilya Pinkhasovich, 398
Pinsk, 11
Pirozhenko (Stavki camp commandant), 129
Pivchenko, Basya, 197
Pivovarova, Varvara Nikiforovna, 411
Plagova, Mery, 326
Platakis, Alexandrovicius, 302, 304, 307
Platov, Ivan, 143
Pliner (Babi Yar victim), 59
Pobyl (Ukrainian policeman), 176, 177, 179
Pochaevskie izvestia (Pochaev News), 357
Podgaets, Sara, 60
poems, 122–23, 124, 126, 127, 129, 131–32
Poganenko, Maria, 178
Pogorclov, Fyodor, 142
pogroms, 12, 21, 153, 167; in Belorussia, 238, 241, 256, 257; Romanian-led, 14, 15; in Ukraine, 100, 187, 188, 191–92, 213
Pohl, Oswald, 40, 41
Polamarchuk (Ukrainian policeman), 190
Poland, 6, 24, 402; extermination camps in, 31; General Government, xv; German invasion of, 3; ghettos in, 11; Hitler-Stalin Pact and, 20, 233, 277; Jewish refugees from, 208, 233; Karaites in, 338; occupation of, xiii, 4; prewar Jewish population of, 13; territories annexed by Soviet Union, 4, 51, 53
Poles, 156, 235, 253; concentration camp inmates, 92, 332; Jews rescued or aided by, xxv, 117, 242, 329; killed for hiding Jews, 286; mistaken for Jews, 250; "reactionaries," 156, 157

Polevoy, Boris, 32
police auxiliaries, xv
Polish language, 156
Polishchuk, Pyotr, 117, 124
Polonsky (Babi Yar victim), 60
Poltava, *xliii*, 23, 101–2, 196, 207–8
Polunova, L., 217
Polyakov family (victims in Crimea), 375
Polyakova, P. I., 137
Ponary, xv, *xlii*, *231*, 278
Ponomarenko, Pantaleymon, 20
Popandopulo, Alexander, 408
Popova, Vasilisa, 220, 221
Postny, Yefim, 375
POWs (prisoners of war), xiv, 339; apparent lack of resistance among, 16; in Belorussia, 236, 237, 261, 262, 264–66; British POWs killed, 38; in Crimea, 368; escaped, 183, 184, 417–19; in Glukhov camp, 407–17; Jewish prisoners, xvii, 406–7, 409–10, 413, 418; in Lithuania, 284; mass graves dug by, 353; Odessa resistance and, 144, 145; rescue from camp in Latonovo, 419–20; staggering numbers of Red Army prisoners, 406; torture of, 168, 313, 320–21, 373, 409
Pozdnev, Georgy, 142
Prague, 331, 333, 396n7
Pravda (Soviet newspaper), xxii, xxviii, 19, 348, 400; Ehrenburg's writing in, 22, 27; fate of Soviet POWs described in, 407; on Nuremberg trial, 32; reports on German atrocities, 21
Pravuk, Vanya, 173
Preyli, *xlii*, 322–28
Pribugski krai [The Bug Region] (newspaper), 135
Prilezhaev, Nikolay, 246–47
Professor Mamlock (film), 19
Prokopovich, Ivan, 142
Pronicheva, Dina, *47*
propaganda, Nazi, xxv, 20, 280, 357
propaganda, Soviet, xxiii, 20
property of Jews, looting of: in Belorussia, 235, 250; in Crimea, 341–42, 344; extent of civilian collaboration and, 13; in Lithuania, 282, 288, 307–8; in Russia, 392; in Ukraine, 214, 222. *See also* apartments, neighbors' takeover of
Proskurov, *xlii*
Protectorate of Bohemia and Moravia, 233
Prozorovsky, V., *381*
Prus (director of orphanage in Simferopol), 366
Prusin, Alexander, 30, 37
Pskov, *xlii*, 384

Pukaylo (survivor in Simferopol), 366
Puritson, Boris, 375
Pushkin, Alexander, 68, 131
Pushkin, city of, *xlii*, 383
Pyatigorsk, *xliii*, 385, 409
Pyatigory, *xlii*, 169–85

rabbis, 118, 162, 271, 305, 309, 310; defiance of Nazis, 303; humiliation and torture of, 302
Rabin, Lyusya, 365–68
Rabinovich, Semyon, 59
Rabinovich, Ya. S., 136
Rabinovich (Babi Yar victim), 60
Radbil (Babi Yar victim), 59
Radetzky, Waldemar von, 43
radio broadcasts, Soviet, xix, 53, 119, 263, 322, 334, 362; appeal to Anglo-American Jews, 20; in Jewish ghettos, 321; in Odessa underground, 143, 144; partisans and, 362; Sovinformburo bulletins, xxi, 400; warnings about Nazi intentions, xx, xxi
Radyansk collective farm, 130
Raihof, Julius, 266–68
railroad boxcars, Jews transported in, 113–14, 124–25, 134, 241, 290
Rajzman, Samuel, 32
Rakhkovsky, Grisha, 199
Rakita family (victims in Crimea), 376
Rakov, 270
Rappaport, Herbert, 19
Rasch, Otto, 43
Rassadin, Viktor Mikhaylovich, 408, 412
Raykis, Shura, 146
Rayzen, Liza, 157
Red Army, xvi, xxviii, 248, 385; approach to German border, 27, 297; Belorussia liberated by, 233, 271, 274; capital cities of Russia defended by, 383; concentration camps liberated by, 21; Crimea liberated by, 363, 365; defense lines overrun in German invasion, 198n73; German retreat from Russia and, 396, 397; as hope of Jews under occupation, 57, 58, 62, 67, 68, 83, 109, 132, 153, 222, 312, 388; Jews in, xvii, 45, 115, 195; *Krasnaya zvezda* newspaper, 25; Latvia liberated by, 317, 322, 328; Lithuania liberated by, 278, 291, 296, 301; occupied territories liberated by, xvii; partisans and, 185, 197; POWs captured by Germans, 6, 406–7; resistance groups and, 148; Ukraine liberated by, 51, 201, 204, 207

440 | Index

registration, of Jews: in Belorussia, 234–36, 243, 254; in Crimea, 345, 359–60, 363, 370; in Ukraine, 213, 223, *226, 227*
Reicher (Babi Yar victim), 59
Reichskommissariat Ostland, xv
Reichskommissariat Ukraine, xv
Rekochinskaya, Tatyana, 120–21
Renk, Andrei, 144
resistance, 16–18, 305; desperate and unarmed, 17; Nazi reprisals, 281; in Odessa, 141–49; against Romanians in Odessa, 110, 116, 133; sabotage, 319, 321. *See also* escapes; partisans
Revich, E. I., 137
Revich, S. I., 137
Reyderman, Isaak, 60
Reynyay camp, 303, 305
Reyzberg family (victims in Crimea), 375
Reyzins, Usiya, 217
Rezekne (Rezhitsa), 328–30
Rezhitsa, *xlii*
Ribayzen (Bukovina survivor), 205
Ribbentrop, Joachim von, 30
Ribenishki, 322, 323, 326
Riderman, Riva, 207
Riga, xv, *xlii*, 30, 290, 317; German capture of, 6, 316; ghettos and labor camps, xvi
Righteous among the Nations title, xvii, xxxviii
Rodoshkovichi, 269
Romanauskas (Lithuanian official), 306
Romania: as ally of Nazi Germany, 13–15; map, *xlii*; postwar reluctance to acknowledge Holocaust, 15–16; prewar Jewish population of, 13; Soviet Ukrainian regions administered by, xv, 53; territories lost to Soviet Union, xv, 51, 53. *See also* Bessarabia; Moldavia; Transnistria
Romanian fascists, 153, 195, 418; in Crimea, 374–75; death camps run by, 129–30; doctors murdered by, 132–37; Jews exterminated by, xv, 53, 138–41; Odessa under rule of, 109–19; resistance against, 142–49; retreat before Red Army, 132; secret police, 205; Tulchin ghetto and, 149, 150
Romanian language, 112, 119
Roosevelt, Eleanor, 41
Rosen, Major A. A., 200
Rosenberg, Alfred, xv, 30
Rosenfeld, Borya, 156
Roseynay, 301–2
Rostov-on-Don, *xliii*, 221, 384
Rotenberg (Babi Yar victim), 59

Rovno, *xlii*, 17, 51
Royanov family (Mariupol), 213, 216, 218, 219
Roytman, Khaim, 161
Rozanov, Vasily, 358
Rozenfeld, David, xxxix, 200, 201
Rozhetsky, Lev, xxxviii, 121–32
Rozner, Moisey, 205
Rubenstein, Joshua, xl
Rubinger, David, 205
Rubinshteyn, B. G., 136
Rubinshteyn, G. M., 137
Rudenko, Daniil Antonovich, 201
Rudkevich, Nikolai Vasilevich, 196
Rühl, Felix, 43
Rumbula Forest, xv, *xlii*, 317
rumors, 196, 210, 217, 310, 353; approach of Red Army, 203, 204, 325, 327, 396; identity of hidden Jews, 388, 395–96; mass extermination, 25, 293, 328, 346, 347, 352; mutilations and torture, 263; Odessa explosion at NKVD building, 110; postwar clemency for Nazis, 41
Rusalkin (Soviet POW), 408
Russia, 337, 383–84; in Bolshevik period, 25, 383; map, *xlii–xliii*; post-Soviet, ix, xxxix, 205n76; Provisional Government (1917), 26n79. *See also specific places in*
Russian language, xxii, xxxvi, 339, 409; ghetto signs in, 237; inscriptions on walls in, 156–57; *100 Letters* in, 25, 26; spoken by Germans, 341, 407, 410, 418; Yiddish accent in, 364n15
Russians, 235, 253; collaborators, xv, 393, 396; credited with defeating fascism, 52; of Crimea, 340, 347; held by Gestapo as hostages, 246; Jewish children hidden by, 259; Jewish spouses of, 216, 255, 275, 350, 353; Jews rescued or aided by, xxv, 77, 117–18, 133, 242, 300, 419; mistaken for Jews, 250, 407; partisans, 261; police auxiliaries, xv; Soviet military decorations awarded to, 18; victims of Nazis, 274; witnesses to slaughter, 251
Rustakov (Soviet POW), 408
Rybakov, Semyon, 59

saboteurs, xiv
St. John, Robert, 13
Sakhnoshvili, Georgy, 419
Saltanov (Babi Yar victim), 59
Samoylovich, B., 218
Sandberger, Martin, 42, 43
Sandberger, SS-Sturmbahnführer Martin, 331

Sandul, Maria Antonovna, 119
sanitation, lack of, 100, 114, 236
Satanovsky (Babi Yar victim), 60
Savchenko, Tsilya, 374
Savchenko (Red Army lieutenant), 373, 374
Savelev, A., 147
Sbitnev (Soviet POW), 408
Schubert, Franz, 34
Schubert, Heinz, 34, 43
Schulz, Erwin, 43
Schwartzbard, Shlomo, 168n59
"The Science of Hatred" (Sholokhov), 407
Sedlets POW camp, 413
Segal, David, 156
Segal family (victims in Crimea), 376
Seibert, Willy, 43
Selbstschutz, 53
Selinov, Mikhail, 146, 147–48
Semibratov (Soviet POW), 408
Seredinin (Russian police chief), 411
Seulescu (Romanian secret police inspector), 143
Sevastopol, *xlii*, 37, 356
Severin, A. A., xxix
Seyfullina, Lidia, xxvi
Shaginyan, Marietta, xxvi
Shakh (Babi Yar victim), 60
Shambadal, M., 317
Shampaner (Babi Yar victim), 60
Shander, Lt. Tot, 403
Shandor, Talatzi, 403
Shapelko (Belorussian doctor), 268
Shapiro, Alexander, 417–19
Shapiro, Nikolai, 59
Shapiro, Rabbi (Kaunas/Kovno), 290
Shapiro, Tsetsilia Mihaylovna, 254–58
Shapiro (Odessa doctor), 137
Shaulyay, Lithuania, xxxviii, 278, 284
Shaus, L., 269–70
Shavli (Shaulyay, Siauliai), *xlii*, 278, 302, 308
Shcherbakov, Alexander, xxi, xxii–xxiii, xxv, 142n39
Shchorbatov (Belorussian witness), 268
Shekhter, Lili, 151
Shendels, Yevgenia, 400–401
Shenfeld, Stepan, xxxviii, xxxix, 89–99
Shepilov, Dmitri, xxxiii
Sheputa, V., 173, 178
Sheremet, Karp Korneevich, 138, 140
Sherman, Eli, 162
Shestopal (Odessa resistance), 143
Sheynis-Rybakova, Sofia, 59
Shimelyovich, Boris, xx, xxxi
Shlemovich, Mira, 307

Shlyakhova, Alexandra Trofimovna, 367
Shma Yisroel prayer, 73, 195
Shmaevsky, Major (Mariupol survivor), 219
Shmaglevskaya, Severine, 32
Shmakov, Alexey, 358
Shmorginsky (Babi Yar victim), 59
Sholokhov, Mikhail, 21–22, 407
Sholokhova, Lyudmila, 327n11
shootings, mass: in Belorussia, 245, 248, 268, 272, 275, 388; in Crimea, 353; in Lithuania, 43, 281, 288; in Ukraine, 121, 128, 138–40, 141, 166, 185–86, 209–11
Shostakovich, Dmitri, 52
Shpitzenburg, Mikhail Borisovich, 398
Shpitzenburg, Vera Osipovna, 398
Shpola, *xlii*, 51, 185–86
Shrayber (victim in Novozybkov), 397
Shtern, Lina, xxiii
Shternsheyn, Fira, 212
shtetls: of Belorussia, 269–70, 271, 275–76; of Latvia, 322–28; of Lithuania, 296–301, 308–12; of Russia, 386–97
Shturko, Lyusya, 375
Shulyak, Grisha, 178
Shuster, Khaya, 296
Shuster, Rasha, 297–301
Shvarts, Khannah, 180
Shwartz, V., 220
Sidelnikov, Fyodor, 141, 142, 143
Sidelnikov, Georgy, 142, 143
Sidelnikova, Yelena, 143
Simferopol, *xlii*, 337, 338, 346–49, 363–65; false documents in, 359–65; German capture of, 338–40; hiding from the Germans in, 349–58; Jewish children in, 365–68; Jews organized and registered by Nazis, 340–45, 359–60, 363; Krimchaks of, 345–46; liberation of, 358–59; as multiethnic city, 339, 348
Simkhes, Yankel, 162
Simonov, Konstantin, xxvi, 23
Sirotskoe, 125–26, 134
Sitinok, Z. I., 177
Six, Franz, 43
Skidel, 269
Sklarenko, Anna Stepanova, 371–72
Sklovsky, Grigory, 59
Skuli, F. G., 141–46, 148, 149
Skupnik, Luiza Petrovna, 109
slave labor, 40, 278, 317, 331
Slavic peoples: anti-fascist committees and, xix, 20n54; enslavement of, xiii
Slavuta POW camp, *xlii*, 165–67, 166, 410, 413

Slipchenko (Kozman), Lidia Maximovna, 109–15
Slivenko (Ukrainian policeman), 128
Slobodka, 295
Slobodyanik, F. K., 177
Slutsk, *xlii,* 270
Smelkin, Khaim, 376
Smetona, Antonas, 280
Smilovitsky, Leonid, 234
Smolar, Hirsh, 18, 46
Smolensk, xxiv, *xlii,* 30, 288; German capture of, 386–87; ghetto in, 384; region of, 386–97, 404
Smorgon, *xlii*
Sobibor death camp, xvi, *xlii*
Solomin, Maks, 363–65, 366
Sonderkommandos, 37, 335
Sorina, B. M., 386–97
Southern Bug River, xv, 14, 121, 128
Soviet Information Bureau (Sovinformburo), xxi, xxii, xxix, xxxviii; Nazi treatment of Jews denounced by, 402; radio bulletins of, 400; resistance groups and, 142, 144–45, 146, 147, 148
Soviet Union: ambivalence toward Final Solution, xxx, 18, 19–29, 30; collapse of (1991), 29; Estonia annexed by, 331; Final Solution in occupied territories of, xiii; German invasion of, xiii, xvii, 4, 5–6, 14, 198n73, 322–23, 383; ghettos in, 11; Jewish population losses, xvii; Nazi administrative areas, xv; Nuremberg trials and, 31, 32; October Revolution anniversary, 251, 408; pact with Germany, 6; refugees in remote parts of, 277; territories annexed by, xv, 13, 20, 51; territories under German occupation, *xlii–xliii;* total war against, xiv; trials of Nazi war criminals in, 29–30, 37, 43, *50;* wartime alliance with western democracies, xix, xxi
Soyfer, Ida, 156
Spanish Civil War, 25
Spector, Shmuel, xl
Speer, Albert, 30
SS *(Schutzstaffel),* Nazi, xiv, 151, 153; in Belorussia, 244, 263, 267, 268; chief physician of, 9; in Estonia, 332; forced labor camps run by, 90–99; Higher SS, xiv, 7; relationship with Wehrmacht, 37; resistance against, 16; Soviet POWs and, 410, 412, 413, 414, 416–17; trials of leaders after war, 33, 40; in Ukraine, 188; Ukrainian militia assistance to, 7; Volksdeutsche and, 53; Waffen SS, xiv. *See also* Einsatzgruppen

Stahlecker, Gen. Walter, 317
Stalin, Joseph, xxv, xxviii, 23, 27, 103n26, 176; as admired figure, 85, 94, 123; antisemitism condemned by, 19, 21; appeal to Jews in Britain and United States, 20; death of, 205n76; JAC trial and, xxxv; Mikhoels's death ordered by, xxxiv, 28; Soviet territorial annexations and, 13; wartime alliance with western democracies, xix
Stalingrad, battle of, *xliii,* 15, 26, 29, 204; German advance halted at, 384; German Sixth Army destroyed at, 396; ghetto Jews' knowledge of, 321; Grossman's reports from, 23
Stalino, *xliii*
Stanislav, *xlii*
Starozhinets, 204–5
Starye Dorogi, *xlii,* 268–69
Staugautis (Catholic bishop), 306
Stavki death camp, 126, 129–30
Stavropol (Voroshilovsk), *xliii,* 384
Steimle, Eugen, 43
Stichproben searches, 292
Stitze (Gestapo agent), 293
Stoklishki, *xlii,* 296–301
Stolyar, Yekaterina Andreevna, 367
Stonoga, Pavel Ivanovich, 138, 139–40
Stonov, Dmitry, xxxviii, 205
The Storm (Ehrenburg), 52
Storozhinets, *xlii*
Stratievsky, Boris, 121
Strauch, Eduard, 11, 43
Stritinin, Yevgeny, 142
Strizhevsky, Avram, 170
Stutthof concentration camp, *xlii,* 317, 331–32
suicides, of Jews, 57, 281, 291; to cheat Nazi executioners, 73, 164–65, 297, 329; in death camps, 129; intellectuals, 117, 124; during Kristallnacht pogrom, 19; raped women, 150; unsuccessful, 109, 204, 385
suicides, of Nazis, 33, 43
Sukhozanet, Vera Petrovna, 77, 83, 87
Sumy, *xlii,* 51, 208–9
Suprun, Olga, 197–200
survivors, xvii, xxxviii, 23, 44; in Belorussia, 234; in Berdichev, 161; of Bogdanovka, 138–41; in Bukovina, 205; in Chudnov (Ukraine), 165; in Debaltsevo, 167–68; of mass shootings, 190–91; in Novo-Zlatopol (Ukraine), 205–7; at war crimes trials, *47*
Suslov, Mikhail, xxxiii
Sutzkever, Abram, 22, 32
Suvorin, Alexei, 358
Sventsyany, 312–13

Svoren (Odessa doctor), 137
synagogues, destruction of, 12, 19; Great Choral Synagogue (Riga), 316–17; in Kovel, 155; in Lithuania, 281
Syrtsov, Ivan, 142, 144

Taberovsky (Babi Yar victim), 59
Taganrog, *xliii*, 221, 419
Tager, Motya, 328, 329
Tallinn, *xlii*, 331, 334
Talmud, 338
Tarabukin, L. N., 384–85
Taranova, Tatyana, 208–9
Tarasevich (Lithuanian rescuer), 297
Tarnopol, 12, 51
Tartu, *xlii*
Tasevich, Matryona, 170
Tatar language, 346
Tatars: in Belorussia, 252; Crimean, xv, 338, 340, 348, 359, 409
Taylor, Telford, 7, 31, 32, 40, 41
Tekst Publishers (Moscow), xxxvii
Telshyay, *xlii*, 303, 308
Temopol, *xlii*
Teplitsky (Odessa doctor), 137
Tereshchenko, Nadezhda, xxxix, 200–202
Teryaeva, Tatyana, 144
Theresienstadt, 331
Third Reich. *See* Nazi Germany (Third Reich)
Thirteenth Symphony (Shostakovich), 52
Timchenko, Valentina, 148
Tipovitskaya, Malka, 207
Tirkltoyd, Ginda, 397
Todt organization, 332
Tokarenko, Yefim, 143
Tonkoshur (Ukrainian police secretary), 192, 194
Torah scrolls, destruction of, 323
Tornbaum (German officer), 284, 286
torture, 16–17, 187, 270, 295, 374–75; "devil's dance," 303–4; skinning alive, 329; of Soviet POWs, 168, 313, 320–21, 373, 409. *See also* burial alive; burning alive
Tovbin (Babi Yar victim), 59
Trainin, Ilya, xxx
Transnistria, xv–xvi, 14, 15; ghettos of, 14; governor of, 138; Jewish survivors in, xvii; Volksdeutsche in, 53
Transylvania, 13, 331
Traugot, Paotukha, 209–11
Treblinka death camp, xvi, *xlii*, 3, 27, 269; Grossman's account of, 24; judgment of history and, 44; survivors of, 32
Trifon, Laszlo, 403

"The Triumph of a Man" (Ehrenburg), 22
Trostyanets, 248, 249
Troyanovskaya, Sosl, 375
Troyanovsky, Abram, 375
Troyanovsky, Alexander, xxix
Truman, Harry, 41
Tseytlin (Babi Yar victim), 60
Tsimmerman (tailor in Libava ghetto), 319–20
Tsiperovich (Babi Yar victim), 60
Tsunts, M., 275
Tsviling, Leah, 205–7
Tsviling, Moisey, 206
Tula, *xliii*
Tulchin, *xlii*, 17–18, 149–51
Turkey, 338
Turok (Babi Yar victim), 59
Tutinyker, Arka, 164
Tvardovsky, Alexander, xxvi
Tver, 384

Ukraine: Crimea transferred to control of, 337n1; Einsatzgruppen in, xiv, 30, 52; German administrative areas of, xv; Jewish population of, 51, 53; map, *xlii–xliii*; massacres in, 52; mobile gas vans in, 10; partisans in, xvii; pogroms in, 12; Romanian occupation, 14; separatist republic (1918–1921), 168n59, 169; Soviet POW escape in, 417–19; western part annexed by Soviet Union, 20. *See also* Babi Yar massacre; *specific places in*
"Ukraine Without Jews" (Grossman), 23
Ukrainian collaborators, xvi, 28, 68, 113, 214; *Black Book* criticized for overemphasizing, xxviii, xxix; camp guards, 209; at execution sites, *228–29*; Jewish resistance and, 17, 18; looting of Jews' property by, 12–13, 187–88, 191; participation in pogroms, 187–88; as "Petlura supporters," 168–69, 170; police, xv, 151, 185, 187, 209–10
Ukrainian language, 72, 78, 190, 339
Ukrainians: concentration camp inmates, 92; Jewish spouses of, 216; Jews rescued or aided by, xvi–xvii, xxv, xxix, 119–20; killed alongside Jews, 190; reaction to German invasion, 54, 170; shot for hiding Jews, 61, 66, 67, 188; Soviet military decorations awarded to, 18; victims of Nazis, 274
Ulman, Fuka, 163
Ulmanis, Karlis, 316
Uman, *xlii*, 51, 186–97
Umansky, Konstantin, xxi
United States, xxi, xxii, xxiii, xxviii, 156; "Jewish

nationalists" in, xxxi, xxxiv; Jewish population of, 20; leniency toward Nazis, 39–42; Mikhoels and Fefer in, xxiii; Nuremberg trials and, 31; publication of *Black Book* and, xxvi, xxvii, xxxi, xxxvi; Soviet ambassador to, xxvii; Soviet films shown in, 19; trials of Nazis in, 43

The Unknown Black Book, xix, 13, 28, 44; map of places indicated in, *xlii–xliii;* post-Soviet publication of, xxxvii–xxxviii; question of resistance and, 16–18; on Romanian atrocities, 14

Upryamtsev, Dr. (Soviet POW), 420
Utyan, *xlii,* 308–12

Vaivara, *xlii,* 331, 332
Vakhnik, Abram Moiseevich, 335
Varshavskaya (Odessa doctor), 137
Varushkina, O., 329
Vasiliev (of Odessa resistance), 143
Vasilievich, Dmitry, 147
Vasilkov (of Odessa resistance), 146
Vasserman, Golda, 149–51
Vaynbern, Moyshe, 207
Vaynshteyn, Srul, 156
Vays, Aron, xl
Vaysblat, Aron, 59
Vaysbreyt, Arkady, 59
Veksler, Boris, 329
Veksler (eyewitness in Lithuania), 301, 304, 306, 308
Velderman (Odessa doctor), 137
Velt, Dr. (Bukovina survivor), 205
vengeance, calls for, 154–57, 190, 270, 272, 288, 295, 321; appeal to Red Army soldiers, 120–21; at Babi Yar, 73, 74; partisans and, xxv, 404; in poetry, 122, 123; written in blood, 288
Verbitsky, A., 248
Veysbrod, A. V., 258
Vichinsky family (victims in Crimea), 375
Vilenchuk, Aron, 287, 290–91
Viliampol ghetto, 291
Vilna (Vilno, Vilnius), xv, xvii, *xlii,* 284; German capture of, 6; ghettos and labor camps, xvi, 11, 32, 308, 331; as "Jerusalem of Lithuania," 277; liberated by Red Army, 291, 386n6; liquidation of ghetto, 295; State Jewish Museum of Lithuania, xxxvi
Vinnitsa, *xlii*
Vinokurov, Lieutenant (Soviet POW), 408, 414, 415
Vital, Sore, 150

Vitebsk, *xlii,* 233, 253, 388, 404
Vladimir-Volynsky POW camp, 413
Vladimirov, Feodosy, 142, 143
Vlasov, Gen. Andrey, 396
Voina i rabochii klass [War and the Working Class] (journal), 27
Voitseshchuk (resident of Slavuta), 165–66
Volga River, 384
Volhynia, 51
Volkischer Beobachter [People's Observer] (Nazi newspaper), 27
Volkov, Pyotr, 181, 182, 184
Volksdeutsche (ethnic Germans), 53
Volman, Rakhil, 60
Volovtseva, Alexandra Yakovlevna, 119–20
Volozhin, 233, 270
Voronezh, *xliii*
Voronovo, 269
Voropaev (Ukrainian policeman), 192, 194
Voznyak (Odessa resistance), 143
Vysotskaya (teacher in Slavuta), 165–66

Waffen SS, xiv
Wannsee Conference, 278, 331
war, front line of, 221–22, 253
war crimes, xiv, 29–30, 31
Warsaw, xxxviii–xxxix, *xlii,* 6, 290, 295, 344
Warsaw ghetto, 3, 4
Wartenberg, Rolf, 33–34, 36, 39
water, lack of, 113, 174, 213, 249, 313; in assembly points, 223; disease epidemics and, 101; no running water, 282; in prelude to execution, 269, 308; shot or beaten for requesting water, 235, 261, 404; women permitted to draw water, 100, 106
Wehrmacht (regular German army), xiv, xix, 3, 8, 284; advance on Moscow, 21; British beliefs concerning, 37; Einsatzgruppen and, xv; in Estonia, 331; expelled from Soviet territory, 23; Final Solution and, 37–38; invasion of Soviet Union, 5–6, 198n73, 383; knowledge of Final Solution, 5; retreat from Russia, 396–97; testimony of German soldiers, 209–11, 266–68
Weinmann, Erwin, 5
Weiss, Shaya, 117
Wells, Leon, 16
Widemann (German officer), 292–93
Wiesel, Elie, 15
Wilhaus, Gustav, 91
Witos, A., 381
Wolf, Friedrich, 19
women: antifascist committee of, xix, 20n54;

Index | 445

childbirth in captivity, 114, 162–63; female prison guards, 117; in forest family camps, 234; hard labor in camps, 334; mourning over dead children, *382*; rape of, 73, 117, 150, 158, 241, 244, 276, 286, 330

World Jewish Congress (WJC), xxvi, xxvii

World War I, 25

World War II, xiii, 13, 383; battles of eastern front, 23; as Great Patriotic War of Soviet Union, xxxv, 155. *See also* Stalingrad, battle of

Yad Vashem, xvii, xix, xxxvi, xxxvii, xl; *Black Book* published by, 28; Righteous among the Nations title and, xxxviii, 279n

Yagotin, 23

Yalovsky, Valentin, 105, 107

Yalta, *xliii*

Yanovsky camp (Lvov), xxxviii, *xlii*

Yaremich, Ivan, 180, 181

Yarmolinskaya, Maria, 296–97

Yarmovskya, Maria Ilinichna, 295

Yaskutelis, Vintsis, 299

Yaskutelis, Yuzus, 301

Yassy (Iasi), *xlii*, 14

Yazhgur (eyewitness in Lithuania), 301, 306, 307

Yedinsty, *xlii,* 157–61

Yefrussi, Polina, 385

Yenin (metalworker in Slavuta), 165–66

Yershova, Alexandra Gnatieva, 87

Yerusalimsky, A., xxxviii

Yerusalimsky, Lazar, 301, 308

Yessentuki, *xliii*, 384–85

Yevpatoria, *xlii,* 338

Yevtushenko, Yevgeny, 28, 52

Yiddish language, xxi, xxv, xxvi, xxxii, 69, 172; diaries in, 322; inscriptions on walls in, 156; newspapers in, 26; poets, 22, 32; Soviet crackdown on Yiddish culture, xxxiv

Yidishe bilder [Pictures of Jewish Life] (journal), 327

Yudelovich, Efraim, 309

Yudkovsky, Boris, 197–98

Yugoslavia, xix

Yukhnikov, Itsik, 313–15

Yurkulov, Mikhail, 141, 142

Yurovsky, Lev, 359–63, 366

Yuzefovich, Joseph, xxvii, xxix

Zabora, Yelena, 147

Zafran, Gitl, 156

Zakharino, 386–87, 388–89, 390, 393

Zakotynsky of Pyatigory, 170

Zaksman, Alexander Borisovich, 119, 120

Zalivansky (Babi Yar victim), 59

Zalkind, Regina, 151

Zaltsman, Motele, 208

Zamels, A. M., 137

Zaporozhe, *xliii,* 205–7

Zarina, Sata, 375

Zarudnitsy camp, 160–61

Zaydberg, Girsh, 315

Zaydelbern, A. A., 137

Zaynfeld (Odessa doctor), 137

Zelenkov, Vasily Ivanovich, 176

Zelenkova, Raisa, 169–85

Zelinsky, Viktor Fyodorovich, 411

Zeltser (head of Simferopol Jewish Committee), 340, 341

Zeyger, Ruvim, 376

Zeyger, Sofia, 376

Zhdanov, Andrei, xxxii

Zheleznova, Miriam, xxxviii, 195

Zhezhmary, 281,

Contributors

Joshua Rubenstein is Northeast Regional Director of Amnesty International USA. He is author of *Tangled Loyalties: The Life and Times of Ilya Ehrenburg,* editor (with Vladimir Naumov) of *Stalin's Secret Pogrom: The Postwar Inquisition of the Jewish Anti-Fascist Committee,* and editor (with Alexander Gribanov) of *The KGB File of Andrei Sakharov.* He is an associate at the Davis Center for Russian and Eurasian Studies at Harvard University.

Ilya Altman is Director of the Center for Holocaust Research and Education in Moscow. He is author of *Zhertvy nenavisti: kholokost v SSSR, 1941–1945* (Victims of Hatred: The Holocaust in the USSR, 1941–1945) and Editor-in-Chief of *Encyclopedia of the Holocaust in the USSR* (in Russian).

Yitzhak Arad is former Director of Yad Vashem. His publications include *Belzec, Sobibor, Treblinka: The Operation Reinhard Death Camps* (Indiana University Press, 1987) and *The Holocaust in the Soviet Union.*

Christopher Morris is co-translator of *Generations of Winter* by Vassily Aksyonov.

www.ingramcontent.com/pod-product-compliance
Lightning Source LLC
Chambersburg PA
CBHW070257240426
43661CB00057B/2570